D1293459

OXFORD MEDIEVAL TEXTS

General Editors

HISTORIA ECCLESIE ABBENDONENSIS

THE HISTORY OF THE CHURCH OF ABINGDON

HISTORIA ECCLESIE ABBENDONENSIS

THE HISTORY OF THE CHURCH OF ABINGDON

Volume II

EDITED AND TRANSLATED BY
JOHN HUDSON

CLARENDON PRESS · OXFORD

OXFORD
UNIVERSITY PRESS

Great Clarendon Street, Oxford OX2 6DP

Oxford University Press is a department of the University of Oxford.
It furthers the University's objective of excellence in research, scholarship,
and education by publishing worldwide in

Oxford New York
Auckland Bangkok Bogotá Buenos Aires Cape Town Chennai
Dar es Salaam Delhi Hong Kong Istanbul Karachi Kolkata
Kuala Lumpur Madrid Melbourne Mexico City Mumbai Nairobi
São Paulo Shanghai Singapore Taipei Tokyo Toronto

Oxford is a registered trade mark of Oxford University Press
in the UK and in certain other countries

Published in the United States
by Oxford University Press Inc., New York

First published 2002

British Library Cataloguing in Publication Data
Data available

Library of Congress Cataloging in Publication Data
Data available
ISBN 0-19-820742-5

1 3 5 7 9 10 8 6 4 2

Typeset in Ehrhardt
by Joshua Associates Ltd., Oxford
Printed in Great Britain
on acid-free paper by
Biddles Ltd., Guildford and King's Lynn

PREFACE

SINCE soon after Joseph Stevenson published his two volumes entitled *Chronicon Monasterii de Abingdon* in 1858, there have been calls for an improved edition. Unfortunately, the ideal editor, Sir Frank Stenton, did not respond to the encouragement he received. So Stevenson's work survived the entirety of the twentieth century. The present is the first of two volumes intended to replace Stevenson's Rolls Series edition. I have chosen to publish the post-1071 volume first, so that my work on the pre-Conquest period might benefit from Susan Kelly's edition of the Abingdon Anglo-Saxon Charters, published by the British Academy in 2000–1. Since my discussion of matters such as editorial principles will appear in my Vol. i, the present Preface will give a brief list of subjects to be dealt with in that introduction, and then provide a short summary of some issues concerning the edition and translation.

The introduction to Vol. i will deal with the following issues relating to the whole period covered by the two volumes: title and authorship; the process of composition; purposes of the text; style; manuscripts; orthography and rubrication; marginalia; editorial principles; illustrations. It will also deal with the following areas primarily in relation to Vol. i: sources; structure; omissions; charters; endowment; personnel; buildings and monastic life.

Here it will be useful to summarize a few of my editorial principles: (i) My text is based on the earlier manuscript, London, British Library, Cotton Claud. C. IX (henceforth referred to as MS C). This probably dates from the 1160s; see below, p. xvii. Appendices I and II print the additions in the later manuscript, London, British Library, Cotton Claud. B. VI (henceforth referred to as MS B). This probably dates from the second quarter or perhaps the middle of the thirteenth century; see below, p. xxxvii. MS B's variant readings for the main text are noted in the *apparatus criticus*.

I do not include a continuation in a different hand in MS C, which covers some of the same period as the continuation in MS B. This is for two reasons: the first is that my aim is to produce an edition concentrating on the work in the main hand of the earliest manuscript, the second that the continuation is available in Stevenson's edition, *CMA* ii. 297–9, and with translation in *English Lawsuits*, no. 570.

I have examined other copies of documents which appear in the text, and footnote any substantial differences. However, only when the document survives as an original do I note all variants in the *apparatus criticus*.

(ii) In minor matters of orthography, for example the use of 'c' or 't', '. . . umque' and '. . . unque', and the spelling of words such as 'litteras', I have standardized usage according to the preferred practice of MS C, even though this manuscript was not always consistent. I have not noted MS B's variants in such matters. In the appendices based solely on MS B, I have followed that manuscript's customary practices, rather than standardizing according to the preferred practice of MS C.

(iii) I have standardized the spellings of personal names according to MS C's preferred forms, and have not footnoted minor variants (for example 'Rotbertus' for 'Robertus', 'Wuillelmus' for 'Willelmus') in either MS C or MS B. This is because each manuscript seems to vary internally in usage, and these variations are not significant. Likewise, where MS B's practice differs from MS C's (e.g. 'Walchelinus' for 'Walkelinus', 'Matilda' for 'Mathilda'), the variations are minor. Significant variants have been noted.

Translating Old English names presents different problems, as we have later twelfth-century Latin versions of names from the preceding hundred years. In order to ensure consistency with Vol. i, I have normally used the standard Old English form (e.g. 'Alfwius' becomes Ælfwig). Sometimes, however, the Latin would allow more than one Old English form, in which case the possibilities are given in footnotes. Where the Latin text gives a name beginning 'Egel-' or 'Egil-', suggesting the twelfth-century vernacular, I retain that form in the translation, whilst footnoting the Old English form beginning Æthel-.

(iv) I have reproduced place-names as they appear in the manuscripts, noting MS B's variants. There are considerable problems in expanding place-names, for example whether 'Abbend'' stands for 'Abbendona', 'Abbendonia', or 'Abbendonensis'. I have sought a solution which neither obscures the sense of the narrative sections of the text by retaining numerous unextended place-names, nor renders the edition unhelpful to those interested in early place-name forms. If MS C gives an abbreviated form, which leaves the core of the place-name clear but removes only the ending, I have adopted MS B's reading when the latter provides a complete word. Otherwise, I have followed MS C's most common usage; for example 'Abbendona' is often, although not invariably, used of the abbey, 'Abbendonia' of the town. This can produce a spurious certainty when the decision is made on the basis of very few instances, for example 'Salesberie' and 'Salesbirie'. In some instances, the text contains no examples of the name in full.

Within documents, I have on occasion adopted the practice, common in charter editing, of not extending the abbreviation if it cannot be told what the correct version would be (e.g. 'Oxen'', when it is unclear whether this means 'Oxeneford' or 'Oxenefordscira'.) This is especially the case in addresses and place-dates.

The ablative of adjectival forms of place-names regularly, although not universally, appears as '-e', not '-i'.

Both manuscripts often use abbreviated forms such as 'Angl' ' in the royal title, leaving a problem as to how the abbreviation should be expanded. My common practice is to extend the abbreviation to 'Anglorum', since MS C regularly uses this form, and it is also quite common in MS B until the collection of Henry I writs, and not unknown thereafter; see fos. 119^{v}, 120^{r}, 121^{v}, 126^{v}, $127^{r,}$ 130^{v}, 132^{r}, 132^{v}, 133^{v}, 134^{r}, 135^{r}, 135^{v}, 136^{r}, 136^{v}, 137^{r}, 137^{v}, 138^{v}, 143^{r}, 145^{v}, 149^{v}, 158^{v}. However, from the time of Henry I MS B quite frequently uses 'Anglie'. I only give MS B's different reading when it is certain from the manuscript, not when it consists simply of the form 'Angl' '. For MS B's additions I extend the abbreviated form to 'Anglie'. Likewise with mention of Normans/Normandy etc. in Henry II's title, my practice has been to expand them to peoples, as opposed to places, unless MS C gives the place word in full. In the appendices, I have followed the practice of MS B in its prevalent use of place-name forms.

For reasons of style and consistency, I have chosen to translate the Latin *uilla* almost invariably as 'village', rather than using the archaic sounding 'vill' or the peculiar sounding—to modern British ears—'township'. This choice risks anachronism in making all *uillae* sound like nucleated settlements, but I hope the word village can be stretched to mean a rural settlement, area, or group of people.

(v) Rubricated headings are represented here in italics. I have introduced chapter numbers, which may prove useful for references. I have simply numbered MS C's rubricated headings, only once introducing an extra chapter number, no. 252. In this instance, the scribe's recognition that a new section was starting is indicated by capitalization within the word 'uenerabilis'. If MS B includes a heading where MS C does not, this is mentioned in the *apparatus criticus*.

(vi) Both manuscripts are inconsistent in the use of figures or words for numbers, although MS C has a slight preference for words. I have therefore standardized usage as words for small numbers, except when referring to amounts of money. In the various administrative lists in the appendices, I follow the practices of those lists.

(vii) The Latin of the *History* is filled with words such as 'predictus', 'supradictus', and so on, which at least to the modern ear give it a rather legalistic sound. This probably was how it sounded in the twelfth century, and I have retained a great many, although not all, of these words in the translation. I have omitted them when they might confuse the reader, or when they make the English sound more stilted than the Latin. See further Vol. i, Introduction, 'Style'.

(viii) The text at various points uses the historic present, but I do not reproduce this in the translation, since it would produce an inconsistent use of tenses, sometimes even within a single sentence (e.g. p. 22).

(ix) Paragraphing is consistent between text and translation. Where possible, sentences in the translation correspond with those in the Latin text, but not infrequently such strict correspondence would lead to a quite inappropriate translation, with an excessively Latinate succession of clauses. The potential problems are clear from the very first sentence of the first paragraph of the text.

(x) I have not tried to make Appendix III, which consists entirely of administrative lists, consistent with the rest of the text, for example with regard to spelling. It seems better to treat the lists on their own terms. Given the nature of these lists, a translation is not necessary.

(xi) I have attempted to provide notes on everyone named in the text, although in some cases this has proved impossible since I have found nothing more about them. I have not, however, provided such notes for people who appear *only* as witnesses of royal or papal documents, since their appearance bears little or no relationship to the history of the abbey of Abingdon. In general, notes are only provided on the first appearance of a person, place, or subject; this first reference can be located through the index.

(xii) I have exercised considerable caution in offering any precise dates for documents, but have cited the more precise dates offered in other editions of relevant texts. My caution reflects the ways in which my work on this edition has revealed the problems in some previous suggestions of dates; see Introduction, below, p. xxxii n. 98.

(xiii) I have provided cross-references to Vol. i by section of the Introduction (e.g. see Vol. i, Introduction, 'Style'), or by chapter number. The chapter numbers take one of two forms: Bk. i, c. 000, is a reference to the main text, based on MS C; Vol. i, c. B000, is a reference to the appendix based on MS B.

I started to think about editing the *History of Abingdon Abbey* when I was a D.Phil. student in the mid-1980s, and have since accumulated many debts. At OMT, I received great initial encouragement and continuing help from Barbara Harvey. I have been singularly fortunate that her successor, John Blair, brought to my aid an immense knowledge of the local history of the Abingdon region. He, and Michael Lapidge and Diana Greenway, also provided a wide range of editorial and other skills. At St Andrews, Rob Bartlett has read the entire typescript, has struggled with rebarbative Latin, and shared innumerable conversations about Norman and Angevin England. Other colleagues and friends at St Andrews have also provided help: Frances Andrews, Esther Pascua, Simone Macdougall, Julie Kerr, Donald Bullough, Clive Sneddon, and Peter King.

Simon Keynes generously shared unpublished work on the manuscripts and provided me with a printout from microfilm. Susan Kelly was invaluable in lending her work on the Anglo-Saxon charters of Abingdon prior to publication. Tessa Webber aided me with her expertise on manuscripts, Roger Rees with his on Latin, Liesbeth van Houts with hers on historical writing, and David Crouch with his on the aristocracy.

I received financial help from the Rubric translation awards, the British Academy Research leave scheme, and the Neil Ker fund. The staff of the British Library have been immensely helpful. I am also grateful to the Berkshire Record Office and Christ's Hospital, Abingdon.

As work on the volume neared completion, many people made generous and swift responses to my cries for help. They include George Garnett, Richard Sharpe, David Bates, Clive Burgess, Ros Faith, Véronique Gazeau, Judith Everard, Derek Keene, Brian Kemp, Martin Brett, Ann Williams, Tony Hunt, Tim Allen, and Jim Holt. M. F. de Beaurepaire, J. le Maho, and Ch. Maneuvrier gave advice on Norman toponyms, members of the English Department at St Andrews on 'Hildehubel'. Visits to London to see the manuscripts were made possible and pleasurable by my late friend Chris Vaughan and by Vanessa and Paul Brand, the last of whom also checked PRO references for me. My wife and small children put up with these pleasurable absences; this volume is dedicated to Ella, who loves the swings that now occupy part of the abbey site at Abingdon.

J.G.H.H.

St Andrews
Oct. 2001

CONTENTS

LIST OF FIGURES

ABBREVIATED REFERENCES

Abingdon Cartularies	*Two Cartularies of Abingdon Abbey*, ed. C. F. Slade and G. Lambrick (2 vols., Oxford Hist. Soc., New Series xxxii, xxxiii, 1990–2)
Acta of Henry II	*The Acta of Henry II*, ed. J. C. Holt, N. Vincent, *et al.* (forthcoming)
Anglo-Norman Dictionary	*Anglo-Norman Dictionary*, ed. L. W. Stone, W. Rothwell, T. B. W. Reid (7 fascicules, London, 1977–92)
Anglo-Norman Families	L. C. Loyd, *The Origins of Some Anglo-Norman Families*, ed. C. T. Clay and D. C. Douglas (Harleian Soc., ciii, Leeds, 1951)
Annales monastici	*Annales monastici*, ed. H. R. Luard (5 vols., London, 1864–9)
Bates, *Regesta*	*Regesta Regum Anglo-Normannorum: the Acta of William I (1066–1087)*, ed. D. Bates (Oxford, 1998)
Benedictine Kalendars	*English Benedictine Kalendars after A. D. 1100*, ed. F. Wormald (2 vols., Henry Bradshaw Soc., lxxvii, lxxxi, 1939, 1946)
Biddle *et al.*, 'Early history'	M. Biddle, G. Lambrick, and J. N. L. Myres, 'The early history of Abingdon, Berkshire, and its abbey', *Medieval Archaeology*, xii (1968), 26–69
BIHR	*Bulletin of the Institute of Historical Research*
Boarstall Cartulary	*The Boarstall Cartulary*, ed. H. E. Salter and A. H. Cooke (Oxford Hist. Soc., lxxxviii, 1930)
Brett, *English Church*	M. Brett, *The English Church under Henry I* (Oxford, 1975)
C.H.	Christ's Hospital, Abingdon, deeds
Charters of Abingdon Abbey	*Charters of Abingdon Abbey*, ed. S. E. Kelly (2 vols., Oxford for the British Academy, 2000–1)
Chatsworth	Chatsworth cartulary, in *Abingdon Cartularies*, ii
CMA	*Chronicon monasterii de Abingdon*, ed. J. Stevenson (2 vols., London, 1858)
Colne	*Cartularium Prioratus de Colne*, ed. J. L. Fisher (Essex Archaeol. Soc., Occasional Pubns., no. 1, 1946)
Complete Peerage	*Complete Peerage of England, Scotland, Ireland,*

	Great Britain, and the United Kingdom, ed. G. E. C[okayne], rev. V. Gibbs, H. A. Doubleday, *et al.* (12 vols. in 13, London, 1910–59)
DB	*Domesday Book seu Liber censualis Wilhelmi Primi Regis Angliae*, ed. A. Farley and H. Ellis (4 vols., London, i–ii 1783, iii–iv 1816)
DMLBS	*Dictionary of Medieval Latin from British Sources*, ed. R. E. Latham *et al.* (London and Oxford, 1975–)
Douglas, 'Early surveys'	D. C. Douglas, 'Some early surveys from the abbey of Abingdon', *EHR* xliv (1929), 618–25
EHD	*English Historical Documents*, i., *c.* 500–1042, ed. D. Whitelock (2nd edn., London, 1979); ii., 1042–1189, ed. D. C. Douglas and G. W. Greenaway (2nd edn., London, 1981)
EHR	*English Historical Review*
English Lawsuits	*English Lawsuits from William I to Richard I*, ed. R. C. van Caenegem (2 vols., Selden Soc., cvi, cvii, 1990–1)
English Register of Godstow	*The English Register of Godstow Nunnery near Oxford*, ed. A. Clark (Early English Text Society, cxxix, cxxx, cxlii (1905–1911)
EPNS	English Place Names Society
Eynsham	*Eynsham Cartulary*, ed. H. E. Salter (2 vols., Oxford Hist. Soc., xlix, li, 1908–9)
Eyton	R. W. Eyton, *Court, Household and Itinerary of King Henry II* (Dorchester, 1878)
Green, *Government*	J. A. Green, *The Government of England under Henry I* (Cambridge, 1986)
Green, *Sheriffs*	J. A. Green, *English Sheriffs to 1154* (HMSO, 1990)
Harvey, *Living and Dying*	B. Harvey, *Living and Dying in England, 1100–1540* (Oxford, 1993)
Heads of Religious Houses	*The Heads of Religious Houses: England and Wales 940–1216*, ed. D. Knowles, C. N. L. Brooke, and V. C. M. London (Cambridge, 1972)
HKF	W. Farrer, *Honors and Knights' Fees* (3 vols., London, 1923)
Hudson, 'Abbey of Abingdon'	J. G. H. Hudson, 'The abbey of Abingdon, its *Chronicle* and the Norman Conquest', *Anglo-Norman Studies*, xix (1999), 181–202
Hudson, *Land, Law, and Lordship*	J. G. H. Hudson, *Land, Law, and Lordship in Anglo-Norman England* (Oxford, 1994)

John of Worcester, *Chronicle*	John of Worcester, *Chronicle*, ed. R. R. Darlington and P. McGurk (3 vols., OMT, 1995–)
Keats-Rohan, *Domesday People*	K. S. B. Keats-Rohan, *Domesday People* (Woodbridge, 1999)
Lambrick, 'Administration'	G. Lambrick, 'Abingdon Abbey administration', *Journal of Ecclesiastical History*, xvii (1966), 159–83
Lyell	Lyell cartulary, in *Abingdon Cartularies*, ii
NMT	Nelson's Medieval Texts
OMT	Oxford Medieval Texts
Orderic, *Ecclesiastical History*	*The Ecclesiastical History of Orderic Vitalis*, ed. M. Chibnall (6 vols., OMT, 1969–80)
Oseney	*Cartulary of Oseney Abbey*, ed. H. E. Salter (6 vols., Oxford Hist. Soc., lxxxix–xci, xcvii–xcviii, ci, 1929–36)
Oxford Charters	*Facsimiles of Early Charters in Oxford Muniment Rooms*, ed. H. E. Salter (Oxford, 1929)
PL	*Patrologia Latina*
Pollock and Maitland	Sir Frederick Pollock and F. W. Maitland, *The History of English Law before the Time of Edward I* (2nd edn., reissued with a new introduction and select bibliography by S. F. C. Milsom, Cambridge, 1968)
PR	*Pipe Roll*
PRO	Public Record Office
Reading	*Reading Abbey Cartularies*, ed. B. R. Kemp (2 vols., Camden Soc., 4th Ser. xxxi, xxxiii, 1986–7)
Red Book	*Liber Rubeus de Scaccario*, ed. H. Hall (3 vols., London, 1896)
Royal Writs, ed. van Caenegem	*Royal Writs in England from the Conquest to Glanvill*, ed. R. C. van Caenegem (Selden Soc., lxxvii, 1958–9)
RRAN	*Regesta Regum Anglo-Normannorum, 1066–1154*, ed. H. W. C. Davis *et al.* (4 vols., Oxford, 1913–69)
Salter, 'Chronicle roll'	H. E. Salter, 'A chronicle roll of the abbots of Abingdon', *EHR* xxvi (1911), 727–38
Salter, *Medieval Oxford*	H. E. Salter, *Medieval Oxford* (Oxford Hist. Soc., 1936)
Saltman, *Theobald*	A. Saltman, *Theobald, Archbishop of Canterbury* (London, 1956)
Sanders, *Baronies*	I. J. Sanders, *English Baronies: a Study of their Origin and Descent* (Oxford, 1960)

Sawyer	P. H. Sawyer, *Anglo-Saxon Charters: an Annotated List and Bibliography* (London, 1968)
Testa de Nevill	Liber Feudorum*: The Book of Fees commonly called* Testa de Nevill *(1198–1293)* (3 vols., London, 1920–31)
TRE	*Tempore regis Edwardi* (in the time of King Edward)
VCH	*Victoria County History*

INTRODUCTION

THE first surviving version of the *History of the Church of Abingdon* comes to an end before the death of Abbot Walkelin in 1164.[1] It was, therefore, most likely completed in the early 1160s, and exists in a manuscript probably written in that decade.[2] Its main concern, as the text immediately states, is the lands of the church, but the abbots themselves, the church buildings, and its treasures also feature prominently. The present introduction is primarily concerned with the treatment of these matters in the *History*, and does not give a complete account of the development of the monastery and its estates; such is a task for a separate book. However, I do draw on other sources to supplement, reinforce, or modify the picture provided by the *History*.

I. SOURCES

1. Sources for the composition of Book II

The composer of the *History* used both written and oral sources. An obvious characteristic of the *History* is its presentation of a large

[1] I take the title from the opening of Book II in MS C, below, p. 2; for discussion of the title, manuscripts, composition, and style of the work, see Vol. i., Introduction. Some historians have dated to after 1164 writs which are included in the first manuscript (see e.g. *Royal Writs*, ed. van Caenegem, no. 98, dating the writ printed below, p. 306, to 1166), but for no compelling reason; it may well be that assumptions about dates of witnesses' appearances, notably John of Oxford, must be modified. That the *History* does not mention an 1162 dispute concerning King's Mead (below p. 97 n. 236) is probably not a sufficiently significant omission on which to base an argument for completion of the work by 1162, given the sketchy nature of the last years of the *History* .

[2] The first manuscript may even be precisely dateable to between early 1166 and 14 June 1170. The scribe wrote a version of the 1166 Abingdon *Carta* concerning knight service; see below, p. 389. In that text and elsewhere he refers to Henry II as 'Henricus iunior', which would be inappropriate after the coronation of Henry the young king on 14 June 1170; for that date, see A. Heslin, 'The coronation of the Young King in 1170', *Studies in Church History*, ii (1965), 165–78, at p. 165 n. 1. In contrast, the continuations of the *History* in both manuscripts refer to Henry II as 'Henricus secundus'. The *terminus ante quem* for MS C therefore seems secure. As for the *terminus post quem*, it is of course possible that the scribe had completed work on the *History* before 1166, only writing up the *Carta* concerning knight service after 1166. See also Hudson, 'Abbey of Abingdon', p. 184, for comments on the dating of the same scribe's version of the *Chronicle* of John of Worcester.

number of documents.[3] It seems likely that some or all of the documents were stored in a chest (*scrinium*) or chests, and either these or further documents were stored in the church's treasury, probably associated with the sacristy.[4] Such arrangements resemble those at other monasteries,[5] and would also fit a possible connection between the *History*'s composer and the sacristy.[6] That some of the documents transcribed were originals is certain. The sealing of a charter of Richard earl of Chester with his mother's seal is not mentioned in the document but only in the accompanying narrative: the writer had seen the original document with its seal.[7]

Almost all the post-Conquest documents are readily acceptable as authentic. A possible exception may be a charter of Henry I. In its heading it is described as concerning Boymill, but it actually also confirms certain other acquisitions. This could simply be a rather awkwardly drafted document, but may have been interpolated.[8] Other documents may have been abbreviated, either by an earlier copyist or by the composer of the *History*. For example, writs of William II and Henry II end rather abruptly without witnesses.[9]

Various of the documents are described as cirographs. Occasionally this term certainly refers to a bi-partite document, of which each party received half.[10] Elsewhere, this is less certain. It is interesting that a 'cirograph concerning the land of Chesterton' did not specify that the parties were each to take a part of the cirograph but rather one of 'two sealed writs of Henry earl of Warwick, of whose fee Chesterton is.'[11] Generally the word 'cirograph' is used in the

[3] Outside the Abingdon and Colne cartularies, very few of the post-Conquest documents survive in additional versions, the most notable being the original of Eugenius III's bull of 1146, below p. 264, which is preserved in Lambeth Palace Library. See also below pp. 302, 372, for documents of Henry II and Richard I preserved in the *Cartæ antiquæ* rolls. The series of originals preserved at Christ's Hospital, Abingdon, begin in the period 1165–75; see below, pp. 317, 321, 359–67.

[4] See below, pp. 50, 200; see also p. 172

[5] M. T. Clanchy, *From Memory to Written Record* (2nd edn., Oxford, 1993), pp. 156–8.

[6] See Vol. i, Introduction, 'Composer', and below, p. xx, on interest in Richard the sacrist.

[7] See below, p. 102.

[8] See below, p. 154; note also the variants in Lyell, no. 122. Henry I's charter for Colne, below p. 86, is unusual in form but cannot be condemned as a forgery. Henry I's general confirmation of Faritius's acquisitions, below, p. 160, may well have been beneficiary drafted, but need not be suspicious.

[9] See below, pp. 40, 310.

[10] See below, p. 250.

[11] See below, pp. 198–200; the phraseology of this document is occasionally rather clumsy, and has a character of its own, distinct from the *History*'s narrative.

rubricated heading, not in the document itself,[12] and sometimes the transaction is simply referred to in terms of a grant rather than, for example, a *conuentio* or *pactum*.[13] On occasion, indeed, the ensuing account looks simply like a narrative put together at Abingdon, rather than a formal document agreed upon by the parties.[14]

So-called cirographs may therefore merge with another type of pre-existing text, that is, written accounts of grants, disputes, or other incidents.[15] Notes of grants not recorded in charters may have been useful not only for their own sake as records but also in obtaining confirmations.[16] The structure and contents of the notes vary. Some have dates, for example beginning with the regnal year of Henry I, some do not.[17] Some simply record the grant concerned, others also specify witnesses.[18] These can resemble charters, but without the address, and without the grantor speaking in the first person.[19] Many grants of tithe, in particular, were recorded as notes rather than charters, and the appearance of a series of such notes at the end of the account of Faritius's acquisitions raises the possibility that they were preserved together in the abbey's muniments.[20] Such notes may relate in some way to entries in the abbey's 'Book of Commemorations',[21] or

[12] See below, pp. 198, 258; below, p. 250 may be an exception, where the rubricated heading may reproduce the word 'Cirographum' written across the document and then cut.

[13] See below, pp. 36, 258; cf. pp. 24, 258.

[14] See below, p. 36.

[15] See also Clanchy, *Memory to Written Record*, pp. 100–1. See below, p. xxxviii, on notices of miracles.

[16] Note e.g. that the grant recorded below, p. 158, appears in Henry I's confirmation below, p. 162. However, other gifts are mentioned only in later grants, not in specific notes in the *History*: see e.g. the gift of Ælfric of Botley first mentioned in Faritius's endowment of obedientiaries, below, p. 216; the gift of Peter the sheriff, below, p. 216. For the closeness of charters and other types of record, see M. Chibnall, 'Charter and chronicle', *Church and Government in the Middle Ages*, ed. C. N. L. Brooke *et al.* (Cambridge, 1976), pp. 1–17, at 1. On notes, see also *Stoke-by-Clare Cartulary*, ed. C. Harper Bill and R. Mortimer (3 vols., Suffolk Charters, iv–vi, 1982–4), iii. 51–3.

[17] See below, pp. 148, 152, 162, 170; cf. e.g. pp. 156, 158.

[18] e.g. cf. below, pp. 148, 154, 162, with pp. 206–12. It seems highly unlikely that names of witnesses, unless they were written down at the time, could have been remembered up to a century later.

[19] e.g. below, p. 84, which contains information that could not be derived from the royal charter, pp. 82–4.

[20] See below, pp. 206–12.

[21] See below, p. 26. No post-Conquest Abingdon *Liber uitae* survives, but for a pre-Conquest example, see J. Gerchow, *Die Gedenküberlieferung der Angelsachsen* (Berlin, 1988), pp. 245–52, 335–8. It is just possible that the phrase 'liber commemorationum' referred not to a *Liber uitae* but to a text recording donations in a way similar to the *History* itself. An analogy would be the *Liber benefactorum* of Ramsey; see *Chronicon Abbatiæ Rameseiensis*,

may have been placed in the abbey's chests along with items used for delivering seisin or for symbolizing some other transaction.[22]

Entries describing disputes too may reproduce or draw upon earlier texts, like the narrative explicitly headed 'record of the agreement between lord Abbot Vincent and Simon the king's dispenser'.[23] Very occasionally a stylistic trait may suggest the insertion of pre-existing text into the narrative: for example, the phrase 'animo bono' occurs three times in the entries concerning Richard the sacrist, and nowhere else in the *History*. This may suggest a tract in praise of Richard.[24] However, some brief passages of narrative would not have required pre-existing notes.[25] Elsewhere, if there were earlier written texts, they have been re-written, to contain phrases such as 'around that time'; or linking passages such as 'these events took place in the time of lord Abbot Vincent; those which follow, on the other hand, took place in the days of his successor Ingulf'; or more fully, to provide stylistic consistency.[26]

We also know that portions of the *History* drew on the composer's own experience,[27] and on oral tradition and testimony. Of one particularly exacting conflict with William Rufus, the *History* states that 'then the resources of the abbey were almost completely consumed, so that this misfortune is complained of to the present day.'[28] This may reproduce a phrase from a text of the earlier twelfth century, but could equally refer to the writer's own day, two generations after the oppression.[29] In addition, the extensive space devoted to this dispute, involving a knight called Rainbald, may

ed. W. D. Macray (London, 1886), pp. 3–5, and J. Paxton, 'Charter and chronicle in twelfth-century England: the house-histories of the Fenland abbeys', Ph.D. thesis (Harvard, 1999), esp. chs. 1 and 4. It should be noted, however, that the initial title *Liber benefactorum* is preserved in a fourteenth-century manuscript of the Ramsey text, but not a thirteenth-century one. It is more likely that the earl of Chester was referring to a commemoration list rather than a house and estate history.

22 See Clanchy, *Memory to Written Record*, esp. pp. 156–7. The five pennies taken from the miller of Culham and placed in the abbey's chest, below, p. 172, surely required some form of written identification.

23 See below, p. 234.

24 See below, pp. 280, 284, 288. Note, however, that other phraseology in the sections on Richard the sacrist resembles that elsewhere in the *History*: cf. e.g. below, p. 280, for 'filio suo quem heredem habuit', with p. 318 for 'cum filio quem heredem habuit'. Other attempts to establish stylistic peculiarities of certain passages must rest on rather limited evidence; one example may be p. 170, which contains two of Book II's three uses of the word 'maxime' and its only use of 'residere' to refer to a court.

25 See e.g. below, p. 292.

26 See below, pp. 181, 249.

27 See below, p. 60.

28 See below, p. 54.

29 See below, p. 70, for information coming from monks of Faritius's time (1100–17).

reflect not only its importance but also the fact that Rainbald's son became a monk of the abbey and thereby further preserved within the abbey memory of the case.[30]

2. Other sources relating to the abbey of Abingdon

Such were the main sources upon which the composer of the *History* drew. What other evidence concerning the abbey do we have with which to supplement his work?[31] *Domesday Book* provides considerable information concerning Abingdon's estates. Otherwise, sources from beyond Abingdon are of limited help. The abbots make only rare appearances as witnesses in royal or ecclesiastical documents.[32] The Pipe Rolls record various scutages and payments to the king,[33] and royal payments to the abbey.[34] A letter of Lanfranc reveals internal strife in the monastery, one of John of Salisbury mentions a dispute not recorded in the *History*.[35] The most useful additional historical work is William of Malmesbury's *Gesta pontificum*.[36] Archaeology provides some guidance as to the form of the post-Conquest church.[37]

For further help, one has to turn to other written sources from Abingdon itself and its daughter house of Colne.[38] First, a later Abingdon kalendar, preserved in a manuscript dated to the late thirteenth century by Francis Wormald, includes amongst the saints' festivals the days of death of various abbots and priors of the house.[39] Second, there is the *De abbatibus Abbendonie* or, to give it

[30] See below, p. 246.

[31] See below, p. cvi, for the works specifically associated with Faritius.

[32] See below, pp. xliv, xlvi, li, lii.

[33] See *PR 31 HI*, p. 123 ('Abbot Vincent of Abingdon renders account of 70m. of silver concerning the plea(s) of Geoffrey of Clinton. In pardon to the same abbot 70m. of silver since he is dead. And he is quit'); *PR 2–4 HII*, p. 35, *PR 5 HII*, p. 37, *PR 7 HII*, p. 52, *PR 9 HII*, p. 52, *PR 11 HII*, p. 74, *PR 12 HII*, p. 121.

[34] See *PR 8 HII*, p. 44.

[35] *The Letters of Lanfranc Archbishop of Canterbury*, ed. H. Clover and M. Gibson (OMT, 1979), no. 28, below, p. ci; *The Letters of John of Salisbury*, ed. W. J. Millor, H. E. Butler, C. N. L. Brooke (2 vols., NMT, 1955; OMT, 1979), i, no. 63 (1153 × 1161), concerning the church of Nuneham Courtenay.

[36] See below, p. civ.

[37] See below, p. cii. See also Vol. i, Introduction, 'Endowment and estates', for geological and archaeological information relevant to the abbey's estates.

[38] Note also Salter, 'Chronicle roll', 727–38; it is unclear what worth should be attached to the small items of additional information this text provides for the period up to Walkelin.

[39] Cambridge, University Library, Kk. i 22, fos. 1^v–7^r; the kalendar, with comments but without the additional obits, is printed in *Benedictine Kalendars*, i. 15–30.

the heading it bears in the thirteenth-century manuscript, 'Excepciones Simonis de primis fundatoribus Abbendoniæ et de abbatibus Abbendoniæ que etiam bona queve mala fecerunt' ('Simon's extracts concerning the first founders of Abingdon, the abbots of Abingdon, and their good and bad actions'). Beginning 'in principio erat Verbum', it gives a general history of early Britain before dealing with the foundation of Abingdon and the abbots up to the time of Hugh (1189/90–*c.*1221).[40] Its account provides useful extra information, particularly on buildings, and some different perspectives.[41] The existing version may well have ended up at Colne, the daughter house of Abingdon, for it is with the affairs of that priory that a lengthy last chapter deals.[42] The *De abbatibus* is usually regarded as a later source than the *History*. The surviving version contains references forward in time, showing that the entries concerned were written or re-written well after the events described: thus the section on Abbot Æthelwold (*c.*954–963) contains references to the Norman Conquest, Abbot Vincent, and the reign of Stephen.[43] Likewise, the Latin definitions of sake and soke and toll and team and infangentheof, included in the section on the Confessor, are probably also later additions.[44]

However, the very idea of the *De abbatibus* as a 'later' source than the *History* may be flawed. The last chapter is rather distinct from the preceding ones, even in its presentation in the manuscript, and may be a Colne addition.[45] It in fact seems likely that what we have is an extended version of a text which once stopped with Ingulf's abbacy (1130–58), that is, earlier than the *History*. His death is contained in a section headed 'Concerning the abbots after Ingulf', which goes on to give only very brief and generally critical mentions of his successors before Abbot Hugh.[46] Notably, the *De abbatibus* presents Abbot

[40] London, British Library, Cotton Vitellius A. XIII, fos. 2[r] (the contents page, which gives the title ending 'fecerint'), 83[r] (where the writing is extremely hard to decipher). Stevenson did not include in his edition (*CMA* ii. 268–95) the general history prior to the foundation of Abingdon; see London, British Library, Cotton Vitellius A. XIII, fos. 83[r]–84[r].

[41] See below, pp. xli, xlvii, li, liii, for additional material and different perspectives.

[42] *CMA* ii. 294–5.

[43] *CMA* ii. 278. The reference to 'today' at *CMA* ii. 284 does not help date the text with any precision.

[44] *CMA* ii. 282.

[45] Notably, it uses frequent, and roughly alternating, red and green initials, unlike the rest of the text.

[46] *CMA* ii. 292–3. It may also be significant that it is stated that the boy who had a vision concerning Faritius's succession lived until the time of Abbot Ingulf; there is even a slight possibility that the phrase replaced one stating that the boy lived 'to this day'; *CMA* ii. 286, and below, p. xlv.

Ingulf in a good light, harmed by the activities of some of his monks; the *History* presents the reverse image, of the convent harmed by its abbot.[47] If a version of the *De abbatibus* was completed during his abbacy, it is very interesting that in the 1150s and 1160s we have two historians operating in Abingdon, one taking the convent's view of Ingulf's time, the other the abbot's.

Next, there is a variety of lists or surveys relating to the abbey's estates and tenants. None of these can be dated with absolute certainty, and none can be identified with a survey mentioned in the *History* in its entry 'Concerning the death of Lord Abbot Faritius, of holy memory': 'Shortly after his death, all the possessions and rents of this church were listed; £300 a year were designated to the royal treasury, and the rest granted to the uses of the church.'[48]

Some of the surveys are related to *Domesday Book*:

(i) MS C fo. 182^r, in a hand of the end of the twelfth century at the earliest, gives a list of Berkshire hidages coinciding generally but not always with those in *Domesday Book* for 1086. Printed by Stevenson, *CMA* ii. 309–10.

(ii) MS C fo. 187^v, in the same hand as the *History*, provides for Berkshire a list of hidages, headed 'Concerning the hundreds and hides of the church of Abingdon in Berkshire, as the writing of the king's treasury contains them, arranged by each hundred'. Whilst the hidages coincide with those for the time of King Edward in *Domesday Book*, it should also be noted that there is some evidence for these figures rather than those for 1086 continuing to be used with reference to Berkshire lands, or for payment having to be made for the use of the reduced 1086 figure. Printed below, App. III, pp. 379–80; also by Douglas, 'Early surveys', 623.[49]

47 See below, p. liii.

48 See below, p. 224.

49 S. P. J. Harvey, 'Domesday Book and its predecessors', *EHR* lxxxvi (1971), 753–73, at pp. 159–60, and F. F. Kreisler, 'Domesday Book and the Anglo-Norman synthesis', *Order and Innovation in the Middle Ages*, ed. W. C. Jordan *et al.* (Princeton, 1976), pp. 3–16, at 13–14, suggest that this may be based on a pre-Domesday geld list. The point cannot be proved or disproved; overall I find Kreisler's analysis of the Abingdon surveys unpersuasive. On later use of *TRE* figures, see *VCH*, *Berkshire*, i. 287, 296; Douglas, 'Early surveys', p. 621 n. 7; D. Roffe, *Domesday: the Inquest and the Book* (Oxford, 2000), pp. 109–11, 140, 172, who suggests that this text appears to be an extract of a hundredally arranged document produced as part of the Domesday process.

(iii) MS C fos. 187^{v}–189^{r}, again in the same hand as the *History*, provides an abbreviated form of *Domesday*, with hidages for the time of King Edward and 1086, for all the counties in which Abingdon held lands. Printed below, App. III, pp. 380–6.

This list is headed 'Also, in the other book of the king's treasury in the time of King William who acquired England, written by his order, is contained an abbreviation of hides and a description, as follows'. The greater detail than in the list at fo. 187^{v} suggests that fos. 187^{v}–189^{r} drew directly upon *Domesday Book*.[50] On the other hand, the Abingdon text states to which hundred lands belonged, even in the case of Oxfordshire for which *Domesday Book* does not provide hundreds. It seems most probable that *Great Domesday* itself is the 'book in the king's treasury' to which the heading refers, and that hundred names were added. The list also includes two gifts of land in Oxfordshire, both made during the abbacy of Faritius.[51]

(iv) MS C fo. 191^{r}, again in the same hand, gives another list of Berkshire hidages, some relating to the figure for the time of King Edward, some to 1086, and some not based on *Domesday*, either because the place is not named in *Domesday*—as in the case of Abingdon—, or because it relates to a post-*Domesday* gift.[52] Printed below, App. III, pp. 391–2.

Other lists, in addition to hidages, contain names of tenants which identify them as twelfth-century texts:

(v) In the same hand, at fos. 189^{v}–190^{r}, comes a list which gives hidages of estates and names of tenants within those estates, together with hidages of their holdings. This list is headed 'Those who hold lands of this church of Abingdon.' Most but not all the hidages correspond to those for the 'the time of King Edward' in *Domesday*. Printed below, App. III, pp. 386–9; also by Douglas, 'Early surveys', 623–5.

(vi) Again in the same hand, on fo. 191^{r} following the list of Berkshire hidages, is a list of tenants and the hidages, but only very occasionally the names, of their holdings. Printed below, App. III, pp. 392–4.

[50] This is the conclusion of Roffe, *Domesday*, p. 111. It also appears to be the conclusion of S. P. J. Harvey, 'Domesday Book and Anglo-Norman governance', *TRHS*, 5th. Ser. xxv (1975), 175–93, at p. 176. She does not comment on the presence of Oxfordshire hundred names, although at p. 179 she takes reference to the presence of such names in a 'Book of the Treasury' to indicate that the book concerned cannot be Domesday; see further, below, p. 170.

[51] The gifts mentioned below, pp. 78, 106, 158.

[52] e.g. Chaddleworth, below, p. 248.

The two lists of tenants have many names in common. Some of those named were already active in the time of Faritius, 1100–17, whilst a few others also appear in the *Cartae baronum* of 1166. Both lists are probably from after 1121, since Hugh son of Berner appears in both, and his father was still alive in 1121.[53] They pre-date the mid-1140s, when William de Pont de l'Arche, mentioned in both lists, ceases to appear in royal documents, quite probably because of his death.[54] There are slight hints that the second of the lists may be the later. For example the first list mentions a Roger Grim, the second a William Grim, a name which also appears in the Abingdon *Carta* of 1166.[55] However, it cannot be certain that the two Williams were the same man.

There are also later lists of knights:

(vii) MS C fo. 190^{r-v}, in the same hand as the *History*, preserves a version of the 1166 Abingdon *Carta* somewhat different from that preserved in the Exchequer records. Notably, it specifies the fractions of knights' fees owed by those whom the Exchequer versions simply list as together owing one and a half knights.[56] The Exchequer, but not the Abingdon, version mentions that Humphrey de Bohun had taken away two hides of the abbey's lands. This dispute is not mentioned in the *History*, and may have been very recent in 1166. Printed below, App. III, pp. 389–91.

(viii) From slightly later comes a list preserved only in MS B, which records those holding 'very small portions which pertain to the chamber of the Lord Abbot.' Assuming that the names are consistent with a specific date, it is notable that many also appear in the *Carta*. However, whereas the *Carta* mentions William Grim, this list mentions his daughters, suggesting a date after 1166. Printed below, App. I, pp. 324–7; also by Stevenson, *CMA* ii. 5–6.

These entries relating to lands pertaining to the abbot's chamber have sometimes been taken to be part of the following list:

(ix) A list headed 'these are the knights holding from Abingdon', which also appears only in MS B. This has sometimes been referred

[53] Below, p. 236. Rainbald, father of John of Tubney, may still have been alive in Abbot Vincent's time, whereas it is John who appears in the second list.
[54] *RRAN* iii, p. xix.
[55] Below, p. 391.
[56] Below, pp. 390–1; *Red Book*, i. 305–6.

to as 'Abbot Adelelm's list of knights', but it in fact must be a list of mixed date; there are some *Domesday* tenants, some who appear in the 1166 *Carta*, and some probably of an even later date.[57] Printed below, App. I, pp. 322–5; by Stevenson, *CMA* ii. 4–5.

(x) In MS C, fo. 182r, in a later hand, a list headed 'The names of knights holding from Abingdon', giving names, places, and hidages. John of St Helen is the only name which also appears in the *Carta*. Others appear to be sons of 1166 tenants, for example Henry son of Pain. Printed by Stevenson, *CMA* ii. 311–12.

Other surveys are of a rather different sort, concerning specific renders or allowances of officials. Stevenson printed some of those in MS C in his appendix III, entitled *De consuetudinibus Abbendoniæ*. However, he did not attempt to date them, nor to date the hands in which they were written, nor even to indicate which were written in the same hand as the *History*.

(xi) The following sections are written in that hand, and can therefore be safely taken to have existed in *c.*1170, although their date of origin cannot be established.[58] They are all contained in MS C, fos. 191v–192v, and are printed below, App. III, pp. 394–8.

'De consuetudinibus lignandi' (*CMA* ii. 321–2);
'De coquina monachorum' (*CMA* ii. 322–4, to 'pro panibus suis');
'De redditu altaris' (*CMA* ii. 324–5);
'De redditu camere' (*CMA* ii. 326–7, to 'quantum opus fuerit').

(xii) Other lists in MS C, fos. 179r–182r, which are probably in late twelfth-century hands, follow an account of the vacancy of 1185.[59] Printed by Stevenson, *CMA* ii. 299–309.

(xiii) MS B also preserves the record produced by an enquiry during the vacancy of 1185 concerning the allowances of the monastery's servants. Printed below, App. II, pp. 358–69. Also by Stevenson, *CMA* ii. 237–43.[60]

(xiv) In MS B, the *History* is followed by the tract *De obedientiariis*,

[57] Herbert son of Herbert and Raerus de *Aure* are examples of 1166 tenants, *Red Book*, i. 305–6. For fuller analysis, see Hudson, 'Abbey of Abingdon', pp. 193–4.

[58] Note that the appearance of the lands of Scalegrai and Roger Haliman suggest a date late in Ingulf's abbacy or after; below, pp. 286–8.

[59] The account of the vacancy is printed in *CMA* ii. 297–9, and translated as *English Lawsuits*, no. 570; see also below, p. 358.

[60] On the use of Old French vocabulary in this text, see Vol. i, Introduction, 'Style'. For the servants mentioned in the list, see further Lambrick, 'Administration', pp. 169–70.

concerning the duties of the monastic officials. Printed by Stevenson, *CMA* ii. 336–417.[61]

Finally there are the Colne cartulary and the two Abingdon cartularies, MSS Oxford, Bodleian Lyell 15, and Chatsworth 71 E.[62] The best version of the Colne cartulary comes from the end of the twelfth century, with a few later additions.[63] It contains some charters phrased as grants to Abingdon, but which do not appear in the Abingdon sources; these documents must have been taken to Colne, or, perhaps, produced there.[64]

MS Lyell 15 dates from the mid-fourteenth century.[65] It is made up of six *particulae* spread over 209 folios. The first five *particulae* are in a bookhand, or more than one, very similar, bookhands. The five contain, in order: papal bulls and privileges; royal writs, charters, and letters patent; episcopal deeds; grants by the abbot and convent to private individuals, or by the abbot to the convent; grants by individuals to the abbey. Only in this last and largest section are grants arranged by the office or 'obedience' to which they refer. The later sixth *particula* was originally a separate volume. It is mostly in fourteenth-century hands, with some later additions, and concerns litigation.

The Chatsworth manuscript consists of 167 folios in various late fourteenth- and early fifteenth-century hands.[66] It includes more than 300 documents, over one-third of which are also in the Lyell

[61] This may date from the end of the twelfth or the beginning of the thirteenth century. It has been noted, for example, that it uses the term *dapifer* for the steward, whereas documents from 1219 consistently use the term *senescallus*, as do some from the earlier thirteenth century; Lambrick, 'Administration', p. 167 n. 7.

[62] On documents appearing in the Abingdon cartularies but not the *History*, see below p. xxxviii.

[63] *Colne*, pp. iv–v; G. R. C. Davies, *Medieval Cartularies of Great Britain* (London, 1958), p. 271.

[64] e.g. *Colne*, no. 64, Hubert de Montchesney's grant of the church of Edwardstone to Abingdon; also nos. 4 (= *RRAN* iii, no. 14), 11 (= Saltman, *Theobald*, no. 79), which are charters of Stephen and Archbishop Theobald concerning Kensington church. For *Colne*, no. 9, being an extremely suspicious document, see below, p. 86. Note that Henry I's charter concerning the church of Kensington, below, p. 82, appears both in the Colne cartulary and the Abingdon *History*, whilst Henry's charter concerning the church of Edwardstone—which might be considered relevant to Colne—does not appear in this cartulary but is included in the *History*; below, pp. 92, 226; note also London, British Library, Cotton Vespasian B. xv (s. xvi), fo. 59^{r}, a transcript of a register of Colne.

[65] For the following discussion, see *Abingdon Cartularies*, i, pp. xxxviii–xlii.

[66] *Abingdon Cartularies*, i, pp. xlv–vi

cartulary. There has been an attempt to arrange the documents, placing papal and episcopal instructions first, followed by other ecclesiastical subjects. Such a plan lasts until fo. 58^{r}; from fo. 61^{r} the arrangement is by 'obedience'. It seems plausible that the Chatsworth cartulary was produced by a convent official, whereas the Lyell manuscript was for the joint use of abbot and monks.

3. Omissions from the *History*'s account.

These supplementary sources reveal that the *History* is not exhaustive in its coverage.[67] Certain incidents involving royalty are omitted. Eadmer's *Historia nouorum* has Henry I at Abingdon on 13 Mar. 1121 for the consecration of Robert bishop of Chester/Coventry. It is strange that the *History* does not mention this, especially if—as seems possible—it was also the occasion for the formal election of Vincent as abbot.[68] Henry was also at Abingdon on at least one other occasion in his reign, as a writ for the abbey concerning toll has Abingdon as the place date.[69] Nor is the Empress Matilda's escape on foot from Oxford to Abingdon in December 1142 mentioned.[70]

This last incident might be omitted as not relevant to the *History*'s main concern, the abbey's lands. However, in this area too there are omissions.[71] As already mentioned, a few documents referring to Abingdon appear in the *Colne* cartulary, but not in the *History*.[72] Likewise the Abingdon cartularies supply some additional documents. These include writs of Henry I, William his son, Stephen, and Henry II,[73] as well as non-royal grants to the church.[74] Only in

[67] See above, p. xxi, on judicial payments and scutages; p. xxv on a dispute with Humphrey de Bohun; p. xxi on a dispute concerning Nuneham Courtenay. Note also below, p. 332, on a dispute concerning the monks' food allowances during the time of Faritius, and the related visit of Ralph archbishop of Canterbury, Roger bishop of Salisbury, and Hugh of Buckland to Abingdon.

[68] Eadmer, *Historia nouorum in Anglia*, ed. M. Rule (London, 1884), p. 293; see also John of Worcester, *Chronicle*, iii. 150.

[69] See below, p. 116. On dating, see below, p. xxxii.

[70] William of Malmesbury, *Historia novella*, bk. iii, c. 79, ed. E. King, tr. K. R. Potter (OMT, 1998), p. 132. See below, p. lii, for Ingulf's presence at the Empress's reception as Lady of England in Mar. 1141.

[71] e.g. some gifts in Wallingford may not be recorded in the *History*, beyond those of Roger Haliman and Æilwin mentioned below, pp. 288–90; see *Testa de Nevill*, i. 110. Some of the writs of Henry I suggest otherwise unrecorded disputes; see e.g. below, p. 120.

[72] See above, p. xxvii; also below, p. xxxix, for writs of Stephen and Henry II included only in MS B.

[73] See Lyell, no. 111, Chatsworth, no. 210 (Henry I's confirmation of the gift of Shippon and Wormsley); Lyell, no. 97 (Henry I's writ concerning freedom from toll; the

[*See opposite page for n. 73 cont. and n. 74*]

one instance is there a problem with the document which may suggest that it was a forgery, perhaps not in existence at the time of the composition of the *History*. A charter of Ralph Basset concerning his grant of Chaddleworth is associated in the *History* with Ralph's death in at the end of the 1120s or early in 1130.[75] It is witnessed by William Basset, abbot of Holme, who held his abbacy between 1127 and 1134.[76] However, it is also witnessed by Hugh of Buckland, and the Hugh who features so prominently in the *History* was probably dead by the 1120s.[77] It is possible, of course, that the witness was another Hugh, but it is particularly curious that the *History* does not include this document. Other omissions seem not to reflect the nature of the documents or the choices of the composer of the *History*. Rather they may reflect the lack of earlier organization in the preservation of documents.

We also know that there were once further documents which were important to the abbey but which do not appear in the *History* and have not survived. Both Eugenius III's statement in his confirmation bull that he was 'following closely in the footsteps of our predecessor of happy memory, Pope Innocent' and another mention of the 'renewal' of the papal privilege suggest that we are missing at least one papal bull.[78] Less surprisingly, the *History* does not contain copies of letters which it mentions as brought by the abbey's opponents.[79]

editors' doubts concerning authenticity seem unnecessary); Chatsworth, no. 319 (William son of Henry I's writ concerning Colnbrook); Chatsworth, no. 347 (Henry II's writ concerning freedom from toll, which can only be dated to before 1172/3, on the basis of the absence of the phrase 'Dei gratia' from the royal title); Lyell, no. 121 (Henry II's writ in favour of Abbot Walkelin and the abbey concerning Kensington church etc.). Chatsworth, no. 100 (concerning the church of Sutton) probably dates from after the completion of the *History*; so too may Lyell, no. 108, Chatsworth, no. 299 (concerning Benham), although the absence of 'Dei gratia' from the royal title renders questionable the editors' dating to ? May 1175; the editors of *Acta of Henry II* date the writ to May 1165 × May 1172.

[74] See e.g. Lyell, no. 245 for a further confirmation of the d'Aubigny grant of Stratton and Holme; Lyell, no. 341, Chatsworth, no. 385 concerning Benson mill (on which see below, p. lxxxvi); Lyell, no. 162, Chatsworth, no. 322 (= *English Episcopal Acta*, xviii. *Salisbury 1078–1217*, ed. B. R. Kemp (Oxford, 1999), no. 42) can only be dated 1142 × 1184. See below, p. cvi, on Chatsworth, no. 212.

[75] Lyell, no. 247, Chatsworth, no. 294. For the grant and Ralph's death, see below, p. 248.

[76] *Heads of Religious Houses*, p. 68.

[77] He last witnessed a royal charter in 1115; *RRAN* ii, no. 1102.

[78] See below, pp. 256, 272.

[79] See below, e.g. pp. 37, 238.

II. STRUCTURE

1. MS C

Abbacies and structure

In terms of words, the amount of space devoted to each abbacy varies considerably:

Abbot	*length of abbacy*[80]	*approx. proportion of words*[81]
Adelelm (1071–83)	*c.*12 years	4%
Reginald (1084–97)	*c.*12½ years	12.5%
Faritius (1100–17)	*c.*16 years	50%
Vincent (1121–30)	*c.*9 years	9%[82]
Ingulf (1130–58)	*c.*28 years	14%
Walkelin (1159–64)	*c.*5 years[83]	7.5%

The remainder—about 2.5%—is accounted for by vacancies. Thus Book II is dominated by Faritius's abbacy, which only lasted for between sixteen and seventeen of the ninety or so years covered. It is also interesting to note that, even aside from the special attention paid to Faritius, the coverage does not increase as the time of composition approaches. The proportion devoted to Ingulf compared with other abbots is explicable in terms of the length of his abbacy, not the thoroughness of the account. Indeed, the later stages of the *History* often involve abrupt transitions between entries, with no attempt to explain connections or development.[84] Such a decline in coherence or

[80] These figures are approximate, and indicate completed years; e.g. Faritius died in the seventeenth year of his abbacy, Vincent in the tenth.

[81] These figures are calculated for the sections bounded by an abbot's installation and his death. Note that, particularly in the case of Vincent, these bounds contain much material not dating from his abbacy; see following note.

[82] Note that approximately one third of this material concerns events outside Vincent's abbacy.

[83] The earlier surviving version of the *History* was completed before his death.

[*See opposite page for n. 84*]

structure is not unique in twelfth-century historical works, William of Malmesbury's *Gesta regum* being another example.

The basic structure of Book II is based upon abbacies, with some cross-referencing from one abbacy to another.[85] However, there are exceptions, with some of the incidents which are described extending beyond one abbacy; such are particularly striking in the sections primarily devoted to Reginald and to Vincent.[86] The structuring of the sections devoted to each abbacy varies, but there are also some consistencies. For example, the sections on Faritius, Vincent, and Ingulf each end with a description of their endowment of the offices of the abbey.

The treatment of Adelelm is basically chronological. Internal affairs are quite frequently mixed with national politics, in a way that does not occur in accounts of later abbacies. The arrangement of the account of Reginald's abbacy too is certainly chronological in its early stages, for it includes reference to abbatial or regnal years.[87] Thereafter, the chronology is less certain, but when dates can be suggested for events, such as the fall of the knight Rainbald, they are not incompatible with a predominantly chronological structure.[88] Three qualifications, however, must be made. First, some entries continue the narrative of incidents beyond Reginald's death, into the time of his successor Faritius.[89] Secondly, a group of grants of tithes are gathered together, suggesting thematic rather than, or in conjunction with, chronological arrangement,[90] and elsewhere similar incidents seem to be placed together.[91] Thirdly, mention of the abbot's favour to his son and William II's initial love of Reginald and his subsequent turning against him are placed just before the abbot's death.

The lengthy part of Book II devoted to Faritius is arranged very differently, and is not chronological. It opens very emphatically, and

[84] See below, p. xxxiv. On the general background to monastic estate histories, see Vol. i, Introduction, 'Structure'.

[85] See below, pp. 78, 308, for cross-reference to events mentioned 'among the deeds (*in gestis*)' of another abbot. Note also how in MS C Faritius's coming to the abbacy is marked by a picture of him in the initial of the relevant section, below, p. 64, whereas there is nothing unusual about the presentation of the section recording the accession of Henry I, below, p. 62; cf. below, p. lxvi, on illustrations of kings in MS B.

[86] See below, and p. xxxiii.

[87] To below, p. 24.

[88] See below, p. 54.

[89] See below, pp. 42, 44, 54 and, I would argue, p. 58 (on which see below, p. 59).

[90] See below, pp. 44–8.

[91] e.g. below, pp. 42–4, 52–8.

immediately provides a character sketch.[92] It then moves on to relics, a subject to which it returns at the end of Faritius's abbacy.[93] Following further discussion of his reforms and conduct, it states that it will turn to Faritius's external accomplishments, dividing these between new acquisitions and resumptions of lost lands.

The basis for the order of the entries recording new acquisitions is unclear, being neither chronological nor obviously geographical. Nor do the acquisitions appear in the same order as in Henry I's confirmation charter. Further, the distinction between acquisitions and resumptions is not maintained. Amongst the entries devoted to new gifts appears a charter of Nigel d'Oilly, recording his 'giving back' to Abingdon the land of *Abbefeld*.[94] Moreover, this is followed by a collection of writs of Henry I, concerned with a wide variety of subjects and not just acquisitions. Again, they are not arranged chronologically. There are some logical sub-groups, for example concerning tolls,[95] but also some strange sequences, for example a writ concerning Fernham dividing two concerning Stanton Harcourt.[96] I have yet to find any general logic to the overall organization of this mini-cartulary, nor any explanation as to why there is a shift to a succession of documents without commentary, nor why certain other writs of Henry in favour of Faritius appear after this collection.[97] One possibility is that the composer was indeed copying out a mini-cartulary which included some but not all of the writs of Henry I in favour of Faritius.[98]

Treatment of acquisitions then resumes, and there may be a limited effort at chronological arrangement, at least amongst those grants which are dated.[99] Other entries are linked by place, for example various entries on Dumbleton.[100] The treatment of acquisi-

[92] See below, p. 64.

[93] See below, pp. 66, 220–4.

[94] See below, p. 110, also p. 163 n. 405; note also below, p. 78 n. 185.

[95] See below, pp. 116–18, although note also p. 130; for another sub-group, see pp. 120–2 on fugitives.

[96] See below, p. 124.

[97] The dating of e.g. below, p. 164, to 1100 × 1107 rules out the possibility that it was the later writs for Faritius which appeared in later sections.

[98] All the writs could be of Faritius's time. There is no reason to follow *RRAN* ii, no. 1258 in dating the writ below, p. 116, to 1121. Certainly Henry was at Abingdon then, but this is only known from a reference in Eadmer, copied by John of Worcester, above, p. xxviii; he may well have paid other, unrecorded visits to Abingdon. Likewise, *RRAN* ii. no. 1510 gives no convincing reason for tentatively dating to 1127 the document below, p. 118.

[99] However, the document below, pp. 102–4, is dated and is earlier than some preceding sections. See also below, p. 154.

[100] See below, pp. 148–54.

tions draws to a close with the 'Charter of King Henry concerning various things which Abbot Faritius acquired', probably issued in 1115, followed by further entries concerning possessions not mentioned in that charter.

There follow disputes concerning various rights of the church other than rights to land. These include a modified treatment of disputes over the churches of Kingston and Peasemore, disputes already discussed in the section devoted to Abbot Reginald.[101] Another acquisition is then mentioned,[102] before the treatment of resumptions begins in earnest. Again there are some sub-groups, for example one of quitclaims of previous unjust alienations from the church,[103] two of disputes with those who had refused homage and service.[104] However, as even the division of the cases concerning homage and service shows, organization was not very tight. A series of exchanges intrudes before a couple more disputes, themselves separated by what seems to be a new gift.[105] There follow a series of entries on acquisition of tithes,[106] before the treatment of Faritius closes with his endowment of church offices, his enquiry into relics, and his death.[107]

The subsequent vacancy is dealt with in strictly chronological fashion, each entry beginning with the date according to the year after Faritius's death. This method is not continued under Vincent. Certainly the account of his time begins with his appointment, but it continues with a series of royal writs which are not in chronological order. Thereafter, the abbacy-by-abbacy structure breaks down to a greater extent than it had even under Reginald. Rather, two disputes, with the king's dispensers and with the Bassets, are dealt with at considerable length and over a period stretching into the reign of Henry II.[108] Conceivably the composer of our version of the *History* slotted later events into an existing account of Vincent's abbacy; more likely he at this stage decided upon the advantages of a case-by-case approach for matters still of recent concern in the 1160s.[109] As with

[101] See below, pp. 176–8, cf. pp. 42–4.
[102] Below, p. 180.
[103] Below, pp. 190–2.
[104] Below, pp. 182–8, 194–8.
[105] Below, pp. 198–202, 204–6.
[106] Below, pp. 206–12.
[107] Below, pp. 214–24.
[108] Below, pp. 234–44, concerning the dispensers; pp. 246–50, concerning the Bassets; pp. 244–6 are brief chapters concerning minor grants and men entering the monastery. See also below, p. xxxviii, on MS B.
[109] Some awkwardness remains. Below, p. 253, begins 'So' and flows more naturally from pp. 244–6 than pp. 246–50; however, it is not the insertion of the *later* material which interrupts the flow, but rather the entire Basset dispute. The link between the sections at p. 246 seems to be that both concern men wishing to take the habit.

Faritius, the section on Vincent's abbacy closes with his endowment of the offices of the monks and finally with his death.[110]

Ingulf's abbacy may well see a return to a basically chronological approach, although the lack of dated entries renders this uncertain. It begins with a brief character sketch and the writ of his appointment.[111] There follows treatment of three matters whose relationship seems random, unless they all occurred before Stephen's accession.[112] Next comes the accession of Stephen, and writs he issued—writs mostly rather more general in concern than those of Henry I.[113] These are followed by two lengthy bulls of Eugenius III.[114] A third, shorter bull is concerned with oppression of the church, and there logically follow a series of incidents relating to losses during Stephen's reign. These losses were reversed by the activities of Richard the sacrist, whose further acquisitions and dealings within the church follow in what amounts to a tract in his praise.[115] In particular, he is implicitly contrasted with the weak and indeed the devious abbot, for the *History* proceeds in a considerably more critical tone concerning Ingulf's unjust alienations of abbey lands.[116] The account of King Stephen seizing money from the church, and the loss of church treasure, may also be a veiled criticism of Ingulf.[117] The critical tone ends with mention of the death of Stephen and the accession of Henry II. There follow, with no linking passage, two documents, lacking any lengthy narrative explanation.[118] They are undated but their positioning strongly suggests that they come from Henry II's reign. The treatment of Ingulf ends with his testament and his death: again, the endowment of the offices of the church features prominently.[119]

The treatment of Walkelin begins with his appointment, followed by a series of royal writs.[120] Any reasons for the ordering of the dispute narratives which follow are unclear. The narratives, particularly that concerning the dispute over Abingdon market, are lengthy, reflecting the composer and his fellow monks' personal knowledge of them.[121] However, this closeness of knowledge does not always lead to

[110] Below, pp. 252–4.
[111] Below, p. 254.
[112] Below, pp. 254–60.
[113] Below, pp. 260–4.
[114] Below, pp. 264–78.
[115] See below, p. cvi, on the festival of the relics; above, p. xx, on vocabulary.
[116] Below, pp. 280–90, 290–4.
[117] Below, p. 292; see also below, p. liii.
[118] Below, pp. 294–6.
[119] Below, pp. 296–8.
[120] Below, pp. 296–306; a brief section of narrative, p. 306, separates the king's writs from the queen's sole one.
[121] Below, p. 308.

clarity, and much is vague, for example in the late entry 'Concerning a certain Richard.'[122] It may even be that there was a deliberate vagueness, to avoid explicit criticism of those still alive.[123] No mention is made of Walkelin's death, strong evidence that this version of the *History* was composed before he died.[124]

Overall, then, there is some limited consistency in the order of entries within abbacies. They start, logically, with the appointment of the abbot, and from the time of Faritius, with a character sketch. Again from Faritius's time, an entry relating to the endowment of the obedientiaries is included shortly before the abbot's death. There are also signs of attempts to gather similar matters in groups, most clearly Faritius's acquisitions, but also, for example, grants of tithes or of houses.[125] More striking, though, is the lack of careful arrangement of entries into groups, and the lack of explanatory links between entries.[126] However, only in the instances of the disputes involving land at Sparsholt and churches at Peasemore and Kingston Bagpuize does the composer's arrangement of material break down to such an extent that matters are repeated.[127]

Documents and narrative

The proportion of the text made up of documents varies between abbacies:

Abbacy[128]	*Proportion documents*[129]
Adelelm	slightly over 10%
Reginald	slightly under 20%, just under half of which is the entry entitled 'Cirograph concerning the church of Sutton', discussed above[130]
Faritius	40%

[122] Below, p. 316. [123] See e.g. below, pp. lv, 318.

[124] Nor does the *History* include a charter of Walkelin which mentions arrangements for his anniversary; Chatsworth, no. 212, on which see also below, p. cvi.

[125] e.g. below, pp. 206–12.

[126] See also above, p. xxxii, and below, p. xxxvi. The rubricated headings sometimes conceal continuity from one section to another: e.g. below, pp. 196, 238.

[127] Below, pp. 42–4, 52, 176–8, 182.

[128] Again, these figures are calculated for the sections bounded by an abbot's installation and his death; see above, nn. 81, 82, for matters concerning other abbacies being included within these bounds.

[129] Again these figures are approximate, hence my use of rounded percentages.

[130] See above, p. xix.

Abbacy	*Proportion documents*
Vincent[131]	slightly over 15% charters; another 20% of entries described in the rubricated headings as agreements or cirographs
Ingulf	slightly over 50%, with 30% being taken up by papal documents, almost 25% by other charters, cirographs, and the abbot's testament
Walkelin	slightly below 50%

The style of many documents, for example royal writs, is distinct from that of the narrative entries. Occasionally, though, one can see verbal influence from document to narrative.[132] The land which Aubrey de Ver gave with the church of Kensington is distinctively described both in Henry I's charter and in the *History*'s narrative as 'two hides of 240 acres'. Narrative could also be used to correct or improve the impression given by a document. Henry's confirmation of the church of Kensington is followed by the statement that 'it should be noted moreover that in these royal letters mention of one virgate is missing. This is so because when this document was drawn up, that grant had not yet been bestowed. But not long after it was strengthened by those same people by whom the above things were paid out, and by royal attestation.'[133]

Frequently the narrative and documentation are skilfully linked, but this is not always the case. In some instances narrative is followed by the relevant document or vice versa, in others the document is integrated into the appropriate narrative.[134] In other instances, in particular the gathering of Henry I's writs, documents are separated from the related narrative, the latter making no mention of the former.[135] In another case, an incident of 1113 × 1114 is followed by a writ 'concerning this land' which comes from before 1107. Whilst no explicit link was made between narrative and document, the arrangement suggests that the composer of the *History* mistakenly believed there was one.[136]

We also have documents for which there is no relevant narrative. This is particularly true of writs within the collection of Henry I documents. For example, we know no more than the writs tell us of a

131 See above, n. 82.
132 See also above, p. xviii, concerning cirographs.
133 Below, pp. 82–4.
134 e.g. respectively below, pp. 10–12, 2–4, 310.
135 Below, pp. 134, 136, 188.
136 Below, pp. 152, 154.

dispute with the men of *Welegrave* or of one between Faritius and the knights of the church over castle-guard service at Windsor.[137] It may be that the composer and his contemporaries in the 1160s could not remember the context of such writs, and lacked further written memorials of them. Certainly the proportion of unexplained royal writs on specific matters is smaller in the later pages of the *History*. However, lack of memory of events cannot explain the absence of explanation of the oppressions mentioned in the third of Pope Eugenius's bulls, nor the lack of context given for certain private charters dating from the later abbacies. Perhaps memory was sufficiently strong to remove the immediate need for clarification through narrative, but such an explanation fits ill with the composer's awareness of his need to preserve knowledge in writing for the benefit of future generations.

2. MS B: Variations and Continuations

MS B was written by a scribe working probably in the second quarter or perhaps in the middle of the thirteenth century. The date of composition of its final sections, and their relationship to the manuscript tradition, is problematic. The version of the *History* ends with Richard I's charter of 1190. Richard, it is reported, was feared by kings both pagan and Christian, indicating that the passage was written after his Crusade. Moreover, he is referred to in the past tense, suggesting that it was written after his death. It is possible, therefore, that MS B is a slightly up-dated copy of an intervening manuscript, written soon after 1190, or a copy of a manuscript written after Richard's death; any such intervening manuscript is now lost. Alternatively, MS B may be primarily a direct copy of MS C, with additions; the evidence of, for example, homœoteleuton is not conclusive.[138]

MS B shows various modifications to Book II, particularly after the death of Faritius, although even then they are limited compared with

[137] Below, pp. 114, 132. Note also e.g. p. 118; see also p. xxviii.

[138] See further Vol. i, Introduction, 'Manuscripts'. The complexities are increased by the possibility that the writer of MS B for the post-Conquest period sometimes went back to the original texts which were copied in MS C; he certainly did so for the Anglo-Saxon period. Some sections, e.g. below, pp. 198–200, require quite frequent textual emendation. However, this cannot be taken as an indication that MS B is a copy of an intervening complete manuscript of the *History*; rather, it may show that the scribe was copying from other sources, perhaps single sheets recording particular incidents. For suggestions as to why a second version of the *History* was produced, see Vol. i, Introduction, 'Composition'.

those in Book I.[139] What is most notable in terms of structure is a more chronological arrangement of the latter part of Book II. The lengthy disputes covered by MS C entirely within its section on Abbot Vincent are now divided between the appropriate abbacies. This makes the development of the disputes considerably harder to follow, as any user of Stevenson's edition will be aware.[140] The inspiration for the change must be uncertain, although it does make the account of Vincent's abbacy more self-contained and in this sense more consistent with those of other abbacies.[141] It also makes the structure more similar to the *De abbatibus*, and other changes in the later version of the *History* also show similarities to that text, most notably interest in the buildings and the ornaments of the church, and sympathy for Abbot Ingulf.[142] However, there are no verbal parallels to suggest that the later version of the *History* drew directly on the *De abbatibus*, or vice versa.[143]

The additional entries in MS B probably derive from the same variety of sources as described above for MS C: writs or charters, narratives or notes, memory.[144] The first insertions are two lists of tenants, discussed above amongst the Abingdon surveys. Both are products of the period after the *History* in MS C had been completed.[145] Next there is a miracle story which greatly expands on MS C's version of the reasons for Robert d'Oilly's restorations to Abingdon, and does so in a somewhat different style, marked, for example, by Biblical quotation.[146] MS B's account of Faritius includes a lengthy description of a conflict with the monks over food assignments. The earlier composer of the *History* may have omitted this since it conflicts with the impression of harmony in the

[139] There are also various other minor differences, see above, Preface; also Vol. i, Introduction, 'Orthography'.

[140] Likewise in the time of Henry II, the narrative concerning the dispute over pigs in 'Kingsfrid' is separated from the relevant writ, again making it harder for the reader to follow; below, p. 304.

[141] At the same time, a greater chronological emphasis makes events fit more neatly within specific reigns, the starts of which in MS B are marked by illustrations of the king concerned; see Vol. i, Introduction, 'Illustrations'.

[142] See below, pp. xlvii, liii, ciii.

[143] Note also e.g. the different versions of the story involving the St Helen family and losses under King Stephen; below, p. liii.

[144] See above, p. xvii.

[145] Above, p. xxvi.

[146] See below, p. 326; for peculiarities of style in the additions to MS B, see also below, p. xxxix, and Vol. i, Introduction, 'Style'. MS B also later contains a passage very close to MS C's briefer account, below, p. 32. When the reduplication was realized, the section in MS B was expunged by a rubricated 'va . . . cat' being added in the margin.

time of Faritius, but MS B shows Faritius in a very good light with regard to the incident.[147] MS B also includes additional entries on the building works and adornment of the church by Faritius, Vincent, and Ingulf.[148] It further reveals that Abbot Vincent obtained the 300 marks necessary for royal help in preserving the abbey's rights to hundred and market by thoroughly stripping the gold and silver retable made by St Æthelwold.[149] Another addition justifies Ingulf's stripping of ornaments of the church.[150]

The remaining additions are writs of Stephen and Henry II.[151] These are not placed in any careful order, and indeed two of them had already appeared elsewhere in both manuscripts.[152] It is unclear why the various writs had not appeared in MS C. Those of Stephen which MS C omits have more specific concerns than those which it includes; conceivably they were considered of little value in the early years of Henry II. As for Henry's writs, not all of them post-date the period covered by MS C; indeed there are probably references to two of them in narratives in the earlier version.[153] It may simply be that the composer of MS C did not find these writs of Henry, or perhaps those of Stephen, in his trawl through the church's records. Given the small size of a writ, particularly when tied up, this need not be surprising, especially if their seals did not survive.

MS B also provides a limited continuation of the earlier version of the *History*.[154] The style of this section differs somewhat from the main text of the *History*, with an increased fondness for quotation or allusion.[155] The continuation mentions abbots and guardians during vacancies, and gives some further royal documents, in addition to the post-1164 writs which had been inserted earlier. It deals with only one land dispute, and that briefly. It omits disputes over Benham and over the advowson of the church of Winterbourne, which are revealed by documents in the cartularies.[156] Nor does it include Alexander

[147] Below, p. 332.

[148] Below, pp. 338, 340, 344. There is no sign that these additional sections are related to the material on the same subject in *De abbatibus*.

[149] Below, p. 338.

[150] Below, p. 344; see below, p. liii.

[151] Below, pp. 340–2, 346–52.

[152] Below, p. 350, concerning Chaddleworth appears twice in MS B, fos. 163^{r}, 171^{v} (see *CMA* ii. 189, 224–5); p. 346 concerning toll is identical except for very minor variation to a second writ of Henry II; MS B, fos. 170^{r}, 171^{r} (*CMA* ii. 218, 221–2).

[153] Below, p. 240.

[154] Below, p. 354.

[155] See below, pp. 354, 358.

[156] See Lyell, no. 108, Chatsworth, no. 299 for Benham (on dating, see above, p. xxix); Lyell, no. 356, Chatsworth, no. 83, Lyell, no. 484 (= *English Lawsuits*, no. 617) for Winterbourne.

III's bulls.[157] Rather its major concern is the dispute over the income of the obedientiaries during the vacancy of 1185, and the extensive statement of these incomes headed 'Concerning the customs of the abbey'.[158] It then swiftly concludes with Richard I's confirmation charter. No attempt has been made to produce a continuation maintaining the level of coverage enjoyed even by Abbot Walkelin in the earlier version of the *History*.

III. PARTICIPANTS IN THE *HISTORY*

1. Abbots

In examining the main characters in Book II of the *History*, let us begin with the abbots, drawing also on supplementary information, particularly from the *De abbatibus*. The writers judged abbots upon various criteria, for example their building works and their treatment of the brethren. Above all, the *History* judges them according to their fulfilment of one of the oaths they swore upon their installation: 'to gather the possessions of the church which had hitherto been unjustly dispersed', as far as he is able, 'and to preserve these for the use of the church, the brethren, and of the poor and pilgrims'.[159]

The Conqueror's first appointee to Abingdon was Adelelm, a monk of Jumièges. He was appointed in 1071 and died on 10 Sept. 1083.[160] The *History* reveals his involvement in Robert Curthose's expedition to Scotland in 1080, whilst other evidence shows him attending the 1072 primacy council and another council at London in 1074 × 1075.[161] The *History* presents Adelelm favourably in general. When at the end of his life he had the opportunity to turn to the internal affairs of the monastery, his activities, including his preparations for rebuilding the church, are noted with apparent approval.[162] Criticism for activities such as the alienation of lands to provide for

[157] *CMA* ii. 313–14, Lyell, nos. 19–22, Chatsworth, no. 87.

[158] See above, p. xxvi. MS C also contains an account of this vacancy, see above, p. xxvi, below, p. 358.

[159] *The Pontifical of Magdalen College*, ed. H. A. Wilson (Henry Bradshaw Soc., xxxix, 1910), p. 81. See also below, p. lxxxix, for the *History*'s criticism of alienation, and pp. 6, 294 for possible echoes of the language of the oath.

[160] Below, pp. 2, 16.

[161] Below, p. 12; *Councils and Synods with other Documents relating to the English Church: I. A.D. 871–1204*, ed. D. Whitelock, M. Brett, and C. N. L. Brooke (2 vols., Oxford, 1981), ii. 604, 615.

[162] Below, p. 16.

knights is muted; such alienation is said not to have started with him, and the difficulty of the times is also mentioned.[163] Adelelm defended the rights of the church, for example taking forceful action against the reeve of Sutton Courtenay.[164] He also made some acquisitions, which the *De abbatibus* refers to as purchases from the king.[165] In the case of Nuneham Courtenay the *History* too describes the acquisition as a purchase, requiring the expenditure of a large chalice. Adelelm's need of money is also revealed by his gaging land for £30 to Robert de Péronne.[166] Again the text does not seem to be criticizing him for this, at least not explicitly. However, he is shown not to have been entirely effective, losing control of Nuneham Courtenay, and the *History* openly criticizes him for succumbing to the flattery of Robert d'Oilly.[167]

Adelelm is much more strongly attacked in the *De abbatibus*, which heads its relevant entry 'The ills which Abbot Adelelm did to Abingdon'.[168] He is accused of sending to Normandy for his relatives, 'to whom he gave and enfeoffed many of the church's possessions'. He typifies the alien and nepotistic abbot familiar from other monastic chronicles.[169] He compounded his faults by his lack of respect for pre-Conquest saints, abusing Æthelwold and Edward. His project to rebuild the church is taken as a lack of respect for Æthelwold's church, his death is presented as a fitting end. He was at table with his relatives and cronies (*notis*), abusing Æthelwold and

[163] Below, pp. 4–8. See also Salter, 'Chronicle roll', p. 729, where Adelelm's alienations to knights were taken to amount to 160 hides. It is unclear how this figure was obtained. One possibility is that the writer had seen the list printed below, p. 392. A calculation based on Domesday Book for Berkshire would also produce a figure not very far from 160 for hides held by tenants.

[164] Below, p. 14.

[165] Below, pp. 10, 12; *CMA* ii. 284.

[166] Below, p. 26.

[167] Below, pp. 12, 10 respectively.

[168] *CMA* ii. 283–4. *De abbatibus* also displays a dislike of monks of Jumièges; *CMA* ii. 278. The analysis of Adelelm provided by S. Ridyard, '*Condigna veneratio*: post-Conquest attitudes to the saints of the Anglo-Saxons', *Anglo-Norman Studies*, ix (1987), 179–206, at pp. 190–3, must be questioned both on account of my suggestions about the composition of the *De abbatibus*, above, p. xxii, and of more recent general discussions of post-Conquest attitudes to pre-Conquest saints.

[169] *CMA* ii. 283; it is unclear what the writer meant when he says that Adelelm gave his relatives seventy of the possessions of the church in one year. Cf. e.g. Hugh Candidus, *Chronicle*, ed. W. T. Mellows (Oxford, 1949), pp. 84–5, on another nepotistic abbot. See also below, p. ci, for Lanfranc apparently criticizing Adelelm's failure to show 'fatherly love' to some of his monks. Adelelm, like his successor Reginald, does not appear in the Abingdon kalendar, but since only abbots from Faritius are regularly included, this need not amount to a criticism; Cambridge, University Library, Kk. i 22, fos. 1^v–7^r.

his works, and saying that the church of English rustics should not stand but be destroyed. After dinner he left to relieve himself, and there cried out. Those who came running found him dead.

The *De abbatibus* has far less to say about Adelelm's successor, Reginald, not even naming him in the heading of the entry in which he appears.[170] However, Reginald was sufficiently widely known that Orderic Vitalis mentions his death in 1097.[171] He had been a royal chaplain, witnessing or signing various of the Conqueror's documents.[172] He then became a monk of Jumièges. Whilst, in the early post-Conquest period, a few other monasteries had abbots who had been monks of Jumièges,[173] nowhere else did the connection persist as at Abingdon. The appointment of Vincent in 1120 meant that three of the first four post-1066 appointees had been monks of Jumièges.

Between 1080 and 1083 William confirmed to Jumièges a house, land, and gardens which Reginald had held of him at Bayeux, as Reginald had become a monk at Jumièges.[174] Still more interesting is a first-person narrative by Reginald concerning the history of this land.[175] However, even if Reginald brought to Abingdon a particular interest in the recording of lands, study of vocabulary establishes no link between the section of the *History* devoted to him and his own memorandum concerning the land in Jumièges.[176]

In the *History*, as opposed to the *De abbatibus*, it is Reginald who appears dangerously blessed with relatives.[177] Royal charters reveal

[170] *CMA* ii. 284–5.

[171] Orderic, *Ecclesiastical History*, bk. viii, c. 8, ed. Chibnall, iv. 170.

[172] He is probably the man appearing in *Recueil des actes des ducs de Normandie de 911 à 1066*, ed. M. Fauroux (Caen, 1961), no. 197; *Regesta*, ed. Bates, nos. 210, 212, 236 (as *clericus*), 244, 246, 251 (as *iunior capellanus*), 266 II, 267 II. *Regesta*, ed. Bates, no. 305 is the sole English document witnessed by Reginald as chaplain, but it is a mid-twelfth-century forgery. See also *Gallia Christiana*, ed. D. de Sainte-Marthe and B. Hauréau (16 vols., Paris, 1715–1865), xi, Instrumenta, col. 328D.

[173] Theodwine at Ely, Robert at Evesham, Godfrey at Malmesbury; *Heads of Religious Houses*, pp. 45, 47, 55.

[174] *Regesta*, ed. Bates, no. 161; the gift is also mentioned in a general confirmation, no. 164. See also no. 59 for a grant by Reginald to La Trinité, Caen, before he became a monk.

[175] *Regesta*, ed. Bates, no. 162 (1080 × 1084); see also his discussion at pp. 33–4.

[176] On tenth- and eleventh-century historical writing at Jumièges, see *The 'Gesta Normannorum Ducum' of William of Jumièges, Orderic Vitalis, and Robert of Torigni*, ed. E. M. C. van Houts (2 vols., OMT, 1992–5), i, pp. xxviii–xxxi.

[177] Reginald was appointed on 19 Jun. 1084 and died 4 Feb. 1097; below, pp. 18, 60.

that Reginald had a brother called William,[178] whilst the *History* records that he had a son, born before he took the habit; a daughter, who married the Abingdon knight Rainbald; a nephew, named Robert; and a niece, who married another Abingdon knight. The *History* calls her the sister of Simon the king's dispenser, although never referring to Simon as Reginald's nephew. He may indeed have been a nephew, the *History* keeping it quiet because of his disputes with Abingdon, or Simon may have been only the niece's half-brother and unrelated to Reginald.[179] The abbot made grants of land to these kin, and the possible genealogy in Figure 1 shows the entanglement of his relatives with the tenants and the opponents of Abingdon.

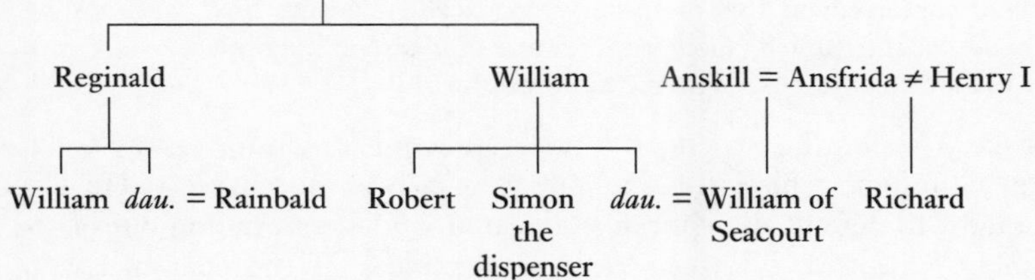

FIG. 1. Possible genealogy of Abbot Reginald's relatives

Yet the *History*'s criticism of Reginald for these alienations is muted. Of his grant of Dumbleton to his nephew Robert it was stated that it 'at the time seemed to him a wise move . . . But not long afterwards the abbot gravely repented of his decisions, for until then he had not known who was the originator of the gift of that land to this monastery.'[180] No obvious criticism is made of Reginald's grants to Rainbald, and there is only quiet criticism of his favour to his son; the grant of Marcham church was made with the convent's permission, but 'in addition he gave some other possessions, of which no mention was made to the convent'.[181]

Rather than as a harmful nepotist, the *History* presents Reginald as a reformer, and an acquirer and defender of possessions. His

[178] *Regesta*, ed. Bates, nos. 161, 164.

[179] Below, pp. 58, 54, 50, 54. See also below, p. lxxii, on the dispensers. J. H. Round, *The King's Serjeants and Officers of State* (London, 1911), p. 187, suggests that Helewise, the wife of Hugh son of Thurstan the dispenser, may have been Reginald's sister; this rests on the assumptions (i) that Simon the dispenser was Hugh's son and (ii) that Simon was nephew of Abbot Reginald.

[180] Below, p. 50.

[181] Below, pp. 54–8.

rebuilding work is accepted, the collapse of the old tower not being represented as divine retribution for the infringement of St Æthelwold's church. Only in the last sentence of the entry on rebuilding is an apologetic note stuck: the collapse of the tower 'was the reason why the monastery which had been constructed by the holy father and bishop Æthelwold was rebuilt'.[182] The writer goes on to praise Reginald for his introduction of the proper payment of tithe, which helped the rebuilding work.[183]

Reginald benefited from Rufus's initial favour: the king

> committed to him his dead father's treasure stored away at Winchester, to be distributed to the use either of churches or of the poor, trustfully expecting that he would perform this most devotedly. From this division, the following were conferred on this monastery: an excellent gospel text, with a silver vessel for the carrying of exorcized water, and also a rough piece of silk, with an ivory incense box made in the form of a ship.[184]

Like Adelelm, he expended money on acquisitions, for example £30 on Shippon, which the *De abbatibus* calls a purchase.[185] He also sought to defend the church's alienated lands from falling out of the abbey's control. Thus he resisted the pleas of the sons-in-law of Gilbert, tenant of Garsington, to be allowed to have their portions of Garsington by hereditary right. However, as was often the case in such defences of church lands, he had to allow the tenants a life-tenure, risking the renewal of claims in future.[186]

Still more of a problem was the fickleness of royal favour. The abbey was hard hit by Rufus turning against two knights of the church, Anskill and Rainbald. In the latter case the abbot had stood surety, according to the *History*, for £300 of the £500 which Rainbald needed to pay the king in order to obtain reconciliation.[187] It may be to these cases, or to a more direct but otherwise unknown conflict, that the *History* refers when stating that 'as time passed, at the instigation of certain men hostile to Reginald, the king's mind was

[182] Below, p. 30; see also p. cii.

[183] Below, p. 34.

[184] Below, p. 58. See F. Barlow, *William Rufus* (London, 1983), pp. 63–4. Reginald witnessed only one of Rufus's surviving charters, *RRAN* i, no. 315, a grant to the bishop of Bath, made at Dover on 27 Jan. 1091.

[185] Below, pp. 24–6; *CMA* ii. 285. Note also the gold mark expended on the confirmation of Chesterton and Hill, below, p. 26; the £20 expended on the acquisition of the church of Sutton, below, p. 36.

[186] Below, p. 48; J. G. H. Hudson, 'Life-grants of land and the development of inheritance in Anglo-Norman England', *Anglo-Norman Studies*, xii (1990), 67–80.

[187] Below, pp. 52, 54. On the plausibility of this figure, see below, p. lxiv.

turned against the abbot, so that grace turned to hatred. Nor did this anger diminish until the end of his life was at hand. This piled further scarcities upon the church.'[188]

Matters declined still further with the death of Reginald and the appointment of Modbert as guardian of the church. The *De abbatibus* calls him 'prior', the *History* 'monk' and '*prepositus*'; *prepositus* may just mean administrator, but it is also the word which the *Rule* and Lanfranc's *Monastic Constitutions* use for prior.[189] It is unclear whether the *History* is trying to conceal that he was prior, or whether Modbert held some other position.[190] Both the *History* and the *De abbatibus* present Modbert the custodian as a servant of the king not the monastery. The *History* criticizes him for his alienations, and for payments to the royal purse. The *De abbatibus* accuses him of nepotistic grants of the abbey's possessions. Only eighteen of the abbey's eighty ploughs remained,[191] only thirty-two out of fifty monks. The church's manors were so ruined that the monks had scarcely anything to eat. The cloister, chapter, and dormitory fell into ruin, so the monks slept (*jacerent*) and held the chapter '*in monasterio*', presumably meaning within the abbey church.

According to the *De abbatibus* the monks, faced with such miseries, resorted to fasts and prayers in order that God and the Virgin Mary might provide a suitable abbot.[192] Whilst others slept, a boy named Nicholas watched at the altar of the holy Trinity, weeping and praying that the Lord help them in such great calamities. A beautiful woman appeared to him, and asked why he was crying. Nicholas answered 'Lady, we don't have a pastor, nor anyone who does any good to us, not even my uncle Modbert. We're in the greatest miseries.' To which the lady replied 'Don't fear. Tell the prior and convent that they are to receive my chaplain, the cellarer of Malmesbury, Faritius by name, and he will provide well for you, for I will be with him.' When, next morning, Nicholas recounted this to the

188 Below, p. 60.

189 *CMA* ii. 285; below, p. 60, see also p. 208; *The Monastic Constitutions of Lanfranc*, revised edn., ed. D Knowles and C. N. L. Brooke, (OMT, 2002), p. 112. For *prepositus* being used in a different sense at Abingdon, to mean a monk living on an estate, see Lambrick, 'Administration', pp. 161, 182.

190 Book II of the *History* only uses the word of Modbert, although it also appears in Book I, notably with reference to Ealdred's position before becoming abbot; see Bk. i. c. 143 (*CMA* i. 482); see also Bk. i, c. 97 (*CMA* i. 357).

191 The precise meaning of this is obscure.

192 *CMA* ii. 285–6.

monks and the prior—it is unclear whether this means Modbert—they praised God and 'our Lady', the Virgin Mary. The prior and two monks went to Henry I, who willingly agreed to appoint Faritius as abbot.[193] The *History* and *De abbatibus* agree that Modbert—or Modred as the *De abbatibus* now calls him—was sent off to the abbey of Milton, Dorset.

Faritius was a noted physician from Arezzo, who had become a monk and cellarer of Malmesbury, itself probably a centre of interest in medicine.[194] Henry I, his queen, and all the leading men of the realm reputedly entrusted themselves to Faritius ahead of any other physician.[195] The *History* describes him as 'especially outstanding in the knowledge of letters', and he wrote a *Life of St Aldhelm*.[196] He also became involved in theological debate. The letters of Theobald of Étampes include one defending himself against Faritius, who had apparently accused him of teaching that unbaptized children could be saved.[197]

Faritius is the hero of Book II of the *History*, and the first entry devoted to him draws parallels with Æthelwold, the great reformer central to Book I. Of him alone does MS C provide a picture at the start of his abbacy.[198] The *History* goes on to present him as the

[193] Faritius was appointed in 1 Nov. 1100 and died 23 Feb. 1117; below, pp. 64, 224.

[194] See E. J. Kealey, *Medieval Medicus: A Social History of Anglo-Norman Medicine* (Baltimore, 1981), p. 14 on Malmesbury, pp. 65–70 on Faritius. Note also John of Worcester, *Chronicle*, iii. 307, where an Abingdon addition to the Worcester chronicle states of Faritius: 'Erat et Romane ecclesie notus cum et in ea tum multis et in aliis ecclesiis per ausonias oras diu deguerit.'

[195] Below, p. 64. Despite the obvious royal favour he received, Faritius was not a frequent witness of Henry I's charters; note *RRAN* ii, nos. 753, 825, 828. For Faritius witnessing two grants by Robert son of Hamo, see below, p. lxix n. 363.

[196] Most easily accessible in *PL* lxxxix. 63–84; note N. R. Ker, *Medieval Manuscripts in British Libraries* (4 vols., Oxford, 1969–92), ii. 939. The *Life* is anonymous, but Faritius's authorship is revealed by the comments of William of Malmesbury, *Gesta pontificum Anglorum*, bk. v, cc. 186–8, ed. N. E. S. A. Hamilton (London, 1870), pp. 330–2, especially p. 332 which clearly refers to *PL* lxxxix. 66. It cannot be precisely dated, although it is often assumed that Faritius must have written it when at Malmesbury (e.g. Ridyard, '*Condigna veneratio*', p. 194); William in the *Gesta pontificum*, bk. v, c. 186, ed. Hamilton, p. 330, ascribes it to Faritius 'abbot of Abingdon', but this may simply reflect the date of composition of the *Gesta pontificum*. On the *Life*, see also Ridyard, '*Condigna veneratio*', pp. 194–5.

[197] *PL* clxiii. 763–4; Theobald describes himself as 'master of Oxford'. On Theobald, see *The History of the University of Oxford*, i. *The Early Oxford Schools*, ed. J. I. Catto (Oxford, 1984), pp. 5–6.

[198] See fo. 144[r].

defender of the church's lands and rights.[199] He generously endowed the monastic officials. He provided the monastery with new buildings and wealthy ornaments, no doubt funded by the newly acquired or resumed possessions. And he increased and organized the abbey's relics.[200]

The *De Abbatibus* supports this triumphant portrayal.[201] Faritius came to Abingdon in 1101, and was honourably received by all.[202] When he reached the bridge over the river Ock, he dismounted from his horse and proceeded barefoot to the church of St. Mary. The text then states that since Anselm was in exile, Faritius placed his pastoral staff on the altar until the archbishop's return to England. However, there is here a problem of chronology, in that Anselm had returned to England on 23 Sept. 1100 and only left again on 27 Apr. 1103; the reason for the confusion is unclear.[203]

According to the *De abbatibus*, Faritius swiftly started his extensive rebuilding of the church and monastic buildings.[204] He increased the number of monks from the twenty-eight whom he found to eighty, and hoped to increase it to 100. He appointed scribes, in addition to the claustral monks, who copied liturgical and theological works.[205] He instituted the practice that the almoner should receive from the cellarer as many loaves as crosses were found in the Martyrology, so that one loaf could be given to the poor for each monk whose death was recorded.[206] He also raised the level of celebration of various feasts.[207]

In addition, *De abbatibus* records Faritius's actions concerning the monks' food, but here its account needs to be compared with that given in an additional entry in MS B of the *History*, both because of the poor condition of the *De abbatibus* manuscript and because of the

[199] See Vol. i, Introduction, 'Anglo-Saxon charters', for suggestions that defence of the abbey during his time may have involved the forging of documents.

[200] See below, pp. lxxxv, cii, civ–vi.

[201] *CMA* ii. 286–90.

[202] Cf. below, p. 64, where the *History* dates his appointment, although not his arrival at Abingdon, to 1 Nov. 1100.

[203] For Anselm's movements, see R. W. Southern, *Saint Anselm: a Portrait in a Landscape* (Cambridge, 1990), pp. xxviii–xxix.

[204] See below, p. cii.

[205] See below, p. cvi.

[206] 'Martyrology' may here be used in a loose sense to mean the obituary list of deceased monks, or indicate that an obit list was bound in a single volume with a martyrology. See also *CMA* ii. 405; Lanfranc, *Monastic Constitutions*, p. 192; Harvey, *Living and Dying*, p. 15, which makes it clear that the provision specified was scarcely generous.

[207] See below, p. civ.

different impression given by much lengthier account in the *History*.[208] According to that entry, one of the monks offered that they give up a quarter of their common bread, to further the abbot's building works. However, Faritius discussed the matter with the monks in the chapter the following day. He promised that he would try not to diminish the monks' bread or their other customs, but rather by restoring and conserving the church's estates would add the weight of half a mark to the afore-mentioned measure of bread. Any left over by those dining would be given to the needy.[209]

The *De abbatibus* specifies that Faritius granted to the eighty monks the same weight of cheese every five days that Æthelwold had allowed forty-three monks every ten days.[210] The addition to the *History* again reveals the background. Certain monks had complained of the diminution of the cheese allowance contrary to Æthelwold's provision, and the dispute reached Henry I. He sent the notably high-powered team of the archbishop of Canterbury, the bishop of Salisbury, and Hugh of Buckland to Abingdon to settle the matter. Faritius defended himself, and explained that the *per capita* diminution in the cheese allowance arose from the increase in the number of monks. He therefore arranged that the allowance be distributed every five days instead of every ten. Once it had been checked that separate provision was made for the abbot's own table, this solution was accepted by all.[211]

According to the *De abbatibus*, Faritius provided everything necessary for the sacrist, cellarer, lignar, and other obedientiaries.[212] A record preserved in MS C, in the same hand as the *History*, records that his endowment of the lignary was intended both to ease the provision of fire and to reduce the burden on the peasantry. Previously they had paid their tithes for the building of the church, and also made payments for the church's wood. Faritius's reform was to draw the money for wood partly from tithes, partly from the other payments.[213]

Apart from a separate mention of the royal grant of Andersey,[214]

[208] On the trustworthiness of MS B's statements about food allowances, see below, p. 334 n. 40.

[209] Below, p. 332. The *De abbatibus* mentions Faritius's increase of the measure of bread; *CMA* ii. 286.

[210] The relevant sentence in the MS ends 'quater xx. monachis in v. diebus concessit'; cf. *CMA* ii. 287, where Stevenson printed 'quarum' instead of 'quater'.

[211] Below, p. 336.

[212] *CMA* ii. 289.

[213] See below, p. 394.

[214] *CMA* ii. 287.

Faritius's acquisitions are gathered under one heading in *De abbatibus*.[215] This begins by stating that many possessions had been taken from Abingdon in the time of the Danes, but that Faritius recovered many of them, by prayer and payment, from King Henry. At the end of his life, he was seeking to purchase Sutton Courtenay from the king, because the men of Sutton were doing great harm to Abingdon. However, the king, then in Normandy, deferred this until his return to England.[216]

De abbatibus gives a lengthy entry on Faritius's death. William, the cantor, on the day of the Purification of the Virgin Mary (2 Feb.) had prepared a *pulmentum*—that is a cereal or vegetable dish—which he took to the abbot sitting at his table in the refectory.[217] Soon after tasting it, Faritius began to feel ill. He rose from the table, and informed the bishop of Salisbury and the abbots of Gloucester, Malmesbury, and Shrewsbury of the day and hour at which he would die. Then he offered on the great altar thirty pounds of gold for gilding a seven-branched candlestick, which he had bought for thirty pounds of silver. All the money he had collected for purchasing Sutton he ordered to be given to the poor. When the hour of his death approached, he meditated upon the words 'Lord, I have loved the habitation of thy house', and then expired.[218]

Thus far we have seen only praise of Faritius, apart from internal monastic rumblings concerning food. However, contrary views appear in descriptions of the election to the archbishopric of Canterbury in 1114, following the death of Anselm in 1109.[219] Eadmer, in his *Historia nouorum*, states that the monks of Canterbury favoured Faritius but that various bishops and magnates blocked his election, since they desired the appointment of a non-monastic bishop or a clerk from the royal chapel. According to the *De abbatibus*, Faritius was elected to the archbishopric, but opposed by the bishops of Lincoln and Salisbury, who protested that there should not be an archbishop who, as a physician, had inspected women's urine—a fastidiousness peculiar in two bishops who had illegitimate children.

215 *CMA* ii. 288.

216 *CMA* ii. 289.

217 For *pulmentum*, see Harvey, *Living and Dying*, pp. 11–12.

218 'Domine, dilexi decorem domus tue'; Ps. 25 (26): 8. Vol. i, c. B207, uses the same passage with reference to Æthelwold; *CMA* i. 344. The *De abbatibus* incorrectly gives 1115 as the year of Faritius's death; *CMA* ii 290.

219 Eadmer, *Historia nouorum*, bk. v, ed. Rule, p. 222; *CMA* ii. 287; below, p. 70; see also William of Malmesbury, *Gesta pontificum*, bk. i, c. 67, ed. Hamilton, pp. 125–6; John of Worcester, *Chronicle*, iii. 307–8; Brett, *English Church*, p. 73.

The *History* does not try to claim that Faritius was elected archbishop, but states that 'the king would have been prepared to put a person of such renown onto the seat of the patriarchate, had not Faritius's inflexible standard of justice been suspect to certain men of higher ecclesiastical rank, disturbing a faction of them'. Thus in the context of the 1114 election, dislike of Faritius's rigour is attributed to churchmen. One entry in the *History* records that laymen felt, or at least argued, that Faritius drove an unfairly hard bargain, a complaint familiar too concerning his illustrious predecessor Æthelwold. Langford mill was one of Faritius's acquisitions, but after the abbot's death the donor, William of Seacourt, complained to the king that the church held it by virtue of the aforesaid abbot's power rather than the donor's wishes. The abbey succeeded in retaining the mill, but William was probably not the only layman for whom Faritius was less than a hero.[220]

The *History* and the *De abbatibus* obviously provide the best evidence for Faritius's later reputation at Abingdon. Faritius's name in the text of the *History* in MS C is almost invariably rubricated; Abbot Vincent enjoyed this privilege only intermittently, Henry I only very rarely.[221] Faritius's name, moreover, was sometimes capitalized, a privilege he shared with the Virgin Mary.[222] In addition, the tract 'Concerning the Obedientiaries' ranks the anniversaries of Vincent and Faritius above those of Walkelin and Ingulf.[223] There is very tentative evidence suggesting a later cult of Faritius. A list of saints' resting places mentions 'Saint Vincente e Saint Caricius en Abindone'. It has been suggested that this is a misspelling of 'Faricius', but if there was any cult, it is extremely surprising that there survives no Abingdon evidence for it.[224]

220 Below, p. 180. See also p. 132 for Faritius having difficulty in forcing his knights to perform castle-guard at Windsor.

221 Faritius: fos. 148^{v} ff.; Vincent: fos. 164^{v}–165^{v}, 167^{r}; Henry I: fo. 159^{r}. Exceptions to the rubrication of Faritius's name occur e.g. fo. 144^{r} (where the name is in capitals), 155^{r}. On rubrication for the pre-Conquest period, see Vol. i, Introduction, 'Manuscripts'.

222 Faritius: e.g. fos. 144^{r}, 146^{v}, etc.; Mary: e.g. fos. 136^{r}, 144^{v}, etc.

223 *CMA* ii. 382; see also ii. 394, 400, 401.

224 L. Butler, 'Two twelfth-century lists of saints' resting places', *Analecta Bollandiana*, cv (1987), 87–103, at pp. 88, 91, 100; the passage concerned is PRO E 164/1, fo. 238^{v}. *CMA* ii. 395, reads 'in duobus anniversariis Sancti Faricii et Vincentii', but 'Sancti' is the editor's mistranscription for 'scilicet'. Nor is there mention of Faritius in e.g. Hugh Candidus's list of saints' resting places, which only mentions Vincent the martyr at Abingdon; Butler, 'Twelfth-century lists', p. 101. It is possible that the French list did mean Faritius, and had brought him in by association with the name Vincent, shared by the martyr and by Faritius's successor; in this case the slip rather resembles that of the

More generally, Faritius was widely noticed amongst chroniclers and historians, and held in high regard. Orderic mentions his appointment to Abingdon. The *Anglo-Saxon Chronicle*, the Margam annals, and the Oseney annals record his death, the last noting that his anniversary is especially commemorated at Abingdon.[225] In the context of the 1114 Canterbury election, both Eadmer and William of Malmesbury comment on his diligence or zeal (*industria*). The latter also notes his *acrimonia*, perhaps best translated as 'severity' and reminiscent of the *History*'s own comment on 'his inflexible standard of justice'.[226] Elsewhere in the *Gesta pontificum*, William is critical of Faritius's *Life* of Aldhelm, but in general he is favourable and includes in his text verses written by another Malmesbury monk, Peter. These emphasize, for example, Faritius's prudence, his work on the church, and his highly regarded medical skills.[227]

Succeeding figures are inevitably diminished by the scale of treatment and the level of praise of Faritius. The vacancy subsequent to his death is presented as a considerable contrast to the custodianship of Modbert. Matters were well handled by Warenger, the prior, and new grants of tithes and success in lawsuits continued.[228] Faritius was eventually succeeded by another monk of Jumièges, Vincent, who was abbot from 1121 until his death on 29 Mar. 1130.[229] The *History* commented that 'everyone loved him since he was munificent and generous'.[230] He again is presented as a benefactor of the obedientiaries, a successful defender of the abbey's rights, and an accumulator of new gifts, although, with the exception of a grant of four hides by Ralph Basset, these tended to be smaller than those under Faritius.[231] The section in the *De abbatibus* is brief, mentioning

CMA's editor. Alternatively 'Caricius' may derive from a corruption of another name, e.g. that of the martyr Cyricus or Cyriacus, of whom Abingdon possessed relics, below, p. 222.

225 Orderic, *Ecclesiastical History*, bk. x, c. 16, ed. Chibnall, v. 298; *ASC*, *s.a.* 1117; *Annales monastici*, i. 10, iv. 17.

226 Eadmer, *Historia nouorum*, bk. v, ed. Rule, p. 222, William of Malmesbury, *Gesta pontificum*, bk. i, c. 67, ed. Hamilton, p. 126; above, p. xlix.

227 William of Malmesbury, *Gesta pontificum*, bk. ii, c. 88, bk. v, cc. 186–8, ed. Hamilton, pp. 192, 330–2. Peter may be identifiable with Peter Moraunt, who was later abbot of Malmesbury; R. Sharpe, *A Handlist of the Latin Writers of Great Britain and Ireland before 1540* (Publications of the Journal of Medieval Latin, i, 1997), p. 429.

228 See below, pp. 224–8; see also Salter, 'Chronicle roll', p. 729.

229 Below, pp. 228, 254.

230 Below, p. 230. Vincent witnessed only one royal charter, *RRAN* ii, no. 1391.

231 See below, p. lxxvii.

certain acquisitions, and his gift of his wool for one year for a great dossal depicting the ten virgins; all the obedientiaries made a dossal depicting the Apocalypse.[232] Above all, it presents Vincent as interested in cleanliness: he was accustomed to fill the washing place (*lauatorium*) with water before the monks rose, and established the monks' baths.[233]

There is no mention of a vacancy between Vincent's death and the appointment of Ingulf, prior of Winchester, abbot from mid-1130 until his death on 19 Sept. 1158.[234] He may have attended the Legatine council at Westminster in December 1138,[235] and William of Malmesbury reports that he was present at Winchester Cathedral, on 3 Mar. 1141, when the Empress Matilda was received as Lady of England.[236] If he was identified as a supporter of the Empress, this may well explain some of his problems with King Stephen, although the sources do not make this explicit.[237]

The *History* emphasizes the difficult circumstances Ingulf faced in Stephen's reign, and his attempt to use papal help as a necessary alternative to ineffective royal aid. However, it grows more critical of Ingulf, for his actions against the wishes of the monks, and for keeping the church's seal under his own control:

some of the church's possessions were taken away with a veneer of propriety, in that the abbot so wished, but unjustly, in that it harmed the church. . . . He kept the seal of the church under his own control and confirmed with it what he wished. Therefore after his death it was ensured that many seal impressions harmfully made by him were broken.[238]

[232] A dossal is an ornamental, usually an embroidered, cloth normally hung at the back of the altar.

[233] *CMA* ii. 290. On monks' baths, see also Lanfranc, *Monastic Constitutions*, p. 14.

[234] Below, pp. 254, 298; also *CMA* ii. 291. See *English Register of Godstow*, p. 28 for Ingulf giving 60s. to Godstow; see also *RRAN* iii, no. 366 where the royal confirmation states only that the gift was by the abbot of Abingdon.

[235] *Councils and Synods: I. 871–1204*, ii. 771.

[236] William of Malmesbury, *Historia novella*, bk. iii, c. 45, ed. King, p. 88.

[237] See below, n. 248, for the difficulty of dating these troubles. Ingulf appeared as the first witness of a charter of Stephen in 1149; *RRAN* iii, no. 455. The other two charters of Stephen which he witnessed would be of 1136 and 1138, but both are of at least dubious authenticity; *RRAN* iii, nos. 284 (where the editors identify as Ingulf the man named as 'Indu . . . Alvendon'), 928. Ingulf witnessed two of Henry I's charters, *RRAN* ii, nos. 1715–16. The charters of Henry II contain no instances of Ingulf witnessing; I would like to thank Judith Everard for conducting this search on the Angevin *acta* collection currently being completed by Sir James Holt, Dr Nicholas Vincent, and herself.

[238] Below, p. 290.

The impression of internal strife is reinforced by the account of his approach to death:

During his lengthy struggle with illness, he had himself brought into the brethren's chapter, for the illness prevented him walking. There he absolved of their sins all subject to him, and humbly asked that they would remit in God's name any sin he had committed towards them.[239]

As remarked earlier, the *De abbatibus* gives a very different impression of Ingulf.[240] It records that he made gifts to the monks' kitchen, and never harmed the chamberlain or kitchener, the latter statement sounding like a defence against accusations. His generosity to the church also included a purchase, matched by the sacrist Richard, of a great bell called 'Hildelhubel', for seventy marks.[241] His building works were also extensive.[242] The later version of the *History* also includes some praise for Ingulf's building work, and his gifts of vestments and hangings to the church.[243]

The church and its ornaments certainly suffered during his abbacy, but the *De abbatibus* provides excuses. The spoliation of Cnut's reliquary of St Vincent was to provide for the poor during famine, as is also mentioned in the later version of the *History*.[244] Ingulf had to break other caskets or reliquaries to pay for King Stephen's demand of £300. The demand arose because Stephen gave the abbey of Chertsey to a monk of Abingdon, named William of St Helen.[245] However, William refused to pay obedience to his diocesan, the bishop of Winchester, and so the bishop excommunicated him. William was released from the excommunication by the pope, and returned to Abingdon. When he heard this, the King demanded from Ingulf the £300 which William had promised him for Chertsey. The

[239] Below, p. 296.

[240] See above, p. xxiii, and *CMA* ii. 291–2 for this and the following paragraphs.

[241] The meaning of the name 'Hildehubel' is not entirely clear. One possibility is that it is a mixture of English and French, Old English 'hilde' meaning 'battle', Old French 'hu' meaning 'clamour', as in 'hue and cry'; perhaps the bell sounded like the clash of metal on metal in battle.

[242] See below, p. ciii.

[243] Below, p. 344.

[244] Below, p. 344. See also Salter, 'Chronicle roll', p. 729.

[245] These events cannot be precisely dated; the only abbot elected to Chertsey in Stephen's reign was the king's nephew Hugh, who became abbot in *c.*1149; *Heads of Religious Houses*, p. 38. How long the abbey had previously been vacant is unclear. See also *English Episcopal Acta*, viii. *Winchester 1070–1204*, ed. M. J. Franklin (Oxford, 1993), no. 34; *Chertsey Abbey Cartularies*, ed. M. S. Giuseppi and P. M. Barnes (2 vols. in 3 parts, Surrey Rec. Soc., xii, 1933–63), ii, p. ix.

later version of the *History* may be referring to a related debt when it explains that Ingulf had to strip twelve reliquaries of their gold and silver in order to retain the service of the land of Richard of St Helen. The knight had fallen foul of King Stephen and 'ought to have been disinherited through Abbot Ingulf'.[246]

Nor, according to the *De abbatibus*, was Ingulf to blame for the plundering of the abbey.[247] Much money was stored in the abbey's treasury, part of it gathered for the restoration of the reliquary of St Vincent. However, a sacrist called Simon Crassus informed the king of this, and Stephen sent William de Ypres there to seize the money. He entered the treasury, feigning prayer, broke into the coffer, and took from it fifty marks of gold and five hundred marks of silver. The sacrist was soon rewarded with an abbacy, but three years later, the writer is pleased to note, died with worms eating away his hands and feet.[248] The later version of the *History* also associates the treasure plundered with the restoration of reliquaries, and blames the abbey's losses on certain 'betrayers of the [abbot's] secret counsel', who went to the king and accused the abbot of improperly acquiring the money.[249]

According to the *De abbatibus*, Ingulf's successor Walkelin, a monk of Evesham, was appointed by Henry II at the intervention of Queen Eleanor.[250] He was abbot from 1159 until his death on 10 Apr. 1164.[251] For the *History*, Walkelin was favoured by the king as a man committed to resuming the losses of his predecessors as abbot, and the *History* goes on to present him as successful in this commit-

[246] Below, p. 346.

[247] The earlier version of the *History*, below, p. 292, attributes this to 'the treachery of certain friends of the abbot'; this may be seen as an excuse for the abbot, or imply blame if the friends were regarded as traitors to the house rather than to Ingulf.

[248] The house was Athelney; *Heads of Religious Houses*, p. 26. The MS refers to it as 'Alignia'. However, there may be problems of chronology. *Two Chartularies of the Priory of St Peter at Bath*, ed. W. Hunt (Somerset Rec. Soc., vii, 1894), no. 61 (pp. 58–9) is a charter of Robert bishop elect of Bath, witnessed by Simon abbot of Athelney, and dated in the cartulary to 1135. Bishop Robert's predecessor, Godfrey, died on 16 Aug. 1135 and Robert was consecrated on 22 Mar. 1136. It is possible that Stephen plundered Abingdon in the first months of his reign, and William de Ypres was present in England early in 1136 (*RRAN* iii, p. 417). Yet the relevant passage in the *History* comes just before mention of Stephen's death (see below, p. 294), and if early 1136 is the correct date, it would also require a reconsideration of our view of Stephen's early rule.

[249] Below, p. 346.

[250] *CMA* ii. 292. A search by Judith Everard of the Angevin *acta* collection has found no instances of Walkelin witnessing.

[251] *Heads of Religious Houses*, p. 25; Cambridge, University Library, Kk. i 22, fo. 3^{r}.

ment.[252] The limited extent of the *History* for his abbacy, however, together with the need for discretion about a still-living abbot, makes it hard to establish the writer's attitude to Walkelin. A criticism may appear in the *History*'s conclusion concerning the dispute over the church of St Aldate, Oxford:

> Moreover, with prelates neglecting the defence of their own possessions, the canons of St Frideswide withhold to this day, and strive to withhold forever, the part of the church which we have said belonged to Nicholas and now by right was ours. The honour of making the presentment, however, is reserved for us, together with our part. I have spoken for this reason, so that some day, through a man given by God, the just resumption of the other part should occur that much more swiftly, because the unjust seizure is found recorded in writing.

It may be that the 'negligent prelates' included Walkelin. If so, it would reinforce the impression, formed from explicit statements concerning Ingulf, that the writer wrote not only on behalf of Abingdon in conflict with outsiders, but also on behalf of the convent in actual or potential conflict with abbots.[253]

The remaining twelfth-century rulers of Abingdon who appear in the *De abbatibus* and the continuation of the *History* will be covered more briefly. Following Walkelin's death, the abbey was vacant for half a year and then entrusted to the custody of Godfrey bishop of St Asaph, a former monk of Coventry.[254] According to the *De abbatibus*, the king removed him after conflict with the monks, whereas Roger of Howden's account of the 1175 Council of Westminster emphasizes the demands of the clerks of St Asaph that he return to his see.[255] The new abbot, Roger, had been prior of Bermondsey, but little can be discovered about his abbacy of Abingdon which lasted from 1175 until 1185.[256] There followed the custodianship of the royal clerk Thomas of Hurstbourne, recorded in MS B, and in a section of MS C

252 Below, p. 298; see also below, p. 314.

253 See also Vol. i, Introduction, 'Composition'.

254 *PR 11 HII*, p. 77; *Heads of Religious Houses*, p. 25. Godfrey had been a monk of Coventry late in Henry I's reign; Saltman, *Theobald*, p. 129.

255 *CMA* ii. 293, which criticizes the insolence of Godfrey's relatives; see also Roger of Howden, *Chronicon*, ed. W. Stubbs (4 vols., London, 1868–71), ii. 77–8, *Gesta regis Henrici secundi Benedicti abbatis*, ed. W. Stubbs (2 vols., London, 1867), i. 90.

256 *De abbatibus* describes him as cruel and suspicious, *CMA* ii. 293; *Heads of Religious Houses*, p. 25. Howden, *Chronicon*, ii. 78, simply refers to him as 'a certain monk'. See *English Register of Godstow*, p. 49, for a grant by Abbot Roger to Godstow.

in a hand later than that of the *History*.[257] Master Thomas performed various administrative duties under Henry II and Richard I, including acting as a royal justice and exacting tallage from the royal demesne.[258] Just before his appointment as custodian of Abingdon, he had shared similar responsibility with Thomas Noel for the bishopric and abbey of Chester.[259] He is presented as threatening the customs of the house, and in particular seeking to control the possessions of the monks as well as those of the chamber of the abbot.[260] However, the monks successfully defended their rights before the justiciar, Ranulf de Glanville. The next abbot, Alfred, formerly prior of Rochester, is simply named in the continuation of the *History*, although the *De abbatibus* comments upon both his virtues and his avarice.[261] The last abbot of the century, Hugh, receives slightly more attention.[262] The continuation of the *History* mentions his obtaining a confirmation charter from Richard I, but does not take events beyond 1190. The *De abbatibus* states that he had been a monk of Abingdon, and praises him for his ever increasing virtues, his undertaking new building work, his gifts to the church, and his replacement of rye with wheat (*frumentum*) as the grain from which the monks' beer was made.[263]

2. Monks of Abingdon

The *De abbatibus* gives us some figures for the number of monks at Abingdon. It states that numbers fell from fifty to thirty-two under Modbert, but recovered from twenty-eight to eighty under Faritius. The latter corresponds well with the *History*'s statement that there was a threefold increase under Faritius. There are no figures for the rest of the twelfth century, but an episcopal deed of *c.*1201 stated that the total was to be increased to eighty again, if suitable candidates could be found. Thus numbers at some point had dropped again.[264]

[257] *CMA* ii. 297–9, and translated as *English Lawsuits*, no. 570.

[258] See e.g. *PR 27 HII*, p. 15, *32 HII*, pp. 7, 17, 27, 35, 65, 77, *33 HII*, pp. 36, 103, 147, 156, 178. Under Richard I he had custody of the archbishopric of York, *PR 7 RI*, pp. 29–33.

[259] *PR 30 HII*, pp. 24–5, *31 HII*, pp. 141–2.

[260] See also M. Howell, *Regalian Right in Medieval England* (London, 1962), p. 43 n. 7, on the *donum* taken from Abingdon during the vacancy; whilst the amount is small, the practice appears to have been unusual under Henry II.

[261] *CMA* ii. 293. Hugh was abbot 1186–1189; *Heads of Religious Houses*, p. 25.

[262] Abbot 1189/90–*c.*1221; *Heads of Religious Houses*, p. 25

[263] *CMA* ii. 293. See *English Register of Godstow*, p. 34, for a grant by Abbot Hugh to Godstow.

[264] Below, p. 72; *CMA* ii. 285, 287; Lyell, no. 166.

We know very little about individual monks. For those other than officials, a few names can be obtained from accounts of their taking the habit,[265] or from witness lists. The latter provide us, for example, with a Benedict, a Robert, and a Godwine, in the time of Faritius or shortly after.[266] From the *De abbatibus*, we know of the monk William of St Helen, who in Stephen's reign aspired to be abbot of Chertsey.[267] There was also a certain Pondius, who was one of those whom MS B recorded as complaining about Faritius's regime.[268]

We know slightly more about some monastic officials.[269] A former prior Ælfric attended the consecration of Kingston Bagpuize church.[270] The *History* praises Warenger, prior since Reginald's time, for his administration during the vacancy after Faritius's death, and he remained prior into Vincent's time.[271] A certain Walter was prior in the mid-1150s,[272] and a Nicholas in the mid-1180s.[273]

265 See below, p. 52, 100; see also p. 90 for Aubrey de Ver receiving the monastic habit on the day before his death.

266 Below, p. 200; see also p. 226 which mentions a William the monk and a William *Brito* who from his place in the witness list may also be a monk. One of these Williams may or may not be identical with the William the monk who appears at p. 156. See also e.g. p. 202. See also *Cartulary of Oseney Abbey*, ed. H. E. Salter (6 vols., Oxford Hist. Soc., lxxxix, xc, xci, xcvii, xcviii, ci, 1929–36), iv, no. 9, a charter of Robert d'Oilly concerning his foundation of Oseney Priory in 1129, which is witnessed by Main' and Walter, monks of Abingdon.

267 See above, p. liii.

268 Below, p. lxxxv.

269 See also below, p. c, on Richard the schoolmaster. Walter the chamberlain of Abingdon, below, p. 148, may have been the monks' or the abbot's chamberlain. William the chamberlain, below, p. 370, almost certainly was the monks'. For the abbot's household, see below, p. lxxxiii. Numerous servants who make no appearance in the main text of the *History* are mentioned in the 1185 survey, below, p. 358.

270 Below, p. 176. For Modbert as a possible prior, see above, p. xlv. The prior mentioned in the account of the collapse of the church tower, below, p. 32, is nameless.

271 Below, pp. 224, 236. Witness lists confirm that he was prior in March 1104 and probably still in early 1111: below, pp. 200, 88; the latter date is based on the assumption that the royal confirmation charter (p. 86) concerning Colne was issued in the same year as Faritius received seisin of all the things mentioned in that charter. For mention of Warenger, see also below, p. 228. Theobald of Etampes's letter to Faritius, *(PL* clxiii. 764) ends by mentioning Abingdon's 'good prior' as 'our inner friend' ('uestrum bonum priorem amicum nostrum interiorem.')

272 Below, p. 294; see also *Historia et cartularium monasterii Sancti Petri Gloucestriae*, ed. W. H. Hart (3 vols., London, 1863–7), ii. 106, for a charter of the archbishop of York witnessed by Walter prior of Abingdon, at Gloucester on 13 Dec. 1157.

273 See below, p. 370. The *De obedientiariis*, *CMA* ii. 367, mentions a sub-prior and a 'third prior'. Lanfranc, *Monastic Constitutions*, p. 112, show that an abbey could have more than one prior at a time even in the eleventh century.

Among sacrists, the prominence of Richard has already been noted. He was vital in the acquisition and resumption of lands, houses, and tithes, apparently through his personality and eloquence. He instituted the festival of the relics, constructed iron doors in the church, and presented a bell and organs, as well as further adornments for the church.[274] Robert the sacrist appears in the *History* only as a witness of a case in 1119, and in a later addition concerning the decoration with gold of a chasuble given by Abbot Vincent.[275] The *De abbatibus* blamed the sacrist Simon Crassus for the ransacking of the abbey's treasury in Stephen's reign.[276]

Early in Faritius's time, the church and abbot are described as being seised of a gift 'through' William the cellarer, his role perhaps linked to Faritius then bestowing part of the gift upon the cellar.[277] A few years later, we again see Ralph the cellarer acting on behalf of the abbot, on this occasion receiving an oath of quitclaim. Ralph was also prominent in a dispute concerning the customs owed by ships of Oxford in 1110 × 1112.[278]

William the cantor appears in the earlier version of the *History* only as a witness in 1104.[279] However, the *De abbatibus* records that he prepared the food on the day Faritius fell mortally ill.[280] There seems to be no criticism intended, but the later version of the *History* has William as one of Faritius's opponents in the dispute over food allowances.[281]

3. Knights holding of Abingdon

The Pipe Rolls show that Abingdon owed a *servitium debitum* of thirty knights, although the *Carta* of 1166 reveals that thirty-three had been enfeoffed before 1135. This can be compared with the sixty owed by the poorer house of Peterborough or the fifteen owed by the richer house of St Augustine's, Canterbury.[282] The abbey contributed substantially to the guard at Windsor castle, and a writ of Henry I

[274] See above, p. xx; below, pp. 280–90.
[275] Below, pp. cvi, 290.
[276] See above, p. liv.
[277] Below, p. 80. William witnessed a document as cellarer in 1104, below, p. 200.
[278] Below, pp. 152, 174.
[279] Below, p. 200.
[280] See above, p. xlix.
[281] See below, p. 332.
[282] See T. Keefe, *Feudal Assessments and the Political Community under Henry II and his Sons* (Berkeley, 1983), pp. 158–60.

indicates even Faritius experiencing difficulties in enforcing this service.[283]

We do not have charters of enfeoffment to show how the obligation was passed on to tenants. Nevertheless, the *History* does provide a plausible and influential account.[284] Initially Abbot Adelelm relied upon household knights. However, he later granted possessions which had belonged to thegns who had fallen at Hastings.[285] A continuing desire to rely upon previously alienated lands is suggested by Abbot Reginald's initial and futile search for 'vavassour's land' with which to endow his nephew Robert; vavassour's land may be the equivalent of thegn's land.[286] Such grants were associated with the coming of knights from overseas, and also with abbatial nepotism.[287] Some knights can indeed be associated with Jumièges, most obviously William de Jumièges, but also possibly the family of St Helen; a Reginald of St Helen made an agreement with the abbot of Jumièges in 1112.[288] *Domesday Book* in general confirms the suggestion that many of the lands alienated after the Conquest had already been granted out in 1066.[289]

Of Abingdon's estates, approximately a quarter had been granted to tenants named in *Domesday*.[290] Working out whether there was any consistency in the size or value of the knights' fees granted is problematic, as we do not have a reliable early list of both holdings and service due. Chew emphasized the widely varying ratio of hidage to knight service, on the basis of MS B's first list of knights.[291] However, if one concentrates only on the minority of entries in this list which are clearly and simply supported by *Domesday*, and if one

[283] Below, p. 132; see also p. 342, for a writ of Stephen ordering that Abbot Ingulf fulfil his castle-guard obligations at Windsor, and below, p. 306, for a writ of Eleanor of Aquitaine ordering the knights and tenants of Abingdon to do Abbot Walkelin the service they owed; also Keefe, *Feudal Assessments*, pp. 77–8.

[284] See e.g. Keefe, *Feudal Assessments*, p. 77. Note also the account provided in Salter, 'Chronicle roll', p. 729.

[285] Below, p. 6; cf. the situation at Bury St Edmunds, *Regesta*, ed. Bates, no. 37. See also below, p. 8.

[286] Below, p. 50.

[287] See below, pp. 6–8, and above, p. xli.

[288] Below, pp. lxv, 136; *Chartes de l'Abbaye de Jumièges*, ed. J.-J. Vernier (2 vols., Paris, 1916), no. liv. Note that one of the witnesses to the agreement was a William Picot; a man named Picot and the St Helen family both had interests in Garsington, below, p. 48.

[289] See e.g. *DB* i, fo. 58^{v} (Seacourt, Shippon, a portion of Barton and Dry Sandford, Bayworth).

[290] See further below, p. lxxv.

[291] H. M. Chew, *The English Ecclesiastical Tenants-in-Chief and Knight Service* (Oxford, 1932), p. 121.

looks at values not hidages, a pattern may emerge. Rainbald owed one knight for Tubney, which had a 1086 value of £4 per annum although being assessed at only one hide; Hubert owed one knight for Wytham, value £4, assessment five hides; Walter Giffard owed one knight for Lyford, value *TRE* £4, in 1086 £5, assessed at seven hides; Walter de Rivers owed two and a half knights for Beedon, value £8, assessed at eight hides. Rather outside this pattern of about £4 per knight's fee is the combined holding of Gilbert Marshal and Sueting, which owed one knight although being worth £6 in 1066, £7 in 1086.

The lack of charters leaves us uncertain of the precise terms on which tenants received lands, but we do have one very useful account from the time of Faritius:

> Abbot Faritius also granted to Robert son of William Mauduit land of four hides in Weston, to hold in fee, which Robert's father had held from the abbot's predecessor. And he was to do the following service therefrom, namely that wherever the church of Abingdon did knight service, he would do that church's service for half a knight, that is, in castle-guard, in military service beyond and this side of the sea, in giving penny coins for a knight, in the king's guard service, and in all other services, as the church's other knights do. He also did homage to Abbot Faritius. This land previously only did three weeks' service each year.

Unfortunately the passage does not reveal the usual duration of service. However, it does indicate both that there was a general notion of the services which all the church's knights did, and that there were variations, as had arisen at Weston.[292]

The *Carta* of 1166 allows us to look more closely at the results of the process of enfeoffment. Jordan of Sandford owed the most service, four knights. John of St Helen and Bohemond of 'Leges' (probably Bessels Leigh) owed three each. Robert of Seacourt, William of Bessels Leigh, and Gilbert de Colombières owed two each, Hugh son of Berner one and a half. Thus these seven owed seventeen and a half of the thirty-three knights' fees. Ten more men held one knight each. Seventeen men made up the remaining five and a half fees.[293]

[292] Below, p. 199; C. W. Hollister, *The Military Organization of Norman England* (Oxford, 1965), pp. 89–100, deals with the duration of military service, but does not cite this evidence. He discusses this passage at pp. 103–4 in the context of service abroad. See also below, p. 134.

[293] *Red Book*, i. 305–6, below, p. 390. The Exchequer version of the *Carta* gives no name for the tenant of Seacourt, but the Abingdon version names Robert. For comment on

Not many of the knights named in the *Carta*, or their predecessors, feature prominently in the *History*. Rather, a few families were predominant in the business of the church, as suggested, for example, by witnessing abbatial acts.[294] Some were tied to abbots by kinship or marriage, and the majority were amongst those owing the larger quotas in 1166: the families of Hugh son of Berner, John of St Helen, and Seacourt.

Berner was the nephew of Robert de Péronne.[295] *Domesday* records him as holding in Berkshire from the abbey five hides in Sunningwell and Kennington, two hides in Boxford, and two hides in Garford, and also Appleton from the bishop of Bayeux's holding.[296] He succeeded Robert in Abbot Reginald's time, and had to give back to the church three hides at Culham in relief.[297] Two years later, Berner challenged this relief, but unsuccessfully. In the *History*'s account of the case, his remaining portion was recorded as owing one and a half knights' service, just as Hugh son of Berner would in the 1166 *Carta*; either continuity from the 1080s to 1166 was great, or the *History*'s account of the 1080s imposed information from the 1160s.[298]

The *History* records Berner bringing this claim in person, but the fact that at the time of his succession he had been brought to the abbot by the bishop of Winchester may suggest that he was quite young. Certainly he was still alive in the early 1120s, and by then his age and position as a long-standing tenant may have reinforced his importance in the affairs of the honour. In Faritius's time and beyond he acted as a witness, for example to the transfer of seisin of Aubrey de Ver's grants to Colne.[299] Early in Vincent's abbacy he is found witnessing together with his son Hugh, but thereafter disappears from the records.[300] Hugh, his son, is slightly less prominent in the *History*, but does appear as a witness to one of the sacrist Richard's

such a preponderance of minor knightly holders, note R. J. Faith, *The English Peasantry and the Growth of Lordship* (London, 1997), p. 198.

[294] Neither documents nor narrative suggests a distinction of these families as 'barons'; a grant by Ingulf was made 'in the presence of our barons and many of our neighbours', but the term does not seem to be used in any precise way. A writ of Henry I addressed 'to the barons of the abbey of Abingdon' is given the rubricated heading 'To the knights of this church'; below, p. 132.

[295] Keats-Rohan, *Domesday People*, p. 167, suggests that the toponym is Péronne (Dept. Somme).

[296] *DB* i, fos. 58^v–59^r, 63^v.

[297] Below, p. 28.

[298] *Red Book*, i. 305, below, p. 390.

[299] Below, p. 80; see also e.g. pp. 44, 202, 226, 228.

[300] Below, p. 236.

resumptions,[301] and as the recipient of one of the grants Abbot Ingulf made without the consent of the convent.[302] As we have seen, he also appears in the 1166 *Carta*. The family thus provides an interesting example of just two generations spanning the period 1086–1166.

The next family derived their name from the manor of Seacourt, amounting to five hides in Cumnor, held from Abingdon. The *Domesday* tenant was Anskill, who also held one hide at Marcham, ten hides at Bayworth with a certain Gilbert, and the area of Sparsholt called Fawler.[303] He first appears in the *History* when his men of Seacourt came into conflict with the abbey over a watercourse at Botley.[304] He later fell out with William Rufus:

> Denunciation from the mouths of his own men so fired the king's anger towards Anskill that he ordered him to be bound in chains and worn down by imprisonment. There he was enfeebled by the unaccustomed harshness and died a few days later.[305]

The king gave Fawler to Thurstan, his dispenser, and Abbot Reginald had to pay Rufus £60 to retain the rest of Anskill's lands for the church. His widow Ansfrida was evicted, his son William banished from his father's holdings. Ansfrida bore an illegitimate son of Henry I, and by Henry's aid recovered Bayworth which had been her dower. William married Abbot Reginald's niece, the sister of Simon the king's dispenser. He eventually recovered Seacourt, the hide at Marcham, and—presumably following his mother's death—land at Bayworth. In 1112 × 1113, he witnessed a quitclaim to the abbey, and following his mother's death gave the mill of Langford to the church.[306] However, after Faritius's death, William resumed the mill through Henry I's support, until the monks managed to persuade the king to the contrary. Perhaps William's grievance against Faritius arose from the latter's acceptance of Hugh son of Thurstan the dispenser as tenant of Fawler.[307] Yet, also in the period after Faritius's death, William was present as a man of the abbey in the

[301] Below, p. 280.

[302] Below, p. 292. He also witnessed C.H., no. 1a, a charter dating from 1165 × 1175.

[303] *DB* i, fos. 58^{v}–59^{r}; see also below, p. 52. A list of Henry I's reign or early in Stephen's has Anskill's son William of Seacourt holding six hides in Bayworth, Robert of Sandford four hides; below, p. 386.

[304] Below, p. 20.

[305] Below, p. 53; see also p. lxvi on royal anger.

[306] Below, pp. 152, 180.

[307] Below, pp. 182–6. The case reopened in the first decade of the thirteenth century, but Robert of Seacourt gave up his claim; *VCH*, *Berkshire*, iv. 314.

county court of Berkshire when the abbey's right of quittance to geld was established.[308] He later acted as a witness on Abbot Vincent's part in the latter's settlement with Simon the king's dispenser, William's own brother-in-law.[309]

Information about William's successors is relatively sparse and hard to interpret. He was most likely followed by Robert, probably his son. A William son of Robert is recorded at the start of Henry II's reign paying forty shillings scutage, the amount appropriate for a holding of two knights' fees. This, however, may not be the successor of Robert son of William son of Anskill, for a later cirograph of Abbot Walkelin was witnessed by a Robert of Seacourt and William his son; it is unclear how many Williams and Roberts succeeded one another between the 1120s and the mid-1150s. The exchequer version of the Abingdon *Carta* of 1166 states only that Seacourt owed two knights, but the version included in MS C gives the name Robert of Seacourt.[310]

The last of our families owed only one knight in 1166 but particularly its first known member, Rainbald, is very prominent in the *History*.[311] He was the son-in-law of Abbot Reginald, and may well have gained most of his lands in the period 1084–6, with some possible further additions by the early 1090s. *Domesday* records that he held one hide from the abbot in Tubney, from which place his family was to take its name, ten hides in Leckhampstead, and one hide in Frilford.[312] He may also have held lands at East Hanney and the mill at Marcham.[313] The untrustworthy list of knights included only in MS B attributes to him further extensive lands.[314] Assuming that the list is not simply misleading, these could be post-*Domesday* acquisitions, otherwise unrecorded sub-tenancies, or holdings of another man of the same name. It is possible that he should be identified with a Rainbald holding lands in Berkshire from the king,

[308] Below, p. 226.

[309] Below, p. 236.

[310] *PR 2–4 HII*, p. 35; below, p. 320; *Red Book*, i. 305, below, p. 390. Note also *English Register of Godstow*, pp. 42–4, 322. C.H., no. 1, a charter of Abbot Roger (1175–1185), confirms a final concord between William of Seacourt and Simon the carpenter and his wife concerning a holding in Abingdon. For William witnessing, see also e.g. Chatsworth, nos. 83, 295.

[311] See above, p. xxi, on why he may feature so prominently in the *History*.

[312] *DB* i, fo. 58^{v}.

[313] Below, p. 190. Marcham mill was on the river Ock, on the south boundary of the parish; *VCH*, *Berkshire*, iv. 354–5.

[314] Below, p. 322.

and different spellings of the same name, such as Rainbold, Reinbald, and Reimbald, also feature in *Domesday Book*.[315]

Whatever the precise extent of his lands, Rainbald, like Anskill, fell out with William Rufus.[316] He was, according to the *History*, to pay £500 for reconciliation, but instead fled, leaving his sureties, most notably the abbot, in deep financial trouble. The figure may be exaggerated,[317] but the royal demands clearly were very burdensome. The abbot resumed the lands at Leckhampstead, Tubney, Frilford, and Hanney, and the mill at Marcham. However, following Rainbald's forgiveness, probably by Henry I, the knight recovered all his lands except Leckhampstead. He went on to surrender the hide at Hanney and the mill at Marcham, because he had them from the monks' demesne without the king and monks' assent. In return he was permitted to hold the remainder of his lands for the accustomed service.[318]

As with assessing his lands, summarizing his later career is hampered by the possible existence of more than one man called Rainbald, and by the inconsistent spelling of names. However, the knight with whom we are presently concerned may well be the Rainbald who witnessed a settlement concerning the church of Peasemore in 1104 × 1105, and two quitclaims to the abbey in 1112 × 1114.[319] It is also possible that his early devotion to the abbey is indicated by one of his sons being named Adelelm. Certainly in the time of Abbot Vincent, Rainbald of Tubney's request that his son of that name be received as a monk of Abingdon was accepted, eased by the gift of half a hide at 'Moor'.[320] In Abbot Ingulf's time we have a John of Tubney active as a witness on behalf of the abbey,[321] and he may well have been Rainbald's heir. Before 1164 he had a son, Richard, who joined him as a witness, but John was still alive in 1166 when he owed one knight.[322]

[315] *DB* i, fo. 57[r]; K. S. B. Keats-Rohan and D. E. Thornton, *Domesday Names: an Index of the Latin Personal and Place Names in Domesday Book* (Woodbridge, 1997), pp. 158, 162.

[316] Below, p. 54.

[317] *PR 31 HI*, pp. 82, 155, records debts of 200m. and 170m. of silver that the king might pardon the debtors for his ill-will.

[318] Below, p. 190.

[319] Below, pp. 44 (Raimbold), 152 (Rainbold), 154 (Rainbald); see also p. 24.

[320] Below, p. 246.

[321] Below, pp. 280, 320.

[322] Below, pp. 320, 390, *Red Book*, i. 306. See also C.H., no. 1a, a document of 1165 × 1175 witnessed by John of Tubney, Henry his son, and Ralph his brother.

Other families appear more occasionally as witnesses to transactions involving the abbey. The St Helen family owed its name to the church of St Helen, close to the abbey, or to the associated lands at 'Helenstow' which Thurstan of St Helen received in an exchange with Faritius.[323] In *Domesday* Reginald was the abbey's tenant for four hides at Frilford and three at Lyford.[324] He may also have held lands at Hendred and at Garsington.[325] He certainly witnessed the settlement between Abbot Reginald and the claimants to the inheritance of Gilbert Latimer, and indeed Reginald of St Helen may have held his land at Garsington not as a direct tenant of the abbey but as a sub-tenant.[326] By 1100 at the latest, he had been succeeded by his son Thurstan, who acquired a hide and a half from Modbert, custodian of the abbey, but later quitclaimed these lands in the presence of Abbot Faritius.[327] It was he who received land at 'Helenstow' in exchange for another holding.[328] By Henry II's reign, his lands had passed to John of St Helen, who witnessed Richard Basset's quitclaim of four hides at Chaddleworth to the abbey.[329] He also appears in the 1155 Pipe Roll as a tenant of Abingdon pardoned 60s. scutage, the amount owed by three knights' fees, and the 1166 *Carta* confirms this as the extent of his holding.[330] Two other men with the toponym 'of St Helen' may well have had some connection with the family. They are the knight Richard and the monk William of St Helen, whom the later version of the *History* and the *De abbatibus* respectively record as falling out with King Stephen and thus bringing great loss upon the abbey.[331]

4. Kings

Abingdon was a monastery with particularly close ties to the king. For the twelfth- and early thirteenth-century historians of the house, this link could be traced back to its original foundation and also to its refoundation in the tenth century.[332] Kings before and after 1066 were fond of staying at their residence on the isle of Andersey, just by

[323] Below, p. 202.
[324] *DB* i, fos. 58^{v}, 59^{r}.
[325] See below, pp. 322, 388.
[326] Below, p. 50.
[327] Below, p. 192.
[328] Below, p. 202.
[329] Below, p. 250.
[330] *PR 2–4 HII*, p. 35. For John, see also *CMA* ii. 305 (holding half a hide at Weston), 311; C.H., no. 1a; on his son, also called John, see *VCH*, *Berkshire*, iv. 417. C.H., no. 2, is a charter of John of St Helen preserved as a single sheet, but oddities of the hand suggest that it is a copy.
[331] See above, pp. liii–iv.
[332] See also Vol. i, Introduction, 'Kings and patrons'.

the monastery.[333] We have already seen the close personal ties of some post-Conquest abbots to kings and queens: the former royal chaplain Reginald, Faritius physician to Henry I and his wife, Walkelin appointed on the advice of Eleanor of Aquitaine.[334] The connections are further exemplified by a writ of Henry II which refers to 'my monks' of Abingdon,[335] and by the illustrations of kings which punctuate MS B.[336]

However, the *History*'s concerns are very much with the local and internal affairs of the church, and therefore it is not especially vivid in its depiction of kings.[337] There is no comment upon William I at his death.[338] In general the tone of Book II towards him is neutral, for example concerning the requirements for knight service, preparations against Danish assault, the enforced grant of land to the maimed knight, Hermer, or even William's taking away of Nuneham Courtenay.[339] This contrasts with criticism of the royal forest and of oppressive royal officials; indeed William I and his queen, like their successors, are presented as the church's defenders against such officials.[340]

For William II, too, there is no general summary of his character. Some explicit criticism does not specifically name the king: 'At that time there was an unspeakable custom practised in England, that if any person among the prelates of churches departed life, the church honour was assigned to the royal treasury.'[341] Other criticism is implicit, for example concerning the king's auctioning his favour to either side in a dispute over Dumbleton.[342] More direct criticism of the king arises from the fluctuations of his favour towards the abbot and the abbot's men, and the ways in which his mind could be swayed against them.[343] His disfavour manifested itself in anger, and—in a rare generalization about a king's character and behaviour—the *History* comments that 'the king acted most severely towards the objects of his anger'.[344]

[333] Below, p. 72.
[334] See above, pp. xlii, xlvi, liv.
[335] Below, p. 248.
[336] See Vol. i, Introduction, 'Illustrations'.
[337] On the *History*'s language concerning kingship and royal power, see Vol. i, Introduction, 'Style'.
[338] For the attitude of the *History* to the Norman Conquest, see Hudson, 'Abbey of Abingdon', pp. 187–92.
[339] Below, pp. 6, 16, 12.
[340] Below, pp. 8, 12, 16. For William II offering protection against forest officials, below, p. 40. For Henry I, see e.g. pp. 116, 166.
[341] Below, p. 60.
[342] Below, p. 50.
[343] See above, p. xliv.
[344] Below, p. 54.

Henry I's early connections to the abbey and the area are mentioned: his stay at the abbey at Easter 1084 and his liaison with Ansfrida, widow of the knight Anskill. So too is his accession: 'his older brother Robert had not yet returned from Jerusalem, where he had gone.' In none of these cases is comment made upon Henry's character or morals.[345] An interesting general comment, though, is made about the changing nature of his rule:

> When King Henry was newly elected to the kingship, numerous men sought to be given many possessions which had belonged to the demesne of his predecessors as king. By prudent council, he gave everything which was sought, being still inferior to his petitioners. But as time passed he considered himself their superior.[346]

Henry's close bond to Faritius as his physician is obvious, and his high opinion of the abbot also apparent in his reported desire to have him as archbishop of Canterbury following Anselm's death.[347] His first queen, Matilda's, connections with the abbot are also clear, as is her piety and generosity to the abbey.[348] Henry himself is praised for his kind reception of the monks of the abbey in 1120, when they went to him to seek a successor for Faritius.[349]

On the other hand, even Faritius could not freely obtain everything he wanted from Henry. Sometimes he had to accept a more limited grant, or needed to make a heavy payment, such as the £60 to have Hugh son of Thurstan the king's dispenser hold Fawler as the abbey's man.[350] It is notable that in this case, when Henry's favour seems to have been hard to obtain, the abbey's opponent was a royal servant.

Henry's anger is also reported. In the time of Abbot Vincent, certain men persuaded the king to take from the church the hundred of Hormer and to prohibit Abingdon market. Unlike Rufus, however, Henry could be brought to recognize the just cause, and Vincent's defence of the abbey's rights and his presentation of Edward the Confessor's privilege was effective: 'The king began to check his

[345] Below, pp. 16, 52, 62.

[346] Below, p. 73.

[347] See above, p. xlix.

[348] Below, pp. 64, 74–6, 140–4. Note also p. 184, for Faritius seeking her aid in the dispute over Fawler.

[349] Below, p. 228. Note that the same entry states that Henry had long been detained in Normandy; this implicitly provides a justification for the length of the vacancy. The description of the vacancy itself, below, p. 224, can be taken as a deliberate contrast with that late in William II's reign.

[350] Below, pp. 96–8, 184.

anger, and to speak more mildly to the abbot.' Once he had been promised 300 marks, he agreed to confirm the abbey's privileges.[351]

The later version of the *History* comments upon King Stephen's piety.[352] Again, however, royal servants could turn him against the abbey.[353] Worst of all was Stephen's plundering of the church's treasure.[354] In general, though, the emphasis is not upon the person of the king but the troubles of his reign and their effect upon the abbey.[355] Stephen is more notable for his lack of direct involvement in the affairs of the abbey, in contrast to Henry I's frequent interventions.[356]

Henry II was associated with the coming of peace: 'Henry the Younger succeeded to the kingdom and the extraordinary war ceased throughout England.'[357] He was also implicitly praised for his desire for the resumption of the church's lands, manifested in his choice of Walkelin as abbot and in the justice he brought against those who had oppressed the church in Stephen's reign.[358] Like the other kings, he could be turned against the abbey, but like his grandfather, he could be persuaded of the rectitude of the abbey's position, most notably in the matter of Abingdon market.[359]

5. Others

Donors

The *History* records a wide range of men and women making grants to Abingdon. Besides kings and queens, major figures who made significant grants include Hugh earl of Chester, Ralph Basset, and the de Ver family.[360] However, it is noteworthy that such grantors are concentrated in the half century after the Conquest. Thereafter, it was lesser, local people who continued their own flow of benefactions.[361] The change may relate to increased competition from the

351 Below, p. 230.
352 Below, p. 346.
353 Below, p. 238.
354 Below, p. 292; see also above, p. liv.
355 See e.g. below, p. 254.
356 e.g. below, pp. 264–92.
357 Below, p. 294.
358 Below, pp. 242, 298, 306–8.
359 Below, p. 308. See *Materials for the History of Thomas Becket*, ed. J. C. Robertson (7 vols., London, 1875–85), i. 213–14, ii. 245, for Eleanor of Aquitaine leaving a foundling to be raised at Abingdon in the time of Bishop Godfrey.
360 Below, pp. 24, 82–90, 246.
361 See e.g. below, pp. 286–8; also E. Cownie, *Religious Patronage in Anglo-Norman England, 1066–1135* (Woodbridge, 1998), ch. 2.

wave of new foundations in the twelfth century, both great houses such as Reading and lesser ones such as Oseney and Littlemore.[362]

Moreover, several of the major donors' gifts were related to attention received from Faritius for sickness:

> Abbot Faritius frequently administered many beneficial treatments to Robert son of Hamo. Therefore, when Robert was approaching the time to pay his debt to death, on the abbot's recommendation he was told that he ought devotedly to render to the monastery of Abingdon some mark of piety, with a view to remembrance of him. He should do so both for the things to come with God and also for Faritius's favour, if he recollected his many services towards him. He heeded these pieces of advice and conferred on that monastery a portion of land between Ackhamstead and Marlow, where a very considerable assart had been cleared.[363]

The *History* also relates to illness new gifts made to Faritius by Geoffrey de Ver, Adelina d'Ivry, Drogo des Andelys, and Miles Crispin, and by Ralph Basset to Abbot Vincent, and by Robert priest of Marcham in the time of Abbot Ingulf.[364] Restorations related to illness were made by Robert d'Oilly and Robert the abbot's nephew to Abbot Reginald, and by William son of Abbot Reginald to Faritius.[365]

Grants could also be associated with the donor's son, the donor himself, or both, taking the monastic habit.[366] This too might be related to illness, as in the cases of Ralph Basset, Drogo des Andelys, and William son of Abbot Reginald.[367] Elsewhere there is no mention of illness: in one case the taking of the habit is simply put down to 'God's calling', but in another arrangements for burial suggest concern with impending death.[368] Further, we have instances of men making arrangements for future gifts in conjunction with being buried at the abbey. When Geoffrey de Mauquenchy took the habit at Abingdon, his son

> Gerard gave himself to this church, so that if he wished to become a monk, he would receive this status from no other monastery but Abingdon. And if it

[362] Cownie, *Patronage*, pp. 50–3.

[363] Below, p. 140. For 'Pharisyus' witnessing two of Robert's grants to Cranborne, see Kealey, *Medieval Medicus*, p. 67.

[364] Below, pp. 82, 98, 106, 142, 246, 286.

[365] Below, pp. 32, 52, 190.

[366] Below, pp. 100, 182, 246. For receipt of spiritual benefits, see also p. 26.

[367] Below, pp. 246, 98, 190.

[368] Below, pp. 256, 246, respectively; see also pp. 52, 90, 234.

happened that he died a layman, and this occurred in England, he would have burial here, together with a one third of all the goods he would then have in England. If he died in Normandy, still a third of his goods in England, as specified, would be the church's.[369]

The *History* also mentions Robert d'Oilly's burial at Abingdon, and the later version specifies that he was buried in the chapter-house, with his wife on his left.[370]

Royal officials

Certain royal officials feature very significantly in the *History*. Most notable are Robert d'Oilly, Hugh of Buckland, and the royal dispensers. Robert d'Oilly received extensive lands following the Conquest, notably in Oxfordshire. He was also a royal constable and castellan of Oxford castle, and quite possibly sheriff of Berkshire, Oxfordshire, and Warwickshire in the course of William I's reign. He died *c.*1093.[371] He appears in the *History* as the addressee of a writ of William I, and in association with the future Henry I when the prince spent Easter 1084 at Abingdon.[372] The earlier version of the *History* presents him abusing his local power to obtain Tadmarton from Abbot Adelelm. The *De abbatibus* includes Tadmarton amongst the lands which Abbot Adelelm gave to his kinsmen, and it is possible that Robert was related to Adelelm.[373] Even with royal help, the abbey could only get the estate back in return for an annual payment of £10 a year to Robert.[374] Eventually, however, illness led Robert to repent, and he became a particular patron of the rebuilding of the abbey church. He remitted the annual payment of £10 and conferred more than £100 'for the emendation of his past misdeeds, and also to help the rebuilding of the monastery'. Despite his repentance, however, he retained his hold on some further lands and meadow.[375] The later version of the *History* adds a frightening vision to the tale of Robert's emendation of his ways, and emphasizes the sound counsel of his wife. To his good deeds is added the rebuilding of other churches, within and outwith the walls of Oxford.

[369] Below, p. 180; see also p. 238.

[370] Below, pp. 34, 330; see also *CMA* ii. 284.

[371] R. V. Lennard, *Rural England* (Oxford, 1959), pp. 70–1; Sanders, *Baronies*, p. 54; Green, *Sheriffs*, pp. 26, 69, 83.

[372] Below, pp. 2, 18.

[373] *CMA* ii. 283.

[374] Below, p. 10.

[375] Below, p. 32.

He and his wife were buried in the northern part of the chapter at Abingdon.[376]

Hugh derived his surname from Buckland in Berkshire, which he held of the abbey. He had already been sheriff of Bedfordshire, Berkshire, and Hertfordshire under Rufus, but is one of the men named by Orderic Vitalis as being raised from the dust by Henry I. Under the latter king he was also sheriff, or perhaps local justice of Buckinghamshire, Essex, London, and Middlesex.[377] The *History*, in which he features very extensively, generally presents him as a friend of the abbey. It describes him as 'a virtuous and wise man, who was sheriff not only of Berkshire but of seven other shires as well—he was so renowned a man and so close to the king'.[378] When the abbey was troubled by the miller of Hennor, 'through the efforts of very many men, and especially through Hugh of Buckland's support (in return for the accompanying spiritual benefit), Abbot Faritius so pressed upon the king's grace that he and the church of Abingdon obtained the lordship of that mill for ever'.[379] Only for his lengthy and 'undeserved' tenure of land at Hanney, obtained by grant of Modbert, was Hugh criticized, and even then the *History* praises his repentance: 'greatly revering the authority of this abbot [Faritius], by which he willingly let himself be advised concerning this, he therefore restored this land to the liberty of this church.'[380]

The abbey's relationship with the king's dispensers was less happy. Following the knight Anskill's forfeiture, William Rufus seized his land in Sparsholt, and granted it to Thurstan his dispenser.[381] Writs of Henry I reveal problems with Thurstan's son Hugh over the payment of services and of geld, whilst the *History* narrates that it cost Faritius a payment of £60 to the king to obtain the land and homage

[376] Below, p. 326. This account particularly emphasizes his possession of the abbey's meadow outside Oxford, but does not mention what happened to it following Robert's vision.

[377] Orderic, *Ecclesiastical History*, bk. xi, c. 2, ed. Chibnall, vi. 16; Green, *Sheriffs*, pp. 25, 26, 28, 39, 47, 57.

[378] Below, p. 172.

[379] Below, p. 96.

[380] Below, p. 192.

[381] Below, p. 52; see also Barlow, *William Rufus*, p. 142. It is unikely that this is the Thurstan referred to in Henry I's writ 'Concerning the lands which Modbert gave or leased', below, p. 126. For Thurstan's ancestors, see Round, *Serjeants*, pp. 186–8; Barlow, *William Rufus*, pp. 141–2, who suggests that he was illegitimate, presumably on the grounds that many of his father's lands passed to Urse d'Abetot. On the possibility that Robert son of Thurstan left an heiress, see *The Beauchamp Cartulary: Charters 1100–1268*, ed. E. Mason (Pipe Roll Soc., New Series xliii, 1980), p. xxi.

of Hugh, together with the service and geld.[382] However, relations were not entirely bad, and following Faritius's death, Hugh and his wife granted the abbey the tithe of all his goods of the manor of Sparsholt.[383]

A further set of disputes involved another royal dispenser named Simon and his son. Simon, as we noted above, may have been Abbot Reginald's nephew.[384] During the vacancy after Faritius's death, Simon suggested to the king in Normandy that various possessions belonged to him by hereditary right as a relative of Abbot Reginald's son William. These were the church of Marcham and two hides and a mill and a dairy farm there; one hide at Garford; one hide at Milton, with a chapel and another half hide; one hide at Appleford; and three and a half hides at Garsington.[385] Abbot Vincent persuaded Simon to surrender all the possessions except Garsington, but in return had to grant him and his heirs the manor of Tadmarton. This settlement seems to have lasted until Stephen's reign, when Simon's son-in-law, the tenant of Tadmarton, failed to perform due service and was disseised by Abbot Ingulf.[386] However, this again turned Simon and his relatives against the church. In 1153 Simon's son Thurstan obtained an order from Stephen to Ingulf that he deliver Thurstan what was his by hereditary right. The abbot delayed, but eventually the sheriff of Oxford seised Thurstan of the church of Marcham and three hides pertaining to it, and one hide in Milton and one in Appleford.[387] Only with the coming of Henry II, the *History* reports, was the church restored to its rights through royal judgment.[388] The Pipe Roll of the fifth year of Henry II reveals Thurstan owing Abingdon half a knight's service and this is confirmed in the 1166 *Carta*.[389]

What we have then is two separate sets of disputes involving the dispensers. The relationship of Hugh son of Thurstan to Simon cannot be established for certain. Round was cautious in his text, but in his family tree made Simon Hugh's son.[390] Given the lack of mention of a relationship in the *History*, this may be doubted. Figure 2 is the best we can do for a genealogy.

382 Below, pp. 132–4, 184.
383 Below, p. 224.
384 See above, p. xliii.
385 Below, pp. 234–8.
386 Below, p. 238.
387 Below, p. 240.
388 Below, p. 240–4, 306–8.
389 *PR 5 HII*, p. 37; *Red Book*, i. 306, below, p. 390.
390 Round, *Serjeants*, pp. 187, 189.

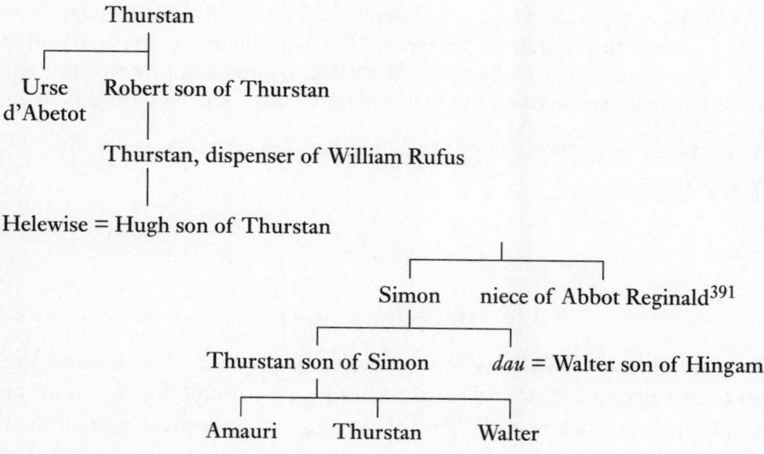

FIG. 2. The dispensers

The disputes with the dispensers emphasize the problems which could arise for a lord when a tenant was also a royal servant. Generally in legal matters the abbots were the ones to benefit from easy access to the king. In this instance, though, it was Simon who benefited from such access, when, with the abbey vacant, he established his claim before Henry I in Normandy.

Popes

The papacy is not very prominent in the *History*. A privilege probably issued by Innocent II does not appear in the text, and does not survive.[392] Alexander III's bulls were not included in the later version of the *History*.[393] Only when the abbey, deprived of royal aid under Stephen, turned to Eugenius III, do papal documents appear, and their impact is not recorded.[394] Papal letters could also be used against the abbey. Thurstan son of Simon the dispenser gave Marcham church to a royal clerk, Ralph of Tamworth. Ralph was unwilling to give up the church when Thurstan was disseised, but found that royal letters did not achieve his aim.[395] He therefore obtained papal letters, which he brought to Walkelin. He had, however, miscalculated.

[391] See above, p. xliii. [392] See above, p. xxix. [393] See above, p. xxxix.
[394] Below, pp. 264–80. [395] Below, p. 244.

[Walkelin] went to the king and showed him how deceitfully his cleric was acting against the church of Abingdon. The king therefore was angry with the cleric and instructed him that if he wished to remain in his court or even in his kingdom, he should strive to make peace with the church of Abingdon.

After 1154, as before 1135, the king, not the pope, was the abbey's best protector.

IV. ESTATES, DISPUTES, AND LAW

1. Abingdon's estates

The abbey had a wide variety of types of income. There were the rents and produce from its lands. There were jurisdictional and other secular rights, such as tolls. And there were ecclesiastical rights, most notably income from tithes which increased markedly during this period. Gifts, confirmations, and resumptions of all these types of right and revenue provide the bulk of the material of the *History*.

Domesday Book gives us our best indication of the estates' annual value.[396]

County	*Approx. annual income*	*Hidage*
(i) 1066		
Berkshire	slightly over £400	just over 510
Oxfordshire	slightly over £60	–
Gloucestershire	£12	–
(ii) 1086		
Berkshire	more than £420 but less than £450	approx. 320
Oxfordshire	slightly over £70	86
Gloucestershire	£9	7·5
Warwickshire	£9 10s	4

Domesday thus suggests a total income *TRE* of about £475, a 1086 income of between £510 and £540 p.a. The increased value came to a small extent from new acquisitions, but more from increased values of

[396] I give rounded figures and ranges because of the problems of making precise Domesday calculations from incomplete or problematic information: note e.g. the absence of a *ualet* for Chilton, *DB* i, fo. 59[r]; the apparent contradiction between *History* and Domesday concerning Shippon, below, pp. 24–6; the absence of an entry for Culham.

existing lands.[397] This made Abingdon probably the eighth wealthiest monastery in England in 1086.[398] Calculations based upon *Domesday* further suggest that just under 75% of the abbey's revenue came from demesne land. This compares with approximately 70% at Glastonbury, 85% at Christchurch Canterbury, 54% at Peterborough, and between about 55 and 60% from many lay tenancies in chief.[399]

The twelfth-century material does not allow us to make such full calculations. Some indications, though, are provided by income during vacancies. According to the *History*, during the vacancy of 1117–20, £300 a year was paid to the treasury, the remaining income comfortably allowing the church to have 'every abundance of provisions and clothing'.[400] This figure seems congruous with the *Domesday* evidence. During the 1164 vacancy, the Pipe Roll records Adam of Catmore rendering account of £87 3s. 10d. for half a year.[401] The Pipe Roll figures for the 1185 vacancy are more in line with those in the *History* for 1117–20. For a single year, but spread over two Pipe Rolls, Master Thomas of Hurstbourne rendered account for a total of £389 9s, of which £252 18s. 8d. came from the farms of the abbey's manors, the remainder from such sources as sales of corn, pleas, and other perquisites.[402]

Geographical Distribution

The abbey's lands were divided into two main groups, one centring on Abingdon itself and stretching westwards, close to the rivers Thames and Ock, the other on the Berkshire downs. There were also some more distant estates, in eastern Berkshire in the area of Windsor Forest, in north Oxfordshire, and in Warwickshire and Gloucestershire. There was no general policy as to the alienation or retention in

[397] Hudson, 'Abbey of Abingdon', p. 198. For general changes of value in Berkshire and Oxfordshire, see also *The Domesday Geography of South-East England*, ed. H. C. Darby and E. M. J. Campbell (Cambridge, 1962), pp. 209, 260; for hidage reduction in Berkshire, ibid., pp. 249–50.

[398] See D. Knowles, *The Monastic Order in England* (2nd edn., Cambridge, 1963), p. 702, although note that his figure for Abingdon is too low. In 1538, when it was dissolved, Abingdon had a net income of about £1876 10s 9d, making it the sixth wealthiest monastery in England; Lambrick, 'Administration', pp. 159, 181.

[399] See N. E. Stacy, 'Henry of Blois and the lordship of Glastonbury', *EHR* cxiv (1999), 1–33, at p. 4. Stacy gives the figure of 73% for Abingdon lands held in demesne in 1086, my own calculations produce the figure of 74%, which excludes Wallingford; such is a rare degree of harmony for Domesday statistics.

[400] Below, p. 224.

[401] *PR 11 HII*, p. 77.

[402] *PR 31 HII*, p. 29, *32 HII*, p. 117.

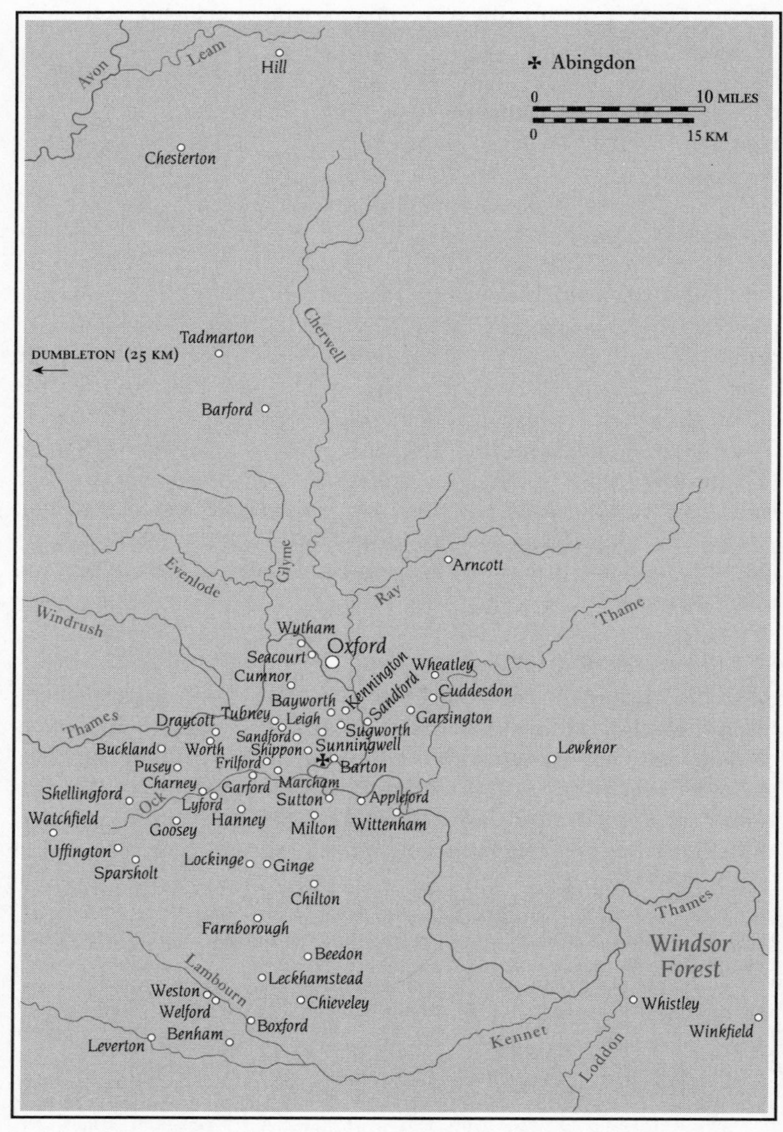

FIG. 3. Abingdon estates named in *Domesday* for 1086

demesne of distant estates. Whistley and Winkfield in eastern Berkshire were kept in demesne. In contrast, Chesterton in Warwickshire was granted to the knight Ansketel to hold in fee, in exchange for Tadmarton in north Oxfordshire. Indeed Tadmarton is a particularly notable instance of an estate repeatedly alienated and resumed.[403] Such distant estates may also have been particularly prone to disputes,[404] but conflicts also arose over lands at the heart of Abingdon's holdings.

Increases after 1086

Mention has already been made of some of the donors to Abingdon after the Norman Conquest, of the increased number of gifts in Faritius's time, and of the decline thereafter.[405] A rough calculation of the extent of post-Conquest acquisitions can be made, although the *History* or charter does not always provide a hidage for the gift. Including the initial endowment of Colne, gifts after 1071 amounted to between twenty and twenty-five hides, approximately two-thirds of which were under Faritius. This represents an increase in hidage of about one twentieth compared with the 1086 figure derived from *Domesday*.

The largest gift in hidage terms was the four hides at Chaddleworth given by Ralph Basset in the time of Abbot Vincent.[406] Next came Thorkell of Arden's gift of three hides at Chesterton and Hill under Adelelm,[407] while three gifts of two hides or slightly more were made under Faritius, two of which became part of the estates of Colne Priory.[408] The initial endowment of Colne was also approximately of

[403] See below, pp. 10, 236, 242; the exchange (below, p. 198) which allowed Ansketel to hold in fee Chesterton in Warwickshire whilst Tadmarton in Oxfordshire was taken back into the abbot's hand cannot really be seen as a significant step in concentrating the abbey's demesne lands close to Abingdon, since Tadmarton was distant in north Oxfordshire, and was later alienated again. Note also below, p. 50, on Abbot Reginald's alienation of Dumbleton, Glos.; although the land was found to have long belonged to the monks' use, its distance from Abingdon may underlie Reginald's decision to grant it to his nephew. Other relatively distant estates were Hill in Warwickshire, South Cerney in Gloucestershire. See above, p. lix, for the pattern of alienation in 1086 resembling that in 1066.

[404] *DB* i, fo. 169^{r} South Cerney; below, p. 26, Chesterton and Hill; below, p. 50, Dumbleton; below, p. 136, Hill; below, pp. 10, 238, Tadmarton; *Red Book*, i. 306 Hill.

[405] See above, p. lxviii.

[406] Below, p. 246.

[407] Below, p. 10.

[408] Below, pp. 82–4 (Kensington—becomes part of Colne's endowment), p. 90 (two carucates at Scaldwell, Northants.—become part of Colne's endowment), p. 158 (Wroxton).

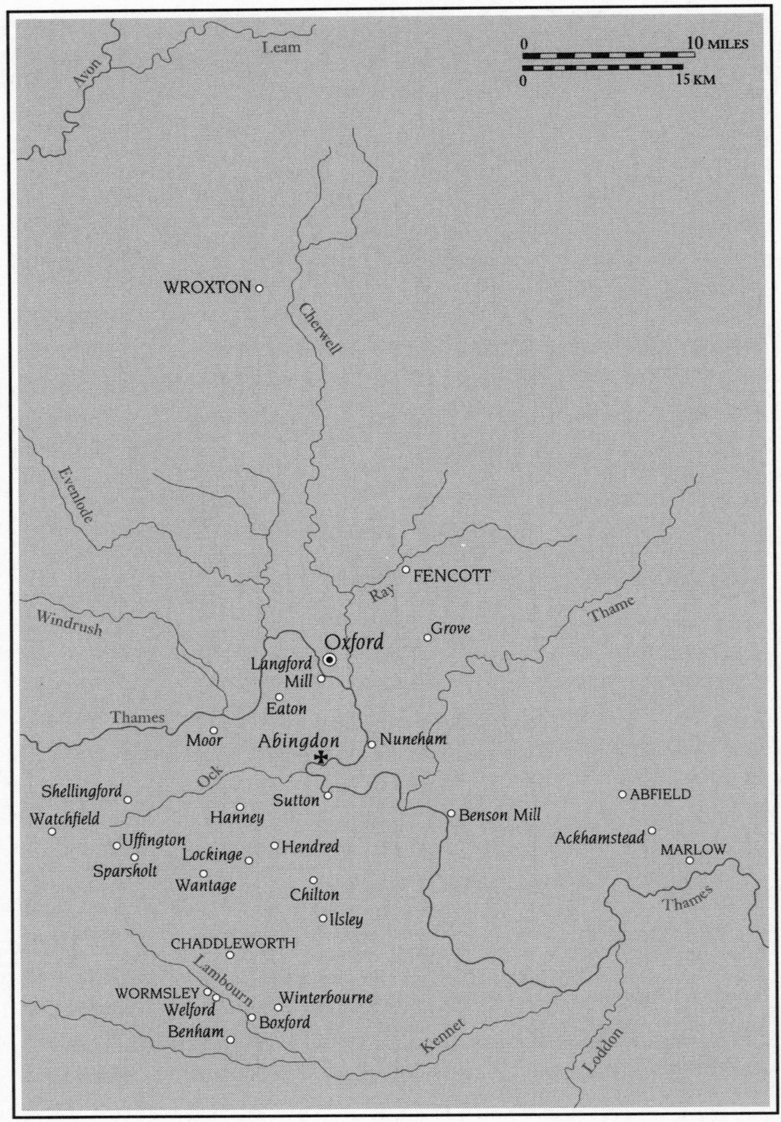

FIG. 4. Abingdon acquisitions after 1086

Acquisitions of a hide or more are in capitals; other acquisitions are in lower case.

NB The island of Andersey and Hennor mill are very close to Abingdon, and are not marked separately. I have omitted *Bulehea* and *Bradendena* as their identification is uncertain.

The acquisitions outside the area of the map were in the following places: Beds.: STRATTON Berks.: Windsor: houses Bucks.: Langley: land Essex and Suffolk: COLNE etc.: endowment of daughter house at Colne Glos.: DUMBLETON Hants.: Winchester: houses Middlesex: London: houses KENSINGTON: lands and church Northants.: STOKE BRUERN SHUTTLEHANGER

this scale. All remaining gifts were of a hide or less, although it should be remembered that some small benefactions could be particularly valuable in monetary or other terms, for example because they included houses or because of their geographical position. These aspects are epitomized by a gift of Henry I's queen, Matilda:

> it was very necessary that the queen bestow this gift on the church: completion of the journey which stretched from Abingdon to London was seen to be wearisome for travellers because of the large number of miles in between, the abbey having no house where a traveller could be suitably put up in mid-journey. That place, fifteen miles distant from London, offers reasonable opportunity for accommodation, since an abundance of woods, meadows, and merchandise exists there.[409]

The *History* protests greatly about the losses which the abbey incurred during Stephen's reign. However, in hidage terms those recorded were not very great. The most serious arose in the dispute with Simon the king's dispenser and his relatives over Tadmarton and other lands.[410] Apart from this, recorded disputes were on a smaller scale, like that over half a hide at Boars Hill.[411] It may be that other disputes were not recorded in the *History*, for example the incursions of William de Beauchamp and others mentioned in a bull of Eugenius III.[412] Alternatively, it may be that the losses were not so much complete deprivations of lands, but rather loss of income from lands harmed in the civil war and losses of money and treasure.[413]

Rights and income other than land[414]

Not many gifts of money or moveable goods are recorded in the *History*, but it does state that Robert d'Oilly 'conferred a sum of over £100 to emend for his past deeds, and to help the rebuilding of the monastery'.[415] Gifts of money may have been particularly welcome since at least some gifts of lands or other rights were made in return for payment. Hugh earl of Chester's charter records that Abbot Reginald gave him £30 of pennies in return for his grant of Shippon;

[409] Below, p. 144.
[410] See above, p. lxxii.
[411] Below, p. 282.
[412] Below, p. 278; the dispute with William Martel may have concerned land at Whistley and Winkfield; see Stephen's writ, below, p. 342.
[413] Below, p. 292.
[414] See also below, p. xcvi, on judicial privileges, p. xci for geld exemption.
[415] Below, p. 32.

the *De abbatibus* states that Abbot Reginald bought it for £30. William Rufus's charter states that he gave the church of Sutton Courtenay to Abingdon, the *History* adds that 'the sum of £20 of the abbey's money, in public coin, was paid to the royal treasury that this might be granted'.[416]

Sutton Courtenay was one of many of the churches in the Abingdon area which the abbey came to control.[417] In addition, the *History* gives a vivid account of Faritius personally supervising the building of a church at Uffington.[418] It has also been suggested that Cumnor church was probably rebuilt by the abbey in the late eleventh or early twelfth century, and that analogies with other churches may suggest that its west tower may have been for the abbot's use.[419] Together with the abbot's provision of a chapel at Whistley, and lay establishment of chapels at Kingston Bagpuize and Peasemore, these building works form part of a notable change in pastoral care in the area.[420] At the same time, the abbey was persistent in its efforts to ensure that its churches did not lose rights or revenues: the *History* includes accounts of the disputes arising from the new churches at Kingston Bagpuize and Peasemore.[421] One potential area of dispute with the establishment of such chapels was the reception of tithe, and tithes also feature very prominently amongst the new gifts to Abingdon from the time of Abbot Reginald.[422] According to both the *History* and the *De abbatibus*, indeed, Reginald was associated with the introduction of the regular payment of correct tithes of the harvest.[423] Grants of tithe to Abingdon continued to be common in the twelfth century, most being from neighbouring or nearby properties.[424]

[416] Below, pp. 24, 36, *CMA* ii. 285. For comment, see Hudson, *Land, Law, and Lordship*, pp. 164–5.

[417] See below, pp. 36–40, *Abingdon Cartularies*, ii, pp. xxv, xxx–xxxi; B. R. Kemp, 'Monastic possession of parish churches in England in the twelfth century', *Journal of Ecclesiastical History*, xxxi (1980), 133–60.

[418] See below, p. 208.

[419] J. Blair, J. Croom, and E. Coleman, 'The early church at Cumnor', *Oxoniensia*, liv (1989), 57–70.

[420] See below, pp. 22, 42, 176; more generally, see e.g. *Minsters and Parish Churches*, ed. J. Blair (Oxford, 1988).

[421] Below, pp. 42–4, 176–8; note also p. 294.

[422] Below, pp. 36, 44–8.

[423] Below, p. 34.

[424] See e.g. below, pp. 76–80, 86, 90, 138, 200, 206–12, 224–6, 244–6, 280, 282; see also Kemp, 'Monastic possession of parish churches'; J. Blair, *Early Medieval Surrey* (Stroud, 1991), pp. 148–50. Cf. B. F. Harvey, *Westminster Abbey and its Estates in the*

Other sources of revenue could also be significant for a monastery, for example income from the town where it was situated. However, if Abingdon was a monastery on the scale of St Albans or Bury, its associated town was much less significant and less assertive.[425] It does not appear by name in *Domesday*, being subsumed within the large manor of Barton. The *De obedientiariis*, of the late twelfth or early thirteenth century, does not give Abingdon any special status, but states that the kitchener 'will possess the vill of Abingdon as lord, freely and quit, and also all the other vills devoted to the kitchen'.[426] The *History* also usually refers to Abingdon as a *uilla*, undistinguished from other settlements, but on one occasion refers to it as a *burgus*.[427] Abingdon did not have burgal status by royal grant, although at least in the thirteenth century it was treated like a borough in having its own presenting jury before the eyre.[428]

Despite these limits to its status, the revenues from the town of Abingdon and in particular its market were worth protecting.[429] *Domesday* reveals something of Abingdon's economic life by recording that 'ten merchants dwelling (*manentes*) in front of the church gate render 40d',[430] and the urban element must have increased in the twelfth century. The abbey faced challenges regarding the market under both Henry I and Henry II. In the first case, opponents of the abbey claimed that of old there had never been a market. Abbot Vincent eventually obtained a royal confirmation of the market, together with the hundred, but only in return for a reported payment of 300 marks—suggestive of the value of these rights.[431] Under Henry II, men of Wallingford and Oxford claimed that in Henry I's reign only a limited range of goods were sold at the market, according to the men of Wallingford nothing except bread and beer, according to those of Oxford a wider range of goods, but not those brought in carts or cargo boats. Eventually the abbey won its case, and Henry 'ordered

Middle Ages (Oxford, 1977), p. 47, on the rarity of gifts of tithe by the laity to Westminster.

[425] On the town of Abingdon, see e.g. *Abingdon Cartularies*, ii, pp. xxxvi–xxxvii.

[426] *CMA* ii. 392; see also ii. 306. On the association of its revenues with the monks' kitchen by 1170, see below, p. 395.

[427] Below, p. 186.

[428] See e.g. *The Roll and Writ File of the Berkshire Eyre of 1248*, ed. M. T. Clanchy (Selden Soc., xc, 1973), pp. xli, 347–9: 'Villa de Abbendon' uenit per xii.'

[429] Below, p. 395 attributes a core payment of £16 a year to the kitchen from Abingdon.

[430] *DB* i, fo. 58^{v}.

[431] Below, pp. 230–2.

that from that day the fullest market should exist at Abingdon, with the sole exception of boats, the abbot using only his own'.[432]

The abbey also had rights to other income from commerce. Particularly notable are the renders of herrings:

From the time of lord Abbot Ordric [1052–66], it has been the custom of this church, that one hundred herrings—or a suitable price for them—be paid each year to the cellarer, in due fashion, from each boat of the city of Oxford which travels southwards by the water of the Thames flowing next to the court of Abingdon. The oarsmen of the boats render them to the cellarer, without being asked, specifically from the time of the Purification of St Mary [2 Feb.] until Easter.

With Henry I's aid, Faritius and the cellarer staged a successful defence of this right against the boatmen of Oxford.[433] The abbey, on the other hand, enjoyed quittance of toll on its own goods, and had this privilege confirmed by a series of royal writs.[434]

Domesday mentions revenues from several fisheries, for example five fisheries at Barton rendering 18s. 4d., that at Whistley rendering 300 eels.[435] The later manuscript of the *History* specifies that approximately 2,400 eels were to be rendered by fisheries.[436] *Domesday* also records the abbey receiving revenue from thirty-two mills, and several more were acquired in the time of Faritius, for example through William son of Aiulf's grant of Boymill.[437] Further mills feature in the endowment of Colne priory.[438] Abingdon benefited considerably from the location of its lands, particularly in the valuable area close to the Thames and its tributaries.

[432] Below, p. 312. Note also *Curia Regis Rolls* (HMSO, 1922–), vi. 296–7, for a later abbot claiming that from the time of the Norman Conquest the abbey had held a 'congregacio' at Shellingford, without the abbot or his men taking toll or other custom from there.

[433] Below, pp. 174, 374. The timing of the render suggests the importance of the fish to the Lenten diet.

[434] Below, pp. 2, 116–18, 300, 342.

[435] *DB* i, fos. 58^{v}, 59^{r}; for eel renders from Whistley, see also below, p. 338. For fish weirs on the Thames and its side streams, see J. Blair, *Anglo-Saxon Oxfordshire* (Stroud, 1994), pp. 123–4; see also *Domesday Geography of South-East England*, pp. 268–9.

[436] Below, p. 338; note also the importance of dairy-farming, on which see further *CMA* ii. 287 (*De abbatibus* on dairy-farms), 308 (kitchener's income; in MS C, list in later hand); below, p. 396 (kitchener's income; in MS C, list in main hand); *VCH*, *Berkshire*, i. 306; *Domesday Geography of South-East England*, p. 280.

[437] Below, pp. 154–6; see also pp. 94–6, 180, 190, 216. From Walkelin's time, see below, p. 316.

[438] Below, pp. 86, 92.

The period after the Conquest, then, did not see a great growth in the extent of Abingdon's estates. However, it did see some acquisitions of land, and also of other revenues. In addition, it appears to have been a period of continuing economic development. The establishment of new churches and conflicts with neighbours over markets may well be signs of economic development, as is competition over mills and meadows.[439] Some of the economic development was probably the work of the abbots themselves. Most notably, the *History* states of Faritius that at

Easter in the year when he took up the abbacy, throughout the church's possessions every plot was devoid of crops. Lest this recur in future, we have seen by his efforts so increased an abundance of crops throughout the abbey's estates, that sometimes three years' grain, often two, was available.[440]

2. Internal arrangement of estates and revenues

Gabrielle Lambrick suggested that in the later Anglo-Saxon period seven central manors were appropriated to the convent for the provision of food supplies: Cumnor, Barton, Marcham, Charney, Uffington, Lockinge with Farnborough, and Milton.[441] Monks lived on these manors, sending in regular contributions. However, such a system is not clear from *Domesday* nor from the *History*. If it was functioning before 1066, it may have been ended as part of a restoration of discipline under Adelelm and Reginald.[442]

After the Conquest, many monasteries saw the gradual emergence of a division of revenues between abbot and convent. The impetus came from various directions: the secular involvement of the abbot; the development of a separate household and separate living quarters for him; internal conflict over alienation of lands; the desire to protect monks during vacancies.[443] At Abingdon, *Domesday* gives only very

[439] For disputes over mills, see below, pp. 20, 94, 172. Note also disputes over meadows, see below, pp. 32, 94, 124, 172, 194, 328.

[440] Below, p. 70.

[441] Lambrick, 'Administration', p. 161; see discussion in Vol. i, Introduction, 'Endowment and estates'.

[442] Lambrick, 'Administration', p. 163; note also ibid., p. 182, for a thirteenth- or fourteenth-century memorandum recording that the monks residing outside monastery lived 'minus ordinate quam deceret', and amongst laymen.

[443] In general see Hudson, *Land, Law, and Lordship*, pp. 234–8 (where I am more cautious about Abingdon's seals); M. Howell, 'Abbatial vacancies and the divided *mensa* in medieval England', *Journal of Ecclesiastical History*, xxxiii (1982), 173–92, esp. pp. 173–81; E. U. Crosby, *Bishop and Chapter in Twelfth-Century England* (Cambridge, 1994). For Abingdon, see also Lambrick, 'Administration', pp. 164–8; below, pp. cii–iii, on the

limited information. The three hides which Wulfwig held in East Hanney were 'of the monks' demesne provisions' before 1066. Also, the *History* backs up *Domesday*'s statement that Hermer held seven hides in Goosey and 'he is on the monks' demesne provisions'.[444] However, such phrases do not prove the existence of a clear division of lands between abbot and monks. During the vacancy of 1117–20, an *ad hoc* arrangement was made, with £300 a year being paid to the royal treasury; had a clear division of revenues existed, such an *ad hoc* arrangement might have been unnecessary. It is notable that the *History* says that Ingulf kept 'the seal of the church under his own control and confirmed with it what he wished'.[445] Probably this was the common seal of the monastery, separate seals for convent and abbot not yet having been created. The earliest surviving impression of an abbot's seal is a fragment of Abbot Roger's (1175–85).[446]

The principle of division is most clearly seen both challenged and confirmed in the vacancy of 1185–6. According to a later addition in MS C, the custodian, Master Thomas of Hurstbourne, 'put it to us that the justices of the lord king had ordered him to seise into the hand of the lord king what is subjected to our obediences as well as the possessions belonging to the chamber of the abbot'.[447] The monks persuaded Ranulf de Glanville of the justice of their case, and he ordered Thomas 'that as our accounts were separated from those of the abbot, as we had clearly proved before him, he only had care of whatever belonged to the chamber of the abbot'. However, the division of revenues was still not complete. Thomas also noted that the monks were accustomed to receive certain unspecified things 'at fixed times by the hand of the abbot'. These may have been revenues from the seven manors named at the start of this section, with some additions. In return, the abbot would provide various supplies for the monks, and fulfil various duties, notably with regard to the expense of lawsuits.[448] The limits of the division of revenues helps to explain certain characteristics of Abingdon

abbot's buildings. Concerning the abbot's household, the *History* contains references to the abbot's chamberlain and the steward; abbot's chamberlain as donor below p. 224, as witness pp. 88, 154, 226; steward / seneschal pp. 348, 360; *CMA* ii. 351.

444 *DB* i, fo. 59ʳ, below, p. 8.

445 Below, p. 290.

446 On seals, see *Abingdon Cartularies*, i, pp. xxxiii–xxxvii.

447 *CMA* ii. 297–8, *English Lawsuits*, no. 570, on which see above, p. xxvi. The account in MS B appears below, p. 358.

448 Lambrick, 'Administration', pp. 173, 182.

administration in the later middle ages, such as the limited importance of the cellarer.[449]

The separation of revenues clearly relates to the endowment of specific monastic offices. These are commonly referred to as obediences, although the Latin term appears only once in the *History*, and that in a document rather than narrative: Abbot Ingulf's testament granted 'to our convent all the customs which it had in each of its offices (*obedientiis*)'.[450] The *History* states that the tithe of East Hendred was given by Robert Marmion in the time of Abbot Reginald, and 'conferred to the care of the almoner, for the reception and service of the poor'.[451] This may be the first grant to a specific office, although it is possible that the bestowal on the almoner was either a later event, or an assumption concerning the original gift based on later arrangements.[452] Lists of endowments of the offices begin with Faritius who made gifts to the sacristy ('the church'), the monks' chamber, the almonry, the refectory, the cellar, and the infirmary.[453] Following Faritius's death, Ralph his chamberlain granted the church a tithe of two hides in Shellingford, and the convent delegated this to the refectorer.[454] Abbot Vincent made grants to the kitchen, the cellar, the refectory, the chamber, the sacristy ('the office of the altar'), and the lignary ('the fuel provision of the brothers').[455] Under Abbot Ingulf, the kitchen acquired Whistley and Winkfield 'for the monks' provision of fat'. His testament also mentions his grant of the rent of the mill of Watchfield, and the *De abbatibus* states that he gave this, Ock mill, and Shippon to the kitchen. A list of the kitchen's revenues probably from before *c.*1170 includes all these grants.[456] Ingulf also granted the sacristy revenues from Milton, and the church of St Aldate, Oxford.

[449] Lambrick, 'Administration', p. 175. For later concern about vacancies, note Lyell, no. 140, Chatsworth, no. 358.

[450] Below, p. 296.

[451] Below, p. 46.

[452] Below, p. 46, the charter of Ralph Rosel is very brief and mentions no special assignment. The warning against infringement of this grant, below, p. 46, may be directed against future abbots as well as Robert Marmion and Ralph Rosel's successors.

[453] Below, pp. 214–16, 394; the tithe of Dumbleton for buying parchment for the abbey's books was, or became, associated with the precentor, *CMA* ii. 328. See also below, p. 80, (for the almonry). Note also below, p. 332. On his grant for the monks' fuel supply, see above, p. xlviii, and below, p. 394.

[454] Below, p. 224.

[455] Below, p. 252.

[456] Below, pp. 296, 395.

The revenue from Milton was probably from tithe, which appears as belonging to the sacristy in a bull of Eugenius III and an early list of the 'rents of the altar'.[457] The *De abbatibus* mentions his grant of twenty shillings in Drayton to the sacrist; conceivably this may be revenue from the Milton tithe, since the two are neighbouring settlements, but the sacrist also received revenues from land in Drayton.[458] The *De abbatibus* attributes to Ingulf the grant of the tithe of Grove and a mill at Benson to the infirmary, but according to the *History*, this mill was received in the time of Abbot Walkelin.[459] In addition Ingulf's testament contained a general confirmation of the offices' customs, 'that is in the cellar, in the refectory, in the almonry, in the maundy, in the sacristy, in the house of the sick, in the kitchen, in the chamber, in the custom of servants, in the court, in the receiving of guests, in the provision of wood, and in the works of the church'.[460]

These grants, together with lists which survive in MS C, including some in the same hand as the *History*, and also the survey undertaken in the vacancy of 1185 reveal the great extent and variety of revenues each office possessed.[461] For example, by Faritius's gift, the chamber had the village of Chieveley (except for thirty-two shillings which pertained to the kitchen), thirty shillings rent from Fencott, twenty-five shillings from the land of Henry d'Aubigny, and five shillings from Egelward of Colnbrook. To these Vincent added Ralph Basset's gift of four hides at Chaddleworth. A further list, in the hand of the author of the *History*, records the chamber also having £37 from the village of Welford and various other rents and possessions.[462] Lambrick points out that Chieveley and Welford were below southern slopes of the Berkshire downs, which certainly later was a good sheep-farming area. It may then have been allotted to the chamberlain for the monks' clothing.[463] The kitchener's estates were much more

[457] Below, pp. 272, 397.

[458] *CMA* ii. 291; see below, pp. 272, 284, for lands in Drayton owing payment to the altar of St Mary.

[459] *CMA* ii. 291; below, p. 314. See also *CMA* ii. 328.

[460] Below, p. 296. Lambrick, 'Administration', p. 169, working from the *De obedientariis*, notes that by the end of the twelfth century, there was also a hostilar, a keeper of works, a gardener, and a pittancer; for the later development of officials, see Lambrick, 'Administration', pp. 174–8. See below, p. cii, on building work related to the specific offices.

[461] For the 1185 survey, see below, p. 358. The lists in MS C which are in the same hand as the *History* summarize the total revenue, for example, of the lignary as £22, that of the kitchen as £82 10s together with extensive renders in kind; below, pp. 395, 396.

[462] Below, pp. 216, 252, 398.

[463] Lambrick, 'Administration', p. 169.

scattered. According to the *History*, Abbot Vincent gave all the rents of Abingdon and a mill on the Ock, and Ingulf added the East Berkshire estates of Winkfield and Whistley.[464] These manors in the more heavily wooded areas of south-east Berkshire were particularly suitable for pig grazing, and hence for provision of fat. The choice of estates with which to endow obedientiaries was based on practical considerations relating to the life of the monastery.

3. Disputes and law

Along with the other monastic chronicles of the period, the *History* is an essential source for the historian of law. It provides information concerning substantive law, disputes, and jurisdiction. Occasional pieces of vocabulary, such as the phrase 'manus inicio', suggest the influence of Roman and canon law,[465] and the latter also appears in the justifications for alienation mentioned in Faritius's excommunication of despoilers of the church.[466] In general, though, the language of the *History*'s narrative does not betray notable learned influence, but rather resembles the regular vocabulary and phraseology of charters and dispute records of the period *c.*1066–1166.

Substantive Law

The *History* is a particularly important source with regard to the law of land-holding, and some issues of land law can helpfully be explained here rather than in footnotes. The *History* is especially interested in the acquisition of lands by the church, and hence is revealing of practices of alienation by the laity.[467] In several instances, the consent of relatives to a grant is mentioned, but this is far from being a standard part of the record.[468] More attention is paid to delivery of seisin, and the witnessing of such delivery. Sometimes the

[464] Below, pp. 252, 296. See further below, p. 395.

[465] Below, p. 182. See also the phrase 'proprio fructuario', below, p. 56. Comparison with other passages suggest that 'proprio' is here an adjective, 'fructuario' a noun, although this cannot be certain. If so, this is an instance of the *History* using a distinctively Romano-canonical word, rather than its more common vocabulary such as 'proprio usui'; see below, pp. 50, 180. This might still be the case if 'fructuario' were an adjective, or the phrase could simply mean 'from the brother's fruitful property'.

[466] Below, p. 220.

[467] For gifts to church involving payment, see above, p. lxxix.

[468] For kin participation in grants, see e.g. below, pp. 24 (wife), 82 (wife and son), 152 (wife), 206 (step-father, mother, mother's brother, daughter), 209 (wife and son), 212 (wife); below, p. xciii, for claims by kin.

donor himself delivered seisin, sometimes an official.[469] Such delivery could also be combined with other ceremonies, notably the placing of a symbol of the gift on the altar, or a new tenant doing homage to the church.[470]

A dying donor might have problems delivering seisin in person, and the incapacitated Robert son of Hamo used his steward for this purpose.[471] In other instances, family participation or rapid confirmation were particularly desirable for death-bed gifts.[472] When the mortally ill Geoffrey de Ver made his grant of the church of Kensington he did so 'with his father Aubrey and his mother Beatrice together with his brothers granting this'. Here, however, the need for consent may also reflect the peculiar situation of an heir making a grant when his father was still alive, and it is notable that Henry I's confirmation attributes the gift to Aubrey himself.[473]

Confirmations, and particularly written confirmations, strengthened the abbey's hold on the gift. In some instances, the *History* provides only a charter of the donor's son, not the donor himself, perhaps as a result of the loss of the earlier document, but perhaps reflecting the increased production of written evidence.[474] For another gift, of a hide at Dumbleton, we have a charter not of the donor but of his lord, Robert count of Meulan. Again it is possible that at this date, 1107 × 1108, the donor did not have a seal of his own.[475] More generally, the lord's confirmation strengthened the abbey's hold on the land, and might remit any services owed from it.[476] If a new lord had taken over the lands of an earlier donor, a confirmation might be particularly necessary.[477] The abbey also obtained many royal confirmations, occasionally of a number of grants, more commonly of specific gifts. As with writs in law cases, some would have been obtained by the abbot in person, others through intermediaries. For example, the count of Meulan was also present at Henry I's confirmation of the gift of a hide at

469 See e.g. below, pp. 78, 88.

470 See e.g. below, pp. 78, 156, 186; also for placing on the altar, see pp. 24, 78, 142, 146, 180, 206, 212, 236.

471 Below, p. 140; note also p. 142. See generally Hudson, *Land, Law, and Lordship*, pp. 195–6.

472 See below, p. 108.

473 Below, pp. 82–4.

474 See below, pp. 80, 148.

475 Below, p. 150.

476 Hudson, *Land, Law, and Lordship*, pp. 218–19; see also below, p. 102.

477 Below, p. 26.

Dumbleton, and may have been responsible for obtaining that confirmation.[478]

So far we have been concerned with grants to the church. What about alienations by the church? These were prohibited, or at the very least restricted, by canon law, and by the oath which the abbot took on his installation.[479] In practice, however, the granting of lands was a necessary and problematic part of the church's existence. Particular problems arose from alienation of lands attributed to the monks' own use,[480] and the difficulties of resuming grants by Modbert and Ingulf feature prominently in the *History*.[481] Especially in the case of Ingulf, the emphasis is on the alienations being made 'against the will of the convent' or 'without the assent of the convent', whereas many charters and cases of the period reveal that the monks' consent to alienation was regarded as proper.[482] Thus when Abbot Faritius gave land at Chesterton to Ansketel, in exchange for his land at Tadmarton, he did so 'by the consent of the monks and on the authority of the knights'.[483] In addition, the king claimed some control over grants of monastic lands, and at Abingdon the knight Rainbald gave back various possessions to Abbot Faritius 'because he had them and many others from the monks' demesne without the king's and monks' consent'.[484]

When land had been alienated, the abbey strove to ensure that the tenurial basis of land-holding from the church was recognized, whereas tenants strove to escape such tenure by not performing homage or services. Nigel d'Oilly failed to do homage and service for his lands held from Abingdon for a long time after the appointment of Faritius. The abbot took court action so that Nigel would do homage to the church and abbot for what he held 'and recognize their lordship of these things for the future'. The terms of his tenure were then spelt out.[485] Henry I ordered Robert Mauduit to perform for Faritius the customary service he owed from the land he held,

[478] Below, p. 152.

[479] See above, p. xl, below, pp. 6, 294; Hudson, *Land, Law, and Lordship*, pp. 231–4.

[480] See e.g. below, p. 8.

[481] See e.g. below, pp. 192, 290–2.

[482] Hudson, *Land, Law, and Lordship*, pp. 238–40.

[483] Below, p. 198.

[484] Below, p. 190. Hudson, *Land, Law, and Lordship*, pp. 247–9.

[485] Below, p. 194. For the 'recognition' of lordship, see also e.g. below, p. 156. For attempts to escape homage and service, see also e.g. p. 188; the settlement arising from this case emphasized that the knight concerned was not free to alienate the land he held of the church.

'and if you do not, then I order that the aforesaid abbot is to do as he wishes concerning his land which you hold'.[486] The phraseology is significant: the land was the abbot's, Robert merely held it. In contrast, the church was only very rarely stated to hold land from someone.[487] The tenurial bond is presented as a feature of lay not ecclesiastical land-holding.[488]

In general, though, the abbey's tenants were fairly secure in their tenure. Failure to perform service led to distraint and court action, but rarely to forfeiture. When William the king's chamberlain had to confess that he had failed to do knight service in 1101, 'it was decided according to the law of the country that he deservedly ought to be deprived of the land, [but] at the intercession of good men who were present the abbot gave him back that land', on specified terms.[489]

The *History* in general is less concerned about inheritance by its tenants than about homage and service. Disputes over men trying to hold onto grants made only for their predecessors' life-time are few.[490] In general, the church seems to have assumed that lands held by its knights would be passed down by inheritance. In return for accepting an inheritance claim, the abbot would receive relief, and in one interesting and rare instance this took the form of surrendering three hides of the claimed holding.[491] When discussing the de Ver family, the *History* mentions primogeniture as the pattern for male heirs.[492] The early pattern for female inheritance is less certain, although it came to be division between heiresses. Late in the eleventh century Gilbert Latimer did divide his lands at Garsington between his daughters, but this occurred in his lifetime and in relation to their marriages, rather than after his death as a matter of inheritance. On the other hand, we have seen that after 1166 the lands of William Grim passed to his daughters, implying division.[493]

486 Below, p. 134. On the significance of pronouns, note also below, p. 56: 'although we have said that these things were [Rainbald's], however he had nothing which he had not acquired by the gift of that abbot [Reginald]. Indeed the more valuable of them were had from the brethren's own lands.'

487 See below, p. 108, cf. p. 100.

488 Note also below, p. xci.

489 Below, p. 186. On forfeiture, see Hudson, *Land, Law, and Lordship*, pp. 33–4.

490 See below, pp. 48, 282.

491 Below, p. 28.

492 Below, p. 82; see also p. 84.

493 Below, p. 48; above, p. xxv, for William Grim. On female inheritance, see also J. C. Holt, 'Feudal society and the family in early medieval England: iv. The heiress and the alien', *TRHS*, 5th Ser. xxxv (1985), 1–28; J. A. Green, *The Aristocracy of Norman England* (Cambridge, 1997), pp. 372–81.

Cases of female succession are, then, too few to draw firm conclusions concerning possible changes in inheritance pattern.

Disputes

The *History* recounts numerous disputes. Whilst it must be remembered that these are *ex parte* accounts, four initial conclusions can safely be drawn. Disputes were generally conducted without violence.[494] Many of the key proceedings took place in court. The king, especially Henry I, was very much involved in the processes of justice. And Stephen's reign provides something of an exception to each of the three preceding conclusions.

Occasionally the *History* will refer to the abbey's opponents only in vague terms, for example 'some greedy-minded men'.[495] In these cases, the writer may not have known the men's precise identity, have considered it unimportant, or have refrained from mentioning their names as an act of discretion. Those of the abbey's opponents who are named or specified by office can be grouped into various, not mutually exclusive, groups. A significant proportion were local royal officials. These included Ælfsige, reeve of the royal village of Sutton Courtenay, who exacted carrying services from the church's men, and brushwood from Abingdon's woods at Cumnor and Bagley.[496] Faritius too had to obtain royal protection against 'the accusations of the king's foresters' regarding these woods,[497] and various of Henry I's writs were directed against his own officials.[498] In the vacancy after Faritius's death, the abbey had to establish the quittance of its demesne hides against the demands of the county geld collectors.[499] In addition, as we have already seen, the abbey came into dispute with another kind of royal minister, the household servant such as the dispensers. In these cases, the disputes arose not over royal demands upon the church but over the tenurial relationship of the abbey and the king's servant.[500]

Tenants of the church formed the second main group of disputants. These cases generally involved failure to perform service,

494 An exception is below, p. 14, although even there the use of force was very specific.

495 Below, p. 104; see also p. 74, on the abbey's rivals in obtaining Andersey.

496 Below, p. 14.

497 Below, p. 166.

498 e.g. below, p. 118; see also above, p. lxxi, on Hugh of Buckland being ordered to restore land to the church.

499 Below, p. 226.

500 See above, p. lxxi; also below, pp. 196–8, involving Herbert, Henry I's chamberlain and treasurer.

disagreement as to the amount of service, and failure to do homage. Such cases may have been particularly common early in abbacies, and certainly there was a cluster in Faritius's first years, following the vacancy of 1097–1100.[501]

Thirdly there were disputes with neighbours. Some were with groups of men, and these often concerned jurisdiction or mills.[502] There were repeated clashes with the men of Sutton Courtenay, over the hundred of Hormer, and over incursions on the abbey's land of Culham in order to take 'turfs of that land for the use of the king's mill and fishery'.[503] In Stephen's reign there seem to have been particular problems with the knights of the honour of Wallingford, and under Henry II the men of Wallingford together with those of Oxford brought the case concerning Abingdon market.[504] Also in Stephen's reign there were disputes with powerful individuals of the region, as is revealed by a bull of Eugenius III addressed to the archbishop of Canterbury and the bishops of Lincoln, Worcester, and Salisbury:

> We have received the serious complaint of the religious brothers of Abingdon that William Martel, Hugh de Bolbec, William de Beauchamp, John Marshal, and their men and also many other men of your dioceses are violently invading their possessions, and seizing and taking away their goods, and demanding from them castle-work services which are not owed.[505]

A different kind of dispute with a neighbour set Abingdon against the church of St Frideswide, over the body of the priest Nicholas:

> the canons of St Frideswide who were present thought him already dead, and they placed their own habit on him without his knowledge, possibly desiring him because of his wealth. Thus they wrongfully seized him by force for their own church.[506]

[501] See e.g. below, pp. 184, 186.

[502] Below, pp. 20, 124, 134.

[503] Below, pp. 166, 170–2; see also *CMA* ii. 289. Bk. i, c. 9, Vol. i, c. B11, and *De abbatibus* present one hundred hides at Sutton as having been part of the early endowment of the abbey, but given away to King Cenwulf of the Mercians; *CMA* i. 21 n., 23, ii. 274. *Charters of Abingdon Abbey*, p. 44, suggests that the hundred hides were not 'at' Sutton, but transferred to the royal vill of Sutton; this contradicts the view of *De abbatibus*. The later version of the *History* states that Ine gave Sutton to the abbey, Vol. i, c. B11 (*CMA* i. 14).

[504] Below, pp. 288, 308, 314.

[505] Below, p. 278.

[506] Below, p. 256; the case clearly demonstrates the desirability of being the last resting place of a potential donor.

A few disputes were with donors or their kin over the continuation of gifts.[507] Richard Basset sought to regain his grandfather's gift of four hides at Chaddleworth.[508] Other challenges came at the time of the gift. When two relatives of a certain Scalegrai heard that he was considering making the church heir of his houses, they moved a hereditary claim to the property, but without success.[509]

The *History* also reveals much of procedure in law cases. Summons to answer in court would mark an important stage in a dispute, and might assert pressure on the abbey's opponent. Failure to perform services led to distraint, as in disputes with William de Jumièges and Ermenold, a burgess of Oxford.[510] Distraint consisted of a temporary taking of the tenant's goods, and sometimes lands, intended to compel the tenant to answer in court, or to perform the services, or both.[511] However, problems in getting people to respond, together with the desire to bring to bear all possible influence, help to explain why Abingdon obtained royal writs.[512] The abbot or another member of the monastery may have had to go to the king in person in order to obtain the writ, or information may have been passed by an intermediary.[513] Not surprisingly, therefore, most of the writs were obtained in southern England, although Henry II's series of writs issued at Rouen is an exception.[514] Some of the writs were couched in terms of confirmations of particular rights, some as orders to participants in disputes. In the latter instances, the writ might conclude with a statement that if the addressee did not obey the order, someone else would enforce it. This could be the sheriff of the relevant county, or a royal justice, or the addressee's lord.[515]

Royal orders were not always effective, and this was the reason the *History* gives for the abbey turning to the pope in Stephen's reign. We can also see delaying tactics being used against royal writs, both by the abbot and the abbey's opponents.[516] Such instances emphasize

[507] See also below, p. 180, discussed above, p. l; below, p. 18. For an heir apparently making a claim out of ignorance of his father's gift, see below, p. 244.

[508] Below, pp. 246–50.

[509] Below, p. 286.

[510] Below, pp. 136, 204.

[511] See Hudson, *Land, Law, and Lordship*, pp. 22–44.

[512] See e.g. below, p. 134; see also pp. 132, 136. For an instance of royal involvement for which no writ survives, and for which no writ need have existed, see below, p. 180.

[513] See e.g. below, pp. 242–4; note also p. 180.

[514] Below, pp. 298–306; note also pp. 346, 372–6.

[515] See below, pp. 116, 126, 134, 248.

[516] See below, pp. 240, 242.

how slow a case might be to reach its conclusion. Moreover, royal support, at least on occasions, required payment. The *History* reports that Abbot Reginald had to give Rufus a total of £70 and two high quality horses to regain Dumbleton, Abbot Faritius £60 to Henry I to regain Sparsholt, Abbot Vincent £200 to Henry for confirmation of the market and hundred.[517] Should we trust these figures? For matters arising in the year 1129–30, the first surviving Pipe Roll reveals that Henry I demanded over £790 for what Judith Green has referred to as 'help in judicial matters'. However, only slightly over £100 of this was actually paid during that year.[518] The *History*'s figures, particularly those concerning Dumbleton and Sparsholt, therefore seem rather high for one-off payments, but more plausible as amounts offered.

Parties in disputes also looked to backers other than the king.[519] Particularly useful to the abbey was the support of Hugh of Buckland, already mentioned in the context of the dispute over Hennor mill.[520] It is notable that he is both addressee and witness to the royal writ concerning the dispute; part of his aid may have been in obtaining the document. Such support need not come free. The custodian Modbert's grant of three hides at Hanney to Hugh was made on the consideration that he was the sheriff and royal justice.[521] When Abbot Ingulf was too old to attend county courts, 'he was long accustomed to give annually 100s. to the sheriff of Berkshire for the following reason, that he treat the abbey's men more leniently and help them in pleas and hundreds, if they had any need'.[522] The *History* only condemns this payment because it became ineffective, but when the abbey's opponents purchased support, the *History* presents it as a matter of corruption.[523]

The main interest of the *History* in disputes concerned Abingdon's claims and the outcome of the dispute. Varying amounts of attention were paid to matters such as procedure and proof.[524] We do hear of 'reasoned pleading and testimony', of the witness of the county or

[517] Below, pp. 50, 184, 230; the last of these conceivably might also be taken as a payment to be free of the king's anger or ill-will, on which see above, p. lxiv.

[518] J. A. Green, '"Preclarum et magnificum antiquitatis monumentum": the earliest surviving Pipe Roll', *BIHR* lv (1982), 1–17, at pp. 9, 17.

[519] See also below, p. 226, for the help received from Ranulf the chancellor.

[520] See above, p. lxxi.

[521] Below, p. 62.

[522] Below, p. 314.

[523] Below, p. 240.

[524] For lack of clear statements as to procedure, see e.g. pp. 188–90, 194.

hundred, of enquiries, and of the use of documents.[525] The overall impression given is that such procedures were more common than reliance on the oath of one party or upon ordeal; indeed there is only one explicit mention of trial by battle, in a section added to MS B.[526]

Court cases often were ended by a judgment tempered with an element of compromise or mercy to the defeated party.[527] The abbey sometimes made payments in order to retrieve lands, a notable example being the £10 a year Abbot Adelelm had to promise Robert d'Oilly for the restoration of Tadmarton.[528] Settlement in or out of court was reinforced by oaths and rituals.[529] Giralmus de Curzun withheld the tithe of West Lockinge from the abbey: 'rebuked by Richard [the sacrist], he did penance and with his own hands broke the bolts of the barn and gave the tithe back to the church, confirming with an oath that he would do nothing similar again.'[530] Nevertheless, he was again to withhold payment, and had to be persuaded by words and concessions before he would again confirm the tithe.

When the normal channels of justice were blocked, for example through the absence of royal support or the particular recalcitrance of the opponent, the abbey might have to rely on spiritual measures or divine intervention, particularly in the form of sickness.[531] In Stephen's reign, William Boterel plundered the abbey's village of Culham.[532] Requests for restoration were ignored.

Thus compelled, Abbot Ingulf (at the order of Theobald archbishop of Canterbury and Jocelin bishop of Salisbury) resorted to the retribution of the

[525] Reasoned pleading and/or testimony: below, pp. 16, 22, 28, 44; witness of county etc.: pp. 4, 172, 308; use of documents: pp. 4, 50, 106, 170 (Domesday); enquiries: pp. 204, 306. For the testimony of a great man, see below, p. 312. For discussion in court, see also below, p. 344. For the possibility that documents were forged to support Abingdon claims, see Vol. i, Introduction, 'Anglo-Saxon charters'; also *Charters of Abingdon Abbey*, pp. 98, 436, 442, 566, 569, 572. It should be noted, however, that the *History*'s accounts of these disputes do not mention such pre-Conquest documents.

[526] Below, p. 344.

[527] See e.g. below, pp. 10, 152, 172. On occasion the *History* may have played down the element of concession, in order to present the case as a victory for the abbey; below, p. 288, could be read thus. Not all cases ended in court. For example, it is possible that failure to do service could result in confiscation of the land without any court judgment: below, p. 238; note also below, p. 56, where the lands had been deserted by their tenant, Rainbald. On other occasions conviction of a crime led to forfeiture; below, pp. 152–4.

[528] Below, p. 10.

[529] See e.g. below, p. 152.

[530] Below, p. 284.

[531] For excommunications issued against future violators of Abingdon lands, see also below, pp. 56, 218.

[532] Below, p. 314.

holy Church and condemned William to the bond of anathema. Yet, despite this condemnation, until the day of his death he neglected to seek forgiveness concerning his misdeed or absolution concerning the anathema. But at long last, by God's just judgment, he received in the aforementioned war a deadly wound, which immediately took away his speech, and rendered him henceforth useless for giving aid or doing harm, and he was despaired of. Feeling compassion for his misery, his brother Peter Boterel came as a supplicant to the abbot, to ask on his brother's behalf that he might obtain forgiveness for the dying man.[533]

Jurisdiction

The judicial affairs recounted in the *History* took place mainly in the abbey's courts and those of the hundred and shire. The *History* mentions a case being conducted 'in the common hallmoot', when relatives challenged a man's gift of houses to the abbey. The hallmoot would be a court for minor tenants and lesser men, and the abbey's estates may have had several such courts, perhaps one for each manor.[534] The abbey also had a court in Oxford, which was confirmed by Henry I, and was presumably for its Oxford tenants.[535] The *History* records the special status of Culham:

From ancient times, that possession, more than others, is so free that no inhabitant is oppressed in any matter by the yoke of any sheriff or royal official, nor is it subject to the shire or hundred but only to the abbot's court in discussing the outcome of cases.[536]

A writ of William II granted that the abbey's land have 'its sake and soke and all its customs', a form re-iterated in a writ of Henry I.[537] Sake and soke jurisdiction may have been similar to that of the hundred court, except perhaps in excluding any rights of capital

533 For sickness, see also below, pp. 52, 328. For 'Divine vengeance', note below, p. 106.

534 Below, p. 286; F. M. Stenton, *The First Century of English Feudalism 1066–1166* (2nd edn., Oxford, 1961), pp. 43–4.

535 Below, p. 232. Another settlement was completed in the 'port-moot' of Oxford. This most likely was the town court; below, p. 206. See below, p. 196, for a plea being held in Oxford on the disputed land itself; p. 114 for Henry I granting that land the abbot received in Oxford through an exchange with the bishop of Salisbury be held 'with sake and soke and toll and team and infangentheof, as the abbot himself had best held that other land which he gave in exchange to the bishop.'

536 Below, p. 29; on which see Bk. i, c. 25, and esp. Vol. i, c. B16 (*CMA* i. 19–21, 91–2); *Charters of Abingdon Abbey*, pp. xlv, ccv–vi, 46–9; *VCH*, *Oxfordshire*, vii. 30–2, 35; A. Thacker, 'Æthelwold and Abingdon', *Bishop Æthelwold: his Career and Influence*, ed. B. Yorke (Woodbridge, 1988), pp. 43–64, at 49.

537 See below, pp. 20, 130.

punishment. The other 'customs' mentioned in these writs may be 'toll and team and *infangentheof*'. The first two are the rights to take tolls and to supervise the processes of proof concerning possession of chattels. *Infangentheof* is the right to execute thieves caught red-handed within the privileged land, after summary trial.[538] All five of these rights are spelt out in a writ of Henry I concerning Oxford and in his writ appointing Abbot Vincent.[539] The latter also includes the rights of 'hamsocn and grithbriche and foresteal over all the abbey's own land'. *Hamsocn* concerns assault on a person's house and the people therein, *grithbriche* breach of special peace, and *forsteal* cases of ambush. To these Henry II added the right of *flemenforthe*, or cases concerning the harbouring of fugitives, and Richard I that of *utfangentheof*, the general right to execute thieves caught red-handed, after summary trial.[540]

The abbot further exercised hundredal jurisdiction in the hundred of Hormer, and from Abbot Vincent's time the king insisted that 'no sheriff or sheriff's officials interfere in anything therein, but they are to have and do their own justice freely'.[541] Some such franchisal jurisdiction, rather than the abbot's own court as lord, may well be the subject of another writ of Henry I: 'Know that I have granted to Faritius abbot of St Mary of Abingdon that he do his justice concerning the thieving priest, who is in his custody at Abingdon. And let him similarly do his justice concerning his other thieves, with the county court looking on.'[542]

Most important of all, though, in the *History* is the honour court. This dealt with the affairs of the abbey and the tenants of its lordship, and generally met in the abbot's presence.[543] It was there, for example, that requests to inherit lands or disputes over services and homage were commonly decided.[544] The core of the gathering was the

538 For these privileges, see J. G. H. Hudson, *The Formation of the English Common Law* (London, 1996), pp. 43–5, 247. The versions given in the *De abbatibus* suggest that knowledge of the precise nature of the rights had faded, at least by the time that text was completed, see *CMA* ii. 282; note also Bk. i, cc. 127–8 (= *CMA* i. 464–5; *Charters of Abingdon Abbey*, no. 148).

539 See above, p. xcvi n. 535, below, pp. 114, 228.

540 See below, pp. 228, 254, 298, 372; Pollock and Maitland, i. 576–80, ii. 453–8.

541 Below, p. 232; see also pp. 20, 166–8, 230, 260, 264, 298, 304, 372; P. Wormald, 'Lordship and justice in the early English kingdom: Oswaldslow revisited', *Property and Power in the Early Middle Ages*, ed. W. Davies and P. Fouracre (Cambridge, 1995), pp. 114–36, at 129.

542 Below, p. 132; see the comment of Hudson, *Formation of the Common Law*, p. 45.

543 See e.g. below, p. 188.

544 e.g. below, p. 204.

abbot's men but others too might attend, at times making it difficult to distinguish the honorial from, say, a shire court. For example, the court which dealt in one day with three cases regarding lands at Bessels Leigh, Beedon, and Benham, may best be described as the honorial court, but the named witnesses were William the sheriff and Ralph Basset, important as royal officials, and Nigel d'Oilly and Hugh of Buckland, both Abingdon tenants, but also important men in their own right.[545]

Apart from control of the hundred of Hormer, and the dispute over Lewknor hundred mentioned earlier, hundredal jurisdiction does not feature very prominently in the *History*.[546] The shire court, on the other hand, is particularly prominent in conflicts with royal officials.[547] An interesting instance is the dispute with the men of Sutton Courtenay, Berkshire, over land at Culham, Oxfordshire, heard before the shire court sitting at Sutton, in the presence of the sheriff, Hugh of Buckland and 'of many men of the three shires who were attending there'.[548] Cases between the abbey and its tenants might also go to the shire. Henry I issued a writ ordering that Faritius return his dry corn and beasts to William de Jumièges, who had, it seems, been distrained; 'concerning the houses, indeed, and the green corn, and the other things, let him do justice by the just judgment of the county.'[549] Shire courts might also be summoned to meet in the presence of royal justices, as in the dispute over Abingdon market early in Henry II's reign.[550]

Various disputes came to court in the presence of the king or queen. King Stephen indeed ordered that the abbey should not plead about its lands, men, and possessions, or concerning any pleas which

[545] Below, pp. 186–8. It is unclear whether below, p. 188, means that the tenant made his concessions in the chamber at Abingdon on the same day as a lengthy hearing—which would indicate that the court should primarily be seen as the abbot's—or whether the concessions were made some time after the initial hearing of the three cases, and not necessarily in the same location.

[546] For one case, see below, p. 172; note also pp. 304–6.

[547] Below, p. 4; see also e.g. pp. 136, 226, 240, 308. Note also the requirement, below, p. 194, that Nigel d'Oilly should serve and help the abbot in the county courts of Berkshire and Oxfordshire; and above, p. xciv, for Ingulf's payment to the sheriff for help in the county court.

[548] Below, p. 172; the three shires were Berkshire, Oxfordshire, and, most likely, Buckinghamshire.

[549] Below, p. 136. On the shire and replevin, see Hudson, *Land, Law, and Lordship*, pp. 40–1. Note also writs which provided that the sheriff was to act if the addressee failed to comply: below, pp. 116, 126, the latter of which first seeks a superior lord to act.

[550] Below, p. 312.

pertained to his crown, except in his presence; unfortunately we do not know the precise circumstances or date of the issue of these writs.[551] Most cases pleaded in the royal court concerned royal rights, or arose from local officials or royal servants taking their case to the king or queen.[552] However, the king's court might hear cases relating to tenants of the abbey other than royal servants:

> A certain knight, Walter, surnamed de Rivers, who held the land called Beedon, died at that time, leaving a very young son of the same name. Because of this, the boy's uncle, named Jocelin, who desired to acquire that possession, appeared in the king's court, then meeting at Beckley, to argue his case concerning this.[553]

It may be that Jocelin was seeking to hold the land directly from the king, or it may be that the location of the king's court, a few miles north-east of Oxford, on this occasion made it a convenient forum. Overall, the impression given by the *History* is that disputants' choice of court did not rest solely upon rules of jurisdictional responsibility.

As for ecclesiastical jurisdiction, episcopal involvement is recorded, for example, in cases relating to the loss of rights through the establishment of chapels.[554] Abingdon was never an exempt abbey in the sense of being free from archiepiscopal and episcopal visitation.[555] However, there is also evidence of Abingdon enjoying some liberties. Culham possessed ecclesiastical as well as secular privileges.[556] It has also been suggested that the 'priests' chapter' gathered at Abingdon which dealt with a burial case could be the court of some kind of immunity.[557] Further, a papal bull, probably of Alexander III (1159–81), prohibited the bishop of Salisbury from coming to the abbey for the sake of assembling synods, celebrating public masses, or various other purposes. The prohibition was issued to protect the abbey's ancient liberty and indemnity.[558] Thus the privileges of Abingdon in the post-Conquest period are not entirely clear. What

[551] Below, p. 262.

[552] See e.g. below, pp. 168, 182–6, 356. Note also the case over geld, below, p. 226, which passed from the county court to a hearing which involved Roger bishop of Salisbury, Robert bishop of Lincoln, Ranulf the chancellor, and Ralph Basset.

[553] Below, p. 30.

[554] See e.g. below, pp. 22–4. Such involvement could take the form of co-operation not conflict between abbot and bishop: below, pp. 42–4, 176–8.

[555] Lambrick, 'Administration', p. 167 n. 4.

[556] *VCH*, *Oxfordshire*, vii. 35, Thacker, 'Æthelwold', p. 49; above, p. xcvi.

[557] Below, p. 178, Brett, *English Church*, pp. 207–8.

[558] Lyell, no. 22, Chatsworth, no. 87.

is certain, however, is that relations with the diocesan play a very limited part in the *History*, in marked contrast with, for example, their prominence in the chronicle of Battle Abbey.

V. MONASTIC LIFE AND BUILDINGS

The *History*'s main concerns are the lands and the external affairs of the abbey and the achievements of its abbots. It pays relatively little attention to learning within the monastery or to spiritual and liturgical life. For example, we know nothing of the liturgical impact of the Conqueror's appointees from Jumièges, although it is notable that a later medieval Abingdon kalendar includes the feast day on 15 Sept. of Aicadrus, abbot of Jumièges.[559] Occasionally internal monastic matters intrude because of a particular incident, for example the collapse of the great tower.[560] On other occasions, they emerge in the context of the leading figures of the *History* and their endowment of the church, as in the case of the establishment of the anniversary of Faritius, or of the sacrist Richard's donation of organs and a bell.[561] We also hear of the contact between liturgical life and the outside world in the context of gifts made on the feast days of St Mary. An agreement concerning a dairy farm at Oxford 'was recorded and confirmed in our chamber, in the presence of our barons and many of our neighbours, who had gathered in our presence on the Nativity of the most blessed Virgin Mary, as is their custom'.[562] Similarly we learn that Robert earl of Leicester recalled having been raised (*nutriretur*) at Abingdon 'in the time of King William', but there is little firm evidence for the abbey providing an external school for laity or clerics.[563]

559 *Benedictine Kalendars*, i. 17.

560 Below, p. 30.

561 Below, pp. 216, 290; above, p. liii.

562 Below, p. 258; note also e.g. p. 142. The *De abbatibus* reveals the presence of the bishop of Salisbury and the abbots of Gloucester, Malmesbury, and Shrewsbury at a feast of the Purification of the Virgin Mary; *CMA* ii. 290.

563 Below, p. 312; cf. D. B. Crouch, *The Beaumont Twins* (Cambridge, 1986), p. 7. A Richard the school-master [*pedagogus*] appears as a witness to a gift in Faritius's time; below, p. 180. F. Barlow, *The English Church, 1066–1154* (London, 1979), p. 231, takes this as evidence for an external school existing at Abingdon in Henry I's time. However, this single act of witness is surely not sufficient evidence, and it cannot even be certain that Richard was schoolmaster at Abingdon. His name follows that of Fulk, an illegitimate son of Henry I, and conceivably his connection was to Fulk, not the abbey. However, for the suggestion that Fulk must have been another illegitimate child of Henry I's mistress Ansfrida, who was the mother of the donor of this gift, see below, p. 53 n. 127. See

The *History* does give some indications of internal conflict, clearest of which are the disputes with Ingulf over alienation of lands.[564] The later version also, as we have seen, mentions conflict in Faritius's time over the monks' food allowances.[565] Further internal troubles are revealed by other sources. For example, we know from a letter of Lanfranc that some monks left the abbey in the time of Abbot Adelelm. Lanfranc rebuked them, and when he found that they wished to return to Abingdon, he agreed to intercede on their behalf. He instructed Adelelm

> that out of love for God and for me you forgive them wholeheartedly whatever injury they have done you and whatever offence they have committed against their monastic profession, and that you receive them back into the positions that they held before their offence: show them from now on such fatherly love that God may show mercy to you.[566]

Lanfranc, the last phrase suggests, considered Adelelm not without fault in the dispute.

The *History* is much more interested in presenting the positive achievements of abbots. Most notable are their building works.[567] The *History* does not deal with these in a very systematic fashion, and here the *De abbatibus* and the additions made to the later version of the *History* are very helpful. The chronology of building derived from the texts complements the suggested plan put together on the basis of the not entirely satisfactory excavation of 1922.[568]

The first two abbots of Abingdon after the Conquest came from Jumièges, an abbey where the Carolingian or post-Carolingian church of St Peter is dwarfed by the church of Notre-Dame dedicated in 1067.[569] This experience surely helps to explain their desire to rebuild at Abingdon, although progress was slow during their abbacies. As we

Materials for the History of Thomas Becket, i. 213–14, ii. 245, for a foundling being raised and learning his letters at Abingdon in the time of Bishop Godfrey.

[564] See above, p. lii.

[565] See above, p. xlvii.

[566] Lanfranc, *Letters,* no. 28.

[567] For church buildings before the Conquest, see Biddle *et al.*, 'Early history', pp. 42–7; Vol. i, Introduction, 'The abbey and its buildings'.

[568] For the excavation, see Biddle *et al.*, 'Early history', pp. 60–2, 65–6.

[569] See *L'Architecture normande au moyen age*, ed. M. Baylé (2 vols., Caen, 1997), ii. 14–15, 32–6. The Abingdon written evidence and excavations do not allow any definite architectural parallels to be drawn between the two churches, for example between the two towers which MS B, below, p. 338, mentions Faritius building at Abingdon and the two massive towers of the west front at Jumièges.

have seen, both the *History* and *De abbatibus* record that Adelelm at the time of his death was intent on rebuilding.[570] By Reginald's time, according to the *History*, 'everywhere in bishoprics and monasteries new buildings were being constructed', and it links his building efforts to reform, notably in the payment of tithe.[571] His first attempt to enlarge the old church led to the collapse of the tower, but soon afterwards new work was begun.[572] Whilst Biddle and others have suggested that the post-Conquest church occupied the same site as Æthelwold's, it has more recently been argued by Fernie that Reginald 'moved the site a few score yards to the north and constructed a longitudinal building of Norman type with an apse, crossing, transept and nave'.[573] An altar of SS Peter and Paul was dedicated before Reginald's death.[574]

The first surviving version of the *History* attributes to Faritius the construction of almost all the church, the enlargement of the sanctuary, the rebuilding from the foundations of almost all the monks' living quarters (*fratrum habitacula*), and of all buildings of the domestic offices (*receptacula officinarum*) to twice their previous size.[575] The later version expands on this. Faritius built the nave of the church, with two towers; the parlour with the chapter house; the dormitory with the refectory; the abbot's chamber with a chapel; and the cloister with the kitchen.[576] The *De abbatibus* confirms this account, stating that he built the cloister, chapter, dormitory, refectory, washplace, cellar, kitchen, and two parlours, one to the east next to the chapter house, one to the west under the abbot's chapel. He also constructed almost all the church, and the tower up to the windows.[577] We also know a little of the logistics of the building process. According to a record preserved in MS C, in the same hand as the *History*, Faritius shifted from using all tithes for the rebuilding of the church to just those of Cumnor and Barton.[578] Materials, and

570 Below, p. 16; *CMA* ii. 284.

571 Below, p. 34.

572 Below, p. 30.

573 Biddle *et al.*, 'Early history', pp. 62–7; E. Fernie, *The Architecture of the Anglo-Saxons* (London, 1983), pp. 108–9.

574 Below, p. 40.

575 Below, pp. 66, 72.

576 Below, p. 338; note also his gift of two large hangings for the choir on the main feast days, below, p. 338. *De abbatibus*, in its section on Vincent, mentions that Faritius made a dossal depicting the Nativity, and another depicting Job; *CMA* ii. 290. For the abbot's chamber, see also below, p. 146.

577 *CMA* ii. 286.

578 See below, p. 394.

especially lead for the roof, were acquired from Andersey.[579] MS B again gives further details:

For all the buildings which that abbot made, he had beams and timber brought from the region of the Welsh, at great expense and with severe toil. He had six wagons for this and for each of them twelve oxen. The outward and return journey lasted six or seven weeks, as it was necessary to cross near Shrewsbury.[580]

The first version of the *History* is uninformative about Vincent's building work, as is the *De abbatibus*.[581] However, the later version of the *History* is more helpful:

he had built the larger tower of the church, and fittingly adorned the court with various and apt outbuildings, that is, the hall of the guests with a chamber, a granary, a brewhouse, a bakehouse, a double stable, an almonry, with three great towers. He also gave two bells, which are struck at the hours on weekdays.[582]

He is also reputed to have founded the hospital of St John, on the western perimeter of the precinct.[583]

The earlier version of the *History* is again uninformative concerning Ingulf. This may have been because of its desire to diminish his standing, for it does mention that Richard the sacrist had the first iron doors constructed in the church.[584] According to the later version of the *History*, Ingulf constructed the infirmary with two chapels, and also the prior's chamber.[585] The *De abbatibus* confirms this information, and adds to it: 'He made a chamber for the abbot above a cellar, and the chapel of St Swithun, and the infirmary, the chapel of St Æthelwold, and the prior's chamber, and the chapel of St Michael'. The form of this statement suggests that each chapel may have been associated with the building mentioned immediately before it.[586]

579 Below, p. 78.

580 Below, p. 338. Faritius was also responsible for the building of at least one parish church, that at Uffington; below, p. 208.

581 See above, p. lii, for *De abbatibus* on Vincent providing the monks with baths. Biddle *et al.*, 'Early history', p. 58 suggests that the baths are likely 'to have been close to the calefactory, probably near the S. end of the dormitory', but such arguments based on analogy with other houses are not always sound.

582 Below, p. 340. Biddle *et al.*, 'Early history', p. 55 suggest that the almonry lay on the western perimeter of the precinct.

583 See Salter, 'Chronicle roll', p. 729.

584 Below, p. 290.

585 Below, p. 344.

586 *CMA* ii. 291. See Biddle *et al.*, 'Early history', p. 48 for additional chapels and altars existing by *c.*1200.

Neither the *History* nor the *De abbatibus* mentions Walkelin undertaking any building work.

The *History* also pays attention to the abbots' concern with increasing the liturgical garments, ornaments and valuable vessels of the church.[587] Amongst these ornaments were reliquaries, and Abingdon had a wide range of relics, both of English saints and of others, for example Roman martyrs.[588] Relics feature especially prominently in connection with Faritius.[589] He was probably present at the translation of Aldhelm's relics at Malmesbury in 1078.[590] Following his arrival at Abingdon, he acquired new relics, including the thigh-bone, part of the head, part of the shoulder-blade, and one tooth of Aldhelm. He was present at Winchester in 1111 when the relics of Æthelwold were translated to a new reliquary, and obtained his shoulder-blade and arm for Abingdon.[591] Late in his abbacy he held an enquiry which produced a relic list preserved in the *History*.[592] The *De abbatibus* reveals that Faritius instituted as feasts 'with twelve

[587] See below, pp. 16, 58, 66, 214, 340, 344. On Faritius, see also the verses of Peter, monk of Malmesbury, William of Malmesbury, *Gesta pontificum*, bk. ii, c. 88, ed. Hamilton, pp. 192–3. Note also, however, the disposal of liturgical equipment to provide money in times of need or for purchases: e.g. below, pp. 12, 344, *CMA* ii. 278.

[588] See also Vol. i, Introduction, 'Monastic life'; Ridyard, '*Condigna veneratio*', pp. 191–2; I. G. Thomas, 'The Cult of Saints' Relics in Medieval England', Ph.D. thesis (London, 1975), pp. 150–7. Thomas, 'Relics', p. 156, suggests that Faritius, being from Italy, may himself have been the source of some relics of the Roman martyrs. Note that the Abingdon kalendars indicate, not untypically, the celebration of the feasts of some saints whose relics are not included in the list in the *History*; see *Benedictine Kalendars*, i. 17 for Aicadrus, Aidan, and Paternus.

[589] See also below, p. 68.

[590] *PL* lxxxix. 84 states that he had seen a man cured at the translation both before and after he was healed; note that according to the *Life* the healed man 'very often told us' about the cure, perhaps a slightly odd statement if Faritius were present at the translation, but not necessarily incompatible with his presence. Thomas, 'Relics', p. 155 suggests that Faritius may have acquired the relics of Aldhelm at the time of the translation. For the date of the translation, see William of Malmesbury, *Gesta Pontificum*, bk. v, c. 267, ed. Hamilton, p. 425. Note also *Benedictine Kalendars*, i. 17 on the observance at Abingdon of the feast of St Paternus, another saint whose cult was important at Malmesbury.

[591] Below, p. 66; *Annales monastici*, ii. 44, which provides the date. Thomas, 'Relics', p. 155 n. 5, suggests that this may have been the same occasion on which Faritius obtained relics of St Swithun and Birinus and perhaps even of St Judoc from New Minster, and Edburga from Nunnaminster.

[592] Below, pp. 220–4. Thomas, 'Relics', pp. 150, 153–4, 156 suggests that Faritius was responsible for the acquisition of many of the relics listed by the enquiry. However, were this the case, it is hard to see why an enquiry would have been needed. The lists may well have been composed from tags attached to or associated with the individual relics; the spelling on such tags is one possible reason why two forms of the name for St Malo appear below, p. 222.

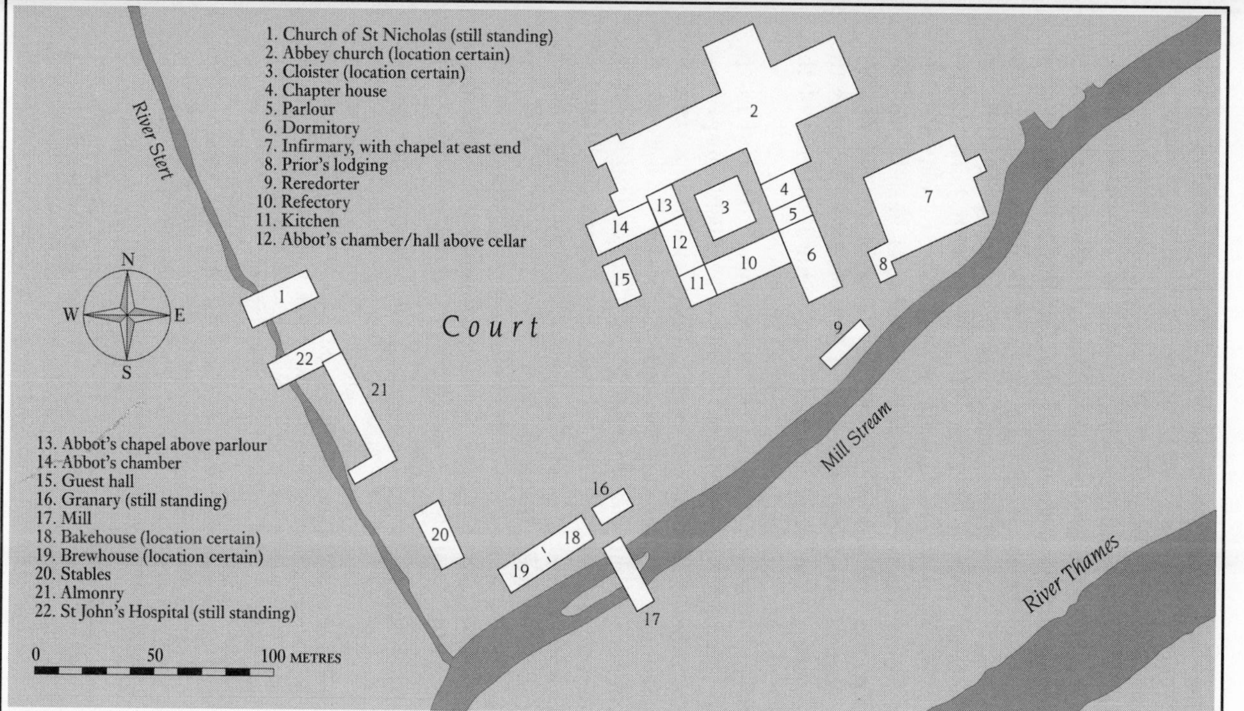

FIG. 5. Plan of the monastic buildings

This plan is highly conjectural, and aims merely to suggest the location of buildings mentioned in this volume. It draws on and interprets the plans in *Abingdon Cartularies*, ii, p. lxiii, and in *Abingdon Abbey: its Buildings and History* (Abingdon, 1993), p. 2. Guesswork plays a large part, for example with regard the stables attributed to Vincent. Even with much conjecture, I do not mark some buildings mentioned in the text, for example the washplace attributed to Faritius.

lessons' those of Saints Apollinaris, John Chrysostom (whose arm he obtained from a Byzantine envoy), Aldhelm, Chad, Mary Magdalene, and Bathild, and to the higher level of feasts 'in copes' those of Saints Vincent (to whom he was especially devoted), of Æthelwold, and of the relics.[593] The *History* contradicts this last point, attributing to Richard the sacrist the institution of the Tuesday immediately after the Easter fortnight as the day for the commemoration of all the church's relics.[594] The relative accuracy or the relationship of the two accounts is impossible to establish. What is certainly notable about the entry in the *History* is its isolation as a reference to relics after the time of Faritius. However, a charter of Abbot Walkelin, probably issued after the completion of the first version of the *History*, mentions that he instituted as feasts to be celebrated in copes the festivals of the Invention of the Holy Cross, the Exaltation of the Holy Cross, St Mary Magdalene, and St Andrew.[595]

The *History* describes Faritius as 'outstandingly learned in the knowledge of letters', and mentions his gift of a valuable gospel text, and of the tithe of Dumbleton, worth thirty shillings a year, for buying parchment for renewing the church's books.[596] However, we must again turn to the *De abbatibus* for a fuller description of his contribution to the library. This records that Faritius instituted six scribes (*scriptores*), besides claustral monks who wrote missals, graduals, antiphonaries, troparies, lectionaries, and other ecclesiastical books.[597] The scribes wrote the following: Augustine's *The City*

593 *CMA* ii. 287; Thomas, 'Relics', pp. 151 (on Apollinaris), 155–6. For the various levels of feast, see *The Monastic Breviary of Hyde Abbey, Winchester*, ed. J. B. L. Tolhurst (6 vols., Henry Bradshaw Soc., lix, lxx, lxxi, lxxvi, lxxviii, lxxx, 1930–42), vi. 146–7; Lanfranc, *Monastic Constitutions*, pp. 2, 12–14, 82–104, 118–20; Knowles, *Monastic Order*, p. 464. Feasts in copes were the second highest level, below the half dozen greatest feasts of all. For Faritius's devotion to St Vincent, see below, p. 70. For the existence by *c.*1200 of a chapel dedicated to St Vincent, see *CMA* ii. 382. Damage to the manuscript of *De abbatibus* at the relevant passage obscures exactly what Faritius did in relation to the daily mass of the dead; London, British Library, Cotton Vitellius A. xiii, fo. 86^{v}. Stevenson's suggested transcription 'in capsa', *CMA* ii. 286, appears wrong.

594 Below, p. 290.

595 Chatsworth, no. 212.

596 Below, pp. 64, 66, 216. Note also R. Gameson, *The Manuscripts of Early Norman England (c.1066–1130)* (Oxford, 1999), p. 147 (no. 818) on Rouen, Bibliothèque Municipale, MS A. 21 (s. xi^{ex}), a Gospel book with a contemporary colophon explaining that Abbot Reginald of Abingdon had commissioned it for Jumièges.

597 *CMA* ii. 289. For such practices, see N. R. Ker, *English Manuscripts in the Century after the Norman Conquest* (Oxford, 1960), pp. 10–11 and n. 1, and Gameson, *Manuscripts of Early Norman England*, pp. 8–9. For the various works, see *English Benedictine Libraries: the Shorter Catalogues*, ed. R. Sharpe, J. P. Carley, R. M. Thomson, A. G. Watson (*Corpus of British Medieval Library Catalogues*, iv, London, 1996), pp. 4–7, on which the following notes rely heavily. There were probably six such scribes at Abingdon (and such is the

of God, his *Treatise on the Gospel of John*, 'and many other volumes of the same doctor'; St Gregory's *Homilies* (probably his *Forty Homilies on the Gospels*), his *Homilies on Ezekiel*, his *Commentary on the Psalter* (which cannot be identified among Gregory's works), 'and many other volumes of the same doctor'; Jerome on the Old Testament (which again cannot be precisely identified), 'Hegesippus', 'and many other volumes of the same doctor';[598] Ambrose's *Concerning Duties*, 'and many other volumes of the same doctor'; John Chrysostom's *On the Letters of Paul*,[599] his *Concerning the Redemption of the Fall* (*De reparatione lapsi*), 'and many other volumes of the same doctor'; Bede's *Homilies*; Cyprian's *Letters*; 'Cassian' *On the Psalter*, which may well be an error for Cassiodorus's *Commentary on the Psalms*; and many books concerning medicine.[600]

In the later eleventh or the earlier part of the twelfth century, Abingdon also had works such as Julian of Toledo's *Prognosticon*, Isidore's *Etymologies*, and Lanfranc's treatise against Berengar of Tours.[601] By the end of the twelfth century there were also copies of works by Origen, lives of Saints, perhaps the *Meditations of Godwin*, and the chronicle of John of Worcester.[602] And the scribe responsible for one of the copies of John of Worcester also wrote a final work we know to have been at Abingdon in the later twelfth century, the *History* of the abbey, Book ii of which is edited and translated in the present volume.

figure given by Ker, for example), but it should be noted that damage to the manuscript, fo. 87^{r}, makes it unclear whether there were further letters before the 'vi'.

[598] The 'many other volumes' probably refers to Jerome. Hegesippus was the common name for the *Historia Iosephi de bello Iudaico et excidio urbis Hierosolymae*; *English Benedictine Libraries*, p. 6. Note also *Medieval Libraries of Great Britain: a List of Surviving Books*, ed. N. R. Ker (2nd edn., London, 1964), p. 3.

[599] *English Benedictine Libraries*, p. 6, suggests that this is John's *Homilies on Hebrews*.

[600] It may be that Faritius gave his own library of medical works, rather than that the scribes copied out many medical tracts.

[601] *Medieval Libraries of Great Britain. Supplement to the Second Edition*, ed. A. G. Watson (London, 1987), p. 1; Gameson, *Manuscripts of Early Norman England*, nos. 410, 445, 708–711.

[602] *Medieval Libraries*, ed. Ker, pp. 2–3; *Medieval Libraries . . . Supplement*, ed. Watson, p. 1. For the *Meditations of Godwin*, written by the precentor of Salisbury at some point in the first third of the twelfth century, see M. T. Webber, *Scribes and Scholars at Salisbury Cathedral, c.1075- c.1125* (Oxford, 1992), pp. 123–9. For the two manuscripts of John of Worcester produced at Abingdon late in the twelfth century, see John of Worcester, *Chronicle*, ii, pp. xli–xlv (on London, Lambeth Palace 42, written by the same scribe as the earlier manuscript of the Abingdon *History*), liii–lix (on Cambridge, Corpus Christi College 92).

MANUSCRIPT SIGLA

B	London, BL, Cotton MS Claudius B. vi
C	London, BL, Cotton MS Claudius C. ix
L	London, Lambeth Palace, Papal Documents no. 1

TEXT AND TRANSLATION

[ii. 1] C fo. 136r B fo. 119v [a]*Incipit Liber Secundus Historie huius ecclesie Abbendonensis.*

1. *De temporibus Adelelmi*[b] *abbatis huius ecclesie.*[a]

[c]At uero ut[c] prelibatum est domno Ealdredo[d] abbate in captione detento, Willelmi regis iussu ipsius abbatis loco Adelelmus[e] preficiendus dirigitur,[1] monachus quidem ex monasterio Gemmeticensi, quod est in Normannia situm.[2] De quo et litteras primoribus[f] regni Anglie huiusmodi transmisit:

2. *Carta Willelmi regis de hac ecclesia.*[3]

Willelmus[g] rex Anglorum Lanfranco[h] archiepiscopo, Roberto de Oilleio, et Rogero de Pistri, et omnibus aliis fidelibus suis totius regni Anglie, salutem.[4] Sciatis me concessisse sancte Marie de Abbendonia et Adelelmo[i] abbati eiusdem loci omnes consuetudines terrarum suarum, quecumque iacent in ecclesia predicta, ubicumque eas habeat, in burgo uel extra burgum, secundum quod abbas iste Adelelmus[j] poterit demonstrare, per breue uel cartam, ecclesiam sancte Marie de Abbendona et predecessorem suum eas consuetudines habuisse dono regis Eadwardi.

[ii. 2] 3. [k]*Carta Willelmi regis de theloneo.*[k][5]

Willelmus[l] rex Anglorum uicecomitibus suis et[m] ministris totius Anglie, salutem. Sciatis quod uolo et precipio ut omnia que ministri monachorum [n]Abbendonie ement ad uictum monachorum,[n] in ciuitatibus et burgis et omnibus mercatis, omnino sint quieta ab

[a–a] *in B, these headings follow this chapter, forming a consolidated heading with* Carta . . . ecclesia [b] Adellelmi *B* [c–c] Vt uero *B*. *C begins with an illuminated initial* A [d] Eldredo *B* [e] Aþellelmus *B* [f] primatibus *B* [g] *B precedes the king's name with an illustration of William I. B has a small* 'a' *above* Willelmus, *and a little* 'c' *above* Quarum *at the start of C's next chapter but one; the intention is to rearrange the order of B's chapters along the pattern of C, and the superscript letters appear to be in the main ink. For another example, see below, p.*18. [h] Lamfranco *B* [i] Aþellelmo *B* [j] Aþellelmus *B* [k–k] *om. B. In B, this chapter follows the chapter headed* De recitatione carte in comitatu. [l] Villelmus *B* [m] *om. B* [n–n] *om. B*

[1] On Ealdred's captivity, see Bk. i, c. 144 (*CMA* i. 486).

[2] On connections between Abingdon and the Norman monastery of Jumièges, see above, p. xlii.

Here begins Book Two of the History of this church of Abingdon.

1. *Concerning the times of Adelelm, abbot of this church.*
When, as mentioned earlier, lord Abbot Ealdred was held in captivity, Adelelm was directed by King William's order to be appointed in his place.[1] Adelelm was a monk from the monastery of Jumièges, situated in Normandy.[2] The king sent the following letters concerning this matter to the leading men of the realm of England:

2. *Charter of King William concerning this church.*[3]
William king of the English to Archbishop Lanfranc, Robert d'Oilly, and Roger de Pîtres, and all his other faithful men of the whole realm of England, greeting.[4] Know that I have granted to St Mary of Abingdon and to Adelelm, abbot of that monastery, all the customs of their lands, which belong to the said church wherever it has them, in borough or out of borough, as the aforementioned Abbot Adelelm can show by writ or charter that the church of St Mary of Abingdon and his predecessor had these customs by gift of King Edward.

3. *Charter of King William concerning toll.*[5]
William king of the English to his sheriffs and officials throughout England, greeting. Know that I wish and order that everything which the officials of the monks of Abingdon buy for the monks' provisions, in cities and boroughs and all markets, be entirely quit of all toll and

[3] *Regesta*, ed. Bates, no. 4, who suggests in his note that the three addressees joined 'to supervise a general enquiry into Abingdon's tenures'. The writ probably dates from soon after Adelelm's appointment in 1071. The text of the writ, and the description of events in the Berkshire county court, are printed, from Stevenson's edition, in *English Lawsuits*, no. 4.

[4] Lanfranc was archbishop of Canterbury 1070–89; *Handbook of British Chronology*, p. 232. On Robert d'Oilly, see above, p. lxx, and below, pp. 32, 326. He may have been addressed in this writ as a sheriff, but perhaps just as a prominent local land-holder. Roger de Pîtres was sheriff of Gloucestershire, and perhaps of Berkshire, during William I's reign; Green, *Sheriffs*, pp. 26, 42. He had died by 1086, but *Domesday Book* reveals that he had held land in Gloucestershire and Herefordshire.

[5] *Regesta*, ed. Bates, no. 6. The writ dates from 1071 × 1083, and—given its position in MS C—possibly from soon after Adelelm's appointment in 1071, although see Bates for comment on its diplomatic form. In MS B, this writ follows the next section, recounting events in the shire court of Berkshire.

omni theloneo et consuetudine. Et prohibeo uobis, sicut me diligitis, ne aliquis uestrum amodo illis inde iniuriam faciat. Teste Eudone[a] dapifero. Apud Bruhellam.[b]

[ii. 1] 4. *De recitatione cartarum in comitatu.*

Quarum recitatio litterarum in Berchescire[c] comitatu prolata pluri-
[ii. 2] mum et ipsi abbati et ecclesie commodi attulit. Siquidem regii officiales illis diebus hominibus in ecclesie possessionibus diuersis locorum manentibus multas inferebant iniurias, nunc has, nunc uero illas consuetudines, eis pati satis graues ingerentes. Sed exhibitis predictis imperialibus mandatis, quibus rectitudines ecclesie per cartam Eadwardi regis et attestatione comitatus, in eodem comitatu
B fo. 120r tunc | publice uentilate, ipsi officiales repulsam sibi aduersam, ecclesie autem commodam suscepere, id uiriliter domno Adelelmo[d] abbate satagente.[6] Cui plurimum auxilii ferebant duo ecclesie huius monachi, germani quidem fratres, quorum maior[e] natu Sacolus, iunior uero Godricus uocabatur, cum quibus et Alfwius[f] presbiter tunc ecclesiam regie uille Suttune hinc uicine gubernans,[7] quibus tanta secularium facundia et preteritorum memoria euentorum inerat,[g] ut ceteri circumquaque facile eorum sententiam ratam fuisse quam edicerent approbarent. Sed et alii plures de Anglis causidici per id tempus in abbatia ista habebantur, quorum collationi nemo sapiens refragabatur.[8] Quibus rem ecclesie publicam tuentibus, eius oblocutores elingues fiebant.

[ii. 3] 5. [h]*De militibus istius ecclesie.*[h]

In primordio autem sui aduentus in abbatiam, non nisi armatorum septus manu militum alicubi[i] procedebat. Et quidem necessario id fieri oportebat, multe enim nouitates coniuratorum in dies passim contra regem et regnum eius ebullientes, uniuersos in Anglia se tueri cogebant.[9] Tunc Walingaforde, et Oxeneforde, et Wildesore,

[a] Eudo *B* [b] Burhellam *B* [c] Berkescire *B* [d] Aþellemo *B* [e] *corr. from* amiori *by erasure C* [f] Alfwinus *B* [g] inereat *B* [h–h] *om. B* [i] alicui *B*

[6] Here and below, p. 50, I translate 'imperialis' as 'imperial', since the writer certainly meant to emphasize the loftiness of the order. He need not have intended to imply that the king of England had any particular emperor-like status. Note also references e.g. to a king entering into his 'imperium', below, pp. 26, 58, 174, 180. Cf. Bk. i, c. 116 (*CMA* i. 442) where it is said that Cnut ruled Denmark, Norway, and England 'imperialiter'; also Bk. i, c. 53 [*Charters of Abingdon Abbey*, no. 60, *CMA* i. 219] for a charter of Eadwig referring to

custom. And I forbid, as you love me, that any of you henceforth do them wrong concerning this. Witness: Eudo the steward. At Brill.

4. *Concerning the reading out of the charters in the county court.*
The reading out of these letters in the county court of Berkshire very greatly profited both this abbot and the church. For in those days royal officials were causing great harm to people living on various of the church's possessions. They made them suffer now some, now other very heavy customs. But when these imperial orders were produced, publicizing in that county court the church's rights by charter of King Edward and witness of the county, the royal officials suffered a reverse harmful to them, but advantageous to the church, through the manful efforts of lord Abbot Adelelm.[6] He was helped greatly by two monks of this church, who were indeed brothers, the older called Sacol, the younger Godric; with these also was Ælfwig, then the priest in charge of the church of the neighbouring royal village of Sutton.[7] These men were so eloquent concerning matters of this world and remembered past events so well that others, on every side, easily approved a judgment they pronounced as correct. In addition, at that time many other English pleaders were retained in the abbey, whose arguments no wise man opposed.[8] With these men protecting the public affairs of the church, its opponents became tongue-tied.

5. *Concerning the knights of this church.*
In the first days of his abbacy, Abbot Adelelm went nowhere unless surrounded by a band of armed knights. Indeed, this was a matter of necessity, for at that time many and widespread rumours of conspiracies against the king and his kingdom boiled up, forcing everyone in England to defend themselves.[9] Then castles were erected at

him as 'imperiali Angol Saxonum diademate infulatus.' 'Imperium' can also mean an order given by the king; see below, pp. 16, 182.

[7] Sutton Courtenay, Berkshire. *DB* i, fo. 57[v], records this as predominantly royal demesne in 1086; fo. 59[r] states that '*Aluui* the priest holds one hide from the abbot' of Abingdon in Sutton. *Alwius* and *Aluui* are forms for the Old English name Ælfwig, or possibly Ælfwine. J. Selden, *Historie of Tithes* (London, 1618), p. 484, saw the assembly which the *Leges Edwardi Confessoris* depicted advising William I on the laws of his realm as including 'the common Lawyers of that time, as Godric and Alfwin.'

[8] On such men, see P. A. Brand, *The Origins of the English Legal Profession* (Oxford, 1992), pp. 9–13.

[9] It is uncertain here whether 'regnum' means 'kingdom' or 'kingship'. Particularly given the external threats which existed at the time, I have opted for the former.

ceterisque locis castella pro regno seruando compacta.[10] Vnde huic abbatie militum excubias apud ipsum Wildesore oppidum habendas regio imperio iussum.[11] Quare, tali in articulo huius fortune, milites transmarini in Angliam uenientes fauore colebantur precipuo.
C fo. 136v Taliter itaque regni tumultuantibus | causis, domnus Adellelmus abbas locum sibi commissum munita manu militum secure protegebat. Et primo quidem stipendiariis[a] in hoc utebatur. At his sopitis incursibus, cum iam regis edicto in annalibus annotaretur quot de episcopiis, quotue de abbatiis, ad publicam rem tuendam milites, si forte hinc quid cause propellende contingeret, exigerentur, eisdem donatiuis prius retentis, abbas mansiones possessionum ecclesie pertinentibus inde delegauit, edicto cuique tenore parendi de sue portionis mansione.[12] Que possessiones ab eis habite fuerant quos tainos[b] dicunt, et in bello Hastingis occubuerant. A quibus uero eedem possessiones primo usui ipsorum distribute sint tainorum,[c] uel cuius rei necessarie gratia, superuacaneum est perscrutari; quandoquidem iam plurima, quod diuino iudicio assistant, tempora
[ii. 4] preterierint, qui solus qua intentione fiant singulorum actus liquido perpendit, et quid inde recte iudicari debeat nouit.[d] Quare mortuis
B fo. 120v his, quicquam calumpniarum oppo|nere desinimus. Vnum tantummodo pro uero edicere possumus: quia perparum illarum fuerit possessionum, quod in solo proprioque seruorum Dei usu et peregrinorum susceptione ac obsequio, ab his qui illas ecclesie distribuerunt, non fuerit delegatum.[13] Porro qui uel parentele, uel secularis alicuius respectu gratie, donatiuo eo abusus fuerit, is uideat an sua consideratio rectior ante Deum, quam donantis ecclesie quod sibi proprium constat, habeatur. Nam benefacta

[a] stipidi ariis *B* [b] tahinos *B* [c] tahinorum *B* [d] *for* noscit ?

[10] Oxford Castle was built by Robert d'Oilly in 1071; *Annales monastici*, iv. 9. Wallingford Castle is mentioned in *DB* i, fo. 56r; see also Bk. i, c. 144 (*CMA* i. 486) for Abbot Ealdred of Abingdon being imprisoned there. *ASC*, *s.a.* 1095, provides one of the first chronicle mentions of Windsor Castle, recording the imprisonment of Robert de Mowbray there; however, as the present text shows, the castle was built in the Conqueror's reign.

[11] On castle-guard, see Stenton, *English Feudalism*, ch. 6; also Keefe, *Feudal Assessments*, pp. 77–8.

[12] This is a rather obscure sentence, as can be seen from previous attempts to translate it; e.g. cf. *EHD* ii, no. 223 with R. A. Brown, *The Norman Conquest* (London, 1984), no. 151. J. Gillingham, 'The introduction of knight service into England', *Anglo-Norman Studies*, iv (1982), 53–64, 181–7, at pp. 57 and 183 n. 36, argues that *annales* should be translated 'rolls', as in administrative records. Note that John of Worcester's *Chronicle*,

Wallingford, Oxford, Windsor, and other places for the defence of the realm.[10] So it came about that this abbey was ordered by royal command to provide knights for guard duty at that Windsor castle.[11] In such circumstances overseas knights coming to England were cherished with particular favour. Therefore, while the affairs of the kingdom were in such upheaval, lord Abbot Adelelm securely protected with an armed band of knights the monastery entrusted to him. At first, indeed, he used paid troops for this. But after the attacks had died down, and when it was noted by royal edict in the annual records how many knights might be demanded for public protection from bishoprics, and how many from abbeys, if by chance compelling cause arose, the abbot then granted manors from the possessions of the church to his followers (who had previously been retained by gifts), laying down for each the terms of subordination for his manor.[12] These possessions had been held by those known as thegns, who had died in the battle of Hastings. By whom indeed these possessions were originally distributed to the use of those thegns, or by reason of what necessity, it is superfluous to investigate, since much time has now passed, and since they stand in the judgment of God, who alone assesses clearly by what intention the deeds of individuals are done, and knew what ought rightly to be judged concerning this. Therefore, with these men dead, we cease to bring any charges. One thing alone can we say for certain, that very few of those possessions had not been given for the sole and particular use of the servants of God and the reception and service of pilgrims, by those who assigned them to the church.[13] Further, let anyone who for reasons of kinship or worldly favour misuses this gift see whether his own decision is, in God's presence, regarded as more just than the decision of the man who gives to the Church what is properly his own. For good things are often accustomed to be exchanged for

which Abingdon possessed, included amongst the material recorded by *Domesday* 'quot feudatos milites', 'how many knights enfeoffed'; John of Worcester, *Chronicle*, iii. 44 (*s. a.* 1086). I have opted for the neutral 'annual records'. Difficulties also arise with the words 'eisdem donatiuis prius retentis', which I have taken to refer back to the stipendiary knights, and 'pertinentibus', which may include various relatives and associates—a historian of the later Middle Ages might well translate it 'affinity'; see also below, p. 140, for a lord issuing a document to 'uniuersis sibi hominibus pertinentibus', the document's address being to 'ministris suis et omnibus aliis suis fidelibus hominibus'. On the rather allusive style of much of this paragraph, see Vol. i, Introduction, 'Style'.

[13] See above, above, p. xl on the abbot's oath to preserve the possessions of the church.

meliorum causa sepe commutari solent. Itaque de his sat dictum; quare stilus ad historiam inchoatam uertatur.[14]

B fo. 121[r] | [a]Tunc temporis[a] milites quidam Abbendonenses regis pro nego-
[ii. 6] tio Normanniam missi, dum maris in medio remigarent a piratis capiuntur, spoliantur, quibusdam etiam manus truncantur, talique infortunio uix uiui abire permissi domum[b] reuertuntur. Quorum unus, Hermerus nomine, necdum alicuius terre portionem adeptus, dum post diffactionem suam ab abbate sibi minus inde intenderetur, regem adiit, quid perpessus sit ostendit, unde in futurum uictitet omnino sumptus sibi deesse conquestus est. Cui rex compatiens, abbati mandauit debere se huiusmodi homini tantum terre aliquorsum prouidere,[c] qua quamdiu uixerit possit sustentari. Paruit abbas imperatis, et possessionem de uictualio monachorum, que Denceswrht[d] dicitur, curie Offentune subiectam, illi delegauit.[15] Ita uir ille priuatus domi sua tantum procurabat, de militie procinctu quoad
[ii. 7] uixit nil exercens. Hoc itaque euentu apud Offentunam dominium abbatie diminutum.

Item[e] in Wichtham, de terra uillanorum curie Cumenore obsequi solitorum, illo ab abbate cuidam militi, nomine Huberto, quinque hidarum portio distributa est.[16]

6. *De quatuor hidis de Winekefeld.*

Preterea de uilla Winekefeld, uersus Wildeshoram sita, regis arbitrio ad forestam illic amplificandam quatuor hide tunc exterminate sunt.[17] Adeo autem saltus ille abbatie noxius illo tempore extitit, quod non solum loca dudum hominum habitacula, nunc ferarum fierent cubilia, uerum et super hoc maior oppidi, quod in uicino super flumen Tamisie locatum, nomen silue continet, duas siluas, quarum una Ierdelea, altera Bacsceat, dicebatur, illi uille Winekefeld[f] attinentes, sibi usurparet.[18] Dicebatur is[g] Walterus filius

[a–a] Item tempore Aþellelmi abbatis *B*. *B precedes this chapter with the heading* De militibus Abbend' qui capti sunt in mare [b] *corr. from* dumum *C* [c] prouiderere *C* [d] Dencheswrþe *B* [e] *initial om. C* [f] Winkefeld *B* [g] his *B*

---

[14] In MS B there follow two lists of knights; below, p. 322.

[15] *DB* i, fo. 59[r], states that 'The abbey itself holds Goosey, and always held it. . . . Of this land of this manor, Hermer holds seven hides and it is from the monks' demesne supply'. Goosey and Denchworth are neighbouring settlements in Berkshire, and these may be two descriptions of the same land; see also *VCH*, *Berkshire*, iv. 281, suggesting that this was the manor of Circourt, on which see further, below, p. 325. *DB* i, fo. 59[r], also states that 'The abbey itself holds Uffington, and always held it.' Assuming it is not

better. So, having said enough about these matters, let our pen return to the history which we have started.[14]

At that time some Abingdon knights were sent to Normandy on the king's business. While rowing in the middle of the sea they were taken by pirates, robbed, and some had their hands cut off. In this unfortunate state, barely alive, they were released and returned home. One of them, named Hermer, had not yet acquired any portion of land. When, after his mutilation, he received little attention in this regard from the abbot, he went to the king and showed what he had suffered. He complained that he was entirely lacking resources to live in future. Pitying him, the king ordered the abbot that he should provide such a man with land somewhere, sufficient to sustain him for the rest of his life. The abbot obeyed the orders and, from the provisions of the monks, granted Hermer a possession called Denchworth, which is subject to the court of Uffington.[15] In this way, the disabled man took care only of his affairs at home, performing none of the knightly duties whereby he had lived. Therefore the abbey's demesne at Uffington was reduced by this incident.

Likewise, an area of five hides in Wytham was given by the same abbot to a knight named Hubert, from the land of the peasants who were accustomed to do suit at the court of Cumnor.[16]

6. *Concerning four hides at Winkfield.*

In addition four hides were then detached by royal will from the village of Winkfield, situated towards Windsor, in order to increase the forest there.[17] Moreover, that incursion was harmful to the abbey, because not only were places which were once dwellings of men now lairs of animals, but in addition the constable of Windsor (which, situated nearby on the river Thames, derives its name from wild wood), usurped for himself two woods pertaining to that village of Winkfield, one called *Ierdelea*, the other *Bacsceat*.[18] That man was

anachronistic, the present text is a very early reference to suit at a manorial court. It may indicate that Denchworth was in some sense a 'berewick' or dependent settlement of Uffington; see e.g. Faith, *English Peasantry and the Growth of Lordship*, pp. 42–7. Such a link suggests the existence in the Anglo-Norman period of complexities of internal arrangements within Abingdon's estates which are otherwise largely hidden.

[16] Berkshire. See also *DB* i, fo. 58^{v}: 'In Wytham Hubert holds 5 hides of the land of the villagers from the abbot.' *VCH*, *Berkshire*, iv. 428, suggests that he was probably the ancestor of the family of Wytham.

[17] Berkshire. See also *DB* i, fo. 59^{r}: 'The abbey itself holds Winkfield, and always held it. . . . Four hides of this land are in the king's forest.'

[18] See also below, p. 192. On *Jerdelea/Virdelea* see also EPNS, *Berkshire*, i. 42.

Oteri.[19] Cuius potestati illo obniti parum profuit, cum esset illius
C fo. 137r castelli et forestarum per comitatum | Berkescire ubique consitarum primas et tutor, et milites nostri penes eum excubias oppidi obseruarent. His itaque causis, quod sibi ille contraxerat, tunc retinuit.

7. *De Tademertuna.*[20]

Robertus de Oileio, et ipse prediues, castelli uero urbis Oxenefordensis oppidanus,[21] dum pro contiguitate monasterii et ipsius castelli, abbati suam inculcaret frequentiam, blandiloquio eorum studium quorum sit secularia potius augere quam monastica, circumuentus
[ii. 8] abbas eidem[a] castellano uillam Tademer|tune inconsiderate dedit.
B fo. 121v Sed post facti penitens, multis sepe ultro citroque uerbis inde habitis, uix ad ultimum regis deliberatione de inuestitura illius terre idem uir demutari ualuit. Restituta ergo abbati terra, oppidani animus adeo egre rem tulit, ut ad pacem reuocari nulla potuisset suasione, si ante ab abbate se munerandum singulis annis non certus foret decem librarum donatiuo. Quare, consultu suorum, abbas huius pacificationis subire remedium impulsus, quoad uixit id uiro postea contulit.

8. *De una hida in Cestretuna et duabus in Hille.*[22]

Turkillus, quidam de Anglis, ualde inter suos nobilis, in partibus Ardene mansitans,[23] abbatis familiaritate et fratrum dum nonnunquam uteretur, de patrimonio suo terras duobus in locis ecclesie Abbendonie concessit, quarum una Cestratuna, altera Hylle[b] nominatur, filio ipsius Siwardo, tunc quidem adolescente, paternum concessum confirmante. De quo tale regis constitit edictum:

[a] idem *B* [b] Hille *B*

[19] Walter held lands in Berkshire, Buckinghamshire, Hampshire, Middlesex and Surrey in 1086; Sanders, *Baronies*, p. 116; Keats-Rohan, *Domesday People*, p. 455; J. H. Round, 'The origins of the FitzGeralds', *The Ancestor*, i (1902), 119–26, at pp. 121–4. He and his heirs were keepers of Windsor forest and constables of Windsor castle. He died in the early twelfth century. For his wife, Beatrice, and his son, William, see below, p. 194.

[20] Oxon. See also above, p. lxx, and *DB* i, fo. 156v, which makes no reference to the dispute, stating simply that 'the abbey holds twenty hides in Tadmarton', and 'a knight holds five hides of this land from the abbot'.

[21] See also below, pp. 32, 326.

[22] Both in Warwickshire. *DB* i, fo. 239r, enters Hill under Abingdon, stating that 'the abbey of Abingdon has two hides in Hill, which the abbot bought from Thorkell's fee. And Warin holds from the abbot'; fo. 241v enters Chesterton under Thorkell, stating that 'from Thorkell, the abbey of Abingdon holds one hide in Chesterton'. Cf. *De abbatibus*, where it is stated that Adelelm bought Chesterton and Hill from the king; *CMA* ii. 284.

called Walter son of Other.[19] There was little benefit in striving against his power, since he was the commander and protector of that castle and of the forests throughout Berkshire, and our knights performed castle-guard service under him. For these reasons, therefore, he then held on to what he had appropriated for himself.

7. *Concerning Tadmarton.*[20]
Robert d'Oilly, an extremely rich man, was castellan of Oxford castle.[21] Because of the proximity of the monastery and castle he forced his company upon the abbot. The abbot was beguiled by the flattery of those eager to further secular rather than monastic interests, and without due consideration he gave that castellan the village of Tadmarton. But afterwards he repented of his deed, and many discussions concerning this took place, back and forth, yet only with difficulty, by the decision of the king, could Robert finally be disseised of that land. When the land was restored to the abbot, the castellan bore the matter with such ill-feeling that no persuasion could have pacified him, had he not beforehand been certain that he would receive a gift of £10 a year from the abbot. On his men's advice, the abbot was compelled to endure the remedy of this settlement, and afterwards conferred this payment on Robert as long as he lived.

8. *Concerning one hide in Chesterton and two in Hill.*[22]
A certain Englishman called Thorkell, very noble among his people, dwelt in the neighbourhood of Arden.[23] Enjoying friendly relations with the abbot and the brethren, he granted the church of Abingdon lands from his patrimony in two places, one named Chesterton, the other Hill. His son Siward, then a youth, confirmed his father's grant. The following royal edict was issued concerning this:

[23] Thorkell of Arden was notable as an Englishman who continued to hold extensive lands from the king after the Conquest; see A. Williams, *The English and the Norman Conquest* (Woodbridge, 1995), esp. pp. 103–5. He may also have been sheriff of Warwickshire. See below, p. 26, on his lands after his death. Professor Crouch (personal communication) informs me that Siward of Arden appeared as a prominent witness in charters of the earls of Warwick, who acquired his father's lands; see below, p. 26. Likewise, in D. B. Crouch, 'The local influence of the earls of Warwick, 1088–1242: a study in decline and resourcefulness', *Midland History*, xxi (1996), 1–22, at p. 5, he states that the Ardens were one of 'a core of dominant local families in the earl's obedience'. A charter of King Stephen for Kenilworth Priory reveals that Siward was dead by 1139; *RRAN* iii, no. 418.

9. *Carta regis de eadem terra.*[24]

Willelmus rex Anglorum Lanfranco archiepiscopo, et Roberto de Oileio, et omnibus baronibus et fidelibus suis, Francis et Anglis, in Warewicensi comitatu, salutem. Sciatis me firmiter et in perpetuum concessisse Adelelmo[a] abbati et ecclesie Abbendonensi ut in dominio habeant, absque ulla calumpnia, unam hidam in Cestretuna et duas in Hylle,[b] sicut Turkillus de Eardene eidem ecclesie in elemosina dedit.

[ii. 9] 10. *De Niweham.*[25]

Dissimile autem quid huic prouectui post accidit. Nam alius nobilium, Leowinus, quandam uillam Niweham de suo patrimonio, trans flumen Tamisie e regione monasterii Abbendonie sitam, ipsi abbati pretio accepto distraxit.[26] In qua distractione et calix pregrandis, magnifici operis argenti aurique, Siwardi pontificis et olim huius loci abbatis, expensus est;[27] cuius uice alterum, sequenti tempore, satis approbandum abbas ipse restituit. Dum hoc fieret, rex Normannie degebat, et Odo frater eius, Baiocensis quidem episcopus, regnum Anglie illo uice regis gubernabat. Cui abbas conquisite rei summam retulit, et apud eum quod egerat licitum sibi fore optinuit. Sed cum tantum odii et discordii inter regem et eundem episcopum non multo post serperet, ut eum in captionem, fauente consultu archiepiscopi Lanfranci, poneret,[28] cuncti qui eius ope se auxiliari rebantur, offensum potius regis quam gratiam merentur. Vnde cum negotium, cuius hic mentio est, illius episcopi concessu actitatum fuisse sciuisset, adeo indignanter rem accepit, ut eandem abbati terram direptam alteri donaret.[29] Ita hanc abbas iacturam perpeti coactus est.

11. *De profectione abbatis ad Scotiam.*[30]

Rex Scotie Malcholmus subesse regi Willelmo eo tempore detrectabat.[31] Quare, coacto in unum exercitu,[c] rex filium suum | Robertum maiorem natu Scotiam sua uice transmisit, cum quo et plures Anglie

B fo. 122r

[a] Adellelmo *B* [b] Hyllæ *B* [c] excercitu *B*

[24] *Regesta*, ed. Bates, no. 5, dating to 1071 × 1083. [25] Oxon.

[26] Leofwine was not a land-holder of Thorkell's stature; for his holdings, see Williams, *The English and the Norman Conquest*, pp. 117–18. *De abbatibus* states that Adelelm bought Nuneham Courtenay from the king; *CMA* ii. 284.

[27] Siward was abbot 1030–44, and then assistant bishop of Canterbury until illness forced him to resign in 1048, and return to Abingdon, where he died late that year; *Heads of Religious Houses*, p. 24, N. P. Brooks, *The Early History of the Church of Canterbury* (Leicester, 1984), pp. 299–300; see also Bk. i. cc. 112–22 (*CMA* i. 434–62).

[28] Odo of Bayeux fell from power in 1082; see D. R. Bates, 'The character and career of Odo, bishop of Bayeux (1049/50–1097)', *Speculum*, l (1975), 1–20, at pp. 15–16.

9. *Charter of the king concerning the same land.*[24]
William king of the English to Archbishop Lanfranc, and Robert d'Oilly, and all his barons and faithful men, French and English, in Warwickshire, greeting. Know that I have firmly and forever granted to Abbot Adelelm and the church of Abingdon that they may have in demesne, without any challenge, one hide in Chesterton and two in Hill, as Thorkell of Arden gave to this church in alms.

10. *Concerning Nuneham Courtenay.*[25]
However, a later event was quite different from this beneficial one. Another of the nobles, Leofwine, in return for payment, sold to this abbot a village from his patrimony, called Nuneham and situated across the river Thames from the locality of the monastery of Abingdon.[26] On this sale was expended a very large chalice of magnificent silver and gold work which had belonged to Bishop Siward, once abbot of this monastery.[27] The abbot later replaced it with another quite acceptable one. While this was happening, the king was in Normandy and in his place his brother Odo, bishop of Bayeux, was governing the kingdom of England. The abbot reported to Odo the price of the acquisition, and in his presence obtained approval for his action. But not long after, such great hatred and discord grew up between the king and the bishop that the king, backed by the advice of Archbishop Lanfranc, placed Odo in captivity.[28] Everyone who had supposed themselves helped by Odo's power received the king's displeasure rather than favour. Therefore, when William learnt that the aforementioned business had been transacted with the bishop's agreement, he was so indignant that he seized the land from the abbot, and gave it to another.[29] In such a way the abbot was compelled to suffer this loss.

11. *Concerning the abbot's departure to Scotland.*[30]
At that time Malcolm king of Scotland was refusing to be subject to King William.[31] Therefore King William gathered an army, and sent his eldest son Robert in his place to Scotland, along with many of the

[29] *DB* i, fo. 159[r], reveals the beneficiary to have been Richard de Courcy; the entry makes no mention of Abingdon's tenure. See also below, p. 78.

[30] This chapter refers to Robert Curthose's expedition to Scotland in 1080; see also A. O. Anderson, *Scottish Annals from English Chroniclers A.D. 500 to 1286* (London, 1908), p. 104 and n. 1. The Abingdon writer's version of the settlement may well impart a later twelfth-century colouring.

[31] Malcolm III (Canmore) was king of Scotland 1058–93; *Handbook of British Chronology*, p. 57.

primates, quorum unus abbas Adelelmus[a] fuit, precipiens eis pacem
armaue offerre—pacem si obtemperantia sibi spondeatur, sin aliter
arma. Verum rex ille, Lodonis occurrens cum suis, pacisci potius
C fo. 137v quam preliari delegit. Perinde ut | regno Anglie principatus Scotie
[ii. 10] subactus foret, obsides tribuit. Quo pacto inito, regis filius cum
exercitu ad patrem hilaris repedauit, a quo sue perfunctionis
premio ipse ceterique secum comitantes, ut quorumlibet dignitatem
decuerat, donatur.

Iterum ad Walos exercitus dirigitur.[32] Quo etiam milites huius pene omnes ecclesie proficisci iubentur, abbate domi remanente. Cuius itineris causa pro uoto regis peracto, ipse Normanniam adiit.[33]

12. *De preposito de Suttune.*[34]

Cum interea prepositus quidam regie uille Suttune uicine huic ecclesie, Alfsi dictus, frequenter contra antiqua ecclesie iura, planis et nemorosis locis, rusticorum uallatus manu, barbare sese inferendo, homines et animalia ita passim exagitabat, ut ab eis regalibus uectationibus summagia fieri exigeret, de nemoribus Bachelea[b] et Cumenore[c] uirgulta quantum uolebat recidi iuberet.[35] Cuius ausum adeo uiua manu tum abbas cohercuit, ut ab eo tempore illius uiri deinceps alter sectator non uenerit. Nam primo, quadam uice dum plumbum regio usui exquisitum, iunctis ecclesie bobus, prepositus idem in curiam regis Suttune carreitare faceret, ipse baculo, quem abbas forte tenebat, non sine dedecore cesus; plumbum disiectum, boues reducti. Secundo, cum de silua Bachelea[d] honustis progredere-tur redis, eadem[e] honera abbas capiens, ipsum equo fugitantem prope molendinum contiguum ponti fluminis Eoche transuadare, ad collum usque humectatum, compulit, uitato timore abbatis ponte.[36] Sed cum ab eo, qui cesus fuerat, penes reginam, per hos dies Wildesore constitutam, querimonia de illata sibi iniuria moueretur, que regis uice Normannie degentis iusticiam rerum ingruentium impendebat,

[a] Aþelelmus *B* [b] Bacheleia *B* [c] Cumenora *B* [d] Bacheleia *B* [e] headem *B*

[32] This probably refers to the Welsh expedition of 1081, on which see R. R. Davies, *The Age of Conquest: Wales 1063–1415* (Oxford, 1991), p. 33.

[33] *Regesta*, ed. Bates, p. 81, suggests that William crossed to Normandy in autumn 1081.

[34] *English Lawsuits*, no. 12. The dispute must have occurred between 1072 and 1083, probably during the king's absence in Normandy in 1081–2.

[35] Both Berks. The *Domesday* entry for Cumnor, *DB* i, fo. 58v, does not mention woods.

[36] Hennor Mill, next to Ock Bridge; see below, p. 94. The most direct route from Bagley Wood to Sutton Courtenay was via Abingdon and Culham, but the reeve would

leading men of England, including Abbot Adelelm. He ordered them to offer peace or armed conflict—peace if obedience were promised him, otherwise conflict. But King Malcolm came into Lothian with his men and chose to make an agreement rather than fight. Accordingly, he gave hostages that the principality of Scotland would be subject to the kingdom of England. Following this agreement, the king's son joyfully marched back with his army to his father, by whom he was rewarded in recompense for his achievement, as were his companions, as befitted their rank.

Also, an army was sent against the Welsh.[32] Almost all the knights of this church were ordered to set out for there, although the abbot remained at home. When the king's desire regarding the aims of the expedition had been fulfilled, he went to Normandy.[33]

12. *Concerning the reeve of Sutton.*[34]
Meanwhile, protected by a band of peasants, a certain reeve, called Ælfsige, of the royal village of Sutton neighbouring this church, frequently and barbarously infringed the church's ancient rights in fields and woods. He harassed men and animals here and there, that he might exact carrying services from them for royal journeys, and ordered that as much brushwood be cut from the woods of Bagley and Cumnor as he wished.[35] The abbot then punished his audacity so firmly that no one thereafter has ever followed the reeve's practice. On a first occasion, when that reeve yoked the church's oxen to cart lead (which he had demanded for royal use) to the king's court at Sutton, to his dishonour he was hit with a staff that the abbot happened to be holding. The lead was scattered, the oxen taken back. On a second occasion, when the reeve set out from Bagley Wood with heavily laden carts, the abbot seized the loads and forced the reeve to flee on horseback. Up to his neck in water, he had to wade across the river Ock, near the mill by the bridge over the river, avoiding that bridge in fear of the abbot.[36] But the man who had been struck brought before the queen a complaint about the injury done him. She was then at Windsor and was doing justice concerning pressing matters, in place of the king who was in Normandy. The abbot did

obviously have wanted to avoid passing so close to the abbey. He therefore presumably was intending to travel via Drayton, which would have involved passing over the Ock Bridge. The present Ock Bridge incorporates the remains of a stone bridge from this period; see J. M. Steane, 'Abingdon Ock Bridge', *Council for British Archaeology Group 9 Newsletter*, x (1980), 99.

abbas nil moratus regium inde preuenit examen, et pecunia exoluit
[ii. 11] quicquid in regis officiali fuerat commissum. Preterea uniuersis tyrannicum[a] excussit exactum prefectorum posteris, nam in contione illa regia, et ratiotinatione[b] et plurimorum testimonio sapientum, peroratum est nequaquam debere ecclesiam Abbendonensem huiusmodi sufferre exactum, quin libertate potiri perpetua. Ea itaque libertas tunc preconata, hodie usque celebris libere defenditur.

13. *De aduentu Danorum.*[37]

Dein fama percrebuit Danos classem qua Angliam oppugnarent
B fo. 122v parasse. Quare militibus, quos soli|darios[c] uocant, undecumque collectis ubique locorum, et in episcopiis et abbatiis, tamdiu administrari uictualia regis imperio iubetur, quoad rei ueritas indice uero predicetur. Cumque plurimum hac in expectatione anni tempus uolueretur, nullaque Danorum impeticio solida certitudine affutura sciretur, solidarii, remunerati regio donatiuo, ad propria remeare sinuntur.

14. *De morte Adelelmi abbatis.*

Inde rixarum et inquietudinum cause per Anglie regnum depresse, pacis quies indulta est. Vnde abbas a forinsecis mentem auertens negotiis, ecclesiasticis intendit studiis, et nunc litterarum suos subditos documentis excolens, nunc mores religionis indens, ornamentis quoque ecclesiam adaugens, disponere queque suis profutura forent sollerter satagebat, preterea a fundamentis ecclesiam renouare, paratis in id exequendum sat copiose sumptibus. Cum itaque huiusmodi instaret exercitiis, inopinata quarto iduum Septembri mensis morte ab hac uita preripitur.[38]

C fo. 138r 15. *De Henrico filio regis.* |

[ii. 12] Adueniente eiusdem anni Paschali festo, regis filius Henricus, tunc quidem adolescens, suis in Normannia cum patre fratribus[d] constitutis, Abbendonie his sollempnibus,[e] uti rex ipse mandauerat, mansit diebus, domno Osmundo Saresbiriensi episcopo, cum Milone de

[a] tirannicum *B* [b] rationatione *B* [c] soli|lidarios *B* [d] fratribus *rep. B* [e] solempnibus *B*

[37] This chapter probably refers to events of 1085; if so, it should have appeared after, not before, the death of Abbot Adelelm.

[38] See above, p. xli, for *De abbatibus* on Adelelm's view of the tenth-century church, and

not delay, but forestalled a royal trial concerning this affair, paying compensation for what had been done to the king's official. But he shook off forever the tyrannical oppression of reeves, for in that royal assembly, by reasoned pleading and the testimony of many wise men it was concluded that the church of Abingdon ought never suffer this type of exaction, but rather enjoy perpetual liberty. So that famed liberty, proclaimed at that time, is freely defended to this day.

13. *Concerning the coming of the Danes.*[37]
Then rumour spread that the Danes had prepared a fleet to attack England. Therefore soldiers whom people call mercenaries were gathered from all about. It was ordered by the king's command that provisions be assembled everywhere, in bishoprics and abbacies, until the truth of the matter be known for certain. And when much of the year had passed in such expectation, and no Danish assault was known to be at hand with absolute certainty, the mercenaries were paid by royal gift and allowed to return home.

14. *Concerning the death of Abbot Adelelm.*
When the causes of contentions and disturbances had been suppressed throughout the kingdom of England, the repose of peace was granted. So the abbot turned his attention from the business of the outside world and concentrated on ecclesiastical pursuits. He strove adroitly to arrange everything for the future good of his men, now tending his charges with literary instruction, now setting in place practices of the religious life, and also improving the church with ornaments. In addition, he was to rebuild the church from its foundations, and sufficient resources had been assigned to do this. When he was pressing on with such business, he was snatched from this life by unexpected death on 10 September [1083].[38]

15. *Concerning Henry, the king's son.*
With Easter that year approaching [31 Mar. 1084], the king's son Henry, then a youth, spent these holy days at Abingdon, as the king ordered; his brothers were in Normandy with their father. Lord Osmund bishop of Salisbury, and Miles of Wallingford, surnamed

on his death. His death is also mentioned in the Abingdon copies of the Worcester chronicle; John of Worcester, *Chronicle*, iii. 307.

Walingaford cognomento Crispin sibi coherentibus;[39] rerum copiam Roberto de Oileio non tantum regalium, sed etiam monasterii huius familie mensis administrante.[40] Que sollempnitas ab incarnatione Dominica celebrata est millesimo octogesimo quarto anno, indictione septima, epacta undecima.[a][41]

B fo. 123v 16. *De Rainaldo abbate.*

[ii. 15] Transacta uero Pentecostes festiuitate, die natalicii sanctorum martirum Geruasii et Prothasii, regimen loci istius a rege Rothomagum[b] constituto Rainaldo, ipsius regis olim capellano, tunc uero Gemmeticensis cenobii monacho, donatur. Qui et Walchelino Wintoniensi episcopo transmittitur, et ut ad locum ipsum perducat ei precipitur, et ecclesiastico more in cura illius designet Dominicum gregem.[42] Fit quod imperatur, et die quinto decimo kalendarum Augustarum, anno solari primo cicli,[c] in abbatia,[d] uictualium affluentia illo referta, recipitur.[43] Et proxima Assumptionis sancte Marie domine nostre et celi regine celebratione, per Osmundum Seresbiriensem episcopum apud eandem pontificalem sedem abbas consecratur.

17. *De hospicio abbatis apud Lundoniam.*

Secundo hinc anno, per Gillebertum[e] de Gant mansio quedam super
[ii. 16] flumen Tamisie sita uia qua Westmonasterium a Lundonia ciuitate itur, ecclesie Abbendonie donatur,[44] cum capella memorie sanctorum Innocentum[f] dicata, eiusdem mansionis preforibus condita. Idem etiam donum antecessoris huius abbatis tempore Adelelmi[g] iste uir

[a] *B follows this with an account of a miracle involving Robert d'Oilly; see below, p. 326. Above the first word of the inserted section is a little* 'b'; *above the first word of the following chapter* (De Rainaldo), *a little* 'a'; *and above the first word of the next chapter* (De hospicio) *a little* 'c'. *It is thus indicated that the inserted section should follow that on Abbot Reginald, but precede that on the abbot's house at London. For another such rearrangement, see above, p. 2*
[b] Rotomagum *B* [c] cidi *B* [d] habatia *B* [e] Gilebertum *B*
[f] Innocentium *B* [g] Aþelelmi *B*

[39] Henry at this time was 15 years old. Osmund was bishop of Salisbury 1078–99; *Handbook of British Chronology*, p. 270. For the possibility that he acted as a tutor to Henry, see C. W. Hollister, *Henry I* (New Haven and London, 2001), pp. 36–7. Miles Crispin was *Domesday* lord of Wallingford. He married Maud/Matilda, daughter of Robert d'Oilly, and died in 1107; Sanders, *Baronies*, p. 93, K. Keats-Rohan, 'The devolution of the Honour of Wallingford, 1066–1148', *Oxoniensia*, liv (1989), 311–18.

[40] This sentence could also read 'Robert d'Oilly administered an abundance not only of royal goods but also from the tables of the community of the monastery'. However, the *History* does not elsewhere use *familia* in this way; cf. below, p. 362, for use of *familia* in an administrative document within the continuation of the *History* in MS B.

[41] In MS B there follows a section concerning Robert d'Oilly, below, p. 326. For dating by indiction and by epact, see *Handbook of Dates for Students of English History*, ed. C. R. Cheney (Cambridge, 1995), pp. 2–3, 8.

Crispin, were attached to Henry.[39] At the tables of this household, Robert d'Oilly administered an abundance not only of royal goods but also those of the monastery.[40] This solemn feast was celebrated in the year of our Lord 1084, in the seventh indiction and the eleventh epact.[41]

16. *Concerning Abbot Reginald.*

After the festival of Pentecost [19 May 1084], on the birthday of the holy martyrs Gervasius and Protasius [19 Jun.], the king, at Rouen, gave control of this monastery to Reginald, formerly his chaplain but at that time a monk of the house of Jumièges. Reginald was sent to Bishop Walkelin of Winchester, who was ordered to lead him to Abingdon and assign the Lord's flock to his care, according to ecclesiastical custom.[42] These orders were followed, and on 18 July in the first solar year of the cycle he was received in the abbey, which was filled with an abundance of provisions for him.[43] And on the next festival of the Assumption of St Mary our Lady and Queen of Heaven [15 Aug.] he was consecrated abbot by Osmund bishop of Salisbury, at his episcopal see.

17. *Concerning the abbot's residence at London.*

In the following year a house, situated on the river Thames, on the road running from London to Westminster, was given to the church of Abingdon by Gilbert de Gant.[44] With it, established at the doors of the house, was a chapel dedicated to the memory of the Holy Innocents. Gilbert had made this gift in the time of the abbot's predecessor, Adelelm, but took it back when he learnt of his death.

[42] Walkelin was bishop of Winchester 1070–98; *Handbook of British Chronology*, p. 276. Reginald's succession is also mentioned in the Abingdon copies of the Worcester chronicle; John of Worcester, *Chronicle*, iii. 307.

[43] For dating by solar year, see *Handbook of Dates*, p. 8: 'The years of the cycle are numbered from I to XIX in direct series and the number for each year is known as the Golden Number. The cycle is computed from the year 1 B.C. and is usually held to begin 1 January in that year. To find the golden number of the year of grace, add 1 to the year of grace and divide by 19. The remainder is the golden number, unless the remainder is 0, when the golden number is XIX.' By my calculation, the *History* has got the solar year wrong, since 1084 plus one and divided by 19 leaves a remainder of 2.

[44] Gilbert was a Fleming, from the area of Ghent, as his name suggests. He may have been present at Hastings, and certainly was rewarded with a large fee in Lincolnshire, and lands in Yorkshire and a dozen other counties. He died in or around 1095; see *Early Yorkshire Charters*, ed. W. Farrer *et al.* (12 vols., i–iii, Edinburgh, 1914–16, iv–xii, Yorkshire Arch. Soc. Rec. Ser. Extra Ser., 1935–65), ii. 431–3. The house was on the south side of the Strand, either on the road itself or possibly on a lane running southwards from the Strand to the river Thames; the latter may be the meaning of 'South Street', below, p. 112. I would like to thank Dr Derek Keene for his help on this point.

contulerat, sed, ipsius obitu cognito, sibi reusurpauit. At modo resipiscens, sub interminatione anathematis, perpetuam possessionem retinendum eidem ecclesie deuote idem restituit. Cui attestationi interfuere Rodulfus eiusdem Gilleberti dapifer, et Robertus de Candos cum Roberto de Armenteres,[45] Hermerus de Ridie[a] cum Roberto filio Osberni, Radulfus et frater illius Hamericus nepotes Roberti, et plures alii.

18. *De morte Willelmi regis senioris.*

Quarto autem aduentus istius abbatis in abbatiam anno, rex apud castellum Madatensium egritudinem incurrens, quinto iduum Septembri mensis diem clausit ultimum, anno Dominice incarnationis millesimo octogesimo septimo, indictione decima.[46] Cui succedens loco, filius eius Willelmus apud Westmonasterium circa sancti
B fo. 124^{r} Michaelis | festum coronatur.[47]

[ii. 17] 19. *Confirmatio carte Eadwardi regis et de hundredo.*[b][48]

Willelmus rex Anglorum[c] uicecomitibus suis in quorum uicecomitatibus abbatia de Abbendona[d] terras habet, salutem. Precipio ut tota terra abbatie de Abbendona[e] ita bene et pleniter habeat sacham suam et socham et omnes consuetudines suas, sicut melius habuit et plenius tempore regis Eadwardi et patris mei, et defendo ne aliquis inde[f] iniuriam faciat. Teste Eudone dapifero, per Radulfum de Languetot.[49] Apud Legam. Et hundredum de Hornimere similiter sicuti tunc temporis habuit. Testibus predictis.

20. *De ductu aque apud Botelea.*[g][50]

Huius regis regni anno secundo, quando ciuitas Rouecestra ab eodem obsidebatur contra tenente ipsam Odone Baiocensi episcopo, eiusdem regis patruo, ductum aque, quem uulgo 'Lacche' appellant, apud
C fo. 138^{v} Boteleam uiri de Suuecurda[h] illicito ausu | fregerunt. Quibus tunc temporis Anskillus dominabatur.[51] Sed eadem in questionem res

[a] *B reads either* Riderie or Riðie, *it being impossible to distinguish whether the third character is an Old English character, or a* d *with an abbreviation mark standing for* er [b] *illustration of William Rufus B* [c] Anglie *B* [d] Abbandona *B* [e] Abbandona *B* [f] *om. B* [g] Boteleia *B* [h] Seuecurda *B*

[45] *DB* i, fo. 56^{v} records that Robert held one house in Wallingford. A Robert—possibly the witness to this charter—or perhaps more than one Robert had various holdings from Gilbert de Gant; *DB* i, fos. 62^{r}, 159^{v}, 227^{v}, 354^{v}, 356^{r}. The *Cartae* of 1166 record that David de 'Armere' held ten knights of old enfeoffment of honour of Gant; *Red Book*, i. 383.

[46] Mantes is in the Vexin (Dept. Seine-et-Oise).

[47] Michaelmas is 29 Sept. Rufus was in fact crowned on Sunday 26 Sept.; see Barlow, *William Rufus*, p. 57 and n. 18.

But now he repented and, under threat of anathema, devoutly restored it to this church to be held as a perpetual possession. Present as witnesses were Rodulf (Gilbert's steward), Robert de Candos with Robert d'Armentières,[45] Hermer de Ridie with Robert son of Osbern, Ralph and his brother Hameric (nephews of Robert), and many others.

18. *Concerning the death of King William the elder.*
In the fourth year of Reginald's abbacy, the king fell ill at the castle of Mantes, and passed away on 9 September in the year of our Lord 1087, in the tenth indiction.[46] In his place succeeded his son William, who was crowned at Westminster around the feast of St Michael.[47]

19. *Confirmation of the charter of King Edward and concerning the hundred.*[48]
William king of the English to all his sheriffs in whose counties the abbey of Abingdon has lands, greeting. I order that all the land of the abbey of Abingdon have its sake and soke and all its customs, as well and fully as it best and most fully had in the time of King Edward and of my father, and I forbid that anyone do harm concerning this. Witness: Eudo the steward, through Ralph de Langetot.[49] At *Lega*. And similarly the hundred of Hormer, as the abbey had it at that time. With the same witnesses.

20. *Concerning the watercourse at Botley.*[50]
In the second year of this king's reign, when he was besieging the city of Rochester which was held against him by his uncle Odo of Bayeux, the men of Seacourt, with improper audacity, broke the watercourse at Botley, commonly called 'the Lake'. Anskill then was their lord.[51]

[48] *RRAN* i, no. 289. The position of the writ in the text suggests that it is from early in William Rufus's reign.

[49] For this phrase, see *Royal Writs*, ed. van Caenegem, pp. 149–51. A Ralph de Langetot was a tenant of Abingdon in the early twelfth century, below, p. 387; see also *Anglo-Norman Families*, p. 53.

[50] Berks. *English Lawsuits*, no. 133.

[51] *DB* i, fo. 58^{v}: of the fifty hides of Cumnor, 'Anskill holds five hides. Norman held them in the time of King Edward as one manor, called Seacourt'; see also *Domesday Geography of South-East England*, p. 244 n. 4, M. Biddle, 'The deserted medieval village of Seacourt, Berkshire', *Oxoniensia*, xxvi/xxvii (1961–2), 70–201, on the later decline of Seacourt. Dr John Blair points out to me that in Oxfordshire dialect Old English *lacu/lace*, meaning stream or pond, normally ends up as 'lake'. The watercourse in this section was later known partly as the Shire Lake Ditch, partly as Seacourt River; it ran southwards from Seacourt to Botley and formed the shire boundary there; see also J. Blair, 'Thornbury, Binsey: a probable defensive enclosure associated with St Frideswide', *Oxoniensia*, liii

[*See p. 22 for n. 51 cont.*]

postea in abbatis presentia posita, non debere fracturam[a] illam eo quo facta est modo fieri ratiotinatione sancitur[b] publica. Vnde ille Anskillus apud abbatem hoc commissum decem pependit solidis. Egit tamen ut tunc indiceretur molendinario loci illius quatinus sibi singulis ab eo redderetur annis duarum summa[c] orarum.[52]

[ii. 18] 21. *De capella apud Wiscelea.*[d][53]

In uilla que Wiscelea appellatur Adelelmi[e] abbatis primordii tempore deerat ecclesia, nam parrochie presbiteri de Sunningis[f] adiacet. Sed quia illic indigenis hieme uadis transitis graue constabat ad Sunningas ecclesiastica[g] audiendi officia conuenire, preterea et abbate eodem hospitandi gratia in illis diuertente partibus locus ipse missarum carebat celebratione capella, tunc primum lignea inibi constituitur, ac per Osmundi episcopi manum in sancti Nicholai memoria dedicatur. Verum, Rainaldo abbate abbatiam gubernante, clericus ecclesie Sunningis[h] apud episcopum preiudicium se pati suarum consuetudinum causa capelle de Wiscelee conqueritur. Quare eadem capella inofficiari ab episcopo prohibetur. In proximo uero Quadragesimali instante ieiunio, episcopus Abbendoniam uenit, ubi cum episcopo istud de ipsa capella abbas pepigit:

22. *Cirographum de eadem capella.*[54]

Hec est conuentio habita inter Osmundum episcopum et Rainoldum Abbendonie abbatem super ecclesia de Wisceleie, quam abbas
B fo. 124v Adelelmus[i] construxit et ab eodem episcopo dedica|ri fecit. Habebit in eadem ecclesia abbas Abbendonensis suum clericum, officiorum Dei curas agentem omnesque oblationes que ad ipsam ecclesiam ab[j] quibuslibet oblatæ[k] fuerint recipientem, et ad usum suum deseruiendo ecclesie reseruantem. Pro quo dabit abba episcopo uno quoque anno ad festiuitatem Omnium Sanctorum dimidiam marcam argenti,
[ii. 19] habente nec minus ecclesia de Sunninge omnes eas consuetudines quas habebat in diebus Eadwardi regis ex uilla de Wisceleæ.[l] Facta est

[a] facturam *B* [b] sanctitur *B* [c] *corr. by erasure from* summarum *B* [d] Wisceleia *B* [e] Aðelelmi *B* [f] Sunnigges *B* [g] *a word such as* causa *may have been omitted here* [h] Sunninges *B* [i] Aðelelmus *B* [j] al *C* [k] oblate *B* [l] Vuisceleia *B*

(1988), 3–20, at p. 7 for a map of the area. On the siege of Rochester, see Barlow, *William Rufus*, pp. 78–81; the siege involving Odo probably lasted from the start of May until mid-Jun. 1088.

52 The ore, or *ora*, was a unit of account most common in Scandinavian areas, and amounted to sixteen pence.

But this matter was later investigated in the abbot's presence, and it was decided by open and reasoned pleading that the breach should not have been made in the way it was. Therefore, in the abbot's presence, Anskill paid for this deed with 10s. However, he contrived that the obligation of rendering him the sum of two *ores* a year then be imposed on the miller of that place.[52]

21. *Concerning the chapel of Whistley*.[53]
When Adelelm was first abbot, there was no church in the village of Whistley, for it is attached to the parish of the priest of Sonning. However, it was known that in winter it was difficult for the inhabitants to cross the fords and to come to Sonning to hear the church offices. In addition, when Abbot Adelelm was travelling in that area and was intent on staying there, mass was not celebrated there. First of all, then, a wooden chapel was built there, and was dedicated by Bishop Osmund's hand in memory of St Nicholas. But during Abbot Reginald's abbacy, the cleric of the church of Sonning complained before the bishop that he was suffering prejudice to his customs because of the chapel of Whistley. Therefore the bishop forbade that the chapel provide liturgical services. However, during the following Lenten fast, the bishop went to Abingdon, where the abbot made the following arrangement with the bishop concerning that chapel:

22. *Cirograph concerning that chapel*.[54]
This is the agreement made between Bishop Osmund and Abbot Reginald of Abingdon concerning the church of Whistley which Abbot Adelelm built and had dedicated by Bishop Osmund. The abbot of Abingdon will have his cleric in the said church, performing the duty of the offices of God, receiving all offerings made by whomsoever to that church, and keeping them for his own use in officiating at that church. In return, each year at the feast of All Saints [1 Nov.], the abbot will give the bishop half a mark of silver. The church of Sonning is to have without reduction all those customs from the village of Whistley which it had in King Edward's days.

[53] Berks.; *DB* i, fo. 59^{r}: 'The abbey itself holds Whistley, and always held it.' Sonning, Berks., neighboured Whistley across the river Loddon. In 1086 it was held by the bishop of Salisbury; *DB* i, fo. 58^{r}. This is one of the earliest references to the proprietor of a mother church providing an outlying chapel in order to improve pastoral care. *Minsters and Parish Churches*, ed. Blair, p. 18 n. 57, states that '"Whistley" church is either now lost or represented by the present church of Hurst.' See also Lennard, *Rural England*, pp. 297–8.

[54] *Salisbury acta: 1078–1217*, ed. Kemp, no. 2.

autem hec conuentio regni Willelmi iunioris anno secundo pridie idus Martii, quando ipse episcopus fuit Abbendone in Quadragesima. Cuius sunt isti testes: ex parte[a] episcopi, Robertus archidiaconus,[55] Heldebrandus frater Raimbaldi, Ricardus de Buro; ex parte abbatis, Walterius[b] monachus Gemm',[c] ⟨G⟩odricus[d] monachus Abbend', Walterius[e] Rufus, Willelmus de Aula.

23. *De Scipena.*[56]

Viculus est burgo Abbendonensi contiguus Scipena dictus. Hunc de abbatia tempore Eadwardi regis quidam ipsius constabulus nomine Eadnotus tenebat. Cuius uiri terrarum metas postea Hugo Cestrensis comes adeptus.[57] Cum didicisset predictum uiculum huius abbatie iuri pertinere, commonitu Rainaldi abbatis, et baronum suorum consultu, tercio regni Willelmi predicti iunioris regis anno, et pridie kalendarum Aprilium, ipse comes in sanctuario ecclesie istius consistens, toto conuentu fratrum ibi presidente, quicquid in illo loco posse uidebatur habere Deo et eius genitrici id optulit, manu cultellum altari superponendo et ut in perpetuum ratum constet
[ii. 20] uerbis illud prosequendo. Affuere illo cum comite Engenulfus et Willelmus uterque nepos ipsius, Godardus etiam de Boiauilla,[58] cum Engerardo et alii plures. De hac ut dictum est re determinata cum primo apud eundem comitem oriretur sermo, litteras abbati inde direxit, quarum huiusmodi extitit textus:

24. *Carta de Scipena.*[f][59]

Hugo Cestrensis comes Rainaldo uenerando abbati et carissimo amico
C fo. 139r suo, salutem. | Mando tibi quod de terra quam erga me petiisti locutus sum cum uxore mea et cum meis baronibus, et inueni in meo consilio quod concedam eam Deo et sancte ecclesie de qua pastoralis cura super te imposita est, tali pacto, quod dones mihi triginta libras

[a] pate *C* [b] ualterus, *with space for initial B* [c] Germ' *B* [d] *initial om. C;* Odricus, *with small* o *in middle of initial B. Such a mistake suggests that B derives from C. The name is almost certainly Godric, perhaps the same Godric as is mentioned above, p. 4* [e] Wualterus *B* [f] Scipenam *B*

[55] J. Le Neve, *Fasti Ecclesiae Anglicanae 1066–1300. 4: Salisbury*, comp. D. Greenway (London, 1991), p. 24, gives this as the only mention of Robert the archdeacon.

[56] Berks. See also *DB* i, fo. 58v: of the sixty hides of Barton, 'Reginald holds in pledge from the abbot one manor, Shippon. Eadnoth the staller held it in the time of King Edward and it was not then the abbey's [*in abbatia*].' On the dating of these events within the period *c.*1086–90, see Hudson, 'Abbey of Abingdon', p. 190. *De abbatibus* states simply that Reginald bought Shippon from Hugh earl of Chester; *CMA* ii. 285, and above, p. xliv. J. H. Round, in *VCH*, *Berkshire*, i. 295, suggested that before 1066 Eadnoth may have encroached on Abingdon's land at Shippon, with Earl Harold's encouragement.

This agreement was made on 14 March in the second year of the reign of William the younger, when Bishop Osmund was at Abingdon during Lent. These are the witnesses of this: from the bishop's side, Robert the archdeacon,[55] Heldebrand brother of Raimbald, Richard de *Buro*; from the abbot's side, Walter monk of Jumièges, Godric monk of Abingdon, Walter Rufus, William de *Aula*.

23. *Concerning Shippon.*[56]

Next to the borough of Abingdon is a hamlet called Shippon. In King Edward's time, a constable of his named Eadnoth held it from the abbey. Afterwards, Earl Hugh of Chester acquired the extent of this man's lands.[57] When he learnt that the aforesaid hamlet belonged to this abbey's property, at Abbot Reginald's urging and advised by his own barons, on 31 March in the third year of King William the younger's reign, the earl stood in the church's sanctuary, with the whole convent of monks there watching, and offered to God and His Mother whatever it seemed he could have in that place. He placed a knife on the altar by hand, and by words expounded that this offering should remain strong for ever. Present there with the earl were Engenulf and William his nephews, and Godard de *Boiauilla*,[58] with Engerard and many others. When discussion first arose in the earl's presence about this matter, which would be settled as above, he sent letters concerning it to the abbot, of which the following text exists:

24. *Charter concerning Shippon.*[59]

Hugh earl of Chester to Reginald, venerable abbot and his very dear friend, greeting. I inform you that I have spoken with my wife and barons about the land which you sought of me, and I have found in my council that I should grant it to God and to the holy church, the pastoral care of which is placed on you, on the following terms: that you give me £30 of pennies from your money, and that I may be your

[57] See C. P. Lewis, 'The formation of the honor of Chester, 1066–1100', *The Earldom of Chester and its Charters*, ed. A. T. Thacker (Jl. of Chester Arch. Soc., lxxi, 1991), pp. 37–68, at 48–9, 55, 67–8. Hugh was earl of Chester 1071–1101 and was one of the largest landholders in England. On Eadnoth the staller, see K. Mack, 'The stallers: administrative innovation in the reign of Edward the Confessor', *Journal of Medieval History*, xii (1986), 123–34, esp. at p. 129.

[58] 'Boiauilla' is probably one of the places named Biville in Normandy.

[59] This document is also printed in *The Charters of the Anglo-Norman Earls of Chester, c.1071–1237*, ed. G. Barraclough (Rec. Soc. of Lancashire and Cheshire, cxxvi, 1988), no. 2. It differs from most of the charters in Book II of the *History* in being addressed solely to the abbot. That it was not primarily intended as a public announcement is also suggested by the absence of a place-name for the land given.

denariorum de tua pecunia, et ut frater uester sim et uxor mea et pater meus et mater mea in orationibus uestris, et ita[a] ut simus scripti omnes in Libro Commemorationum, et ut sit factum tale obsequium pro nobis quale debet fieri pro uno fratre de ecclesia, ubicumque moriamur.[60]

Quicquid itaque pro illa terra exactum est nil fieri relictum, nam et pecunia data et cetera quesita omnino impensa.

25. *De Cestretuna et Hilla.*

B fo. 125r In comitatus supplementum Henrici Warewicensi comitis, | regis Willelmi iunioris in sui imperii principio dono, patrimonium terrarum Turkilli de Eardene[b] adiectum est.[61] Quare idem comes de
[ii. 21] terra diebus Adelelmi[c] abbatis ecclesie a predicto uiro Turkillo donata uerbum Rainaldo abbati intulit, dicens ut alias possessiones illius uiri ita et illam quam ecclesia[d] habebat sui iam iuris esse.[62] At, ut ipsum comitem abbas sibi ecclesieque beniuolum et muneris Turkilli concessorem et confirmatorem efficeret, eidem marcam auri optulit. Quam gratanter comes suscipiens, coram huius ecclesie sanctuario et monachorum cetu hic cohabitantium, horum quoque suorum baronum presentia, quod petebatur sua auctoritate et ipse roborauit: Ricardi filii Osberni, Turstini de Mundford, Herlewini presbiteri, Willelmi Sorel, Ricardi capellani, Godrici Interpretis, et aliis pluribus.[63]

26. *De Bernero.*[64]

Mutuande necessitate pecunie cuius constabat summa triginta librarum, abbas Adelelmus[e] Roberto de Pirronis terre quantitatem quam quesiuit in uadem posuit.[65] Sed non longe post, abbatis uite finis accidit. Cumque Rainaldus in pastorali succederet cura, et predictus Robertus paruam inde subnecteret moram[f] moriendi,[g] Walchelinus Wintoniensis episcopus Bernerum defuncti nepotem abbati adducens, hunc iure loco illius contestatur subrogari in his

[a] *om. B* [b] Ardene *B* [c] Aðelelmi *B* [d] ecclesiam *B* [e] Aðelelmus *B*
[f] *poorly corrected to* moram, *perhaps from* curram *C;* curam *B* [g] *C is damaged along the edge of this column, so where necessary the text is completed from B*

[60] On the Book of Commemorations, see above, p. xix. On burials, see above, p. lxix. On receipt of confraternity by a secular person, see Lanfranc, *Monastic Constitutions*, p. 170.

[61] Henry was created earl *c.*1088, and died in 1119. He was the son of Roger de Beaumont and brother of Robert count of Meulan and earl of Leicester. See Sanders, *Baronies*, p. 93, Crouch, 'Influence of earls of Warwick'.

[62] See above, pp. 10, 26.

brother, and my wife and father and mother be in your prayers, and in such a way that we all be written in the Book of Commemorations, and that, wherever we die, there be such a funeral for us as there might for one of the brethren of the church.[60]

Whatever was demanded for this land, nothing remained to be done, for the money was given and the other requirements completely fulfilled.

25. *Concerning Chesterton and Hill.*

The patrimony of the lands of Thorkell of Arden was added as a supplement to the earldom of Henry earl of Warwick, by gift of King William the younger at the start of his dominion.[61] The earl therefore raised with Abbot Reginald the issue of the land given by the aforesaid Thorkell to the church in Abbot Adelelm's days, saying that Thorkell's other possessions, and the land which the church had, were now his property.[62] But the abbot offered the earl a mark of gold to ensure his good will towards himself and the church, and that he grant and confirm Thorkell's gift. The earl gratefully accepted this, and in the sanctuary of the church, in the presence of a gathering of the monks living here, he reinforced with his own authority what was sought, in the presence of the following of his barons: Richard son of Osbern, Thurstan de Montfort, Herluin the priest, William Sorel, Richard his chaplain, Godric the interpreter, and many others.[63]

26. *Concerning Berner.*[64]

Needing to borrow money amounting to £30, Abbot Adelelm placed in gage with Robert de Péronne some land which Robert was seeking.[65] But not long after, the abbot's life came to its end. When Reginald succeeded to the pastoral care, and Robert died not long thereafter, Walkelin bishop of Winchester brought Berner, nephew of the deceased, to the abbot, and asserted that Berner should by right succeed Robert in those possessions which he enjoyed when Reginald

[63] On Richard son of Osbern, Thurstan de Montfort, and William Sorel, see Crouch, 'Influence of earls of Warwick', pp. 5, 16 n. 15. Professor Crouch (personal communication) points out that Herluin the priest also occurs as a prebendary of the collegiate church of Warwick, with a prebend at Brailes and Coten End; Ctl. St Mary Warwick, London, Public Record Office, E164/22, fo. 8^{r}. He is presumably the same Herluin the priest who appears in a charter of Henry, earl of Warwick, below, p. 202. For a Godric the interpreter (Latunarius) holding in Kent, see A. Ballard, *An Eleventh-Century Inquisition of St Augustine's, Canterbury* (London, 1920), p. 30.

[64] On Berner and Robert de Péronne, see above, p. lxi.

[65] For the gaging of land, see Pollock and Maitland, ii. 117–19.

quibus cum in abbatiam uenisset fungebatur. Abbas autem hinc creditum eius qui mortuus erat unde redderet non habens, illinc interpellantis se et diligentis auctoritatem intuens, nequaquam obniti
[ii. 22] quesitis funditus quiuit. Sed tamen ad hoc uertit responsum, ut que petebatur partim annueret, alia denegaret. Nam sine releuatione id se non permissurum, nec aliam nisi tres quas de uilla Culeham habebat hidas recepturum, dixit.[66] Si has abiuraret, cetera sibi remanerent. Ille cum id ab episcopo, cuius presentia patrocinabatur, fructuosum agendum fore, quia in aliud diuerti animus abbatis fixus erat nolle, acciperet, remissum unde pulsabatur, fide sua interposita ut nec per se nec per alterum unquam mentio alicuius inde machinationis moueretur, exsoluit. Dictorum horum et factorum Wintonie in hospicio abbatis extra urbis meridianam portam sito locus fuit.[67] Vbi interfuerunt Richerus de Andelei,[68] Rannulfus Baiocis, Robertus Floriaci, Gaufridus conestabulus, Droardus, Robertus Ermenoldeuille, et plures alii.

27. *De tribus hidis apud Culeham.*

Transcursis postea duobus annis, idem Bernerus sue oblitus sponsionis, constitutis episcopo predicto et abbate ipso apud Apelford, discrimen preiudicii sibi illatum pro illa qua carebat terre portione conqueritur.[69] Super quo abbas non ultra debere quamlibet mouere causam eundem per testes ostendit idoneos, nec se illi intendere.
B fo. 125v Qua | re tunc omnino deliberatum est nil causarum inde deinceps |
C fo. 139v agitari, sed dominicis monachorum reliquo euo usibus terram illam deputari, et merito. Nam adeo pre ceteris possessionibus illa a priscis temporibus libera habetur, ut nemo illic inhabitantium cuiuslibet uicecomitis aut regii officialis iugo in aliquo deprimatur, nec uicecomitatus siue hundredi, sed solius abbatis curie in dis-
[ii. 23] cutiendis causarum euentibus subiciatur.[70] Bernerus uero de portione sibi remanente militis et dimidii seruitium consuetudinaliter prosequatur. Et hic interfuere Robertus de Rosel, Robertus nepos

[66] Oxon. Culham is not named in *Domesday Book*.

[67] Identification of this house is difficult. The Winchester survey of *c.*1110 does not include the south suburb, and for a lack of completeness in the 1148 survey, see below, p. 164 n. 405. One possibility is that the abbot first had a residence outside the South Gate, and then moved to one outside the North, see below, p. 1640; another is that the abbot—at least for a period—had residences at both gates. (I would like to thank Dr Derek Keene for his help on these points). Note also below, p. 272, for Eugenius III confirming to Abingdon land worth half a mark outside the south gate of Winchester.

came to the abbacy. Now not only did the abbot lack the wherewithal to repay the dead man's loan, but also he had regard for the authority of the person attentively interceding with him, and he was quite unable to resist by any means what was sought. However, he resorted to the following answer: he would agree to some requests, reject others. He said that he would not permit this succession without payment of a relief, nor would he accept any relief except the three hides which Berner had from the village of Culham.[66] If Berner abjured these, the rest would remain to him. Berner learnt from the bishop (whose presence acted as a defence) what it would be fruitful to do, since the abbot's mind was set and not to be swayed in any way. He made the required concession, pledging his faith that neither he nor anyone else would ever suggest any deceit concerning this. These words and deeds took place in the abbot's house in Winchester, outside the south gate of the city.[67] Present there were Richer des Andelys,[68] Ranulf de Bayeux, Robert de Fleury, Geoffrey the constable, Droard, Robert d'*Ermenoldeville*, and many others.

27. *Concerning the three hides at Culham.*

Two years later, Berner forgot his oath. When Bishop Walkelin and Abbot Reginald were together at Appleford, he complained that the decision was prejudicial to him with regard to the portion of land of which he was deprived.[69] Concerning this, the abbot showed by suitable witnesses that Berner ought to bring no further case, and that he should not pay attention to him. Therefore it was conclusively and with good cause decided then that no case should henceforth be started concerning this, but the land should be assigned to the demesne uses of the monks for the rest of time. For from ancient times that possession, more than others, is so free that no inhabitant is oppressed in any matter by the yoke of any sheriff or royal official, nor is it subject to the shire or hundred but only to the abbot's court in discussing the outcome of cases.[70] From his remaining portion, Berner would carry out the service of one and a half knights in accordance with custom. Present here were Robert de Rosel, Robert

[68] See *DB* i, fo. 52^r, for a Richer des Andelys having the customary dues of four houses in Southampton by grant of King William; this is his sole appearance under this name in *Domesday Book*. Note also Keats-Rohan, *Domesday People*, p. 368.

[69] Berks. *DB* i, fo. 59^r, states that 'the abbey itself holds Appleford in demesne'.

[70] See above, p. xcvi.

Gotmundi,[a] Rannulfus Flambard, et frater eius Osbernus, et plures alii.[71]

Miles quidam Walterus, cognomen habens de Ripario, et terram que Bedena dicitur tenens, ea tempestate obiit, cui paruulus relictus est filius eiusdem nominis.[72] Hac pro re istius patruus pueri, Godcelinus nomine, predictam adipisci ambiens possessionem, in regis curia apud Becceleam tunc constituta argumentari inde exorsus est.[73] Sed Rainaldo abbate puerum manutenente,[b] et contra illum ratiocinante,[c] suo frustratus est conatu. Tunc desistente obnisu, supplicatur quatinus, quoad puer maioris foret etatis, sue manui eadem possessio permittatur;[74] daturus fidem nil se interim malitie in eo ad opus ipsius quesiturum, preterea et trium militum exhibiturum,[d] qui inde exiguntur, suo in loco more solito seruitium. Fit ei quod petịit, se cuncta integre seruaturum ut spopondit fidem abbati dedit. Sed tamen isdem puer cum adoleuisset, in his que sibi ratiocinatu competebantur publico nequiuit admitti, nisi prius diuersis inde habitis questionibus.[75]

28. *De renouatione huius ecclesie.*

Interea, dum prospera sibi succederent, abbas ueteris ecclesie oratorium amplificare disposuit.[76] Iactoque fundamento operis, dum turri ueteri quod nouiter operabantur incautius quam expedi-
[ii. 24] ebat unire pararent a parte orientali, qua disiecta porticus innixa fuerat, undique fundamento ipsius terebrato et conuulso,[77] anno ab incarnato Verbo millesimo nonagesimo primo, die Veneris quarte ebdomade Quadragesime, indictione quarta decima, fratribus uigiliis

[a] Godmundi *B* [b] manu tenente *B* [c] rationante *B* [d] exibiturum *B*

[71] It is uncertain how, if at all, Robert de Rosel was related to the Ralph de Rosel, mentioned below, p. 46. Ranulf Flambard was the leading administrator of William II and then bishop of Durham 1099–1128; see R. W. Southern, *Medieval Humanism and Other Studies* (Oxford, 1970), pp. 183–205; J. O. Prestwich, 'The career of Ranulf Flambard', *Anglo-Norman Durham 1093–1193*, ed. D. Rollason, M. Harvey, M. Prestwich (Woodbridge, 1994), pp. 299–310.

[72] Beedon, Berks. *DB* i, fo. 58[v], states that 'Walter de Rivers holds Beedon from the abbot', and that 'the same Walter holds two hides in Benham' from Abingdon. On the Rivers family, see also below, p. 157, and Keats-Rohan, *Domesday People*, pp. 236, 453; she suggests that their toponym may derive from La Rivière-Thibouville (Eure), but I adopt the practice for such toponyms of using the modern English Rivers. This section appears in *English Lawsuits*, no. 145; it is discussed in S. F. C. Milsom, 'The origin of prerogative wardship', *Law and Government in Medieval England and Normandy*, ed. G. S. Garnett and J. G. H. Hudson (Cambridge, 1994), pp. 223–44, at 235. The section has no heading in

nephew of Gotmund, Ranulf Flambard and his brother Osbern, and many others.[71]

A certain knight, Walter, surnamed de Rivers, who held the land called Beedon, died at that time, leaving a very young son of the same name.[72] Because of this, the boy's uncle, named Jocelin, who desired to acquire that possession, appeared in the king's court, then meeting at Beckley, to argue his case concerning this.[73] But he was frustrated in his attempt by Abbot Reginald who supported the boy and pleaded against Jocelin. Then Jocelin abandoned this effort and begged that he be allowed to take that possession into his own hand until the boy was older.[74] He would pledge his faith that he would not in the mean time seek anything maliciously for his own benefit in this, but in Walter's place would do the service of the three knights who are demanded therefrom, in the customary way. He was granted what he sought, and gave his word to the abbot that he would maintain everything entirely as he promised. But when Walter grew up, he could not gain admission to these possessions which belonged to him by this public plea, until various proceedings had been held on the matter.[75]

28. *Concerning the rebuilding of this church.*

Meanwhile, as good times continued, the abbot decided to enlarge the old church.[76] The foundations of the work were laid and they were preparing, with less than proper caution, to join the new work to the old tower from the eastern side, where a porticus chapel had once been attached but since demolished. Then its foundations were cut through and violently displaced on all sides,[77] and in the year 1091 from the Incarnation of the Word, on the Wednesday of the fourth week of Lent, in the fourteenth indiction [26 Mar. 1091], while the

MS C, and therefore I have not provided it with a distinct number; MS B provides just a line of red pen-strokes.

[73] Beckley, Oxon., about five miles north-east of Oxford; in 1086 it was held by Roger d'Ivry, *DB* i, fo. 158^{v}.

[74] Presumably until he reached the legal age of majority; for legal development on this matter, see Pollock and Maitland, ii. 438–9.

[75] See also below, p. 157.

[76] On this section, note Biddle *et al.*, 'Early history', p. 45. 'Oratorium ecclesie' probably does not refer to a specific part of the church building; see also below, pp. 66, 92.

[77] The statement that the foundations were cut through on all sides is not obviously reconciled with the previous emphasis on the new work being from the eastern side of the tower. Perhaps what happened was that the base [*fundamentum*] of the tower was weakened from the east, but the result was a violent displacement and then collapse on all sides.

nocturnalibus[a] instantibus ac responsorio tercie lectionis terminato,[b] loco quo capitulum tenebatur, casum mirabilem eadem turris dedit.[78] Nam cum ad easdem celebrandas in ecclesia conueniretur uigilias, et diuino mentem inspiratus prior instinctu conuentui inde abscedere, et capitulum turri proximum subire, innueret, subito ruens tam densissimam de fragmentis[c] cementi nebulam sparsit, ut luminaria ubi fratres psallebant ardentia cuncta extinguerentur. Sonitu et nebula presentes turbati, nil nisi mortem opperientes,
B fo. 126r terre quique prosternuntur. Sed euanescente | paulatim nebula, et reaccensis luminaribus, alter ab altero requisitus, nemo lesus reperitur, cum quibusdam in locis obdormitantibus seruientibus, caput pene supra pregrandes corruissent lapides, nil tamen quislibet eorum mali passus. Recollectis inde in unum monachis,[d] matutinale inceptum officium in claustro peragitur, non enim tum diuerti alias liberius posse inueniebatur. Ab incepto ergo opere oratorii tunc desitum, et aliud post Paschale festum exordiri coactum. Et hec fuit causa qua monasterii edificationem, a sancto patre et antistite Æthelwoldo[e] olim constructam, renouari contigit.[79]

29. *De Roberto de Oili.*[f][80]

Cum itaque operi instaretur, Robertus de Oileio in egritudinem incidit, in qua integro decubuit anno. Qui adeo huius ecclesie |
C fo. 140r renouationi intendit tunc, ut eam toto illo anno suorum ope
[ii. 25] sumptuum fabricantes ulla sine penuria accelerarent. Decem uero librarum reditum,[g] quas Ædelelmi[h] abbatis illuc usque dono exegerat, omnino remittens, contestatur suarum post se rerum possessores, ne inde quicquam exactionis ultra quereretur;[81] simul et amplius quam centum librarum summam, suorum pro emendatione preteritorum commissorum, pro iuuanda quoque monasterii reedificatione istic confert. Sed de prato extra urbis Oxenefordis murum sito, collato sibi dudum ut cetera tanquam regis constabulus tueretur, nichil actum.[82] Preterea et de tribus hidis, quorum una apud Sandford[i] ultra

[a] nocturnialibus *B* [b] terminata *B C* [c] frangmentis *B* [d] manachis *C* [e] Aðeluuoldo *B* [f] *in B, the beginning and end of this section have respectively the letters* ua *and* cat *in the margin in red in the main hand. The section was thus to be cancelled, because of the presence of the earlier extended section on Robert d'Oilly which is peculiar to this manuscript; below, p. 326* [g] redditum *B* [h] Aðelelmi *B* [i] Samford *B*

[78] This prior cannot be identified. It could be Warenger who is later referred to as prior since Abbot Reginald's time, below, p. 224; see also above, p. lvii.

[79] See above, p. cii, for interpretation of the rebuilding.

brethren were devoting themselves to the night vigils in the place where the chapter was held, and the responsory of the third reading had been completed, in wondrous fashion the tower collapsed. For though it was appropriate to celebrate these vigils in the church, the prior, inspired by divine prompting, beckoned the convent to leave there and go into the chapter next to the tower.[78] The tower suddenly crashed down and scattered so very thick a cloud of fragments of mortar that all the lights, burning where the brethren were chanting the psalms, were extinguished. Disturbed by the sound and the cloud, those present threw themselves to the ground, awaiting nothing save death. But as the cloud dispersed little by little, and the lamps were lit again, each inquired after the other, and no one was found to have been harmed. The largest stones fell almost on top of the heads of some servants falling asleep in their places, but no one suffered any ill. The monks regathered, and the morning's service, already begun, was completed in the cloister, as the most freely accessible place. The work begun on the church therefore was then abandoned, and after Easter new work had to be begun. And this was the reason why the monastery which had been constructed by the holy father and bishop Æthelwold was rebuilt.[79]

29. *Concerning Robert d'Oilly.*[80]

When this work was under way, Robert d'Oilly fell ill and was bed-ridden for an entire year. He was then so enthusiastic about the rebuilding of this church that with the assistance of his expenditure throughout that year the builders were able to speed up the work without any shortages. He entirely remitted the £10 rent which until then he had demanded by gift of Abbot Adelelm, and solemnly declared that those possessing his property after him would henceforth seek no exaction therefrom.[81] At the same time he also conferred a sum of over £100 to emend for his past misdeeds, and to help the rebuilding of the monastery. But nothing was done concerning the meadow situated outside the wall of the town of Oxford, conferred on him some time before, like the others, on the grounds that as the king's constable he might provide protection.[82] Also he was then silent about the three hides granted to him and Roger d'Ivry by the

[80] Cf. the version in MS B, below, p. 326. For caution about the abruptness of Robert's conversion to a more holy life, see Lennard, *Rural England*, p. 71; Robert's change of attitude seems more specifically to have concerned Abingdon.

[81] For the £10 rent, see above, p. 10.

[82] It is possible that this is King's Mead, mentioned below, p. 96.

Tamisiam, due uero in Earnicote habentur, a predicto Adelelmo[a] abbate sibi et Rogero de Iureio concessis, tunc tacitum.[83] Iste ille est cuius studio pons Oxenefordis factus est.[84] Qui mense Septembrio obiens, hic[b] in loco sepulturam accepit.[c][85]

Considerans autem abbas grande opus grandibus oportere sumptibus iuuari, et, quia ubique locorum in episcopiis et monasteriis ea tempestate noua conderentur edificia, ideoque quosque uicinorum auxilio niti tunc et ipse huiusmodi in suis commentatur opificum,[86] pro lege per abbatie[d] loca rusticis deputabatur, ut quislibet eorum, cui uel inuidia uel cupiditas alterius adipisci rem inerat, prepositi impleta manu mercature beneficio, posset alium de sua mansione expellere. Item et aliud plebeiorum incommodum: cum aliquis filios et uxorem habens, et agrorum fortunatus frugiferorum, domino suo iura inoffense persolueret, et is[e] debito fine quiesceret, nulla filiis aut uxori eius gratia rependebatur, sed illis eiectis in defuncti lucrationibus extraneus, data pecunia, inducebatur. His diebus raro a quoquam decima messium, ut lege precipitur, in abbatia ipsa dabatur, sed aut
[ii. 26] de hidagio quadraginta manipuli, quos uulgo garbas uocant, aut decima sue culture acra porrigebantur.[87] Vnde de uicis singulis

[a] Aðelelmo *B* [b] *om. B* [c] *followed by rubricated heading of minims B* [d] abatie *B* [e] his *B C*

[83] Both in Oxfordshire; see also *DB* i, fo. 156ᵛ, which states that in Sandford 'Robert and Roger hold one hide from the abbot' and that 'Robert d'Oilly and Roger d'Ivry hold . . . Arncott from the abbot, from the fee of the church. There are two hides here.' This section of the *History* is distinguishing Sandford-on-Thames from Dry Sandford in Berkshire. *De abbatibus* includes Sandford, Arncott, a meadow next to Oxford, and Whitchurch, amongst the possessions Abbot Adelelm granted to his kinsmen, and which the abbey still lacked at the time of writing; *CMA* ii. 283–4. Apart from Arncott's appearance in the papal confirmation below, p. 266, there is no other evidence for Abingdon lordship there in the twelfth century or afterwards. The land was probably given by Robert d'Oilly and Roger d'Ivry to the church of St George in Oxford Castle. St George's held Arncott and Sandford when Henry I confirmed the church's possessions, probably in the mid-1120s, and both estates then passed to Oseney Abbey in *c.*1149; see *RRAN* ii, no. 1468, *VCH*, *Oxfordshire*, v. 19, 268–9. See also above, pp. lxx, 10, on Tadmarton. On Whitchurch, Oxon., see Bk. i, c. 138 (*CMA* i. 477–8), *DB* i, fo. 159ʳ, where the 1086 tenant was Miles Crispin.

Roger d'Ivry was William I's butler and a close associate and 'sworn brother' of Robert d'Oilly: see *The Domesday Monachorum of Christ Church Canterbury*, ed. D. C. Douglas (London, 1944), pp. 56–7; Keats-Rohan, *Domesday People*, pp. 403–4; *Oseney Cartulary*, iv. 1. For his widow giving land at Fencott to Abingdon, see below, p. 106.

[84] See Lennard, *Rural England*, p. 71 n. 2: 'The *Magnus Pons* was evidently Folly Bridge and the causeways leading to it, as the name "Grandpont" was in the Middle Ages "often used of the part of Oxford between South Gate and Folly Bridge"', citing Salter, *Medieval Oxford*, p. 15. For more recent archaeological and other investigation, see

aforesaid Abbot Adelelm, one at Sandford beyond the Thames and two in Arncott.[83] He was the man by whose efforts Oxford bridge was built.[84] He died in September, and received burial here.[85]

Moreover, the abbot then was considering that great work must be helped by great expenditure and (since at this time new buildings were everywhere being constructed in bishoprics and monasteries) that these expenditures must therefore be supported by the aid of neighbours.[86] So, regarding his own business of this sort, he thought about the aid of those who work. It used to be considered as law for peasants throughout the abbey's estates that any of them, into whom entered envy or desire of acquiring another's possession, could expel the other from his holding, after filling the reeve's hand with a gift of goods. Likewise, another hardship of the ordinary people: when anyone who had sons and a wife, who prospered with fertile fields, and who paid his dues to his lord without any offence, found rest in his due end, no grace used to be allowed to his sons and wife, but they were expelled and an outsider, who paid money, was inserted into the profitable possessions of the dead man. In these days, rarely did anyone in that abbey's lands give the tithe of the harvest, as the law orders, but from each hide were offered either forty bundles—commonly called sheaves—or the tenth acre of his cultivated land.[87] In this connection, the abbot summoned the inhabitants of

B. Durham *et al.*, 'The Thames crossing at Oxford: archaeological studies 1979–82', *Oxoniensia*, xlix (1984), 57–100, at pp. 87–95.

[85] Robert's building of the bridge, his gift of £100, and his burial in the chapter of Abingdon are also recorded in *De abbatibus*; *CMA* ii. 284.

[86] This whole section is somewhat obscure, and perhaps for that reason has drawn surprisingly little comment by historians of tithe or of land law. Within the text of the *History* it is peculiar in certain ways. For example, it lacks a rubricated heading, despite being only linked most tenuously, if at all, to the previous chapter on Robert d'Oilly. Likewise some of the vocabulary, for example 'opificum' and 'plebeiorum', appears only in this section; see also next note. The essence of the section seems to be that, in return for the proper payment of tithe, Reginald instituted security of peasant tenure and inheritance, replacing tenancy and inheritance at the will of the reeve.

[87] This presumably means that the produce of every tenth acre was offered. As *DMLBS*, fasc. iv, s.v. *hidagium*, points out, the meaning of *hidagium* in this sentence is rather unusual and perhaps obscure. On tithe, see also *Leges Edwardi Confessoris*, cc. 7–8, in B. O'Brien, *God's Peace and King's Peace: the Laws of Edward the Confessor* (Philadelphia, 1999), p. 164. A parallel passage concerning forty sheaves from each hide occurs in *De abbatibus*; *CMA* ii. 284–5. The sheaves presumably were church-scot, which here appears to be presented, very unusually, as an alternative to tithe; see also below, pp. 78, 208. Cf. the payment of forty-eight sheaves per hide 'scrifcorn' to Leominster; B. R. Kemp, 'Some aspects of the *parochia* of Leominster', in *Minsters and Parish Churches*, ed. Blair, pp. 83–95, at 87–8.

B fo. 126v incolas abbas | aduocat, seruilitatis iam dicte graue eis assuetum imponi iugum compatiendi modo proponit, inde libertatis remedium promittit, dum modo rectas suarum messium decimas in operis restaurande ecclesie auxilium donarent. Illi talibus allecti promissis parent; quisque dum meteret decimam quesitam donat. Multum ergo ab hoc tempore operibus fabricandis ipsa affabilitas abbatis oratioque[a] prestitit.

30. *De ecclesia de Suttuna.*[88]
Ecclesia uille regalis Suttune per hos dies regis dominio constabat soli subdita. Hanc ipse rex Willelmus iunior, a Rainaldo petitus abbate, ecclesie Abbendone concessit, istas ad comitatum Berchescire inde litteras dirigens:

31. *Carta de [b]ecclesia eadem.*[b][89]
Willelmus rex Anglorum Gilleberto de Britteuilla,[c] et omnibus fidelibus suis, Francigenis et Angligenis, de Berchescira,[d] salutem.[90] Sciatis me dedisse sancte Marie Abbendonensis ecclesie, et abbati Rainaldo, et monachis eius, ecclesiam de Suttuna, cum terris et decimis et consuetudinibus, sicut predicta ecclesia eas melius habuit tempore patris mei. Testibus Roberto[e] filio Haimonis,[f] et Roberto[g] cancellario, et Croco[h] uenatore.

[ii. 27] Vt autem id concederetur, ex abbatie pecunia, summa uiginti librarum publice monete in regio thesauro appensa est. Nec[i] longe post abbati alias litteras misit rex, precipiens ut clericus ecclesie Suttune, Alwinus nomine, ita honorifice ab eo tractaretur uti[j] ei constiterat dum proprie sub rege deguerat.[91] Erat enim legibus patrie optime institutus, et preter illius sue ecclesie iura de abbatia unam[k] in
C fo. 140v eadem uilla hidam ad illud usque tempus | tenuerat. His causis, is[l] pro mandato acceptius suscipitur.

32. *Cirographum de ecclesia Suttune.*[m]
Tempore nobilissimi Anglorum regis Eadwardi et antecessorum suorum habuit abbas ecclesie sancte Marie Abbendonensis duas

[a] oratio *B C* [b–b] eadem ecclesia *B* [c] Brittewilla *B* [d] Berkascira *B* [e] *initial om. C* [f] Hamonis *B* [g] *initial om. C* [h] Droco, *the wrong initial apparently having been added B* [i] *initial om. C* [j] ut *B* [k] *followed by* ut *with expunction marks under it B* [l] his *B* [m] de Suttun *B*

[88] The gift is also recorded in *De abbatibus*; *CMA* ii. 284.
[89] *RRAN* i, no. 359; Lyell, no. 78; the writ dates from the chancellorship of Robert

each village, made a proposal to show his compassion concerning their customary and burdensome yoke of servility, and promised the remedy of liberty therefrom, provided they gave the correct tithes of their harvests to help the work of rebuilding the church. Enticed by such promises, they obeyed; each gave the requisite tithe when harvesting. From this time, then, the abbot's affability and prayer did much for the building works.

30. *Concerning the church of Sutton.*[88]
At that time the church of the royal village of Sutton was accepted to be subject only to the king's lordship. At Abbot Reginald's request, King William the younger granted it to the church of Abingdon, sending these letters concerning it to the county court of Berkshire:

31. *Charter concerning this church.*[89]
William king of the English to Gilbert de Bretteville and all his faithful men, French and English, of Berkshire, greeting.[90] Know that I have given to the church of St Mary of Abingdon, and to Abbot Reginald, and to his monks the church of Sutton, with lands, and tithes, and customs, as the aforesaid church best had them in my father's time. Witnesses: Robert son of Hamo, and Robert the chancellor, and Croc the huntsman.

Moreover, the sum of £20 of the abbey's money, in public coin, was paid to the royal treasury that this might be granted. Not long afterwards, the king sent the abbot further letters, ordering that the cleric of the church of Sutton, named Ælfwig, be treated by him as honourably as had been established when he lived directly under the king.[91] For he was very well informed on the laws of the land, and, besides the rights of his own church, had hitherto held one hide in that village from the abbey. For these reasons, Ælfwig was received more cordially, as ordered.

32. *Cirograph concerning the church of Sutton.*
In the time of the most noble king of England Edward and his ancestors, the abbot of the church of St Mary of Abingdon held two

Bloet, who was in office by Jan. 1091 and ceased to act around Feb. 1094: Barlow, *William Rufus*, p. 147.

[90] Gilbert was probably sheriff of Berkshire in the period 1090 × 1094: Green, *Sheriffs*, p. 26, although the sole evidence cited there is this Abingdon writ. He was a tenant-in-chief in Berkshire, *DB* i, fos. 61^v–62^r, and also held lands in Hampshire, Oxfordshire, and Wiltshire.

[91] These further letters do not survive. On Ælfwig, see also above, p. 4.

portiones decime cuiusdam uille regis que uocatur Suttun, et unam hidam terre in eadem uilla, quam sub abbate presbiter eiusdem uille tenebat, sibi uidelicet inde seruiendo.[92] Hec omnia similiter in diebus Willelmi regis, successoris Eadwardi, possedit abbas prefati monasterii. Willelmus autem rex iunior, filius Willelmi regis senioris, cum post obitum patris successisset in regnum, dedit ecclesie sancte Marie Abbendonensis et Rainaldo abbati omnibusque fratribus in eodem loco Deo seruientibus, ecclesiam scilicet suprascripte uille Suttune, cum omnibus que eidem ecclesie adiacebant. In illis diebus, tenebat eandem ecclesiam sub rege presbiter quidam Alfwi nuncupatus, cui rex concessit ut quamdiu uiueret de abbate et fratribus Abbendonensis loci illam ecclesiam teneret, eodem modo quo de se ante illud
[ii. 28] tempus tenuerat; et iussit ut post eius decessum in commune abbatis et fratrum rediret. Cum rex hec ita precepisset, uenit prefatus presbiter ad abbatem Rainaldum et requisiuit[a] ab eo et a fratribus
B fo. 127r eiusdem loci monasterium suum, ut sicut rex pre|ceperat ab eis monasterium suum habere posset.[93] Post hec autem iterum rogauit idem presbiter abbatem, uidelicet Rainaldum, et fratres prescripte congregationis, ut ecclesiam illam quam de eis tenebat filio suo tunc puero concederent, quatinus eam et ipse quamdiu uiueret habere posset.[94] Cuius petitioni abbas Rainaldus et omnes fratres, quia fidelis eis extiterat, libenter assensum dederunt, eumque in capitulum cum filio suo iusserunt uenire; ibique sibi omnia que petebat concesserunt, scilicet ut, sicut ipsam predictam ecclesiam cum omnibus ad eam pertinentibus et queque alia de abbate et fratribus Abbendonie ante tenuerat, ita puer quamdiu uiueret eadem omnia haberet, extra capellam Middeltunæ[b] et que ad eam pertinent,[95] quam in manu abbatis idem presbiter dimisit pro concessu quem fecit filio eius de ecclesia Suttune ceterisque rebus ad eam pertinentibus. Necnon quinque libras denariorum dedit presbiter abbati, quibus quandam situlam argenteam deuadimonizauit que inuadimoniata fuerat pro centum solidis. Et quia nulli finis uite sue agnitus est, talem conuentionem abbas cum presbitero fecit: scilicet ut si puer ante

[a] requiuit *C* [b] Middeltune *B*

[92] The retention of two thirds of the tithe would appear to be in line with II *Edgar* 2, which laid down that a thegn who had on his bookland a church with a graveyard, was to pay it a third of his demesne tithe; *Die Gesetze der Angelsachsen*, ed. F. Liebermann (3 vols., Halle, 1903–16), i. 196. Sutton would here be the equivalent of the thegn's church—even though it is referred to below as a *monasterium*—and Abingdon would be the mother church.

parts of the tithe of a royal village called Sutton, and one hide of land in the same village, which the village priest held under the abbot, by doing service to him for it.[92] The abbot of the aforementioned monastery possessed all these in similar fashion in the days of King William, Edward's successor. But when King William the younger, son of King William the elder, had succeeded to the kingdom after his father's death, he gave to the church of St Mary of Abingdon and to Abbot Reginald and to all the brethren serving God in that monastery, the church of the above village of Sutton with everything pertaining to that church. In those days, a priest called Ælfwig held that church under the king, and the king granted him that, as long as he might live, he would hold that church from the abbot and brethren of the monastery of Abingdon, in the same way as Ælfwig had previously held from the king. He ordered that after Ælfwig's death, it would return to the common property of the abbot and brethren. When the king had given these orders, the aforementioned priest came to Abbot Reginald and sought his minster from him and the monks of Abingdon, as the king had ordered he could have his minster from them.[93] Next, moreover, the priest asked Abbot Reginald and the brethren of the above congregation that they grant the church he was holding from them to his son, who was then a boy, that he could have it as long as he lived.[94] Abbot Reginald and all the brethren willingly assented to his request, as he had remained faithful to them, and ordered him to come with his son into the chapter. There they granted him everything he sought; that is, that just as he had previously held the aforesaid church, with everything pertaining to it, and anything else from the abbot and brethren of Abingdon, so his son, as long as he lived, would have all these things, except the chapel of Milton and its appurtenances.[95] These latter Ælfwig surrendered into the hand of the abbot, because of the grant which the abbot made to his son of the church of Sutton and the other things pertaining to it. And the priest gave the abbot £5 in coin, with which he redeemed from pledge a silver vessel which he had pledged for 100s. And since no one knows when his life will end, the abbot made the following agreement with the priest: if the son

[93] In the eleventh century, *monasterium* and *mynster* 'could be used for any kind of religious establishment with a church'; *Minsters and Parish Churches*, ed. Blair, p. 1.

[94] On sons succeeding to benefices, see e.g. B. R. Kemp, 'Hereditary benefices in the medieval English Church: a Herefordshire example', *BIHR* xliii (1970), 1–15.

[95] Milton, Berks. *DB* i, fo. 59^r, states that 'The abbey itself holds Milton, and always held it', but makes no mention of the chapel.

patrem moreretur, pater quamdiu uiueret monasterium suum haberet; si uero puer superuiueret patrem, haberet et ipse sui patris monasterium sicut superius scriptum est; et post eiusdem pueri decessum, in abbatis et fratrum manu esset cui et quomodo eandem ecclesiam locarent. Hec autem facta sunt coram his testibus: ex parte abbatis Rainaldi, totus conuentus, de laicis Ricardus filius Rainfridi[96]
[ii. 29] et multi alii; ex parte presbiteri Alwini, Siwardus nepos eius, cum pluribus[a] aliis.

33. *De dimidia hida apud Winekefeld.*[b][97]

Operis renouande ecclesie structura capiente augmentum, episcopus Osmundus dedicandi in memoriam apostolorum Petri et Pauli altaris gratia, ab abbate Abbendoniam rogatus uenit. Dies quarte ebdomade Quadragesime erat tunc Dominicus. Cum ecce, inter benedictionum sacra pontificalium, legati a Waltero filio Oteri missi in presentia eiusdem episcopi et abbatis assunt, contestantes quod dimidiam hidam apud Winekefeld,[c] ab eodem diu possessam ecclesie et abbati nunc relictam, promiserit reliquo deinceps euo se suosque heredes inde nunquam intromittere uelle, ideoque eam perpetualiter reddiderit illis liberam.

34. *De Winekefeld.* |

C fo. 141r Predicte autem uille Winekefeld[d] regis forestarii plurimum infesti fiebant. Quod cum ipsi regi abbatis ex parte deferretur, illorum molestiam huiusmodi cohercuit mandato, Waltero eidem taliter scribens:

35. *De silua apud Winekefeld.*[98]

[ii. 30] Willelmus rex Anglorum Waltero Oteri filio, salutem. Mando tibi et precipio ut abbati Abbendone permittas habere suam terram et suam
B fo. 127v siluam omnino | liberam, preter[e] siluestrem siluam, et pascua suorum hominum habeat in predicta silua.[99] Et uide ne amplius de hac silua uel uilla iniuriam abbati facias.

[a] multis *B* [b] Winkefeld *B* [c] Winkefeld *B* [d] Winkefeld *B*
[e] *erased in C, in an attempt to conceal this restriction to the grant*

[96] A Richard son of Reinfrid was a man of Miles Crispin according to *Regesta*, ed. Bates, no. 167; see also Keats-Rohan, *Domesday People*, p. 364. On the day he died, he gave two hides at Wroxton to Abingdon; below, p. 158.

died before the father, the father would have his minster as long as he lived; but if the son outlived the father, he would have his father's minster as described above; and after the son's death, it would be up to the abbot and brethren whom they would appoint to that church, and in what way. This took place in the presence of the following witnesses: from Abbot Reginald's side, the whole convent, and from the laymen Richard son of Reinfrid[96] and many others; from Ælfwig the priest's side, Siward his nephew, with very many others.

33. *Concerning half a hide at Winkfield.*[97]

With the rebuilding of the church advancing, Bishop Osmund came to Abingdon at the abbot's request to dedicate an altar in memory of the apostles Peter and Paul. It was the Sunday of the fourth week of Lent. Then behold! Present with the bishop and abbot in the middle of the sacred rituals of the pontifical blessings was a deputation sent by Walter son of Other. They testified that Walter promised for ever more that neither he nor his heirs would ever wish to interfere concerning half a hide at Winkfield, which Walter had long possessed but had now been left to the church and abbot, and that thus he gave it back to them free in perpetuity.

34. *Concerning Winkfield.*

However, the king's foresters were growing extremely hostile to the aforesaid village of Winkfield. When the king was informed of this on behalf of the abbot, he checked their harassment with a writ of the following sort, writing to Walter thus:

35. *Concerning the wood at Winkfield.*[98]

William king of the English to Walter son of Other, greeting. I instruct and order you that you allow the abbot of Abingdon to have his land and his wood completely free, except for the tree-covered woodland, and let him have his men's pastures in the aforesaid wood.[99] And see that you do no further harm to the abbot concerning this wood or village.

[97] See also above, p. 8.

[98] *RRAN* i, no. 391, dating to 1087 × 1097; *Royal Writs*, ed. van Caenegem, no. 31.

[99] The translation of 'siluestrem siluam' is uncertain. I follow *Royal Writs*, ed. van Caenegem, p. 428, who suggests that it would be in such woodland that the king preserved his hunting rights.

36. *De ecclesia de Kingestuna.*[100]

Ecclesie de Wrda,[a] tempore Eadwardi regis, parrochiani erant qui in uilla Kingestuna degebant. At Osmundo apud Saresbiriam pontificali fungente infula, eiusdem loci domini, Adelelmus et Radulfus cognomento Bachepuiz, ibidem capellam constituentes, dedicari cum cimiterio illam per predictum fecerunt episcopum,[101] promittentes omnem se amputaturos inde apud rectorem Abbendonensis loci et fratres, insuper apud clericum eorum ecclesie de Wrde,[b] querelam, ut non nisi unita de eis deinceps predicaretur concordia. Quare postea Abbendoniam expetunt, singulis annis duas oras[c] (id est triginta duos denarios) monachorum usibus sese impensuros promittunt, et terminum reddendi Pentecosten ponunt. Clerico quoque de Wrda[d] duas acras, duos porcos, et duos caseos annuatim constituunt, de hoc toto istius considerata ratione diuisionis, ut medietatem unus, reliquam uero alter persolueret. Hec res hucusque deducta Rainaldi abbatis diebus, sequens Faritii eiusdem successoris constitit peracta. Defuncto ergo Radulfo de Bachepuiz, Henricus filius eius heres illi et successor extitit rerum, sed nequaquam morum, quandoquidem uotum, quo se pater obstrinxerat ecclesiastice respectui unitatis, filius
[ii. 31] iste conseruare neglexit. Sed illo post paruo tempore defuncto, frater eius Robertus ei successit. Qui fraterni euentus timidus ad abbatiam currit, pro defuncti commisso[e] intercedit, se uero quoad uixerit paterni pacti redditorem non defore promittit. Quod tercio decimo regni Henrici regis anno, et diebus Quadragesimalibus accidit, in presentia horum: Nigelli de Oileio,[102] Ricardi de Ledecumba, et multorum aliorum.

37. *De ecclesia de Pesimara.*[103]

Item, in Pesimaro capella cum cimiterio, per prefatum Osmundum episcopum dedicata, eo tenore extitit: ne ecclesia que apud Ciueleam

[a] Wrða *B* [b] Wrðe *B* [c] horas *B* [d] Wrða *B* [e] commissio *B*

[100] See *VCH*, *Berkshire*, iv. 352–3; see also below, pp. 176–8, and above, p. xxxv. For Abingdon's possession of Longworth, Berks., and its church, see *DB* i, fo. 59[r–v]; for Kingston Bagpuize, Berks., see *DB* i, fo. 60[v] (Ralph's holding from Henry de Ferrers) and fo. 61[r] (Adelelm's holding from William son of Ansculf). *VCH*, *Berkshire*, iv. 350, takes the former to be the southern part, the latter the northern.

[101] For Ralph's family, see J. H. Round, 'A Bachepuz charter', *The Ancestor*, xii (1905), 152–5; *Anglo-Norman Families*, p. 10; *Facsimiles of Royal and other Charters in the British Museum*, i. *William I–Richard I*, ed. G. F. Warner and H. J. Ellis (London, 1903), no. 49. In 1166 the *Carta* of William de Ferrers records Robert de Bagpuize holding three knights' fees; *Red Book*, i. 337. On Adelelm's successors at Kingston in the thirteenth century and

36. *Concerning the church of Kingston.*[100]

In King Edward's time there were parishioners of the church of Longworth who lived in the village of Kingston. But when Osmund was enjoying the episcopal symbols of office at Salisbury, the lords of Kingston, Adelelm and Ralph, surnamed Bagpuize, set up a chapel there, and had it dedicated, with a cemetery, by that bishop.[101] They promised they would remove any complaint concerning this in the presence of the ruler of the monastery of Abingdon and the brethren, and in addition of the cleric of their church of Longworth, so that a wholly unanimous agreement about these matters might thereafter be announced. Therefore, they afterwards went to Abingdon and promised to pay each year to the monks' use two *ores* (that is 32d.), setting the time for this payment at Pentecost. Also, they assigned to the cleric of Longworth two acres, two pigs, and two cheeses a year. They decided upon the following division of all these payments, that each would pay half. Thus far this affair took place in Abbot Reginald's time, but the following conclusion was reached in that of his successor, Faritius. When Ralph de Bagpuize died, his son Henry was his heir and successor with regard to his possessions but not his standards of conduct, in that the son neglected to preserve the vow whereby his father had bound himself in respect of ecclesiastical unity. But a short while later he died, and his brother Robert succeeded him. Fearing for his brother's fate, he rushed to the abbot and interceded concerning the dead man's misdeed. He promised that indeed as long as he lived he would not fail in fulfilling his father's agreement. This happened in Lent in the thirteenth year of King Henry's reign [19 Feb.–5 Apr. 1113], in the presence of these men: Nigel d'Oilly,[102] Richard of Letcombe, and many others.

37. *Concerning the church of Peasemore.*[103]

Similarly in Peasemore a chapel with a cemetery, dedicated by the aforesaid Bishop Osmund, existed on the following terms: that the

beyond, see *VCH*, *Berkshire*, iv. 351. Note how the *History* refers to Adelelm and Ralph as the lords of Kingston, despite *Domesday* recording them as holding from tenants-in-chief.

[102] Heir of Robert d'Oilly, although their relationship is not certain. He succeeded possibly *c.*1093, and died possibly *c.*1115; see Sanders, *Baronies*, p. 54, Green, *Government*, p. 265 n. 326. He may have been a local justiciar in Oxfordshire; see the writ addresses below, pp. 114, 134.

[103] See also below, p. 176, and above, p. xxxv. *DB* i, fo. 62^r, records Richard as holding Peasemore, Berks., from Gilbert de Bretteville. Note also the other entries relating to Peasemore, *DB* i, fos. 60^r, 62^v; also *VCH*, *Berkshire*, iv. 81. Despite the chronicler's presentation of the outcome as a success for the abbey, Peasemore was afterwards a parish, and the advowson appears to have remained in Richard's family; *VCH*, *Berkshire*, iv. 84.

sita est in aliquo consuetudinibus sibi debitis priuaretur.[104] Ab antiquo enim tempore, ille de Pesimaro locus ecclesie de Ciuelea[a] iuri obnoxius[b] fuit. Sed dedicatione peracta, Ricardus, eiusdem tunc dominus uille, parum duxit mandatis sibi intendere. Ita ad quintum regis Henrici annum sub abbate Faritio a dedicate capelle termino sub abbatis Rainaldi[c] regimine habite, uir ille tali in obstinatione perdurans, sed tunc in sese reuertens, presentie ipsius abbatis et monachorum Abbendone sistitur, tenacitatis hactenus sue huiusmodi penitens, hanc spondet correctionem: quod quoto deinceps anno ecclesie Abbendonensis altari duos solidos, et clerico qui ecclesie de
B fo. 128r Ciuelea deseruit duas | annone acras, unam triticeam, alteram auenaceam, persolueret.[105] Causa dilate tamdiu huius deliberationis et modo exhibite[d] bifaria[e] fuit: quia Saresbiriensis sedis auctoritas, super hoc requisita, sanciuit[f] ut illa capella ab officio suspenderetur
[ii. 32] diuino, nisi se matri olim ecclesie reconciliando coaptaret; et quia idem iam debilis uite petebat occasum, fractus senio. His ratiociniis in medium,[g] hec talis tunc prolata sententia. Que a filio eiusdem, Felice
C fo. 141v | dicto, illa hora approbata, et inde ab utroque indeficienter tenenda promissa; coram his testibus: Gaufrido[h] filio Haimonis,[i] Bernero, Raimboldo,[j] et multis aliis.[106]

38. *De decima de Westlakinga.*[k] [107]

Viuente predicto Rainaldo abbate, trium[l] decimationum ecclesie huic facta est. Vna ab Huberto de uilla sua Lakinz appellata, Henrici de Ferrariis milite, scilicet frugum, agnorum, caseorum, uitulorum, et porcellorum. Quod et Robertus filius eiusdem, post patris mortem, confirmans, concedente domino suo predicto Henrico, Abbendoniam uenit, pro patris et sui suorumque salute, prefatam[m] hic decimationem perpetualiter tradidit sibi, fratribus suis germanis Huberto et Stephano in his fauentibus, etiam istis amicis suis uidentibus: Quirio

[a] Ciueleia *B* [b] obnoxia *B C* [c] Reinaldi *B* [d] exibite *B* [e] bafaria *B C* [f] sancciuit *B* [g] *a word appears to have been om.* [h] *initial om. B* [i] Hamonis *B* [j] Raimbaldo *B* [k] West Lakinga *B* [l] *a word such as* donatio *may have been om. in this sentence* [m] prephatam *C*

[104] Chieveley, Berks. *DB* i, fo. 58v, states that 'the abbey itself holds Chieveley and always held it'.

[105] As above, p. 35, this presumably means the produce of two acres.

church situated at Chieveley would not in any way lose customs owed it.[104] For Peasemore had from long ago been subject to the authority of the church of Chieveley. But after the dedication, Richard, then lord of that village, paid insufficient attention to his obligations. He persisted in such obstinacy from the time of the dedication of the chapel under the rule of Abbot Reginald to the fifth year of King Henry under Abbot Faritius [5 Aug. 1104–4 Aug. 1105]. But then coming to his senses, he presented himself before the abbot and monks of Abingdon, repented of his previous stubbornness, and promised the following way of righting his wrong: that henceforth he would pay 2s. annually to the altar of the church of Abingdon, and two acres of arable (one of wheat, the other of oats) to the cleric officiating at the church of Chieveley.[105] The cause of his decision, long delayed, but now granted, was twofold: the authority of the see of Salisbury, which had been sought on this matter, ordained that the chapel would be suspended from divine office unless it complied in being reconciled to its former mother church; and, broken by old age, he was now moving towards the end of feeble life. Following these proceedings, this decision was then pronounced in public. His son, called Felix, approved it at this time, and both of them promised to keep it unfailingly; in the presence of these witnesses: Geoffrey son of Hamo, Berner, Rainbald, and many others.[106]

38. *Concerning the tithe of West Lockinge.*[107]

When Abbot Reginald was alive, gifts of three tithes were made to this church. One was by Hubert, a knight of Henry de Ferrers, from his village called Lockinge, consisting of crops, lambs, cheeses, calves, and piglets. After his death, his son Robert confirmed this, and, with the consent of his lord Henry de Ferrers, came to Abingdon and here handed over the aforesaid tithe in perpetuity, for the salvation of his father, himself, and his relatives. His brothers Hubert and Stephen approved this, and the following friends of his also looked on: Quirius

[106] A Geoffrey son of Hamo also witnessed Abbot Faritius's receipt of seisin of Aubrey de Ver's gifts to Colne; below, p. 88. For Berner and Rainbald, see above, pp. lxi, lxiii.

[107] *DB* i, fo. 60^{v}, records that Henry de Ferrers held West Lockinge, Berks., and Hubert held it from him. Hubert is the ancestor of the Curzon family; his sons were Robert, Hubert, and Stephen. Next came Giralmus, who is mentioned below, p. 282. See *Red Book*, i. 338, for the 1166 *Carta* of William, earl of Ferrers, which shows Hubert de Curzon having held three knights' fees and Stephen, his grandson, holding two. See *VCH, Berkshire*, i. 289, iv. 308; *Anglo-Norman Families*, p. 37. Income from the tithe of Lockinge was devoted to the monks' wood supply and the sacristy; below, pp. 394, 397.

de Moenais, et fratre eius Hugone, et Roberto filio Aldulfi[a] de Betretuna.[108]

39. *De decima Hildeslee.*[b][109]

Altæra[c] a Seswalo de uilla sua Hildeslea, caseorum scilicet et uellerum suarum ouium. Quod et heres et filius eius Frogerus post eum deuote confirmauit.[d] Que utreque decimationes luminaribus et ministeriis altaris sancte Marie ab eo die specialiter delegate, hucusque in hoc expenduntur.

[ii. 33] 40. *De decima de Henreda.*[e][110]

Tercia[f] a Roberto, cuius erat cognomen Marmion, et a filio ipsius Helto de uilla sua Henreda,[g] frugum omnium sue proprie lucrationis. Sed et post illos a Radulfo, cognomento Rosel, idem concessum, cuius littere suis tunc hominibus ab ipso illuc transmisse hunc continuere modum:

41. *Carta de eadem decima de Henreda.*[h]

Ego Radulfus, agnomento Rosellus, concedo, uolo, atque precipio seruientibus meis ut segetes meas de Henreth[i] deciment ad hostium grancie mee, que ibidem habetur, et ipsam decimam recte et fideliter seruienti sancte Marie deliberent.

Hec iccirco recitauimus, ut noscatur ubi[j] eadem decima et quomodo debeat decimari, eorum consideratione qui ab initio illam Deo contulerunt. Que sub elemosinarii cura, pauperum susceptioni et officio, collata est. Vnde uideant utrum melius locari qui ipsa istic concesserunt potuerint, quandoquidem pars solius Dei, pars egenorum usibus deputate sunt. Ideoque ad quorum dominatum ipsorum amodo pertinuerit locorum dispositio, augere Deo donata potius studeant quam diminuere. Potest enim ipse omnium distributor sibi largita augmentantibus illis multa superaddere beneficia, et
B fo. 128v minuentibus suorum | merita diminutionum rependere.[111]

[a] Addulfi *B* [b] Hildesleia *B* [c] Altera *B* [d] firmauit *B* [e] Henriþa *B* [f] Teria *B* [g] Henreða *B* [h] Henriþa *B* [i] Henreðe *B* [j] tibi *B*

[108] Betterton is in the parish of Lockinge, Berks. (*VCH*, *Berkshire*, iv. 307). *DB* i, fo. 57r, mentions a Robert as a tenant in the king's holding at Betterton.

[109] *DB* i, fo. 62r, records Seswal as holding Ilsley, Berks., from Geoffrey de Mandeville. Seswal was ancestor of the Osevill family: note *Rotuli Chartarum in Turri Londinensi Asservati, 1199–1216*, ed. T. D. Hardy (Record Commission, 1837), p. 16; also *Testa de*

de *Moenais* and his brother Hugh, and Robert son of Ealdulf of Betterton.[108]

39. *Concerning the tithe of Ilsley.*[109]
A second tithe was given by Seswal from his village of Ilsley, consisting of cheeses and the fleeces of his sheep. After him, his son and heir Froger devotedly confirmed this. Both these tithes were from that day specifically delegated to the lights and liturgical furnishings of the altar of St Mary, and are still spent on it.

40. *Concerning the tithe of Hendred.*[110]
The third tithe, of all the crops of their harvest, was given by Robert, surnamed Marmion, and his son Helto from their village of Hendred. After them it was also granted by Ralph surnamed Rosel, whose letter, which he then sent his men concerning this, contained this message:

41. *Charter concerning the same tithe of Hendred.*
I, Ralph, surnamed Rosel, grant, wish, and order my servants that they pay the tithe of my fields of Hendred at the door of my barn there, and that they deliver this tithe rightly and faithfully to the servant of St Mary.

We have related this, therefore, so it may be known where and how that tithe should be paid, by the decision of those who first conferred it on God. The tithe was conferred to the almoner's care, for the reception and service of the poor. Whence let those who granted these things here see whether they could have been better assigned, since part were granted to the profit of God alone, part to that of the poor. Therefore, let those to whose lordship pertains henceforth the disposal of these places, be eager to increase rather than diminish what has been given to God. For the Distributor of all things can add many benefits for those who increase gifts bestowed on Him, but for those who reduce them, He can weigh out just deserts for their reductions.[111]

Nevill, e.g. i. 298. The list of rents of the altar in MS C in the same hand as the *History*, below, p. 397, does not include this tithe.

[110] East Hendred, Berks. This is the manor known as Framptons, because it later passed to the abbey of Caen's cell at Frampton, Devon; *VCH*, *Berkshire*, iv. 299. The history and lands of the Marmion family only become clearer from the time of Roger Marmion, who certainly held Lincolnshire lands in 1115–18. Roger may have been Robert's successor. On the Marmion family, see Sanders, *Baronies*, p. 145, *Complete Peerage*, viii. 505–22.

[111] See above, p. lxxxv.

[ii. 34] **42.** *De eadem decima.*

Tempore itaque Danorum, fuit quidam eorum qui possidens septem hidas in Henreda,[a] propter uicinitatem Abbendonie et amorem sancte Marie uirginis et aliorum sanctorum qui inibi digniter coluntur, dedit decimam de dominio eiusdem terre ecclesie sancte Marie Abbendonensi in elemosinam pauperum, hoc est de quatuor hidis. Quam terram Helto Marmiun[b] Deo et sancto Stephano Cadomi dedit; ecclesie uero Abbendonensi decima de dominio predicto in euum permansit.[112]

43. *De Gersendona.*[113]

Dono abbatis Adelelmi[c] apud Gersendunam Gillebertus, qui cognominabatur Latemer (id est Interpres), septem hidas et dimidiam habuit.[114] Hic filiis carebat, filiabus uero tribus potitus, quas maritis tradidit, data portionis tantumdem[d] de eadem Gersenduna eisdem, quantum locus ipse patiebatur. Earum maritorum primus Radulfus Percehai, alter Picotus, tercius Willelmus appellabantur.[115] Regente[e] autem abbatiam Rainaldo abbate, unus iam dictorum, Radulfus,
C fo. 142[r] moritur. Quem et ipse socer eius Gillebertus | deinde ad hoc subsequitur. Quo defuncto,[f] Picotus et Willelmus, cum quibus et uiduata uiro una filiarum Gilleberti, abbatem adeunt, terrarum portionibus quibus uxorati fuerant ut liceat sibi iure hereditario perfrui expetunt, astipulantes secum ita sic fuisse compactum cum earum conubio inducerentur.[116] Abbas dum ignorasse econtra se que fatentur respondet, quandoquidem Gillebertus dum uiueret nec
[ii. 35] unum sibi uerbum super his fecisset, nil ideo modo eorum requisitioni uelle satisfacere; illi instare, precari, ut quoad uiuerent petitis saltem fruerentur. His talibus orationibus abbas tum benignius flexus, Picotum in hominem, id est homagium suscepit,[g] eo tenore ut militis unius seruitium ab eo ubique ecclesie debitum inde exhiberet,[h] scilicet ceteris Willelmo et uxore Radulfi defuncti de suis portionibus

[a] Henreða *B* [b] Marmium *B* [c] Aðelelmi *B* [d] tantunden *C* [e] *initial om. B, although a small* r *in the main ink was included for the rubricator* [f] defucto *B* [g] succepit *B* [h] exiberet *B*

[112] Henry I's general confirmation to Caen, *RRAN* ii, no. 1575, included 7 hides in East Hendred. See *DB* i, fo. 63[v], for the seven hide holding in East Hendred in 1066. Book I of the *History* does not record the grant of tithe 'in the time of the Danes', and the phrase is sufficiently vague to raise suspicion about a very unusual reference to a pre-Conquest grant of tithe away from their local destination.

[113] *DB* i, fo. 156[v], states that 'Gilbert holds seven and a half hides from the abbot in Garsington', Oxon.; see also below, p. 324.

42. *Concerning the same tithe.*
In the time of the Danes, one of them (who possessed seven hides in Hendred) gave the tithe from the demesne of that land, that is from four hides, to the church of St Mary of Abingdon in alms for the poor, because of its proximity to Abingdon and because of his love of the holy Virgin Mary and the other saints who are worthily venerated there. Helto Marmion gave this land to God and to St Etienne of Caen, but the tithe from that demesne has remained to the church of Abingdon for ever.[112]

43. *Concerning Garsington.*[113]
By gift of Abbot Adelelm, Gilbert, surnamed Latimer (that is, Interpreter), had seven and a half hides at Garsington.[114] He had no sons but three daughters, whom he handed in marriage to husbands, giving to each as large a portion of Garsington as the place permitted. The first of the husbands was named Ralph *Percehai*, the second Picot, the third William.[115] However, when Abbot Reginald was ruling the abbey, one of them, Ralph, died. Then his father-in-law, Gilbert, followed him. After Gilbert's death, Picot and William, and with them the widowed daughter of Gilbert, went to the abbot and sought permission to enjoy by hereditary right the portions of land with which they had been endowed at marriage, asserting that this had been agreed when they were brought into marriage with the daughters.[116] The abbot answered to the contrary that he was ignorant of what they said, since Gilbert had in his lifetime spoken to him not one word concerning this. He was therefore totally unwilling to meet their request now. They pressed on, begging that they might enjoy at least for life what they sought. These prayers made the abbot look more kindly on the situation, and he received Picot as his man, that is received his homage, on the terms that he should do anywhere the service of one knight owed therefrom by him to the church; William and the widow of Ralph were to help him from

[114] On interpreters, see C. Bullock-Davies, *Professional Interpreters and the Matter of Britain* (Cardiff, 1966), pp. 8–10.

[115] Ralph may be the same man whom *DB* i, fo. 56^{v}, records holding seven sites in Wallingford. William is presumably the William of *Botendon* mentioned below, p. 258. *Botendon* cannot be identified with certainty; 'Botendone' is the Domesday form for Boddington, Northants., *DB* i, fo. 224^{r}, 224^{v}. However, the toponym could refer to other places with similar names, for example Boddington in Glos.

[116] See above, p. xc.

suam opem illi conferentibus.[117] Super id, ut morientibus eisdem siue uiris siue feminis, de aliqua predicte terre portione nulla eorum progenies quid proprii sibi in posterum uendicaret. Quibus tunc propositionibus iidem[a] fide et sacramento consensum prebuere. His testibus in presentia constitutis: Rainaldo[b] de Sancta Helena, Goisfrido Rogeri presbiteri filio, et multis aliis.[118]

44. *De Dumeltona.*[119]

Habebat Rainaldus abbas nepotem forinsecorum studiorum prudentem, Robertum nomine. Cui, cum nullam terrarum uauassorum hereditarie dandam repperisset, ad uillam que Dumeltun uocatur, bene sibi tunc uisus agere, suum transtulit consultum, et eidem illam donauit.[120] Nec tamen multo post grauiter penituit talia se fecisse, nam hactenus inscius[c] extiterat, quis donatiui auctor illius terre ad
B fo. 129r hunc locum fuerit. | At postquam scripto coram se recitato, quod in huius ecclesie scrinio continetur, Alfricum archiepiscopum et deuotum Deo famulum largitorem, et ne ab usu monachorum proprio aliquorsum transponeretur interdictorem uehementem perpendit,[121] predictum suum nepotem aduocat, precatur sibi ab eo misereri,
[ii. 36] restituendo loco quod inconsulte ipsemet ei dederat, ne tante auctoritatis uiri maledictionibus uterque subiacerent. Cumque plurimum temporis in hoc supplicando abbas inaniter consumeret, ac nepotis in nullo assensum sibi inclinare potuisset, ad ultimum apud regni principem cum oblationibus orationum, etiam pecunie mercede, adeo institit, ut imperiali decreto terra eadem ecclesie libertati redderetur. Summa uero eiusdem pecunie computata est quinquaginta librarum monete publice fuisse, cum duobus equis regiis usibus aptis. Sed Roberto triginta postea regi ut rehaberet terram que sibi auferebatur offerente, hac necessitate abbas compulsus, ad supradictam a se datam summam uiginti libras adiecit.[122] Nec tamen uir ille a

[a] hiidem *B* [b] *initial om. B* [c] incius *B, which involves a correction*

[117] Cf. 'Ranulf de Glanvill', *Tractatus de legibus et consuetudinibus regni Anglie*, bk. vii, c. 3, ed. G. D. G. Hall (NMT, 1965), p. 76: 'Younger daughters or their husbands are . . . bound to do their service for their tenements to the chief lord by the hand of the eldest daughter or her husband.'

[118] On Reginald, and the St Helen family, see above, p. lxv. For the later history of Garsington, see below, pp. 130, 258.

[119] *English Lawsuits*, no. 146. *DB* i, fo. 166r, records that 'St Mary's church of Abingdon holds Dumbleton', Glos.; in addition, various men held lands in 'Littleton' in Dumbleton; fos. 167v William Breakwold, 168v Ralph holds of Durand of Gloucester; see also below, p. 149, on William Goizenboded. For the suggestion that this dispute may provide the

their portions.[117] In addition, when these husbands or wives died, none of their offspring were thereafter to claim for themselves any ownership concerning any portion of the aforesaid land. They then consented to these proposals with a statement of good faith and an oath. With these witnesses present: Reginald of St Helen, Geoffrey son of Roger the priest, and many others.[118]

44. *Concerning Dumbleton.*[119]

Abbot Reginald had a nephew named Robert who had a good understanding of studies external to the cloister. Since the abbot found no vavassours' land to give him hereditarily, he shifted his plan to the village called Dumbleton, which at the time seemed to him a wise move, and gave it to Robert.[120] But not long afterwards the abbot gravely repented of his decisions, for until then he had not known who was the originator of the gift of that land to this monastery. But afterwards, a text, kept in the church chest, was read out in his presence, and he understood that Ælfric, archbishop and devout servant of God, was the benefactor and had vehemently forbidden that the land be transferred anywhere from the monks' own use.[121] He summoned his nephew and implored that he take pity on him by restoring the place which Reginald had unadvisedly given Robert, lest they both suffer the curses of a man of such authority. After spending much time unprofitably in this beseeching, and quite unable to persuade his nephew to agree, in the end the abbot so pressed his case before the prince of the realm, with offers of prayers and also payment of money, that by imperial decree the land was returned to the liberty of the church. The amount of this payment was calculated at £50 of public money, together with two horses suited for royal use. But afterwards Robert offered the king £30 that he might have back the land which had been taken from him, so the abbot was forced to add £20 to the amount he had given.[122] However, Robert was not

context for the reworking of earlier documentation concerning Dumbleton, see *Charters of Abingdon Abbey*, p. 99.

[120] On the phrase 'vavassours' land', see above, p. lix.

[121] See also above, pp. xviii, xliii. Ælfric had been a monk of Abingdon before rising to be archbishop of Canterbury. He was consecrated in 991, transferred from Ramsbury in 995, and died in 1005; *Handbook of British Chronology*, pp. 214, 220. The relevant document is Ælfric's will, Bk. i, c. 105 (*CMA* i. 416–19), *Charters of Abingdon Abbey*, no. 133, Sawyer, no. 1488, *EHD* i, no. 126.

[122] The financial arithmetic is unclear. It may be that Robert offered the king £70, rather than £30; the slip would be easy to make in Roman numerals, 'xxx' being written instead of 'lxx'.

sua intentione deflecti uoluit, donec graui adeo molestia paralisis[a] inuaderetur, ut totius[b] careret corporis conamine, priuatus etiam lingue officio. In cuius incommodi detentione in se reuersus, nutibus quibus poterat ecclesie et in ea cohabitantium indulgentiam deuote multum atque suspiriis expetiit. Cui et deuotius commissa fratres indulgentes, eum infra monasterii septa, dato sibi sacri habitus indumento receperunt Deo gratias referentem, et quamdiu post hec uixit sincera uoluntate illi seruientem. Ex illo autem tempore eadem Dumeltuna libere dominio fratrum remansit.

45. *De Anskillo milite huius ecclesie.*[123]

Optimatum huius loci ea tempestate uirorum Anskillus erat unus, cuius iuri pertinebant Suuecurda et Speresholt et Baiewrda[c] partim, et apud Merceham hida una.[124] Hunc contra, suorum delatione
C fo. 142[v] osorum, | ita regis exarsit iracundia ut uinculis artatum carcerali
[ii. 37] preciperet custodie macerandum.[125] Vbi insolito rigore deficiens, post dies paucos interiit. Ad cuius mox uillam, que Spereshot[d] dicitur, rex manum immittens, suo dispensatori Turstino ipsam donauit.[126] Quam et ille quamdiu uixit, et deinde filius eius Hugo ad regimen usque abbatis Faritii tenuere,[e] retracto inde ecclesie in hoc temporis spacio seruitii omni genere. Sed et reliquam portionem terre eiusdem uiri ipse rex distraxisset, ni maturius abbas Rainaldus, datis ei sexaginta libris, impetrasset ne a loci usu ea aliena haberentur. Cum hec agerentur, uxore Anskilli iam defuncti domo exclusa, filio uero eius, nomine Willelmo, a rebus paternis funditus eliminato,[127] eadem mulier fratrem regis Henricum (tunc quidem comitem) suffragiorum suis incommodis gratia frequentans, ex eo concepit, et filium pariens Ricardum uocauit. Quamobrem ipsius comitis pa-
B fo. 129[v] tronio[f] Baieiwrdam,[g] qua dotata fuerat, recipiens, deinceps | secure

[a] paralisi *B C* [b] tucius *B* [c] Baigeuurða *B* [d] Speresholt *B* [e] tenure *B* [f] patrocinio *B* [g] Bæiewrðam *B*

[123] See below, p. 182, for further mention of this incident in the context of Sparsholt; also above, p. lxii.

[124] All were in Berkshire. See above, p. 21, for Seacourt; *DB* i, fo. 58[v], states that 'Anskill and Gilbert hold ten hides from the abbot in Bayworth', and that 'Anskill holds one hide' from Abingdon at Marcham. *DB* i, fo. 59[r], names as Fawler his holding which the *History* describes as Sparsholt; 'Anskill holds Fawler from the abbot.' Fawler was one of the three manors in the pre-Conquest estate of Sparsholt, the others being Sparsholt and Kingston Lisle, EPNS, *Berkshire*, ii. 372–3. See above, p. xliii, for a Seacourt family tree; also below, p. 322, for another statement of his holding.

[125] See above, p. lxvi, on royal anger.

willing to be diverted from his purpose until he was afflicted by such serious paralysis that he lacked the power to move any of his body and was deprived even of use of his tongue. In the grip of this affliction, he came to his senses and with such bowing of his head as he could manage and with sighs he very devoutly sought the indulgence of the church and those living therein. The monks still more devoutly forgave him his misdeeds, gave him the garment of the sacred habit, and received him within the confines of the monastery, as he gave thanks to God. For as long as he lived thereafter, he served Him with a sincere will. From that time, moreover, Dumbleton has remained freely in the brethren's demesne.

45. *Concerning Anskill, a knight of this church.*[123]

At this time, Anskill was one of the leading men of this neighbourhood. Seacourt, Sparsholt, part of Bayworth, and a hide at Marcham were his property.[124] Denunciation from those who hated him so fired the king's anger towards Anskill that he ordered him to be bound in chains and worn down by imprisonment.[125] There he was enfeebled by the unaccustomed harshness and died a few days later. Soon the king sent a band of men to the village called Sparsholt, and gave it to Thurstan, his dispenser.[126] Thurstan held it as long as he lived, and then his son Hugh did so until the abbacy of Faritius, and during this period they withheld from the church all types of service therefrom. The king would also have taken away the remainder of Anskill's land had not Abbot Reginald very quickly given him £60 and sought that the land not be separated from the monastery's use. During these events, Anskill's widow was barred from her home, and indeed his son, named William, was completely banished from his father's possessions.[127] The widow frequently visited the king's brother Henry, then a count, for aid in her troubles. She conceived by him and gave birth to a son called Richard. Therefore, by the count's patronage, she received and henceforth securely possessed

[126] On Thurstan and the other dispensers, see above, p. lxxi.

[127] Her name was Ansfrida, see below, p. 180; William of Malmesbury, *Gesta regum Anglorum*, bk. v, c. 419, ed. R. A. B. Mynors, R. M. Thomson, and M. Winterbottom (2 vols., OMT, 1998–9), i. 760, refers to her as a 'prouincialis femina'. See also G. H. White's Appendix D to *Complete Peerage*, xi, ' Henry I's illegitimate children', esp. p. 107, for a brief biography of Richard son of Ansfrida and Henry; p. 110 for Fulk, whom White suggests may have been a son of Ansfrida, on the perhaps not very strong grounds that he witnessed a grant by her and William son of Anskill, below, p. 180; and p. 114 for the suggestion, on still more tenuous evidence, that 'it is not unlikely' that Ansfrida was the mother of a third illegitimate child of Henry, Juliana.

possedit. At filius illius Willelmus et ipse sororem Simonis dispensatoris regis et neptem predicti abbatis in uxorem ducens, ad Suuecurdam, que sibi iure hereditario competebatur, et ad hidam de Merceham, libere peruenit, dispensatore eodem deliberationem[a] sibi inde procurante. Multorum tamen dierum mora ut hec ad istum finem uenirent longa protensa.

46. *De Rainbaldo*[b] *milite.*[128]

Alter quoque miles, Raimbaldus appellatus, gener eiusdem abbatis, a rege ratiociniis uehementer oppositis impetitur, carceris ei ergastulum diuturnum inferendum comminatur, nisi quingentas illi libras
[ii. 38] reconciliandi se gratia, quo iuberet, expenderet, et inde fideiussores ad medium deduceret. Ille minata preterea et ampliora pertimescens, (nam erga quos infestus erat seuerissimum[c] se pretendebat), eos qui secum illo accesserant gementis modo flagitabat ne se desererent, fideiussores sui potius de pecunia que exigebatur fierent, se apud amicos et notos sic sollicite procuraturum, ut nullam suspicarentur sibi affore noxam. Subeuntibus ergo abbate et amicis Rainbaldi[d] apud regem pro eo fideiussorium, abbas uidelicet trecentarum librarum, amici ducentarum, dum a curia ad sua remeant, ille portum Dorbernensem festinato itinere, nullo sciente, petit, mare transit, Flandrensem comitem adit,[e] se eius tuitioni committit.[129] Que res tunc fide susceptoribus illis satis maximum intulit detrimentum, cum ab eis totam sibi pactam pecuniam absque ulla[f] remissione rex exigeret. Vnde plures illorum supremam[g] id induxit ad penuriam. Tunc abbatie uires pene absumpte adeo ut usque ad presens illud conqueratur infortunium.[130]

Preterea et sequenti anno uectigal quatuor solidorum de hida, patriotis cunctis nimium ferre ponderosum, in augmentum mali, per Angliam illatum;[131] quod de primo restabat forte consumendum miseriarum incendio, id in subsequenti penitus exhausit. Quare infra monasterii limina, uasorum altaris diuersorum argenteorum pro his plurima elata atque confracta; forinsecus uero pecora abducta, pre oculis abbatis et monachorum, ministrorum ui regalium; et ab eis ad libitum cuncta distracta sunt.

[a] liberationem *B* [b] Raimbaldo *B* [c] seruerissimum *C* [d] Raimbaldi *B* [e] adiit *B* [f] *corr. from* ullam *C* [g] suppremam, *with second* p *interlin. B*

[128] The dispute probably began in 1095, because the reference later in the section to heavy taxation in the following year would fit 1096; below, n. 131. *English Lawsuits*, no. 147. For Rainbald and his lands, see above, p. lxiii.

[129] Count Robert II, 1093–1111.

Bayworth, which had been given to her as dower. Also, her son William married the sister of Simon the king's dispenser, niece of Abbot Reginald. He came into possession of Seacourt, which belonged to him by hereditary right, and of the hide at Marcham; Simon the king's dispenser obtained livery for him. However, it took a considerable time for these matters to reach such a conclusion.

46. *Concerning the knight Rainbald.*[128]
Another knight, named Rainbald, was Abbot Reginald's son-in-law. He was fiercely assailed with hostile pleas by the king, who threatened to throw him into prison for a long time, unless he paid him £500 for reconciliation, as the king ordered, and in the mean time produced sureties for this. Terrified, in addition, of even greater threats (for the king acted most severely towards the objects of his anger), with groans he begged those who had accompanied him there not to desert him but rather to be his sureties concerning the money demanded. He would attend to his interests so carefully in the presence of his friends and acquaintances that they need not suspect themselves to be risking any harm. The abbot and Rainbald's friends therefore went to the king as surety for him, the abbot for £300, the friends for £200. As they were returning home from court, unbeknown to anyone Rainbald rushed to the port of Dover, crossed the sea, went to the count of Flanders, and entrusted himself to the count's protection.[129] This affair, then, very greatly harmed his sureties, for the king demanded from them all the money pledged to him, without any remission, thereby bringing many of them to the worst depths of poverty. The resources of the abbey were then almost completely consumed, so that people complain of this misfortune to the present day.[130]

Adding to the troubles, in the following year an especially heavy tax of 4s. per hide was imposed throughout England, to bear on all inhabitants.[131] What happened to survive being devoured by the first fire of miseries was completely consumed in the next. Therefore within the confines of the monastery, very many of the silver altar vessels were taken away and broken up for this. Outside, indeed, royal officials took away livestock by force, before the abbot and monks' very eyes. And the officials disposed of all these things as they pleased.

[130] See above, p. xx.

[131] 'The following year' was probably 1096: see the *Anglo-Saxon Chronicle* for that year. For the Church's demesne lands being affected by the tax of 1096, see *Leges Edwardi Confessoris*, 11.2, O'Brien, *God's Peace and King's Peace*, p. 168.

47. *De Lecamstede.*[a] [132]

Cum hec geruntur, abbas manum ad possessiones quas Rainbaldus
[ii. 39] habuerat mittens, sue proprie ditioni subiecit. Quarum scilicet nomina et mansiones sunt: in Lecamstede[b] decem hidarum; in Tobbeneia unius hide; in Frigeleford duarum hidarum; in Hannia unius hide; cum uno molendino apud Merceham,[c] duodecim soli-
C fo. 143r dorum reddibili.[133] Et quanquam huius uiri ista fuisse dixerimus, |
B fo. 130r nulla | tamen habuerat que non ipsius abbatis dono adeptus sit.[134] Potiora uero eorum de proprio fratrum fructuario habebantur, et precipue uilla Lecamstede.[d] [135] Quam per hos dies ipsis fratribus restituit, publico eis interminato maledicto qui ultra iam eandem ab eorum usu dominico eliminare satagerent. Cui restitutioni[e] Rannulfus, regis tunc quidem capellanus et regni Anglie iusticiarius, postmodum Dunelmen episcopus, interfuit. Coram quo abbas ipse, stola amictus sancta, anathema id executus est, et scripto eodem momento in sacro Euuangeliorum textu memorie posterorum commendari precepit, cuius forma hec est:

48. *Excommunicatio de Lecamstede.*[f] [136]

Ego Rainaldus abbas et omnis conuentus Abbendonensis ecclesie ex auctoritate Dei Patris omnipotentis et Filii et Spiritus Sancti, et sanctissime uirginis Marie matris Dei, et omnium sanctorum Dei, excommunicamus et anathematizamus et a liminibus sancte matris ecclesie sequestramus omnes, siue homines siue feminas, qui in hoc facto uel consilio erunt, ut uilla, que Lechamstede uocatur, a dominio eiusdem ecclesie aliquo ingenio aut pacto extrahatur. Et qui hoc fecerint sint cum Iuda traditore Domini, et Pilato, et Herode perpetualiter dampnati, nisi penituerint et ad satisfactionem peruenerint.

[ii. 40] Hac tali deliberatione disposita,[137] instare pecunie regie exactores penes abbatem sepe cepere, supradictum moleste exigentes debitum. Qua molestia mente consternatus, et unde se pulsantibus satisfaceret non habens, prefatam terram Lecamstede,[g] quia precipue Rainbaldi causa (cuius hec terra ut predictum est fuerat) sibi hec inferebantur,

[a] Lechamstede *B* [b] Lechamstede *B* [c] Mercham *B* [d] Lechamstede *B*
[e] restitutionis *B C* [f] Lechamstede *B* [g] Lechamstede *B*

[132] Berks. [133] All in Berks.
[134] See above, p. xc. [135] See above, p. lxxxvii n. 465.
[136] For such excommunications, see L. K. Little, *Benedictine Maledictions* (Ithaca, NY, 1993).

47. *Concerning Leckhampstead.*[132]

The abbot, meanwhile, sent a band of men to Rainbald's former possessions, and placed them under his own control. The names and extents of these are: in Leckhampstead ten hides; in Tubney one hide; in Frilford two hides; in Hanney one hide; with a mill in Marcham which can render 12s. rent.[133] Although we have said that these were this man's possessions, however he had nothing which he had not acquired by gift of that abbot.[134] Indeed the more valuable of them were had from the brethren's own possession, and especially the village of Leckhampstead.[135] The abbot then restored this to the brethren, with a public malediction threatened against those who henceforth strove to remove it from their demesne use. Present at this restitution was Ranulf, then the king's chaplain and justiciar of the kingdom of England, afterwards bishop of Durham. In his presence the abbot, clothed in his holy stole, laid down this anathema and at the same time ordered it to be committed to writing in the holy text of the Gospels, for the memory of those to come. This is its form:

48. *Excommunication concerning Leckhampstead.*[136]

I, Abbot Reginald, and all the convent of the church of Abingdon, by the authority of Omnipotent God the Father and the Son and the Holy Spirit and of the most holy Virgin Mary mother of God and of all the saints of God, excommunicate and anathematize and cut off from the thresholds of the Holy Mother Church all, whether men or women, who will act or counsel that the village called Leckhampstead be taken from the demesne of this church by any trick or agreement. And anyone who does this is to be perpetually damned with Judas the betrayer of the Lord, and Pilate, and Herod, unless they repent and come to satisfaction.

After this conveyance had been settled,[137] the exactors of royal revenue began to press frequently upon the abbot, vexatiously demanding the aforementioned debt. The abbot was dismayed by such vexation and did not have the wherewithal to satisfy those afflicting him. Therefore, since these difficulties were brought upon him particularly by the affair of Rainbald (whose land Leckhampstead had been, as stated above), he leased that land to a certain Hugh,

[137] I take 'deliberatio' to mean the delivery or conveyance of the land by the abbot to the monks, in a sense similar to the various words based on 'liberare' in *Domesday Book*; see *DMLBS*, fasc. iii, s.v. *deliberatio* (definition 3 b).

Hugoni cuidam quem cognominabant de Dun pro uiginti libris ad denominatum dierum terminum credidit. Itaque hec[a] in uadimonio credita abbatis usque obitum ipsius permansit. Paucis deinde labentibus annis, comes Flandrensis ad regis colloquium Angliam appulsus, et multum ab eo honoratus, Rainbaldo secum adducto, adeo regis eiusdem offensam leniuit, ut cuncta ab eo retro habita sibi restitui imperaret.[138] Restituuntur ergo ei uniuersa preter Lechamstede, que uadis debito subiacebat. De hoc itaque uiro et de iamdicta terra, hoc loco sat relatum sufficiat.[139]

49. *De Willelmo filio abbatis Rainaldi.*

Ante susceptum sacre religionis habitum, huic abbati filius natus, nomine Willelmus, et scolis traditus litteris instituebatur. Cumque abbatie honorem fuisset adeptus, eidem suo filio ecclesiam de Merceham,[b] optænta[c] conuentus inde permissione, donauit, cum omnibus que Ælfricus clericus ibidem antea tenuerat constitutus et eidem ecclesie uidebantur competere, adiectis insuper quibusdam aliis rebus, conuentui quidem illi tacitis, de quibus in sequentibus tractabimus.[140]

[ii. 41] **50.** *Qualiter rex abbatem dilexerit.*

B fo. 130v Ipsum abbatem rex idem Willelmus iunior in primordio regni | sui precipuo coluerat honore, ita ut cum[d] in imperium ascisceretur, eidem patris sui defuncti thesaurum Wincestre reconditum, uel ecclesiarum uel pauperum usibus dispertiendum, spe credula deuotius id ipsum tractaturum intendens, commendaret.[141] Ex qua particione, hec—scilicet euuangelicus textus optimus, cum situla argentea aque exorcizate gestatoria, uillosum etiam quoddam sericum cum acerra eburnea in nauicule modum parata—ad hunc locum collata sunt. Testantur quoque et litterarum monimenta sue gratie erga abbatis affectum indicia, quas Petro uicecomiti de Oxeneford, pro quibusdam sub illius manu degentibus et abbati iniuriam inferentibus, transmisit, ita iubendo:[142]

[a] hoc *C* [b] Mercham *B* [c] optenta *B* [d] eum *B C*

[138] There may here be a problem of chronology, and of confusion on the part of the writer. It seems likely that Rufus last met Count Robert in England in the summer of 1093; Barlow, *William Rufus*, p. 325. Count Robert was on Crusade from 1096, setting off home

surnamed de Dun, for a set term of days in return for £20. This remained gaged by the abbot until his death. Then, after a few years had passed, the count of Flanders landed in England for a conference with the king and was much honoured by him. He brought Rainbald with him, and so reduced the king's animosity to him that the king ordered to be restored to Rainbald all he had previously had.[138] So everything was restored to him besides Leckhampstead, which was subject to the debt of gage. Therefore enough has been said here about this man and the aforementioned land.[139]

49. *Concerning William, son of Abbot Reginald.*

A son named William was born to this abbot before he received the habit of the holy religious life. William was sent to the schools and educated in letters. And when Reginald acquired the honour of the abbacy, after obtaining the convent's permission he gave his son the church of Marcham, with everything which Ælfric, the previous cleric appointed there, had held and which was seen to belong to that church. In addition he gave some other possessions, of which no mention was made to the convent; these we shall treat later.[140]

50. *How the king loved the abbot.*

At the start of his reign, King William the younger cherished that abbot with outstanding honour, so that when he came to power, he committed to him his dead father's treasure stored away at Winhester, to be distributed to the use either of churches or of the poor, trustfully expecting that he would perform this most devotedly.[141] From this division, the following were conferred on this monastery: an excellent gospel text, with a silver vessel for the carrying of exorcized water, and also a rough piece of silk, with an ivory incense box made in the form of a ship. Also testifying to his grace towards the abbot's affection are records of letters which he sent to Peter sheriff of Oxford, concerning certain men living under his power and doing harm to the abbot, ordering this:[142]

in 1100; Orderic, *Ecclesiastical History*, bk. ix, c. 3, bk. x, c. 12, ed. Chibnall, v. 34, 278. It seems possible, therefore, that the king whom Robert met was in fact Henry I; see also above, p. lxiv.

[139] See below, p. 190, for further developments concerning Rainbald.

[140] See below, p. 190.

[141] See Barlow, *William Rufus*, pp. 63–4.

[142] Peter was sheriff of Oxfordshire, possibly throughout William II's reign; see Green, *Sheriffs*, p. 69.

51. *De consuetudinibus huius ecclesie.*[143]

Willelmus rex Anglorum Petro de Oxeneford, salutem. Sciatis quod uolo et precipio ut abbas Rainaldus de Abbendona et monachi ecclesie sue ita bene et honorifice et quiete habeant et teneant omnes consuetudines suas, ubique in omnibus rebus, sicut melius habuerunt tempore regis Eadwardi et tempore patris mei; et nullus homo eis
C fo. 143v inde amplius | iniuriam faciat. Teste Rannulfo capellano. Et fac abbati predicto plenam rectitudinem de Eadwi preposito tuo et aliis ministris tuis, qui monachis suis iniuriam fecerunt.[144]

[ii. 42] Verum procedenti tempore, quorumdam abbati infestorum instigatione eo regius erga ipsum immutatus est animus, ut gratia uerteretur[a] in odium, nec eadem deficeret commotio, quoad uite instaret determinatio. Quod ad penuriarum ecclesie cumulum exaggeratio fuit. Qua de re iterum abbatie reliquie superioribus in malis superstite absumuntur, nec ulla miseris et pauperibus ecclesie hominibus respiratio a perdito suarum rerum conceditur. Cuius periculi illati auctores par uidi postero[b] tempore tolerasse[c] infortunium. Nam et priuatarum exhautus[d] pecuniarum et dominiorum inter suos commanipulares minorem amicitiam uel raram perferre coacti sunt.

52. *De morte Rainaldi abbatis.*

Contigit interea regem Normanniam adire. Vbi eo demorante, abbas egritudinem incurrens, anno Dominice incarnationis millesimo nonagesimo septimo uitam finiuit.[145] Ea tempestate, infanda usurpata est in Anglia consuetudo ut si qua prelatorum persona ecclesiarum uita decederet, mox honor ecclesiaticus fisco deputaretur regio.[146] Vt itaque de ceteris, sic et de ecclesia Abbendonensi actum.

53. *De Motberto huius ecclesie preposito.*[147]

Positio ergo loci Abbendonensis in census redditione post abbatis Rainaldi obitum quatuor et paulo plus dimidii annorum ad tempus computata est.[148] In quo spacio, Motbertus ecclesie huius monachus curam rerum infra extraue ministrabat, non ecclesie prouectibus sed

[a] reuerteretur *B* [b] posteri *B C* [c] tollerasse *B* [d] exhaustus *B*

[143] *RRAN* i, no. 390, dating to 1087 × 1097.

[144] Salter, *Medieval Oxford*, p. 47, suggests that Eadwig was the town-reeve, and that in the twelfth century it may have been the custom for the sheriff to nominate one of the two town-reeves.

[145] *Heads of Religious Houses*, p. 24: 4 Feb. 1097. Reginald's death is also mentioned in the Abingdon copies of the Worcester chronicle; John of Worcester, *Chronicle*, iii. 307.

51. *Concerning the customs of this church.*[143]
William king of the English to Peter of Oxford, greeting. Know that I wish and order that Abbot Reginald of Abingdon and the monks of his church have and hold all their customs, everywhere in all things, as well and honourably and undisturbed as they best had them in the time of King Edward and in the time of my father. And let no man do further harm to them concerning this. Witness: Ranulf the chaplain. And do the aforesaid abbot full justice concerning Eadwig your reeve and all your other officials who have harmed his monks.[144]

But as time passed, at the instigation of certain men hostile to Reginald, the king's mind was turned against the abbot, so that grace turned to hatred, and nor did this anger diminish until the end of his life was at hand. This piled further scarcities upon the church. As a result of this, again the remnants of the abbey which had survived the above evils were consumed, and no breathing-space was granted to the weak and poor men of the church from loss of their possessions. I saw the perpetrators of the damage which was inflicted suffer equal misfortune at a later time. For deprived of the plundered goods and of their lordships, they were compelled to maintain lowlier friendship among their barrack-mates, and that only rarely.

52. *Concerning the death of Abbot Reginald.*
It happened meanwhile that the king went to Normandy. While he was there, the abbot fell ill and ended his life in the year of our Lord 1097.[145] At that time there was an unspeakable custom practised in England, that if any person among the prelates of churches departed life, the church honour was assigned to the royal treasury.[146] And this was done with the church of Abingdon, as with others.

53. *Concerning Modbert, administrator of this church.*[147]
The assignment of the monastery of Abingdon to rendering royal revenue, therefore, was calculated as a period of just over four and a half years after the death of Abbot Reginald.[148] In that time, Modbert, a monk of the church, dealt with internal and external business, not for the profits of the church but for payments into the royal purse. It

[146] See M. Howell, *Regalian Right in Medieval England* (London, 1962), ch. 1.
[147] *De abbatibus* says that Modbert was prior when he undertook care of the monastery; *CMA* ii. 285. See above, p. xlv, for the account of the vacancy in *De abbatibus* and the meaning of *prepositus*.
[148] In fact the vacancy stretched from 4 Feb. 1097 to 1 Nov. 1100, just over three and a half years.

[ii. 43] regii marsupii mercibus.[a] Cuius noticie insinuatum est quia Hugo de Dun de terra Lechamstede, que sibi ad tempus credita fuerat, suggereret regi quatinus, accepto pretio, sibi ea libere uti et suis posteris eius dono permitteretur.[149] Quare comitis Mellentis Roberti senioris ope adiutus, regi tantundem census quantum in uadimonio eadem terra fuerat posita (id est uiginti libras) dedit,[150] et eo dato terram edicto regio recepit, predicto Hugone habente quicquid exituum inde processerat dum in manu eandem tenuisset. Itaque postea, causa consultuum suorum negotiorum, Herberto regis cubiculario et thesaurario, delegatione commendaticia, assignauit, et hoc quamdiu publicam huius loci actionem procuraret.[151] Similiter et Hugoni de Bochelanda tres hidas apud Hanni eadem consideratione commisit, eo quod et Berchescire uicecomes et publicarum iusticiarius compellationum a rege constitutus existeret.[152]

Quadam itaque die rex Willelmus, dum cibatus, uenatum exerceret, suorum unus militum quasi ad ceruum sagittam emittens, regem econtra stantem, sibique non cauentem eadem sagitta in corde percussit.[153] Qui mox ad terram corruens expirauit, regnique iura frater ipsius Henricus minor natu optinuit. Nam frater eius Robertus, maior quidem natu, nondum ab Ierusalem, quo iuerat, regressum habuerat.

[ii. 44] **54.** *De Henrico rege.*

Motbertus uero monachus, cum accessisset ad Henricum regem nouiter insignitum, ab eo honorationis gratia ad monasterium Middeltunense, quod pastore uacabat, missus eundem locum procuraturus;[154] sed ibidem non multo post, lecto inualitudinis detentus, defunctus est.

[a] *B lacks a folio here, lost after the first numbering of folios; it seems likely that it was removed for the picture of Henry I which it would have contained*

---

[149] See above, p. 58, below, p. 126.

[150] Robert count of Meulan was a leading aristocrat under William the Conqueror, William Rufus, and Henry I, until his death in 1118; see *Complete Peerage*, vii. 523–6; Crouch, *Beaumont Twins*. He held extensive estates in England, particularly in Warwickshire and Leicestershire. His connection to Modbert is not explained; for further relations with Abingdon, see below, pp. 114, 150. The *History*, below p. 312, has his son, Robert earl of Leicester, recall his up-bringing at Abingdon.

[151] Probably to be identified with the Herbert *camerarius* who appears in Hampshire *Domesday* and elsewhere; on Herbert, see further C. W. Hollister, *Monarchy, Magnates and Institutions in the Anglo-Norman World* (London, 1986), pp. 211–15; Keats-Rohan, *Domes-*

was brought to his notice that Hugh de Dun was suggesting to the king that, in return for a payment, he and his descendants be permitted to enjoy freely by the king's gift the land of Leckhampstead which had been loaned to him for a set time.[149] Therefore Modbert, helped by the power of Robert count of Meulan the elder, gave the king the same amount of money for which that land had been gaged, that is £20.[150] After giving this, he received the land by royal command, while Hugh de Dun retained whatever the land had produced while he had held it in his possession. Afterwards, for as long as he looked after the public activity of this monastery, he assigned it as a grant in return for protection to Herbert, the king's chamberlain and treasurer, for the sake of his advice in matters of business.[151] Likewise he entrusted three hides at Hanney to Hugh of Buckland on the same consideration, that he was appointed by the king sheriff of Berkshire and justice of public accusations.[152]

One day, then, King William, having eaten, was hunting. One of his knights loosed an arrow as at a stag, but instead that arrow struck in the heart the king, who had been standing not looking out for himself.[153] He fell to the ground and soon died, and his younger brother Henry acquired the rights of the kingdom, for his older brother Robert had not yet returned from Jerusalem, where he had gone.

54. *Concerning King Henry.*

When the monk Modbert went to Henry, newly invested as king, as an honour he was sent by Henry to the monastery of Milton, where there was a vacancy, to administer that place.[154] But there, not long afterwards, he was confined to his sickbed and died.

day People, p. 249. For his disputes and subsequent settlement with Abingdon, see below, pp. 196–8; also p. 126.

[152] On Hugh of Buckland, see above, p. lxxi. *DB* i, fo. 59^{r}, states that 'Ulfwi holds three hides' at Hanney 'which were from the monks' demesne supplies in the time of King Edward.' Ulfwi is the man the *History*, below, pp. 192, 208, refers to as Wulfwig 'Bullock's Eye'; see also EPNS, *Berkshire*, ii. 478, on the area of East Hanney and Grove called 'Bullocks', and note *VCH*, *Berkshire*, iv. 287–8.

[153] See Barlow, *William Rufus*, pp. 420–4 for the king's death on 2 Aug. 1100.

[154] Milton is in Dorset.

55. *De uenerando Faritio abbate huius ecclesie, qui distractas possessiones reuocauit, et inuenta tota sagacitate accumulauit.*[155] |

C fo. 144r Anno[a] ergo ab incarnatione Christi millesimo centesimo, predicto Henrico regnante, quarto mense principatus ipsius, id est Nouembri die celebritatis Omnium Sanctorum, per manum episcopi Lincoliensis Roberti, domnum Faritium, ex Malmesbiriensi cenobio monachum, Abbendoniam direxit, et ut debitam illi subiectionem deferrent monachis mandauit,[156] utiliorem eis fore nusquam, ut rebatur, posse se prouidere patronum contestans. Hec estimatio quantum sit in re applicita, quamdiu ecclesie huius aliquid durauerit monimentum, tamdiu eadem uera processisse predicabitur.

Hic itaque genere Tuscus, urbis Arætie ciuis, probatissimus officio medicus, adeo ut eius solius antidotum confectionibus rex ipse se crederet sepe medendum,[157] seculari prudentia quod hoc tempore regimini ecclesiarum pernecessarium fit cautissimus, litterarum adprime scientia optime eruditus. Huic etiam sese pre ceteris medicis
[ii. 45] regina, sed et totius Anglie maiores natu crediderunt.[158] Tante uero affabilitatis et urbanitatis erat ut perparum uideretur auditoribus prolixum ipsius eloquium. Agilis ipse ad queque exercitia, mire frigoris et caloris patiens, sobrietatis integre a puero ad uite finem studens, ac per hoc memorie predicabilis et perspicacis. Quod uero multis honore colligitur, diuitum scilicet consanguinitate potiri, parentum caterua in prelatione ambiri, quia talibus obsequiis citius occurritur, id totum iste refutans, sola prudentie disciplina constipatus, tam ecclesiasticis quam secularibus in tantum circumspecte uiris occurrebat, ut multo amplius ipsum unicum quam quemlibet popularem uideres omnes honorare, seruire, et circa eum quasi pro admiratione morum et dictorum nobilium multitudinem coire. Coram rege constitutus seria honestatis mox inserebat, nec erat difficile impetratu que fieri ab eo querebat, adeo cuncta que agebat eidem conueniebant. Et quidem hec Dei gratia uniuersa ei pie

[a] *the initial in C is large and contains an illustration of Faritius*

[155] For the account in *De abbatibus* of the choice of Faritius, and his coming to the monastery, see above, p. xlvii.

[156] Robert Bloet was bishop of Lincoln 1093–1123; *Handbook of British Chronology*, p. 255. 1 Nov. 1100 was in fact within three months of Henry I coming to the throne. A very similar sentence appears in an Abingdon copy of the Worcester chronicle, the manuscript of which is preserved in Lambeth Palace library; John of Worcester, *Chronicle*, iii. 307.

[157] See Kealey, *Medieval Medicus*, pp. 65–70; C. H. Talbot and E. A. Hammond, *The*

55. *Concerning the venerable Faritius, abbot of this church, who recalled its dispersed possessions, and very wisely built up what he found.*[155]

Therefore in the year 1100 from the Incarnation of Christ, with Henry ruling, in the fourth month of his reign, that is November, on the day of the festival of All Saints [1 Nov. 1100], by the hand of Bishop Robert of Lincoln, the king appointed to Abingdon lord Faritius, a monk from the monastery of Malmesbury, and ordered the monks that they show him due obedience.[156] He asserted that nowhere, in his opinion, was there a more advantageous patron whom he could provide for them. As to the accuracy of this judgment in reality, so long as any record of this church remains, it will be declared to have turned out to be true.

This man, then, was a Tuscan by birth, a citizen of the town of Arezzo, a most esteemed physician by practice, to the extent that the king often believed himself only curable by the compounds of his antidotes.[157] He was very circumspect in worldly prudence, which at this time was essential for the governing of churches, and especially outstandingly learned in the knowledge of letters. The queen too entrusted herself to him before other physicians, as also did the more highly born men of all England.[158] He was of such affability and urbanity that his speech seemed not at all drawn-out to his listeners. He was agile for any exercise, tolerant of extraordinary cold and heat, and entirely committed to sobriety from his boyhood to the end of his life, and through this, he was of praiseworthy and keen memory. What many amass together with honour—obtaining the kinship of rich men, being surrounded in a position of authority by a band of relatives—since he was very swiftly met with such services, all this he rejected, supported by the discipline alone of prudence. He met with ecclesiastics and lay men so discreetly that you would see everyone honour and serve him without equal, much more than any popular man, and a crowd gather around him as it were out of admiration for his conduct and his noble sayings. He soon raised serious matters of virtue in the king's presence, and it was not difficult for that abbot to obtain what he was seeking that the king do, so agreeable to the king was everything which the abbot did. And indeed by the grace of God

Medical Practitioners in Medieval England: a Biographical Register (London, 1965), pp. 45–6. A similar passage appears in an Abingdon copy of the Worcester chronicle, the manuscript of which is preserved in Lambeth Palace library; John of Worcester, *Chronicle*, iii. 307.

[158] See also the verses by Peter, monk of Malmesbury, in William of Malmesbury, *Gesta pontificum*, bk. ii, c. 88, ed. Hamilton, p. 192.

contulerat, que prouectibus ecclesie quam regendam susceperat omnino fideliter impendebat. Nec quisquam prelatorum a tempore sancti patris Ædelwoldi uel studiosissimi abbatis Wlfgari eo procuratius circa huius loci utilitates intrinsecus siue forinsecus prefuit, nec in his quamdiu uixit torpuit.[159]

Infra quidem monasterium huiusmodi se studio contulit, ut cuncta pene fratrum habitacula, que aut nimium uetustate diruta aut minus erant capacia, a fundamentis reedificauit,[a] amplitudine et qualitate satis honestiora contexeret.[160] Sanctuarium oratorii quam procuratius ualuit augmentauit. Testatur id sancte Dei genitricis imago per eum reuerenter compacta, et sanctorum reliquiis cauato loco insignita, a domno uero Radulfo Cantuariorum archiepiscopo sacrata.[161] Textus
[ii. 46] quoque euuangelicus, aurificio optime redimitus opere; de argento puro quedam, alia ex argento et desuper deaurata, uasa officio altaris plura; pallia ex serico plurima, alia ad hornandos ipsos ecclesie ambitus, reliqua induendorum sacerdotum, leuitarum, cantorumque usibus congrua: idem conspicientibus testificantur.

Accedit ad hec et sancti patris nostri Adelwoldi pium patrocinium, spatula scilicet eius cum brachio. Que dum eius sacre reliquie a ueteri in nouam capsam per uenerabilem eiusdem sedis antistitem, Wil-
C fo. 144v lelmum cognomento Giffardum, sollempniter | pontificum et abbatum et regni primatum in presentia transponerentur, ab eodem abbate
B fo. 131r prius mul|tis[b] precibus exquisita et nunc impetrata, huc magno cum tripudio allata fuerunt.[162]

De sancto Aldelmo quoque Meldunensi episcopo, quem precipue eximius Anglorum doctor Beda in *Historia* eiusdem gentis commendat, hancia integra, cum parte capitis, et dente uno, et parte spatule.[163] Nec mirandum huius sancti tanta abbatem percepisse pignera, cum in loco obdormitionis eius mundialem ipse habitum deposuerit, et fratribus inibi degentibus in multis utilitatibus sue cum

[a] *corr. from* reedificat *C* [b] *B resumes half way through this word*

[159] Æthelwold was abbot *c.*954/5–963, Wulfgar 990–1016; *Heads of Religious Houses*, pp. 23–4. 'Procuratius' is a very unusual word, with only two appearances in the *History*, both in this section; see also Vol. i, Introduction, 'Style'.

[160] On Faritius's building works, see also below, p. 338 for an additional section in MS B, and above, p. xlvii, for the account of his abbacy in *De abbatibus*.

[161] Ralph d'Escures was archbishop of Canterbury 1114–22; *Handbook of British Chronology*, p. 232.

[162] William Giffard was nominated bishop of Winchester in 1100, only consecrated in 1107, and died in 1129; *Handbook of British Chronology*, p. 276. The Winchester annals date the translation of relics to 1111; *Annales monastici*, ii. 44.

the king had piously conferred on Faritius everything which the latter faithfully devoted entirely to the profits of the church which he had undertaken to rule. And none of the prelates from the time of the holy father Æthelwold or the most zealous Abbot Wulfgar was more attentively in charge of the internal or external well-being of this monastery than him, and as long as he lived he did not slacken in these matters.[159]

Within the monastery, indeed, he devoted himself to business of the following kind. To provide shelter of improved size and quality, he rebuilt from the foundations almost all the brethren's living quarters, which had either fallen into ruin through excessive age or were too small.[160] He enlarged the sanctuary of the church as attentively as he could. Witness to this is the image of the holy mother of God, reverently constructed through his efforts, adorned with a hollowed-out space for the relics of saints, and consecrated by lord Ralph archbishop of Canterbury.[161] Also testifying for those who look are a Gospel text, excellently bound with goldsmith's work; many vessels for the service of the altar, some of pure silver, others of silver and gilded; very many cloths of silk, some for adorning the very walls of the church, the rest suitable for garbing priests, deacons, and choir monks.

To these he also added a holy relic of our father St Æthelwold, that is his shoulder-blade with his arm. While Æthelwold's sacred relics were being solemnly transferred from an old into a new reliquary by the venerable bishop of Winchester, William surnamed Giffard, in the presence of bishops and abbots and the great men of the realm, Abbot Faritius obtained what he had previously sought with many prayers, and they were brought here with great jubilation.[162]

He also acquired the whole thigh-bone, with part of the head, one tooth, and part of the shoulder-blade, of St Aldhelm, bishop of Malmesbury, whom Bede, the outstanding scholar of the English, especially praises in his *History* of that people.[163] Nor is it any wonder that the abbot acquired such great relics of this saint because he shed his worldly garb in the monastery where Aldhelm fell asleep, and he provided many benefits for the brethren living there during his

[163] See Bede, *Historia ecclesiastica*, bk. v, c. 18, ed. B. Colgrave and R. A. B. Mynors (OMT, 1969), p. 514; *The Oxford Dictionary of Saints*, ed. D. H. Farmer (Oxford, 1978), pp. 10–11. His feast on 25 May appears in the Abingdon kalendar; *Benedictine Kalendars*, i. 23.

eis conuersationis tempore profecerit.[164] Quibus in fraterne largitatis uicissitudinem supplicantibus, eis de sancti Iohannis Crisostomi brachio partem contulit.[165]

Qualiter autem et illud sacratissimum brachium habuerit, opere pretium est breui recitare. Constantinopolitanus imperator Alexius litteras et dona Henrico regi et Mathilde regine per hos dies Angliam direxit.[166] Ipsa legatione Wlfricus, genere Anglus, Lincolie urbis natiuus, ut tante dignitatis directorem decuerat, magna cum pompa
[ii. 47] functus est. Is plurimum familiaritatis ausum circa eundem imperatorem habens, predictas beati Iohannis reliquias ob sue patrie subleuationem petens et ab ipso accipiens, Abbendoniam commendaturus se fratrum orationibus uenit, et eadem sanctuaria cum puluere qui de sepulchro[a] sancti Iohannis euuangeliste miro modo fertur scaturire,[b] et de sanctis partim ossibus Macharii et Antonii abbatum, deuotissime inibi deposuit.[167] Abbas autem eandem suscipiens, digne solito sibi more condiuit.

56. De sancto Wilfrido spatula.[168]

Ipsam[c] tempore Eadwardi regis, ditissimi Dani, dignitate potiti huscarlii, capellanus taliter sibi uendicarat. Cum ad Eboracensem prouinciam quadam uice tunc dominum suum comitaretur, orandi gratia in itinere ad quoddam diuerterunt hora diuini sacrificii oratorium, in quo eedem deuote a loci presbitero reliquie seruabantur.[169] Sed cum forte presbiter tunc abesset, capellanus edituo loci locutus, de his, que ibi uenerabantur, sciscitans est edoctus. Dein[d] cum eo exegit sacra ipsa licere sibi efferri. Nec ambiguum cuiquam de his que dicuntur fiat, cum illo in tempore raro ecclesia usquam illis in partibus fuerit. Nam a paganis uicino mari egressis, non multo ante, scilicet patris sui Ædelredi[e] regis regni primordio, ubique predata illic

[a] sepulcro *B* [b] scaturire *written twice C* [c] Ipam *B* [d] Deinde *B* [e] Æðeredi *B*

---

[164] A reference to Faritius's time at Malmesbury; see above, p. xlvi.

[165] Lived 347–407, archbishop of Constantinople; *Oxford Dictionary of Saints*, pp. 217–18. His feast on 27 January appears in the Abingdon kalendar; *Benedictine Kalendars*, i. 19. See above, p. cvii, for Faritius having works of John Chrysostom copied.

[166] Alexius I Comnenus, 1081–1118; see M. Angold, *The Byzantine Empire, 1025–1204* (2nd edn., London, 1997), chs. 8 and 9.

[167] Two fourth-century Egyptian abbots called Macarius were canonized; see *Bibliotheca Hagiographica Latina*, ed. Socii Bollandiani (2 vols., Brussels, 1898–1901), nos. 5093–9. Their feast days are 2 Jan. and 15 Jan., but these do not appear in the Abingdon kalendar; *Benedictine Kalendars*, i. 19. Anthony, particularly prominent amongst monastic saints in the medieval period, was a solitary, a monk, and an abbot in Egypt from the later third to

monastic life with them.[164] To those men, who humbly begged reciprocation of their brotherly generosity, he gave part of the arm of St John Chrysostom.[165]

It is worthwhile, moreover, to record briefly how he obtained that very sacred arm. Emperor Alexius of Constantinople at that time sent to England letters and gifts for King Henry and Queen Matilda.[166] In that embassy, Wulfric, an Englishman by birth, native of the town of Lincoln, performed with great pomp, as befitted the guide of such a dignity [i.e. the relic]. He was very bold in his close relations with that emperor, and sought and received from him these relics of the blessed John, with a view to the uplifting of his homeland. He went to Abingdon to commend himself to the brethren's prayers, and there most devotedly deposited these relics, together with the dust which is said to have marvellously burst forth from the tomb of St John the Evangelist, and a part of the bones of Macarius and Anthony the abbots.[167] The abbot, moreover, received this and enshrined it fittingly in the way customary with him.

56. Concerning the shoulder blade of St Wilfrid.[168]

In the time of King Edward [1042–66], the chaplain of a very rich Dane who held the rank of housecarl, claimed this for himself in the following way. Once, when he was accompanying his lord to the province of York, they turned *en route* to a church, to pray at the hour of divine mass, in which church these relics were devotedly kept by the priest of the place.[169] But since the priest happened to be away then, the chaplain spoke with the sacrist of the place and, on enquiring, learnt about what was venerated there. Then he demanded that he be allowed to take these holy objects away with him. And let no one doubt what is said, since at that time there was rarely a church anywhere in those regions. For not long before, that is with the start of the reign of King Æthelred, King Edward's father, the dwellings of men throughout the area had been plundered and destroyed by the

the mid-fourth centuries; *Oxford Dictionary of Saints*, pp. 19–20. His feast on 17 Jan. appears in the Abingdon kalendar; *Benedictine Kalendars*, i. 19.

[168] Although not rubricated, this is clearly intended as a heading. Wilfrid was a seventh-century abbot and bishop; *Oxford Dictionary of Saints*, pp. 402–3. His feast on 12 Oct. appears in the Abingdon kalendar; *Benedictine Kalendars*, i. 28.

[169] The Yorkshire church was presumably Ripon. Although Canterbury claimed the relics of Wilfrid as translated by Archbishop Oda, this seems to have been contested by Ripon, as is suggested by the account of St Oswald's enshrinement of Wilfrid's relics there; see N. Brooks, *The Early History of the Church of Canterbury* (Leicester, 1984), pp. 227–31, *Vita Oswaldi*, in *The Historians of the Church of York*, ed. J. Raine, (3 vols., London, 1879–94), i. 462.

et diruta hominum habitacula.[170] Est et illuc ueridicum quia huius eui homines de sanctuariis ecclesiasticis nullo modo fallere sciebant, nec etiam tam pro Deo tam pro seculo ausum fallendi capere dignabantur. Regiminis itaque domni Faritii ad tempora, capellanus idem, multum
[ii. 48] iam ueteranus sed adhuc tamen sospes, eadem pignora[a] sancta sibi contulit, iureiurando fidem presentibus faciens seriem uti digessimus pro uero debere teneri.

B fo. 131v Item.[b] | De sancte Marie Magdalene[c] capillis. De ossuum particulis sanctarum uirginum et martirum Margarete et Fidis, in marsupio purpureo inuoluta,[d] sanctuaria contulit.[171]

Sancti Vincentii sollempnem[e] diem pre cunctis antecessoribus suis magnificentius extulit, et tanto martiri[f] deuote sese assidue commendare studuit.[172] Vnde in plurimis suis negotiis pie inuocatis eius suffragiis, sepe consolari et iuuari promeruit. Cuius sacre reliquie, a tempore Eadgari regis, maxima habentur ueneratione hoc in monasterio, ab ipso (ut illorum hominum dierum ore audiuimus) exquisite et a fratribus tunc hic degentibus sollerti uigilantia procurate,[g] ut secum ob remedium tanti testis patrocinii posteris cunctis prouidentes locarentur.[173]

C fo. 145r Cotidianum autem ipsius abbatis exer|citium non nisi ecclesie huius prouectibus militabat. Quare tante opinionis personam, uenerabili archiepiscopo Anselmo hac ab uita migrato, patriarchatus ipsius sedem parasset rex substituere, nisi norma equitatis eius inflexibilis quibusdam etiam maioris ordinis ecclesiastici suspecta, ipsorum factione id tum perturbaretur.[174]

Anno uero suscepte abbatie regende, omnis per possessiones ecclesie area Paschale ad festum segetibus uacua fuit. Idem ne in posterum procederet, tantam eius industria ubique locorum abbatie copiam segetum multiplicatam conspeximus,[h] ut aliquando trium annorum, sepe annona duorum, in promtu haberetur. Quod utique

[a] *corr. from* pignera *C* [b] *rubricated B* [c] Magdaliene, *because of attempted correction C* [d] uel ob *interlin. C* , *i.e.* obuoluta *meant as alternative for* inuoluta [e] sollemnem *B* [f] martirii *B* [g] procuratum *B C* [h] compleximus *B*

[170] Æthelred reigned 978–1016.

[171] Mary Magdalene's feast on 22 Jul. appears in the Abingdon kalendar; *Benedictine Kalendars*, i. 25; see also *Oxford Dictionary of Saints*, pp. 270–1. St Margaret of Antioch, whose feast on 20 Jul. appears in the Abingdon kalendar; *Benedictine Kalendars*, i. 25; *Oxford Dictionary of Saints*, pp. 260–1. St Faith, virgin and martyr, whose feast on 6 Oct. appears in the Abingdon kalendar; *Benedictine Kalendars*, i. 28; *Oxford Dictionary of Saints*, pp. 146–7. See also below, p. 222, 224 for Mary Magdalene and Margaret.

[172] See above, p. cvi. St Vincent, d. 304, was the protomartyr of Spain; see *Oxford*

pagans who had disembarked from the neighbouring sea.[170] It is also true since men of that period neither knew how to practise deception in any way concerning church shrines, nor thought it proper to dare to be deceitful with regard God or the world. And so, at the time of the abbacy of lord Faritius, the same chaplain, now very old but still healthy, bestowed those holy relics on him and with an oath pledged his faith that the account, as we have set it out, should be taken as true.

Likewise, concerning hairs of St Mary Magdalene. He bestowed relics of pieces of the bones of the holy virgins and martyrs, Margaret and Faith, wrapped in a purple pouch.[171]

More than any of his predecessors, he raised to particular magnificence the solemn day of St Vincent, and strove devotedly to recommend himself constantly to the great martyr.[172] Therefore he deserved frequent consolation and help when he piously invoked the saint's support in his many matters of business. Vincent's holy relics, held in the greatest veneration in this monastery from the time of King Edgar, were sought out by him (as we have heard from the mouths of men of those days), and tended with resourceful vigilance by the brethren then living here, so that they, together with the abbot, might be considered as prudent men in future generations, because of the remedy of the support of so great a witness [to the faith].[173]

The abbot's daily exertion, moreover, fought only for the profit of this church. Therefore, when the venerable Archbishop Anselm departed this life, in his place the king would have been prepared to put a person of such renown onto the seat of the patriarchate, had not Faritius's inflexible standard of justice been suspect to certain men of higher ecclesiastical rank, by a faction of whom this proposal was overturned.[174]

At the festival of Easter in the year when he took up the abbacy, throughout the church's possessions every plot was devoid of crops. Lest this recur in future, we have seen by his efforts so increased an abundance of crops throughout the abbey's estates that sometimes three years' grain, often two, was available. This certainly is worthy of

Dictionary of Saints, p. 391. His feast day on 22 Jan. appears in the Abingdon kalendar; *Benedictine Kalendars*, i. 19. See also *De abbatibus*; *CMA* ii. 287.

[173] Edgar reigned 957/9–975.

[174] A near identical sentence appears in an Abingdon copy of the Worcester chronicle, the manuscript of which is preserved in Lambeth Palace Llibrary; John of Worcester, *Chronicle*, iii. 307–8. Anselm died on 21 Apr. 1109; for Faritius as his potential successor, see above, p. xlix.

mirandum: cum sepissime tot aduentantium turme hospitum, scilicet
[ii. 49] archiepiscoporum, episcoporum, et regni primatuum cum tota familia, uti in proprio constituto gratis collecte, aliquando per plures dies simul omni genere alerentur.[175] Ad hoc et trifariam fratrum infra claustralia numerus quem illo repperit sub se multiplicatus, ad sufficientiam cotidie reficeretur.[176] Pallia serica amplius quam sexaginta uidimus eum emisse, et ad ecclesiastica ea ornamenta uarios per usus distribuisse. Ipsam ecclesiam fere totam construxit, et receptacula officinarum a fundamentis omnia duplo maiora quam inuenit effecit.[177]

Et quia de eius studiis infra monasterium patratis aliqua iam disseruimus, ad forinseca facta stilum uertamus, ea tamen discretione: quatinus primo que aliena antea uidebantur et eo procurante ecclesie propria effecta sunt; deinde que olim propria sed ab aliquibus minus utilibus rectoribus loci distracta et funditus iuri abbatie alienata, per eum [a]nunc uero[a] restituta, singula ordinatim concinnentur.[178] Prime itaque discretio partis sint hec:

57. *De insula Andresia.*[179]

B fo. 132r Insula quedam [b]australem ad plagam[b] monasterii illo in tempo|re sita, Andresia a nomine apostoli Andree cuius inibi ecclesia habebatur nuncupata, diuersis in girum domunculis multiplici decore constipata erat. Quo in loco Willelmus rex senior et filius eius Willelmus rex iunior post patrem sepe hospitari, cum in hanc prouinciam deuerterent, delegerant, quandoquidem oblectamento non paruo hospes ibi frueretur, hinc aqua circumfluente perspicua, illinc pratorum uiridantium demulcente illecebra. Vbi ipse rex Willelmus senior et sanguinis diminutione et antidoti perceptione se recreare solebat. Qua de causa huius dominium mansionis potestas regia sibi uendicarat.

[ii. 50] Rege ergo Henrico ad regnum nouiter electo, cum multa que antecessorum suorum regum dominio pertinuerant multi sibi donari petiuissent, et ipse prudenti usus consultu cuncta petita distribueret,

[a–a] uero nunc *B* [b–b] ad australem plagam *B*

[175] On the reception of guests, see the *Rule of St Benedict*, c. 53.

[176] *De abbatibus* states that he increased the number from 28 to 80, and wished it to reach 100; *CMA* ii. 287, 289. On supplies to the monks, see above, p. xlvi.

[177] See above, p. cii.

[178] *De abbatibus* lays its emphasis on lands lost in the time of the Danes and recuperated by Faritius from Henry I 'both by prayer and by payment'; *CMA* ii. 288.

wonder: when, very frequently, numerous parties of guests arrived—archbishops, bishops, and leading men of the kingdom with their whole households—they were received free of charge, in accordance with our own rule, and together were nourished in every way, sometimes for many days.[175] Also, although the number of brethren whom he found within the cloisters there multiplied threefold under him, yet still they ate sufficiently every day.[176] We saw him buy more than sixty silk cloths and distribute these ecclesiastical adornments to various men for their use. He constructed almost all of this church, and completed from the foundations all the buildings of the domestic offices, on twice the scale he found them.[177]

Now we have recounted some of his accomplishments within the monastery, let us turn our pen to his deeds outside, making this distinction: each is to be arranged in order, first those things which previously were deemed to belong to others, and by his endeavour became the church's own; then those which had once been the church's own, but which had been dispersed by other less sound rulers of the monastery, and were completely alienated from the abbey's property, but were now restored by him.[178] The following, then, are of the first type:

57. *Concerning the island of Andersey.*[179]

To the south of the monastery was situated an island called Andersey, from the name of the apostle Andrew, whose church was there. At that time it was crammed on all sides with sundry small buildings of varied quality. King William the elder and after him his son King William the younger had often chosen to stay there when making a detour into this region, since a guest here enjoyed no little pleasure, with on one side the crystal-clear water flowing around and on the other the soothing charm of verdant meadows. King William the elder was accustomed to restore himself there both by letting of blood and by receiving a remedy. For this reason royal authority claimed for itself lordship of this holding.

When King Henry was newly elected to the kingship, numerous men sought to be given many possessions which had belonged to the demesne of his predecessors as king, and by prudent council, he gave

[179] Berks. The island lies between two branches of the Thames, near Abingdon. On the buildings there, see Bk. i, c. 136 (*CMA* i. 474–5), *The History of the King's Works: the Middle Ages*, ed. R. A. Brown, H. M. Colvin, and A. J. Taylor (2 vols., London, 1963), ii. 895–6. *De abbatibus* records that Faritius obtained the island, with all its royal buildings, from the king, at the intervention of the queen; *CMA* ii. 287.

utpote petitoribus adhuc inferior; sed processu temporis superior fieri cogitans, nonnulli locum predictum ab ipso principe temptabant adipisci, uerum regina Mathildis pre ceteris hunc impetrandi facultatem assecuta est. Nec multo post regia eam primo contigit prole grauari. Mandatur mox medicis ei curam impendere, pronostica edicere, ne in aliquo periclitetur. Quorum primus abbas Faritius, secundus Grimmaldus,[a] uterque gentis et lingue unius, ac per hoc plurimo inter se deuincti amore fuere.[180]

Tali comite abbas de ecclesie sancte Marie Abbendonensis reedificatione, coram regina, quadam die intulit sermonem, quia multa uidelicet tanto operi, tam in parietum quam tectorum structura, conueniret stipendia impendere, illam uero de Dei gratia posse ualde confidere, si in aliquo sua regina liberalitate id processum operationis caperet. Sciscitante tum regina quid necessarium magis, quidue aptius ipsa consulere ualeret, de insula prefata Abbendonie
C fo. 145v sita abbas refert, quia nec Deo in ea seruiatur, | nec hominibus eius usus habeatur, a principio sue fundationis habitore uacua, nisi cum raro dominum Anglie transcursim hospitem reciperet, ob uetustatem autem et incuriam rimis undique parietum patula. Quod si eius benignitati placeret, pro regis tuitione et salute suaque, Deo concedente, permitteret quicquid in ipsis edificiis haberetur edificio ecclesie sancte Dei genitricis Marie imponi, ubi fructus pietatis inde caperetur. His rationibus, quod solet sepe animos demulcere, de donatiuo pariter interserens tante persone congruo, id responsi recepit, se hac uice plumbi quo uniuersa habitacula ibi cooperta erant sibi concedere tollendi facultatem, tectum uero sue ecclesie ex eo
[ii. 51] contegendum, et de ceteris spe bona inniti. Itaque sue largitatis huius apices uicecomiti Berchescire destinauit, ista continentes:

Mathildis regina Anglorum Hugoni de Bochelanda, salutem. Per-
B fo. 132v mitte | Faritium abbatem de Abbendona habere plumbum de domibus de Andresia ad opus ecclesie sue Abbendone. Testibus Radulfo de Tuin et Bernardo clerico. Apud Suttunam.[181]

[a] Grimbaldus *B*

---

180 On Grimbald, another Italian and leading physician of Henry I, who was also a frequent witness of royal charters, see Kealey, *Medieval Medicus*, esp. pp. 70–4; Talbot and Hammond, *Medical Practitioners*, pp. 67–8. M. Chibnall, *The Empress Matilda* (Oxford, 1991), p. 9 dates the birth of the queen's first child, the future Empress Matilda, to *c.*7 Feb. 1102.

181 *RRAN* ii, no. 565; this gives the first witness as Ralph of Tew, but the suggested reading of 'Tiuu' is incorrect. The writ dates from the queen's pregnancy with the Empress Matilda, and before either of the following two writs.

everything which was sought, being still inferior to his petitioners. But, as time passed he considered himself their superior, and when some men tried to acquire Andersey from Henry, Queen Matilda, before anyone else, got authorization to obtain it. Not long afterwards it happened that she was first pregnant with royal child. Soon physicians were ordered to devote their care to her and to pronounce a prognosis, lest she be exposed to danger in any way. The first of these physicians was Abbot Faritius, the second Grimbald, both of one people and language, and thereby bound together by very great love.[180]

In the queen's presence, the abbot one day had a conversation with this companion about the rebuilding of the church of St Mary of Abingdon: great expenditure was appropriate for work of such magnitude, on the building of both walls and roofs, yet he was extremely confident that by the grace of God this was possible if the queen by her generosity gave some support to the progress of the work. The queen then asked what was needed most, and what she could most suitably provide. The abbot mentioned that no service was performed to God at the aforesaid island situated at Abingdon, nor was it held for the use of His men. It had been empty of inhabitants since its first foundation, except occasionally when it received the lord of England as a passing guest. Furthermore, because of old age and neglect, it gaped all over with cracks in the walls. If it were pleasing to her kindness, God granting, she would, for the protection and salvation of the king and herself, permit that whatever was contained in those buildings be assigned to the building of the church of St Mary the mother of God, where the benefit of her piety concerning this would be received. Because he was highly accustomed to softening minds, he added in the same manner to these arguments concerning a gift appropriate for so great a person, and received the following answer: that at this point she granted him the right of taking the lead which covered all the dwellings, with which the roof of his church could certainly be covered, and that he had good reason to be hopeful concerning other matters. So she sent a letter concerning her largesse to the sheriff of Berkshire, containing the following:

Matilda queen of the English to Hugh of Buckland, greeting. Permit Faritius abbot of Abingdon to have the lead from the houses of Andersey for the building-work of his church of Abingdon. Witnesses: Ralph of *Tuin* and Bernard the cleric. At Sutton.[181]

Confidentiam deinde bonitatis Dei animo abbas captans, iteratis reginam precibus sollicitat, quatinus ad reliquam operis sancte Marie constructuram siquid necessarium in insula relictum fuerat, scilicet lapides et fustes, ipsa permittente, assumere ualeret. Que non solum petitum permisit, uerum regis inde auctoritatem et fauorem suo interpellatu addidit, ita ut non tantum lapidum et fustium, sed et ipsius insule dominio abbatia Abbendonensis perpetuo frueretur. [a]Quanti autem de hoc emolumenti monasterii contigerit,[a] hinc pensetur, cum ii, qui[b] insulam adipisci pridem cupiuerant,[c] aut defensionis obstaculum ibi instituere, aut personas religionis primi siue secundi sexus intromittere, disponebant. Et hec quidem fama per ora multorum tunc spargebatur. Dein fraterno uideatur intuitu quantum hec congregatio his debeat esse obnoxia, quorum talia patrociniis annichilata fuere molimina.

Predictarum uero rerum concessionis ad comitatum Berchescire huiusmodi descriptum extitit:

Mathildis regina Anglorum Hugoni de Bochelanda et omnibus
[ii. 52] fidelibus suis de Berchescira, Francis et Anglis, salutem. Sciatis me dedisse Faritio abbati Abbendonie domos et omnia edificia de insula sancte Marie,[d] ad reficiendum monasterium ipsius sancte Marie, et ipsam insulam predicto monasterio in perpetuum reddidisse.[182] Et hoc totum dominus meus rex Henricus mihi predictoque abbati, meipsa interueniente, concessit. Testibus Rogero cancellario et Grimaldo medico.[183]

Henricus rex Anglorum Hugoni de Bochelanda uicecomiti de Berchescira et omnibus baronibus et fidelibus suis, Francis et Anglis, de eadem scira, salutem. Sciatis me dedisse sancte Marie de Abbendona et Faritio abbati capellam sancti Andree de insula, et omnes domos eiusdem insule, scilicet plumbum, lapides, et ligna, et quicquid edificii habetur in eadem insula, ad faciendum opus ecclesie sancte Marie eiusdem uille; et ipsam insulam reddidi sancte Marie et monachis perpetuo habendam in suo dominio. Testibus Mathilde regina uxore mea, et Rogero cancellario, et Herberto camerario, et

[a–a] *this clause perhaps should read* Quantum autem de hoc emolumentum monasterio contigerit [b] hii *B* [c] cupierant, *corr. from* cupiuerant *B* [d] *corr. to* sancti Andreæ *by a much later hand C*

[182] Conceivably with the transfer to Abingdon, an attempt was made to change the name to the 'island of St Mary'. More likely, the writ should have read 'of St Andrew', the wrong name being written by the scribe who was used to following 'St' with 'Mary'.

Confident of God's goodness, the abbot then pressed the queen with repeated requests, that if anything necessary for the remaining building work of St Mary—that is, stones and sticks—had been left on the island, he might acquire it by her permission. She not only granted his request, but by her own intercession added the king's authority and favour, so that the abbey of Abingdon enjoyed not only the stones and sticks but also the island itself in perpetual lordship. Moreover, the scale of the resultant benefit to the monastery may be gauged from the following: those men who had previously desired to acquire the island were intending either to set up a defensive obstruction there, or to send in religious persons, male or female. And this rumour indeed was spread by many mouths. Then let it be seen by a brotherly look to what degree this congregation should be subject to these men, whose efforts were rendered nothing by our protectors.

A record exists of the grant of the aforesaid possessions, for the county of Berkshire, as follows:

Matilda queen of the English to Hugh of Buckland and all her faithful men of Berkshire, French and English, greeting. Know that I have given to Faritius abbot of Abingdon the houses and all the buildings of the island of St Mary for rebuilding the monastery of St Mary herself, and have granted back the island itself to the aforesaid monastery in perpetuity.[182] And my lord husband, King Henry, granted all this to me and the aforesaid abbot, at my intercession. Witnesses: Roger the chancellor and Grimbald the physician.[183]

Henry king of the English to Hugh of Buckland sheriff of Berkshire and all his barons and faithful men, French and English, of that shire, greeting. Know that I have given to St Mary of Abingdon and to Abbot Faritius the chapel of St Andrew of the island, and all the houses of that island, that is the lead, the stones, and the wood, and whatever building exists on that island, for using on the work of the church of St Mary of that place. And I have given back the island itself to St Mary and to the monks to hold perpetually in their demesne. Witnesses: Queen Matilda my wife, and Roger the

[183] *RRAN* ii, no. 567, dating to after Roger became chancellor, by early Sept. 1101, and probably to before the birth of the Empress Matilda. Roger was a leading administrator of Henry I. He was nominated as bishop of Salisbury in 1102 and elected in 1103, only consecrated in 1107, and died in 1139. For his career, see E. J. Kealey, *Roger of Salisbury* (Berkeley, 1972).

Nigello[a] de Oilleio, et Arsone de Abetot, et Radulfo Basset. Apud Windresoras.[184]

58. *De ecclesia de Niweham.*[185]

Willelmus de Curceio, regis dapifer, hunc plurimo excolere abbatem solebat amore.[186] Huius uilla erat Niweham, trans fluuium Tamesim sita, uille uero que Culeham dicitur contermina, de qua in gestis
C fo. 146r abbatis Adelelmi[b] | fit mentio.[187] Idem itaque regis dapifer eiusdem
[ii. 53] sue possessionis ecclesiam, cum terra, id est una hida, et decimis siue cyrcsceattis, reliquisque suis consuetudinibus, abbati Faritio et mona-
B fo. 133r chis in Abben | donia perpetuo dono concessit, preter duas portiones sue proprie decime ex eadem uilla;[188] huius autem rei donationem cum sua coniuge altari sancte Marie imposuit, atque coram his testibus confirmauit: Serlone episcopo de Sais, Nigello abbate de Bertona, et multis aliis.[189]

59. *De decima eiusdem uille.*

Non multo post uero tempore, predictus abbas cum eodem Willelmo de duabus suprascriptis portionibus decime sermonem habuit, et de quadam piscatione que Anglice nominatur Sotiswere, quatinus et ista cum predicta donatione ecclesie sancte Marie et sibi condonaret.[190] De his quoque rebus dum abbas se intromitteret, apud eundem uirum per uiginti marcas argenti finem fecit, ita ut ipse concessum cum litteris sigillatis regis prefati de omnibus iam dictis donationibus requireret, et requisitum Abbendoniam deferret, et die festiuitatis Romani Rothomagi archiepiscopi, coram omni conuentu monachorum et presentia horum laicorum, super altare sancte Marie offerret: Willelmi regis camerarii, Wini, et multorum aliorum.[191]

Et misit ipse Willelmus dapiferum suum Goisfredum et saisauit

[a] *initial om. C* [b] Aðelelmi *B*

---

[184] *RRAN* ii, no. 550, dating to probably 3 Sept. 1101, on grounds of the place and the witnesses.

[185] The church of Nuneham Courtenay is listed amongst Faritius's acquisitions in *De abbatibus*; *CMA* ii. 288. No mention is here made of the earlier loss of the village; see above, p. 12.

[186] William was younger son of Richard de Courcy, who held Nuneham Courtenay at the time of *Domesday Book* (see above, p. 13). He married a daughter of William de Falaise and his wife, Geva. His elder brother inherited the family's continental lands. William attested royal charters down to 1111 or soon after, suggesting that this may have been the time of his death; see *HKF* i. 103–5; *RRAN* ii, p. xxii.

[187] See above, p. 12.

[188] On church-scots, see Brett, *English Church*, pp. 224–5; N. Neilson, *Customary Rents*

chancellor, and Herbert the chamberlain, and Nigel d'Oilly, and Urse d'Abetot, and Ralph Basset. At Windsor.[184]

58. *Concerning the church of Nuneham.*[185]
William de Courcy, the king's steward, was accustomed to revere this abbot with the greatest love.[186] His village of Nuneham Courtenay was across the river Thames, next to the village called Culham, which was mentioned in the deeds of Abbot Adelelm.[187] So this steward of the king granted to Abbot Faritius and the monks in Abingdon by perpetual gift the church of this possession of his, together with one hide of land, and the tithes (or church-scots), and the rest of his customs, save two portions of his own tithe from this village.[188] Moreover, with his wife he placed the gift of this possession on the altar of St Mary and confirmed it in the presence of these witnesses: Serlo bishop of Sées, Nigel abbot of Burton, and many others.[189]

59. *Concerning the tithe of that village.*
Not long afterwards, Abbot Faritius spoke with William about the aforementioned two portions of tithe and about a fishing place which in English is called *Sotiswere*, that he might give these with the previous gift to the church of St Mary and to Faritius.[190] While dealing with these matters, the abbot also made an agreement with William by means of twenty marks of silver, that William would seek to obtain King Henry's grant and sealed letters concerning all the donations. He brought what he obtained to Abingdon, and on the day of the feast of Romanus, archbishop of Rouen [23 Oct.], offered it on the altar of St Mary, in the presence of the whole convent of monks and of these laymen: William the king's chamberlain, Wini, and many others.[191]

William also sent his steward Geoffrey and seised the church and

(Oxford Studies in Social and Legal History, ii, 1910), pp. 193–6; J. H. Round, '"Churchscot" in Domesday', *EHR* v (1890), p. 101; above, note 87.

[189] Serlo was bishop of Sées 1091–1123, *HKF* i. 104; Nigel was abbot of Burton 1094–1114, *Heads of Religious Houses*, p. 31.

[190] See also below, p. 386. On fishing in this area, see *VCH*, *Oxfordshire*, v. 242.

[191] William the chamberlain's identity is not entirely certain, although he may be William de Houghton, *RRAN* ii, p. xv, or William Mauduit: Hollister, *Monarchy, Magnates and Institutions*, pp. 211–12. Wini may be the same man who appears as Win, below, p. 210, and could also be the father of Henry son of Oini, below, pp. 202, 324; see below, p. 146, for Oini appearing as a witness to a gift of Henry d'Aubigny, named in a marginal addition in MS C, in the main text in MS B. St Romanus was bishop of Rouen from 630 until his death in *c*.640; *Oxford Dictionary of Saints*, pp. 347–8. His feast day on 23 Oct. appears in the Abingdon kalendar; *Benedictine Kalendars*, i. 28.

inde ecclesiam et abbatem per Willelmum cellararium.[192] Piscationi predicte[a] adiacent septemdecim acre telluris. Que tali ipse abbas decretione monasterii officinis locauit: capellam predicte uille cum rebus suis uniuersis edituo,[193] duas uero decime dominii partes elemosinario, piscariam cellarario impertire curauit.

[ii. 54] **60.** *Confirmatio regis Henrici.*[194]

Henricus rex Anglorum[b] Roberto episcopo Lincolie, et Willelmo uicecomiti de Oxenef', et omnibus baronibus, Francis et Anglis, de Oxenefordscira, salutem. Sciatis quod concedo sancte Marie de Abbendona et monachis eiusdem loci perpetuo habendam ecclesiam de Niweham, et terram et decimam totam ipsius manerii, et alia que ad ipsam ecclesiam pertinent, et piscariam, cum omnibus sibi pertinentibus, sicut Willelmus de Curci dapifer meus eis dedit et concessit. Testibus Rannulfo episcopo Dunelmensi, et Rogero Bigod, per Goisfridum Peccatum. Apud Corneberiam, in die sancti Luce euuangeliste.

Post mortem autem istius Willelmi, filius eius Willelmus donationem patris sui taliter confirmauit:[195]

61. *Carta Willelmi iunioris de Curci de ecclesia de Niweham.*

Ego Willelmus de Curceio reddo Deo, et sancte[c] Marie, et ecclesie Abbendonie, elemosinam quam pater meus dedit predicte ecclesie, scilicet[d] ecclesiam de Niweham, et unam hidam terre, et omnem decimam de dominio meo et totius uille, et unam piscariam, cum omnibus sibi pertinentibus, et pasturam ccc. ouium, et octo boum, et decem uaccarum in mea dominica pastura, et unum pratum quod uocatur Cumed, unde ego accreui[e] elemosinam patris mei, consilio
[ii. 55] et uoluntate fratris mei Roberti, et militum meorum.[196] Et uolo ut ecclesia predicta teneat ista in pace, et quiete, et libere, et honorifice, et ut nullus eam inde inquietet. Qui uero hanc

[a] *om. B* [b] Anglie *B* [c] beate *B* [d] scllicet *C* [e] acreui *B C*

[192] See above, p. lxxxvii, on transfers of seisin.

[193] See also below, p. 214.

[194] *RRAN* ii, no. 699; Lyell, no. 112; Chatsworth, no. 111. The writ must date between 1101, the return of Ranulf Flambard, and 1107, the death of Roger Bigod; *RRAN* suggests 18 Oct. 1105 for this and other writs issued at Cornbury. MS B and the Chatsworth Cartulary (no. 110), but not MS C, include confirmations by King Stephen; the Chatsworth Cartulary (no. 100) also includes a confirmation by Henry II.

[195] William the younger is a rather obscure figure compared with his father, for example not appearing as a witness of royal charters; see *HKF* i. 105. See also *HKF* i. 112 for a

abbot of the gift through William the cellarer.[192] Seventeen acres of land pertain to the aforesaid fishery. The abbot divided these possessions among the domestic offices of the monastery as follows: he took care to bestow the chapel of Nuneham with all its lands and rights on the sacrist,[193] the two parts of the tithe of the demesne on the almoner, and the fishery on the cellarer.

60. *Confirmation of King Henry.*[194]
Henry king of the English to Robert bishop of Lincoln, and William sheriff of Oxford, and all the barons, French and English, of Oxfordshire, greeting. Know that I grant to St Mary of Abingdon and to the monks of that monastery to have perpetually the church of Nuneham, and the land and the whole tithe of that manor, and the other things which pertain to that church, and the fishery with everything pertaining to it, as William de Courcy, my steward, gave and granted to them. Witnesses: Ranulf bishop of Durham and Roger Bigod, through Geoffrey Pecche. At Cornbury, on the day of St Luke the Evangelist [18 Oct.].

Moreover, after the death of this William, his son William confirmed his father's donation thus:[195]

61. *Charter of William de Courcy the younger, concerning the church of Nuneham.*
I, William de Courcy, give back to God, and to St Mary, and to the church of Abingdon the alms which my father gave to the aforesaid church, that is the church of Nuneham, and one hide of land, and all the tithe from my demesne and of the whole village, and one fishery with everything pertaining to it, and pasture of 300 sheep and of eight oxen and of ten cows in my demesne pasture, and one meadow which is called Cowmead, whereby I have increased my father's alms, by the counsel and approval of my brother Robert and my knights.[196] And I wish that the aforesaid church may hold these in peace and undisturbed and freely and honourably, and that no one may disturb

dispute between Abingdon and the widow of William de Courcy III over the advowson of Nuneham church.

[196] Unlike William the grantor, Robert probably did become a royal steward, as his father had been. The doubt arises from the fact that there were two branches of the Courcy family, both of which had members called Robert at this time; Green, *Government*, pp. 242–3. For Cowmead, see also the map of 1707 copied in *VCH*, *Oxfordshire*, v. 235, for its position between the Abingdon Road and the river Thames; also EPNS, *Oxfordshire*, i. 184. The Domesday entry for Nuneham mentions 40 acres of meadow and 10 acres of pasture; *DB* i, 159[r].

redditionem uel donationem actu uel consilio uiolauerit, maledic-
B fo. 133v tionem Dei et eiusdem genitricis Marie sustineat.[197] Huic | autem redditioni uel donationi interfuerunt testes: Robertus de Curceio, Philippus[a] dapifer, Willelmus de Estuna, Hugo Walensis, Berengerius,[b] Robertus presbiter, Godefridus presbiter, Willelmus nepos, Rogerius de Lillebona, Ricardus filius Fulconis, Mainardus de Niweham.[c][198]

62. *De ecclesia de Kinsentona.*[199]

Gosfredus[d] de Ver, Albrici senioris filius, Albrici iunioris frater,
C fo. 146v suorum fratrum in | nascentia primus, ac ideo in hereditate paterna successor futurus, tam morum quam parentum generositate admodum inclitus, abbatem medendi se gratia ad Faritium contulit; erat enim graui irretitus morbo. Tribus ergo ab abbate ei cura mensibus impensa, ea qua pulsabatur conualuit molestia. Sed quia contra mortem nulla est medicina, alius morbus hunc occupat, cogens decedere uita.[200] Itaque instante temporis ipsius articulo, idem eger ecclesiam sui patrimonii de uilla Kinsuetuna, patre suo Albrico et matre sua Beatrice, una cum fratribus suis, idem concedentibus,
[ii. 56] perpetua donatione Abbendonensi monasterio contulit, cum duarum hidarum duodecies uiginti acris terra disterminata, et insuper unius uirgate[e] portione. Cuius doni auctoritatem regis quoque huiusmodi confirmauit edictum:

63. *Carta regis de ecclesia de Kunsentuna.*[f][201]

Henricus rex Anglorum Mauritio Lundoniensi episcopo, et Gilleberto abbati Westmonasterii, et Hugoni de Bochelanda, et omnibus baronibus suis et ministris, Francis et Anglis, de Lundonia et de Middelsexo, salutem.[202] Sciatis me concessisse, in tempore Faritii abbatis, ecclesie sancte Marie in Abbendonia ecclesiam de

[a] *initial om. C* [b] Berengerus *B* [c] Neweham *B* [d] Godefridus *B* [e] uirgata *B* [f] Kinsentun *B*

[197] Cf. the excommunication below, p. 218; also above, p. 56, concerning Leckhampstead.

[198] See *Red Book*, i. 308, for a Walter the Welshman who was probably a relative of Hugh; i. 225 for a Berenger holding half a knight of William de Courcy in 1166. For the family of Milton Lilborne, see *HKF* i. 136–7.

[199] Middlesex; see also *DB* i, fo. 130v: Aubrey de Ver holds Kensington from the bishop of Coutances. Aubrey de Ver the elder was a prominent *Domesday* land-holder. He died *c.*1112, and was succeeded by his son Aubrey II who lived until probably 1140; see *Complete Peerage*, x. 193–9, Green, *Government*, p. 276, Keats-Rohan, *Domesday People*, pp. 131–2. Beatrice's background is uncertain. The church of Kensington is listed amongst

the church in respect thereof. Whoever, indeed, violates this restoration or gift, by act or counsel, is to suffer the curse of God and His mother Mary.[197] Present as witnesses for this restoration and gift were Robert de Courcy, Philip the steward, William of Eston, Hugh the Welshman, Berenger, Robert the priest, Godfrey the priest, William the nephew, Roger of Milton Lilborne, Richard son of Fulk, Mainard of Nuneham.[198]

62. *Concerning the church of Kensington.*[199]
Geoffrey de Ver, son of the elder Aubrey and brother of the younger Aubrey, the first-born amongst his brothers and so the future successor to the paternal inheritance, was very famous for the nobility of his conduct as much as of his parentage. Ensnared by a serious illness, he had recourse to Abbot Faritius to be cured. The abbot took care of him for three months, and he regained his health regarding the attack of that affliction. But as there is no medicine against death, another illness seized Geoffrey, and compelled him to depart from life.[200] So with this moment imminent, and with his father Aubrey and his mother Beatrice together with his brothers granting this, the sick man conferred by perpetual gift to the monastery of Abingdon a church of his patrimony, in the village of Kensington, together with land of two hides divided into 240 acres, and in addition a portion of a virgate. An edict of the king also confirmed the authority of this gift, as follows:

63. *Charter of the king concerning the church of Kensington.*[201]
Henry king of the English to Maurice bishop of London, and Gilbert abbot of Westminster, and Hugh of Buckland, and all his barons and officials, French and English, of London and Middlesex, greeting.[202] Know that I have granted to the church of St Mary in Abingdon, in

Faritius's acquisitions in *De abbatibus*; *CMA* ii. 288. It is now St Mary Abbot's, linking it to its earlier history.

[200] F. Getz, *Medicine in the English Middle Ages* (Princeton, 1998), pp. 13–14, 98 n. 82, suggests that the writer here was probably 'echoing Faritius's words of comfort', and compares the phrase with a statement of Seneca, 'Ne medicina quidem morbos insanabiles uincit'. The sentiments are similar but the verbal parallels limited, and it is probably best to take the Abingdon phrase as one version of a proverb.

[201] *RRAN* ii, no. 702; the writ must date to before 1107, the death of Maurice bishop of London. For a further copy, see *Cartularium prioratus de Colne*, ed. J. L. Fisher (Essex Arch. Soc. Occasional Publications, i, 1946), no. 3. For later confirmations, preserved in the Colne Cartulary, but not in the present text, see *RRAN* iii, no. 14, Saltman, *Theobald*, no. 79, *Colne*, nos. 4, 11.

[202] Gilbert Crispin was abbot of Westminster ?1085–1117/18; *Heads of Religious Houses*, p. 77.

Chensuetuna et quicquid ad eam pertinet; et terram in ipsa uilla inter ecclesiam et terram aliam duarum hidarum de duodecim uiginti acris, quam Albricus de Ver dedit predicte ecclesie pro anima Goisfredi filii sui defuncti. Et eam ecclesiam cum terra predicta Abbendonensis ecclesia in pace inperpetuum et quiete teneat. Testibus Mathilde regina, et Eudone dapifero, et Willelmo de Curceio, et Nigello de Oileio, et Vrsone de Abetot, et Roberto Malet. Apud Corneberiam.

Notandum autem quod in his regiis litteris[a] unius uirgate mentio deest. Quod ideo fit, quia quando eadem descriptio composita fuit, nondum eius collatio impertita, sed non multo post tempore ab eisdem a quibus et superiora repensa, et regia attestatione roborata fuit.[203]

[ii. 57] **64.** *De ecclesia de Colas.*[b][204]

Predictus itaque Goisfredus mundo demigrans, in huius monasterii cultiori loco sepelitur. Quare eius parentes eundem locum diligere, seque Deo et fratrum beneficiis ibidem precipue postea commendare. Et quia in Eastsexe regione, que ab Abbendonia pluribus distat miliariis, frequentiori commoratione degere solebant, nec istic ideo totiens adesse quotiens id affectabant, ubi sui nati memoria continetur, poterant, communi consilio [c]pater et mater, fauente adhoc
B fo. 134r Albrico iuniore filio[c] eorundem (quem tunc | sibi heredem substituerant), abbatis quoque Faritii et conuentus fratrum sibi commissi consensu, monasterium in proprio fundo, cui Colas uocabulum est, construere delegerunt, quod loco Abbendonensi in omnibus foret perpetuo summissum, et monachi inde assumpti illic locarentur. Ibi enim ad opus cohabitantium copiose de suis rebus se collaturos, ibi se suosque posteros post decessum requieturos corpore, promittebant. Itaque deliberatum consultum regia auctoritate et episcopi Mauritii (ex cuius diocesi locus ille habebatur)[205] confirmantes, Abbendonenses fratres ad se uenire rogant, et locum ipsum eis designant. Cui rei indicium carta regis inde pretendit, que ea tempestate talibus annotata est apicibus:

[a] litteriis *B C* [b] Colum *B* [c–c] *om. B*

[203] See above, p. xxxvi. This is the text's only use of 'rependere' to refer to a grant, and it perhaps means that the grant was made partly as a repayment for the medical care Geoffrey had received.

[204] The church of Colne, Essex, is listed amongst Faritius's acquisitions in *De abbatibus*,

the time of Abbot Faritius, the church of Kensington, and whatever pertains to it, and the land in that village between the church and the other land of two hides of 240 acres which Aubrey de Ver gave the aforesaid church for the soul of Geoffrey his dead son. And let the church of Abingdon hold that church with the aforesaid land in peace and undisturbed in perpetuity. Witnesses: Queen Matilda, and Eudo the steward, and William de Courcy, and Nigel d'Oilly, and Urse d'Abetot, and Robert Malet. At Cornbury.

It should moreover be noted that in these royal letters mention of one virgate is missing. This is because when the document was drawn up, that grant had not yet been bestowed. But not long afterwards, it was bestowed by those same people by whom the above things were given as repayment, and strengthened by royal attestation.[203]

64. *Concerning the church of Colne.*[204]

When the aforesaid Geoffrey departed this world, he was buried in the better appointed part of this monastery. Therefore his parents loved this monastery and afterwards especially commended themselves to God and the spiritual benefits of the brethren here. However, since they were accustomed to spend more time in the region of Essex, very many miles distant from Abingdon, they could not be as often as they desired at that monastery where the memory of their child is maintained. Therefore by common counsel, and with the support of their son Aubrey the younger (whom they had then substituted as heir to themselves), and also with the consent of Abbot Faritius and the convent of brethren entrusted to him, his father and mother chose to build a monastery in their own estate called Colne. This would forever be subject to the monastery of Abingdon in all matters, and monks taken from Abingdon would be placed at Colne. They promised that they would make a plentiful grant from their own possessions for the use of those living together there, and that after death they and their posterity would rest there in body. They confirmed their considered decision with royal authority and that of Bishop Maurice (in whose diocese Colne was),[205] and asked brethren of Abingdon to come to them and assigned that monastery to them. The king's charter sets out proof on this matter, which at that time was noted down in the following letter:

which adds that he placed six monks there, later increasing the number to twelve; *CMA* ii. 288.

[205] Maurice was bishop of London 1085–1107; *Handbook of British Chronology*, p. 258.

65. *Carta regis de ecclesia de Colas.*[a][206]

Omnibus ecclesie Dei fidelibus sub regimine meo, notum fieri uolo
[ii. 58] quod ego Henricus, Dei gratia Anglorum rex, pro peccatorum meorum remissione et anime mee salute, Deo et sancte[b] Marie in Abbendonensi ecclesia, et sancto Andree in Colensi ecclesia, que ut filia matri, ut membrum[c] capiti, subiecta et coherens est ecclesie
C fo. 147r Abbendonensi, concedo et in | eternum permanere auctorizo omnes illas donationes quas Albricus de Ver et uxor eius Beatrix, et eorum filius Albricus, cum fratribus suis, eorumque homines iam fecerunt uel facturi sunt supradicte ecclesie, tam in ecclesiis quam in terris, hominibus et decimis, molendinis, siluis et pratis, pascuis et exitibus, quarum nomina rerum subnexa leguntur, scilicet: in Cola, ecclesiam sancti Andree, cum terra Rannulfi presbiteri, et cum omnibus ad ecclesiam pertinentibus, et sexies uiginti acras de dominio, et uiridarium quod est ultra aquam cum uiuario; et terram quam Serlo habuit, sicut melius et largius unquam habuit ipse uel aliquis antecessorum illius, in pascuis et siluis[d] et campis; et duas siluas, scilicet Dodepoliso[207] et Northwde;[e] et terram Gode decem solidorum de gablo; et terram Eadwini quinque solidorum de gablo; et uiginti acras de dominio que cambite fuerant pro terra Blachemanni; et unum hominem, cum quinque acris; et terram Ælmari longi;[208] et terram Wlfwini forestarii; et molendinum; grangias; et ecclesiam de Duurecurt,[f][209] cum triginta acris terre, et cum omnibus sibi pertinentibus. In maneriis, scilicet, Hethingeham,[g] Belcheam, Laureham, Aldeham, Duurecurt,[h] Bonecleida, Rodingas,[210] duas partes decime de omnibus rebus, et unum hominem cum quinque
[ii. 59] acris. In Walda et Wadana,[211] medietatem decime, et unum hominem cum quinque acris. In Hethingeham, duo molendina que Aldwinus molendinarius tenebat.[212] De terra Adelelmi[i] de Burgata

[a] Colum *B* [b] beate *B* [c] menbrum *B* [d] siluiis *B* [e] Noðwde *B* [f] Duuercurt *B* [g] Hethingaham *B* [h] Duuercurt *B* [i] Adelelmi *B*

[206] *RRAN* ii, no. 981; the regnal year establishes that the document was issued before 5 Aug. 1111. For Colne versions, see *RRAN* ii, no. 981 and *Colne*, nos. 1, 2. In *Colne*, no. 1, the most notable differences from the version printed here are different witnesses and the replacement of the dating clause with sentences stating privileges. In *Colne*, no. 2, there are more extensive rearrangements, and again the dating clause is replaced with the privileges, but the witnesses are identical to the Abingdon version. Note that *Colne*, no. 1, is a later addition to the cartulary, and the text printed here is preferable. The present text is somewhat unusual in form, and may be treated with suspicion, but cannot be firmly condemned as a forgery. Note also *Colne*, no. 9, which purports to be Ralph archbishop of Canterbury's confirmation, but is very suspicious. It survives as a supposed original,

65. *Charter of the king concerning the church of Colne.*[206]

To all the faithful of the church of God under my rule, I wish it to be known that I, Henry, by the grace of God king of the English, for the remission of my sins and the salvation of my soul, grant and authorize to remain for ever to God and to St Mary in the church of Abingdon, and to St Andrew in the church of Colne, which is subject and attached to the church of Abingdon as daughter to mother, as limb to head, all those gifts which Aubrey de Ver and his wife Beatrice and their son Aubrey, with his brothers, and their men, have now made or will make to the aforesaid church, both in churches and in lands, men and tithes, mills, woods and meadows, pastures and revenues, the names of which are listed below, that is to say: in Colne, the church of St Andrew with the land of Ranulf the priest, and with everything pertaining to the church, and 120 acres of demesne, and the green, which is beyond the water, with the fish-pond; and the land which Serlo had, as well and extensively as he or any of his ancestors ever held it, in pastures and woods and fields; and two woods, that is *Dodepoliso*[207] and Northwood; and the land of Goda, of 10s. rent; and the land of Eadwine, of 5s. rent; and twenty acres of demesne, which were exchanged for the land of Blaccheman, and one man with five acres; and the land of Ælmar the tall;[208] and the land of Wulfwine the forester; and the mill; the granges; and the church of Dovercourt,[209] with thirty acres of land, and with everything pertaining to it. In the manors of Hedingham, Belchamp Walter, Lavenham, Aldham, Dovercourt, Great Bentley, Beauchamp Roding,[210] two parts of the tithe of all things, and one man with five acres. In Wold and Wadenhoe[211] half the tithe and one man with five acres. In Hedingham, two mills which Ealdwine the miller held.[212] 10s. worth of land

(Chelmsford, Essex County Record Office D/DPr 150) but in a hand of the mid-twelfth century at the earliest. It also is closely related to the second modified version of the Henry I's charter, *Colne*, no. 2. I would like to thank Dr Martin Brett for sharing with me his text of and notes on Archbishop Ralph's charter which will appear in the *English Episcopal Acta* series.

[207] A rental of *c.*1385 mentions 'Dodepollyshoo' close to the north-west border of the parish; *Colne*, p. 57 n. 1, and map at p. 95.

[208] Alternatively, 'Longus' could be an inherited byname, rather than one based on a personal characteristic, in which case one might call him Ælmar Long. The name Ælmar could derive from either the OE Ælfmær or the OE Æthelmær.

[209] Essex.

[210] Castle Hedingham, Belchamp Walter, Dovercourt, Great Bentley, and Beauchamp Roding are all in Essex, Lavenham and Aldham in Suffolk.

[211] Northants; see also *DB* i, fo. 220^{v}.

[212] Sible Hedingham, Essex.

decem solidatas;[213] dimidiam decimam Demiblanc de Cola;[214] et terciam partem decime Rannulfi Mangui.[a][215] Et ecclesiam de Campis,[216] et ecclesiam de Bonecleta, et ecclesiam de Bellocampo,[b] cum omnibus eis pertinentibus. Et siluam de Litehaia,[217] cum uiginti acris terre. Hec donationum concessio facta est a serenissimo rege Anglorum Henrico anno Dominice incarnationis millesimo cente-
B fo. 134v simo undecimo, indictione quarta, | anno uero regni sui undecimo, coram his testibus: Roberto Lincoliense episcopo, et Iohanne da Baiocis, et Gilleberto capellano, et Goisfredo[c] de Diua, et Hamone dapifero, et Rannulfo Meschino, et Willelmo Peurello[d] de Notingeham, et Hugone de Bochelanda. Apud Radingas.

66. *Item de Colas.*[e]

Omnium uero rerum que per cartam istam regis notantur, abbas Faritius apud Colas, Quadragesimali tempore et die festi sancti Cuthberti, constitutus inuestituram (id est saisitionem) accepit, per manum Picoti dapiferi Albrici, iubente eodem Albrico et uxore eius Beatrice, concedentibus id Albrico iuniore et ceteris eorum filiis, cum suis uniuersis militibus, qui huic donationi interfuerunt, idem uidentes et annuentes.[218] Quorum nomina hec fuerunt: filiorum,
[ii. 60] iam nominatus Albricus, Rogerus, Robertus, Willelmus; militum uero, Aluredus[f] uicecomes, Goisfredus filius Haimonis, Haimon de Lamara, et multi alii.[219] Item, Adelelmus[g] de Burgate, qui eo die, coram his omnibus testibus, sese per manum abbatis predicti in eodem loco Deo et sancto Andree optulit, ut ibi post mortem sepeliretur, et quia de sua terra decem solidatorum prouideret, sicut et fecit, et de ea monachos ibidem commanentes saisiuit, Thihelo et Willelmo tunc id concedentibus. Item affuit Goisfredus de Ruelent.[220] Ex parte abbatis affuerunt Garengerius[h] prior, Benedictus, et Robertus, et Godwinus, et Willelmus monachi; milites uero, Bernerus, et Robertus de Sandford,[i] Radulfus camerarius[j] abbatis; Rogerus clericus.[221]

[a] magni *B* [b] Bellocambo *B* [c] Gossfredo *C* [d] Peuerello *B*
[e] Colum *B* [f] Alfredus *B* [g] Aðelelmus *B* [h] Warengerius *B*
[i] Samford *B* [j] camerrarius *B*

[213] Adelelm was prominent as a tenant of Aubrey de Ver in Suffolk; see Keats-Rohan, *Domesday People*, p. 124. His toponym is drawn from Burgate, Suffolk; see *DB* ii, fo. 419r. See also *Colne*, no. 87.

[214] The *Domesday* tenant of one hide at White Colne, *DB* ii, fo. 77r, was called 'Dimidius Blancus'; see also *DB* ii, fos. 78r, 106r.

[215] The name obviously gave the scribes trouble; *Colne* offers 'Mengui', MS B

of Adelelm of Burgate.[213] Half the tithe of Demiblanc, from Colne;[214] and a third part of the tithe of Ranulf *Mangui*;[215] and the church of Camps,[216] and the church of Great Bentley, and the church of Belchamp Walter, with everything pertaining to them, and the wood of Littley,[217] with twenty acres of land. This grant of gifts was made by Henry the most serene king of the English in the year of our Lord 1111, the fourth indiction, in the eleventh year indeed of his reign, in the presence of these witnesses: Robert bishop of Lincoln, and John de Bayeux, and Gilbert the chaplain, and Geoffrey de Dives, and Hamo the steward, and Ranulf Meschin, and William Peverel of Nottingham, and Hugh of Buckland. At Reading.

66. *Likewise concerning Colne.*

Abbot Faritius was present at Colne in Lent on the feast day of St Cuthbert [20 Mar.] and by the hand of Picot, Aubrey's steward, received investiture (that is seisin) of all the possessions recorded by the king's charter. Aubrey the elder ordered this, and his wife Beatrice and Aubrey the younger and their other sons granted it, together with all their knights, who were present at this gift and saw and agreed to it.[218] Their names were these: the sons, the aforementioned Aubrey, Roger, Robert, William; and the knights Alfred the sheriff, Geoffrey son of Hamo, Hamo of *Lamara*, and many others.[219] Likewise, Adelelm of Burgate did the same, since he was providing 10s. worth of his land, and seised of this the monks living there; on that day Adelelm also offered himself to God and St Andrew in that monastery, through the hand of the aforesaid abbot, in the presence of all these witnesses, so that he might be buried there after his death. Thihel and William then granted his gift. Also present was Geoffrey de *Ruelent*.[220] Present from the abbot's side were Warenger the prior, the monks Benedict, and Robert, and Godwine, and William; and the knights Berner and Robert of Sandford, Ralph the abbot's chamberlain; Roger the cleric.[221]

'magni'. The last may be the most plausible, on the analogy of 'longus' above; note also *DB* ii, fo. 30r, for a pre-Conquest tenant at Colne called Ælfric Big.

216 Castle Camps, Cambs.; see also *VCH*, *Cambridgeshire*, vi. 45.

217 Essex.

218 See above, p. lxxxvii, on transfers of seisin.

219 Presumably Alfred was sheriff of Essex; Green, *Sheriffs*, pp. 26, 40.

220 Thihel is perhaps the same man as the Thiel, knight of Aldham, Essex, mentioned in *Colne*, no. 25 (a charter of 1141 × 50), and accompanying note at p. 67.

221 On Warenger, see above, p. lvii. Robert was tenant of the abbey's lands at Sandford-on-Thames, Oxon. According to a survey from Henry I's reign, he also held four hides in Bayworth from the abbey; below, p. 386. A Robert of Sandford founded Littlemore Priory, Sandford, in the mid-twelfth century; *VCH*, *Oxfordshire*, ii. 75. A list in MS C, in a later

[*See p. 90 for n. 221 cont.*]

67. *De Albrico de Ver.*

His ita determinatis, non multorum post decursum annorum, idem Albricus senior ante sui obitus diem religionis habitum in eodem loco recipit, et defunctus sepulture traditur. Vbi et Willelmus filius eius, suorum iunior fratrum, paruo tempore superstes patri effectus, tumulatur. Pro cuius memoria frater eius, Albricus scilicet iunior,
C fo. 147v terram[a] duarum carrucarum in Scaldeswlla[b] | Deo et sancto Andree perpetua largitione contulit, presente predicto abbate Faritio.[222] Aderat enim ibidem, et funeris defuncti exequias agebat. Horum[c] itaque sepultorum epitaphium[d] hic annexuimus.

Cedunt e uita uotis animisque cupita,
Barbarus et Scita, gentilis et Israhelita.
Has pariter metas habet omnis sexus et etas:
En puer, en senior, pater alter, filius alter:
[ii. 61] Legem, fortunam, terram uenere sub unam.
Non iuueni tote quas epotauit Athene,
Non uetulo note uires uel opes ualuere.
Sed ualuere fides, et predia que memoramus,[e]
Vt ualeant, ualeant, per secula cuncta precamur.[223]

Cum autem uicini eundem orationis gratia locum frequentarent, ad usum inhabitantium[f] sua beneficia respectu premiorum supernorum largiri cepere. Quorum ea tempestate aliquos hic subnominamus: Hubertus enim de Monte Canesi acram unam prati; item Goisfredus et Robertus fratres, et filii Odeline, alteram acram prati; ad hos et
B fo. 135r Walterus, cognomento Macerel, de|cimam totius sue pecunie uille sue Colis, de feudo Eustachii comitis Bolonensis, pratumque Suunul contiguum molendino illius loci paruulum; Ricardus quoque de Buris, de eadem sua uilla, id est Buris, decimam tam mobilium quam immobilium rerum totam Deo et sancto Andree illic contulerunt.[224]

[a] terrarum *B* [b] Scaldewlla *B* [c] *this and the next nine lines start with relatively large capitals in the margin C. The lines in B also start with capitals, but only the last five are in the margin* [d] epitafium *B* [e] *erasure before* memoramus *C*; commemoramus *B* [f] inhabitatium *B*

---

hand, has a Richard of Sandford holding four hides in Bayworth; *CMA* ii. 311. For Ralph the chamberlain see also below, p. 154.

[222] Scaldwell is in Northants.; see also *VCH*, *Northamptonshire*, iv. 214. *Colne*, nos. 1, 2, 9, all include lands at Scaldwell worth 40s. a year in the original gift; see above, p. 86 n. 206, on these charters.

67. *Concerning Aubrey de Ver.*

After these matters had been concluded thus and a few years had passed, Aubrey the elder, before the day of his death, received the habit of the religious life in that monastery, and when he died he was handed over for burial. Also buried there was his son William, youngest of the brothers, who survived his father for a short time. In memory of him, his brother Aubrey the younger conferred on God and St Andrew by perpetual donation two carrucates of land in Scaldwell, in the presence of Abbot Faritius.[222] For he was there and conducted the funeral rites of the deceased. We have therefore here added the epitaph of those who had been buried:

They withdrew from life, desired in their wishes and hearts,
Barbarian and Scythian, Gentile and Israelite.
Each sex and age equally has these limits:
See the boy, see the older man, the one father, the other son.
They came beneath one law, one fortune, one land.
Not all Athens, which he drank up, availed for the young man,
Not famous strength or wealth for the old man.
But their faiths availed, and the estates which we record [here].
Let us pray that they may avail, may avail for ever more.[223]

Moreover, local people, frequenting that monastery for prayer, began to make their own gifts for the use of the inhabitants, for the sake of heavenly rewards. Some of the men who made grants to God and St Andrew at that time we here name: Hubert de Montchesney, one acre of meadow there; likewise, the brothers Geoffrey and Robert, sons of Odelina, another acre of meadow; also Walter, surnamed Macerel, a tithe of all his goods of his village of Colne from the fee of Eustace count of Boulogne, and the tiny meadow of *Suunul* next to that monastery's mill; also Richard of Bures, from his village, that is Bures, the whole tithe of his moveable and immoveable possessions.[224]

[223] For the form of this obituary verse, see Vol. i, Introduction, 'Style'.

[224] Hubert was a significant tenant of Robert Malet and also a lesser tenant-in-chief in Suffolk in 1086; for him and his family, see Keats-Rohan, *Domesday People*, pp. 256–7, *Rotuli de dominabus*, ed. J. H. Round (Pipe Roll Soc., xxxv, 1913), pp. xliv–xlv. For Count Eustace holding land in Colne, see *DB* ii, fo. 30^{r}; his tenant in 1086 was called Robert. For Bures, Essex, see *DB* ii, fos. 39^{v}–40^{r}, 40^{v}; also *Colne*, no. 2 and note on p. 58.

68. *De ecclesia Eadwardestune.*[225]

In comitatu Suthfolc[a] habetur uilla Eadwardestun appellata, cuius dominus Hubertus de Monte Canesi dicebatur. Hic familiaritate abbatis Faritii adductus, ecclesiam predicte uille, cum omnibus sibi pertinentibus, monasterio Abbendonensi iure perpetuo donauit, et coram Deo et altari sancte Marie in Abbendonensi oratorio, et coram abbate et fratribus eiusdem ecclesie, et testibus Albrico scilicet iuniore
[ii. 62] de Ver, et Ricardo Bisceat, et multis aliis, donationem ipsam confirmauit, anno quinto decimo regni Henrici regis,[226] eo scilicet tenore, ut locus ille semper monachili consistorio frueretur et seruiretur,[227] nullaque capellano eiusdem[b] domini foret licentia ibidem indicere[c] uel suscipere, etiam presente eodem domino siue ipsius familia, aliquid, nisi quod uelle monachorum illic degentium concederet.[d] Quid uero aut quantum cum eadem ecclesia tunc temporis collatum fuerit, regie ad comitatum Suthfolc[e] tunc directe littere attestantur, quarum forma hec fuit:

69. *Littere regis de ecclesia Eadwardestun.*[228]

Henricus rex Anglorum Herberto episcopo de Norwic,[f] et uicecomitibus de Suthfolc[g] et de Eastsexa, et omnibus baronibus suis, Francis et Anglis, de utraque scira, salutem.[229] Sciatis quia ego concedo Deo et sancte Marie in Abbendonensi ecclesia, et Faritio abbati et omnibus successoribus suis, et monachis eiusdem loci, elemosinam illam quam Hubertus de Monte Canesi dedit predicte ecclesie, scilicet ecclesiam de Eadwardestuna, cum terris et decimis et omnibus sibi pertinentibus iure, et insuper duas acras terre iuxta ecclesiam, et duas partes decime omnium rerum de Stauretona et de Stanesteda, et decimam de [h]redditibus molendinorum[h] et nemorum, et ubicumque porci sui fuerint in pasnagio, erunt dominici porci abbatis sine pasnagio, preter haiam de Stanestede;[i] et decimam redditus turbarum de Stauretona,

[a] Suðfolc *B* [b] eiudem, *followed by* locum *struck out B* [c] indicem *B*, *arising from form of C's abbreviation. Such a mistake again suggests that B derives from C* [d] *corr. from* concederetur *B* [e] Suðfolc *B* [f] Norðwic *B* [g] Suðfolc *B* [h–h] reditibus molendonorum *C* [i] Standestede *B*

[225] *DB* ii, fo. 304[r], records that Hubert held Edwardstone from Robert Malet. Amongst the acquisitions of Faritius, *De abbatibus* records that Hubert de Montchesney granted the church of Edwardstone with all its appurtenances to the church of Colne, to sustain two monks who would always intercede for his own salvation and that of his successors; *CMA* ii. 288. Hubert's charter is preserved in *Colne*, no. 64; see also nos. 65, 66, his son and grandson's confirmations.

[226] Neither Aubrey nor Richard appear as witnesses to *Colne*, no. 64, Hubert de Montchesney's charter recording his gift of the church of Edwardstone to Abingdon. I have

68. *Concerning the church of Edwardstone.*[225]
In the county of Suffolk is a village named Edwardstone, the lord of which was called Hubert de Montchesney. Brought here by his close relationship with Abbot Faritius, he gave to the monastery of Abingdon by perpetual right the church of Edwardstone with everything pertaining to it, and he confirmed that gift in the presence of God and the altar of St Mary in the church of Abingdon, and in the presence of the abbot and the brethren of that church, and with Aubrey de Ver the younger and Richard *Bisceat* and many others witnessing, in the fifteenth year of King Henry's reign [5 Aug. 1114–4 Aug. 1115].[226] He did so on the following condition, that the monastery always enjoy the proceeds and employ them for the monks' meals;[227] and that the lord's chaplain have no permission to impose or receive anything there, even with his lord or his lord's household present, except what the monks residing there might willingly grant. What, indeed, or how much was then conferred with that church is attested by royal letters which were then sent to the county court of Suffolk, of the following form:

69. *Letters of the king concerning the church of Edwardstone.*[228]
Henry king of the English to Herbert bishop of Norwich, and the sheriffs of Suffolk and Essex, and all his barons, French and English, of both shires, greeting.[229] Know that I grant to God, and to St Mary in the church of Abingdon, and to Abbot Faritius, and to all his successors, and to the monks of that monastery, that alms which Hubert de Montchesney gave to the aforesaid church, that is the church of Edwardstone, with the lands and tithes and everything pertaining to it by right; and in addition two acres of land next to the church, and two parts of the tithes of all things of Staverton and of Stanstead, and the tithe of the rents of the mills and woods; and wherever his own pigs have been in pannage, the demesne pigs of the abbot will be without pannage, with the exception of the enclosure of Stanstead; and the tithe of the rent of the turfs of Staverton, and

been unable to identify Richard Bisceat, but Professor Crouch (personal communication) has suggested that he may in fact be Richard Basset.

[227] For texts related to Abingdon using *consistorium* in this unusual sense, see *DMLBS*, fasc. ii, s.v. *consistorium*.

[228] *RRAN* ii, no. 1089, after the king's return to England in Jul. 1115.

[229] Herbert was bishop of Norwich 1090/1–1119; *Handbook of British Chronology*, p. 261. The identity of the sheriffs of Essex and Suffolk cannot be certain; Green, *Sheriffs*, pp. 39–40, 77.

et quicquid pro Dei amore accrescere uoluerit.[230] Testibus Rannulfo cancellario, et Grimaldo medico, et Iurardo archidiacono, et Waltero[a]
[ii. 63] archidiacono, et Willelmo de Abinni,[b] et Rogero filio Ricardi, et Nigello de Oilli, et Radulfo Basset, et Goisfredo filio Pagani. Apud Wodestocam.[c]

Descripta est autem huius concessionis carta anno ab incarnatione Dominica millesimo centesimo quinto decimo.

Sed et de mansione illic monachorum Abbendonensium, Radulfi
C fo. 148r archiepiscopi | Cantuariensis ad Norwicensem episcopum huiusmodi littere tunc temporis transmisse fuerunt:

70. *Littere archiepiscopi Cantuariensis.*[231]

Frater Radulfus, indignus Cantuariensis ecclesie minister, uenerabili domino et confratri Herberto, Norwicensi Dei gratia episcopo,
B fo. 135v salutem, et a|micitiam, et fideles orationes pro posse. Quia notam sancte prudentie uestre non ignoramus reuerentiam et religiositatem domni abbatis Abbendonensis[d] Faritii et totius congregationis illi a Deo commisse, non est opus uobis eam intimare. Pro his igitur oratam esse uolumus caritatis uestre bonitatem, quatinus gratia Dei (cuius sunt) et nostri (qui uester sum), et ipsorum etiam qui amici uestri et filii esse profitentur, quosdam fratres ecclesie in quadam ecclesia a quodam parrochiano uestro illis in elemosinam concessa paterna suscipiatis benignitate, et consilium et auxilium, prout potestis et scitis, amicabiliter prebeatis. Quod faciendo, Deus omnipotens diu conseruet incolumem[e] sanctam paternitatem uestram, nostri memorem. Valete.

[ii. 64] **71.** *De molendino quod dicitur Enora.*[f][232]

Ad exitum burgi Abbendonensis pons, quo transitur cum fluuius Eoche exundat, habetur, iuxta quem australi in parte situm est molendinum, ab incolis Einore appellatum, regio per id tempus fisco deditum. Huius molendinarius prata in uicino posita, que abbatie iuris erant, summergebat;[g] aque etiam ductum, quamdiu

[a] Wualtero *B* [b] Abini *B* [c] Wdestocam *B* [d] Abbendonensi *B C* [e] incolumen *C* [f] Henora *B* [g] submergebat *B*

[230] See *DB* ii, fos. 88r, 325r, for Hubert holding Stanstead Hall, Essex, and Staverton, Suffolk, of Robert Malet. Both the sense and comparison with *Colne*, no. 64, suggest that either the Latin text is misleading in the section concerning pannage, or that the word *pannagium* is used in the first instance to mean the right of feeding, in the second to mean payment for feeding. Hubert must have meant that, with one specific exception, wherever his own pigs had had the right to feed, the abbot's pigs were henceforth to have the same.

whatever he may wish to add for love of God.[230] Witnesses: Ranulf the chancellor, and Grimbald the physician, and Everard the archdeacon, and Walter the archdeacon, and William d'Aubigny, and Roger son of Richard, and Nigel d'Oilly, and Ralph Basset, and Geoffrey son of Pain. At Woodstock.

Moreover, the charter of this grant was written down in the year of our Lord 1115.

Also concerning the monks of Abingdon's holding there, letters of Ralph archbishop of Canterbury were sent to the bishop of Norwich at that time, as follows:

70. *Letters of the archbishop of Canterbury.*[231]
Brother Ralph, unworthy servant of the church of Canterbury, to the venerable lord and fellow brother Herbert, by the grace of God bishop of Norwich, greeting, and friendship, and faithful prayers to his utmost power. Since we are not unaware that the reverence and devoutness of lord Faritius abbot of Abingdon and of all the congregation entrusted to him by God is known to your holy prudence, there is no need to inform you of it. On behalf of these, therefore, we beseech the goodness of your love, by the sake of God (whose they are), and of us (who are yours), and indeed of those who are avowed to be your friends and sons, that you may support by your fatherly goodness and in friendly fashion provide counsel and aid, as far as you can and know how, for certain brethren of the church, in a certain church which has been granted to them in alms by one of your parishioners. For doing this, may almighty God long preserve your holy fatherhood safe and mindful of us. Farewell.

71. *Concerning the mill which is called Hennor.*[232]
There is a bridge at the way out from the borough of Abingdon, by which the river Ock is crossed when it floods, next to which on the south side is situated a mill, called Hennor by the locals. Throughout that time it was devoted to the royal treasury. Its miller used to submerge the meadows situated in the area, which were the abbey's property; often he used to block the watercourse for as long as he was

[231] This is a curiously vague letter, the penultimate sentence having the ring of a set form into which the specifics have yet to be entered. See *Colne*, no. 14, for Bishop Herbert's own, much more specific charter.

[232] 'The mill of Hennor' is listed amongst Faritius's acquisitions in *De abbatibus*; *CMA* ii. 288.

poterat, ne molendinum abbatis inferius positum moleret, sepe recludebat.[233] Quare cum ob istiusmodi insolentiam frequenter notaretur, nec ideo ab hac[a] proteruitate descisceret, abbas inde remedium, et futurum posteris loci Abbendonensis hac de causa prouectum multum utile et durabile, acquisiuit. Nam plurimorum industria uirorum, et precipue Hugonis de Bochelanda, suo pro beneficio comitante sibi suffragio, adeo apud regis gratiam institit, ut dominatum ipsius molendini perpetuo ipse et ecclesia Abbendonensis, ea libertate qua hactenus[b] constiterat, potiretur. Quo percelebrato, illud idem molendinum usibus elemosinarii monasterii, pro pauperum sustentatione, delegauit. Cuius rei testes sunt apices ea tempestate regis ad comitatum Berchescire directe, quarum iste extitit textus:

72. *Carta regis de molendino Enora.*[c][234]

Henricus rex Anglorum Rogero episcopo Salesbirie,[d] et Hugoni de Bochelanda, et omnibus baronibus et fidelibus suis, Francis et Anglis, de Berchescira, salutem. Sciatis me dedisse et perpetuo possidendum
[ii. 65] concessisse Deo et sancte Marie in Abbendonensi ecclesia, ad opus elemosine ipsius ecclesie, quoddam molendinum quod uocatur Enora,[e] quod situm est super flumen Eoche, cum omnibus sibi pertinentibus, scilicet terra, prato, aqua, pascuis, et cum omnibus consuetudinibus suis, sicuti ego ipse melius et liberius et quietius illud molendinum unquam tenui in dominio meo. Testibus Rogero episcopo Salesbir', et Roberto episcopo Lincol', et Iohanne episcopo Bathense,[f] et Willelmo de Curci, et Willelmo de Albini pincerna, et Nigello de Oilli, et Thoma de Sancto Iohanne,[235] et Radulfo Basset, et
B fo. 136r Hugone de Bochelanda, et Waltero[g] | de Gloecestria, et Goisfredo de Clinctuna.[h] Apud Wdestoca in parco, in anno quo rex filiam suam Romano imperatori dedit.

73. *De prato quod[i] dicitur Kingesmed.*[236]

Pratum quoddam situm est iuxta urbem Oxeneford, Kingesmad[j] appellatum, regi quidem pertinens, pernecessarium autem hominibus de uilla abbatie que Hangestesi dicitur, pasturarum quippe suorum

[a] ac *B* [b] actenus *B* [c] Henora *B* [d] Salesbirie *B* [e] Henora *B* [f] Batense *B* [g] Wualtero *B* [h] Clintona *B* [i] qui *B C* [j] Kingesmed *B*

[233] For Hennor Mill, on the south bank of the river Ock, see EPNS, *Berkshire*, ii. 437; also above, p. 12.

able, so that the abbot's mill, lower down, would not grind.[233] Since the miller was frequently mentioned because of such arrogant acts and would not abandon his impudence, the abbot acquired a remedy concerning this, which would very usefully and durably profit later men of the monastery of Abingdon. For through the efforts of very many men, and especially through Hugh of Buckland's support (in return for accompanying spiritual benefit), the abbot so pressed upon the king's grace that he and the church of Abingdon obtained lordship of that mill for ever, with the same liberty established hitherto. Once this had become thoroughly well known, he delegated that mill to the uses of the almoner of the monastery, for the sustenance of the poor. Letters of the king sent to the county court of Berkshire at this time witness this matter, of which the following text exists:

72. *Charter of the king concerning the mill of Hennor.*[234]
Henry king of the English to Roger bishop of Salisbury, and Hugh of Buckland, and all his barons and faithful men, French and English, of Berkshire, greeting. Know that I have given and granted to God and to St Mary in the church of Abingdon to be possessed for ever, for the use of the alms of that church, a mill called Hennor, which is situated on the river Ock, with everything pertaining to it, that is land, meadow, water, pastures, and with all its customs, as I myself best, most freely, and undisturbedly ever held that mill in my demesne. Witnesses: Roger bishop of Salisbury, and Robert bishop of Lincoln, and John bishop of Bath, and William de Courcy, and William d'Aubigny the butler, and Nigel d'Oilly, and Thomas of St John,[235] and Ralph Basset, and Hugh of Buckland, and Walter of Gloucester, and Geoffrey of Clinton. At Woodstock in the park, in the year in which the king gave his daughter to the Roman emperor [1110].

73. *Concerning the meadow which is called King's Mead.*[236]
A certain meadow called King's Mead is situated next to Oxford. It belonged indeed to the king but was essential to the men of the abbey's village of Hinksey, as they were seen to be short of pasture for

[234] *RRAN* ii, no. 958, dating to 1110.

[235] Joint sheriff of Oxfordshire with Richard de Monte, at least between 5 Aug. 1110 and 4 Aug. 1111; Green, *Sheriffs*, p. 69. He continues to feature significantly below, pp. 108, 170, 196.

[236] King's Mead lay west of Oxford; see the map in Salter, *Medieval Oxford*, between pp. 66 and 67. *VCH*, *Oxfordshire*, iv. 282, states that it was later called Botley Mead. See also *VCH*, *Oxfordshire*, iv. 283, for an arrangement concerning this meadow in 1162.

pecudum indigentes cernuntur.[237] Vnde cum apud regis prefectum et illius procuratorem[a] loci pro illa pastura habenda multis in supplicationibus constituerentur, et nunc priuato munere delinitus uix
C fo. 148v audiret, nunc alias intendens, | sese quasi surdum petitoribus preberet, abbas Faritius, tum pro releuatione huius penurie suorum hominum, tum pro eiusdem prepositi proterua exactione, a rege inde remedium quesiuit. Sed quia illud sibi funditus appropriare nequiuit, saltem effecit ut pro uiginti solidis in anno reddendis in regis expensis
[ii. 66] regis pratum illud in feudo firmam perpetuo continerent, eo tenore adeo libere, quatinus nullus uicecomitum super eos ad censum predictum amplius abinde imponeret, aut aliquid aliud consuetudinis pro hoc ab eis preter statutam pactionem exigeret. De qua concessione regis, littere huiusmodi ad comitatum Oxenefordscire ab eo tunc temporis sunt directe:

74. *Carta [b]Henrici regis[b] de Kingesmed.*[238]

Henricus rex Anglorum Roberto episcopo Lincol', et Willelmo uicecomiti de Oxenefordescira, et omnibus baronibus suis inde, Francis et Anglis, salutem. Sciatis me concessisse ecclesie sancte Marie de Abbendona et monachis eiusdem ecclesie pratum nomine Kingesmed, quod homines de Hancstesia soliti sunt habere ad firmam de Tillinc, in perpetuum habendum pro uiginti solidis in unoquoque anno, ita quod nullam aliam consuetudinem inde reddant. Et in potestate eorum sit ut inde faciant quicquid uoluerint. Testibus Rogero episcopo Salesbir', et Roberto episcopo Lincol', et Haimone dapifero, et Willelmo de Curci, et Willelmo uicecomite de Oxenefordscira, et Hoeldo capellano, et Radulfo Basset, et Aluredo[c] de Lincolis. Apud Westmoster.[d]

[ii. 67] 75. *De Wdemundeslea.*[e][239]

His diebus nobiliorum quidam militum de Nigelli de Oilli feudo tenentium, Droco nomine, egritudine captus, monasterium ad hoc

[a] procuratoris *B C* [b–b] regis Henrici *B* [c] Alfredo *B* [d] Westmuster *B*
[e] Wdemundesleia *B*

[237] Hinksey, Berks., is not mentioned in *Domesday Book*. It almost certainly formed part of the assessment of Cumnor; see *VCH*, *Berkshire*, iv. 406. There is no sign that North and South Hinksey were separated at this time.

[238] *RRAN* ii, no. 970, dating to 1102 × 1110, as William ceased to be sheriff in *c.*1110. See also below, p. 160.

[239] Oxon. In 1086, Hugh earl of Chester held nine hides in Weston, and Robert held from him; *DB* i, fo. 157r; *Domesday* does not specify that Drogo was Robert's tenant there,

their cattle.[237] Often, in the presence of the king's reeve and guardian of that place, they humbly requested to have that pasture, and on one occasion, bribed by a private gift, he would scarcely listen, on another he would direct his attentions elsewhere and behave as if deaf to the petitioners. Abbot Faritius, therefore, sought a remedy from the king both to relieve his men's shortage and regarding this reeve's shameless exaction. He was unable to appropriate the king's meadow for them completely, but he at least obtained that they keep it perpetually in fee farm, for 20s. a year to be rendered to the king's revenues, on the following terms: so freely that no sheriff make an imposition on them beyond the aforesaid rent therefrom, or in return for this demand from them any other custom beside the fixed agreement. The following letters were then sent by the king to the county court of Oxfordshire concerning his grant:

74. *Charter of King Henry concerning King's Mead.*[238]
Henry king of the English to Robert bishop of Lincoln, and William sheriff of Oxfordshire, and all his barons there, French and English, greeting. Know that I have granted to the church of St Mary of Abingdon and to the monks of that church the meadow named King's Mead, which the men of Hinksey were accustomed to have at farm from Tillinc, to have in perpetuity for 20s. each year, thus that they render no other custom therefrom. And let it be in their power that they do whatever they wish with it. Witnesses: Roger bishop of Salisbury, and Robert bishop of Lincoln, and Hamo the steward, and William de Courcy, and William sheriff of Oxfordshire, and Theulf the chaplain, and Ralph Basset, and Alfred of Lincoln. At Westminster.

75. *Concerning Wormsley.*[239]
In those days Drogo, one of the noblest knights holding from the fee of Nigel d'Oilly, was seized by illness. He came to this monastery, put

but for that possibility see *VCH*, *Oxfordshire*, viii. 254. A man or men named Drogo held three houses in Wallingford; Shirburn and Hardwick, Oxon., from Robert d'Oilly; Ardley, Oxon., from Robert d'Oilly who in turn held from Hugh earl of Chester; and lands in Buscot, Berks., directly from Earl Hugh, as well as various lands in Cheshire; *DB* i, fos. 56^{v}, 60^{r}, 157^{r}, 158^{r}, 264^{r-v}. Drogo's surname suggests that he was from Les Andelys, Eure; on his family, see also *HKF* ii. 244–8. For a further confirmation of these lands in the second half of the twelfth century, see Lyell, no. 239. NB Lyell, no. 111, Chatsworth, no. 210, a writ of Henry I which does not appear in the *History*, and is also absent from *RRAN*. It confirms Hugh earl of Chester's gift of Shippon, Drogo des Andelys's gift of Wormsley, and Richard earl of Chester's acquitting of the latter of its service; see also above, p. xxviii.

sese contulit, et religionis habitum, abbate Faritio tribuente, illic induit et ipse quamdiu superuixit infra claustri septa deguit.[240] Qui, ut eius inter benefactorum monasterii specialius apud posteros haberetur memoria, suis de possessionibus aliquid beneficii inibi curauit conferre. Dedit itaque fratrum usibus unam hidam in loco qui dicitur Wdamundaslea, de uilla Westuna, liberam quidem et quietam omnium quarumlibet questionum, uel geldorum, uel militaris exactionis, quanquam ad ipsam diuerse dominationes diuerso respectu intenderent. Siquidem feudi comitis Cestrensis deputatur,
B fo. 136v de quo tunc | temporis Nigellus de Oilli eandem hidam simul cum nonnullis aliis possessionibus, et per Nigellum Droco, tenebat. Sed Drocone monachatum subeunte, Rogerus filius Radulfi, filiam ipsius in coniugium ducens, quarumlibet ille rerum potiebatur dum seculo militaret summam ipse adipiscitur.[241] Qui, quoniam ingenio callebat, Nigelli de Oilli consensum sibi traduxit, quatinus de comite in capite (ut uulgo loquatur) teneret, homo ipse comitis effectus. Dum ergo Nigelli iuris predicta terra fuisset, quicquid Droco de ea disposuit libenter fieri annuit, hocque modo suis litteris auctorizauit:

76. *Carta de Wdemundeslea.*[a]

Ego Nigellus de Oilli concedo et auctorizo Deo et sancte Marie et monachis in Abbendonensi ecclesia in perpetuum habendam unam
[ii. 68] hidam in Oxenefortscira,[b] in loco qui dicitur Wdemundelai,[c] quam Droco de Andelai[d] concessit eidem ecclesie licentia mea; ita solidam et quietam concedo sicut idem Droco melius unquam habuit tempore fratris mei Roberti et meo. Testibus Faritio abbate, et Rogero de Casneio,[e] et Luuello de Peri, et Aedrico homine eiusdem Droconis.[242]

Consequenter rex quoque idem subscribens, ita confirmauit:

77. *Carta regis de eadem terra.*[243]

Henricus rex Anglorum Roberto Lincoliensi[f] episcopo, et Willelmo uicecomiti de Oxenefortscira,[g] et omnibus baronibus suis, Francis et |
C fo. 149r Anglis, salutem. Sciatis me concessisse Deo et sancte Marie in

[a] Wdemundesleia *B* [b] Oxenefordscira *B* [c] Wdemundesleia *B* [d] Andelia *B* [e] Canesio *B* [f] Lincolniensi *B* [g] Oxenefordscira *B*

[240] See above, p. lxix.

[241] On Roger son of Ralph, see *HKF* ii. 244–5. The rest of the present chapter is rather terse, but it soon becomes clear that Roger's craftiness probably involved his making a claim on the land, below, p. 102.

[242] Mention of Faritius is an unusual instance of a beneficiary also acting as a witness. Roger de Chesney may have been a *Domesday* tenant of Robert d'Oilly, as a Roger is

on the habit of religious life bestowed by Abbot Faritius, and resided within the confines of the cloister for the rest of his life.[240] There, so that future men might hold his memory in special esteem amongst the monastery's benefactors, he took care to confer something profitable from his possessions. So he gave for the use of the brethren one hide in the place called Wormsley, of the village of Weston, free indeed and quit from all types of soke or gelds or military exaction, although various lordships had claims upon it in various respects. It was reckoned as of the fee of the earl of Chester, from whom Nigel d'Oilly then held that hide together with some other possessions, and Drogo held it through Nigel. But when Drogo became a monk, Roger son of Ralph married his daughter and himself acquired the entirety of what Drogo used to possess while he lived a knight's life in the world.[241] Since he was crafty by nature, Roger brought Nigel d'Oilly to agree with him that he might hold from the earl in chief (as may be said in common language) and himself became the earl's man. While therefore the aforesaid land had been Nigel's property, he willingly agreed and in his letters authorized as follows that whatever Drogo disposed concerning the land should be done:

76. *Charter concerning Wormsley.*
I, Nigel d'Oilly, grant and authorize to God, and to St Mary, and to the monks in the church of Abingdon, to have in perpetuity one hide in Oxfordshire in the place called Wormsley, which Drogo des Andelys granted to that church by my permission. I grant it as firm and quit as Drogo himself ever best held it in the time of my brother Robert and myself. Witnesses: Abbot Faritius, and Roger de Chesney, and Lovell of Perry, and Eadric, Drogo's man.[242]

Subsequently, the king also endorsed and confirmed the grant thus:

77. *Charter of the king concerning the same land.*[243]
Henry king of the English to Robert bishop of Lincoln, and William sheriff of Oxfordshire, and all his barons, French and English, greeting. Know that I have granted to God, and to St Mary in the

recorded holding lands from Robert which were in the Chesney family in the twelfth century; see *Eynsham Cartulary*, ed. H. E. Salter (2 vols., Oxford Hist. Soc., xlix, li, 1907–8), i. 411–12. He married Alice de Langetot, who may have been the daughter of Ralph de Langetot, mentioned above, p. 20. See also *Facsimiles of Early Charters in Oxford Muniment Rooms*, ed. H. E. Salter (Oxford, 1929), nos. 86 and 87, for Chesneys witnessing d'Oilly grants. Perry is most likely Waterperry, Oxon., held by Robert d'Oilly in 1086, *DB* i, fo. 158^{v}; see *VCH*, *Oxfordshire*, v. 296, *Oseney Cartulary*, iv, pp. 372–3.

[243] *RRAN* ii, no. 693. The writ can be dated to *c.*1105 × 1106.

Abbendonensi ecclesia et Faritio abbati unam hidam terre in Westuna, in loco qui dicitur Wdemundeslea, quam Droco de Andeleio dedit eidem ecclesie, et Nigellus dominus eius concessit; ita solutam et quietam concedo predicte ecclesie sicut unquam melius fuit tempore patris et fratris mei. Testibus Mathilde[a] regina et Goisfredo Peccatum. Apud Ailesberiam.[b]

Comes autem Cestrensis Ricardus, cum sua matre et melioribus suorum baronum secum, postea Abbendonia in uilla hospicio receptus,[244] abbate Faritio interpellante, et comitissa, matre scilicet eiusdem comitis, et eis[c] qui simul aderant cunctis id fauentibus et consultantibus, quicquid de predicta terra Wdemundeslea actitatum
[ii. 69] extitit, comes ipse benefactum extulit, et suo descripto roborauit. Quod descriptum, sigillo quidem matris signari constitit, nondum enim militari baltheo cinctus, materno sigillo littere quolibet ab eo directe includebantur. Hac de re quod eo annotatur, comitisse potius quam comitis sigillo signatur. Cuius forma hec fuit:

78. *Carta comitis Cestrensis de eadem terra.*[245]
Ricardus Cestrensis comes et Ermentrudis comitissa mater eius Nigello de Oilli, et Rogero filio Radulfi, et omnibus baronibus de Oxenefordscira, salutem et amicitiam. Sciatis quia, pro amore Dei,
B fo. 137r et anima patris mei, et remissione[d] | nostrorum peccatorum, concedimus hidam illam quam Droco de Andeleia[e] dedit ecclesie Abbendonensi, que est in loco qui dicitur Wdemundeslai.[f] Nos eidem ecclesie concedimus et auctorizamus perpetuo habendam, solidam et quietam ab omni nostro seruitio. Et Rogerus filius Radulfi et successores eius sint quieti in nostro seruitio, quantum ad illam hidam pertinet. Et defendimus ut nullo modo Rogerus, uel alius per eum, inquietet habitantes in terra illa. Hoc autem fecimus et testimonio nostrorum baronum, scilicet Willelmi filii Nigelli, et Hugonis filii Normanni, et Ricardi Balaste, et Willelmi filii Anskitilli, et Ricardi filii Nigelli, et domni Goisfridi capellani, et aliorum.[246]

[a] Gatilde *B* [b] Ailesbiriam *B* [c] ii *C*, hii *B* [d] remissionem *B C*
[e] Andelia *B* [f] Wdemundesleia *B*

[244] Richard was earl of Chester, 1101–20. Ermentrude was daughter of Hugh count of Beauvais; *Complete Peerage*, iii. 165–6.

[245] *Chester Charters*, no. 6, which notes other MSS.

[246] William son of Nigel was Richard's constable; see *Sir Christopher Hatton's Book of Seals*, ed. L. C. Loyd and D. M. Stenton (Northants. Rec. Soc. and Oxford, 1950), no. 515n.; Lewis, 'Formation of the honor of Chester', pp. 59–60; *Chester Charters*, nos. 3

church of Abingdon, and to Abbot Faritius, one hide of land in Weston, in the place which is called Wormsley, which Drogo des Andelys gave to that church, and Nigel his lord granted. I grant it to the aforesaid church as unburdened and quit as it ever best was in the time of my father and brother. Witnesses: Queen Matilda and Geoffrey Pecche. At Aylesbury.

Moreover, Richard earl of Chester, together with his mother and the better among his barons, afterwards received lodging in the town of Abingdon.[244] At Abbot Faritius's beseeching, and with the countess (that is the earl's mother) and all present favouring and advising this, the earl approved and strengthened by his document whatever had been transacted concerning the aforesaid land of Wormsley. Also, it was agreed that this document be sealed by his mother's seal, for he was not yet girded with the belt of knighthood, and letters sent anywhere by him were closed by his mother's seal. Consequently, that which is recorded about this matter is sealed with the countess's seal rather than the earl's. This was its form:

78. *Charter of the earl of Chester concerning the same land.*[245]
Richard earl of Chester and countess Ermentrude, his mother, to Nigel d'Oilly, and Roger son of Ralph, and all the barons of Oxfordshire, greeting and friendship. Know that for the love of God and the soul of my father and the remission of our sins, we grant that hide which Drogo des Andelys gave to the church of Abingdon, which is in the place called Wormsley. We grant and authorize that church to have it perpetually, unburdened and quit of all our service. And let Roger son of Ralph and his successors be quit in our service, as much as pertains to that hide. And we forbid that Roger or anyone through him disturb in any way those living on that land. Moreover we have done this by witness of our barons, that is, William son of Nigel, and Hugh son of Norman, and Richard Balaste, and William son of Ansketel, and Richard son of Nigel, and lord Geoffrey the chaplain, and others.[246] This was done in the sixth year of King

and 28. For Hugh son of Norman, see Lewis, 'Formation of the honor of Chester', pp. 56, 60, 61n, D. Crouch, 'The administration of the Norman earldom', *Earldom of Chester*, ed. Thacker, p. 76 (who states that Hugh son of Norman was the earl's steward); also *Chester Charters*, nos. 3, 8, 28. Richard Balaste may be the same as Richard Banaste/Banastre, who appears in *Chester Charters*. nos. 3, 13, 28. For Richard son of Nigel, see also *Chester Charters*, nos. 3, 12, 13, 28. For Geoffrey the chamberlain, see also *Chester Charters*, nos. 12 & 13.

Hoc actum est in sexto anno regni Henrici regis, in mense Maio, in die Pentecostes.

[ii. 70] 79. *De confirmatione eiusdem terre.*

Ista ergo comitis hinc regi intimata concessio, eius edicto et auctoritate confirmatur, uti in carta est uidere que compilationem rerum exquisitarum per abbatem Faritium continet.[247] Inde non multo post, census[a] qui geldum dicitur per comitatum Oxenefordscirǽ[b] passim a burgensibus et uillanis solutio per officiales huic negotio deputatos, uti alias ita ab incolis predicte terre exigitur. Quod ipse non passus, rem regi innotuit, ratiocinando[c] quod ab antiquo tempore usu consuetudinario eadem terra non debeat ulli huiusmodi exactioni subici. Quare rex uicecomiti eiusdem comitatus inde litteras misit, id continentes:

80. *Littere regis.*[248]

Henricus rex Anglorum Willelmo uicecomiti de Oxenefordscira, salutem. Precipio tibi ut illa hida quam Droco de Andelei dedit sancte Marie de Abbendona ita sit quieta de hoc geldo et de omnibus consuetudinibus sicut melius fuit quieta in tempore patris mei et fratris mei, et nichil aliud aduersum eam requiras. Testibus Waldrio cancellario et Grimaldo[d] medico. Apud Romesi.

[ii. 71] 81. *De eadem terra.*[249]

Adhuc, ad posterorum cautelam, quiddam de eodem loco dignum putauimus subnectendum. Quidam cupide[e] mentis homines illius terre portione frui nitebantur. Quod cuidam plurimum callenti ingenio actitandum commisere, cui nomen Benedictus, qui causis comitis consulendis sepius interesse solebat.[250] Ille dum promitteret
C fo. 149v quod ad finem propositum eorum, uti rebatur, | deduceret, in spe arrecti expectabant rei exitum. Machinari itaque cepit, ut primo insueta a loco exigerentur, deinde, cum exacta non redderentur, queque illic reperta forent abducerentur. Et hec quidem abbatis Faritii post obitum contigerunt. Talia itaque cum sepius ingererentur, eorum qui publicam monasterii rem gubernabant consultu,

[a] *there is confusion in both manuscripts between* census *and* censum. *Certainly in B and perhaps C,* census *was corr. to* censum [b] Oxenefordscire *B* [c] raciocinando *B* [d] Grimbaldo *B* [e] cupite *B C*

[247] See below, p. 160. Note also above, p. xxviii n. 73 on another charter of Henry I.

[248] *RRAN* ii, no. 758, dating the document to between 13 May 1106, when the earl of Chester's grant was made, and the end of Jul. 1106, since the *Anglo-Saxon Chronicle* records that the king crossed for Normandy before Aug.

Henry's reign, in the month of May, on the day of Pentecost [13 May 1106].

79. *Concerning the confirmation of this land.*
The king was informed of the earl's grant, and it was confirmed by his edict and authority, as can be seen in the charter containing a compilation of the possessions acquired through Abbot Faritius.[247] Not long after, specifically appointed officials demanded payment of the tax called geld throughout Oxfordshire, from burgesses and peasants, from the inhabitants of the aforesaid land as from elsewhere. Faritius would not allow this, but notified the king, pleading that from ancient times by customary usage this land should not be subject to any such exaction. Therefore the king sent letters concerning the matter to the sheriff of this county, containing the following:

80. *Letters of the king.*[248]
Henry king of the English to William sheriff of Oxfordshire, greeting. I order you that the hide which Drogo des Andelys gave to St Mary of Abingdon be as quit of the current geld and of all customs as ever it was best quit in the time of my father and my brother, and you are to seek nothing against it. Witnesses: Waldric the chancellor and Grimbald the physician. At Romsey.

81. *Concerning the same land.*[249]
Further, as a warning for men in future, we have thought that something else concerning this place warranted inclusion. Some greedy-minded men strove to enjoy the proceeds of part of that land. They entrusted this task to a certain man of extremely crafty nature, named Benedict, who was a particularly frequent participant in those of the earl's affairs requiring counsel.[250] When he promised that he would achieve their proposed end, as he supposed, they awaited the outcome with their hopes raised. He began to plot that first of all unaccustomed dues would be demanded from the place, then, when the demands were not rendered, whatever was to be found there would be taken away. And so indeed it happened after the death of Abbot Faritius. Since therefore such oppressions were too frequent, one of the church's servants was sent to the earl's court, by the advice of those governing the public affairs of the monastery. He was

[249] *English Lawsuits*, no. 217. The incident can be dated to 23 Feb. 1117 × 25 Nov. 1120, that is between the deaths of Faritius and Ranulf earl of Chester.

[250] The earl of Chester's charters reveal no more about Benedict, despite his prominence here.

comitis ad curiam unus de ecclesie seruientibus mittitur, cum[a] carta secum ferenda assignatur, ipsiusque comitis auctoritatem libertatis
B fo. 137v totius de illa | terra exactionis protestatur. Legatus ergo, itinere confecto, curiam adire sibi imperatam intrat, coram arbitrum maioribus de causa sibi dicendi imposita conqueritur, cartam libertatis pro attestatione rerum dictarum ad medium effert. Aderat is[b] de quo supra intulimus, dictorum et responsorum finem opperiens. Iamque communi in audientia litteris recitatis, rogat ille sibi easdem porrigi, parumper adhuc percepturus earum intellectum. Quibus porrectis, sinum mox in suum inuoluit. Quo breuigerulus uiso, miratus factum, stupidus primo hesit. Tum deinde cum repeteret porrectum, nil ab
[ii. 72] eodem inuasore rehabuit nisi risum. At assidentes, quibus iustum placebat, pro hoc indignari, alii uero ad contrarium illecti cachinnari. Ita infecto negotio, legatus ille cum tali detrimento domum reuertitur, labore tristiciaque confectus. Dei autem miseratio hanc ipsam fortunam, et si ad tempus quidem aliquantisper contrariam, postmodum tamen uertit in prosperam. Illum itaque Benedictum predictum dignatio diuina priuat amicitia comitis, huncque expellit qui sic quandoque latorem scripti fefellit, uellet nolletue, relicti. Pressus uero sub fasce ruine, ultio diuina penas eidem ingessit. Monachique, Deum precibus stimulantes, scripta, que pridem perdiderant, receperunt. Caueant ergo omnes periuri fraudes, caueantque tali legato mittere breue fraudis amico.

82. *De terra de Fencota unius hide.*[251]

Nobilis quedam matrona, [c]Athelina de Iwreio[c] uocata, Abbendonensi in uilla lecto egritudinis diu irremediabiliter decubans, apud locum qui Faincote dicitur, hidam unam, pro sui remedio perpetuo, ea per omnia libertate et usu quibus et ipsa ad illud tempus potita ibidem est, ad monasterii utilitatem ubi decubabat, perpetualiter contulit. Est quidem ipsa pecudum pasturis habilis. Dies huius donationis[d] his extitit quando sancti Augustini Cartaginensis episcopi memoria

[a] *for* cui ? [b] his *B C* [c–c] Aðelina de Hiuerio *B* [d] dominationis *B*

[251] Oxon. *DB* i, fo. 224v, has Roger d'Ivry holding Charlton-on-Otmoor from Hugh de Grandmesnil; Fencott is a hamlet in the parish of Charlton. Adelina was a daughter of Hugh de Grandmesnil and wife of Roger I d'Ivry; see *DB* i, fo. 160r–v, for her holding in 1086; *VCH*, *Oxfordshire*, i. 386–7 and note; Orderic, *Ecclesiastical History*, bk. viii, c. 15, ed. Chibnall, iv. 230; Keats-Rohan, *Domesday People*, p. 443. Her daughter, Adeliza, was also a patron of Reading Abbey; *Reading Abbey Cartularies*, ed. B. R. Kemp (2 vols.,

detailed to take the charter with him, and to bear witness to the earl's own authority regarding the freedom from all exaction from that land. The representative completed his journey and entered the court which he had been ordered to visit. In the presence of the greater of the suitors, he made his complaint concerning the plea entrusted to him, and displayed the charter of liberty as witness of the things pleaded. Benedict, about whom we commented above, was present, awaiting the end of the statements and responses. When the letters had been read out in everyone's hearing, he asked that they be handed to him so that he might quickly improve his grasp of their meaning. When they were handed to him, he at once wrapped them in a fold of his clothing. The bearer of the letter saw this, was amazed at his action, and at first stood stunned. Then, when he sought back the letters, he received nothing from that predator except laughter. As to those sitting in court, some—whom justice pleased—reacted with indignation, but others—attracted to the contrary—with guffaws. With the business thus unfinished, the representative returned home defeated and worn out by his toils and despondency. But if fortune had for some time been rather hostile, God's mercy afterwards rendered her favourable. So divine grace deprived that Benedict of the earl's friendship, and expelled this man who had thus once tricked the bearer of that document, abandonded whether he wished it or not. Therefore Benedict was crushed under the burden of ruin and Divine vengeance heaped punishments on him. Urging God with prayers, the monks received back the document they had previously lost. So let all guard against the frauds of a perjurer, and guard against sending a letter to the friend of fraud by such a representative.

82. *Concerning one hide of land at Fencott.*[251]

A certain noble matron called Adelina d'Ivry for a long time lay incurable in her sick bed in the town of Abingdon. For her eternal cure she conferred perpetually one hide at the place called Fencott for the profit of the monastery where she was lying sick, with the same freedom and usage in every respect with which she had possessed it hitherto. This land indeed is suitable for cattle pasture. The day of this donation was when the memory of St Augustine, the Carthaginian bishop, is celebrated, by the calculation of five concurrents

Camden Soc., 4th Ser. xxxi, xxxiii, 1986, 1987), i, no. 602 (where, however, the note is misleading).

celebratur, concurrentium[a] quinque per computationem.[252] Post emensum uero annum, ipsa defungitur. Cuius die defunctionis, presente clero, plebe plurima, immo abbate Faritio, nondum etiam
[ii. 73] defuncte cadauere tumulatum exposito, filia eiusdem, Adeliz dicta, maternum confirmauit donum sancte Marie in eius ecclesia Abbendonie deuote id conferendo.[253] Hec autem donatio facta est anno undecimo regni Henrici regis. Rex quoque idem confirmatum subscripsit ita:

83. *Carta regis de Fencota.*[254]

Henricus rex Anglorum Roberto episcopo Lincolie,[b] et Thome de Sancto Iohanne, et omnibus baronibus suis, et omnibus fidelibus suis, Francis et Anglis, de Oxenefordscira, salutem. Sciatis me concessisse Deo et sancte Marie Abbendonensi in ecclesia terram que est in
B fo. 138r Feincota, scilicet unam hidam[c] cum | pratis, et pascuis, et omnibus sibi pertinentibus, quam Adelina de Iureio eidem[d] ecclesie in elemosina dedit, et Adeliz filia sua auctorizauit. Et uolo et precipio ut ipsa ecclesia in pace et quiete et solute illam terram, cum omnibus
C fo. 150r sibi pertinentibus, | in perpetuum possideat. Testibus Nigello de Oilli, et Thoma de Sancto Iohanne, et Hugone de Euremou, et Goisfredo filio[e] Pagani, et Goisfredo[f] de Magnauilla, et Rogero de Oilleio, et Roberto de Dunestauilla, et Radulfo[g] de Ansgeriiuilla. Apud Wodestoch,[h] in Quadragesima.

84. *Item [i]littere regis de terra[i] de Fencota.*[255]

Henricus rex Anglorum[j] R. uicecomiti de Oxenef' et Rainero de
[ii. 74] Bada,[k] salutem.[256] Precipio quod Faritius abbas Abbendone ita bene et quiete teneat hidam terre de Fencota,[l] quam tenuit de Adelina de Iuri, cum omnibus rebus que[m] ad eam pertinent, sicut melius et quietius tenuit. Et si inde dissaisitus[n] est, resaisiatur, et bene et in pace teneat. Et siquid inde captum est, cito[o] inde similiter resaisiatur.

[a] cuncurentium *C* [b] Lincolnie *B* [c] hydam *C* [d] eiusdem *B* [e] filius *B* [f] Goisfredus *B* [g] Ead' *B* [h] Wdest' *B* [i–i] *om. B* [j] Anglie *B* [k] Baða *B* [l] Fencote *B* [m] quem *B* [n] dissiatus *B* [o] sito *B*

[252] On concurrents, see *Handbook of Dates*, p. 9: 'To each year was allotted by the computists a number (1 to 7) which represents the concurrents, or the number of days between the last Sunday in the preceding year and 1 January. . . . It will be noticed that the concurrents are counted as 7 when the preceding year ends on a Sunday.' Thus, if 31 Dec. was a Sunday, the concurrents were counted as the seven days intervening between Mon. 1 Jan. and Sunday 24 Dec. in the previous year, not the one day from Sunday 31 Dec. up

[28 Aug. 1110].[252] After a year passed, she died. On the day of her death, and with her corpse still lying out unburied, her daughter, called Adeliza, confirmed her mother's gift and devoutly conferred it on St Mary in her church of Abingdon, in the presence of clergy, of very many common people, and also of Abbot Faritius.[253] This gift was made in the eleventh year of King Henry. The king also endorsed the confirmation thus:

83. *Charter of the king concerning Fencott.*[254]
Henry king of the English to Robert bishop of Lincoln, and Thomas of St John, and all his barons and all his faithful men, French and English, of Oxfordshire, greeting. Know that I have granted to God and to St Mary in the church of Abingdon the land in Fencott, that is one hide, with meadows and pastures and everything pertaining to it, which Adelina d'Ivry gave to that church in alms, and her daughter Adeliza authorized. And I wish and order that the church itself possess that land in peace and undisturbed and unburdened, with everything pertaining to it, in perpetuity. Witnesses: Nigel d'Oilly, and Thomas of St John, and Hugh d'Envermeu, and Geoffrey son of Pain, and Geoffrey de Mandeville, and Roger d'Oilly, and Robert de Dunstanville, and Ralph d'Angerville. At Woodstock, in Lent.

84. *Likewise, letters of the king concerning the land of Fencott.*[255]
Henry king of the English to Richard sheriff of Oxford and Rainer of Bath, greeting.[256] I order that Faritius abbot of Abingdon hold the hide of land of Fencott, which he held from Adelina d'Ivry, with everything which pertains to it, as well and undisturbed as she best and most undisturbedly held. And if he has been disseised of this, let him be reseised and hold well and in peace. And if anything has been

to and including Mon. 1 Jan. 1 Jan. 1110 was a Saturday, the preceding Sunday was 26 Dec. 1109, so the writer counted the intervening days as the five concurrents. On such forms of dating, see also Vol. i, Introduction, 'Style'.

[253] See above, p. lxxxviii on death-bed gifts.

[254] *RRAN* ii, no. 973; Lyell, no. 113. Assuming that Henry's confirmation followed soon after the original gift, this document can be dated to 15 Feb.–2 Apr. 1111.

[255] *RRAN* ii, no. 1133; *Royal Writs*, ed. van Caenegem, no. 76; Lyell, no. 114; the document presumably was issued after Henry's confirmation charter of Lent 1111, and certainly before Apr. 1116, his last departure for Normandy before the death of Faritius.

[256] Richard de Monte, probably sheriff of Oxford between *c.*1110 and 1117; Green, *Sheriffs*, p. 69, and below, p. 174. A Rainer of Bath was sheriff of Lincolnshire 1128–30, and was one of the men whom Orderic Vitalis described as having been raised from the dust—that is, his power and status were the creation of Henry I; Green, *Government*, p. 233, *Sheriffs*, p. 55.

Et mihi faciat, quod iuste facere debet. Teste Nigello de Albinni. Apud Wincestram.

85. *Cartam Nigelli de Oili de terra Abbefeld.*[257]
Notum sit omnibus Christi amatoribus quod ego Nigellus de Oilli reddidi Deo et sancte Marie in Abbendonensi ecclesia terram de Abbefelda, quam Algarus tenebat,[258] quietam ab omni querela successorum meorum, perpetuo in dominio habendam, pro animabus fratrum meorum et meorum remissione peccatorum, et salute uxoris mee Agnetis et meorum filiorum. Et hoc ego feci in domo mea apud Stuntesfeldam, in presentia abbatis Faritii, in cuius manus hanc terram reddidi, et in presentia uxoris mee et Roberti filii mei, quorum rogatu et consensu hoc peregi,[259] et in presentia W. capellani mei, et Manaserii Arsi, et Radulfi Basset, et Rogeri de Casneto, et Gilleberti[a] Basset, et Rogeri Radulfi filii, et Luuelli de Braio, quorum testimonio hanc redditionem firmaui.[260] Quicumque autem hoc mutare uoluerit, non habeat partem in regno Christi et Dei. Amen.

86. *Littere regis de eadem terra Abbefeld.*[261]
Henricus rex Anglorum[b] Roberto episcopo Linc', et W. uicecomiti de Oxenef', et baronibus suis, Francis et Anglis, de Oxenefordscira,
[ii. 75] salutem. Sciatis me concessisse sancte Marie in Abbendonensi ecclesia, ad usum monachorum, terram quam Algarus tenet in uilla de Abbefeld, sicut Nigellus de Oilli reddidit predicte ecclesie et auctorizauit. Testibus Mathilde regina, et Eudone dapifero, et Willelmo de Curci, et Vrsone de Abetot, et Roberto Malet, et Albrico de Ver. Apud Corneberiam.

[a] G. *C* [b] Anglie *B*

---

[257] Lyell, no. 237; the charter is presumably from before the royal confirmation, probably datable to 18 Oct. 1105. See *VCH*, *Oxfordshire*, viii. 104; A. Morley Davies, 'Abefeld and Ackhamstead: two lost places', *Records of Buckinghamshire*, xv (1947–52), 166–71. *Abbefeld* lay between Lewknor, Stokenchurch, and Aston Rowant, and included parts of estates in all three. The Lewknor portion was largely held by Abingdon. It is not named in *Domesday*, but was probably attached to Lewknor: *DB* fo. 156v states that 'the abbey of Abingdon holds Lewknor. There are seventeen hides there'; fo. 158r that 'Peter holds one hide in Lewknor from Robert [d'Oilly]'. *Abbefeld* could be the latter hide, or one of those attributed to Abingdon but later obtained by the d'Oilly family; note that Nigel's charter refers to him giving *back* the land. *CMA* ii. 309 shows that the kitchener later held land there, of the fee of Drogo des Andelys, who was a tenant of Nigel d'Oilly, see p. 98. *Abbefeld* is listed amongst Faritius's acquisitions in *De abbatibus*; *CMA* ii. 288.

[258] None of the references elsewhere to a man/men named Ælfgar can be tied with certainty to the man mentioned here.

[259] Stonesfield is in Oxfordshire. On Robert d'Oilly II, see Green, *Government*, pp. 264–5, Sanders, *Baronies*, p. 54. He married Eda or Edith, daughter of Forne, and died in 1142.

taken therefrom, let him likewise be swiftly reseised of it. And let him do me what he should justly do. Witness: Nigel d'Aubigny. At Winchester.

85. *Charter of Nigel d'Oilly concerning the land of Abbefeld.*[257]
Let it be known to all who love Christ that I, Nigel d'Oilly, have given back to God and to St Mary in the church of Abingdon the land of *Abbefeld*, which Ælfgar held,[258] to have perpetually in demesne, quit of all plea by my successors; for the souls of my brothers and the remission of my sins, and the salvation of my wife, Agnes, and my sons. And I have done this in my house at Stonesfield in the presence of Abbot Faritius, into whose hands I gave back this land, and in the presence of my wife and Robert my son, at whose request and with whose consent I carried this out,[259] and also in the presence of W. my chaplain, and Manasser Arsic, and Ralph Basset, and Roger de Chesney, and Gilbert Basset, and Roger son of Ralph, and Lovell of Bray, with whose testimony I strengthened this restoration.[260] Moreover, let whoever wishes to change this have no share in the kingdom of Christ and God. Amen.

86. *Letters of the king concerning the same land of Abbefeld.*[261]
Henry king of the English to Robert bishop of Lincoln, and William sheriff of Oxford, and his barons, French and English, of Oxfordshire, greeting. Know that I have granted to St Mary in the church of Abingdon, for the use of the monks, the land which Ælfgar holds in the village of *Abbefeld*, as Nigel d'Oilly gave back and authorized to the aforesaid church. Witnesses: Queen Matilda, and Eudo the steward, and William de Courcy, and Urse d'Abetot, and Robert Malet, and Aubrey de Ver. At Cornbury.

[260] Ralph Basset was a leading administrator of Henry I. He died at the end of the 1120s or early in 1130; see *Basset Charters c. 1120 to 1250*, ed. W. T. Reedy (Pipe Roll Soc., New Series l, 1995), pp. xxviii–xxx. Gilbert Basset was probably a brother of Ralph; see *Boarstall Cartulary*, p. 324. Manasser Arsic held lands in Oxfordshire, notably being lord of Cogges; see Sanders, *Baronies*, p. 36, Keats-Rohan, *Domesday People*, pp. 294–5, J. Blair and J. M. Steane, 'Investigations at Cogges, Oxfordshire, 1978–81', *Oxoniensia*, xlvii (1982), 37–125, at pp. 43–7. Roger son of Ralph may be the same man as the son-in-law of Drogo des Andelys mentioned above, p. 100. Lovell is almost certainly the same man as Lovell of Perry, above, p. 100; see *VCH Buckinghamshire*, iv. 81, 127, *Boarstall Cartulary*, p. 314, *Oseney Cartulary*, iv. 373, *Rotuli curiae regis*, ed. F. Palgrave (2 vols., London, 1835), i. 22–3. *PR 31 HI*, p. 101 records Lovell of Bray accounting for a forest render in Buckinghamshire.

[261] *RRAN* ii, no. 700, Lyell, no. 109. The writ can be dated to 1100 × *c.*1106 when Robert Malet's attestations cease; *RRAN* suggests 18 Oct. 1105.

87. *Littere regis de domibus abbatis Lundonie.*[262]

Henricus rex Anglorum[a] R. episcopo Lund', et Hugoni de Bochelanda, et baronibus suis omnibus et fidelibus Londonie[b] et Mid-
delsexe, salutem.[263] Sciatis me concessisse ecclesie sancte Marie de
Abbendona et Faritio abbati perpetuo habenda hospicia sua de
B fo. 138v Londonia[c] in Westmenstrestret, | cum omnibus rebus pertinentibus
ad hospicia, omnino ab omnibus quieta, sicut melius unquam illa
ecclesia et quietius habuit tempore patris et fratris mei. Testibus
Grimaldo[d] medico et Nigello de Albini. Apud Windr'.

88. *De terra quam rex dedit abbati Faritio apud Lundoniam.*[264]

Henricus rex Anglorum[e] Ricardo episcopo Lond',[f] et Hugoni de
Bochelanda, et omnibus baronibus suis, Francis et Anglis, de
Londonia[g] et de Middelsessa,[h] salutem. Sciatis me dedisse sancte
Marie de Abbendona[i] et Faritio abbati unam mansam terre, que fuit
[ii. 76] Aldewini, in Suthstreta[j] iuxta hospicium abbatis predicti. Et uolo et
precipio ut bene et quiete et honorifice teneat illam terram, sicut
quietius tenet ibi aliam terram suam. Testibus Rogero episcopo
Salesb', et Gilliberto[k] de Aquila, et Otuero filio[l] comitis, et Grimbaldo medico, et Waltero de Bellocampo. Apud Westmoster.

89. *Item de eadem terra.*[265]

Henricus rex Anglorum[m] Hugoni[n] de Bochelanda, et omnibus
ministris suis Londonie, et Reinero preposito, salutem.[266] Volo et
firmiter precipio ut Faritius, abbas de Abbendona, ita bene et quiete
C fo. 150v habeat terram quam accreui ei ad hospicium suum, | sicut dedi ei per
breue meum. Testibus Roberto episcopo Linc' et Iohanne capellano[o]
Baioc'. Apud Radingas.

[a] Anglie *B* [b] Lundonie *B* [c] Lundonia *B* [d] Grimbaldo *B* [e] Anglie *B* [f] Lundonie *B* [g] Lundonia *B* [h] Middelsexsa *B* [i] Abbendonia *B* [j] Suthtreta *C* [k] Gilleberto *B* [l] filius *B* [m] Anglie *B* [n] Hugo *B* [o] cappellano *B*

[262] *RRAN* ii, no. 980. The writ can only be dated to between 1108, when Richard became bishop of London, and 1116, Henry's final departure for the Continent before the death of Faritius. See also above, p. 18 and n. 44 for the location of these houses. Houses in London for himself and his successors are listed amongst Faritius's acquisitions in *De abbatibus*; *CMA* ii. 288. Hugh of Buckland was probably addressed as sheriff of London; Green, *Sheriffs*, p. 57.

[263] Richard was bishop of London 1108–27; *Handbook of British Chronology*, p. 258.

87. *Letters of the king concerning the abbot's houses in London.*[262]
Henry king of the English to Richard bishop of London, and Hugh of Buckland, and all his barons and faithful men of London and Middlesex, greeting.[263] Know that I have granted to the church of St Mary of Abingdon and to Abbot Faritius to have in perpetuity their houses in London in Westminster Street with all possessions pertaining to the houses, entirely quit of everything, as that church best and most undisturbedly ever held in the time of my father and brother. Witnesses: Grimbald the physician and Nigel d'Aubigny. At Windsor.

88. *Concerning the land at London which the king gave to Abbot Faritius.*[264]
Henry king of the English to Richard bishop of London, and Hugh of Buckland, and all his barons, French and English, of London and Middlesex, greeting. Know that I have given to St Mary of Abingdon and to Abbot Faritius one messuage of land which was Aldwin's in South Street next to the aforesaid abbot's house. And I wish and order that he hold that land as well and undisturbed and honourably as he most undisturbedly holds his other land there. Witnesses: Roger bishop of Salisbury, and Gilbert de l'Aigle, and Otuer son of the earl, and Grimbald the physician, and Walter de Beauchamp. At Westminster.

89. *Likewise, concerning the same land.*[265]
Henry king of the English to Hugh of Buckland, and all his officials of London, and Rainer the reeve, greeting.[266] I wish and firmly order that Faritius abbot of Abingdon may have the land which I added to his house for him, as well and undisturbed as I gave to him by my writ. Witnesses: Robert bishop of Lincoln and John de Bayeux, the chaplain. At Reading.

[264] *RRAN* ii, no. 972. The writ can be dated to between 1108, when Richard became bishop of London, and *c.*1114–16, the death of Gilbert de l'Aigle and Henry's final departure for the Continent before the death of Faritius. For the location of the property, see above, p. 19 n. 44.

[265] *RRAN* ii, no. 982. The writ can be only be dated to after the previous writ.

[266] See Green, *Sheriffs*, p. 57: Hugh certainly was sheriff of London and Middlesex early in Henry I's reign. Here it may be that Hugh was acting as justice, rather than sheriff, in which case Rainer was sheriff, but there is no evidence to support this. Rainer may have been the reeve of Abingdon Abbey.

90. *Littere regis de quadam terra in Oxeneford.*[267]

Henricus rex Anglorum Roberto episcopo Linc', et Thome de Sancto Iohanne, et Nigello de Oilleio, et omnibus baronibus, Francis et Anglis, de Oxenefordscira, salutem. Sciatis me concessisse escambium terre de Oxeneford iuxta ecclesiam sancte Fridesuithe, quod fecerunt Rogerus episcopus Salesbirie et Faritius abbas de Abbendona, uidelicet ut abbas predictus et ecclesia sua teneat et habeat illam terram quam predictus episcopus ei escambiauit, ita liberam et quietam ab omnibus consuetudinibus, cum soca et saca et tol et team et infangentheof, sicut ipse abbas melius tenuerat illam aliam
[ii. 77] terram quam episcopo escambiauit. Testibus Roberto episcopo Linc', et Herueo episcopo de Heli, et Rannulfo cancellario, et Roberto filio regis, et Rannulfo Meschino. Apud Radingas.

91. *De hominibus de Welegraue.*[a][268]

Henricus rex Anglorum[b] Roberto et Aluredo, ministris comitis de Mellent de Welegraua,[c] salutem. Precipio uobis ut custodiatis omnes terras abbatis de Abbendona que circa uos sunt. Et ne patiamini ut aliquis, per uos siue per alium, quicquam in eis forisfaciat. Et ad minus[269] uolo et precipio ut ipse ita bene et quiete et libere teneat predictas terras, sicuti erant solute et libere et quiete quando manerium de Welegraua[d] erat in manu mea. Et homines sui sint in pace et sine calumpnia. Testibus Rannulfo cancellario et Iohanne de Baiocis. Apud Niweberiam.

92. *De terra de Langelea.*[e][270]

Henricus rex Anglorum[f] W. de Montefichet, salutem. Permitte esse in pace terram de Langelega,[g] quam regina Mathilda uxor mea dedit
B fo. 139r in elemosinam[h] sancte Marie de Abben|dona,[i] sicut melius unquam fuit in pace tempore antecessoris tui. Et quicquid inde super hoc

[a] Wellegraue *B* [b] Anglie *B* [c] Wellegraue *B* [d] Wellegraua *B* [e] Langeleia *B* [f] Anglie *B* [g] Langeleia *B* [h] helemosinam *B* [i] Abbendonia *B*

[267] *RRAN* ii, no. 1128, dating to 1113 × Apr. 1116 on the basis of Robert the king's son and Ranulf Meschin witnessing. For a map of Abingdon's Oxford possessions, see C. J. Bond, 'The reconstruction of the medieval landscape; the estates of Abingdon Abbey', *Landscape History*, i (1979), 59–75, at p. 72; however, the land exchanged here cannot be precisely identified with any certainty.

[268] *RRAN* ii, no. 983. The place concerned is uncertain, particularly in the context of a Beaumont connection. One possibility is Wargrave, Berks., close to the Abingdon possession of Whistley; for the name form, see EPNS, *Berkshire*, i. 119, *Reading*, ii, no. 771. The writ can be dated to between Ranulf becoming chancellor in *c.*1107 and Henry's departure to the Continent in Apr. 1116.

90. *Letters of the king concerning certain land in Oxford.*[267]
Henry king of the English to Robert bishop of Lincoln, and Thomas of St John, and Nigel d'Oilly, and all barons, French and English, of Oxfordshire, greeting. Know that I have granted the exchange of land of Oxford next to the church of St Frideswide, which Roger bishop of Salisbury and Faritius abbot of Abingdon made, that is, that the aforesaid abbot and his church may hold and have that land which the aforesaid bishop gave in exchange to him, as free and quit of all customs, with sake and soke and toll and team and infangentheof, as the abbot himself had best held that other land which he gave in exchange to the bishop. Witnesses: Robert bishop of Lincoln, and Hervey bishop of Ely, and Ranulf the chancellor, and Robert the king's son, and Ranulf Meschin. At Reading.

91. *Concerning the men of Welegrave.*[268]
Henry king of the English to Robert and Alfred, the count of Meulan's officials of *Welegrave*, greeting. I order you that you guard all the lands of the abbot of Abingdon which are around you. And do not allow anyone, through you or anyone else, to do any wrong therein. And at least[269] I wish and order that he hold the aforesaid lands as well and undisturbed and freely as they were unburdened and free and undisturbed when the manor of *Welegrave* was in my hand. And let his men be in peace and unchallenged. Witnesses: Ranulf the chancellor and John de Bayeux. At Newbury.

92. *Concerning the land of Langley.*[270]
Henry king of the English to William de Montfichet, greeting. Allow to be in peace the land of Langley which Queen Matilda my wife gave in alms to St Mary of Abingdon, as best it ever was in peace in your ancestor's time. And give back whatever you have taken from there

[269] This is an unusual and rather surprising phrase to find in this position in a writ. It seems likely to be a mis-transcription, but the more obvious alternatives, notably 'Et similiter' ['And likewise'], are not easily mis-read as the existing text.

[270] Langley Marish, Bucks.; see also below, p. 142. *RRAN* ii, no. 1402, dating to 1120 × 1123; *Royal Writs*, ed. van Caenegem, no. 38. The dating of the writ must be uncertain. Its position in the *History* suggests that it is from the time of Faritius, and after Abingdon acquired Robert Gernon's lands, below, p. 142; only the assumption that William of Buckland cannot have been a sheriff before the death of his father, Hugh, points to a later date. Langley Marish formed part of Wraysbury manor, held by Robert Gernon in 1086, *DB* i, fo. 149^{v}. William de Montfichet acquired most of Robert Gernon's lands; see note accompanying *Charters in the British Museum*, ed. Warner and Ellis, no. 17. See below, p. 142 n. 340, for a writ of William son of Henry I to William de Montfichet.

cepisti, redde. Et nisi feceris, Willelmus de Bochelanda faciat fieri, ne audiam inde clamorem amplius pro penuria recti et iusticie.[271] Teste Nigello de Albini. Apud Warengeford.[a]

[ii. 78] **93.** *Ad Aret[b] falconarium.*[272]

Henricus rex Anglorum[c] Aret[d] falconario et omnibus forestariis suis, salutem. Volo et precipio ut omnia ligna et uirgas, que fuerint data uel uendita hominibus abbatis Faritii de Abbendona ad opus suorum operum, sine omni impedimento et disturbatione possint ea conducere in pace quocumque uoluerint. Teste Rogero[e] Bigod. Apud Wincestram.

94. *Littere regis de carreio ecclesie.*[273]

Henricus rex Anglorum[f] baronibus suis, et uicecomitibus, et ministris suis, salutem. Prohibeo ne aliquis disturbet ullo modo carreiam sancte Marie de Abbendona, nec aliquid aliud quod sit dominicum abbatis uel monachorum eius, uel per terram uel per aquam, disturbet. Sed in pace eat et redeat quicumque rem suam, siue uictum siue aliquod aliud quod ad opus ecclesie pertineat, conduxerit. Teste Willelmo cancellario. Apud Londoniam.[g]

95. *De theloneo.*[274]

Henricus rex Anglorum[h] omnibus uicecomitibus, et prepositis, et omnibus ministris suis totius Anglie et portuum maris, salutem.
[ii. 79] Precipio quod omnia que ministri monachorum de Abbendona emerint, ad uictum et uestitum et utensilia monachorum, in ciuitatibus et burgis et omnibus aliis mercatis Anglie, sint quieta de theloneo et passagio et omni consuetudine, unde homines sui affidare poterint suas esse dominicas. Et nullus eos uel res illas inquietet uel iniuste disturbet, super decem libris forisfacture. Testibus cancellario et Milone de Gloecestria. Apud Abbendoniam.

96. *Item de theloneo.*[i][275]

Henricus rex Anglorum[j] Hugoni de Bochelanda et omnibus uicecomitibus et ministris totius Anglie, salutem. Precipio quod omnes res

[a] Walingeford *B* [b] Ared *B* [c] Anglie *B* [d] Ared *B* [e] *initial om. B*
[f] Anglie *B* [g] Lundoniam *B* [h] Anglie *B* [i] teloneo *B* [j] Anglie *B*

[271] William was probably acting as sheriff of Buckinghamshire, although this is the only evidence that Green, *Sheriffs*, p. 28, has for him holding that position. William was the son of Hugh of Buckland, and was still acting as a royal official in 1130; see Green, *Government*, p. 237.

[272] *RRAN* ii, no. 855, dating to 1100 × 1107, the *terminus ante quem* being the death of

contrary to this. And if you do not, William of Buckland is to ensure that it is done, so that I do not hear further complaint concerning this for want of right and justice.[271] Witness: Nigel d'Aubigny. At Wallingford.

93. *To Aret the falconer.*[272]
Henry king of the English to Aret the falconer and all his foresters, greeting. I wish and order that the men of Abbot Faritius of Abingdon can collect all the wood and sticks which are given or sold to them for use on his works, without any impediment or disturbance, in peace, wherever they wish. Witness: Roger Bigod. At Winchester.

94. *Letters of the king concerning transport of the church.*[273]
Henry king of the English to his barons, and sheriffs, and officials, greeting. I forbid that anyone disturb in any way transport of St Mary of Abingdon, nor disturb anything else which may belong to the lordship of the abbot or his monks, whether by land or by water. But whoever collects their property, whether provisions or anything else which pertains to the use of the church, may go and return in peace. Witness: William the chancellor. At London.

95. *Concerning toll.*[274]
Henry king of the English to all sheriffs, and reeves, and all his officials of the whole of England and of sea-ports, greeting. I order that everything which the officials of the monks of Abingdon buy for the monks' provisions and clothing and necessaries, in cities and boroughs and all other markets in England, be quit of toll and transport due and every custom, concerning which goods their men can pledge their faith that they belong to their own lordship. And let no one disrupt or unjustly disturb them or their goods, on £10 of forfeiture. Witnesses: the chancellor and Miles of Gloucester. At Abingdon.

96. *Likewise concerning toll.*[275]
Henry king of the English to Hugh of Buckland and all the sheriffs and officials of the whole of England, greeting. I order that all the

Roger Bigod. Aret was a huntsman of William II and Henry I and a tenant at least of the latter; *RRAN* i, no. 347, ii, nos. 673, 854, 856, 956, 961; see also *DB* i, fo. 160^{v}.

[273] *RRAN* ii, no. 520, dating to 1100 × 1101, the *terminus ante quem* being the date when William ceased to be chancellor.

[274] *RRAN* ii, no. 1258; for the dating of this writ, see above, p. xxxii.

[275] *RRAN* ii, no. 938. The writ can only safely be dated to 1100 × 1116, although *RRAN* suggests 10 Apr. 1110

C fo. 151r proprie abbatis et monachorum de Abbendona, | quod ministri sui uendiderint et emerint, sint quiete de theloneo et consuetudine et passagio, unde homines sui affidare poterint quod sue sint. Et prohibeo ne aliquis eos disturbet super decem libras forisfacture. Teste cancellario. Apud Merleberiam.

97. *Littere regis ad prepositum de Hamtona.*[276]
Henricus rex Anglorum[a] Warino preposito Hamtone et ministris suis, salutem. Precipio quod uictus et uestitus abbatis de Abbendona, et quicquid homines eius poterint affidare esse suum proprium, sit quietum de omni theloneo et lestagio et consuetudine et passagio.[277] Et siquid inde captum super hoc est, cito reddatur. Teste W. de Tanc', per Willelmum de Calna. Apud Windr'.

[ii. 80] **98.** *Item ad Warinum prepositum.*[278]
Henricus rex Anglorum[b] Warino preposito Hamtune et ministris suis, salutem. Precipio quod cito reddatis quicquid cepistis de proprio corredio abbatis Abbendonie de theloneo uel consuetudine, et amodo nichil capiatis de theloneo uel consuetudine uel passagio de corredio suo, uel rebus quas homines eius poterint affidare esse suas proprias.
B fo. 139v Teste Thoma de Sancto Iohanne. | Apud Wodestocha.[c]

99. *De consuetudinibus ecclesie.*[279]
Henricus rex Anglorum[d] W. uicecomiti de Oxeneford, salutem. Precipio ut permittas et facias sancte Marie Abbendone habere omnes illas consuetudines in hominibus suis, et nominatim de uerberatione quam frater Atselini et scutiger Anskitilli fecerunt inter eos, quas melius et plenius habuit tempore patris et fratris mei.[280] Et nullus sit ausus ei inde super hoc iniuriam facere. Teste Vrsone[e] de Abetot. Apud Warengeford.[f]

100. *Vt nemo hospitetur in hac uilla.*[281]
Henricus rex Anglorum[g] omnibus constabulis et omnibus fidelibus suis de curia, salutem. Prohibeo ne aliquis hospitetur in uilla Abbendune,[h] nisi licentia [i]Faritii abbatis.[i] Teste Grimaldo[j] medico. Apud Oxeneford.

[a] Anglie *B* [b] Anglie *B* [c] Wdestocha *B* [d] Anglie *B* [e] *initial om. C*
[f] Walengeford *B* [g] Anglie *B* [h] Abbendunæ *B* [i–i] abbatis Faritii *B*
[j] Grimbaldo *B*

---

[276] *RRAN* ii, no. 1612, dating to 1100 × 1129. On Warin, see Green, *Government*, p. 278.
[277] Lastage was a duty or toll levied on goods by the load or 'last'.
[278] *RRAN* ii, no. 1510; on dating, see above, p. xxxii.

goods belonging to the abbot and monks of Abingdon which their officials sell and buy, be quit of toll and custom and transport due, concerning which goods their men can pledge their faith that they are their own. And I forbid that anyone disturb them, on £10 of forfeiture. Witness: the chancellor. At Marlborough.

97. *Letters of the king to the reeve of Southampton.*[276]
Henry king of the English to Warin the reeve of Southampton and his officials, greeting. I order that the provisions and clothing of the abbot of Abingdon, and whatever his men can pledge their faith to be their own, be quit of all toll and lastage and custom and transport due.[277] And if anything has been taken therefrom contrary to this, let it be swiftly given back. Witness: William de Tancarville, through William of Calne. At Windsor.

98. *Likewise, to Warin the reeve.*[278]
Henry king of the English to Warin the reeve of Southampton and his officials, greeting. I order that you swiftly give back whatever you have taken from the abbot of Abingdon's own goods in relation to toll or custom, and henceforth take nothing as toll or custom or transport due from his goods, or from the things which his men can pledge their faith to be their own. Witness: Thomas of St John. At Woodstock.

99. *Concerning the customs of the church.*[279]
Henry king of the English to William sheriff of Oxford, greeting. I order that you allow and make St Mary of Abingdon have all those customs in respect of her men, and specifically concerning the brawl between Atselin's brother and Ansketel's squire, which she best and most fully had in the time of my father and brother.[280] And let no one dare to do her any harm in this matter contrary to this. Witness: Urse d'Abetot. At Wallingford.

100. *That no one may lodge in this town.*[281]
Henry king of the English to all his constables and faithful men of the court, greeting. I forbid that anyone lodge in the town of Abingdon without the permission of Abbot Faritius. Witness: Grimbald the physician. At Oxford.

[279] *RRAN* ii, no. 724. The writ can be dated to William's shrievalty, *c.*1100 × 1110.

[280] In 1086 Abingdon had a tenant called Atselin at Milton; *DB* i, fo. 59^{r}. Ansketel may be the man mentioned below, p. 198.

[281] *RRAN* ii, no. 1037. The writ can only be safely dated to 1100 × 1116, although *RRAN* suggests Feb./Mar. 1114.

[ii. 81] **101.** *Vt nemo hospitetur in Watelea.*[282]

Henricus rex Anglorum[a] Nigello de Oillei[b] et omnibus uenatoribus et mariscalcis[c] suis de curia, salutem. Prohibeo ne aliquis uestrum hospitet in Wateleia, terra sancte Marie de Abbendona, quia clamo eam quietam de hostagio, pro anima patris mei et matris mee. Testibus Grimaldo[d] medico et Areto falconario. Apud Corneberiam.

102. *De fugitiuis ecclesie.*[283]

Henricus rex Anglorum omnibus uicecomitibus et ministris suis totius Anglie in quorum baillia fugitiui abbatie de Abbendona inuenti fuerint, salutem. Precipio uobis quod plene et iuste faciatis habere abbati Abbendone omnes fugitiuos suos, cum tota pecunia et catallo suo, ubicumque[e] ipsi inuenti fuerint. Et prohibeo ne aliquis eos ei, uel pecuniam suam, super hoc iniuste detineat, super decem libras forisfacture. Teste cancellario. Apud Wodestoc'.[f]

103. *Item de fugitiuis.*[284]

Henricus rex Anglorum Hugoni de Bochelanda, et Roberto de Ferrariis, et Willelmo uicecomiti de Oxeneford, et Nicholao de Statford, salutem.[285] Precipio uobis ut iuste et sine mora faciatis
[ii. 82] redire ad abbatiam de Abbendona omnes fugitiuos suos, et cum tota pecunia sua, ubicumque[g] sint, et ita ne inde amplius clamorem audiam pro recti penuria. Et nominatim hominem qui est in terra Roberti de Ferrariis, et cum tota pecunia sua. Teste Rogero filio Ricardi. Apud Warengeford.[h]

104. *De fugitiuis de Weliford.*[i][286]

Henricus rex Anglorum omnibus uicecomitibus, et ministris, et fidelibus suis, Francis et Anglis, totius Anglie, salutem. Precipio uobis ut sine aliqua mora faciatis habere Faritio abbati de Abbendona omnes homines suos qui de terra sua exierunt de Walifort[j] propter

[a] Anglie *B* [b] Oilli *B* [c] marescalcis *B* [d] Arimbaldo *B* [e] ibicumque *C* [f] Wdestoc' *B* [g] ibicumque *C* [h] Walengeford *B* [i] Welliford *B* [j] Walingeford *B*

[282] *RRAN* ii, no. 961. The writ can only safely be dated to 1100 × *c.*1115, the *terminus ante quem* being the death of Nigel d'Oilly, although *RRAN* suggests 1110. Wheatley, Oxon., is not named in *Domesday*; see below, p. 324, for Sueting holding one and a half hides in Wheatley, and note the comments of *VCH*, *Oxfordshire*, v. 109–10.

[283] *RRAN* ii, no. 1799, dating to 1100 × 1133, although probably of Faritius's time; *Royal Writs*, ed. van Caenegem, no. 112; Lyell, no. 126. On fugitives, see P. R. Hyams, *Kings, Lords, and Peasants in Medieval England* (Oxford, 1980), esp. pp. 224–5, 229.

[284] *RRAN* ii, no. 726; *Royal Writs*, ed. van Caenegem, no. 108. The writ can be dated to William's shrievalty, *c.*1100 × 1110.

101. *That no one may lodge in Wheatley.*[282]
Henry king of the English to Nigel d'Oilly and all his huntsmen and marshals of the court, greeting. I forbid that any of you lodge in Wheatley, the land of St Mary of Abingdon, since I quitclaim it of the duty of providing lodging, for the soul of my father and my mother. Witnesses: Grimbald the physician and Aret the falconer. At Cornbury.

102. *Concerning the fugitives of the church.*[283]
Henry king of the English to all his sheriffs and officials of the whole of England in whose jurisdiction fugitives of the abbey of Abingdon are found, greeting. I order you that you fully and justly make the abbot of Abingdon have all his fugitives with all their goods and chattels, wherever they are found. And I forbid that anyone unjustly detain from him these men or their goods contrary to this, on £10 of forfeiture. Witness: the chancellor. At Woodstock.

103. *Likewise, concerning fugitives.*[284]
Henry king of the English to Hugh of Buckland, and Robert de Ferrers, and William sheriff of Oxford, and Nicholas of Stafford, greeting.[285] I order you that you justly and without delay have returned to the abbey of Abingdon all its fugitives with all their goods, wherever they may be, in such a way that I do not hear further complaint concerning this for want of justice. And namely the man who is in Robert de Ferrers' land, together with all his goods. Witness: Roger son of Richard. At Wallingford.

104. *Concerning the fugitives from Welford.*[286]
Henry king of the English to all his sheriffs, and officials, and faithful men, French and English, of the whole of England, greeting. I order you that without any delay you make Faritius abbot of Abingdon have all his men who left his land of Welford because of the lodging of my

[285] Robert de Ferrers was the son of Henry de Ferrers. He was created earl of Derby in 1138 and died in 1139; Sanders, *Baronies*, p. 148. The family had significant Berkshire and Oxfordshire lands. Nicholas of Stafford succeeded his father Robert of Stafford in *c.*1088, and himself lived until the mid or late 1130s; Sanders, *Baronies*, p. 81. The family had lands in Oxfordshire and Berkshire. *DB* i, fos. 60^{v}, 62^{r}, shows both families having lands at South Denchworth, Berks., very close to Abingdon's possessions, and this could be the place to which the fugitive had gone.

[286] *RRAN* ii, no. 856, dating to 1100 × 1107, the *terminus ante quem* being the death of Roger Bigod, whom *RRAN* suggests is the witness; *Royal Writs*, ed. van Caenegem, no. 110. The spellings on the earlier manuscript show the land concerned to be at Welford, not Wallingford. On Henry's attempts to control his household, see Green, *Government*, p. 27.

herberiam curie mee, uel propter alias res, et cum omni pecunia sua ubicumque sint. Teste Rogero Big',[a] per Aretum[b] falconarium. Apud Westmuster.

105. *De terra uasta apud Weliford.*[c] [287]

C fo. 151v Henricus rex Anglorum Rogero episcopo Salesbirie,[d] et Hugoni | de Bochelanda, et omnibus ministris et baronibus, Francis et Anglis, de Berchescira, salutem. Sciatis me concessisse Faritio abbati de Abbendona terram uastam de Waliford,[e] ut eam excolet sicut Crocus |
B fo. 140r uenator et Aluredus[f] de Lincolia ei monstrauerunt.[288] Testibus Aluredo[g] de Lincolia, et Droco uenatore, et Hugone[h] de Falesia. Apud Westmoster, in Natale Domini.

[ii. 83] **106.** *De terra uasta apud Weliford*[i] *et Ciuele.*[289]

Henricus rex Anglorum[j] Croco uenatori, salutem. Permitte lucrari terram monachorum Abbendone de Ciuelea et Waliford,[k] illam scilicet que non noceat foreste mee, et quod non sit de foresta mea. Teste Aluredo[l] de Lincolia. Apud Westmoster.

107. *De bosco apud Waliford.*[290]

Henricus rex Anglorum Hugoni de Bochelanda et ministris suis de Berchescira, salutem. Prohibeo ne aliquis capiat quicquam de bosco abbatis[m] de Abbendona, quod pertinet manerio suo de Waliford,[n] nisi licentia sui. Et ne patiamini ut aliquis quicquam inde capiat. Teste cancellario. Apud Niweberiam.

108. *De terra quam Rannulfus episcopus dedit Roberto de Calm'.*[291]

Henricus rex Anglorum Hugoni de Bochelanda, salutem. Precipio tibi ut sine mora facias habere ecclesie sancte Marie de Abbendona terram

[a] *apparent corr. from* pig. *to* big. *C*; pig' *B* [b] *initial om. B* [c] Welliford *B* [d] Saresberie *B* [e] Waliegeford *B* [f] Alfredus *B* [g] Alfredus *B* [h] Augone *B* [i] Welliford *B* [j] Anglie *B* [k] de Walieford, *corr. from* Walingeford *B* [l] Alfredo *B* [m] *followed by* de abbatis *struck out B* [n] Weliford, *corr. from* Walingford *B*

[287] *RRAN* ii, no. 615. After Roger became bishop of Salisbury and before the death of Faritius, Henry was at Westminster for Christmas in 1102, 1103, 1105, 1107, and 1109.

[288] *DB* i, fos. 49r, 74v, records Croc as holding lands in Hampshire and Dorset. He witnessed various documents of William II and Henry I, and had responsibilities concerning forest affairs in the New Forest and Berkshire, together with, presumably, duties regarding royal hunting; see e.g. *RRAN* i, nos. 319, 361; ii, p. xx, no. 754. Alfred of Lincoln may well have brought the relevant information to the king, as he acted as first witness.

[289] *RRAN* ii, no. 616, which suggests the same date as the previous writ. *DB* i, fo. 58v: 'The abbey itself holds Chieveley [Berks.], and always held it.'

court or for other reasons, with all their goods, wherever they may be. Witness: Roger *Pig'*, through Aret the falconer. At Westminster.

105. *Concerning the waste land at Welford.*[287]
Henry king of the English to Roger bishop of Salisbury, and Hugh of Buckland, and all officials and barons, French and English, of Berkshire, greeting. Know that I have granted to Faritius abbot of Abingdon the waste land of Welford, as Croc the huntsman and Alfred of Lincoln showed him, so that he may cultivate it.[288] Witnesses: Alfred of Lincoln, and Drogo the huntsman, and Hugh de Falaise. At Westminster, at Christmas.

106. *Concerning the waste land at Welford and Chieveley.*[289]
Henry king of the English to Croc the huntsman, greeting. Permit the land of the monks of Abingdon at Chieveley and Welford to be cultivated, that is such land as would not harm my forest nor be of my forest. Witness: Alfred of Lincoln. At Westminster.

107. *Concerning the wood at Welford.*[290]
Henry king of the English to Hugh of Buckland and his officials of Berkshire, greeting. I forbid that anyone take anything from the abbot of Abingdon's wood which pertains to his manor of Welford, except with his permission. And do not allow anyone to take anything therefrom. Witness: the chancellor. At Newbury.

108. *Concerning the land which Bishop Ranulf gave to Robert de Calzmont.*[291]
Henry king of the English to Hugh of Buckland, greeting. I order you that without delay you make the church of St Mary of Abingdon have

[290] *RRAN* ii, no. 984. Hugh was sheriff until at least 1110, and possibly beyond; see Green, *Sheriffs*, p. 26.

[291] *RRAN* ii, no. 721, dating to 1100 × 1105, when a blow took away Robert son of Hamo's senses at the time of his capture, or at latest 1107 when Robert died; *Royal Writs*, ed. van Caenegem, no 73. W. the chancellor could be either William Giffard, chancellor 1100–1, or Waldric, chancellor 1103–7. The following writ shows the land concerned to have been in Wytham. A list in MS C in the same hand as the *History*, below, p. 388, mentions a Richard de *Calmont* holding one and a half hides in the large estate of Cumnor; his name follows that of Robert of Wytham. Another list, below, p. 326, mentions the land of William *Chaumum* at Wytham owing a quarter of a knight. *Red Book*, i. 306, has Richard de *Caumund* contributing to making up one and a half knights owed to Abingdon in 1166; the Abingdon version of the *Carta*, below, p. 390, specifies that Richard *Calmunt*'s contribution was one quarter of a knight. Another list, *CMA* ii. 312, has Beatriz *Kalemund* holding one and a half hides in Wytham. See also *Testa de Nevill*, ii. 853. It seems likely, therefore, that all were members of the same family. I have not been able to identify the family's toponym with any certainty; it most likely is a Calmont or Caumont in Normandy.

quam Rannulfus episcopus dedit Roberto de Calzmont, si illa terra est de dominio predicte ecclesie, quia nolo ut ecclesia quicquam perdat quod habere debeat. Testibus W. cancellario et R. filio Haimonis. Apud Westmoster.[a]

[ii. 84] **109.** *Confirmatio eiusdem terre.*[b][292]

Henricus rex Anglorum Hugoni de Bochelanda, et Willelmo uicecomiti de Oxeneford, et omnibus fidelibus suis de Berchescira et Oxeneford, salutem. Volo et concedo ut ecclesia et monachi de Abbendona habeant et teneant in dominio illam terram suam de Witteham quam Rannulfus Dunelmensis episcopus tenuit, sicuti predicta ecclesia et monachi predicti unquam melius tenuerunt et habuerunt, cuicumque terram de Estantona dedero. Et nulla iniuria eis super hoc fiat. Teste Roberto Linc' episcopo. Apud Wincestram, in Pascha, per ipsum Willelmum de Oxeneford.

110. *De hominibus de Fernham qui fenum abbatis acceperunt.*[293]

Henricus rex Anglorum Rogero episcopo Salesb', salutem. Mando tibi quod plenum rectum teneas abbati de Abbendona de hominibus meis de Fernham, de feno suo quod ui ceperunt de prato suo. Teste G. filio Pagani. Apud Wodestoc.[c]

111. *De una uirgata apud Estuna.*[294]

Henricus rex Anglorum[d] Hugoni de Bochelanda et Willelmo uicecomiti de Oxeneford, salutem. Precipite ex mei parte hominibus uestrorum uicecomitatuum ut ipsi, sicut me diligunt, ueritatem omnino dicant de tribus uirgatis terre quas Rualucus de Abrincis
[ii. 85] reclamat.[295] Et si pertinent ad manerium quod ego ei dedi de Estantona, habeat ipse. Sin autem, habeat ipsa abbatia de Abbendona. Teste Rogero[e] cancellario, per ⟨P⟩agen' Basset. Apud Grentebruge.

[a] Westmuster *B* [b] ecclesie *B* [c] Wdestoc' *B* [d] Anglie *B* [e] *initial om. C*

[292] *RRAN* ii, no. 527. This writ and the next document but one date to 1101 × 2. This and later mentions of Stanton probably refer to Stanton Harcourt, across the river Thames from Wytham.

[293] *RRAN* ii, no. 1800, dating to *c.*1107 × 1133, between Geoffrey's earliest attestation and Henry's final departure from England. Fernham, Berks., is not named in *Domesday* but was probably included in the large royal estate of Shrivenham, *DB* i, fo. 57[v].

the land which Bishop Ranulf gave to Robert de *Calzmont*, if that land is of the demesne of the aforesaid church, since I wish the church to lose nothing which it ought to have. Witnesses: W. the chancellor and Robert son of Hamo. At Westminster.

109. *Confirmation of the same land.*[292]
Henry king of the English to Hugh of Buckland, and William sheriff of Oxford, and all his faithful men of Berkshire and Oxford, greeting. I wish and grant that the church and monks of Abingdon have and hold in demesne their land of Wytham which Ranulf bishop of Durham held, as best the aforesaid church and monks ever held and had, to whomsoever I give the land of Stanton. And let no harm be done to them contrary to this. Witness: Robert bishop of Lincoln. At Winchester, at Easter, through William of Oxford himself.

110. *Concerning the men of Fernham who seized the abbot's hay.*[293]
Henry king of the English to Roger bishop of Salisbury, greeting. I instruct you that you do full justice to the abbot of Abingdon in relation to my men of Fernham concerning his hay, which they took by force from his meadow. Witness: Geoffrey son of Pain. At Woodstock.

111. *Concerning one virgate at Stanton.*[294]
Henry king of the English to Hugh of Buckland and William sheriff of Oxford, greeting. On my behalf, order the men of your counties that, just as they love me, they are to speak entirely the truth concerning three virgates of land which Rualon d'Avranches claims back.[295] And if they pertain to the manor of Stanton which I gave him, let him have them. If not, however, let the abbey of Abingdon have them. Witness: Roger the chancellor, through Pain Basset. At Cambridge.

[294] *RRAN* ii, no. 528; *Royal Writs*, ed. van Caenegem, no. 138. This writ probably dates to after the previous document but one, i.e. *RRAN* ii, no. 527. For the identification with Stanton Harcourt, see also *VCH*, *Oxfordshire*, xii. 274.

[295] Rualon was one of Henry I's most important military leaders. He married Maud, daughter of Emma, who was heiress of the honour of Folkestone. However, it is uncertain how much of that honour he possessed; Green, *Government*, pp. 271–2.

112. *De terra quam Radulfus de Chaureha dedit.*[296]

Henricus rex Anglorum Iordano de Sacceuilla, salutem.[297] Precipio tibi ut plenum rectum facias Faritio abbati et ecclesie de Abbendona de terra quam abstulisti eis, quam Radulfus de Chaisnesham[a] dedit ecclesie in elemosina. Et nisi sine mora feceris, precipio quod Walterus Giffardus faciat.[298] Et si ipse non fecerit, Hugo de Bochelanda faciat, ne inde clamorem audiam pro recti penuria. B fo. 140v Teste | Goisfredo[b] de Magnauilla. Apud Wodestoc'.

113. *Item de eadem terra.*[299]

Henricus rex Anglorum Waltero Giffardo et Agneti matri sue, salutem. Precipio ut teneatis plenum rectum Faritio abbati de Abbendona de terra quam Radulfus Chauresham[c] posuit ad Abbandonam[d] uestra concessione, et unde ecclesia fuit saisita.[e] Et ita facite, ne inde clamorem audiam pro recti penuria. Teste ⟨R⟩annulfo cancellario. Apud Windr'. |

[ii. 86] 114. *De terris quas Motbertus[f] dedit uel prestitit.*[300]

C fo. 152r Henricus rex Anglorum Hugoni de Bochelanda, salutem. Precipio tibi ut eas Abbendonam, et de omnibus terris, quas Modbertus dedit uel prestitit uel emit ab aliquo et dedit alii, resaisias ecclesiam et iuste facias habere, sicut de Herberto camerario et Warino Caluo et Turstino et Hugone et omnibus aliis; ita ne amplius inde pro recti penuria audiam clamorem.[301] Testibus Willelmo[g] cancellario et Rogero capellano. Apud Londoniam.[h]

115. *De dominiis huius ecclesie.*[302]

Henricus rex Anglorum Rogero episcopo Salesb', et Roberto episcopo Linc', et Hugoni de Bochelanda, et Willelmo de Oxeneford, et

[a] Caisnesham *B* [b] Goisfredi *B* [c] Kauresham *B* [d] Abbendonam *B* [e] saisiata *B* [f] Modbertus *B* [g] W. *C* [h] Lundoniam *B*

[296] *RRAN* ii, no. 974; *Royal Writs*, ed. van Caenegem, no. 36. The writ can only safely be dated to 1100 × *c.*1116, although *RRAN* suggests 1111, before Apr. 2. Van Caenegem suggests that the land involved in the dispute may itself have been in Caversham, but this is uncertain. Certainly Walter Giffard was lord of Caversham (below, n. 298), and he may be invoked later in the writ as tenant in chief of the land concerned. However, Hugh of Buckland is presumably invoked as sheriff in the county concerned. He was not sheriff of Oxfordshire, but of Berkshire, where Walter Giffard also held certain lands close to those of Abingdon, in West Hanney and Long Wittenham; see *DB* i, fo. 60r–v.

[297] See J. H. Round, *Peerage and Pedigree* (2 vols., London, 1910), i. 288, for Jordan's genealogy.

[298] Walter Giffard I was a cousin of William the Conqueror. His son Walter II, the *Domesday* tenant of Caversham (*DB* i, fo. 157v; then Oxon., now Berks.), was created earl

112. *Concerning the land which Ralph of Caversham gave.*[296]
Henry king of the English to Jordan de Sackville, greeting.[297] I order you that you do full justice to Abbot Faritius and the church of Abingdon concerning the land which you took away from them, which Ralph of Caversham gave to the church in alms. And if you do not do this without delay, I order that Walter Giffard is to do it.[298] And if he does not do it, Hugh of Buckland is to, so that I do not hear complaint concerning this for want of justice. Witness: Geoffrey de Mandeville. At Woodstock.

113. *Likewise, concerning the same land.*[299]
Henry king of the English to Walter Giffard and Agnes his mother, greeting. I order that you perform full justice to Faritius abbot of Abingdon concerning the land which Ralph of Caversham presented to Abingdon by your grant and whereof the church was seised. And do it in such a way that I do not hear complaint concerning this for want of justice. Witness: Ranulf the chancellor. At Windsor.

114. *Concerning the lands which Modbert gave or leased.*[300]
Henry king of the English to Hugh of Buckland, greeting. I order you that you go to Abingdon and reseise the church concerning all the lands which Modbert gave, or leased, or bought from someone and gave to another, and make the church have them justly, concerning Herbert the chamberlain, and Warin the bald, and Thurstan, and Hugh, and all others; in such a way that I do not hear further complaint concerning this for want of justice.[301] Witnesses: William the chancellor and Roger the chaplain. At London.

115. *Concerning the demesnes of this church.*[302]
Henry king of the English to Roger bishop of Salisbury, and Robert bishop of Lincoln, and Hugh of Buckland, and William of Oxford,

of Buckingham in *c.*1093. He married Agnes, sister of Anselm de Ribemont, and died in 1102, leaving Walter III, who died without offspring in 1164; Sanders, *Baronies*, p. 62. At the time of this case he was presumably still a minor, hence his mother being included in the address of the next writ.

[299] *RRAN* ii, no. 979. The writ can only be safely dated to between *c.*1107, when Ranulf became chancellor, and 1116, although *RRAN* suggests 1111, probably before Aug. 4.

[300] *RRAN* ii, no. 521, dating to 1100 × 1101, the *terminus ante quem* being when William ceased to be chancellor; *Royal Writs*, ed. van Caenegem, no. 71. For Modbert's grants, see above, p. 62.

[301] Probably Thurston of St Helen; below, p. 192. Hugh must be Hugh de Dun, despite the mention of his alienating lands. See above, pp. lxxi, 52, 58, 62.

[302] *RRAN* ii, no. 613. After Roger became bishop of Salisbury and before the death of Faritius, Henry was at Westminster for Christmas in 1102, 1103, 1105, 1107, and

[*See p. 128 for n. 302 cont.*]

baronibus suis omnibus et fidelibus, Francis et Anglis, de Berchescira et Oxenefordscira, salutem. Sciatis me concessisse et in perpetuum firmiter reddidisse Deo et sancte Marie de Abbendona, et Faritio abbati et omnibus successoribus suis, omnia dominia, quicumque tenet ea, quocumque modo, et ubicumque, sicut eadem ecclesia habebat ea die quando pater meus rex Willelmus dedit Rainaldo abbati abbatiam de Abbendona. Testibus Mathilde regina, et Rogero episcopo Salesb', et Rainaldo cancellario, et W. Werelwast. Apud Westmoster, in Natale Domini.

[ii. 87] **116.** *Carta de dominiis huius ecclesie.*[303]
Henricus rex Anglorum[a] Roberto Linc', et Rogero Salesb' episcopo, et Hugoni de Bochelanda, et Willelmo de Oxeneford, et omnibus baronibus suis, Francis et Anglis, de Berchescira et de Oxenefordscira, salutem. Sciatis me reddidisse et in perpetuum firmiter concessisse Deo et sancte Marie de Abbendona, et Faritio abbati et omnibus successoribus suis, omnia dominia,[b] quicumque tenet ea, quoquomodo teneat, et ubicumque sint, sicut ipsa abbatia ea habebat ea die qua pater meus rex Willelmus dedit Rainaldo abbati abbatiam de Abbendona. Et uolo et firmiter precipio ut in pace et honorifice teneat, et nulli a dominio monachorum ea dominia extrahere liceat. Testibus Mathilde regina et Rogero episcopo Salesb'. Apud Westmoster, in Natale Domini.

117. *Carta de Winekefeld.*[c][304]
Henricus rex Anglorum Hugoni de Bochelanda, et Godrico, et baronibus de Berchescira, Francis et Anglis, salutem. Volo et precipio ut ecclesia sancte Marie de Abbendona habeat et teneat terram suam de Winicfelda,[d] cum omnibus sibi pertinentibus, ita bene et honorifice et in firma pace, sicut melius eam tenuit tempore patris[e] et fratris mei. Et precipio ut calumpnia quam God',
[ii. 88] prepositus de Windresores, super eam terram facit[f] de haia omnino et perpetualiter remaneat.[305] Testibus Rogero Bigod et Grimaldo[g] medico. Apud Norhamtonam. |

[a] Anglie *B* [b] domina *B* [c] Winkefeld *B* [d] Winkefelda *B* [e] patris mei *B* [f] faciat *B* [g] Grimbaldo *B*

1109. *RRAN* treats this and the following writ as basically the same document, of which the latter is the fuller version in that it includes extra clauses at the end. Given the order in which the bishops appear at the start of the writ, it is conceivable that the first was to the court of Berkshire, the second to that of Oxfordshire.

and all his barons and faithful men, French and English, of Berkshire and Oxfordshire, greeting. Know that I have granted and firmly given back in perpetuity to God, and to St Mary of Abingdon, and to Abbot Faritius, and to all his successors, all demesnes, whoever holds them in whatever way and wherever, as that church had them on the day when my father King William gave the abbey of Abingdon to Abbot Reginald. Witnesses: Queen Matilda, and Roger bishop of Salisbury, and Reginald the chancellor, and William Warelwast. At Westminster, at Christmas.

116. *Charter concerning the demesnes of this church.*[303]
Henry king of the English to Robert of Lincoln, and Roger bishop of Salisbury, and Hugh of Buckland, and William of Oxford, and all his barons, French and English, of Berkshire and of Oxfordshire, greeting. Know that I have given back and firmly granted in perpetuity to God, and to St Mary of Abingdon, and to Abbot Faritius, and to all his successors, all demesnes, whoever holds them, in whatever way he holds and wherever they are, as that abbey had them on the day on which my father King William gave the abbey of Abingdon to Abbot Reginald. And I wish and firmly order that the abbey hold in peace and honourably, and no one is to be permitted to remove these demesnes from the monks' demesne. Witnesses: Queen Matilda and Roger bishop of Salisbury. At Westminster, at Christmas.

117. *Charter concerning Winkfield.*[304]
Henry king of the English to Hugh of Buckland, and Godric, and the barons of Berkshire, French and English, greeting. I wish and order that the church of St Mary of Abingdon have and hold its land of Winkfield, with everything pertaining to it, as well and honourably and in secure peace as it best held it in the time of my father and brother. And I order that the claim which God' the reeve of Windsor makes on this land concerning a hedge be completely and perpetually stayed.[305] Witnesses: Roger Bigod and Grimbald the physician. At Northampton.

303 *RRAN* ii, no. 613.
304 *RRAN* ii, no. 736; Lyell, no. 81, Chatsworth, no. 176; *English Lawsuits*, no. 171. The writ dates to 1100 × 1107, the *terminus ante quem* being the death of Roger Bigod; *RRAN* suggests 1 × 7 Feb. 1106.
305 Lyell, no. 81, calls the reeve 'Godefridus'.

B fo. 141r **118.** *Carta de sale apud Wiche.*[a] [306]

Henricus rex Anglorum Vrsoni[b] de Wirecestra uicecomiti, salutem.[307] Precipio tibi ut salem monachorum de Abbendona permittas esse ab omni theloneo et consuetudinibus quietum, et bene precipias tuis ministris de Wice ne supradictorum monachorum rebus forisfaciant, et ita ne amplius clamorem inde audiam. Teste Hugone de Bochelanda. Apud Suttunam.

119. *Confirmatio carte regis Eadwardi.*[308]

Henricus rex Anglorum omnibus uicecomitibus suis et omnibus suis fidelibus totius regni[c] Anglie, salutem. Sciatis me concessisse sancte Marie Abbendonie omnes consuetudines terrarum suarum, quecumque iacent in ecclesia predicta, ubicumque eas habeat, in burgo uel extra burgum, secundum quod monachi eiusdem loci poterunt demonstrare, per breuem[d] uel cartam, ecclesiam sancte Marie de Abbendona habuisse dono regis Eadwardi, et secundum quod pater meus et frater concesserunt per breuia sua. Teste Eudone[e] dapifero. Apud Westmoster, in nuptiis meis.

[ii. 89] **120.** *De consuetudinibus huius ecclesie.*[309]

Henricus rex Anglorum[f] omnibus uicecomitibus suis [g]in quorum uicecomitatibus[g] et ministeriis abbatia Abbendone terras habet, |
C fo. 152r salutem. Precipio ut tota terra abbatie de Abbendona ita plene[h] et pleniter habeat sacam suam et socam et omnes consuetudines suas, in burgo et extra burgum, sicut melius habuit et plenius tempore regis Eadwardi et patris mei, et latronem similiter sicuti tunc temporis habuit.[310] Et defendo ne aliquis ei inde iniuriam faciat. Teste Eudone dapifero. Apud Westmoster, in nuptiis meis. Et etiam sicuti frater meus per breuem[i] suum precepit. Teste eodem.

121. *De terra Perchehaia.*[311]

Henricus rex Anglorum Ricardo de Monte et omnibus baronibus, Francis et Anglis, de Oxenefordsira,[j] salutem.[312] Sciatis quia uolo et

[a] Winkefeld *B* [b] Vrsone *B C* [c] *om. B* [d] breue, *with* m *at end erased B* [e] Eudo *B* [f] Anglie *B* [g–g] *om. B*, suis *having been interlined* [h] *for* bene ?; *cf. above, p. 20* [i] breue, *corr. from* breuem, *by deletion in red ink B* [j] Oxenefordscira *B*

[306] *RRAN* ii, no. 566. The writ can be dated to 1100 × 1108, the *terminus ante quem* being the death of Urse. For general background, see D. Hooke, 'The Droitwich salt industry', *Anglo-Saxon Studies in Archaeology and History*, ii, ed. D. Brown, J. Campbell, and S. C. Hawkes (*British Archaeological Reports*, British Series, xcii, 1981), 123–69.

[307] Urse d'Abetot was probably sheriff of Worcestershire by 1069 and remained so until his death in 1108; Green, *Sheriffs*, p. 87.

118. *Charter concerning the salt at Droitwich.*[306]
Henry king of the English to Urse sheriff of Worcestershire, greeting.[307] I order you that you permit the salt of the monks of Abingdon to be quit of all toll and customs, and that you order effectively your officials of Droitwich that they do no wrong to the possessions of the said monks, and in such a way that I do not hear further complaint concerning this. Witness: Hugh of Buckland. At Sutton [Courtenay].

119. *Confirmation of the charter of King Edward.*[308]
Henry king of the English to all his sheriffs and all his faithful men of the whole realm of England, greeting. Know that I have granted to St Mary of Abingdon all the customs of their lands which belong to the aforesaid church, wherever it has them, in borough or out of borough, as the monks of that monastery can show by writ or charter that the church of St Mary of Abingdon had by gift of King Edward and as my father and brother granted by their writs. Witness: Eudo the steward. At Westminster, at my wedding [11 Nov. 1100].

120. *Concerning the customs of this church.*[309]
Henry king of the English to all his sheriffs in whose counties and jurisdictions the abbey of Abingdon has lands, greeting. I order that all the land of the abbey of Abingdon have its sake and soke and all its customs, in borough and out of borough, as full and fully as it best and most fully had in the time of King Edward and of my father, and likewise rights over theft as they then had.[310] And I forbid that anyone do it harm concerning this. Witness: Eudo the steward. At Westminster, at my wedding. And also as my brother ordered by his writ. Witness: the same.

121. *Concerning Percehai's land.*[311]
Henry king of the English to Richard de Monte and all the barons, French and English, of Oxfordshire, greeting.[312] Know that I wish

[308] *RRAN* ii, no. 499; Lyell, no. 73; for the charter of Edward the Confessor probably referred to here, see above, Bk. i, cc. 127–8 (*CMA* i. 464–5 = *Charters of Abingdon Abbey*, no. 148).

[309] *RRAN* ii, no. 499; Lyell, no. 74.

[310] Rights over theft may have been equivalent to infangentheof, on which see above, p. xcvii.

[311] *RRAN* ii, no. 1132, dating to between 1110, when Richard was sheriff of Oxford, and 1116. I take 'Percehaia' to be Ralph de *Percehai*, who married one of the daughters of Gilbert Latimer, above, p. 48; *RRAN* ii, p. 133, suggests that it means the daughter herself.

[312] The addressee is Richard sheriff of Oxford.

precipio ut abbas Faritius et abbatia de Abbendona in pace et sine calumpnia[a] omnium hominum teneant terram in Gersendona quam Perchehaia tenebat. Et nulli inde respondeant, et ita bene teneant sicut abbatia tenuit tempore patris et fratris mei et meo. Testibus Iohanne episcopo Luxouii et Gilleberto filio[b] Ricardi. Apud Windres'.[c]

[ii. 90] **122.** *De presbitero latrone.*[313]
Henricus rex Anglorum Hugoni de Bochelanda, et Albrico, et omnibus baronibus, Francis et Anglis, de Berchesira[d] salutem.[314] Sciatis me concessisse Faritio, abbati sancte Marie de Abbendona, ut ipse faciat iusticiam suam de presbitero latrone, qui in captione sua in Abbendona est. Et de aliis latronibus suis, faciat iusticiam suam similiter, uidente comitatu. Teste Rogero Bigod, per Walterum Hosatum. Apud Bruhellam.

123. *Ad[e] milites huius ecclesie.*[315]
Henricus rex Anglorum omnibus baronibus abbatie de Abbendona, salutem. Volo et uobis firmiter precipio ut faciatis wardam meam de Windresores, sicut solebatis facere tempore Rainaldi abbatis et tempore fratris mei, et sicut abbas Faritius uobis preceperit;[f] et sitis ei obedientes. Et multum me piget de hoc, quod preceptum
B fo. 141v eius | non facitis, uti facere deberetis. Teste Vrsone[g] de Abetot. Apud Wareng'.

124. *[h]Carta ut[h] Hugo filius Turstini faciat quod terre sue pertinet.*[316]
[ii. 91] Henricus rex Anglorum Faritio abbati de Abbendona, salutem. Si Hugo filius Turstini noluerit facere seruitium quod terre sue tibi pertinet, in operatione parcorum et pontium, et de omnibus aliis rebus, tunc precipio ut tu ipse inde iusticiam facias, ut omnia que facere debet faciat. Teste cancellario. Apud Pontem Arcarum.

125. *Vt Hugo filius Turstini geldat.*[317]
Henricus rex Anglorum Hugoni filio Turstini, salutem. Precipio tibi ut ita geldas cum Faritio abbate de Abbendona, sicut geldare solebas,

[a] calumnia *B* [b] filius *B* [c] Windresores *B* [d] Berchescira *B* [e] De *B* [f] precepit *B* [g] *initial om. C* [h–h] Quod *B*

[313] *RRAN* ii, no. 695; *English Lawsuits*, no. 169; the writ can only be dated to 1100 × 1107, the *terminus ante quem* being the death of Roger Bigod, although *RRAN* suggests Oct. 1105. See also above, p. xcvii.
[314] Aubrey is probably Aubrey de Ver, and may be addressed as the local justiciar.
[315] *RRAN* ii, no. 725; *EHD* ii, no. 243. The writ can be dated to 1100 × 1108, the

and order that Abbot Faritius and the abbey of Abingdon are to hold the land in Garsington which *Percehai* held, in peace and unchallenged by any man. And they are to answer to no one concerning it, and are to hold as well as the abbey held in the time of my father and brother and myself. Witnesses: John bishop of Lisieux and Gilbert son of Richard. At Windsor.

122. *Concerning the priest who is a thief.*[313]
Henry king of the English to Hugh of Buckland, and Aubrey, and all the barons, French and English, of Berkshire, greeting.[314] Know that I have granted to Faritius abbot of St Mary of Abingdon that he do his justice concerning the thieving priest who is in his custody at Abingdon. And let him similarly do his justice concerning his other thieves, with the county court looking on. Witness: Roger Bigod, through Walter Huse. At Brill.

123. *To the knights of this church.*[315]
Henry king of the English to all the barons of the abbey of Abingdon, greeting. I wish and firmly order you that you do my guard service concerning Windsor as you were accustomed to do in the time of Abbot Reginald and the time of my brother, and as Abbot Faritius orders you; and you are to be obedient to him. And it displeases me greatly that you do not carry out his order concerning this, as you ought to do. Witness: Urse d'Abetot. At Wallingford.

124. *Charter that Hugh son of Thurstan do what pertains to his land.*[316]
Henry king of the English to Faritius abbot of Abingdon, greeting. If Hugh son of Thurstan is unwilling to do the service which pertains to you for his land, in work on parks and bridges and concerning all other things, then I order that you yourself do justice concerning this, so that he does everything which he ought to do. Witness: the chancellor. At Pont de l'Arche.

125. *That Hugh son of Thurstan pay geld.*[317]
Henry king of the English to Hugh son of Thurstan, greeting. I order you that you pay geld with Faritius abbot of Abingdon in the way you

terminus ante quem being the death of Urse d'Abetot. See above, p. 6 n. 11, on castle-guard.

[316] *RRAN* ii, no. 789, suggesting a date of 1106.

[317] *RRAN* ii, no. 576. The document may date to before the settlement with Hugh son of Thurstan in 1105, below, p. 184; *RRAN* suggests Jul. 1102 on the basis of Wolverhampton being on the way to Bridgnorth, besieged by Henry in 1102.

et ita ne amodo terra sua sit esnamiata pro terra tua, super decem libras forisfacturam meam. Quod nisi cito feceris, Albricus de Berchesira[a] te constringat per pecuniam tuam ut cito facias, et ita ne inde amplius clamorem audiam, super decem libras forisfacture.[318] Teste Roberto episcopo Linc'. Apud Wlnrunehamtonam.[b]

126. *De terra Roberti Maledocti.*[319]
Henricus rex Anglorum[c] Roberto Maledocto, salutem. Precipio tibi ut abbati Faritio facias seruitium terre quam tenes, sicut tui antecessores fecerunt tempore Adelelmi abbatis. Et nisi feceris, tunc precipio ut abbas predictus de terra sua, quam tenes, suam uoluntatem faciat. Teste Ricardo de Retueris.[d] Apud Becchelegam.[e]

[ii. 92] **127.** *De Budena.*[320]
Henricus rex Anglorum Gotselino de Riparia, salutem. Precipio ut faciatis Faritio abbati de Abbendona tale seruitium de feudo quod de eo et de abbatia sua tenes, quale fratres tui fecerunt antecessori suo A. Quod nisi feceris,[f] ipse abbas inde te constringat per feudum tuum. Teste Roberto filio Hamonis, per W. de la Rochella. Apud Lundoniam.

128. *De exclusa quam homines de Estona fregerunt.*[321]
Henricus rex Anglorum Nigello de Oilli et Willelmo uicecomiti de Oxen', salutem. Precipio uobis ut faciatis abbati de Abbendona
C fo. 153r plenariam rectitudinem de exclusa sua quam | homines de Estantona fregerunt, et ita ne amplius inde clamorem audiam pro recti penuria, et hoc super decem libras forisfacture. Teste Rannulfo cancellario. Apud Westmoster.

129. *De hominibus de Stantona qui fregerunt exclusam abbatis.*[322]
Henricus rex Anglorum Willelmo uicecomite de Oxeneford, salutem. Fac cito et sine mora plenam iusticiam Faritio abbati de hominibus de
[ii. 93] Stantona qui fregerunt exclusam suam, et ita ne inde amplius pro

[a] Berchescira *B* [b] Wlfrunehamtune *B* [c] Anglie *B* [d] Retueres *B* [e] Becceleam *B* [f] feceritis *B*

[318] Aubrey of Berkshire is probably Aubrey de Ver, and may be acting as local justiciar.

[319] *RRAN* ii, no. 697, dating to ?Oct. 1105 on the grounds that William Mauduit probably died in or before 1105. Certainly it must be from before the death of Richard de Redvers in 1107. Robert Mauduit was a chamberlain of Henry I; see *Beauchamp Cartulary*, ed. Mason, p. xxvi. This writ probably concerns Weston, Berks., for which Robert was Abingdon's tenant; below, p. 198. *DB* i, fo. 58v, states that 'William [Mauduit holds] four hides in Weston' from Abingdon.

[320] *RRAN* ii, no. 553. The resultant case was one of three heard in a single day in 1103,

were accustomed to pay geld, and in such a way that his land may henceforward not be distrained for your land, on my forfeiture of £10. If you do not do this swiftly, Aubrey of Berkshire is to distrain you by your goods that you do it swiftly, and in such a way that I do not hear further complaint concerning this, on £10 of forfeiture.[318] Witness: Robert bishop of Lincoln. At Wolverhampton.

126. *Concerning the land of Robert Mauduit.*[319]
Henry king of the English to Robert Mauduit, greeting. I order you that you do Abbot Faritius service for the land which you hold, as your ancestors did in the time of Abbot Adelelm. And if you do not, then I order that the aforesaid abbot is to do as he wishes concerning his land which you hold. Witness: Richard de Redvers. At Beckley.

127. *Concerning Beedon.*[320]
Henry king of the English to Jocelin de Rivers, greeting. I order that you do Faritius abbot of Abingdon such service from the fee which you hold from him and his abbey as your brothers did his predecessor A[delelm]. If you do not do this, let the abbot himself distrain you concerning this by your fee. Witness: Robert son of Hamo, through W. de la Rochelle. At London.

128. *Concerning the sluice which the men of Stanton broke.*[321]
Henry king of the English to Nigel d'Oilly and William sheriff of Oxford, greeting. I order you that you do the abbot of Abingdon full justice concerning his sluice which the men of Stanton broke, and in such a way that I do not hear further complaint concerning this for want of justice, and this on £10 of forfeiture. Witness: Ranulf the chancellor. At Westminster.

129. *Concerning the men of Stanton who broke the abbot's sluice.*[322]
Henry king of the English to William sheriff of Oxford, greeting. Swiftly and without delay do full justice to Abbot Faritius concerning the men of Stanton who broke his sluice, and in such a way that I do

see below, p. 188. One of them was started by *RRAN* ii, no. 651, (below, p. 136), which dates to the summer of 1103; the present writ is likely to be from a similar date. Beedon had been held by Walter de Rivers from Abingdon in 1086; see above, p. 30 n. 72.

321 *RRAN* ii, no. 814; *Royal Writs*, ed. van Caenegem, no. 141. The writ dates from between 1107, when Ranulf became chancellor, and 1110 when William ceased to be sheriff. The sluice would presumably be on the Thames. It cannot be certain why Nigel d'Oilly was included in the address; one possibility is that he was a local justice.

322 *RRAN* ii, no. 815, dating to after the previous writ; *Royal Writs*, ed. van Caenegem, no. 142.

recti penuria clamorem audiam, super decem libras forisfacture.[a] Teste Eudone dapifero. Apud Corneberiam.

130. *De terra quam tenuit Willelmus Gemmeticensis.*[323]
Henricus rex Anglorum Hugoni de Bochelanda et Albrico, salutem. Sciatis quod uolo ut Faritius abbas de Abbendona reddat Willelmo Iemmeticensi totam pecuniam suam, scilicet in annona sicca et in pecudibus, quam apportauit ad terram suam de terris aliis. De domibus uero et annonis uiridis et ceteris aliis rebus, fiat rectitudo iusto iudicio comitatus. De terra autem illa, faciat predictus abbas
B fo. 142r suam uoluntatem, sicut | ei per breue[b] meum concessi, et nulli inde super hoc respondeat. Teste Waldrico[c] cancellario. Apud Brantonam.

131. *De terra de Hylle.*[324]
Henricus rex Anglorum H. comiti de Warewic et W. uicecomiti, salutem.[325] Si Goslinus[d] quid clamauerit in terra sancte Marie de Abbendona quam habet apud Hyllam, precipio ut ipse Goslinus eat in curiam abbatis, et ipse abbas sit ibi[e] ei ad rectum. Et[f] defendo ipsi abbati quod non respondeat inde Goslinus in alio loco. Testibus Waldrico cancellario et Grimaldo[g] medico. Apud Westmoster, in Natale Domini.

[ii. 94] **132.** *De quinque hidis apud Wrtha.*[326]
Henricus rex Anglorum Rogero episcopo Salesbirie, et Hugoni[h] de Bochelanda, et omnibus fidelibus suis de Berchesira,[i] salutem. Sciatis me omnino quietas clamasse quinque hidas terre de Wrda[j] de terra monachorum de omnibus consuetudinibus meis, scilicet de geldis et placitis et aliis rebus, ad opus elemosine ipsius ecclesie. Et nullus sit ausus predicte terre, uel hominibus in ea manentibus, ullomodo[k] super hoc iniuriam aliquam facere. Quod siquis fecerit, mihi

[a] forisfactione *B* [b] *corr. from* breuem *B C* [c] *initial om. B*
[d] Goscelinus *B* [e] *om. B* [f] *written twice in B, at end and start of line*
[g] Grimbaldo *B* [h] Hugo *B* [i] Berchscira *B* [j] Wrða *B* [k] ullo modo *B*

323 *RRAN* ii, no. 651, dating to summer 1103, after Waldric became chancellor about Sept. 1102, and before the death of Serlo abbot of Gloucester (see below, p. 191), on 3 Mar. 1104; this leaves mid-1103 as the only time when there would have been significant green corn in the fields; *Royal Writs*, ed. van Caenegem, no. 5. The writ concerns a dispute about Bradley, see below, p. 188. William's toponymic surname suggests he had links with Abbot Adelelm or Reginald, both of whom came from Jumièges. A Thomas de 'Gimeges' held half a fee at Bradley in 1242–3; *Testa de Nevill*, ii. 844, 846, 853. See also above, p. lix.

324 *RRAN* ii, no. 654; *Royal Writs*, ed. van Caenegem, no. 6; *English Lawsuits*, no. 165.

not hear further complaint concerning this for want of justice, on £10 of forfeiture. Witness: Eudo the steward. At Cornbury.

130. *Concerning the land which William de Jumièges held.*[323]
Henry king of the English to Hugh of Buckland and Aubrey, greeting. Know that I wish that Faritius abbot of Abingdon give back to William de Jumièges all his goods—that is dry corn and beasts—which he took to his own land from other lands. Concerning the houses, indeed, and the green corn, and the other things, let him do justice by the just judgment of the county. Concerning that land, moreover, let the aforesaid abbot do his will, as I granted him by my writ, and concerning this let him answer to no one contrary to this. Witness: Waldric the chancellor. At Brampton.

131. *Concerning the land of Hill.*[324]
Henry king of the English to Henry earl of Warwick and William the sheriff, greeting.[325] If Jocelin claims anything in the land of St Mary of Abingdon which it has at Hill, I order that Jocelin himself go to the abbot's court, and let the abbot himself there do justice to him. And I forbid that Jocelin answer to the abbot concerning this elsewhere. Witnesses: Waldric the chancellor and Grimbald the physician. At Westminster, at Christmas.

132. *Concerning five hides at Longworth.*[326]
Henry king of the English to Roger bishop of Salisbury, and Hugh of Buckland, and all his faithful men of Berkshire, greeting. Know that I entirely quitclaim of all my customs—that is gelds and pleas and other things—five hides of land at Longworth, the monks' land, for the use of the alms of that church. And let no one dare to do any harm in any way to the aforesaid land or the men living on it, contrary to this. If anyone does, he will be in forfeiture to me. Witnesses: Queen

During Waldric's chancellorship, Henry was at Westminster for Christmas in 1102, 1103, and 1105. Van Caenegem takes Jocelin to be Jocelin de Rivers, but there is no secure evidence for this identification. Hill is listed amongst Faritius's acquisitions in *De abbatibus*; *CMA* ii. 288. See also above, p. 10.

[325] The identity of William sheriff of Warwickshire is uncertain, with William son of Corbucio and William de Cahaignes being possibilities; Green, *Sheriffs*, p. 83.

[326] *RRAN* ii, no. 722, dating to 1102 × 1105, between Roger becoming bishop of Salisbury and Robert son of Hamo's loss of his senses, or at the latest Robert's death in 1107. The place concerned is Longworth, not Littleworth in Faringdon, as *RRAN* suggests. Cf. below, p. 166. 'Five hides in Longworth' are listed amongst Faritius's acquisitions in *De abbatibus*; *CMA* ii. 288.

forisfactus sit. Testibus Mathilde regina et [a]Roberto filio[a] Haimonis, per Reinerum de Carisburc.[b] Apud Ceat.

133. *De decima foreste de Windlesores.*[327]
Henricus rex Anglorum W.[c] filio Walteri, et Croco uenatori, et Ricardo seruienti, et omnibus ministris de foresta Windresores,[d] salutem.[328] Sciatis me concessisse Deo et sancte Marie de Abbendona totam decimam de uenatione que capta fuerit in foresta de Windesores. Testibus Roberto episcopo Linc' et Eudone[e] dapifero. Apud Bruhellam.[f]

134. *De hominibus de Wisselea.*[329]
Henricus rex Anglorum W. Osato, salutem. Precipio tibi ut dimittas
[ii. 95] in pace homines abbatis de Abbendona qui sunt in Wisseleia, quos requiris, quia ego clamo eos quietos. Teste Rogero Bigod.[g] Apud Wind'.

135. *De consuetudine nauium per Tamisiam transeuntium.*[330]
Henricus rex Anglorum Rogero episcopo Salesbirie, et Roberto Lincolie episcopo, et Hugoni[h] de Bochelanda, et Willelmo uicecomiti de Oxeneford, et omnibus baronibus et ministris suis de utraque scira, salutem. Volo et precipio ut ecclesia de Abbendona et monachi habeant suas consuetudines in nauibus transeuntibus, scilicet in accipiendis allecibus et in mercatis faciendis, sicuti unquam melius et plenius habuit, tempore regis Eadwardi et patris[i] et fratris mei, et meo tempore. Teste Willelmo episcopo Exonie. Apud Merlebergam. Et testibus Eustachio de Britoil et Patricio de Cadurcis.

136. *Item de consuetudine nauium.*[331]
Henricus rex Anglorum Hugoni[j] de Bochelanda et Willelmo de Oxeneford uicecomiti, salutem. Precipio uobis ut faciatis Faritio abbati de Abbendona et omnibus monachis Abbendone habere omnes consuetudines in omnibus rebus quas habere debent per aquam Tamisie, ubicumque habere debent. Et ita ne pro penuria

[a–a] Robertus filius *B* [b] Kerisburc *B* [c] Willelmo *B* [d] Windesor' *B* [e] Eudo *B* [f] Burhellam *B* [g] Bigot *B* [h] Hugo *B* [i] mei *add. B* [j] Hugo *B*

[327] *RRAN* ii, no. 696; Lyell, no. 82. The writ can only safely be dated to 1100 × 1116, although *RRAN* suggests Oct. 1105, partly on the grounds that 'Croc the huntsman does not appear to attest later than 1106'. This tithe is listed amongst Faritius's acquisitions in *De abbatibus*; *CMA* ii. 288.

[328] William was the son of Walter son of Other, mentioned above, p. 10. William was

Matilda and Robert son of Hamo, through Reiner of Carisbrooke. At Chute.

133. *Concerning the tithe of the forest of Windsor.*[327]
Henry king of the English to William son of Walter, and Croc the huntsman, and Richard the sergeant, and all his officials of the forest of Windsor, greeting.[328] Know that I have granted to God and to St Mary of Abingdon the entire tithe of game which is taken in the forest of Windsor. Witnesses: Robert bishop of Lincoln and Eudo the steward. At Brill.

134. *Concerning the men of Whistley.*[329]
Henry king of the English to W. Huse, greeting. I order you that you leave in peace the men of Abingdon who are in Whistley, whom you claim, since I quitclaim them. Witness: Roger Bigod. At Windsor.

135. *Concerning the customs of boats passing along the Thames.*[330]
Henry king of the English to Roger bishop of Salisbury, and Robert bishop of Lincoln, and Hugh of Buckland, and William sheriff of Oxford, and all his barons and officials of either shire, greeting. I wish and order that the church of Abingdon and the monks have their customs in passing boats, that is in receiving herrings and making purchases, as they ever had them best and most fully in the time of King Edward and of my father and brother, and in my time. Witness: William bishop of Exeter. At Marlborough. Also witnesses: Eustace de Breteuil and Patrick of Chaworth.

136. *Likewise, concerning the custom of boats.*[331]
Henry king of the English to Hugh of Buckland and William sheriff of Oxford, greeting. I order you that you make Faritius abbot of Abingdon and all the monks of Abingdon have all customs in all things which they ought to have on the water of the Thames, wherever they ought to have them. And thus that the church itself

constable of Windsor; see Green, *Government*, p. 254, Round, 'Origins of FitzGeralds', pp. 124–5.

[329] *RRAN* ii, no. 857, dating to 1100 × 1107, the *terminus ante quem* being the death of Roger Bigod. *RRAN* gives the addressee the name William, but provides no reason for so doing.

[330] *RRAN* ii, no. 937. The writ can only safely be dated to between 1102, when Roger became bishop of Salisbury, and *c.*1110, when William ceased to be sheriff of Oxford; *RRAN* suggests 10 Apr. 1110, on the grounds that Henry was at Marlborough at Easter 1110.

[331] *RRAN* ii, no. 854, dating to 1100 × 1107, the *terminus ante quem* being the death of Roger Bigod; Chatsworth, no. 209. See below, p. 174, for further mention of this writ.

iusticie uestre ipsa ecclesia uel monachi quicquam perdant, super decem libras.[a] Teste Rogero Bigod,[b] per Aret[c] falconarium. |

[ii. 96] 137. *De terra inter Hamstede et Merlaue.*[332]

C fo. 153v Roberto filio Haimonis multa medele beneficia abbas Faritius fre-
B fo. 142v quenter impenderat.[333] | Quare ipse morti debitum soluendi tempori appropinquans, cum abbatis summonitu, suam ob memoriam aliquod pietatis uestigium, prouenturis cum Deo, tum quoque si recordaretur sua circa se plurima officia, pro sua gratia, monasterio Abbendonensi indiceretur pie debere deferre; intendit monitis, et quandam terre portionem, in qua plurimum sarti extirpatum fuisset, inter Hamstede et Merlaue, eidem monasterio contulit, scribens inde uniuersis [d]sibi hominibus[d] pertinentibus hoc modo:

138. *Carta de eadem terra.*[334]

Robertus filius Haimonis ministris suis et omnibus aliis suis fidelibus hominibus de Merlaue, salutem. Sciatis me dedisse terram sancte Marie et monachis eius de Abbendonia, quam abbas et monachi a me requirebant, terram scilicet de Merlaue, sicut Gillebertus dapifer meus eam monachis liberauit, testimonio Huberti de Sancto Quintino, et Roberti Sor, et Rogeri filii Gotze.[335] Valete.

Rex quoque idem confirmatum subscripsit ita, quia terram illam sancte Marie Abbendonie quam Robertus filius Haimonis dedit ecclesie, que est inter Hamstede et Merlauam,[e] sicut Gillebertus dapifer eius et Hubertus de Sancto Quintino et Robertus Sor cum multis aliis diuiserunt, ipse rex concesserit, testimonio Willelmi episcopi Wintoniensis, et Eudonis dapiferi, et Haimonis dapiferi, et Rogeri Bigod, et Rogeri filii[f] Ricardi, et Willelmi de Curci. Apud
[ii. 97] Westmoster, in Pentecostes. Existente[g] Lincolis episcopo Roberto Bloet, et Oxenefordscire uicecomite Willelmo.[336]

[a] forisfacture *add. B* [b] Bigot *B* [c] Ared *B* [d–d] hominibus sibi *B*
[e] Merlaua *B* [f] fili *B* [g] Existentes *B*

[332] Ackhamstead is a lost village site, formerly in Oxon., now in Bucks.; see below, p. 292, on it being a member of Lewknor. Marlow is in Bucks., see *VCH*, *Buckinghamshire*, iii. 70.

[333] Robert son of Hamo was a prominent supporter of William Rufus and Henry I. He held extensive lands, particularly in Gloucestershire, and took a leading part in the conquest of south Wales; see the *DNB* entry by T. F. Tout. A blow to the temple led to the loss of his senses in 1105; see William of Malmesbury, *Gesta regum*, bk. v, c. 398, ed. Mynors, Thomson, and Winterbottom, i. 722, ii. 361. He died in 1107, to which time the present gift probably dates. It is notable that the Abingdon writer gives no hint of any mental incapacity on the donor's part.

[334] Lyell, no. 243.

or the monks may not lose anything for want of justice by you, on £10 [of forfeiture]. Witness: Roger Bigod, through Aret the falconer.

137. *Concerning the land between Ackhamstead and Marlow.*[332]
Abbot Faritius frequently administered many beneficial treatments to Robert son of Hamo.[333] Therefore, when Robert was approaching the time to pay his debt to death, on the abbot's recommendation he was told that he ought devotedly to render to the monastery of Abingdon some mark of piety, with a view to remembrance of him, and he should do so both for the things to come with God and also for Faritius's favour, if he recollected the abbot's many services to him. He heeded these pieces of advice and conferred on that monastery a portion of land between Ackhamstead and Marlow, where a very considerable assart had been cleared. Concerning this he wrote to all men pertaining to him, in the following way:

138. *Charter concerning the same land.*[334]
Robert son of Hamo to his officials and all his other faithful men of Marlow, greeting. Know that I have given to St Mary and to her monks of Abingdon the land which the abbot and monks were seeking of me, the land that is of Marlow, as Gilbert my steward delivered it to the monks, by witness of Hubert de Saint-Quentin, and Robert Sor, and Roger son of Gotze.[335] Farewell.

The king also endorsed this confirmation in such a way that he himself granted to St Mary of Abingdon that land between Ackhamstead and Marlow which Robert son of Hamo gave to the church, as Gilbert his steward and Hubert de Saint-Quentin and Robert Sor with many others apportioned it, by witness of William bishop of Winchester, and Eudo the steward, and Hamo the steward, and Roger Bigod, and Roger son of Richard, and William de Courcy. At Westminster, at Pentecost. With Robert Bloet being bishop of Lincoln and William sheriff of Oxfordshire.[336]

[335] Gilbert was a member of the d'Amory family, later members of which also acted as stewards to Robert son of Hamo's successors, the earls of Gloucester; see Green, *Aristocracy of Norman England*, pp. 208–9. In Henry I's charter, below, p. 156, Hubert de St Quentin appears as Herbert. Members of his family also witnessed charters of the earls of Gloucester; see e.g. *Earldom of Gloucester Charters*, ed. R. B. Patterson (Oxford, 1973), nos. 43, 71. Robert Sor witnessed two surviving charters of Earl Robert of Gloucester; *Earldom of Gloucester Charters*, nos. 42, 157. Gotze may be a derivative of *Goscelinus*, i.e. Jocelin.

[336] *RRAN* ii, no. 816, dating to 2 Jun. 1107, soon after the death of Robert son of Hamo, but before that of Roger Bigod in the same year.

139. *De terra de Colebroc quam Milo Crispin dedit.*[337]

Milo Crispin, pro seruitio quod abbas Faritius ei in sua infirmitate impenderat, dedit in elemosina ecclesie sancte Marie et monachis in Abbendonia quoddam hospicium in uia Lundonie apud Colebroc, in quo manebat quidam uocabulo Ægelwardus,[338] et dimidiam hidam terre, pariter cum omnibus illi adiacentibus pratis, pascuis, et siluis. Et misit Abbendonie suum dapiferum, Gillebertum Pipard, cum capellano suo, Warino, et per eorum manus donum[a] huius rei super altare sancte Marie imponi iussit, in presentia domni abbatis et totius conuentus ecclesie, anno uidelicet septimo Henrici regis.[339]

140. *De terra*[b] *Roberti filii Heruei.*[340]

Rege in Normannia degente, Mathildis regina mensis Augusti diebus per Abbendoniam transiens,[341] [c]imminente solempni[c] die Assumptionis celi regine, illuc suum ea de causa iter deflexit. Sacris itaque misteriis pro tanti festi competenti[d] annisu celebratis, abbate uero Faritio, ut tantam decuerat hospitam quam in his exceperat,
[ii. 98] affabiliter et ubertim in officiis sese exhibente[e] humanitatis, regina, eadem abbatis exoratu, Robertum quendam filium Heruei, in uicino calcete Colebrocensis degentem,[342] cum tota ipsius terra quam tunc tenebat sancte Marie in loco Abbendonensi perpetue dominationi contulit, domino eiusdem uiri id fieri concedente, simili quidem uocabulo Roberto scilicet, sed cognomine diuerso, id est Gernone,[343]
B fo. 143r sub | inferentibus illius filiis idem sibi ualde placuisse—Aluredo uidelicet et Mathathia, cum nepotibus Goisfredo, Fulcone, et Pagano.[344] Preterea ad hoc et curtillagium adiectum est terre predicti Roberti, in quo commanebat Rannulfus, eiusdem Roberti germanus,

[a] domum *B* [b] terre *B C* [c–c] imminete sollempni *B* [d] competentia *B C* [e] exibente *B*

[337] Colnbrook, Bucks. The tenant is referred to below, p. 156, as 'of Sutton', which is very close to Colnbrook. Miles died in 1107. For a dispute in the reign of Henry II and probably concerning this land, see below, p. 350.

[338] Egel-/Egil- names developed from the Old English Æthel-, in this case Æthelweard.

[339] For the Pipard family, see *Boarstall Cartulary*, pp. 308–9.

[340] The land concerned is Wraysbury, Bucks., which is very close to Colnbrook; below, p. 268, this land is referred to as in Colnbrook. The *History* does not include a writ of William son of Henry I concerning a dispute between Abingdon and William de Montfichet in *c.*1119 which probably concerned this land, although the writ calls it Colnbrook. The writ was addressed to William de Montfichet, and ordered him to reseise the abbey of Abingdon of the alms of Colnbrook which the queen had given, as on the day Faritius was alive and dead and Queen Matilda was alive and dead; see Chatsworth, no. 319, and also cf. above, p. 115.

139. *Concerning the land of Colnbrook, which Miles Crispin gave.*[337]
For the service which Abbot Faritius devoted to him in his illness, Miles Crispin gave in alms to the church of St Mary and to the monks in Abingdon a house (in which lived a man called Egelward)[338] at Colnbrook on the road to London, and half a hide of land, together with all the attached meadows, pastures, and woods. And he sent his steward Gilbert Pipard to Abingdon, with Warin his chaplain, and he ordered the gift of this possession to be placed on the altar of St Mary by their hands, in the presence of the lord abbot and the whole convent of the church, in King Henry's seventh year [5 Aug. 1106–4 Aug. 1107].[339]

140. *Concerning the land of Robert son of Hervey.*[340]
During the month of August, while the king was in Normandy, Queen Matilda was passing through Abingdon,[341] and because the feast day of the Assumption of the Queen of Heaven was at hand [15 Aug.], she diverted her journey there. The sacred mysteries were celebrated with the effort appropriate to so great a festival, and Abbot Faritius was affable and generous in carrying out the duties of kindness, as befitted such a great guest whom he had welcomed in these mysteries. Then the queen, entreated by the abbot, conferred on St Mary in the monastery of Abingdon, as a perpetual lordship, a certain Robert son of Hervey who lived close to the causeway of Colnbrook,[342] together with all his land which he was holding then. His lord (who had the same first name, that is Robert, but a different second name, that is Gernon) granted this transaction,[343] and his sons, namely Alfred and Mattathias, and his nephews, Geoffrey, Fulk, and Pain, added that this pleased them greatly.[344] A further addition was a plot of the aforesaid Robert's land on which lived his brother Ranulf, which in turn was not far from the holdings of the

[341] *RRAN* ii, no. 674, argues that this must be 15 Aug. 1104, on the grounds that this gift must be earlier than that of Miles Crispin just mentioned, since otherwise Abingdon would not have been in need of a lodging in the area.

[342] Colnbrook lies on four channels of the Colne; *VCH*, *Buckinghamshire*, iii. 246. Later they were individually bridged, but the present text suggests an embanked causeway crossing the streams and a broad, shallow floodplain.

[343] On Robert Gernon's holding of Wraysbury, see above, p. 115. He also held lands as a tenant-in-chief in several other counties; see Keats-Rohan, *Domesday People*, p. 388.

[344] Mattathias (see Luke 3: 26), Matthias, and Matthew are all developments of the same name; see E. G. Withycombe, *The Oxford Dictionary of English Christian Names* (3rd edn., Oxford, 1977), p. 213. I have chosen the form closest to the Latin, since other documents also use forms such as 'Matheus', which should be translated Matthew.

non ab inuicem ipsi longe dispositi mansionibus.[345] Et quidem ipsa regine donatio ecclesie impendi ualde erat necessaria. Nam iter quod ad urbem Lundoniam ab Abbendonia porrectum est, pro milium numerositate interpositorum, itinerantibus laboriosum peragi uide-
C fo. 154r batur, siquidem deerat propria | mansio, ubi apte hospitari potuisset, huius itineris in medio. Locus autem predictus quindecim miliariis ab urbe Lundonia distans, hospitandi non minimam prebet oportunitatem, cum sit illic siluarum, pratorum, mercimoniorumque copia.[346] De hac itaque regine donatione, eiusdem littere ad comprouinciales publicarum administrationum exactores directe fuere, hunc modum continentes:

141. *Carta regine de eadem terra.*[347]
Mathildis [a]Anglorum regina[a] Roberto Linc'[b] episcopo, et Hugoni de Bochelanda, et omnibus baronibus, Francis et Anglis, de Buchingehamscira, salutem. Sciatis me dedisse et concessisse Deo et ecclesie sancte Marie de Abbendona Robertum filium Heruei cum tota terra sua in elemosina, quia Robertus Gernon[c] ita dedit mihi. Et uolo et
[ii. 99] precipio ut ipsa ecclesia de Abbendona ita bene et honorifice et quiete teneat terram illam, cum prato et pastura et nemore, et cum omnibus consuetudinibus que ad illam terram pertinebant, uel sicut melius et quietius predicta abbatia tenet alias [d]suas terras,[d] quas quietius tenet. Et uidete ne inde clamorem amplius audiam. Testibus Rogero de Curcellis, et Roberto Malet, et Odone Moire. Apud Lundoniam.

142. *Confirmatio regis Henrici de eadem re huiusmodi textum habet:*[348]
Henricus rex Anglorum[e] Roberto episcopo Linc', et Hugoni de Bochelanda, et omnibus baronibus, Francis et Anglis, de Buchingehamscira, salutem. Sciatis me concessisse sancte Marie de Abbendona, et Faritio abbati, et monachis de ipsa abbatia de Abbendona, in perpetuo possidendum terram Roberti filii Heruei de Wirettesberia, quam Robertus Gernon[f] dedit Mathildi regine uxori mee.[349] Et precipio ut ita bene et honorifice teneat illam terram, sicut melius

[a–a] regina Anglorum *B* [b] Lincolniensi *B* [c] Gernun *B* [d–d] terras suas *B*
[e] Anglie *B* [f] Gernun *B*

[345] The translation deliberately reproduces the somewhat allusive nature of the Latin. It appears to mean that the additional plot was close to the holdings of Robert son of Hervey who had been given to Faritius.

[346] Colnbrook is, in fact, slightly over fifteen miles from London. This is very early evidence for the road-route from Abingdon to London; for an illustration of the route, see J. Ogilby, *Britannia*, i (London, 1675), pl. 14.

man who had been granted to Abingdon.[345] Moreover, it was very necessary that the queen bestow this gift on the church: completion of the journey which stretched from Abingdon to London was seen to be wearisome for travellers because of the large number of miles in between, the abbey having no house where a traveller could be suitably put up in mid-journey. That place, fifteen miles distant from London, offers reasonable opportunity for accommodation, since an abundance of woods, meadows, and merchandise exists there.[346] Concerning the queen's gift, letters of the following form were sent to the local officials of public administration:

141. *Charter of the queen concerning this land.*[347]
Matilda queen of the English to Robert bishop of Lincoln, and Hugh of Buckland, and all the barons, French and English, of Buckinghamshire, greeting. Know that I have given and granted in alms to God and to the church of St Mary of Abingdon Robert son of Hervey together with all his land, since Robert Gernon gave it thus to me. And I wish and order that the church of Abingdon hold that land, as well and honourably and undisturbed, with meadow and pasture and wood, and with all customs which used to pertain to that land, or as best and most undisturbedly as the aforesaid abbey holds its other lands which it holds most undisturbed. And see that I do not hear further complaint concerning this. Witnesses: Roger de Courseulles, and Robert Malet, and Odo Moire. At London.

142. *King Henry's confirmation concerning the same matter has the following text:*[348]
Henry king of the English to Robert bishop of Lincoln, and Hugh of Buckland, and all the barons, French and English, of Buckinghamshire, greeting. Know that I have granted in alms to St Mary of Abingdon, and to Abbot Faritius, and to the monks of that abbey of Abingdon, to possess in perpetuity the land of Robert son of Hervey of Wraysbury which Robert Gernon gave to Queen Matilda, my wife.[349] And I order that she [i.e. St Mary] hold that land as well and

[347] *RRAN* ii, no. 674; for the date of the queen's gift, see above, p. 143 n. 341. Lyell, no. 116 provides the heading 'Concerning the land of Wraysbury', but for this and the next writ gives the address as Berkshire, not Buckinghamshire.

[348] *RRAN* ii, no. 676; Lyell, no. 117, where the address is to Berkshire, not Buckinghamshire. The document probably dates to soon after the previous writ.

[349] Lyell, no. 117, here adds 'et ipsa regina dedit sancte Marie et monachis suis de Abbend.' Et uolo . . .', i.e. 'and the queen gave [it] to St Mary and her monks of Abingdon. And I wish . . .'

tenet totam aliam terram suam, et cum eisdem consuetudinibus. Teste Rogero de Curcellis. Apud Sanctum Dionisium in Leons.

143. *Carta item de eadem terra.*[350]

Henricus rex Anglorum[a] Roberto Gernon,[b] salutem. Precipio tibi ut permittas esse ita in pace Robertum filium Heruei cum tota terra sua et pecunia, sicut melius et quietius tenebat eam die qua dedisti eam
[ii. 100] terram regine, et ipsa eam terram dedit in elemosina[c] ecclesie sancte Marie de Abbendona. Et uide ne inde amplius clamorem audiam. Testibus regina et Roberto comite de Mellent. Apud Rochingeham.

144. *De terra quam Henricus de Albinei dedit huic ecclesie.*[351]

B fo. 143v Henricus de Albeneio dedit | sancte Marie, in presentia domni Faritii abbatis et totius conuentus Abbendonensis, unam hidam et unam uirgatam in Bedefordensiscira, que terra uocatur Stretune, et quam Waldef de illo tenuerat.[352] Dedit autem eam ita quiete habere, ut nulli inde aliquod seruitium faciamus, excepto quod de geldo regali, secundum totius terre morem, procuremus. Et hanc donationem in capitulo feria quinta in ebdomada Pasche, anno septimo regni Henrici regis.[d] Post hec, eodem anno die apostolorum Philippi et Iacobi, manente eodem Henrico adhuc in ista uilla, creuit donum superius dictum, una uidelicet uirgata et dimidia eo loco quo antea dederat. Factaque est ipsa datio unius hide et dimidie et unius[e] uirgate. Vadem autem huius posterioris doni per manum sui capellani Gilleberti super altare imponendum transmisit, in conspectum omnium monachorum et plurimorum laicorum.[f] Hec omnia postea in conspectu suorum prudentum hominum, Nigelli de Wast et Arfast, idem
[ii. 101] Henricus, et in presentia domni[g] Faritii abbatis, confirmauit in camera ipsius abbatis, quatinus et ipsi in posterum[h] testes inde existerent.[353] Henrico uero defuncto, Robertus filius eius taliter eandem donationem sigillo proprio confirmauit: |

[a] Anglie *B* [b] Gernun *B* [c] helemosina *B* [d] *a word such as* fecit *has been omitted or is understood in this sentence* [e] *over erasure, perhaps of* dimidie *C*; dimidie *B* [f] + Oini. Rainbald. W de Fauarcis *in brown ink in margin, possibly in one of the hands providing guidance for B's rubricator, and with an + in the text to mark the insertion C*; Oini, Rainbaldi, et Warini de Fauarcis *add. B* [g] domini *B* [h] posterium *B*

---

[350] *RRAN* ii, no. 742; *Royal Writs*, ed. van Caenegem, no. 35; Lyell, no. 118. The writ can only be safely dated to 1104 × 1116, although *RRAN* suggests Feb. 1106.

[351] Henry was the son of Nigel d'Aubigny, a *Domesday* tenant-in-chief of various lands in Bedfordshire, including Cainhoe. Henry succeeded his father by 1107; Sanders, *Baronies*, p. 26; L. C. Loyd, 'The origin of the family of Aubigny of Cainhoe', *Bedfordshire Historical Records Society*, xix (1937), 101–9. The date of Henry's death is uncertain.

[352] *DB* i, fo. 214v seems to record this land as in Holme, Beds., a hamlet close to

honourably as best she holds all her other land, and with the same customs. Witness: Roger de Courseulles. At Lyons-la-Forêt.

143. *Likewise, a charter concerning the same land.*[350]
Henry king of the English to Robert Gernon, greeting. I order you that you permit to be in peace Robert son of Hervey with all his land and goods, as he best and most undisturbedly held on the day on which you gave that land to the queen and she gave it in alms to the church of St Mary of Abingdon. And see that I do not hear further complaint concerning this. Witnesses: the queen and Robert count of Meulan. At Rockingham.

144. *Concerning the land which Henry d'Aubigny gave to this church.*[351]
In the presence of lord Abbot Faritius and the whole convent of Abingdon, Henry d'Aubigny gave to St Mary one hide and one virgate in Bedfordshire, which land is called Stratton, and which Waltheof had held from him.[352] Moreover he gave this for us to have so undisturbedly that we are to do no one any service therefrom, except to make provision concerning royal geld according to the practice of the whole land. And [he made] this gift in the chapter on the Thursday in Easter week in the seventh year of King Henry's reign [18 Apr. 1107]. After this, in the same year, on the day of the apostles Philip and James [1 May], Henry d'Aubigny was still staying in this town [Abingdon] and increased the gift mentioned above with one and a half virgates in the same place as his previous gift. The completed gift was thus of one and a half hides and one virgate. He further sent a gage of the later donation to be placed on the altar by the hand of his chaplain Gilbert in the sight of all the monks and very many laymen. Afterwards Henry confirmed all these things in the sight of his prudent men Nigel de *Wast* and Arfast, in the presence of the lord Abbot Faritius, in the latter's chamber, that in future they too might stand as witnesses of this.[353] Following Henry's death, Robert his son confirmed this gift with his own seal in the following way:

Stratton; *VCH*, *Bedfordshire*, ii. 211. Note also *De abbatibus*, *CMA* ii. 288, which mentions an acquisition by Faritius of land in Bedfordshire, but damage to the manuscript prevents identification of the location.

[353] Nigel held various lands in Buckinghamshire from Nigel d'Aubigny in 1086; *DB* i, fo. 214^{r-v}; his family may be from Le Vast in the Cotentin; Loyd, 'Aubigny of Cainhoe', pp. 107–8. Arfast or Erfast held various lands in Bedfordshire from Nigel d'Aubigny, *DB* i, fo. 214^{r-v}.

C fo. 154v **145.** *Carta Roberti filii Henrici de eadem terra.*[354]

Notum sit et certum omnibus presentibus et futuris, clericis et laicis, quod ego Robertus de Albeneio concessi finaliter Deo et ecclesie sancte Marie de Abbendona terram quam pater meus Henricus libere dederat eidem ecclesie, unam scilicet hidam et dimidiam et uirgatam unam in Stretona, et hoc breui meo confirmaui, perpetualiter solutam esse et quietam ab omni requisitione et seruitio, et liberam ab omnibus rebus preter ea que communiter totus comitatus per communes summonitiones regis facturus est. Testibus his Radulfo priore ecclesie de Cothes, Waltero camerario de Abbendona, Cezilia[a] matre mea, Nigello fratre meo, Hugone[b] capellano, Roberto capellano, Willelmo filio Nigelli, Henrico de Broi, Iohanne de Charun, Roberto de Cothes, Rogero de Standene.[355] Hec concessio et confirmatio facta est feria quinta Pasche, apud Cahenno.[356]

146. *Confirmatio regis Henrici eiusdem terre.*[357]

Henricus rex Anglorum[c] Roberto episcopo Linc', et Hugoni de Bochelanda, et omnibus fidelibus suis, Francis et Anglis, de Bedefortscira,[d] salutem. Sciatis me concessisse ecclesie sancte Marie de
[ii. 102] Abbendona terram quam Henricus de Albinni[e] dedit predicte ecclesie, uidelicet unam hidam terre ad Holmum et dimidiam uirgatam terre, et dimidiam hidam in Estratona de hundredo de Bicheleswatere. Testibus Roberto episcopo Linc', et[f] Rogero episcopo Salesb', et Hamone[g] dapifero, et W. de Albinni,[h] et Nigello de Albinni,[i] et Grimbaldo medico. Apud Westmoster.

147. *De una hida apud Dumeltun quam Willelmus dedit.*[358]

Anno octauo regni Henrici regis, Faritio abbate et omnibus monachis in capitulo residentibus, Willelmus Guizenboeth dedit sancte Marie

[a] Cecilia *B* [b] Iug' *B* [c] Anglie *B* [d] Bedefordscira *B* [e] Albini *B* [f] *in margin,* [R]ainfridi et . . ., *the remainder being illegible, possibly in the same hand as the marginalia in the last section but one C* [g] Haimone *with* i *interlin. B* [h] Albini *B* [i] Albini *B*

[354] Lyell, no. 244. Lyell, no. 245, is another confirmation charter by this man's son, also called Robert, who succeeded his father in 1191; Sanders, *Baronies*, p. 26.

[355] Ralph, prior of the church of 'Cothes', cannot be identified. *Heads of Religious Houses*, p. 228, suggests that the church may be identified with the Hospital at Cotes, Northants. Another possibility is an unknown priory at Westcotts, Beds., or—most likely—that the charter has been wrongly transcribed, and that 'priore' should read 'presbitero'. Henry de *Broi* may well have been a descendant of Osbert de *Broilg*, who in 1086 held land in Bletsoe and Sharnbrook, Beds., from Hugh de Beauchamp; see *DB* i, fo. 213r–v, *VCH*, *Bedfordshire*, iii. 40. The toponym may be Brouay or possibly Breuil, both Dept. Calvados; *Anglo-Norman Families*, pp. 20–1; Keats-Rohan, *Domesday People*, p. 318.

145. *Charter of Robert son of Henry concerning the same land.*[354]
Let it be known and certain to all, present and future, cleric and lay, that I, Robert d'Aubigny, have granted forever to God and to the church of St Mary of Abingdon the land which my father Henry had freely given to that church, that is one and a half hides and one virgate in Stratton. And by this my writ I have confirmed that it be perpetually unburdened and quit from all demand and service, and free of all things except those which the whole county will do in common, by common summons of the king. Witnesses: Ralph, prior of the church of *Cothes*, Walter the chamberlain of Abingdon, Cecilia my mother, Nigel my brother, Hugh the chaplain, Robert the chaplain, William son of Nigel, Henry de *Broi*, John de *Charun*, Robert of *Cothes*, Roger of *Standene*.[355] This grant and confirmation was made on Easter Thursday at Cainhoe.[356]

146. *Confirmation of King Henry of the same land.*[357]
Henry king of the English to Robert bishop of Lincoln, and Hugh of Buckland, and all his faithful men, French and English, of Bedfordshire, greeting. Know that I have granted to the church of St Mary of Abingdon the land which Henry d'Aubigny gave to the aforesaid church, namely one hide of land at Holme and half a virgate of land, and half a hide in Stratton, of the hundred of Biggleswade. Witnesses: Robert bishop of Lincoln, and Roger bishop of Salisbury, and Hamo the steward, and William d'Aubigny, and Nigel d'Aubigny, and Grimbald the physician. At Westminster.

147. *Concerning one hide at Dumbleton, which William gave.*[358]
In the eighth year of King Henry's reign [5 Aug. 1107–4 Aug. 1108], with Abbot Faritius and all the monks present in the chapter, William

Note also *Red Book*, i. 324, where Roger de 'Bray' shares with two others in owing a knight to Robert d'Aubigny, as does Ranulf de 'Charun'; *Cartulary of the Abbey of Old Wardon*, ed. G. H. Fowler (Beds. Hist. Rec. Soc., xiii, 1930), pp. 352–4, and also Fowler's pedigree no. 9; *HKF* i. 74. *Cothes* could be Westcotts, Beds., a holding of Nigel d'Aubigny in 1086; *DB* i, fo. 214^{r}. *Red Book*, i. 320, mentions a Robert of 'Cotes' as a Bedfordshire tenant of Simon de Beauchamp in 1166. *Standene* may be Stondon, Beds.

[356] Beds., head of the Aubigny honour; Sanders, *Baronies*, p. 26.

[357] *RRAN* ii, no. 812; Lyell, no. 119; Chatsworth, no. 318. The writ probably dates to fairly soon after Henry d'Aubigny's gift on 1 May 1107.

[358] *DB* i, fo. 167^{r}: William Goizenboded held one hide there. William also held other lands in Gloucestershire and Wiltshire as a tenant-in-chief; *DB* i, fos. 167^{r}, 177^{v}. It is not certain when or how lordship of his lands passed to the count of Meulan. William probably had an English mother and a Norman father. His second name means 'cursed, or foretold, by a witch'; see A. Williams, *The Gloucestershire Domesday* (London, 1989), pp. 35, 37. For a further note on the family, see Crouch, *Beaumont Twins*, p. 110. See also above, p. 50.

B fo. 144r de Abbendona unam hidam, | quietam ab omni calumpnia, quam habebat in uilla Dumeltuna;[a] et hoc dedit concessu domini sui Roberti, comitis de Mellent, de cuius uidelicet feudo hidam illam tenuerat.

148. *Carta comitis de Mellent de eadem hida.*[359]
Ego Robertus comes de Mellent rogatus fui a Willelmo Guizenboeth,[b] et ab amicis suis, et baronibus meis, ut concederem Deo et sancte Marie in Abbendonensi ecclesia quandam hidam terre que est in uilla Dumeltuna, in hundredo de Gretestan, quam idem Willelmus ante me et meos barones dederat in elemosina[c] perpetuo habendam supradicte ecclesie. Quod libenter annui et uoluntarie concessi, quia de feudo meo erat, pro remissione peccatorum meorum et anime mee
[ii. 103] salute. Hoc denique feci coram subscriptis testibus, et me rogantibus, scilicet eodem Willelmo, et Ricardo[d] capellano, et Goisfredo medico, et Nigello de Oileio, et Roberto filio Ansketilli, et Gosfredo[e] Ridello, et Radulfo uicecomite, et Roberto filio Ercenboldi,[f] et Roberto filio Rogeri, et Rodulfo de Furcis, et Rogero[g] filio Rodulfi nepote Nigelli, Luuello de Peri, et Willelmo nigro homine eiusdem W. Guizenboeth, et Rogero Frangelupum, et aliis multis, et Warino homine abbatis, et Rainaldo,[h] et Lamberto.[i][360] Hec omnia acta sunt coram me et per me, scilicet comitem de Mellent, et ante omnes suprascriptos fecit Willelmus Guizenboeth[j] donum istud, pro se et filio et uxore et omnibus heredibus suis, et promisit auctoritatem omnium se esse facturum.

149. *Carta regis de eadem hida.*[361]
Henricus rex Anglorum Samsoni episcopo, et Waltero uicecomiti, et omnibus baronibus suis, Francis et Anglis, de Gloecesterscira, salutem.[362] Sciatis me concessisse Deo et sancte Marie ecclesie Abbendone hidam terre que est in uilla Dumeltuna in hundredo de Gretestan, quam Willelmus Goizenboeth dedit predicte ecclesie. Et

[a] Dumeltona *B* [b] Guizenboeht *B* [c] helemosina *B* [d] *initial om. B* [e] Goisfredo *B* [f] Ercenbaldo *B* [g] Oggero *B* [h] Lainaldo *B* [i] *initial om. C* [j] Goizenboeth *B*

359 Lyell, no. 246.
360 On Richard the chaplain, see Crouch, *Beaumont Twins*, pp. 148–9. Robert son of Ansketel may well be a member of the Harcourt family, on whom see Crouch, *Beaumont Twins*, pp. 120–7. Geoffrey the physician does not appear in Talbot and Hammond, *Medical Practitioners*. Geoffrey Ridel was the same man who was a royal justice, mentioned below, p. 170. He was one of four men called 'justiciars of the whole of England' by Henry of Huntingdon, *De contemptu mundi*, c. 17, in Henry, archdeacon of Huntingdon, *Historia*

Goizenboded gave to St Mary of Abingdon one hide which he had in the village of Dumbleton, quit of all claim. And he gave this by grant of his lord, Robert count of Meulan, from whose fee, that is, he had held that hide.

148. *Charter of the count of Meulan concerning that hide.*[359]
I, Robert count of Meulan, have been asked by William Goizenboded and by his friends and by my barons, that I grant to God and to St Mary in the church of Abingdon a hide of land which is in the village of Dumbleton, in the hundred of Greston, which that same William had given in the presence of me and my barons to the above-mentioned church to have perpetually in alms. For the remission of my sins and the salvation of my soul, I gladly agreed to this and willingly granted it since it was of my fee. This, lastly, I did in the presence of the witnesses listed below and at their request, that is, William himself, and Richard the chaplain, and Geoffrey the physician, and Nigel d'Oilly, and Robert son of Ansketel, and Geoffrey Ridel, and Ralph the sheriff, and Robert son of Ercenbold, and Robert son of Roger, and Rolf de *Furcis*, and Roger son of Rolf nephew of Nigel, Lovell of Perry, and William the black the man of William Goizenboded, and Roger *Frangelupum*, and many others, and Warin the abbot's man, and Reginald, and Lambert.[360] All these things have been done in my presence and through me, that is the count of Meulan, and before all the above-mentioned William Goizenboded made this gift for himself and his son and his wife and all his heirs, and he promised that he would establish himself as authority of all these things.

149. *Charter of the king concerning the same hide.*[361]
Henry king of the English to Bishop Samson, and Walter the sheriff, and all his barons, French and English, of Gloucestershire, greeting.[362] Know that I have granted to God and to St Mary of the church of Abingdon a hide of land which is in the village of Dumbleton in the hundred of Greston, which William Goizenboded gave to the

Anglorum, ed. D. E. Greenway (OMT, 1996), p. 614. He died in the White Ship in 1120; see Green, *Government*, pp. 169–70. Ralph the sheriff's identity, and the county of which he was sheriff, is uncertain; see Green, *Sheriffs*, p. 26.

[361] *RRAN* ii, no. 893; Lyell, no. 120. The gift which the writ confirms was given between 5 Aug. 1107 and 4 Aug. 1108; the confirmation may well date from before Henry crossed the Channel prior to Aug. 1108.

[362] Samson was bishop of Worcester 1096–1112; *Handbook of British Chronology*, p. 278. Walter was sheriff of Gloucestershire *c.*1093–*c.*1126; Green, *Sheriffs*, p. 42.

C fo. 155r hoc concedo perpetuo | firmiter habendam, ita quiete et in pace in omnibus sicut habet aliam terram in eadem uilla.[363] Testibus comite de Mellent, et Vtuer, et Gosfrido filio[a] Pagani, et Aluredo[b] de Lincola. Apud Wintoniam.

[ii. 104] **150.** *De Radulfo filio Walterii fossatarii.*[364]

Radulfus filius Walteri fossatarii tenebat de ecclesia et de abbate Faritio unam hidam in uilla Dumeltuna, quam Willelmus Guizenboeth olim quietam ecclesie et predicto abbati dimiserat. Et contigit ipsum Radulfum furti crimen admittere, propter quod suam legalitatem perdidit, et more iudicii Anglie suis omnibus rebus cum uita debuit carere.[365] Sed regis Henrici, qui tunc in Normannia erat, misericordia de his requisita, regine etiam, que in Anglia remanserat, Abbendoniam uenit, domni Faritii abbatis similiter pietatem quesiturus. Cui abbas, pro sua bonitate, et in equi et in denariorum et tritici donatione tanta largitus est, ut non solum terram quam hactenus tenuerat ecclesie dimitteret, sed etiam sacramento super sancta euuangelia confirmaret, quod nunquam a se uel ab aliquo suo
B fo. 144v herede aliquid calumpnie uel requisitionis super | eam inferretur. Et huic eius sacramento isti interfuerunt: Radulfus cellararius, qui istud sacramentum loco abbatis suscepit, Hubertus prior de Walingaford, Rainboldus, Willelmus de Seuecurda, cum multis aliis, anno tercio decimo regni Henrici regis.[366]

151. *De hida quam Walterus fossatarius*[c] *tenebat.*[367]

Anno quarto decimo Henrici regis, Walterius fossatarius cum coniuge sua dimisit et clamauit quietam dimidiam hidam apud uillam
[ii. 105] Dumeltuna[d] in manu Faritii abbatis, tam a se quam ab omnibus suis heredibus. Forisfecerat enim eam multis in causis, et ideo se purgare non ualens per singula, consilio sapientum quod tenebat ecclesie et abbati predicto, ut dictum est, dimisit, et abbas dedit ei triginta solidos et quatuor somas segetum pro hac re.[368] Et hoc factum est coram his testibus: Grimmundo abbate Wincelcumb'; de uicinis

[a] filius *B* [b] Aluered *B* [c] fossarius *B* [d] Dumeltona *B*

[363] See above, p. 50, for other land in Dumbleton.

[364] *English Lawsuits*, no. 192, dating to between 5 Aug. 1112, the start of the thirteenth year of Henry's reign, and Jul. 1113 when Henry returned from the Continent.

[365] See above, p. xcv.

[366] On Ralph the cellarer, see above, p. lviii.

[367] *English Lawsuits*, no. 195.

aforesaid church. And this I grant perpetually to be had firmly, as undisturbed and in peace in all things as it has other land in that village.[363] Witnesses: the count of Meulan, and Otuer, and Geoffrey son of Pain, and Alfred of Lincoln. At Winchester.

150. *Concerning Ralph son of Walter the ditcher.*[364]
Ralph son of Walter the ditcher held from the church and from Abbot Faritius one hide in the village of Dumbleton, which William Goizenboded had once surrendered quit to the church and that abbot. And it happened that Ralph committed the crime of theft, because of which he lost his lawfulness, and by the custom of judgment of England he ought to have lost all his possessions together with his life.[365] But after seeking mercy concerning these matters from King Henry, who was then in Normandy, and also from the queen, who had remained in England, he came to Abingdon to request in similar fashion the compassion of lord Abbot Faritius. Because of his goodness, the abbot bestowed on Ralph such a gift of a horse and of money and wheat, that he not only surrendered to the church the land which he had hitherto held, but also confirmed by oath on the holy Gospels that no claim or suit would ever be brought concerning this by himself or by any of his heirs. And present at this oath were the following: Ralph the cellarer, who received this oath in place of the abbot, Hubert prior of Wallingford, Rainbold, William of Seacourt, together with many others, in the thirteenth year of King Henry's reign [5 Aug. 1112–4 Aug. 1113].[366]

151. *Concerning the hide that Walter the ditcher held.*[367]
In King Henry's fourteenth year [5 Aug. 1113–4 Aug. 1114], Walter the ditcher, with his wife, surrendered and quitclaimed in the hand of Abbot Faritius half a hide at the village of Dumbleton, both from himself and from all his heirs. He had forfeited it in many cases, and was unable to clear himself on the individual matters. Therefore he followed the counsel of wise men and surrendered to the church and to the aforesaid abbot what he was holding, as has been said, and the abbot gave him 30s. and four loads of grain for this possession.[368] This was done in the presence of these witnesses: Grimmund abbot of

[368] A *soma* or seam of corn was a measure usually equivalent to eight bushels; R. E. Zupko, *A Dictionary of Weights and Measures for the British Isles: the Middle Ages to the Twentieth Century* (American Philosophical Soc., Philadelphia, 1985), pp. 369–71.

Abbendone, Radulfo Basset, Ricardo de Grai; de hominibus abbatis Faritii, Rainbaldo, Radulfo camerario.[369]

152. *Regis littere de eadem terra ita se habent:*[370]
Henricus rex Anglorum Samsoni episcopo Wigornensi, et Waltero uicecomiti de Gloecesterscira,[a] et omnibus baronibus, Francis et Anglis,[b] de Gloecesterscira, salutem. Sciatis quod concedo sancte Marie de Abbendona, et Faritio abbati, et monachis, perpetuo habendam terram Walterii[c] fossatarii, quam habet in uilla Dumeltuna. Testibus Roberto episcopo Lincoliensi, et Rannulfo episcopo Dunelmensi, et Rogero Bigod, et Dauid fratre regine, et Nigello de Oili, et Rogero de Oili, et Willelmo de Hoctuna, et Droco uenatore. Apud Corneberiam.

153. *De Leseboimilne.*[371]
Willelmus filius Aiulfi et uxor eius Mathildis, cum Ricardo filio
[ii. 106] eorum, in capitulo Abbendonense, in presentia Faritii abbatis et totius conuentus, et[d] concesserunt Deo et ecclesie Abbendonensi, communi consensu, molendinum quod Anglice uocatur Leseboie mylne,[e] cum omnibus sibi pertinentibus, tam in aquis quam in agris et pascuis, et omnes domos quas in burgo habebant, perpetuo et hereditario iure in supradicta ecclesia permanere,[372] astantibus his testibus: monachis omnibus, Serlone presbitero, et multis aliis, anno septimo Henrici regis.

154. *Carta regis de eodem molendino.*[373]
Henricus rex Anglorum Roberto episcopo Linc', et Nigello de Oili, et Hugoni de Bochelanda, et Willelmo uicecomiti de Oxeneford, et omnibus baronibus suis et fidelibus suis de Oxenefordscira et de Buchingehamscira, salutem.[374] Sciatis me concessisse Deo et sancte

[a] Glouecesterscira *B* [b] Anglss *C* [c] Walteri *B* [d] *it seems probable that this word should have been preceded by the verb* dederunt [e] milne *B*

[369] Grimmund, or Girmund, was abbot of Winchcombe 1095–1122; *Heads of Religious Houses*, p. 79. Richard de Grey may be the same man whom a charter of Henry I, dated to Christmas 1109, records as having granted tithes in Oxfordshire to Eynsham in connection with his son's entry to that monastery, *RRAN* ii, no. 928. *DB* i, fo. 161[r], records an Ansketel holding six hides in Brighthampton, Oxon. This was probably Standlake, to which the Richard de Grey mentioned here succeeded Ansketel, and was in turn succeeded by his own son, also called Ansketel. Richard may, therefore, also be the man who stood surety for Ermenold, below, p. 204. For Ralph the chamberlain, see above, p. 88.

[370] *RRAN* ii, no. 701. The writ must date between 1101, the return of Ranulf Flambard, and 1107, the death of Roger Bigod; *RRAN* suggests 18 Oct. 1105. On problems of the relationship between the preceding narrative and this writ, see above, p. xxxvi.

Winchcombe; from the neighbours of Abingdon, Ralph Basset, Richard de Grey; from the men of Abbot Faritius, Rainbald, Ralph the chamberlain.[369]

152. *Letters of the king concerning this land are as follows:*[370]
Henry king of the English to Samson bishop of Worcester, and Walter sheriff of Gloucestershire, and all his barons, French and English, of Gloucestershire, greeting. Know that I grant to St Mary of Abingdon, and to Abbot Faritius, and to the monks to have perpetually the land of Walter the ditcher, which he has in the village of Dumbleton. Witnesses: Robert bishop of Lincoln, and Ranulf bishop of Durham, and Roger Bigod, and David the queen's brother, and Nigel d'Oilly, and Roger d'Oilly, and William of Houghton, and Drogo the huntsman. At Cornbury.

153. *Concerning Boymill.*[371]
William son of Aiulf and his wife Matilda, with their son Richard, in the chapter of Abingdon in the presence of Abbot Faritius and the whole convent, by common consent granted to God and to the church of Abingdon the mill which in English is called Boymill, with everything pertaining to it, both in waters and in fields and pastures, and all the houses they had in the borough, to remain in the above-mentioned church perpetually and by hereditary right.[372] With these witnesses present: all the monks, Serlo the priest, and many others, in King Henry's seventh year [5 Aug. 1106–4 Aug. 1107].

154. *Charter of the king concerning the same mill.*[373]
Henry king of the English to Robert bishop of Lincoln, and Nigel d'Oilly, and Hugh of Buckland, and William sheriff of Oxford, and all his barons and faithful men of Oxfordshire and Buckinghamshire, greeting.[374] Know that I have granted to God, and to St Mary of

[371] For the location of Boymill, on a side-stream of the Cherwell, south of Magdalen Bridge, see *Cartulary of the Monastery of St Frideswide at Oxford*, ed. S. R. Wigram (2 vols., Oxford Hist. Soc., xxviii, xxxi, 1895–6), i, map at end. In 1086 it may have been the mill worth 40s. included in Leofwine's holding at Cowley; *DB* i. 160^{v}. It had been acquired by Godstow by 1138, when a papal document states that it had been given by Roger bishop of Salisbury; *VCH*, *Oxfordshire*, v. 82.

[372] Note that the royal confirmation below avoids such use of inheritance language and substitutes that of alms; see Hudson, *Land, Law, and Lordship*, p. 90. The borough mentioned is Oxford.

[373] *RRAN* ii, no. 813; Lyell, no. 122; Chatsworth, no. 317; see above, p. xviii. The writ can be dated to 2 Jun. 1107, after the original gift and before the death of Roger Bigod. The *Anglo-Saxon Chronicle* confirms that Henry was at Westminster at Pentecost 1107.

[374] Lyell, no. 122, omits Buckinghamshire from address.

Marie de Abbendona et monachis molendinum illud quod uocatur Boiemylna,[a] cum omnibus rebus sibi pertinentibus, tam in terris quam in pratis et in aquis, et quinque domos que sunt infra burgum, que Willelmus filius Aiulfi et uxor sua dederunt supradicte
C fo. 155v ecclesie perpetuo in elemosina. | Et terram illam quam Robertus filius Haimonis dedit eidem ecclesie, que est inter Hemmestedam et Merlauam, sicut Gillebertus dapifer eius et Herbertus de Sancto
B fo. 145r Quintino et Robertus | Sorus, cum multis aliis diuiserunt.[375] Et similiter concedo Alwordum de Suttona[b] cum tota terra sua, quam Milo Crispinus et uxor eius dederunt predicte ecclesie perpetuo in
[ii. 107] elemosina.[376] Et similiter concedo terram Roberti filii Heruei de Writeberia, quam regina Mathildis dedit predicte ecclesie in elemosina,[c] et Robertus Gernon[d] dedit ei.[377] Testibus Willelmo episcopo Wintonie, et Rogero episcopo Salesbirie, et Eudone dapifero, et Raim'[e] dapifero, et Rogero Bigod, et Willelmo de Curci, et Nigello[f] de Oili, et Rogero filio Ricardi. Apud Westmoster, in Pentecoste.

155. *De duabus[g] hidis apud Benneham.*[378]

Humfridus de Bohun,[h] consistens cum abbate Faritio apud uillam suam, Wochesi nominatam, ecclesie de Abbendona et abbati predicto duas hidas de Benneham ab omni clamore in perpetuum clamauit quietas.[379] Et precepit Walterio de Ripario, qui easdem hidas de se ante hoc tempus recognouerat et tenuerat, postea de ecclesia Abbendonensi et de abbate recognosceret et in perpetuum teneret, et inde abbati, qui aderat, homagium faceret. Paruo post hoc interposito tempore, isdem Humfridus misit Serlonem capellanum suum cum Willelmo monacho, et per eum de hac sua concessione saisiuit ecclesiam et abbatem de Abbendona. His ita peractis, Walterius de Ripario (de quo superius diximus) Abbendoniam uenit, ibique abbati

[a] Boiemilne *B* [b] Suttuna *B* [c] helemosina *B* [d] Gernun *B* [e] *for* Ham' *?, as Chatsworth, no. 317; the initial in C is in green, and is probably a mistake* [f] Rigello *C* [g] duobus *B* [h] Boun *B*

[375] See above, p. 140.

[376] See above, p. 142. Lyell, no. 122, omits this sentence concerning Egelward; presumably the scribe's eye slipped to the second use of 'Et similiter'.

[377] See above, p. 142.

[378] This is almost certainly Hoe Benham, Berks.; see *Charters of Abingdon Abbey*, pp. 304–5, on the complex development of land-holding within what must once have been a single land-unit of Benham. Abingdon's tenure of Benham before the Norman Conquest had been troubled, but for Walter de Rivers holding two hides there from Abingdon in

Abingdon, and to the monks that mill which is called Boymill, with everything pertaining to it, both in lands and in meadows and in waters, and five houses which are within the borough, which William son of Aiulf and his wife gave to the above-mentioned church perpetually in alms. Also that land which Robert son of Hamo gave to the same church, which is between Ackhamstead and Marlow, as Gilbert his steward and Herbert de Saint-Quentin and Robert Sor, with many others, apportioned it.[375] And likewise I grant Egelward of Sutton with all his land, which Miles Crispin and his wife gave to the aforesaid church perpetually in alms.[376] And likewise I grant the land of Robert son of Hervey of Wraysbury, which Queen Matilda gave to the aforesaid church in alms, and Robert Gernon gave to her.[377] Witnesses: William bishop of Winchester, and Roger bishop of Salisbury, and Eudo the steward, and Hamo the steward, and Roger Bigod, and William de Courcy, and Nigel d'Oilly, and Roger son of Richard. At Westminster, at Pentecost.

155. *Concerning two hides at Benham.*[378]

Humphrey de Bohun, whilst staying at his village of Oaksey with Abbot Faritius, quitclaimed in perpetuity to the church of Abingdon and to that abbot two hides at Benham, free from all claim.[379] He ordered that Walter de Rivers, who had previously recognized his lordship of these hides and held them from him, hereafter should recognize the lordship of and in perpetuity hold from the church of Abingdon and from the abbot, and do homage concerning this to the abbot, who was present. Shortly after this, Humphrey sent his chaplain Serlo with William the monk, and through him he seised the church and abbot of Abingdon concerning this his grant. After the completion of these matters, Walter de Rivers (about whom we have spoken above) came to Abingdon and there did homage to Abbot

1086 see above, p. 30 n. 72. It would seem that at some point after 1086 Humphrey de Bohun acquired this land, perhaps on the death of the *Domesday* tenant which resulted in a problematic succession, above, p. 30. The Walter here would seem to be the nephew of the *Domesday* tenant. It is unclear when Walter son of the *Domesday* tenant regained control of the land, as is implied above, p. 30. For continuing trouble under Henry II, see below, p. 390. Benham is listed amongst Faritius's acquisitions in *De abbatibus*; *CMA* ii. 288.

[379] Humphrey de Bohun was son of Humphrey *cum barba* who arrived in England with William I. He married Maud, daughter and heiress of Edward of Salisbury, thereby gaining extensive estates. He was dead by the end of the 1120s; Sanders, *Baronies*, p. 91. Oaksey is in Wiltshire.

Faritio pro predicta terra homagium fecit, et eam de ecclesia recognoscendam et tenendam suscepit.[380]

156. *Carta Henrici regis de eadem terra.*[381]

Henricus rex Anglorum Rogero episcopo Salesbirie, et Hugoni de
Bochelanda, et omnibus baronibus suis, Francis et Anglis, de
[ii. 108] Berchescira, salutem. Sciatis me concessisse sancte Marie in Abbendonensi ecclesia, et abbati Faritio,[a] et monachis duas hidas terre que
sunt in Beneham,[b] quas Walterus filius Gotselini[c] de la Riuera tenuit
de Vnfrido de Bohun, quas idem Vnfridus tenebat et in presentia mea
reddidit predicte ecclesie perpetue remansuras. Et uolo et precipio ut
ita bene et honorifice illam terram teneat, sicut melius et honorabilius
tenet alias terras ecclesie. Testibus Waltero de Meduana, et Widone
de Clermunt, et Radulfo de Todeneio, et Drocone de Monceio,[382] et
Duhello[d] de Brielual, et Ricardo de Merei,[383] et Willelmo de Albinni,[e]
et Roberto de Dunestanuilla, et Areto falconario, et Patricio de
Cadurcis. Apud Romesiam, in anno quando rex dedit filiam suam
imperatori.

157. *De duabus hidis apud Brochestan.*[f][384]

Ricardus filius Reinfridi, ad diem mortis perueniens, in die scilicet
sancti Leonardi confessoris, dimisit huic ecclesie pro sua anima
decem et nouem solidorum redditionem singulis annis, preter illud
quod pro anima sue uxoris, prius defuncte et hoc[g] in loco sepulte,
iam dederat, id est sex solidos. Post hec, abbas Faritius de his
requisiuit heredem ipsius Ricardi, filium scilicet eiusdem Hugonem[h]
nomine, quatinus alicubi de suis terris prospiceret aliquam |
B fo. 145v portionem, quam ecclesie huic concederet, ut elemosinam, quam
pro sua anima concesserat eius pater, ipsius filius stabilem efficeret,
ex illius terre uidelicet persolutione quam eum abbas ecclesie
monebat prouidere. Quod et fecit. Nam in loco qui dicitur Broche-
[ii. 109] stan duarum hidarum terram sancte Marie dedit, quam Willelmus
Clemens de se tenebat, unde et isdem quindecim solidos sibi singulis
annis reddebat. Et hoc fecit consensu domini sui Brientii et domine
sue Mathildis, apud Wottesdunam, in horum testium presentia:

[a] *om. B. The abbot's name is included in Lyell, no. 107 and Chatsworth, no. 298* [b] Benneham *B* [c] Gotscelini *B* [d] Luhello *with the* h *interlined, probably in the ink used on this page to provide guidance for the rubricator B* [e] Albini B [f] Brokestal *B* [g] *corr. from* huc *C*; huc *B* [h] Hugonem *rep. B*

[380] See above, p. 30.

Faritius for the aforesaid land, and undertook to recognize the lordship of, and hold it from, the church.[380]

156. *Charter of King Henry concerning the same land.*[381]
Henry king of the English to Roger bishop of Salisbury, and Hugh of Buckland, and all his barons, French and English, of Berkshire, greeting. Know that I have granted to St Mary in the church of Abingdon, and to Abbot Faritius, and to the monks two hides of land which are in Benham, which Walter son of Jocelin de Rivers held from Humphrey de Bohun, which that Humphrey was holding and in my presence gave back to the aforesaid church to remain perpetually. And I wish and order that she [i.e. St Mary] hold that land as well and honourably as she best and most honourably holds the church's other lands. Witnesses: Walter de Mayenne, and Guy de Clermont, and Ralph de Tosny, and Drogo de *Moncei*,[382] and Duhel de *Brielval*, and Richard de *Merei*,[383] and William d'Aubigny, and Robert de Dunstanville, and Aret the falconer and Patrick of Chaworth. At Romsey, in the year when the king gave his daughter to the emperor [1110].

157. *Concerning two hides at Wroxton.*[384]
Richard son of Reinfrid, coming to the day of death, on the day that is of St Leonard the Confessor [6 Nov.], for his soul surrendered to this church an annual rent of 19s., besides what he had already given (that is 6s.) for the soul of his wife, who had died earlier and was buried in this monastery. Concerning these matters, Abbot Faritius afterwards asked Richard's heir, that is his son named Hugh, that he look out for a portion of his lands somewhere which he might grant to this church. From the revenue of the land which the abbot advised him to provide for the church, the son would make stable the alms which his father had granted for his soul. And he did this. For in a place called Wroxton he gave to St Mary land of two hides which William Clemens was holding from him and from which he rendered him 15s. each year. And he did this at Waddesdon, by the consent of his lord Brian and his lady Matilda, in the presence of these witnesses:

[381] *RRAN* ii, no. 956; Lyell, no. 107; Chatsworth, no. 298.

[382] 'Moncei' cannot be identified with certainty. One possibility may be Moncy (Dept. Orne). It seems likely that the man's first name should be 'Juhel', not 'Duhel'.

[383] 'Merei' cannot be identified with certainty. One possibility might be Merri (Dept. Orne).

[384] Oxon.; see *VCH*, *Oxfordshire*, ix. 177–8. Wroxton is listed amongst Faritius's acquisitions in *De abbatibus*; *CMA* ii. 288. Lyell, no. 320, is a confirmation by Richard son of Reinfrid's grandson.

Ruellent dapiferi, Gisleberti[a] Pipard, Radulfi Foliot, Hugonis filii Milonis, et multorum aliorum.[385]

C fo. 156r **158.** *Carta Henrici regis | de diuersis rebus quas abbas Faritius adquisiuit.*[386]

Licet omnia mundi regna sint transitoria, per ea tamen conquiruntur eterna, si eorum diuitie rite tractentur et iuste dispensentur. Felix sane commercium ubi pro transitoriis semper manentia, pro terrenis celestia, commutantur. Vnde ego Henricus Dei gratia rex Anglorum et dux Normannorum—inter cetera que (Deo auctore) pro salute anime mee et parentum meorum, uxoris mee et filiorum,[387] in diuersis iam locis feci—consilio baronum meorum, hec que infra leguntur Deo et sancte genitrici eius concessi, in Abbendonensi ecclesia perpetuo iure manenda. Videlicet quinque hidas terre, quietas omnibus geldis et placitis et aliis rebus mihi pertinentibus, in manerio eiusdem ecclesie quod dicitur Wrda,[b] ad opus elemosine.[388] Et quoddam meum molendinum proprium, cum terris, et aquis, et consuetudinibus, aliisque rebus sibi pertinentibus, quod uocatur Henoura, positum super flumen Eccam in manerio de Suttuna.[389] Et duas hidas terre que sunt in Beneham, quas Vnfridus de Bohun, in presentia mea et multorum baronum,[c] reddidit et concessit predicte
[ii. 110] ecclesie.[390] Et quoddam pratum, nomine Kingesmeda, in feudo firma perpetuo habendum, pro uiginti solidis reddendis unoquoque ⟨anno⟩,[d] quod ante reddebat tantum quindecim prepositis meis.[391] Et terram quam Algarus tenet in Abbefeld, quam Nigellus de Oilleio reddidit eidem ecclesie in dominio habendam.[392] Et unam hidam in Westona, in loco qui dicitur Wdemundesleia, quam Droco de Andeleia dedit ecclesie, et comes Ricardus de Cestra fecit quietam de omni seruitio suo, pro anima patris sui.[393] Et ecclesiam de Niweham, cum terra sibi

[a] Gilleberti *B* [b] Wrþa *B* [c] meorum *add. B* [d] *suppl. ed.*

[385] Those consenting are presumably Brian fitzCount and Matilda, either daughter or widow of Miles Crispin; see Keats-Rohan, 'Devolution of the Honour of Wallingford'. Brian was constable of Henry I and controlled the Honour of Wallingford until late in Stephen's reign; he probably died in the late 1140s. See Green, *Government*, pp. 247–8. Waddesdon, of which Brian fitzCount was lord, is in Buckinghamshire. See above, p. 142, for Gilbert Pipard being steward of Miles Crispin; the manuscript here, however, definitely intends the word steward to describe Ruellent, not Gilbert. Ralph was a member of the family of Foliot of Chilton, Wilts.; see *HKF* iii. 234. Hugh son of Miles could, but need not, be an illegitimate son of Miles Crispin. A Hugh son of Miles appears with Richard son of Reinfrid in *Regesta*, ed. Bates, no. 167, and see accompanying note.

[386] *RRAN* ii, no. 1092; Lyell, no. 123. The charter may well date to the Westminster Council of 16 Sept. 1115. It must be after the consecration of Theulf as bishop of

Ruellent the steward, Gilbert Pipard, Ralph Foliot, Hugh son of Miles, and many others.[385]

158. *Charter of King Henry concerning various things which Abbot Faritius acquired.*[386]

Although all kingdoms of the world are transitory, through them, however, may be acquired eternal kingdoms, if their riches are rightly employed and justly spent. It is a very happy transaction when things ever-lasting are received in return for the transitory, heavenly ones for earthly. Therefore I, Henry, by the grace of God king of the English and duke of the Normans—amongst other things which (with God the author) I have already done in various places, for the salvation of my soul and my parents, my wife and my children[387]—by the counsel of my barons have granted to God and to his holy mother these possessions which are listed below to remain in the church of Abingdon by perpetual right. Namely, five hides of land, quit of all gelds and pleas and other things pertaining to me, in the church's manor called Longworth, for the use of alms.[388] And a mill of mine, with lands and waters and customs and other things pertaining to it, which is called Hennor, positioned on the river Ock in the manor of Sutton.[389] And two hides of land which are in Benham, which Humphrey de Bohun gave back and granted to the aforesaid church in my presence and that of many barons.[390] And a meadow named King's Mead to have perpetually in fee farm for 20s. to be rendered annually, which previously only rendered 15s. to my reeves.[391] And the land which Ælfgar holds in *Abbefeld*, which Nigel d'Oilly gave back to this church to have in demesne.[392] And one hide in Weston in the place called Wormsley, which Drogo des Andelys gave to the church, and Earl Richard of Chester made quit of all his service, for the soul of his father.[393] And the church of Nuneham,

Worcester on 27 Jun. 1115 (*Handbook of British Chronology*, p. 278), whilst William bishop of Exeter was sent to Rome after that council. For the form of the charter, see above, p. xviii n. 8. The proem expresses sentiments often found in Anglo-Saxon charters, including those of Abingdon, but is not based on any surviving Abingdon example. More generally for such sentiments, see S. D. White, *Custom, Kinship, and Gifts to Saints: the Laudatio Parentum in Western France, 1050–1150* (Chapel Hill, NC, 1988).

[387] The meaning of 'filiorum' may be either 'children' or 'sons'; certainly in the latter case Henry would be including his illegitimate sons as well as his legitimate son and heir, William. 'Filiorum' does appear in other charters of Henry I in this context; see e.g. *RRAN* ii, no. 1347.

[388] See below, p. 160.

[389] See above, p. 96.

[390] See above, p. 158.

[391] See above, p. 98.

[392] See above, p. 110.

[393] See above, p. 98.

pertinente, et decimam eiusdem uille, et unam piscariam cum rebus
sibi pertinentibus, sicut Willelmus de Curceio predicte ecclesie dedit
in elemosina.[394] Et unam hidam in Feincotam[a] cum pratis et pascuis,
et omnibus sibi pertinentibus, sicut Adelina de Iureio dedit ecclesie in
elemosina, et Adeliza filia concessit.[395] Et sartum quod Robertus filius
Haimonis dedit ecclesie, quod est inter Merlauam et Hamestede,
sicut designatum fuit per barones ipsius Roberti.[396] Et terram
Alwardi de Suttuna, iuxta Colebroc, quam Milo Crispinus et uxor
B fo. 146r eius Mathildis dederunt ecclesie in elemosina.[397] Et | terram Roberti
filii Heruei, cum consuetudinibus quibus eam tenebat a Roberto
Gernone domino suo, qui eam dedit regine Mathildi uxori mee, et
ipsa cum eo iam dicte ecclesie dedit in elemosina.[398] Et unam hidam
cum dimidia uirgata in uilla que dicitur Holm, et dimidiam hidam in
Estratona,[b] sicut Henricus de Albinneio[c] concessit ecclesie.[399] Et
unam hidam in uilla Dumeltune, quam Willelmus Goizenboeth[d]
[ii. 111] dedit ecclesie, et comes Robertus de Mellent ex cuius feudo erat
ante me auctorizauit.[400] Et in eadem uilla, dimidiam hidam quam ego
ipse concessi ecclesie in elemosina.[401] Et in uilla Chinsuetona[e]
ecclesiam et duas hidas de[f] duodenis uiginti acris, et unam uirgatam,
quas Albricus[g] de Ver et uxor eius Beatrix et filii eius dederunt
ecclesie, pro anima Gaufridi filii sui.[402] Et hospicia sua que sunt
Lundonie in Westminsterstret.[h][403] Et terram quam Ricardus filius
Reinfredi dedit ecclesie, et Willelmus Clemens ab eo tenebat, quam
Brientius et [i]Mathildis uxor eius[i] concesserunt ecclesie.[404] Signum
regis Henrici +.[j] Signum regine Mathildis +. Signum Willelmi filii
regis. Signum Radulfi archiepiscopi Cantuariensis +. Signum Tur-
stani archiepiscopi Eboracensis +. Signum Willelmi episcopi Wintonie +. Signum Willelmi episcopi Exonie[k] +. Signum Teoldi[l]
episcopi Wirecestrie +. Signum Rogeri abbatis Fiscanni +. Signum
Rannulfi cancellarii Henrici regis +. |

C fo. 156v **159.** *De hospicio abbatis apud Wintoniam.*[405]

Anno quinto decimo Henrici regis, Willelmus Wintoniensis episcopus, dum ecclesiam apud Clares dedicaret, concessit ecclesie sancte

[a] Feincote *B* [b] Estratuna *B* [c] Albineio *B* [d] Goinzenboeth *B* [e] Kinsuetona *B* [f] *erased B* [g] Abbericus *B* [h] Westminster stret *B* [i–i] uxor eius Macthildis *B* [j] *crosses om. in B. The cross for the king's son was accidentally omitted in C* [k] Oxonie *B* [l] Theoldi *B*

[394] See above, p. 78. [395] See above, p. 106. [396] See above, p. 140. [397] See above, p. 142. [398] See above, p. 142. [399] See above, pp. 146–8. [400] See above, pp. 148–50. [401] See above, p. 154. [402] See above, p. 82.

with the land pertaining to it, and the tithe of that village, and one fishery, with the things pertaining to it, as William de Courcy gave to the aforesaid church in alms.[394] And one hide in Fencott, with meadows and pastures and everything pertaining to it, as Adelina d'Ivry gave to the church in alms, and Adeliza her daughter granted.[395] And the assart between Marlow and Ackhamstead which Robert son of Hamo gave to the church, as specified by Robert's barons.[396] And the land of Egelward of Sutton, next to Colnbrook, which Miles Crispin and his wife Matilda gave to the church in alms.[397] And the land of Robert son of Hervey, with the customs with which he used to hold it from Robert Gernon his lord, who gave it to Queen Matilda my wife, and she with him gave it to the aforesaid church in alms.[398] And one hide with half a virgate in the village which is called Holme, and half a hide in Stratton, as Henry d'Aubigny granted to the church.[399] And one hide in the village of Dumbleton, which William Goizenboded gave to the church, and Count Robert of Meulan, of whose fee it was, authorized before me.[400] And in the same village, half a hide which I myself granted to the church in alms.[401] And in the village of Kensington the church and two hides of 240 acres, and one virgate, which Aubrey de Ver and his wife Beatrice and his sons gave to the church for the soul of Geoffrey their son.[402] And their houses which are in London, on Westminster street.[403] And the land which Richard son of Reinfrid gave to the church, and William Clemens held from him, which Brian and Matilda his wife granted to the church.[404] Mark of King Henry +. Mark of Queen Matilda +. Mark of William the king's son. Mark of Ralph, archbishop of Canterbury +. Mark of Thurstan archbishop of York +. Mark of William bishop of Winchester + . Mark of William bishop of Exeter +. Mark of Theulf bishop of Worcester +. Mark of Roger abbot of Fécamp +. Mark of Ranulf, chancellor of King Henry +.

159. *Concerning the abbot's house at Winchester.*[405]

In King Henry's fifteenth year [5 Aug. 1114–4 Aug. 1115], while he was dedicating a church at Kingsclere, William bishop of Winchester granted to the church of St Mary of Abingdon, and to Abbot Faritius,

[403] See above, p. 112.

[404] See above, p. 158.

[405] See *Winchester in the Early Middle Ages*, ed. M. Biddle (Oxford, 1976), p. 389. The property is not mentioned in the Winchester surveys of *c.*1110 and 1148. In the first case, this is probably because the grant came after the survey, although it is not absolutely certain that the present text indicates a new gift rather than a confirmation and

[*See p. 164 for n. 405 cont.*]

Marie Abbendonie, et abbati Faritio et omnibus successoribus eius post eum, et monachis ipsius ecclesie, locum sui hospicii quod est extra murum ciuitatis Wintonie, iuxta portam scilicet septemtriona-
[ii. 112] lem eiusdem[a] urbis, ab omni questu et consuetudine omnino[b] in perpetuum quietum, preter redditum duodecim denariorum, qui ad festum sancti Michaelis officiali ipsius episcopi in eadem ciuitate sunt reddendi.[406] Huic conuentioni affuit prior monachorum de episcopatu domnus Gaufridus, cum Antonio suo monacho, et concessis fauit, ita ut libenter episcopi preceptum reciperet quo iussit in capitulo monachis suis hec ab ipso referri et confirmari.[407] Hii testes interfuerunt: Henricus archidiaconus eiusdem episcopi, Stephanus[c] archidiaconus, Richerus et Alfricus archidiaconi, et multi alii.[408]

160. *Carta de eodem hospicio apud Wintoniam.*[409]
Henricus rex Anglorum Willelmo de Pontearcharum et preposito et collectoribus Wintonie, salutem.[410] Volo et precipio quod domus Faritii abbatis de Abbendona, quam habet in Wintonia, sit quieta ab omnibus geldis, scottis, et auxiliis, et omnibus rebus. Teste Waltero de Gloecestria.

161. *Carta de hospicio apud Windlesores.*[411]
Henricus rex Anglorum[d] Waltero filio Walteri de Windresore, salutem. Sciatis quod concedo Faritio abbati et ecclesie Abbendone
B fo. 146v terram illam et | domum de Windresores que fuit Alberti, sicut Rainerius eam sibi concessit.[412] Teste Rogero Bigod. Apud Londoniam.[e]

[a] eiudem *B* [b] omnio *B* [c] *initial om. C* [d] Anglie *B*
[e] Lundoniam *B*

exemption. One possible reason for the omission in the 1148 survey is that Henry I's writ, which follows this entry in the *History*, freed the property of all dues, including the rent to the bishop. For the approximate location of the abbot's house, see D. Keene, *Survey of Medieval Winchester* (2 vols., Oxford, 1985), i. 71 (fig. 3), where the bishop's soke corresponds approximately to his lands there in the twelfth century, and hence to the area from which the house was granted to Abbot Faritius. (I would like to thank Dr Keene for his help on these points.) Houses in London and Winchester for himself and his successors are listed amongst Faritius's acquisitions in *De abbatibus*; *CMA* ii. 288.

[406] Kingsclere is in Hampshire.

[407] Geoffrey was prior 1111–26; J. Le Neve, *Fasti Ecclesiae Anglicanae 1066–1300. 2: Monastic Cathedrals*, comp. D. Greenway (London, 1971), p. 88.

[408] On Henry, Stephen, and Richer, see *Fasti: Monastic Cathedrals*, pp. 91–2; *Winchester acta: 1070–1204*, ed. Franklin, pp. lv–lvii. Winchester diocese probably at this time, as

and to all his successors after him, and to the monks of that church, the site of his house which is outside the wall of the city of Winchester, next to the northern gate of that town, completely quit in perpetuity of all levy and custom, except a rent of 12d. to be rendered at Michaelmas [29 Sept.] to that bishop's official in the city.[406] Lord Geoffrey, prior of the monks of the bishopric, with Anthony his monk, was present at this agreement, and approved these grants, so that he willingly received the bishop's order whereby the bishop instructed that these matters were to be related and confirmed by him [i.e. Geoffrey] to his monks in the chapter.[407] These witnesses were present: Henry the bishop's archdeacon, Stephen the archdeacon, Richer and Ælfric the archdeacons, and many others.[408]

160. *Charter concerning this house at Winchester.*[409]
Henry king of the English to William de Pont de l'Arche and the reeve and collectors of Winchester, greeting.[410] I wish and order that the house of Abbot Faritius of Abingdon, which he has in Winchester, be quit of all gelds, scots, and aids, and all things. Witness: Walter of Gloucester.

161. *Charter concerning a house at Windsor.*[411]
Henry king of the English to Walter son of Walter of Windsor, greeting. Know that I grant to Abbot Faritius and to the church of Abingdon that land and house of Windsor which was Albert's, as Rainer granted it to them.[412] Witness: Roger Bigod. At London.

later, had only two archdeaconries. Richer and perhaps also Ælfric may have been assistant archdeacons, of the kind who would later be called 'sub-archdeacons' or 'vice-archdeacons'. This distinction would fit with the presentation of Richer and Ælfric as a distinct pair. Richer went on to become a full archdeacon, but if Ælfric did not do so it would explain why I have been unable to discover more about him. I would like to thank Professor Brian Kemp for his help on this point.

[409] *RRAN* ii, no. 1110; the writ can be dated to 1114 × 1116, between the making of the gift and Henry's last departure from England before the death of Faritius. The absence of a place date at the end of the writ is quite, although not very, unusual at this time.

[410] William was probably addressed as sheriff of Hampshire. Prominent as an administrator of Henry I, he became a tenant of Abingdon for lands in Weston, following the death of Robert Mauduit later in Henry I's reign; see Green, *Government*, pp. 267–9.

[411] *RRAN* ii, no. 858, dating to 1100 × 1107, the *terminus ante quem* being the death of Roger Bigod.

[412] *DB* i, fo. 56^{v}, has an Albert *clericus* holding one and a half hides in Windsor from the king; J. H. Round, *The Commune of London* (Westminster, 1899), pp. 36–8, suggests that the *Domesday* Albert can be identified with Albert of Lotharingia. For Walter, and the possibility that the reading should be William, see Round, 'Origins of FitzGeralds', p. 126. This may be the source of the rent later attributed to the kitchen, below, p. 395.

[ii. 113] **162.** *De quinque hidis apud Wrda.*[413]
Henricus rex Anglorum Roberto episcopo, et Herberto camerario, et Hugoni de Bochelanda, salutem. Sciatis quod clamo quietas quinque hidas abbatis Faritii de Abbendona de elemosina de Wrða[a] de omnibus rebus, et nominatim de isto auxilio quod barones mihi dederunt; et hoc, dico, sicut clamaui quietas eas per aliud breue meum in omni tempore.[414] Testibus Eudone dapifero, et Hamone dapifero, et Willelmo de Curci, et Nigello[b] de Oili.[c] Apud Corneberiam.

163. *De Bacgelea.*[d]
Siluas de Bachelea[e] et Cumenora iste abbas Faritius a regis forestariorum causationibus funditus quietas, et in eis capreorum uenationem, regio optinuit decreto.

164. *Carta de siluis Bacgelea[f] et Cumenora.*[415]
Henricus rex Anglorum Rogero episcopo Salesbirie, et Hugoni de Bochelanda, et omnibus baronibus, Francis et Anglis, de Berchescira[g]
[ii. 114] salutem. Sciatis quod concedo ecclesie sancte Marie de Abbendona, et Faritio abbati, et monachis, perpetuo in custodia eorum habendam siluam de Cumenora et Bagelega,[h] et omnes capreolos quos ibi inuenire poterint accipiant. Et ceruos et ceruas non accipiant, nisi mea licentia, et ego nemini licentiam dabo ibi uenandi nisi illis. Et omnes foresfacturas sartorum condono[i] eis. Testibus Roberto Linc' episcopo, et Rannulfo[j] episcopo Dunelm', et Rogero Bigod, et Nigello de Oili,[k] et Dauid fratre regine, et Rogero de Oili,[l] et Gosfrido[m] Ridel, et Droco uenatore, et W. de Hoctona. Apud Corneberiam.

165. *De [n]hundreto Hornimere.[n]*[416]
Comitatus Anglie ubique per centenos, quos hundred uocamus, determinatur. Hec autem ecclesia unum hundred in Sandford[o] adeo libere antiquitus continet, ut nulli alteri, nisi soli abbati, sit obnoxium.[417] Cui regis homines de Suttuna iuxta Abbendonam semper infensi, multociens sue potestati illud subdere, sunt, sed abbatis

[a] Wrþa *B* [b] *initial om. B* [c] Oilli *B* [d] Baggeleia *B* [e] Bacchleia *B* [f] Baggelea *B* [g] Bercscira *B* [h] Baggeleia *B* [i] concedo *B* [j] Rannulf *B* [k] Oilli *B* [l] Oilli *B* [m] Goisfr' *B* [n–n] hundredo Hornimera *B* [o] Samford *B*

[413] *RRAN* ii, no. 959; the writ may well be referring to the aid granted for the marriage of the king's daughter in 1110. On the identification of the place, see above, p. 137. Lyell, no. 105, gives Hubert, not Herbert, as the name of the second addressee.

162. *Concerning five hides at Longworth.*[413]
Henry king of the English to Bishop Robert, and Herbert the chamberlain, and Hugh of Buckland, greeting. Know that I quitclaim from all things Abbot Faritius of Abingdon's five hides of alms at Longworth, and namely from that aid which my barons have given me. And this, I say, as I quitclaimed them for all time by another writ of mine.[414] Witnesses: Eudo the steward, and Hamo the steward, and William de Courcy, and Nigel d'Oilly. At Cornbury.

163. *Concerning Bagley.*
Abbot Faritius obtained by royal decree the woods of Bagley and Cumnor, absolutely quit of accusations by the king's foresters, and the hunting of roe deer in them.

164. *Charter concerning the woods of Bagley and Cumnor.*[415]
Henry king of the English to Roger bishop of Salisbury, and Hugh of Buckland, and all barons, French and English, of Berkshire, greeting. Know that I grant to the church of St Mary of Abingdon, and to Abbot Faritius, and to the monks to have perpetually in their custody the wood of Cumnor and Bagley, and they may take all the roe deer which they can find there. And they are not to take red deer stags and hinds, except by my permission, and I shall give no one except them permission to hunt there. And I pardon them all forfeitures concerning assarts. Witnesses: Robert bishop of Lincoln, and Ranulf bishop of Durham, and Roger Bigod, and Nigel d'Oilly, and David the queen's brother, and Roger d'Oilly, and Geoffrey Ridel, and Drogo the huntsman, and William of Houghton. At Cornbury.

165. *Concerning the hundred of Hormer.*[416]
The county in England is everywhere divided into 'centeni', which we call 'hundreds'. Moreover, this church from of old holds one hundred in Sandford, so freely that it is subject to no one but the abbot.[417] The king's men of Sutton, next to Abingdon, were always threatening this, frequently attempting to subject it to their own

[414] Presumably *RRAN* ii, no. 722, above, p. 136.

[415] *RRAN* ii, no. 703; Lyell, no. 76; the writ must date to between 1101, the return of Ranulf Flambard, and 1107, the death of Roger Bigod; *RRAN* suggests 18 Oct. 1105 for this and other writs issued at Cornbury.

[416] 'The liberties of the hundred of Hormer' are listed amongst Faritius's acquisitions in *De abbatibus*; *CMA* ii. 288.

[417] i.e. Dry Sandford, in Hormer hundred. It is unclear why the hundred is referred to in this way.

prudentia, nunc regiis litteris, nunc qualibet alia cautela, assidue obuia,[a] in manu propria libere id usque hodie contra cunctos defendit.[418]

[ii. 115] **166.** *Carta regis de eodem hundreto.*[b][419]
Henricus rex Anglorum Rogero Salesbiriensi episcopo, et Hugoni |
C fo. 157r de Bochelanda, et omnibus baronibus suis, Francis et Anglis, de
Berchescira, salutem. Sciatis quod uolo et concedo et precipio ut abbatia de Abbendona, et Faritius abbas, et monachi, habeant et teneant ita firmiter et honorifice et quiete in perpetuum hundredum de Hornimera, sicut melius habuerunt et tenuerunt in tempore Eadwardi regis et Willelmi patris et Willelmi fratris mei. Testibus Roberto filio Haimonis et Rogero Bigod. Apud Legam.[420]

167. *Carta de hundredo Hornimere.*[421]
Henricus rex Anglorum Hugoni de Bochelanda, et iusticiariis suis, et omnibus baronibus suis, Francis et Anglis, de Berchescira, salutem.
Precipio quod abbas de Abbendona habeat hundredum suum de
B fo. 147r Hornimera | bene et in pace et honorifice, sicut unquam antecessores
sui melius habuerunt tempore patris mei, et fratris mei, et meo. Et nominatim placitum de equa, unde Osbertus calumpniatus fuit. Teste cancellario. Apud Wintoniam.

168. *De Leuechenora.*[422]
Homines de hundredo Peritune moliebantur manerium huius ecclesie
[ii. 116] Leueconore[c] appellatum suo iuri mancipari, sed is[d] abbas, in castello
Wincestre, coram episcopis Rogero Salesbiriense,[e] et Roberto Lincoliense,[f] et Ricardo Lundoniense, et multis regis baronibus, ratiocinando ostendit declamationem eorum iniustam esse.[423] Quare, iusticiariorum regis iudicio, optinuit ut illud manerium nulli alteri hundredo, nisi proprio, debeat in aliquo fieri obnoxium.[424] Sed quia rex tunc in Normannia erat, regina, que tunc presens aderat, taliter hoc sigillo suo confirmauit:

[a] obuius *B C* [b] hundredo *B* [c] Leuecenore *B* [d] his *B*
[e] Saresbiriense *B* [f] Lincolniense *B*

[418] *De abbatibus* states that Faritius unsuccessfully sought to buy Sutton from Henry I; *CMA* ii. 289–90.

[419] *RRAN* ii, no. 728; Lyell, no. 88; Chatsworth, no. 345. The writ must date to 1102 × 5, between Roger becoming bishop of Salisbury and Robert son of Hamo's loss of his senses, or at the latest his death in 1107.

[420] Berks., now Oxon.

power. But the abbot, in his prudence, assiduously confronted them, now with royal letters, now with some other precaution, and maintained this hundred in his own hand freely against all to this day.[418]

166. *Charter of the king concerning this hundred.*[419]
Henry king of the English to Roger bishop of Salisbury, and Hugh of Buckland, and all his barons, French and English, of Berkshire, greeting. Know that I wish, and grant, and order that the abbey of Abingdon, and Abbot Faritius, and the monks have and hold in perpetuity the hundred of Hormer, as firmly and honourably and undisturbed as they best had and held it in the time of King Edward and William my father and William my brother. Witnesses: Robert son of Hamo and Roger Bigod. At Bessels Leigh.[420]

167. *Charter concerning the hundred of Hormer.*[421]
Henry king of the English to Hugh of Buckland, and his justiciars, and all his barons, French and English, of Berkshire, greeting. I order that the abbot of Abingdon have his hundred of Hormer well and in peace and honourably, as best as his predecessors ever had it in the time of my father, my brother, and myself. And namely the plea concerning a mare, wherein Osbert was accused. Witness: the chancellor. At Winchester.

168. *Concerning Lewknor.*[422]
The men of the hundred of Pyrton were striving to subject to their authority this church's manor called Lewknor, but in the castle of Winchester, in the presence of Bishops Roger of Salisbury, Robert of Lincoln, and Richard of London, and many of the king's barons, Abbot Faritius showed by pleading that their claim was unjust.[423] Therefore, by judgment of the king's justiciars he obtained that that manor ought not be subject in anything to any hundred except its own.[424] But since the king was currently in Normandy, the queen, who was then present, confirmed this with her seal thus:

[421] *RRAN* ii, no. 1111; Lyell, no. 89; *Royal Writs*, ed. van Caenegem, no. 8; *English Lawsuits*, no. 199; the writ must date to 1100 × 16, and before Hugh ceased to be sheriff of Berkshire.

[422] Oxon. *English Lawsuits*, no. 189; trans. *EHD* ii, no. 201. Lewknor is listed amongst Faritius's acquisitions in *De abbatibus*; *CMA* ii. 288.

[423] Note Biddle, *Winchester in the Early Middle Ages*, pp. 304–5, on the location of the treasury in the castle at Winchester.

[424] i.e. the hundred of Lewknor.

169. *Carta regine de Luuechenora.*[a][425]

Mathildis Anglorum regina Roberto episcopo Lincoln', et Thome de Sancto Iohanne, et omnibus baronibus, Francis et Anglis, de Oxenefordscira, salutem. Sciatis quod Faritius abbas de Abbendona, in curia domini mei et mea, apud Wintoniam in thesauro, ante Rogerum episcopum Salesbiriensem, et Robertum episcopum Lincolniensem, et Ricardum episcopum Lundoniensem, et Will'[b] de Curceio, et Adam de Porto, et Turstino capellano,[c] et Waltero de Gloecestria, et Herebertum[d] camerarium, et Willelmum de Oileio,[e] et Gosfr' filium Herberti, et Will' de Enesi, et Radulfo Basset, et Goisfr' de Magnauilla, et Goisfr' Ridel, et Waltero archidiacono de Oxeneford, et per Librum de Thesauro disratiocinauit quod Leuecanora manerium suum nichil omnino debet in hundredo de Peritona[f] facere.[426] Sed omnia que debet facere, tantummodo in hundredo de Leuecanora[g] facere debet, in quo hundredo habet ecclesia de
[ii. 117] Abbendona decem et septem hidas.[427] Testibus Rogero episcopo Salesb', et Willelmo de Curci, et Adam de Porto. Apud Wincestram.

170. *De Culeham.*[428]

Anno decimo regni Henrici regis, apud Suttunam residente plenarie scira, et maxime pro causa que sequitur, disrationauit domnus abbas Faritius et monachi de Abbendona terram de Culeham, solidam et quietam de omnibus consuetudinibus et de omnibus hominibus, ad opus ecclesie Abbendonensis, et maxime de quadam uiolentia[h] quam homines de supradicto manerio Suttune inferebant illi terre, scilicet in accipiendis glebis illius terre ad opus molendini et piscarie regis. Vnde, sicut antecessor illius Adelelmus abbas

[a] Leuechenora *B* [b] Willelmo *B* [c] cappellano *B* [d] Herbertum *B* [e] erleio *C* [f] Perituna *B* [g] Leuacanora *B* [h] uioilentia *C*

[425] *RRAN* ii, no. 1000; Lyell, no. 127, which omits the 11 names after William de Courcy. The charter dates to Henry's absence between Aug. 1111 and Jul. 1113; *RRAN* suggests the Michaelmas meeting of the exchequer in 1111.

[426] Adam de Port was a royal steward; see Green, *Government* p. 39. Thurstan the chaplain was elected archbishop of York in mid-August 1114; *Handbook of British Chronology*, p. 281. Walter of Gloucester was a royal constable, with responsibilities in Wales. He may have died by 1126; see Green, *Government*, pp. 53, 257. William d'Anisy was a royal dispenser; see Green, *Government*, p. 228, *Anglo-Norman Families*, p. 4. William d'Oilly and Geoffrey son of Herbert do not appear elsewhere in the surviving charters of Henry I. Geoffrey de Mandeville was probably of the Mandeville family of Marshwood, Dorset. He witnessed various of Henry I's charters early in his reign, and was probably sheriff of Devon; *RRAN* ii, no. 769n., Green, *Sheriffs*, p. 35. J. Le Neve, *Fasti Ecclesiae Anglicanae 1066–1300. 3: Lincoln*, comp. D. Greenway (London, 1977), p. 35 states that this is Walter archdeacon of Oxford's first appearance as archdeacon. Unless

169. *Charter of the queen concerning Lewknor.*[425]

Matilda queen of the English to Robert bishop of Lincoln, and Thomas of St John, and all the barons, French and English, of Oxfordshire, greeting. Know that Abbot Faritius of Abingdon, in the court of my lord and myself in the treasury at Winchester, before Roger bishop of Salisbury, and Robert bishop of Lincoln, and Richard bishop of London, and William de Courcy, and Adam de Port, and Thurstan the chaplain, and Walter of Gloucester, and Herbert the chamberlain, and William d'Oilly, and Geoffrey son of Herbert, and William d'Anisy, and Ralph Basset, and Geoffrey de Mandeville, and Geoffrey Ridel, and Walter archdeacon of Oxford, by the Book of the Treasury proved that his manor of Lewknor ought to do nothing at all in the hundred of Pyrton.[426] But everything which it ought to do, it ought to do only in the hundred of Lewknor, in which hundred the church of Abingdon has seventeen hides.[427] Witnesses: Roger bishop of Salisbury, and William de Courcy, and Adam de Port. At Winchester.

170. *Concerning Culham.*[428]

In the tenth year of King Henry's reign [5 Aug. 1109–4 Aug. 1110], the shire was fully present and sitting at Sutton, primarily for the case which follows. Lord Abbot Faritius and the monks of Abingdon deraigned the land of Culham for the use of the church of Abingdon, firm and quit of all customs, and of all men, and especially of certain violence which the men of the above-mentioned manor of Sutton were inflicting on that land, that is taking turfs from that land for the use of the king's mill and fishery. Therefore, just as his predecessor

perhaps there were two successive and indistinguishable archdeacons called Walter, he died before 6 Feb. 1152. He is most famous as the man who presented Geoffrey of Monmouth with his 'old book'; see *The Historia Regum Britannie of Geoffrey of Monmouth, i. Bern Burgerbibliothek, MS. 568*, ed. N. Wright (Cambridge, 1985), p. 1. The 'Book of the Treasury' is usually taken to be *Domesday Book*, but Harvey, 'Domesday Book and Anglo-Norman governance', p. 179 argues that it must be some other treasury document, 'for information on hundreds is absent from the relevant section' of *Domesday*. See also above, p. xxiv, and below, p. 378, for an Abingdon list based on *Domesday Book* which supplies the names of the hundreds containing its Oxfordshire lands.

[427] A figure confirmed by *Domesday Book*, above, p. 110 n. 257. The abbey held no other lands in that hundred.

[428] *RRAN* ii, no. 952; *English Lawsuits*, no. 185. The mention of Adelelm's defence of Culham is not entirely clear, although it may well refer to his firm actions against the reeve of Sutton, above, p. 14. Froger was sheriff of Berkshire 1066 × 86, probably soon after 1066; Green, *Sheriffs*, p. 26, and see above, Bk. i, c. 144 (*CMA* i. 486) for his oppressions. 'A portion of Culham' is listed amongst Faritius's acquisitions in *De abbatibus*; *CMA* ii. 288.

tempore Willelmi senioris regis et tempore Frogerii uicecomitis terram supradicte uille Culeham a tali uiolentia quietauit, sic et iste abbas Faritius eo die et eo tempore quo supradictum est quietauit eam a supradicta uiolentia et omnibus consuetudinibus, in presentia Hugonis uicecomitis, probi et sapientis uiri, qui non solum Berchescire[a] sed etiam aliis septem sciris preerat uicecomes—adeo erat nominatus uir et carus regi—et in presentia multorum hominum trium scirarum ibi assistentium. |

C fo. 157ᵛ Post istam disratiocinationem, cum in eorum non fuisset ausum[b] hominum quod pridem egerant iam publico in conspectu iterare, clanculo id repetunt. De qua re cum certi nuncii relatio abbati esset perlata, uicecomitatum tunc Berchescire regenti, Hugoni de Bochelande eandem retulit, cuius et iussu in hundredo ipsi, Suttune
[ii. 118] predicte regis uille adiacenti, rectum de hac iniusticia ecclesie et abbati, per iudicium eiusdem hundredi, huiusmodi persolutum fuit. Erat eo tempore molendinarius molendini quod situm est super flumen Tamisie ad orientalem partem predicte uille regis, nomine Gamel, qui horis, ex altera parte fluminis de terra uille Culeham pertinenti glebas clam effodiens pro reficiendo molendino, nocturnis, cuius curam habebat, exportare solebat. Et cum, de hac sua temeritate in hundredo ipso interpellatus, negare nequiuisset, et pro hoc iure legis subactus esset, decreuerunt iusticiarii hundreti debere eum abbati et ecclesie emendationem quinque mancusarum denariorum exsoluere.[429] Quod et fecit. Sed cum eedem mancuse ab ipso molendinario exhibite[c] abbatis presentie fuissent, de singulis mancusis unum denarium solummodo accipiens, pro sua clementia ceteros illi remisit, testibus omnibus qui in hundredo erant. Predictos autem quinque denarios iussit abbas, pro memoria huius emendationis, in ecclesie scriniis reseruandos locari.[430]

171. *De clausura apud Cudesdunam.*[431]

Homines episcopi Lincolniensis Roberti de uilla Middeltuna fregerant pro suis pratis clausuram molendini abbatie apud uillam suam Cuthesduna,[d] duabus uicibus, per diuersa tamen tempora.[432] Sed,

[a] Berchescirę *B* [b] *for* ausu ? [c] exibite *B* [d] Cudesduna *B*

[429] An Old English unit of account, worth 30d.

[430] For later events relating to this mill, see *VCH*, *Oxfordshire*, vii. 32; *Curia Regis Rolls*, vii. 390–1.

[431] *DB* i, fo. 156ᵛ, states that 'the abbey holds Cuddesdon [Oxon.]. . . . a mill and two fisheries, twelve shillings'. 'The mill of Cuddesdon' is listed amongst Faritius's acquisitions in *De abbatibus*; *CMA* ii. 288.

Abbot Adelelm had freed from such violence that land of the village of Culham in the time of King William the elder and of Froger the sheriff, so too did Abbot Faritius free it from the above-mentioned violence and all customs, on the day and at the time mentioned above. He did so in the presence of Hugh the sheriff, a virtuous and wise man, who was sheriff not only of Berkshire but of seven other shires as well—he was so renowned a man and so close to the king—, and in the presence of many men of the three shires who were attending there.

After that court victory, the men of Sutton dared not repeat their previous deed in public view, so they returned to it in secret. When a trustworthy messenger's report concerning this reached the abbot, he conveyed it to Hugh of Buckland, then ruling the shrievalty of Berkshire. At Hugh's order, in the hundred pertaining to the king's village of Sutton, justice was done by judgment of that hundred to the church and abbot concerning this wrong, as follows. There was at this time a miller of the mill situated on the river Thames to the east of the king's aforesaid village, and he was named Gamel. During the hours of darkness he was accustomed secretly to dig up turfs from the land belonging to the village of Culham on the other side of the river, and to remove them for repairing the mill of which he had care. When he was accused in the hundred court of Sutton concerning this reckless deed of his, he could not deny it and was convicted of this by right of law. The justiciars of the hundred decreed that he ought to pay the abbot and church an emendation of five *mancuses* of pennies.[429] And he did this. But when the miller produced these *mancuses* in the abbot's presence, the abbot only took one penny from each *mancus*, and by his clemency remitted the rest to the miller, with everyone in the hundred court witnessing. Moreover, the abbot ordered the aforesaid five pennies to be placed for safe-keeping in the church chests, in memory of this emendation.[430]

171. *Concerning the enclosure at Cuddesdon.*[431]

Bishop Robert of Lincoln's men from the village of Milton on two different occasions broke the dam of the abbey's mill in its village of Cuddesdon, for the benefit of their meadows.[432] But since this is

[432] Great Milton, Oxon., which *DB* i, fo. 155^{r-v}, confirms was a possession of the bishop of Lincoln in 1086. Given the sense of the passage, I have translated 'clausura' as dam, and see the men of Milton as trying to flood their water-meadows. However, *DMLBS*, fasc. ii, s.v. *clausura*, gives '(enclosing) fence, hedge, wall, ditch or sim.' as the meaning for this passage; see also *Local Maps and Plans from Medieval England*, ed. R. A. Skelton and P. D. A. Harvey (Oxford, 1986), p. 204, for the use of 'clausum' in a fifteenth-century map; and cf. 'exclusa' in *Curia Regis Rolls*, vi. 390.

quia contra legem consuetudinariam id est, episcopus ipse, ratione et amore istius abbatis et ecclesie, ab eisdem suis hominibus de Middeltuna fecit reficere eandem quam fregerant clausuram, millesimo centesimo [a]quinto primum, posterius uero millesimo centesimo[a] octauo ab incarnatione Dominica anno.

[ii. 119] **172.** *De consuetudine nauium.*[433]

Consuetudo huius ecclesie est a tempore domni Ordrici abbatis ut de unaquaque naui Oxeneforde ciuitatis que transitum fecerit per aquam Tamisie prope curiam Abbendonensem, uersus australem scilicet partem diffluentem, cellarario centum allecia omni anno more debito reddantur, aut pro eis condignum pretium,[434] ita ut nauium remiges, non interrogati, eadem cellarario deferant, a tempore uidelicet Purificationis sancte Marie usque ad Pascha. Quod si eorum aliquis hanc consuetudinem detinuisse inuentus fuerit, huiusmodi nauem cellararius, ne per aquam transeat ecclesie, iure detinet, donec sibi rectum faciat. Hanc ecclesie consuetudinem, tempore domni Faritii abbatis, naute predicte ciuitatis moliti sunt ecclesie abripere, sed cito eos ab hac temeritate disratiocinatione iusta idem abbas repressit, ita ut eadem regi Henrico allegaret, et rex per sua
B fo. 148ʳ breuia iusticiariis suis et | uicecomitibus Berchesire[b] et Oxenefordscire preciperet, quatinus rectam iusticiam inde facerent, ne ecclesia ultra huiusmodi consuetudine sua careret.[435] Itaque, eodem rege regnante, anno imperii sui undecimo, et Thoma de Sancto Iohanne ac Ricardo de Monte Oxenefordscire uicecomitibus constitutis, apud
C fo. 158ʳ eandem Oxeneford | ciuitatem in domo Hardingi presbiteri, de hac re placitum habitum est;[436] et maiorum eiusdem loci communi iudicatum est decreto Abbendonensem[c] ecclesiam iustam rem[d] exigere, et
[ii. 120] eam a ciuitatis totius nauigio debere omni anno persolui.[e] Sequenti[f] quoque post hoc anno, Radulfus cellararius, eisdem[g] coadunatis Oxeneforde primoribus, questus est quod de quibusdam eorum nautis necdum iam decretam consuetudinem habuisset. Quibus ilico accersitis, precipitur manibus[h] eiusdem cellararii debitum idem[i] ecclesie coram reddere. Et ita factum est, cunctis qui aderant testibus.

[a–a] *om. B, an omission which suggests that B derives from C* [b] Berchescire *B* [c] Abbendunensem *B* [d] *corr. from* rex *C* [e] persoluere *B C* [f] sequente *B C* [g] eiusdem *B* [h] nauibus *B* [i] ei dem, *involving erasure B*

[433] *English Lawsuits*, no. 191. 'One hundred herrings from the boats which cross through the fish-garth', that is an enclosure on a river for preserving or taking fish, are

against customary law, Bishop Robert, with good reason and from love of that abbot and church, made his men of Milton repair the enclosure which they had broken, first in the year of our Lord 1105, later indeed in the year of our Lord 1108.

172. *Concerning the custom of boats.*[433]

From the time of lord Abbot Ordric [1052–66], it has been the custom of this church that one hundred herrings—or a suitable price for them—be paid each year to the cellarer, in due fashion, from each boat of the city of Oxford which travels southwards by the water of the Thames flowing next to the court of Abingdon.[434] The oarsmen of the boats render them to the cellarer, without being asked, specifically from the time of the Purification of St Mary [2 Feb.] until Easter. If any of them is found to have withheld this custom, the cellarer by right prevents their boat from crossing through the church's water until justice has been done to him. In the time of lord Abbot Faritius, the sailors of Oxford were striving to take this custom away from the church, but the abbot swiftly stopped them from this reckless act by bringing a just plea. He cited their attempts to King Henry, and the king by his writs ordered his justiciars and sheriffs of Berkshire and Oxfordshire that they do proper justice concerning this, so that the church no longer be deprived of its customs of this sort.[435] Therefore with Henry reigning in the eleventh year of his dominion [5 Aug. 1110–4 Aug. 1111] and with Thomas of St John and Richard de Monte as sheriffs of Oxfordshire, a plea concerning this matter was held at Oxford in the house of Harding the priest.[436] It was judged by common decree of the greater men of Oxford that the church of Abingdon's demand was just, and that it ought to be paid each year by the shipping of all the city. In the following year, when the same leading men of Oxford had gathered, Ralph the cellarer complained that he did not yet have from some of their boatmen the custom as adjudged. These men were summoned immediately and ordered to render publicly into the cellarer's hands what was due to the church. And this was done, with all present acting as witnesses. At this plea

listed amongst Faritius's acquisitions in *De abbatibus*; *CMA* ii. 288. See also above, Bk. i, c. 141 (*CMA* i. 481).

[434] For the area of the monastic precinct known as the court, see Plan, p. cv.

[435] See above, p. 138.

[436] *Eynsham*, i, no. 7, records a man called Harding as having houses at Oxford, but he was dead by 1109, having died at Jerusalem. Nevertheless, it is possible that after his death his property could still have been referred to as 'the house of Harding the priest'.

Ad hanc disratiotionem fuerunt hi[a] presentes: Ricardus de Monte tunc uicecomes, Walterus archidiaconus, et multi alii.

173. *De ecclesia Pesimare.*[437]

Ricardus et filius eius Philippus de Pesimari ecclesiam habent in eadem uilla, quam dedicare[b] et cimiterium illic benedici per domnum Osmundum episcopum fecerunt, tempore Rainaldi abbatis. Sed eiusdem uille parrochia iuri[c] ecclesie de Ciuelea[d] antiquitus pertinet. Et quanquam abesset capituli Abbendonie et presbitero de Ciuelea,[e] dedicatio tamen illa concelebrata est.[f] Quare, istius abbatis postea tempore, inde questione mota, pater cum filio, qui facti huius auctores extiterant, pro emendatione duos solidos quoque[g] anno monachis Abbendonie, et ecclesie de Ciuelea duas acras, se promiserunt reddere.

174. *De ecclesia Kingestuna.*[h][438]

Ecclesia de Kingestuna[i] subest parrochiali ecclesie de Wrde,[j] et hoc ab antiquo iure. Iccirco cum ecclesia ipsa de Kingestuna dedicaretur cum cimiterio per domnum Osmundum episcopum, duo ex monachis
[ii. 121] nostris, Alfricus scilicet quondam prior et Motbertus,[k] illic ceterorum fratrum loco consistentes, episcopo calumpniati sunt consuetudines matris ecclesie que est apud Wrdam.[l][439] Quo tempore Rainaldus[m] preerat ecclesie abbatis regimine. Itaque huiuscemodi imposita calumpnia, postea a primis predicte uille senioribus consultum est, uidelicet Radulfo de Bachepuz[n] et Athelelmo,[o] quatinus annuatim ecclesie Abbendonie ad Pentecosten ab eis utrisque donarentur sexdecim denarii, id est due ore, et ad ecclesiam de Wrda[p] similiter a singulis una acra,[440] unus porcus, et unus caseus. Sed mortuo Radulfo, cum eius filius Henricus sibi succederet, predictam persoluere pactionem neglexit. Verum eo tempore non multo post improuisa morte sublato ex hac uita, frater eius Robertus heres illi factus est suarum rerum. Qui tempore Quadragesimali Abbendoniam
B fo. 148v ueniens, regnante tunc Henrico rege et domno Fa|ritio existente abbate, promisit coram multis testibus ab illo deinceps se redditurum predictam pactionem.

[a] his *B C* [b] fecit *add. B* [c] uiri *B* [d] Ciuileia *B* [e] Ciuileia *B* [f] *although the meaning of this sentence is clear, at least one word appears to have been omitted, and there may also be grammatical mistakes* [g] *possibly corr. to* quoquo *C* [h] de Kingestuna *B* [i] Kingestona *B* [j] Wrþe *B* [k] Modbertus *B* [l] Wrþam *B* [m] Rainnaldus *B* [n] Bakepuz *B* [o] Adellelmo *B* [p] Wrþa *B*

[437] See above, p. 42.

were present Richard de Monte, then sheriff, Walter the archdeacon, and many others.

173. *Concerning the church of Peasemore.*[437]
Richard and his son Philip of Peasemore had a church in that village, which they had dedicated and the cemetery there blessed by lord Bishop Osmund in the time of Abbot Reginald [1084x97]. But of old the parochial obligations of this village belonged to the jurisdiction of the church of Chieveley. And although [no representative] of the chapter of Abingdon nor the priest of Chieveley was present, that dedication was still celebrated. Therefore, after Abbot Reginald's time, a complaint was raised concerning this. The father and son, who were responsible for this deed, promised that in emendation they would render 2s. annually to the monks of Abingdon, and two acres to the church of Chieveley.

174. *Concerning the church of Kingston.*[438]
The church of Kingston is subject to the parish church of Longworth, and this by ancient right. Therefore, when that church of Kingston, with its cemetery, was dedicated by lord Bishop Osmund, two of our monks, namely Ælfric (once the prior) and Modbert, who were present there representing all the other brethren, put a claim to the bishop for the customs of the mother church at Longworth.[439] At that time Reginald controlled the church in the office of abbot. After the claim had been brought, the foremost lords of Kingston, namely Ralph de Bagpuize and Adelelm, decided that at Pentecost every year 16d. should be given by each of them to the church of Abingdon (that is two *ores*), and similarly by each one acre,[440] one pig, and one cheese to the church of Longworth. But when Ralph died, his son Henry succeeded him and failed to fulfil that agreement. However, he was soon after taken from this life by unforeseen death, and his brother Robert was made heir of his possessions. While King Henry was reigning and lord Faritius was abbot, Robert came to Abingdon at Lent, and in the presence of many witnesses promised that henceforth he would restore the aforesaid agreement.

[438] Cf. above, p. 42. This account, compared with the earlier one, makes Robert's restoration seem rather less voluntary.

[439] Ælfric may be specified as ex-prior because there were two monks of that name; below, p. 200. Modbert may well be the monk who held the church as guardian between 1097 and 1100.

[440] Presumably the produce of one acre.

175. *Littere episcopi de ecclesia Kingestuna.*[a] [441]

Rogerus episcopus Salesbirie[b] Adelelmo de Kingestuna et Roberto de Bacepuiz,[c] salutem. Precipio uobis quod reddatis ecclesie de Abbendona rectitudines quas illi debetis de ecclesia uestra de Kingestuna. Et nisi feceritis, Ilbertus decanus interdicat diuinum officium apud Kingestona.[d] Apud Westmoster.

176. *De quadam mortua.*

Contigit etiam per hos[e] dies, ut presbiter de manerio Pesi[f] parro-
[ii. 122] chianam ecclesie de Wrda[g] quandam mortuam apud suam ecclesiam illicite sepeliret.[442] Sed per hunc abbatem, in capitulo presbiterorum apud Abbendonam tunc constituto, proposita declamatione, decretum datur idem corpus iam sepultum effodiri a presbitero de Pesi, ac referri ad ecclesiam de Wrda[h] sepeliendum debere, sacramento quod idem esset de quo agebatur ab eodem premisso.[443] Quod et factum est, anno uidelicet quarto decimo regni Henrici regis.

177. *De Walchelino Visus lupi.*[444]

Walchelinus quoque, cognomento Visus lupi, terram de rege tenet iuxta Boxore,[i] cuius terre redditus ecclesiasticus attinet ad parrochiam que est in predicto loco. Quem redditum cum idem uir retraheret,[j]
C fo. 158v abbatis huius rationibus | rectis auditis, consensum attribuit, et omnia que contra tenuerat Deo, et sancte Marie, et abbati predicto in perpetuum quieta clamauit, et ut ecclesia de Boxore omnes suas consuetudines de suo tenore ab illo die in reliquum tempus haberet, sicut unquam melius habuit, promisit, uidelicet de gildis, de cera, de unctione et uisitatione infirmorum, de corporibus omnium mortuorum de sua terra sepeliendorum,[k] et singulis de aliis quibusque consuetudinibus ecclesie pertinentibus.[445]

[a] de Kingestun *B*   [b] Saresbirie *B*   [c] Bachepuz *B*   [d] Kingestuna *B*
[e] os *B*   [f] Pesie *B*   [g] Wrþa *B*   [h] Wrþa *B*   [i] Boxora *B*
[j] retraeret *B*   [k] sepeliendum *B*

[441] See *Salisbury acta: 1078–1217*, ed. Kemp, no. 5, which dates the document to 'prob. Lent 1113 or shortly before'; Kealey, *Roger of Salisbury*, pp. 230–1. Kealey says that nothing else is known of Ilbert, but he was probably a rural dean in Berkshire.

[442] Pusey was in Berkshire, although now Oxon. *DB* i, fos. 59v (Gilbert holds Pusey from the abbot), 60v, 62v, show lordship of Pusey to have been divided between Abingdon, Saint-Pierre-sur-Dives, Henry de Ferrers, and Roger d'Ivry; only the last entry mentions a church.

[443] See above, p. xcix.

175. *Letters of the bishop concerning the church of Kingston.*[441]
Roger bishop of Salisbury to Adelelm of Kingston and Robert de Bagpuize, greeting. I order you that you give back to the church of Abingdon the rights which you owe it from your church of Kingston. And if you do not, Ilbert the dean is to prohibit divine office at Kingston. At Westminster.

176. *Concerning a certain dead woman.*
Also at that time it happened that the priest of the manor of Pusey wrongly buried at his church a dead woman, a parishioner of the church of Longworth.[442] But in the priests' chapter which was then gathered at Abingdon a claim was brought by Abbot Faritius, and the following decision was given: that the body which had already been buried should be dug up by the priest of Pusey and returned to the church of Longworth for burial, with the priest giving an oath that it was the body under dispute.[443] And this was done, in the fourteenth year of King Henry's reign [5 Aug. 1113–4 Aug. 1114].

177. *Concerning Walkelin Visdelou.*[444]
Also Walkelin, surnamed Visdelou, held land from the king next to Boxford, its ecclesiastical dues belonging to the parish which is in that place [i.e. Boxford]. Walkelin withheld these dues, but after hearing just reasons from Faritius, he granted his consent and quitclaimed in perpetuity to God, and to St Mary, and to the aforesaid abbot everything which he had withheld, and promised that the church of Boxford would have all its customs on its own terms from that day forth for the rest of time as best it ever had them, that is concerning guilds, candle-wax, unction and visitation of the sick, bodies of all dead people from its land to be buried, and each and every other custom pertaining to the church.[445]

[444] *DB* i, fo. 63^{r}, shows Humphrey Visdelou holding Boxford, Berks., in chief of the king; fo. 58^{v} states that 'Berner [holds] two hides in Boxford' from Abingdon; *VCH, Berkshire*, iv. 45, identifies Humphrey's holding as Westbrook. *VCH, Berkshire*, iv. 47, suggests that Walkelin, Humphrey's son, was seeking to give the dues to the church of Speen, in which parish were most of his lands. Walkelin later killed a knight, and forfeited a significant part of his fee. See further *HKF* i. 54–60, on the lordship of Visdelou; also *VCH, Berkshire*, iv. 103–4. Abingdon claimed Boxford as part of its early endowment, Bk. i, c. 11, *CMA* i. 26, *Charters of Abingdon Abbey*, no. 9; however, certainly by the later tenth century it was out of the abbey's control.

[445] See Brett, *English Church*, p. 227 on burial dues; J. R. H. Moorman, *Church Life in England in the Thirteenth Century* (Cambridge, 1945), p. 129 on candle-wax; also C. R. Cheney, *From Becket to Langton* (Manchester. 1956), pp. 152–3.

178. *De molendino*[a] *de Langeford.*[446]

Circa idem tempus defuncta Ansfrida, qua concubine loco rex ipse Henricus usus ante suscepti imperii monarchiam filium, Ricardum
[ii. 123] nomine, genuit, ac per hoc celebri sepultura a fratribus est tumulata.[b][447] Quare Willelmus filius eiusdem, quem de[c] Anskillo marito suo, ante regis predicti filii partum iam mortuo, pepererat, molendinum de Langeford, quod sui fundum iuris pertinuerat, triginta solidorum persolutorium, proprio monachorum usui habendum, concessit, apud pontem Oxeneford positum, quod hactenus Baiewrde[d] adiacuerat, cum omnibus sibi pertinentibus. Et ut inperpetuum firmum istud staret, idem Willelmus super altare sancte Marie donum huius concessionis posuit. Testibus domno Faritio abbate et toto conuentu, et Fulcone filio[e] regis, et Ricardo pedagogo, et multorum aliorum testimonio.[448]

B fo. 149r [f]Post obitum uero abbatis Faritii, | conquestus est idem Willelmus regi, tunc in Normannia posito, de supradicto molendino, quia uidelicet ui potestatis predicti abbatis potius quam sue proprie uoluntatis ecclesia habebat.[g][449] Quare regis mandato saisitus est inde. Sed postea legatione monachorum per Walterum, capellanum Willelmi de Bochelande, ueritatem rex cognoscens, precepit resaisiri[h] ecclesiam. Qua propter postea Willelmus ipse de Seuecurda suam iniusticiam recognoscens, correxit quod egerat, ita ut in capitulo in perpetuum omnem calumpniam de ipso molendino clamaret quietam, et in ecclesia super altare donum per baculum illic impositum confirmaret.[450]

[ii. 124] 179. *De terra de Stoches.*[i][451]

Gaufridus[j] de Malchenceio, cum uxore sua Ermentrude,[k] in capitulo coram Faritio abbate et toto conuentu, concessit huic ecclesie in elemosina unam hidam in uilla sua Stoches,[l] ita libere in perpetuum habendum ab omni negotio et suo seruitio, preter solum regis gildum,[m] sicut unquam ipsemet liberius eam habuerat.[452] Ex suo

[a] molendina *B* [b] uidelicet in claustro ante hostium ecclesie ubi fratres intrant in ecclesiam et exeunt *add. B* [c] *om. B* [d] Baiewrðe *B* [e] filius *B* [f] De morte Faritii abbatis *rubricated heading add. in B* [g] habeat *B* [h] resaisiari *B* [i] Stokes *B* [j] Galfridus *B* [k] Ermentrudæ *B* [l] Stokes *B* [m] geldum *B*

[446] Salter, *Medieval Oxford*, p. 15 states that this was also known as Weirs Mill, close to the Abingdon Road at Hinksey, one mile from Folly Bridge. *VCH*, *Berkshire*, iv. 408, distinguishes between Weirs Mill and Langford Mill. 'The mill of Langford' is listed amongst Faritius's acquisitions in *De abbatibus*; *CMA* ii. 288.

178. *Concerning the mill of Langford.*[446]
Around that time died Ansfrida, by whom, his concubine, King Henry had produced a son named Richard, before he exercised the monarchy of the dominion he acquired. As a result, she was interred by the brethren in a renowned tomb.[447] Therefore William, her son by Anskill her husband (who was already dead before the birth of the king's aforesaid son), granted the mill of Langford, which had been his property, situated at the bridge of Oxford, and until then belonging to Bayworth. Paying 30s., it was to be held for the monks' own use, with everything pertaining to it. So that this might stand firm in perpetuity, William placed the gift of this grant on the altar of St Mary. Witnesses: lord Abbot Faritius and all the convent, and Fulk the king's son, and Richard the schoolmaster, and by witness of many others.[448]

After the death of Abbot Faritius, however, William complained about this mill to the king, who was then in Normandy, specifically that the church held it through Faritius's power rather than William's wishes.[449] Therefore he was seised of it by the king's order. But afterwards the king learnt the truth by an embassy of the monks through Walter, chaplain of William of Buckland, and ordered the church to be reseised. William of Seacourt himself afterwards recognized his unjust act and made good what he had done, thus that in the chapter he quitclaimed in perpetuity all claim concerning this mill, and in the church confirmed the gift on the altar by a staff placed there.[450]

179. *Concerning the land of Stoke.*[451]
In the chapter in the presence of Abbot Faritius and the whole convent, Geoffrey de Mauquenchy, with his wife Ermentrude, granted to this church in alms one hide in his village of Stoke, to have in perpetuity as free from all obligations and from his service as he himself had ever most freely had it, except only the king's geld.[452]

[447] MS B here adds an extra phrase—'that is in the cloister before the door of the church where the brethren enter and leave the church.' See above, p. 52.

[448] For Fulk, see above, p. 53 n. 127; for Richard, see above, p. c n. 563.

[449] 1117×20. See also above, p. l, for perceptions of Faritius.

[450] A list in MS C in the same hand as the *History*, below, p. 398, includes the mill of Langford among the revenues of the chamber.

[451] Stoke Bruern, Northants., a Mauquenchy holding. The land reappears in a papal privilege below, p. 274, as Shuttlehanger, which is one mile west of Stoke Bruern, and in Stoke Bruern parish. It too was a Mauquenchy holding; see *HKF* iii. 413.

[452] For later members of the Mauquenchy family, see *HKF* iii. 413, *Anglo-Norman Families*, pp. 56–7.

quoque prato quatuor acras concessit, libertatem etiam omnibus pecoribus monachorum in suis communiter pascuis eundi, et porcis eorum sine pasnagio in sua silua, uti ipsis monachis uelle fuerit, et ad necessitatem curie ipsorum quantum opus erit de ipsa silua accipiendi. Non multo post, cum filius eius Girardus de ultra mare uenisset, eo presente et uxore sua Ermentrude, monachatum[a] suscepit, et suo predicto dono adiecit dimidiam hidam in eadem uilla, ipso Girardo cum matre sua hoc confirmante coram patre suo. Insuper pro amore ipsius sui patris, seipsum huic ecclesie dedit, ita ut si monachus fieri uelit, a nullo alio loco nisi ab isto id suscipiet, et si forte laicus defunctus fuerit et hoc in Anglia contigerit, hic sepulturam habebit cum tercia parte totius sue pecunie quam in Anglia tunc habuerit. Quod si in Normannia id contigerit, tercia tamen, ut dictum est, pars sue pecunie de Anglia ecclesie erit.[453] Eadem in conuentione et mater eius se per omnia dedit. Similiter et homines eius Robertus filius predicti Gaufridi, Willelmus filius eius, Goisfredus nepos eius, Willelmus nepos eius, Warinus dapifer eius, Radulfus de Munteneio,[454] Turstinus miles, qui etiam testes affuerunt his.[455] |

[ii. 125] **180.** *De Speresholt.*[456]

C fo. 159r Prope montem ubi ad Album Equum scanditur,[457] ab antiquo tempore ecclesia ista manerium Offentun appellatum in dominio possidet, iuxta quod uilla decem hidarum adiacet ex iure ecclesie, quam Speresholt nominant.[b] Hanc miles, Anskillus nomine, de ecclesia tempore Rainaldi abbatis pro unius militis seruitio tenebat. Verum hunc contigit et ipsius abbatis regisque iunioris Willelmi inimicitias adeo incurrisse postea, ut in regia poneretur captione,
B fo. 149v ibique moreretur. Quare rex | manus ad ecclesie possessionem mox iniciens, Turstino suo dispensatori illam dedit.[458] Quo mortuo, filius eius Hugo eadem ratione per regem in ipsa successit.[459] Eratque in hoc negotio quod maxime abbatiam tedebat. Nam nullum more militum seruitium exhibebatur[c] inde, et si quando regio imperio

[a] monacatum *B* [b] nominauit *B* [c] exibebatur *B*

[453] On bequests of moveables, and other instances of the specification of a third being bequeathed, see M. M. Sheehan, *The Will in Medieval England* (Toronto, 1963), pp. 289–91; note also below, p. 238.

[454] The toponym is probably one of the places in Normandy called Montigny or Montagny.

[455] Cf. A. Murray, *Reason and Society in the Middle Ages* (Oxford, 1978), p. 347.

[456] See also above, p. 52. This chapter marks the start of the second *discretio* of

He also granted four acres from his meadow, and freedom for all the monks' livestock to go communally onto his pastures, and for their pigs without pannage to go into his wood, as the monks wished, and to gather from that wood as much as would be required for the needs of their court. Not long afterwards, when his son Gerard came from overseas, in his presence and that of his wife Ermentrude, Geoffrey received the monk's habit, and added to his aforesaid gift half a hide in the same village. Gerard, together with his mother, confirmed this in his father's presence. In addition, because of his love of his father, Gerard gave himself to this church, so that if he wished to become a monk, he would receive this status from no other monastery but Abingdon. And if it happened that he died a layman, and this occurred in England, he would have burial here, together with a third of all the goods he would then have in England. If he died in Normandy, still a third of his goods in England, as specified, would be the church's.[453] In this agreement, his mother also gave herself in all respects; likewise his men, Robert son of the aforesaid Geoffrey, William his son, Geoffrey his nephew, William his nephew, Warin his steward, Ralph de *Munteneio*,[454] Thurstan the knight, who were also present as witnesses to these matters.[455]

180. *Concerning Sparsholt.*[456]

Close to the hill rising to the White Horse,[457] this church has from long ago possessed in demesne the manor called Uffington, next to which lies a village of ten hides, of the church's property, which people call Sparsholt. A knight named Anskill used to hold this from the church in the time of Abbot Reginald, for the service of one knight. But it happened that this man later incurred such enmity of both that abbot and King William the younger that he was placed in royal captivity, and there he died. Therefore the king soon laid his hands on the church's possession, and gave it to Thurstan his dispenser.[458] When Thurstan died, his son Hugh succeeded to it through the king, on the same basis.[459] This business was particularly annoying to the abbey, for the customary knight service was not performed from there, and, if ever geld was taken by royal order, the

Faritius's activities relating to the abbey's estates, his resumptions; see above, p. 72. Sparsholt is listed amongst Faritius's acquisitions in *De abbatibus*; *CMA* ii. 288.

457 See *VCH*, *Berkshire*, i. 188–91, iv. 544. This is the earliest known reference to the White Horse; see EPNS, *Berkshire*, ii. 380.

458 See above, p. lxxxvii, on the phrase 'manus inicio'.

459 On Hugh the king's dispenser, see above, p. lxxi.

gildebatur,[a] obolum ad ualens, nolente predicto Hugone reddere, homines de Offentuna cum suo etiam ipsius gildum exoluere[b] cogebantur. Quam iniusticiam cum pater uenerabilis Faritius, abbatiam postea regens, comperisset, nunc apud regem, nunc apud reginam, tum apud regni consultores, se multis uicibus circumferens, petendo, munerando, ad hoc laborem suum perduxit, ut et terram ipsam et ipsius Hugonis homagium, cum antiquo seruitio et gildum decem hidarum suarum, sollerti industria ad ecclesie libertatem optineret, datis regi sexaginta libris[c] argenti. Regis itaque[d] littere de hac re sic se habent:

[ii. 126] 181. *Carta regis de Speresholt.*[460]

Ego Henricus Dei gratia rex Anglorum, consilio et assensu Mathildis uxoris mee baronumque meorum, tam presulum quam laicorum, reddo atque concedo et in perpetuum confirmo Deo, et ecclesie sancte Marie de Abbendona, et abbati, monachisque eiusdem cenobii, decem hidas in Espereshołt, que et alio nomine uocatur Flagaflora, uidelicet quas tenet inpresentiarum Hugo filius[e] Turstini, curie mee dispensator. Vnde uolo et precipio ut ipse Hugo, et quicumque post eum eas habuerit, hominium inde ecclesie et abbati ac fidelitatem faciat. Et tale seruitium inde faciat predicte ecclesie atque abbati quale factum fuit ab Anskillo eidem[f] ecclesie tempore regis Willelmi patris mei, et tempore Adelelmi eiusdem loci abbatis. Et hoc, pro animabus patris matrisque mee, et fratris mei regis Willelmi, et[g] anime mee, necnon pro salute uxoris mee Mathildis regine, omniumque fidelium Dei defunctorum, facio, et propria manu confirmo et consigno. Testibus subscriptis:

+ Ego Henricus rex redditionem et donationem hanc signaui.
Ego[h] Rannulfus Dunelmensis episcopus interfui. +
Ego Iohannes Batoniensis episcopus interfui et confirmaui. +
Ego Herueus Pangornensis episcopus interfui. +
Ego Robertus Lincoliensis[i] episcopus interfui et confirmaui. +
Ego Rogerus electus Salesbiriensis episcopus interfui et confirmaui. +
[ii. 127] Ego Willelmus de Werelwast interfui. +
Ego Waldricus regis cancellarius interfui et confirmaui. +
Ego Grimbaldus medicus interfui. +

[a] geldebatur *B* [b] exsoluere *B* [c] libras *B C* [d] ita *B* [e] *om. B*
[f] eiusdem *B* [g] *it seems likely that the words* pro salute *should appear here; they have either been omitted, or mistakenly placed before the mention of Queen Matilda* [h] *each cross precedes* Ego *B* [i] Lincolniensis *B*

aforesaid Hugh was unwilling to make payment to the value of half a penny, and the men of Uffington were compelled to pay his geld together with their own. When later the venerable father Faritius was ruling the abbey, he learnt of this injustice, and he travelled about on many occasions, now to the king, now to the queen, now to the counsellors of the kingdom. By asking and by giving, he concluded his labour as follows: after giving the king £60 of silver, he obtained by his resourceful industry both the land and the homage of Hugh himself for the church's liberty, together with the old service and the geld of his ten hides. The king's letters about this matter are as follows:

181. *Charter of the king concerning Sparsholt.*[460]

I, Henry, by the grace of God king of the English, by counsel and assent of Matilda my wife and of my barons, both prelates and laymen, give back and grant and in perpetuity confirm to God, and to the church of St Mary of Abingdon, and to the abbot, and to the monks of that monastery, ten hides in Sparsholt (which also has the alternative name of Fawler), that is, those which Hugh son of Thurstan, the dispenser of my court, at present holds. Therefore I wish and order that Hugh himself and whoever has these after him is to do homage and fealty concerning this to the church and abbot. And let him do such service therefrom to the aforesaid church and abbot as was done by Anskill to that church in the time of King William my father, and in the time of Adelelm, abbot of that monastery. And this I do for the souls of [my] father and my mother and my brother King William and my own soul, and also for the salvation of my wife Queen Matilda, and of all the deceased faithful of God, and I confirm and sign it by my own hand. With these witnesses written below:

+ I King Henry have signed this restoration and gift.
I Ranulf bishop of Durham was present. +
I John bishop of Bath was present and confirmed. +
I Hervey bishop of Bangor was present. +
I Robert bishop of Lincoln was present and confirmed. +
I Roger bishop elect of Salisbury was present and confirmed.+
I William de Warelwast was present. +
I Waldric, the king's chancellor, was present and confirmed. +
I Grimbald the physician was present. +

[460] *RRAN* ii, no. 683, dating to Feb. 1105 when Henry was at Romsey. See above, p. 52 n. 124, on the relationship between Fawler and Sparsholt. See above, p. 132, for other writs concerning Hugh son of Thurstan. See *VCH*, *Berkshire*, iv. 314, for early thirteenth-century disputes concerning Fawler.

Nos[a] dapiferi Henrici regis Eudo,[b] Rogerius Bigod, Haimo[c] interfuimus et concessimus. +
Ego Vrso de Abetot interfui. + [d]Ego Walterus filius Ricardi interfui. + Ego Rogerus de Oilei constabulus interfui.[d] Hoc actum est anno Dominice incarnationis millesimo centesimo quinto, indictione tercia decima, anno uero Henrici serenissimi regis quinto in curia eiusdem regis[e] apud Romesei.

B fo. 150r Igitur[f] eodem | anno idem Hugo Abbendoniam uenit, et domno abbati Faritio homagium cum fidelitate et ecclesie pro eadem terra fecit, secundum hunc tenorem, ut ipse omne seruitium faceret quod Turstinus de Trubbeuilla[g] et post eum Anskillus sub abbate Ade-
C fo. 159v lelmo fecerunt.[461] Hac pactione sic confirmata, idem Hugo | abbatem et monachos requisiuit, quatinus sibi animeque sui patris indulgerent, eo quod contra eorum uoluntatem de terra ipsa diu egerant. Cuius precibus cum fratres annuissent, ipse in manibus textum euuangeliorum accepit, et promisit pro sibi concessis rebus omni anno [h]tam ipsum quam omnes suos posteros[h] quinque solidos in Natiuitate sancte Marie Abbendoniam deferre, et monachis loci illius donare. In testimonium affuerunt Ricardus filius Reinfredi, Aredus falconarius regis, et multi alii.

[ii. 128] **182.** *De terra de Lea[i] quam Willelmus camerarius tenebat.*[462]

Est iuxta Abbendonie burgum unius militis mansio que Lea[j] uocatur.[463] Hanc Willelmus regis camerarius de Lundonia tenebat, sed nullum inde seruitium militis uel homagium domno Faritio abbati, cum abbatiam primo suscepisset, impendere uolebat. Et contigit interea ut rex Henricus contra fratrem suum Robertum, Normannie comitem, super se in Anglia cum exercitu uenientem, totius regni sui expeditionem dirigit.[464] Tum abbas a Willelmo representationem[k] militis expetens, nec ab eius inportunitate impetrans, prudenter id sustinet, et militem ipse quesitum alterum supponit. Verum rege fratri suo pacis firmatione unito, abbatis

[a] Gos, *rubricator having added wrong initial B* [b] *initial om. B* [c] Iaimo *B*
[d–d] *om. B* [e] regis *written twice C* [f] *initial om. C* [g] Turbeuilla *B*
[h–h] tam ipse quam omnes sui posteri *B C* [i] Leia *B* [j] Leia *B*
[k] representionem *B C*

[461] It would seem probable that Thurstan de *Trubbeuilla* is Thurstan the dispenser, but I have been unable to link the dispenser with a suitable place in Normandy.

[462] Bessels Leigh, Berks., now Oxon. This and the following two sections are *English Lawsuits*, no. 164. *DB* i, fo. 58v, states that 'William holds [Bessels] Leigh from the abbot'. A William the former chamberlain of London appears in the 1130 Pipe Roll, *PR 31 HI*,

We, Eudo, Roger Bigod, and Hamo, King Henry's stewards, were present and granted. +
I Urse d'Abetot was present. + I Walter son of Richard was present. + I Roger d'Oilly the constable was present. This was done in the year of our Lord 1105, in the thirteenth indiction, and the fifth year of the most serene King Henry, in the king's court at Romsey.

Therefore in the same year, Hugh came to Abingdon and did homage with fealty to lord Abbot Faritius and the church for this land, according to these terms: that he would do all the service which Thurstan de *Trubbeuilla* and, beyond him, Anskill did under Abbot Adelelm.[461] When the agreement had been confirmed in this way, Hugh asked the abbot and monks that they forgive him and his father's soul for long contradicting the monks' will concerning this land. When the monastic brethren agreed to his prayers, he took the text of the Gospels in his hands and promised for himself that each year both he and all his posterity would bring 5s. to Abingdon at the Nativity of St Mary and give them to the monks of that monastery, for what was granted. Present to witness were Richard son of Reinfrid, Aret the king's falconer, and many others.

182. *Concerning the land of Bessels Leigh which William the chamberlain held.*[462]

Near to the borough of Abingdon is a manor of one knight which is called Bessels Leigh.[463] William the king's chamberlain of London held this, but he was unwilling to pay any knight service or homage therefrom to lord Abbot Faritius when he first took over the abbey. And it happened, meanwhile, that King Henry directed the military service of his whole realm against his brother Robert, count of Normandy, who was coming with an army against him in England.[464] Then the abbot sought that William present a knight, but failed in his request because of William's persistent opposition. Prudently he suffered this and himself substituted another knight as required. But once the king had been united to his brother in confirming peace,

p. 145, and is probably the addressee of a writ of 1120 × 1122, *RRAN* ii, no. 1377, but it is uncertain whether all these Williams are the same man, relatives of the same name, or even unrelated. Bessels Leigh is listed amongst Faritius's acquisitions in *De abbatibus*; *CMA* ii. 288.

[463] See above, p. lxxxi, on Abingdon being described as a borough.

[464] 1101. See above, p. lx, on knight service.

testibus coram deductis quod militem hec possessio tempore senioris regis Willelmi et abbatis Adelelmi inuenit, nunc uero eum regnanti regi Henrico et eodem indigenti retentum palam fuerit, tamdiu, in presentia sapientum, hanc rem uentilari fecit, ut ille neutram negaret,[a] immo fateri sic esse, uera ratione cogeretur. Vnde cum lege patrie decretum processisset ipsum exortem terre merito debere fieri, interpellatione bonorum qui intererant uirorum, reddidit[b] terram illam illi, eo tenore quod Willelmus effectus est homo ipsius, et decem libras pro emendatione dedit, et seruitium unius militis facere debet in omni loco ubi ceteri homines ecclesie faciunt seruitium militum, et nulli unquam debet illam terram uendere, uel uadimonizare, uel in feudo dare siue in feudo firma. Pascua etiam debet in illa terra hominibus abbatis [c]qui sunt ibi circumpositi ex
[ii. 129] omni parte, sicut erat tempore Adelelmi abbatis, et Willelmus debet habere abbatis illas consuetudines pro pascuis quas habebant sui decessores, qui fuerunt tempore Adelelmi abbatis et suorum predecessorum. Hoc actum est coram his testibus: Nigello de Oili, Hugone de Bochelande, Willelmo uicecomite, Radulfo Basset,[c] et multorum aliorum.[465]

183. *De Bydena.*[d][466]

Disrationauit etiam eo die, abbas Faritius contra Godselinum[e] de Riueria seruitium unius militis de Bedena. Idem dicebat se non
B fo. 150v debere facere seruitium nisi duorum | militum pro feudo quem tenebat de ecclesia, et abbas et sui dicebant eum debere seruitium trium militum. Tandem uero uadimonizauit et seruitium et rectum abbati et firmauit et omnino concessit se et debere facere, et de cetero facturum trium militum seruitium. Et hoc actum est in Abbendonensi camera, coram abbate Faritio, multorum testimonio.

184. *De Bradelea.*[467]

Illa die qua predictum placitum finem accepit, coram isdem[f] testibus illius placiti, Willelmus de Gemmetico reddidit et quietas clamauit

[a] regnaret *B* [b] reddit *B* [c–c] *six and a half lines in somewhat compressed letters, over erasure, with an extensive erasure in margin B* [d] Bidena *B* [e] Godcelinum *B* [f] hisdem *B C*

[465] On the court hearing this case, see above, p. xcviii. William was presumably the sheriff of Oxford.

[466] Lyell, no. 162, Chatsworth, no. 322, *Salisbury acta: 1078–1217*, ed. Kemp, no. 42, a charter of Jocelin bishop of Salisbury (1142–84), records that Walter de Rivers gave one third of Beedon to Abingdon in alms, and asked the bishop to confirm his gift. If I am right to conclude that Bomund of 'Ledis' in the Abingdon *Carta* of 1166, below, p. 390, was

the abbot produced witnesses that in the time of King William the elder and Abbot Adelelm this possession found a knight, yet now it was common knowledge that the knight had been denied to the reigning King Henry who required him. The abbot had the matter discussed for so long in the presence of wise men that William denied neither point, but rather was compelled by truthful reasoning to admit it was thus. Therefore, after it had been decided according to the law of the country that he deservedly ought to be deprived of the land, at the intercession of good men who were present the abbot gave him back that land, on these terms: that William was made his man; gave £10 by way of emendation; ought to do the service of one knight everywhere the other men of the church did knight service; and should never sell, or gage, or give that land in fee or fee farm to anyone. He should also allow pasture in that land for the abbot's men, who neighbour there on all sides, as in the time of Abbot Adelelm, and for the pastures William ought to have those customs of the abbot which his predecessors had, who were alive in the time of Abbot Adelelm and his predecessors. This was done in the presence of these witnesses: Nigel d'Oilly, Hugh of Buckland, William the sheriff, Ralph Basset, and many others.[465]

183. *Concerning Beedon.*[466]

On the same day, Abbot Faritius also deraigned the service of one knight from Beedon, against Jocelin de Rivers. Jocelin was saying that he ought only do the service of two knights for the fee which he was holding from the church, and the abbot and his men were saying that Jocelin owed the service of three knights. At length, indeed, he pledged and confirmed and utterly granted that he ought to do both service and justice to the abbot, and that in future he would do the service of three knights. And this was done in the chamber at Abingdon, in the presence of Abbot Faritius, by the testimony of many.

184. *Concerning Bradley.*[467]

On the day on which the aforesaid plea was settled, in the presence of the same witnesses as that plea, William de Jumièges gave back and

Jocelin's successor, the abbey succeeded in establishing the quota of three knights. Note also that the list of knight service added in MS B has Walter de Rivers owe two and a half knights for Beedon, while a marginal annotation adds 'according to others three knights'; below, p. 324.

[467] Bradley, Berks., is not named in *Domesday*, but note that the entry for Chieveley states that William holds five hides in Chieveley from the abbot, *DB* i, fo. 58^{v}, and these lay in Bradley; see EPNS, *Berkshire*, i. 242.

abbati Faritio quinque hidas terre, quas Rainaldus abbas iniuste ei dederat, quia de dominio erant in uilla Ciuele,[a] in loco qui dicitur Bradelea;[b] et omnia que in illa terra erant concessit abbati.

[ii. 130] **185.** *De una hida in Hannie.*[468]

[c]Item, eodem anno Rainbaldus miles abbatis de Abbendona reddidit
abbati Faritio unam hidam terre in Hannie, quam[c] Toroldus[d] tunc
habebat ad usuram pro uiginti quatuor solidis, et unum molendinum
C fo. 160r prope Merceham quod[e] tunc reddebat duodecim solidos, et | unum
pratum.[469] Eo tenore reddidit sibi ista solide, et quiete, et omni tempore, sine omni calumpnia,[f] ut posset alia que tunc tenebat ab abbate tenere, pro solito seruitio. Et hec ideo reddidit quia hec et alia plura habebat de dominio monachorum sine consensu regis et monachorum, et [g]rex reddidit[g] ecclesie et abbati omnia dominia sicut fuerant tempore Adelelmi abbatis. Hec redditio Rainbaldi facta est in manu Faritii abbatis Abbendonie, coram abbate Serlone Gloecestrense, et coram multis aliis testibus.[470]

186. *De Willelmo filio abbatis Rainaldi.*[471]

Eodem etiam anno, Willelmus filius abbatis Rainaldi unam hidam in Appelford, et alteram in Middeltuna,[h] et unam wicham que[i] in prepositura Merceham sita est, reddidit predicto abbati Faritio; et quia de dominio esse iudicata fuerant, eidem abbati in omni tempore quieta ab omni calumpnia clamauit. Ecclesiam uero de Merceham, sicut predecessor eius Alfricus presbiter, in seruitio abbatis et monachorum deseruiuit, ita et ipse per omnia quamdiu uiueret
eodem seruitio deseruiret, et post finem uite sue hominum nullum
[ii. 131] de ea seu de terra Gersenduna, quam tunc tenebat, heredem faceret,
aut, si uxorem duceret, non eam de his ullomodo[j] dotaret, sed, eo mortuo, omnia ecclesie, abbati et monachis dimitteret[k] quieta et libera. Inde fidem suam dedit, et fideiussores eidem abbati inuenit. Euolutis uero non multis annis, uenit Abbendonam, cogente infirmitate in qua

[a] Ciuelea *B* [b] Bradeleia *B* [c–c] *three lines over erasure, with extensive erasure in margin B* [d] Thoroldus *B* [e] qui *B C* [f] calumnia *B* [g–g] reddidit rex, *extending into central margin B* [h] Middeltona *B* [i] quem *B* [j] ullo modo *B* [k] dimittet *B*

---

468 See above, p. 56, on Rainbald and Hanney. Hanney is listed amongst Faritius's acquisitions in *De abbatibus*; *CMA* ii. 288. On consent to alienation of church lands, see above, p. lxxix.

469 The phrase 'ad usuram' is an extremely unusual and rather surprising one, given the ecclesiastical prohibition of the charging of interest. *DB* i, fo. 60r, records a Thorold the priest holding the church of Hanney with one hide from Walter Giffard. It is uncertain

quitclaimed to Abbot Faritius five hides of land which Abbot Reginald had given him unjustly, since they were from the demesne in the village of Chieveley, in the place called Bradley. And he granted to the abbot everything which was on that land.

185. *Concerning one hide in Hanney.*[468]
Likewise, in the same year, Rainbald, a knight of the abbot of Abingdon, gave back to Abbot Faritius one hide of land in Hanney, which Thorold then held for interest for 24s., and one mill next to Marcham which then rendered 12s., and one meadow.[469] He gave back these things on these terms, securely and undisturbed, and without ever any claim, so that he could hold for the accustomed service the other possessions he was then holding from the abbot. And he gave them back thus because he had them and many others from the monks' demesne without the king and monks' consent, and the king had given back to the church and abbot all their demesnes as they had been in the time of Abbot Adelelm. Rainbald's restoration was made in the hand of Abbot Faritius of Abingdon in the presence of Abbot Serlo of Gloucester and of many other witnesses.[470]

186. *Concerning William, son of Abbot Reginald.*[471]
In the same year, too, William son of Abbot Reginald gave back to the aforesaid Abbot Faritius one hide in Appleford, and another in Milton, and a dairy-farm which is situated in the reeveship of Marcham, and since this had been adjudged to be from the demesne, he quitclaimed it to the abbot for all time, from every claim. But he officiated at the church of Marcham, like his predecessor the priest Ælfric, in the service of the abbot and monks, in such a way that as long as he lived he would officiate by the same service in all respects. After the end of his life he would make none of his men heir of this or of the land at Garsington which he then held, or if he took a wife, he would not in any way give her dower from these possessions, but at his death he would surrender them all, undisturbed and free, to the abbot and monks. He gave his faith concerning this and found guarantors for the abbot. A few years later, he came to Abingdon, compelled by the illness of which he died. There he took the monk's

whether this is the same Thorold as appears in the text here and below, p. 208; the later text makes it seem somewhat unlikely, since it mentions Thorold allotting tithe to a further priest, but it could be that the married Thorold had another priest carry out his duties.

470 Serlo was abbot 1072–1104; *Heads of Religious Houses*, p. 52.

471 See above, p. 58, for the grant to William.

obiit, et monachatum ibidem accepit, et reddidit ecclesiam quam tenuerat et terram de Gersenduna ecclesie et abbati Faritio et monachis quieta et libera.

187. *De una hida apud Cernei et dimidia ad Moram.*[472]

Turstinus etiam filius Rainaldi de Sancta Helena per Motbertum monachum habuerat unam hidam apud Cernei,[a] et dimidiam ad More, quas clamauit quietas ab omni reclamatione in reliquum
B fo. 151r tempus in presentia Fa | ritii abbatis. Requisiuit autem isdem abbatem quatinus molendinum suum apud Merceham[b] sibi permitteret habere, et abbas eo tenore hoc ei concessit, ut ita de suo illo molendino procuraret, ne abbatis[c] molendinum in illa uilla in aliquo damnum pateretur.[473]

188. *De terra de Hanni.*

Hugo de Bochelanda per Motbertum monachum[d] diu tenuerat immerito terram quam [e]Wlfui Bullochesege[e] olim per conuentum Abbendonie ad tempus habituram susceperat, in uilla scilicet Hanni uocitata.[474] Quocirca huius auctoritatem abbatis, qua se de hoc commoneri libenter ferebat, plurimum reuerens, restituit ecclesie
[ii. 132] libertati eandem. Verum et miles nomine Osbernus, qui sibi de ea hactenus seruierat, ecclesie et abbatis homo effectus est unius militis seruitii ad singula militum officia pactione.[475]

189. *De siluis apud Winekefeld.*[f] [476]

Walterus filius Oteri, castellanus de Wildesore, reddidit abbati Faritio duas siluas uocatas Virdelæ et Bacsceat apud Winekefeld nostram uillam, que pertinuerant ecclesie Abbendonie, sed eas per predecessores huius abbatis, uidelicet Adelelmum et Rainaldum, hucusque tenuerat. Hanc redditionem primo apud castellum Wildesores abbati eidem reddidit, et deinde ad Natiuitatem sancte Marie uxorem suam

[a] Cerneia *B* [b] Mercham *B* [c] abbas *B* [d] monacum *B* [e–e] Wlfuui Bullokes ege *B* [f] Welliford *B*

[472] Charney Basset, Berks. *DB* i, fo. 59v, states that 'the abbey itself holds Charney'. Moor is probably the place now called Draycott Moor or Southmoor; EPNS, *Berkshire*, ii. 404–5. *DB* i, fo. 59r, states that 'the abbey itself holds Draycott and always held it'.

[473] On the St Helen family, see above, p. lxv. Thurstan held land at Frilford, the neighbouring settlement to Marcham, *DB* i fo. 58v, and his mill was presumably upstream on the river Ock from the abbot's own mill at Marcham. *DB* i, fo. 58v, mentions only one mill at Marcham, none at Frilford.

[474] See above, p. 62 and n. 152.

[475] For this holding see also below, p. 208, where it is revealed that Osbern was nephew

habit, and gave back to the church and Abbot Faritius and the monks, undisturbed and free, the church which he had held and the land at Garsington.

187. *Concerning one hide at Charney and half at Moor.*[472]
Through the monk Modbert, Thurstan son of Reginald of St Helen had had one hide at Charney and half a hide at Moor, which he quitclaimed in the presence of Abbot Faritius from all further claim for the remainder of time. He moreover requested the abbot that he permit him to have his mill at Marcham, and the abbot granted this to him on the following terms, that he administer his mill in such a way that the abbot's mill in the same village suffer no loss.[473]

188. *Concerning the land of Hanney.*
Undeservedly, through the monk Modbert, Hugh of Buckland had long held the land in the village called Hanney which Wulfwig 'Bullock's Eye' had formerly received as a temporary holding through the convent of Abingdon.[474] He greatly revered Abbot Faritius's authority, and on this matter willingly let himself be advised by that authority, and therefore he restored this land to the liberty of the church. In addition, the knight named Osbern, who hitherto had served him from the land, was made the man of the church and the abbot on the terms of one knight's service for each knight's duty.[475]

189. *Concerning the woods at Winkfield.*[476]
Walter son of Other, the castellan of Windsor, gave back to Abbot Faritius two woods called *Virdelea* and *Bacsceat* at our village of Winkfield. These woods had belonged to the church of Abingdon, but Walter had hitherto held them through this abbot's predecessors, that is Adelelm and Reginald. He first made this restoration to the abbot at Windsor castle and then sent his wife Beatrice with their son William to Abingdon at the Nativity of St Mary [8 Sept.], so that they

of Modbert, custodian of the church following the death of Abbot Reginald. A list in MS C in the same hand as the *History*, below, p. 393, records Osbern of Hanney holding three hides. *DB* i, fo. 60^{r}, records an Osbern as one of two tenants of Walter Giffard in W. Hanney. The phrase 'ad singula militum officia' is very unusual, and therefore somewhat obscure. *Officia* may have overtones from canon law, but its sense remains uncertain. The phrase perhaps means that Osbern held only part of a fee, and was to do the appropriate proportion of the service. Note that in 1166, below, p. 391, a hide at Hanney owed one fifth of a knight's service.

[476] 'Two woods in the forest of Windsor' are listed amongst Faritius's acquisitions in *De abbatibus*; *CMA* ii. 288. See also above, p. 8, where the first of the woods is called *Ierdelea*.

Beatricem cum filio suo Willelmo Abbendoniam transmisit, ut quod ipse domi fecerat ipsi Abbendonie confirmarent. Quod et factum est.

190. *De Nigello de Oili.*[a][477]

Nigellus de Oilio tenebat unum pratum apud Oxeneford, et unam
hidam in Sandford, et alteram in Earnecote, de feudo scilicet
Abbendonie, sed nullum homagium uel seruitium longo post tempore
aduentus ipsius Faritii abbatis ad Abbendoniam inde ecclesie fecerat.
C fo. 160v | Quapropter abbas contra ipsum disratiocinando egit, ut et ecclesie
et sibi pro his que tenebat homagium faceret, et hoc tenore eadem in
posterum recognosceret, scilicet ut in omni regis gildo ipsa quietet, et
abbati sicut suo domino ubique seruiat. In uicecomitatibus Berchescire et Oxenefordscire, quandocumque abbas eum mandauerit,
[ii. 133] ad auxiliandum sibi et seruiendum paratus aderit, nec excusabitur ab
ecclesie seruitio nisi regis eum detinuerit[b] executio. Quod si ita
constiterit, pro se de melioribus suis hominibus in abbatis obsequium
transmittet.[c] In curia etiam regis, si abbati placitum aliquod forte
habendum contigerit, ipsius abbatis parti idem aderit, nisi contra
regem placitandum forte fuerit. Ad eandem curiam uenienti abbati
procurabit hospicium, et si aptum illi non inuenerit, suum proprium
cedet ipsius receptui.[d][478]

191. *De quadam terra in Oxeneford.*[479]

Eodem mense quo et ista uentilata est causa, abbas contra eundem
Nigellum de Oili disratiocinauit quandam terre portiunculam infra
Oxeneforde[e] ciuitatem sitam, in uia scilicet qua itur a sancti Michaelis
ecclesia ad castellum. Que terra manerio Tademertune ab antiquo
B fo. 151v adiacet | tempore. Verum hec precedenti tempore in neglectum
uenerat, adeo ut de hac nullam exhiberet[f] tunc Nigellus ecclesie
recognitionem. Itaque ipsius abbatis iuste rationi se idem submittens,
tali post illud tempus tenore de ecclesia predicta terram suscepit
tenendam, ut gablum antiquitus consuetum inde persolui, id est sex
denarios, et ipse Nigellus singulis annis ad Natiuitatem sancte Marie
illi collectori in eadem uilla redderet,[g] qui aliud ecclesie gablum illic

[a] Oilli *B* [b] ditinuerit *B* [c] trasmittet *B* [d] respectui *B*
[e] Oxenefordæ *B* [f] exiberet *B* [g] ut *add.* *B*

[477] *English Lawsuits*, no 206. See above, p. 34, and *Charters of Abingdon Abbey*, p. 463, on these lands.

[478] I here retain use of the present and future tenses, since the *History* may be reproducing an earlier record of the agreement.

could confirm at Abingdon what he had done at home. And this was done.

190. *Concerning Nigel d'Oilly.*[477]

Nigel d'Oilly held one meadow at Oxford, and one hide in Sandford and another in Arncott, from the fee of Abingdon, but had done no homage or service therefrom to the church for a long time after Abbot Faritius's coming to Abingdon. Therefore the abbot proceeded against him by court action, so that he would do homage to the church and Faritius for what he was holding, and recognize their lordship of these things for the future, on these terms, that is, that he discharge them of all the king's geld, and serve the abbot everywhere as his lord. Whenever the abbot instructs him, he will come to help and serve him in the county courts of Berkshire and Oxfordshire, and he will not excuse himself from the service of the church unless performance of the king's business detains him. If this happens, he is to send in his place one of his best men for the abbot's service. Also, if by chance it happens that the abbot has a plea in the king's court, he will be present on the abbot's side, unless by chance the abbot is pleading against the king. He will provide lodging for the abbot when he comes to that court, and if he finds nothing suitable for the abbot, he shall give up his own lodgings for his accommodation.[478]

191. *Concerning certain land in Oxford.*[479]

In the same month as that case was heard, the abbot also deraigned against Nigel d'Oilly a small portion of land situated within the city of Oxford, on the road which goes from St Michael's church to the castle. From of old this land has belonged to the manor of Tadmarton. However, this connection had since been neglected, so that Nigel was then displaying to the church no recognition of its lordship of the land. Nigel submitted to the just reasoning of Abbot Faritius, and received the land to hold thereafter from the aforesaid church on the following terms: that as of old the accustomed rent be paid therefrom, that is 6d., and Nigel himself should render it annually at the Nativity of St Mary [8 Sept.] to the collector who collects the church's other

[479] *English Lawsuits*, no. 207. The church concerned is St Michael at the South Gate, which no longer exists. Salter, *Medieval Oxford*, p. 25 n. 1, suggests that this was a *Domesday* holding 'apparently on the site of Pembroke College'; see also his *Survey of Oxford* (2 vols., Oxford Hist. Soc., New Series, xiv, xx, 1960, 1969), ii. 83–4 (SW99). John Blair suggests to me that another possibility would be to take this road as the present Brewer Street which ran outside the city wall, and the land concerned perhaps to be the tenements mentioned in Salter, *Survey*, ii. 37–8 (SW35–37).

collegeret. Quod placitum factum est super eandem terram coram multis testibus.

192. *De Waltero Giffar.*[a] [480]

Walterus comes iunior, cognomine Gifardus,[b] manerium septem
[ii. 134] hidarum quod uocatur Linford tenebat, et est ex iure ecclesie huius, sed ipse comes inde seruitium debitum contra tenere moliebatur.[481] Qua re industria abbatis Faritii tantum in hoc preualuit, ut idem comes, coram episcopis[c] Rogero Saresbiriensi ac Roberto Lincoliensi,[d] et multis regis baronibus, ecclesie et abbatis homo efficeretur, eo tenore ut ex illa terra militis unius seruitium omnimodo reddat, quo alii ecclesie milites seruitia exhibent.[e] Hec omnia disratiocinata[f] fuere, precepto Henrici regis, apud Oxeneford in domo Thome de Sancto Iohanne, ubi abbas tunc curiam suam fecit, eo quod ille Thomas suus homo erat.

193. *De Lechamsted.*[g] [482]

In huiusmodi contentionibus[h] nemo sic ipsi abbati impedimento obstitit, ut Herebertus regis cubicularius atque thesaurarius. Siquidem per abbatem Rainaldum unam hidam in Ferneburga,[i] itemque per Motbertum[j] monachum in eodem manerio portionem terre que Kingescumbe uocatur, et uillam Lecamstede[k] appellatam possederat, nec de his seruitium aliquod reddebat.[483] Volens itaque is[l] patrem sepe nominandum hunc donationes illas sibi confirmare, per reginam, per maiores regni, tum abbatem, tum monachos, multotiens de ea re interpellabat. Verum quia longum foret exequi quanta uir ille contra ecclesiam ac abbatem machinatus est, eo quod uelle suo obsistebant, ideo his omissis finalem inde exsoluamus.

194. *De Herberto cubiculario.*

Constantia abbatis in ecclesie negotii defensione predictus uir cognita,
[ii. 135] ipsemet solis comitatus suis amicis uenit Abbendoniam, et ipsi abbati

[a] Giffard *B* [b] Giffardus *B* [c] *om.* *B* [d] Lincolniensi *B* [e] exibent *B* [f] disratinata *B* [g] Lechamsteda *B* [h] contentionis *B C* [i] Ferneburgam *B C* [j] Mortbertum *B* [k] Lechamstede *B* [l] his *B C*

---

[480] *English Lawsuits*, no. 162, which presumes 'Earl Walter the younger' to be Walter II Giffard, and therefore dates the case to between 29 Sept. 1102 (Roger's nomination as bishop of Salisbury) and the end of 1102 (the death of Walter II); however 'Walter the younger' may refer to Walter III, who succeeded his father Walter II. See above, p. 126 n. 298, on the Giffards.

[481] *DB* i, fo. 59^{r}, records that 'Walter Giffard holds Lyford [Berks.] from the

rent there. This plea was held on that land in the presence of many witnesses.

192. *Concerning Walter Giffard.*[480]

Earl Walter the younger, surnamed Giffard, was holding a manor of seven hides which is called Lyford, and is the property of this church, yet that earl strove to withhold the service due therefrom.[481] Abbot Faritius's efforts concerning this matter so prevailed that, in the presence of Bishops Roger of Salisbury and Robert of Lincoln and many of the king's barons, the earl was made the man of the church and abbot, on the terms that he render the service of one knight from that land in every way in which the church's other knights do service. All these matters were deraigned by King Henry's order at Oxford in the house of Thomas of St John, where the abbot then held his court, because Thomas was his man.

193. *Concerning Leckhampstead.*[482]

No one created such difficulties for Abbot Faritius in this type of conflict as Herbert, the king's chamberlain and treasurer. Through Abbot Reginald he had possessed one hide in Farnborough, and likewise through the monk Modbert a portion of land called Kingscombe in the same manor, and the village called Leckhampstead, and he rendered no service from these.[483] He wished, therefore, that this father, whom it has often been necessary to mention [i.e. Faritius], should confirm these gifts to him, and he often brought requests concerning this matter, sometimes to the abbot, sometimes to the monks, through the queen and through the greater men of the realm. But as it would be long-winded to continue with the extent of that man's plotting against the church and abbot, in that they resisted his will, we omit these things and explain the outcome.

194. *Concerning Herbert the chamberlain.*

When Herbert recognized the abbot's constancy in defence of the church's business, he came to Abingdon accompanied only by his

abbot. . . . Then and now seven hides'. A survey from the time of Henry I or Stephen, below, p. 387, has Ralph de Langetot hold seven hides in Lyford; he may have been the sub-tenant. Lyford is listed amongst Faritius's acquisitions in *De abbatibus*; *CMA* ii. 288.

[482] Leckhampstead is listed amongst Faritius's acquisitions in *De abbatibus*; *CMA* ii. 288. On the headings for this and the following section, see above, p. xxxv n. 126.

[483] *DB* i, fo. 59r, states that 'the abbey itself holds Farnborough', Berks. EPNS, *Berkshire*, ii. 501, states that 'it seems likely that this . . . is Coombe F[ar]m in Farnborough, perhaps called *Kinges-* because held for a time by a royal official'.

ac ecclesie libere se restituere hidam in Ferneburga cum Kingescumba, sed et unius militis omnino seruitium de terra Lechamstede ex illo iam tempore exhibiturum,[a] atque pro hac concessione marcam
C fo. 161r auri oblaturum, simul promisit, solummodo | abbas et monachi tali tenori beniuoli efficerentur. Cuius rationi sapientum consultu plurimorum abbas tum annuens, et que offerebantur ad ecclesie fructum et utilitatem recepit, et uillam Lechamstede illi, homagium ecclesie et
B fo. 152r sibi facienti, predicta pactione habere | concessit.

195. *De Westona.*[484]

Concessit etiam abbas Faritius Roberto filio Willelmi Maledocti[b] terram quatuor hidarum in Westuna in feudum tenendam, quam pater suus tenuerat ab antecessore ipsius. Et hoc seruitium inde faciet, scilicet quod, ubicumque ecclesia Abbendonensis fecerit seruitium militum, ipse pro dimidio milite seruitium faciat eiusdem ecclesie, scilicet in custodia castelli, in expeditione ultra et citra mare, in dandis nummis pro milite, in custodia regis, et ceteris aliis seruitiis, sicut alii milites ecclesie faciunt.[485] Homagium quoque fecit eidem abbati. Hec terra prius seruitium trium ebdomadarum tantum faciebat per annum.

196. *De una uirgata[c] in Dreituna.*[d][486]

Anno duodecimo Henrici regis, Warinus Mancus clamauit quietam
[ii. 136] unam uirgatam terre apud Dreitunam, et unam mansionem hospicii in hac uilla, tam uidelicet a se quam ab omnibus suis heredibus, ecclesie sancte Marie Abbendonensi. Et hoc factum est coram domno Faritio abbate et coram multis testibus.

197. *[e]Cirographum de terra de Cestretona.[e]*[487]

Campsio terrarum que infra legitur, facta est consensu omnium monachorum et bonorum hominum ecclesie Abbendonensis, inter domnum Faritium abbatem eiusdem ecclesie et Anskitillum suum hominem de Tademertuna.[488] Idem Anskitillus, cum filio suo Roberto

[a] exibiturum *B* [b] *corr. from* Maledicti *C* [c] terre *add. B* [d] Draituna *B*
[e–e] Cirographum de Cestrætona *B*

[484] See also the writ, above, p. 134. [485] On knight service, see above, p. lx.

[486] Berks.; probably East Drayton, on which see *VCH*, *Berkshire*, iv. 341–2, *Charters of Abingdon Abbey*, pp. 322–3. *Domesday* may conceal extensive Abingdon holdings there, as given by Kings Eadwig and Edgar (*Charters of Abingdon Abbey*, nos. 78, 85—ten and twenty hides respectively) and revealed in twelfth-century documents, below, p. 387, *CMA* ii. 310 (eighteen and twenty hides respectively). Alternatively or additionally, lands there may have been lost before 1066 and regained after 1086. *DB* i, fo. 61v, records that Hascoit Musard held Drayton in 1086 for one hide, and that Godwine had held it 'in alodio' from

friends, and promised that he would restore the hide in Farnborough together with Kingscombe freely to the abbot and the church; that he would henceforth fully perform the service of one knight from the land of Leckhampstead; and that he would offer a mark of gold for this grant, merely that the abbot and monks be made agreeable to such a stipulation. On the advice of very many wise men the abbot then agreed to his argument and received what was offered to the benefit and advantage of the church; on the aforesaid terms he granted the village of Leckhampstead to Herbert as he did homage to the church and abbot.

195. *Concerning Weston.*[484]

Abbot Faritius also granted to Robert son of William Mauduit land of four hides in Weston, to hold in fee, which Robert's father had held from the abbot's predecessor. And he was to do the following service therefrom, namely that wherever the church of Abingdon did knight service, he would do that church's service for half a knight, that is, in castle-guard, in military service beyond and this side of the sea, in giving penny coins for a knight, in the king's guard service, and in all other services, as the church's other knights do.[485] He also did homage to Abbot Faritius. This land previously only did three weeks' service each year.

196. *Concerning one virgate in Drayton.*[486]

In King Henry's twelfth year [5 Aug. 1111–4 Aug. 1112], Warin Mancus quitclaimed to the church of St Mary of Abingdon one virgate of land at Drayton and one tenement of a house in the same village, both from himself and from all his heirs. And this he did in the presence of lord Abbot Faritius and many witnesses.

197. *Cirograph concerning the land of Chesterton.*[487]

The exchange of lands which is declared below was made between lord Faritius abbot of that church and Ansketel his man of Tadmarton, by the consent of all the monks and good men of the church of Abingdon.[488] Ansketel came with his son Robert and his

King Edward as a manor for three and a half hides. The Musard family are not heard of again in this context. For Hascoit, see also Keats-Rohan, *Domesday People*, p. 246. See also *DB* i, fo. 60[r], for Earl Hugh's holding at Drayton.

[487] See above, pp. lxxv–vi, on the consolidation of estates.

[488] MS B's list of knights, below, p. 322, includes an Ansketel owing two knights for Bessels Leigh and Chesterton. For another mention of an Ansketel, see above, p. 118. A Robert son of Ansketel witnesses a charter of the count of Meulan above, p. 150, but these need not be men of the same family.

et cum amicis, uenit in capitulum Abbendonense, coram omni
conuentu et militibus et seruientibus ecclesie et multis uicinis, et
reddidit cum filio suo in manu abbatis quicquid terrarum et domorum
ecclesie et uiridariorum que ante aliquomodo possederat in Tademertuna, et omni calumpnia uocauit quieta omni tempore, ipse et
heredes eius. Et abbas, consensu omnium monachorum et auctoritate
militum, dedit sibi pro illa in campsione terram de Cestretuna,[a] cum
omnibus sibi pertinentibus, hereditario iure in feudo habendam, ut,
sicut ipse illam de Tademertuna in feudo habuerat, ita haberet illam
de Cestretona,[b] et illud omne seruitium quod faciebat ecclesie
Abbendonensi de Tademertuna,[c] omne illud faceret de Cestretona.
Terra autem de Tademertuna[d] quietat se in gildo regis pro quinque
hidis, Cestretuna uero[e] pro una sola hida. Et quia graue erat abbati et
monachis[f] tantum gildum reddere, donauit Anskitillus[g] omnem
decimam omnium segetum sui dominii de Cestretuna[h] ecclesie de
Abbendonia omni tempore, et heredes eius in perpetuum post eum.
[ii. 137] Hoc actum est in quarto anno Henrici Dei gratia Anglorum
strenuissimi regis, die nonarum Martiarum, in capitulo Abbendonensi, coram his testibus: eodem scilicet abbate, Warengerio priore,
Alfrico et alio Alfrico, Halawino, Kitello et alio Kitello, Sagaro,[i]
Sarico, [j]Roberto, Willelmo cantore, Willelmo cellarario, Benedicto,[j]
Roberto diacono, Rainaldo, Nicholao iuuenibus, Augustino, Milone,
et Willelmo pueris, ceterisque; clericorum: Roberto sororio Lamberti
B fo. 152v presbi|tero, Roberto presbitero de Merceham,[k] et aliorum pluri-
morum;[489] laicorum: eodem Anskillo cum filio suo Roberto, et
Ansgero suo homine, et multorum aliorum. Vt autem hec campsio
firma foret ad opus Anskitilli,[l] firmata est duobus breuibus sigillatis
Henrici comitis de Warewic, ex cuius feudo est Cestretuna. Ex quibus
sigillis, unum est in thesauro Abbendonensi et aliud habet Anskitillus.[490]

198. *Carta comitis Warwicensis*[m] *de eadem terra.* |
C fo. 161v Henricus comes Dei gratia de Warwic[n] Faritio abbati de Abbendona
et omnibus suis monachis, salutem et amicitiam. Sciatis me concessisse, pro amore Dei et uestro, illam campsionem quam fecistis
cum Ansketillo homine uestro de Cestretuna pro terra sua de
Tademertuna,[o] eo scilicet tenore, ut, sicut ipse tenuit illam de

[a] Cestratuna *B* [b] Cestretuna *B* [c] Tademertona *B* [d] Tademertona *B*
[e] et *add. B* [f] monakis *C* [g] Ankitillus *B* [h] Cestratuna *B* [i] Saga *B*
[j–j] *om. B* [k] Mercheam *B* [l] Ankitilli *B* [m] Warewicensis *B*
[n] Warewic *B* [o] Tadmertuna *B*

friends to the chapter of Abingdon, and with his son, in the presence of the whole convent and the knights and servants of the church and many neighbours, gave back into the abbot's hand whatever of the church's lands and houses and greens he had previously possessed in Tadmarton in any way, and on behalf of himself and his heirs he vouched that they would be quit forever of all claim. And by the consent of all the monks and on the authority of the knights, the abbot gave him in exchange for that the land of Chesterton to have in fee by hereditary right with everything pertaining to it, so that just as he had had the land of Tadmarton in fee so he would have that of Chesterton, and he would do all the service from Chesterton which he used to do for the church of Abingdon from Tadmarton. But the land of Tadmarton acquits itself in the king's geld for five hides, Chesterton for only one hide. And since it was burdensome for the abbot and monks to render so much geld, Ansketel gave the entire tithe of all the crops of his demesne of Chesterton to the church of Abingdon for all time, and his heirs would do so in perpetuity after him. This was done in the fourth year of Henry by the grace of God most vigorous king of the English, on 7 March [1104], in the chapter of Abingdon, in the presence of these witnesses: namely, this abbot, Warenger the prior, both Ælfrics, Halawin, both Ketels, Sagar, Saric, Robert, William the cantor, William the cellarer, Benedict, Robert the deacon, Reginald and Nicholas the young men, Augustine, Miles and William the boys, and others; of clerics: Robert the priest (brother-in-law of Lambert), Robert priest of Marcham, and of many others;[489] of laymen: the same Anskill [i.e. Ansketel] with his son Robert, and Ansger his man, and of many others. Moreover, so that this exchange be firm for Ansketel's benefit, it was confirmed by two sealed writs of Henry earl of Warwick, of whose fee Chesterton is. One of these seals is in the treasury of Abingdon, and Ansketel has the other.[490]

198. *Charter of the earl of Warwick concerning this land.*
Henry by the grace of God earl of Warwick to Faritius abbot of Abingdon and all his monks, greeting and friendship. Know that, for God's love and your love, I have granted that exchange which you made with Ansketel your man concerning Chesterton in return for his land of Tadmarton, that is, on the following terms: that just as he

[489] See above, p. lvii, on various of these monastic witnesses. Saric conceivably is Saric the cook, mentioned below, p. 284. Robert priest of Marcham could just conceivably be the man mentioned below, p. 286.

[490] See above, p. xviii.

Tademertuna[a] a uobis et seruiuit, ita teneat a uobis et a successoribus uestris illam de Cestretuna, et seruiat omni tempore ecclesie de
[ii. 138] Abbendona. Hoc factum est coram his testibus: ex parte comitis: Herlewino scilicet presbitero, et Wih capellano,[b] et Roberto dapifero;[491][c] ex parte abbatis: Ælfrico[d] monacho, Bernerio, et Rainaldo, et Anskitillo, et alio Rainaldo,[492] militibus. In presentia comitis et abbatis, in uilla Bragels, in quarto anno Henrici Anglorum strenuissimi regis.

199. *De Turstino de Sancta Helena.*[493]

Turstino etiam de Sancta Helena escambiuit idem abbas, pro terra que a ponte Yccheford ad ecclesiam tendentibus sinistrorsum[e] continetur, cum omnibus sibi adiacentibus, terram que ueteri gurgiti adiacet, in loco qui Anglice dicitur Helenestou, inferius scilicet.

200. *De Bernero milite.*

Bernero uero, pro terra que a Bertona curiam uersus itinerantibus dextrorsum est, terram que Blachegraue dicitur, cum hospicio quod Goisfredi cementarii fuerat.[494]

201. *De Henrico filio Oini.*

Henricum etiam filium Oini fecit heredem de omnibus que fuerant patris sui dum uiueret, eo tenore ut unius militis seruitium per omnia faceret.[495] De hida uero quam in uilla Draituna habet, que de dominio ecclesie est, si abbas ipsi auferre uoluerit, pro illa campsionem ei restituat.

[a] Tadmertuna *B* [b] cappellano *B* [c] et *add. B* [d] Alfrico *B*
[e] sinistror *B*

[491] Professor Crouch (personal communication) suggests that 'Wih' the chaplain is probably a William *capellanus* associated with the earl of Warwick who appears e.g. in the cartulary of Kenilworth Abbey, London, British Library, Harl. 3605, fo. 11[r]. For a list of the stewards of the earls of Warwick, see Crouch, 'Earls of Warwick', pp. 21–2.

[492] The two Reginalds cannot be identified with any certainty.

[493] On Thurstan see above, p. lxv. EPNS, *Berkshire*, ii. 400, identifies the bridge at *Yccheford* as Ock Bridge. 'Helenstow' means 'the holy place of Helen', and is land associated with the church of St Helen; EPNS, *Berkshire*, ii. 439, and note Vol. i, c. B7 (*CMA* i. 7); see also the street map of medieval Abingdon in *Abingdon Cartularies*, ii, p. lxvii, fig. 5.

[494] Blagrove was in the manor of Wootton, Berks.; see EPNS, *Berkshire*, ii. 462, and below, p. 292. *DB* i, fo. 58[v], states that 'the abbey itself holds Barton in demesne'; Barton, Berks., contained the borough of Abingdon, which is not named in *Domesday*. For the area of the monastic precinct known as the court, see Plan, p. cv.

[495] Henry may be the son of the 'Wini', mentioned above, p. 78; see above, p. 146, for

held that land of Tadmarton from you and did service, so he is to hold from you and your successors the land of Chesterton and for all time is to do service to the church of Abingdon. This was done in the presence of these witnesses: from the earl's side: Herluin the priest and *Wih* the chaplain, and Robert the steward;[491] from the abbot's side: Ælfric the monk, and the knights Berner and Reginald and Ansketel and the other Reginald.[492] In the presence of the earl and abbot in the village of Brailes, in the fourth year of King Henry the most vigorous king of the English.

199. *Concerning Thurstan of St Helen.*[493]
In return for the land which is enclosed on the left from the bridge of *Yccheford* for those proceeding to the church, together with everything belonging to that land, the same abbot also exchanged with Thurstan of St Helen the land lying near the old weir, in the place called in English *Helenstow*, which is lower down the river.

200. *Concerning Berner the knight.*
He exchanged with Berner the land which is called Blagrove, together with the house which was Geoffrey the mason's, in return for the land which is to the right for those travelling from Barton towards the court.[494]

201. *Concerning Henry son of Oini.*
He also made Henry son of Oini heir of everything which had been his father's while he was alive, on the terms that he would do the service of one knight for everything.[495] Moreover, if the abbot wished to take away from him the hide which he had in the village of Drayton, which is from the church's demesne, he was to give him an exchange for it.

Oini appearing as a witness to a gift of Henry d'Aubigny, named in a marginal addition in MS C, in the main text in MS B. On Abingdon's lands at Drayton, see above, p. 198. What other lands passed to Henry is uncertain. A list from Henry I or Stephen's time, below, p. 387, mentions Henry son of Oini holding one hide in Dry Sandford, Berks., and, p. 387, a Henry holding one hide in Drayton. Another list, of the same period, mentions a 'Henricus filius Idini' holding three hides, below, p. 393; this may be the same man. The list of knights in MS B, below, p. 324, has a Henry son of Oini holding three hides in Abingdon, and two hides in Hill, Warw. The *Testa de Nevill*, ii. 845, 848, 853, mention a Hugh son of Henry holding a knight's fee in Abingdon, Drayton, and Sandford. *Testa de Nevill*, ii. 953, mentions a Hugh of Abingdon holding one sixth of a knight's fee from the abbot at Hill. For further discussion of the family, see A. E. Preston, *The Church and Parish of St Nicholas, Abingdon* (Oxford Hist. Soc., xcix, 1935), pp. 403–9; for the location of their lands in Abingdon, known as FitzHarris, see the map in *Cartularies*, ii, p. lxvi.

[ii. 139] **202.** *De Godrico de Celuesgraue.*[a][496]

Egilwinus filius Godrici de Celuesgraue celauit abbati Faritio quantum terre habebat.[497] Dicebat etiam non nisi duodecim acras in campo se habere, sicut ei in conuentione factum fuerat in capitulo monachorum. Sed ipse abbas, inquisitione certa de hoc facta, inuenit aliter istud se habere, et multo amplius terre illum cum predictis duodecim acris tenuisse. Vnde iudicatum est pro hoc forisfacto in curia eiusdem abbatis, ut predictus uir singulis annis sex sextarios mellis redderet,[498] sicut antea duos reddiderat, et cetera seruitia sicut antea fecerat monachorum usui persolueret.

203. *De Rogero Maledocto.*[b][499]

Rogerus Maledoctus, cum sua coniuge nomine Odelina, uenit in capitulum monachorum Abbendone, et pro animarum suarum reme-
B fo. 153r dio dederunt sancte Marie et huic ecclesie ter | ram cum domibus quas in Oxeneforde[c] habebant, et talem finis uite sue conuentionem fecerunt: ut uidelicet, cum quis ipsorum moreretur, huc se sepeliendum deferri preciperent, et centum solidos de suo pro sua anima tunc ecclesie donaret. Que conuentio facta est in presentia domni Faritii abbatis, sub istorum laicorum testimonio: Raineri medici, Turstini Basset, et aliorum plurimorum.[500]

[ii. 140] **204.** *De Ermenol burgensi.*[501]

Ermenol,[d] burgensis de Oxeneford,[e] tenebat de abbate[f] wicham[g] que est iuxta pontem Oxeneford, pro quadraginta solidis ad gablum, et contigit ut gablum detineret anno uno. Quare abbas, sequenti anno messis tempore, quicquid pecunie desuper terram illam inueniri poterat namari iussit, et terram prohiberi. At ipse Ermenoldus pro se Walterum archidiaconum de Oxeneford et [h]Rac' de Standlac[h] abbati transmisit,[502] et pecuniam suam eorundem plegio recepit, die statuto placitandi et plegio quietandi. Dies postea statutus uenit, nec placitor, nec plegius quietandus affuit. Vnde abbas predictos plegios

[a] Cheluesgraue *B* [b] Maledicto *B* [c] Oxeneford *B* [d] Ermenold *B* [e] Oxeford *B* [f] Faritio *add. B* [g] wicam *B* [h–h] Ricardum de Stanlache *B*

[496] *English Lawsuits*, no. 208. The place-name could be Chalgrove, Oxon., or Chalgrave, Beds. It was probably carelessness on the part of the rubricator which made the heading mention Godric rather than Egilwin.

[497] Egel-/Egil- names developed from the Old English Æthel-, in this case Æthelwine.

[498] A sester of honey was generally four gallons, but occasionally five to six gallons; Zupko, *Weights and Measures*, p. 374.

[499] I have been unable to identify with certainty either the donors or the precise location of the lands and houses in Oxford which Roger gave to Abingdon.

202. *Concerning Godric of Celvesgrave.*[496]

Egilwin son of Godric of *Celvesgrave* concealed from Abbot Faritius how much land he had.[497] For he said he only had twelve acres in the field, as had been made over to him in an agreement in the monks' chapter. But the abbot made a specific enquiry concerning this, and found that it was otherwise, in that Egilwin held much more land with the aforesaid twelve acres. Therefore it was commanded in the abbot's court that for this wrong Egilwin should render six sesters of honey,[498] as previously he had rendered two, and pay the other services for the monks' use as he had previously done them.

203. *Concerning Roger Mauduit.*[499]

Roger Mauduit, with his wife named Odelina, came to the chapter of the monks of Abingdon, and for the cure of their souls they gave to St Mary and to this church the land and houses which they had in Oxford, and made the following agreement concerning the end of their lives: namely, they ordered that when either of them was dying, they were to be brought here for burial, and would then give the church 100s. of their own for their soul. This agreement was made in the presence of lord Abbot Faritius, under the witness of these laymen: Rainer the physician, Thurstan Basset, and many others.[500]

204. *Concerning the burgess, Ermenold.*[501]

Ermenold, a burgess of Oxford, held from the abbot a dairy-farm next to Oxford bridge, for 40s. rent, and it happened that one year he withheld the rent. Therefore, the following year at harvest time, the abbot ordered the seizure of whatever livestock could be found on that land and forbade him access to it. But Ermenold sent Walter archdeacon of Oxford and Richard of Standlake to the abbot on his behalf;[502] he received back his livestock on their surety, and a day was set for pleading and for the acquitting of surety. Afterwards, the specified day came, and neither the pleader nor the surety to be acquitted was present. Therefore the abbot initiated a complaint

[500] This is the sole mention of Rainer to appear in Kealey, *Medieval Medicus*, pp. 32, 142; he does not appear in Talbot and Hammond, *Medical Practitioners*. Thurstan may be Ralph Basset's son, also mentioned below, pp. 248, 250.

[501] *English Lawsuits*, no. 209; see Hudson, *Land, Law, and Lordship*, pp. 27, 30, 32. The contemporary existence of more than one Ermenold makes it difficult to say more about the protagonist; see *Oseney*, i, no. 40, witnessed by 'duobus Ermenoldis'. See also above, p. xciii.

[502] For the possible identification of Richard of Standlake with Richard de Grey, see above, p. 154 n. 369.

ascitos mouit de habita re questionem. Et quia in amore familiares ei
C fo. 162r erant, eorum internuntio mediante inter se | et ipsum Ermenoldum actum est ut iste uir misericordiam abbatis quereret, et hoc de suis rebus abbati et ecclesie Abbendone concederet, ut quicquid terre habebat sua procuratione in burgo et deforis burgo, siue sibi proprie, siue in uadem posite (nec tamen esset regis, baronis, aut episcopi), totum simul ecclesia haberet. Creditores autem terre, si possent ab abbate suam terram ex uadimonio quietare, reciperent eam; sin uero, abbati et monachis permaneret.[a] [503] At uero abbas eidem uiro concessit, ut si uellet monachus fieri, monachum in Abbendona eum faceret. Quod si mallet in uilla Abbendonie laicus degere, hospicium ei procuraretur conueniens, et uictus unius monachi et
[ii. 141] unius seruientis sibi daretur. Hoc factum est in domo predicti Ermenoldi, sua coniuge et filio[b] Willelmo annuente, coram predicto Waltero et [c]Rac' de Standlac,[c] et multis aliis. Sed et postea in portmannimot ostensum et concessum eodem modo et eadem conuentione est.[504]

205. *De decima [d]uille que dicitur Bulehea.*[d] [505]

Anno quinto regni Henrici regis intrante, Willelmus de Sulaham[e] dedit Deo, et sancte Marie, et abbati Faritio, et monachis in Abbendona, decimam sue uille que Bulehea uocatur, die uidelicet Assumptionis eiusdem sancte Marie.[506] Eodem etiam die, confirmauit donum de alia decima quam antea dederat de uilla Cildestuna,[f] que ad hereditatem Leodseline priuigne sue pertinebat,[507] ipsa puella coram monachis concedente donum, et cum ipso Willelmo et cum matre sua super altare idem imposuit, coram his testibus: abbate predicto et omni conuentu, Iohanne fratre coniugis eiusdem
B fo. 153v Willelmi, Hum|frido eiusdem militis,[g] Hugone Conred.

[a] permanerent *B C* [b] suo *add. B* [c–c] Ricardo de Stanlac *B* [d–d] de Offentona *B* [e] Suleham *B* [f] Childestuna *B* [g] *for* milite ?

[503] The Latin is not entirely clear, but it would appear that Ermenold had received land as gages (securities) for loans; hence the distinction between his own lands and those placed in gage. Those who had gaged the lands are now given the chance to redeem them.

[504] *VCH*, *Oxfordshire*, iv. 336, states that this is the first mention of the Oxford town court, and traces the twelfth-century development.

[505] *Boarstall Cartulary*, p. 325, correctly states that it is hard to identify where these tithes were. On place-name grounds (see EPNS, *Oxfordshire*, i. 73–4) a possibility may be Bolney, Oxon., close to Harpsden; the latter was another manor of Miles Crispin. See also *VCH*, *Berkshire*, iv. 63, the basis for which analysis is very unclear.

concerning this matter against the sureties who had been summoned. And since they were his close friends, it was arranged by their mediation between him and Ermenold that the latter should seek the abbot's mercy, and grant to the abbot and church of Abingdon concerning his own possessions that the church should have all the land he held for his maintenance, inside or outside the borough, whether his own or placed in gage, but not, however, land belonging to the king, a baron, or a bishop. Moreover, those who had received credit for land were to receive the land back from the abbot if they were able to acquit it from the gage; if not, it would remain to the abbot and monks.[503] Further, the abbot granted to Ermenold that if he wished to become a monk, the abbot would make him a monk in Abingdon. If he preferred to live as a layman in the town of Abingdon, he would provide him with an appropriate lodging and give him the provisions of one monk and a servant. This took place in Ermenold's house, with the agreement of his wife and his son William, in the presence of the aforesaid Walter and Richard of Standlake, and many others. Afterwards it was publicized and granted in the same fashion and with the same terms in the portmoot.[504]

205. *Concerning the tithe of the village which is called Bulehea.*[505]
At the start of the fifth year of King Henry's reign, William of Sulham gave to God, and to St Mary, and to Abbot Faritius, and to the monks in Abingdon the tithe of his village which is called *Bulehea*, on the day of the Assumption of St Mary [15 Aug. 1104].[506] On the same day he also confirmed the gift of another tithe which he had previously given from the village of Chilton, which pertained to the inheritance of Leodselina his step-daughter.[507] The girl herself granted the gift in the presence of the monks, and with William himself and her mother she placed this on the altar in the presence of these witnesses: the aforesaid abbot and all the convent, John (brother of William's wife), Humphrey his knight, Hugh Conred.

[506] *DB* i, fo. 61^r, records William de Cailly holding Sulham, Berks., from the king, fo. 61^v records a William holding one hide in Sulham from Miles Crispin. See also *Boarstall Cartulary*, p. 325, Keats-Rohan, *Domesday People*, p. 489, for further information on William 'son of Turold' and his family, and for other lands held from Miles.

[507] Presumably Chilton, Berks. In 1086, Abingdon and Walter son of Other each had five hides in Chilton, *DB* i, fos. 59^r, 61^v.

206. *De quadam decima in Hanneia.*[a] [508]

Osbernus, nepos Motberti monachi quondam prepositi abbatie, promisit donaturum se omni anno Deo, et sancte Marie, et monachis in Abbendonia, decimam sua[b] de terra quam de Hugone de Boche-
[ii. 142] lande tenet, que fuit olim Bulluchesege[c] in uilla Hannie, scilicet de lucro sue dominice carruce, de agnis et porcellis.

207. *De decima Turoldi in Hanneia.*[d] [509]

Similiter Turoldus de eadem uilla dedit Deo et sancte Marie de Abbendona, coram Faritio abbate et omni conuentu in capitulo, decimam omnium suarum possessionum, porcellorum scilicet, agnorum, uellerum, sed decimam carruce sue tantummodo ita discreuit, ut duas istius decimationis partes huic loco, terciam uero partem presbitero sibi seruienti concederet, hoc idem concedente et confirmante uxore sua Hugulina,[e] et filio suo Willelmo. Et hanc donationem donauit anno quinto Henrici regis.

208. *De decima de Offentona.*[510]

Eodem anno, cum uenisset abbas Faritius in uillam suam Offentunam, ut opus ecclesie quod ibi lapideum a fundamento inchoauerat ad perfectum determinaret, congregauerunt se homines sui ex eadem uilla, et optulerunt communi deuotione et concessione decimam suam totius uille eiusdem sancte Marie, et ipsi abbati, et[f] loco Abbendonie,[g] ab illo in reliquum tempus, ut uidelicet abbas de suo proprio ecclesiam eiusdem alacrius construendo perficeret, et ipsi mererentur in fraternitate loci annumerari. Hanc expeticionem cum abbas audisset, inquisiuit utrum ecclesie eiusdem uille antiquitus decima
[ii. 143] ab illis hominibus daretur, nolens scilicet eam sua rectitudine minuere pro alicuius donatione sibi suoque loco oblata. Dictumque est hoc esse moris uille, ut a singula uirgata ecclesie illi uiginti quatuor [h]garbas pro decima numeratas donarentur.[h] [511] Quod sciens abbas, statuit ante ipsos homines ut, sicuti ipsimet uoluerant et optulerant, reciperet eorum decimam, ea determinatione assignata inter ipsum
C fo. 162[v] abbatem et ecclesiam eiusdem | uille, scilicet ut tempore colligendarum decimationum, abbas ipse mitteret Offentonam quem uellet de

[a] Hannia *B* [b] suam *B* [c] Bullukes ege *B* [d] Hannie *B* [e] Hulina *B* [f] in *B* [g] et *add. B* [h–h] *the text should read either* garbas pro decima numeratas donarent *or, more likely,* garbe pro decima numerate donarentur

[508] See also above, p. 192.

[509] See Kemp, 'Monastic possession of parish churches', pp. 142, 144–5, esp. n. 50, for

206. *Concerning a certain tithe in Hanney.*[508]
Osbern, nephew of the monk Modbert who was once administrator of the abbey, promised to give annually to God, and to St Mary, and to the monks in Abingdon tithe from his land in the village of Hanney held from Hugh of Buckland, which once was 'Bullock's Eye''s, that is from the produce of his demesne plough, from lambs and piglets.

207. *Concerning Thorold's tithe in Hanney.*[509]
Similarly from the same village, Thorold gave to God and to St Mary of Abingdon, in the presence of Abbot Faritius and all the convent in the chapter, the tithe of all his possessions, that is of piglets, lambs, and fleeces, but merely divided the tithe of his plough, granting two parts of it to this monastery, but the third part to the priest who served him; his wife Hugolina and his son William granted and confirmed this. And he gave this gift in King Henry's fifth year [5 Aug. 1104–4 Aug. 1105].

208. *Concerning the tithe of Uffington.*[510]
That same year, Abbot Faritius came to his village of Uffington so that he could round off perfectly the stone-work of the church which he had begun there from the foundations. His men from that village gathered, and out of common devotion offered by a common grant to St Mary, and to the abbot, and to the monastery of Abingdon their tithe of all that village, thenceforth and for the rest of time, so that the abbot might from his own resources complete their church by building more swiftly, and so that they might deserve to be numbered amongst that monastery's fraternity. When the abbot heard their intention, he inquired whether of old they gave the tithe to the church of that village, as he was unwilling to diminish it in its rights through any gift offered to himself and his monastery. And it was said that the village custom was for twenty-four sheaves from each virgate to be given to that church as a tithe.[511] In this knowledge, the abbot ordained in the villagers' presence that he would accept their tithe as they had wished and offered, with the following division fixed between himself (the abbot) and the village church, that is, that at the time of the collecting of tithes, the abbot himself would send to

lay gifts of tithe and in particular divisions of tithe between monastery and parish priest. For Thorold and Hanney, see also above, p. 190.

[510] See also below, p. 394.

[511] See Brett, *English Church*, pp. 224–5; also Round, 'Churchscot', p. 101, who pointed out that twenty-four sheaves made up a 'thrave', each sheaf being three feet round.

suis, et ipse reciperet a singulis, secundum singulorum possessionem, rectam decimationem, et post illam totam collectam, de singula uirgata illius uille tot manipulos presbitero illius ecclesie tribueret quot superius diximus ei deberi, reliqua uero decimationis abbati seruaret.[512]

Aderat[a] et Droco illic, qui de feudo Roberti de Britteuilla[b][513] in eadem uilla tres hidas terre tenebat, et pro sua decima omni anno promisit se daturum duos solidos, quousque decimam ipsius terre, quam illic habebat, ualeret, adiutorio eiusdem abbatis ab illo loco
B fo. 154r quietare, quo data a suo predicto domino fuerat, uidelicet cano|nicis sancti Georgii de castello Oxeneford.[514]

[c]His omnibus[c] in manu abbatis uadimonizatis, concessit illis omnibus, ex parte sui totiusque conuentus, Abbendonie beneficia eiusdem loci, presentibus his testibus: ⟨G⟩irardo[d] preposito eiusdem uille, Mantino,[e] et multis aliis.

[ii. 144] **209.** *De decima Willelmi de Wecenesfeld.*[f][515]

Willelmus de Wecenesfeld[g] dedit suam decimam ex omni sua pecunia sancte Marie et monachis in Abbendona, de tribus uidelicet hidis in Wecensfeld[h] et duabus de Boxore, excepto una acra que ecclesie[i] de Boxore adiacet. Hoc donum dedit in presentia domni Faritii abbatis, anno septimo Henrici regis.

210. *De decima de Ættuna.*[j][516]

Rogerus etiam filius Aluredi[k] dedit decimam suam Deo et huic ecclesie de uilla sua Ættuna, que est proxima Cumenore,[l] de suo uidelicet dominio, etiam et de piscationibus suis illic adiacentibus. Et promisit quod cum Osmundo et aliis suis hominibus de illa uilla[m] faceret, [n]ut et[n] ipsi de suo tenore similiter decimam ecclesie huic concederent, coram his testibus: Warino capellano Milonis,[517] Wino, et multis aliis.

[a] *preceded by a line of red minims, supplied by the rubricator B* [b] Brittewilla *B* [c–c] Hec omnia *B C* [d] *initial om. C.* Ricardo *B* [e] *initial om. C* [f] Wenekefeld *B* [g] Wechenesfeld *B* [h] Wechenesfeld *B* [i] exclesie *C* [j] Wtuna *B* [k] Alfredi *B* [l] Cumenoræ *B* [m] *a word such as* rectum *may be omitted here* [n–n] et ut *B*

[512] On this division of tithe, see G. Constable, *Monastic Tithes from their Origins to the Twelfth Century* (Cambridge, 1964), p. 105 and n. 2, who suggests that 'production had presumably increased between the time when the tithe was fixed and when it was granted to the monks, who collected the difference'.

[513] There are several places in Normandy called Bretteville .

[514] *DB* i, fo. 59r, states that 'the abbey itself holds Uffington [Berks.], and always held it. . . . Of this land Gilbert holds six hides from the abbot'; this could be Gilbert de

Uffington a chosen man of his. That man would receive from each villager the just tithe according to their individual possession, and after the whole tithe had been collected, from each virgate of the village he would assign to the priest of the church as many bundles as we said above were owed to him, the rest of the tithe being kept for the abbot.[512]

Also present there was Drogo, who held three hides of land in the same village from the fee of Robert de Bretteville.[513] Regarding his own tithe he promised he would give 2s. annually, in so far as he could with the abbot's help acquit the tithe of his land there in respect of the place to which it had been given by Robert his lord, namely the canons of St George in Oxford castle.[514]

When all these had been pledged in his hand, the abbot granted on his own behalf and that of the whole convent of Abingdon the benefits of this monastery to all the grantors, with these witnesses present: ⟨G⟩erard the reeve of this village, *Mantin*, and many others.

209. *Concerning the tithe of William of Watchfield.*[515]
William of Watchfield gave his tithe from all his goods to St Mary and to the monks in Abingdon, that is from three hides in Watchfield and two of Boxford, except one acre which belongs to the church of Boxford. He gave this gift in the presence of lord Abbot Faritius, in King Henry's seventh year [5 Aug. 1106–4 Aug. 1107].

210. *Concerning the tithe of Eaton.*[516]
Also, Roger son of Alfred gave to God and to this church his tithe from his village of Eaton, which is next to Cumnor, that is from his demesne and also from his fisheries belonging to the village, and he promised that he would make an arrangement with Osmund and his other men of Eaton, that they too would similarly grant the tithe to this church on their own terms; in the presence of these witnesses: Warin (Miles's chaplain),[517] Win, and many others.

Bretteville, see also below, p. 224, but is more likely Gilbert de Colombières; see below, p. 324. Henry I's confirmation for the church of St George, dating from 1123 × 33, does not specify any interest in Uffington; *RRAN* ii, no. 1468.

[515] *DB* i, fo. 59^{r}, states that 'the abbey itself holds Watchfield [Berks.] and held in the time of King Edward. . . . Gilbert holds three hides and one virgate from the abbot, Wimund one hide.'

[516] *DB* i, fo. 61^{v}, shows that Miles Crispin was tenant-in-chief of Eaton, Berks., in 1086; Alfred is recorded as his tenant. The entry mentions two fisheries, of 18s. On Roger son of Alfred, see *Boarstall Cartulary*, p. 323.

[517] Presumably Miles Crispin.

211. *De quadam decima apud*[a] *Waliford.*

Ad festum etiam Natiuitatis sancte Marie, anno nono Henrici regis, Aldred et Luured,[518] homines ecclesie de Waliford, [b]dederunt monachis huic[b] ecclesie suas decimas, de omnibus uidelicet suis pecoribus, et de agrorum suorum cultura, in capitulo coram toto conuentu.

[ii. 145] **212.** *De decima de Bradandena.*[519]

Quidam etiam miles, Radulfus nomine, in capitulo coram abbate Faritio et omni conuentu, omnem decimam de uilla sua Bradendene Deo et sancte Marie dedit, et donum huius rei super altare sancte Marie confirmando imposuit. Promisitque quod suum dominum Robertum de Insula requireret, de quo uidelicet ipsam terram tenebat, quatinus illius permissione et concessu suo hoc confirmaret, ut hec ecclesia ipsius decime donatione firmius in posterum potiretur. Et hoc fuit factum anno nono regis Henrici. Et hii testes affuerunt: Milo presbiter, Warinus de Fauarcis,[520] Lambertus, et multi alii.

213. *De decima quadam in Benneham.*[521]

Hugo filius Wichtgari[c] de Bennaham, cum uxore sua, recepit fraternitatem huius loci ad Natiuitatem sancte Marie anno decimo Henrici regis,[d] et dedit Deo et sancte Marie in perpetuum suam decimam habendam, et fecit conuentionem de se et uxore sua, quod post mortem hic requiescerent.

214. *De decima quadam in Waneting'.*[e] [522]

Quidam etiam miles, nomine Gillebertus Basset, unum ex filiis suis, nomine Robertum, monachum in hac Abbendonensi ecclesia fecit.
[ii. 146] Cum quo etiam inperpetuum dedit quandam decimam de terra quam habebat in uilla que uocatur Waneting ad usum pauperum, et unum
B fo. 154v pensum casei de sua[f] wicha, et decimam uelle|rum et agnorum. Solebat autem de pullis decimam dare quos de haratio suo apud Bernecestriam habebat.[523]

[a] aput *B* [b–b] *the text should probably read either* monachis et huic ecclesie *or* monachis huius ecclesie [c] Witgari *B* [d] *om. B* [e] Wanetinga *B* [f] de sua *written twice B*

[518] The name Luvred probably derives from the OE Leofred.

[519] I have been unable to identify this place with certainty. However, a plausible candidate may be Broad Dean in North Stoke, Oxon.; EPNS, *Oxfordshire*, i. 50. In 1235–6 a Robert 'de Lill'' (= 'de Insula') held one knight's fee in Stoke, from the honor of the earl of Giffard; *Testa de Nevill*, i. 446, 557.

[520] See above, p. 146, for Warin de *Favarcis* appearing as a witness to a gift of Henry d'Aubigny, named in a marginal addition in MS C, in the main text in MS B.

211. *Concerning a certain tithe at Welford.*
Also, at the feast of the Nativity of St Mary in King Henry's ninth year [8 Sept. 1108], in the chapter in the presence of the whole convent, Ealdred and Luvred,[518] men of the church from Welford, gave to the monks of this church their tithes, that is of all their livestock and of the tilling of their fields.

212. *Concerning the tithe of Bradendena.*[519]
Also, in the chapter in the presence of Abbot Faritius and all the convent, a certain knight named Ralph gave all the tithe of his village of *Bradendena* to God and to St Mary, and in confirmation he placed the gift of this possession on the altar of St Mary. And he promised that he would ask his lord Robert de Insula, from whom he held that land, that he confirm this by his permission and grant, so that this church would possess the gift of this tithe most firmly in future. And this was done in the ninth year of King Henry [5 Aug. 1108–4 Aug. 1109]. And these witnesses were present: Miles the priest, Warin de *Favarcis*,[520] Lambert, and many others.

213. *Concerning a certain tithe in Benham.*[521]
Hugh son of Wigar of Benham, with his wife, received the fraternity of this monastery on the Nativity of St Mary in King Henry's tenth year [8 Sept. 1109]. He gave to God and to St Mary his tithe to have in perpetuity, and made an agreement concerning himself and his wife, that after death they would rest here.

214. *Concerning a certain tithe in Wantage.*[522]
Also, a certain knight named Gilbert Basset made one of his sons, named Robert, a monk in this church of Abingdon. With Robert, he also gave in perpetuity a tithe from the land he had in the village called Wantage, for the use of the poor, and one weight of cheese from his dairy-farm, and the tithe of fleeces and lambs. Moreover, he was accustomed to give the tithe of foals which he had from his stud at Bicester.[523]

[521] *DB* i, fo. 63^{v}, records a certain Wigar holding two hides in Benham, Berks., from the king. On the complex nature of Benham, see above, p. 156.

[522] For lands in Wantage, Berks., passing from the royal demesne to the Basset family via Robert d'Oilly, see *VCH*, *Berkshire*, iv. 323.

[523] *DB* i, fo. 158^{r}, records Robert d'Oilly holding Bicester, Oxon., as two manors. In MS B, there follows an additional passage on Faritius's works as abbot; below, p. 332.

[ii. 150] **215.** *Hec sunt que abbas Faritius contulit ad singula officia monasterii.*[a] [524] |
C fo. 163r Hec sunt que domnus abbas[b] Faritius ecclesie contulit: ecclesiam scilicet sancti Martini de Oxeneford, et ecclesiam de Mercham, ecclesiam de Offentuna, ecclesiam de Witteham, ecclesiam de Cudesduna, ecclesiam de Niweham.[525]

[ii. 151] **216.** *De ornamentis ecclesie.*[526]

Hec etiam contulit ad ornatum ecclesie. Duo brachia polita argento[c] et lapidibus. Scrinium paruulum argenteum. Textum unum.[527] Calices quinque.[528] Patenam unam sine calice.[529] Ampullam[d] unam argenteam et deauratam. Turibula tria, unum argenteum et duo de cupro deaurato.[530] Duas acerras argenteas. Duo paria bacinorum de argento. Vasculum[e] unum in modum patene, in quo hostie deferuntur in refectorio pro communione sancta.[531] Imaginem sancte Marie. Casulas tres.[532] Stolas tres sine fanonibus, et unam cum fanone politam aurifrixo.[533] Albas tres de serico, cum uno tantum superhumerali, et alias[f] albas lineas pallio politas[g] decem.[534] Dalmaticas quatuor.[535] Tunicas tres. Cappas uiginti nouem, de his sexdecim cum tassulis, relique[h] sunt adhuc sine eis.[536] Pallia parua ante altaria duo, et pallia per ecclesiam pendentia quatuordecim. Cortinas septem. Tapetia sex. Dossalia sex.[537] Banchalia[i] in festis per chorum dependentia undecim, et unum ad supersedendum. Duo paria candelabrorum de argento, et unum magnum septem brachiorum. Signa ad pulsandum duo maiora, et tria minora. Pixidem de argento ad Eucharistiam.[538]

[a] *below this, in dry point, quite probably in the same hand as the dry point headings provided for the rubricator in B,* De operibus Faricii abbatis et maxime de ecclesia, *C. B has the heading* De operibus . . . ecclesia here *instead of* Hec . . . monasterii *for the present section. It also has it at fo. 154v for a section not in C; see below, p. 338* [b] *om. B* [c] argenteo *B* [d] *initial om. B* [e] *initial om. B* [f] *repeated on next line, but struck out by rubricator C* [g] pollitas *B* [h] reliqui *B C* [i] Lanchalia, *the wrong initial having been added by the rubricator B*

---

[524] See above, p. lxxxv, for the endowment of obedientiaries; also below, p. 394, for lists in MS C in the same hand as the *History*.

[525] For Marcham, see above, p. 192, below, p. 234; for Uffington, above, p. 208; for Nuneham, above, p. 80.

[526] Cf. above, p. civ; also below, p. 338.

[527] Probably a Gospel text.

[528] A chalice is a cup for consecrated eucharist wine. For liturgical vessels and vestments, see e.g. *A New Dictionary of Liturgy and Worship*, ed. J. G. Davies (London, 1986).

[529] A paten is a plate for eucharist bread, usually of silver, sometimes gold.

[530] A censer is the incense-burning vessel, or thurible.

[531] This was presumably to carry the hosts through the refectory, possibly from the

215. *These are the things which Abbot Faritius conferred on each office of the monastery.*[524]

These are the things which lord Abbot Faritius conferred on the church: namely, the church of St Martin of Oxford, and the church of Marcham, the church of Uffington, the church of Little Wittenham, the church of Cuddesdon, the church of Nuneham.[525]

216. *Concerning the ornaments of the church.*[526]

He also conferred these things, for the decoration of the church. Two arm-shaped reliquaries embellished with silver and stones. A very small silver box-reliquary. One text.[527] Five chalices.[528] One paten without a chalice.[529] One gilded silver flask. Three censers, one silver and two of gilded copper.[530] Two silver incense boxes. Two pairs of silver basins. One vessel in the manner of a paten, on which the hosts are carried in the refectory for holy communion.[531] An image of St Mary. Three chasubles.[532] Three stoles without maniples, and one decorated one with a gold-bordered maniple.[533] Three silk albs, with only one amice, and ten other linen albs decorated with a *pallium*.[534] Four dalmatics.[535] Three tunics. Twenty-nine copes; of which sixteen are with tassels, the rest still without them.[536] Two small cloths hanging before the altars and fourteen cloths hanging throughout the church. Seven curtains. Six hangings. Six dossals.[537] Eleven cushions hanging throughout the choir at festivals and one for sitting on. Two pairs of silver candlesticks and one large one of seven arms. Two larger bells for striking, and three smaller ones. A silver pyx for the Eucharist.[538]

kitchen where the eucharistic bread may have been made, or perhaps to the infirmary; see Plan, above, p. cv.

[532] A sleeveless mantle, the outermost vestment worn by the celebrant at the eucharist.

[533] A stole is a vestment consisting of a narrow strip of silk or linen, worn over the shoulders and hanging down to the knee or below. A maniple is a eucharistic vestment consisting of strip of cloth worn over the left wrist and hanging down.

[534] An alb is a white vestment, reaching to the ankles, with tight fitting sleeves and held in by a girdle at the waist. It was worn at performance of mass. An amice is a square or oblong of white linen worn round the neck of the celebrant priest. *Pallium* normally refers to the narrow circular band, of white wool, which was worn over the chasuble and hanging down like a scarf, and which was a mark of metropolitan office within the church. However, this surely is not the meaning here, and it may signify the embroidered cloth panels sometimes used to decorate albs; cf. e.g. *PL* clxvi. 1509 for 'albas . . . sine pallio, auro uel argento'.

[535] An over-tunic worn at mass by deacons and sometimes by bishops.

[536] A cope is a semi–circular cloak worn at liturgical functions when the chasuble was not used.

[537] A hanging, especially for the back of an altar.

[538] A small box for carrying the sacrament. MS B here contains a further short passage; see below, p. 338.

[ii. 152] **217.** *De camæra*[a] *monachorum.*

B fo. 156r Ad ministerium camere addidit uillam que uocatur Ciuelea, ex|cepto triginta duobus solidis qui[b] pertinent ad coquinam monachorum, et de aliis reditibus[c] quos[d] ipse adquisiuit sexaginta solidos.[539] Predicti denarii inde redduntur: de Faincota, id est de terra Atheline[e] de Iuri triginta solidi; de terra Henrici de Albinio uiginti quinque solidi; de Ægelwardo de Colebroc quinque solidi.[540]

218. *De elemosina.*

Ad ministerium elemosine addidit sex solidos que[f] redduntur de terra Alfrici de Boteleia apud Oxeneford foris burgum. Hanc terram filius eiusdem Alfrici, nomine Æilwinus, clamauit quietam abbati Faritio et ecclesie in perpetuum.[541] Dedit etiam unum molendinum, quod uocatur Henora, et duas partes decime de Niweham de dominio, et quinque hidas apud Wrda quietas ab omni placito uel seruitio, et terram quam dedit Hugo filius Ricardi pro anima patris sui, reddentem quindecim solidos.[542]

219. *De refectorio.*

Ad ministerium refectorii, decimam de Cestretuna appreciatam octo solidos.

[ii. 153] Ad[g] pergamenum[h] emendum, pro librorum ecclesie renouatione, concessit decimam de Dumeltuna, que ualet per annum triginta solidos.[543]

220. *De anniuersario abbatis Faritii.*

Die quo primum in capitulo nouo conuentus concessum acceperunt, predictus abbas Faritius uiginti septem solidorum redditus, quos sua industria in Oxeneforda urbe adquisiuit, in caritatis largitione eidem conuentui optulit, de terra scilicet Rogerii[i] Maledocti quindecim solidos, et de[j] Petri quondam uicecomitis nouem solidos, de Dermanni[k] uero tres solidos.[544] Et cellerariis precepit ut omni anno, ad memoriam huius rei et temporis, ex hac donatione conuentui ubertim seruirent, ut et presentibus et posteris sui laboris executio fieret largitatis fraterne recompensatio. Verum quia nemo

[a] camera *B* [b] que *B C* [c] redditibus *B* [d] quas *B C* [e] Adeline *B*
[f] qui *B C* [g] *preceded by* Ad parcamenum *as rubricated heading B*
[h] parcamenum *B* [i] Rogeri *B* [j] *om. B* [k] Dermani *B*

[539] Cf. a list in MS C in the same hand as the *History*, below, pp. 395, 398.

217. *Concerning the chamber of the monks.*
To the office of the chamber he added the village called Chieveley (except the 32s. which pertain to the monks' kitchen), and 60s. from other rents he acquired.[539] The aforesaid money is rendered from the following: 30s. from Fencott, that is the land of Adelina d' Ivry; 25s. from the land of Henry d'Aubigny; 5s. from Egelward of Colnbrook.[540]

218. *Concerning alms.*
To the office of alms he added 6s. which are rendered from the land of Ælfric of Botley, at Oxford outside the borough. Ælfric's son, named Æilwin, quitclaimed this land to Abbot Faritius and the church in perpetuity.[541] The abbot also gave one mill which is called Hennor, and two parts of the tithe of Nuneham from the demesne, and five hides at Longworth quit of all plea or service, and the land which Hugh son of Richard gave for the soul of his father, rendering 15s.[542]

219. *Concerning the refectory.*
To the office of the refectory, the tithe of Chesterton valued at 8s.

For buying parchment for renewing the church's books, he granted the tithe of Dumbleton, which is worth 30s. each year.[543]

220. *Concerning the anniversary of Abbot Faritius.*
On the day on which the convent first received a grant in the new chapter, the aforesaid Abbot Faritius offered it in a gift of love 27s. of rent, which by his efforts he had acquired in the town of Oxford, that is 15s. from the land of Roger Mauduit, 9s. from that of Peter (once the sheriff), and 3s. from that of Deormann.[544] And he ordered the cellarers that each year, in remembrance of this event and occasion, they serve the convent copiously from this gift, so that the performance of their labour may be fitting repayment for his brotherly generosity to men present and future. But as no one

[540] For these pieces of land, see above, pp. 106, 146, 142; also below, p. 398, a list in MS C in the same hand as the *History*.
[541] The name Æilwin could derive from either the OE Æthelwine or the OE Ælfwine.
[542] See above, pp. 94, 78, 136, 158.
[543] See above, p. cvi.
[544] For Roger Mauduit's grant, see above, p. 204; for Peter the sheriff, see above, p. 59. For a Deormann holding in Oxford, see *DB* i, fo. 154[r], where he holds one dwelling at 12d., and a share of another valued at 16d. Note also *Cartulary of St Frideswide*, i, no. 163, for a late twelfth-century grant of 'all the land which was of Stephen the priest son of Dermann the cleric in Oxford.'

sue nouit uite terminum, idem pater, pro se sollicitus, fratres hortatus est, ut suum post obitum in anniuersarii sui die hec eadem transmutaretur caritas, 'quia consideratis', ait, 'in predecessoribus meis anniuersariis, ad usus uestros et ad eorum memoriam, nichil huiusmodi hactenus fuisse delegatum. Vos proinde exoro mei memores existere, cum ad id temporis peruentum fuerit.'[545]

[ii. 154] **221.** *De domo infirmorum.* |

C fo. 163v Quia infirmi fratres, et qui opus habebant minui sanguine, igne carebant, idem abbas Faritius, consensu totius capituli, concessit omnes redditus eis mansionum subnotatarum quas in Oxenefordia ipsemet emerat, quatinus cum necessarium foret ignis exhibitio[a] domui infirmorum presto adesset. Et hoc concessit pro sue anime redemptione et infirmorum compassione, et quicumque hoc irritum faceret anathematizauit. He[b] sunt ille mansiones, cum redditibus: terra Wlfwi piscatoris quinque solidos et octo denarios; terra Rualdi quinque solidos et duos denarios; terra Dermanni presbiteri septem solidos et duos denarios; terra Colemanni octo solidos; terra Eadwini monetarii et fratris eius quinque solidos.[546] Deo itaque alienus et
B fo. 156v regno eius exors in perpetuum habeatur, qui | collatum hoc beneficium infirmis auferat.

222. *De excommunicatione.*

Ex quo igitur uir uenerabilis (de quo plura iam diximus) abbas Faritius huic ecclesie iure abbatis prefuit, multis et diuersis rebus eam sua industria decorauit. Que cum fratres sibi in Christo subiecti cernerent, atque, negligentias quorumdam eius antecessorum coram mentis oculis[c] ponendo, nequitias futurorum pastorum, si (quod absit) boni non fuerint, ualde pertimescerent, crebro supplicabant eum ut grauissimam in eos maledictionem uibraret, quorum actu uel
[ii. 155] consilio istinc auferrentur,[d] que [e]ipse huic[e] ecclesie procurauit.[547]
Quorum preces benigne amplectens, ex auctoritate sancte et indiuidue Trinitatis, ac inuocatione beate Dei genetricis et perpetue uirginis Marie, necnon omnium electorum Dei, excommunicauit perpetuo et sequestrauit a consortio cunctorum fidelium omnes qui

[a] exibitio *B* [b] Hee *B* [c] occulis *B C* [d] auferentur *B* [e–e] huic ipse *B*

[545] Cf. 1 Cor. 11: 2 'Laudo autem uos fratres quod per omnia mei memores estis', 'Now I praise you, brethren, that ye remember me in all things.'

[546] *DB* i, fo. 154r, records Wulfwig the fisherman holding 1 dwelling in Oxford at 32d. *Eynsham*, i, no. 64, mentions a Ruald holding in Oxford from Robert d'Oilly II, but

knows when his life will end, the same father, careful on his own behalf, urged the brethren that after his death this boon be transposed to his anniversary, 'since', he said, 'you consider that nothing of this sort has hitherto been assigned for your use and their memory on the anniversaries for my predecessors. I accordingly entreat that you remember me when it comes to that time.'[545]

221. *Concerning the house of the sick.*
Since the sick brethren, and those who needed to be bled, lacked a fire, Abbot Faritius, by the consent of the whole chapter, granted them all the rents of the holdings recorded below, which he himself had bought in Oxford, so that when necessary fire would be readily provided in the house of the sick. He granted this for the redemption of his soul and in compassion for the sick, and he anathematized whoever would render this null. These are the holdings, with rents: the land of Wulfwig the fisherman, 5s. 8d.; the land of Ruald, 5s. 2d.; the land of Deormann the priest, 7s. 2d.; the land of Colemann, 8s.; the land of Eadwine the mint worker and his brother, 5s.[546] And so let whoever takes away this benefit conferred on the sick be held for ever a stranger to God and one with no share in His kingdom.

222. *Concerning excommunication.*
So, the venerable man Abbot Faritius (of whom we have already said very much) was in charge of this church by right of being abbot, and by his toils glorified it with many and various possessions. When the brethren subject to him in Christ perceived these, and picturing the negligent acts of certain of his predecessors, they became extremely frightened of the profligacies of future pastors if (let it not be so) they were not good men. They frequently begged him that he brandish the severest malediction against those by whose deed or counsel are taken away from this church what he had provided for it.[547] He welcomed their prayers kindly, and, by authority of the holy and indivisible Trinity and the invocation of the blessed mother of God and ever Virgin Mary, and also of all the elect of God, he forever excommunicated and removed from the community of all the faithful everyone

specifies that Robert gave all that land to Eynsham. *DB* i, fo. 154^{r}, records Colemann as having had three dwellings in Oxford at 3s. 8d. There is no known Oxford moneyer called Eadwine issuing coins in the first half of Henry I's reign. Two possibilities arise: one is that he was a moneyer but from elsewhere, perhaps London or Winchester; the other is that he had a position in mint administration different from that of the men named on coins. I would like to thank Dr Mark Blackburn for advice on this point.

[547] Cf. the curse in William de Courcy the younger's charter, above, p. 82.

uiolenter siue fraudulenter aut quocumque molimine abstulerint aliquid post[a] obitum eius de rebus quas ipse uel eum diligentes quoad uixit isti ecclesie contulerunt, nisi publica satisfactione et restitutione penituerint; his tribus conditionibus exceptis, captiuorum redemptione, et terrarum huius ecclesie ac famis necessitate.[548] Hec fecit abbas Faritius, et hec scribere iussit ne posteri se de ignorantia excusent, constringens et eos maledictione perpetua qui ea arroganter uel fraudulenter aboleuerint.[549]

223. *De reliquiis huius ecclesie.*[550]
Nomina sanctorum subscripta reliquiarum sunt in Abbendonensi ecclesia perscrutatarum[b] a pie memorie[c] Faritio abbate, unacum senioribus ecclesie eiusdem,[d] sub[e] incarnationis Christi millesimo centesimo sexto decimo. De sudario Domni nostri Iesu Christi et de cruce eius.[551] Particula claui crucifixionis eius. [f]De mensa eius, et de sepulchro eius.[f] [552]

[ii. 156] **224.** [g]*De uestimentis sancte Marie.*[g]

225. [h]*De apostolis.*[h]
De ossibus sancti Iohannis Baptiste. De barba sancti Petri apostoli. De cruce eius, et de uestimentis eius, et Pauli apostoli similiter. Os et dens de sancto Andrea apostolo, et de cruce eius. Os de sancto Iacobo, fratre Domini, et de uestimentis eius. Os de sancto Barthomeo[i] apostolo.

226. *De martiribus.*
Os de sancto Stephano prothomartire, et de stola et dalmatica eius, et de capillis eius, et de lapidibus unde lapidatus est. De sancto Vincentio brachium, et hanca, et pars spatule, et costa eius. De sancto Laurentio leuita et martire digitus et pars coste eius. De sancto Victore martire brachium eius, et costa integra, et pars alterius coste, et alia plura ossa. Digitus et dens sancti Sebastiani martiris. Pars[j]

[a] quod *B*; post *added in margin in dry-point in a different hand B* [b] perscrutarum *B* [c] me memorie *B*, *the duplication being caused by a change of line* [d] ecclesie *add. B* [e] anno *interlined add. B* [f–f] *initial of* De *om., and whole line over erasure B* [g–g] *followed by* De uestimentis matris Dei, *which was then expunged*; *i.e. the rubricated version was added to replace that in ordinary ink C; om. B* [h–h] *over erasure B* [i] Bartholomeo *B* [j] Dars, *resulting from a mistake by the rubricator (distracted by the surrounding initials all being D) C*

[548] For the justification of alienation of church lands on grounds of necessity or utility, see Hudson, *Land, Law, and Lordship*, p. 231 and the canons cited there. The exact wording of the exception here has no obvious basis in any canonical collection which might

who after his death violently or deceitfully or by whatever sort of effort took away anything from the possessions which he or those who loved him conferred on this church in his life-time, unless they repent with public penance and restitution. These three circumstances were excepted: the redemption of captives, or the needs of the lands of this church, or of hunger.[548] Abbot Faritius did these things and ordered that they be written down, lest men in future excuse themselves by reason of ignorance, and he bound with perpetual malediction those who arrogantly or deceitfully destroy them.[549]

223. *Concerning the relics of this church.*[550]
Written below are the names of the relics of saints in the church of Abingdon, investigated by Abbot Faritius of holy memory, together with the older men of this church, in the year 1116 from the Incarnation of Christ. Part of the *sudarium* of our Lord Jesus Christ and of His cross.[551] A small piece of a nail of His crucifixion. Of His table and of His tomb.[552]

224. *Of the clothes of St Mary.*

225. *Concerning the apostles.*
Of the bones of St John the Baptist. Of the beard of St Peter the apostle. Of his cross and his clothes, and likewise of Paul the apostle. A bone and a tooth of St Andrew the apostle, and of his cross. A bone of St James, brother of the Lord, and of his clothes. A bone of St Bartholomew the apostle.

226. *Concerning the martyrs.*
A bone of St Stephen the protomartyr, and of his stole and dalmatic and of his hairs, and of the stones with which he was stoned. Of St Vincent, an arm and a thigh-bone, and part of his shoulder-blade, and his rib. Of St Laurence the deacon and martyr, a finger and part of his rib. Of St Victor the martyr, his arm and a whole rib and part of another rib, and very many other bones. A finger and tooth of St Sebastian the

have been available to Faritius. I would like to thank Dr Martin Brett for his help on this point.

[549] See above, p. xxxvii.

[550] Almost all of these saints appear in *Oxford Dictionary of Saints*; I here footnote only those who are not contained therein. On Faritius and saints, see also above, p. civ.

[551] The *sudarium* is the cloth with which St Veronica wiped the face of Christ after the weight of the cross caused him to fall on the way to Calvary; see *New Catholic Encyclopedia* (17 vols., New York, 1967–79), xiv. 625, entry for 'Veronica'.

[552] The list assumes the word 'part' before each phrase beginning 'of'.

C fo. 164r minoris ossis brachii | de sancto Dionisio et digitus eius. Dens et digitus sancti Georgii. De capite sancti Pancratii[a] martiris [b]et de osse
[ii. 157] eius.[b] De brachio sancti Firmini martiris.[c] Digitus sancti Ypoliti martiris. Dens sancti Eusebii martiris, cuius memoria est undeuicensimo kalendas Septembris. Ossa de Innocentibus. De camissia[d] sancti
B fo. 157r Eadmundi regis et martiris sanguino|lenta, quam uestitam habuit hora passionis eius, et de ligneo eius sarcofago, et de theca puluinaris eius, et de dolaturis de buxu unde plenum fuit.[553] De sancto Eadwardo pars plurima.[554] De his sanctis martiribus: Iohannis et Pauli, Tiburtii, Valeriani, Cosme et Damiani, Fabiani, Simplicii, Nerei et Achillei, Simphoriani,[e] Ciriaci, Sixti episcopi et martiris, Christofori, Bonefacii, Leodegarii, Eustachii.

227. [f]*De confessoribus.*

De sancto Ceadda,[g] episcopo et confessore, capud,[h] et maxillia, et brachium, cum aliis ossibus. De sancto Aldelmo,[i] episcopo et confessore, de capite eius, et dens, et pars scapule, et integra hanca eius. De sancto Adelwoldo spatula integra, et brachium,[j] et digitus, et de capillis eius. Brachium[k] sancti Iohannis Crisostomi.[555] De costa et aliis ossibus sancti Bertini abbatis. De barba sancti Cutberti.[l] De costa sancti Audoeni. [m]De his confessoribus ossa:[m] de manu sancti Martini, Nicholai, Siluestri, Gregorii, Benedicti, Mauri abbatis, Germani
[ii. 158] episcopi, Augustini, Ambrosii, Medardi, Vedasti et Amandi, Gaugerici,[556] Winwaloe, Wandregisili, Wilfridi, Columbani, Samsonis, Hylarii; costa sancti Swithuni, Birini, Machuti, Sulpicii, Guthlaci, Caurentini, Iudoci, Egidii, Leonardi, Antonii, Macharii, Cholumchille;[n][557] digitus Macloe contestoris.[o][558]

228. *De uirginibus.*[559]

De capillis sancte Marie Magdalene. De[p] capite sancte Cecilie et digitus eius. De capillis sancte Lucie. Duo brachia et maxilla cum dentibus sancte Balthildis.[q] De ossibus istarum uirginum: Agathe,

[a] Pancraci *B* [b–b] *om. B* [c] De brachio sancti Firmini martiris *squeezed in margin, and also at bottom of column in ink in one of the hands providing guidance for rubricator B* [d] camisia *B* [e] Simforiani *B* [f] De sancto Cedd' *rubricated add. B* [g] Cedda *B* [h] caput *B* [i] Abdelmo *C* [j] c *erased B* [k] *initial* B *at distance in margin, rubricator having failed to add C* [l] Chutberti *B* [m–m] De hiis confessoribus ossa *as rubricated heading B* [n] Columkilne *B* [o] *for* confessoris ? [p] *initial om. B* [q] Baltildis *B*

[553] For this relic, see Herman's *De miraculis sancti Eadmundi*, in *Memorials of St Edmund's Abbey*, ed. T. Arnold, (3 vols., London, 1890–6), i. 53.

martyr. Part of the lesser bone of the arm of St Denis, and his finger. A tooth and finger of St George. Of the head of St Pancras the martyr and a bone of his. Of the arm of St Firmin the martyr. A finger of St Hippolytus the martyr. A tooth of St Eusebius the martyr, whose memorial day is 14 August. Bones from the Innocents. Of the blood-stained shirt of St Edmund, king and martyr, which he was wearing at the hour of his passion, and of his wooden coffin, and of the reliquary of his pillow and of the shavings of box-wood of which it was full.[553] The greatest part of St Edward.[554] Of these holy martyrs: John and Paul, Tiburtius, Valerian, Cosmas and Damian, Fabian, Simplicius, Nereus and Achilleus, Symphorian, Cyricus, Sixtus the bishop and martyr, Christopher, Boniface, Leger, Eustace.

227. *Concerning the confessors.*
Of St Chad, bishop and confessor, the head and jaw-bones, and arm with other bones. Of St Aldhelm, bishop and confessor, of his head and a tooth and part of the shoulder-blade and his whole thigh-bone. Of St Æthelwold, his whole shoulder-blade and an arm and a finger and of his hairs. The arm of St John Chrysostom.[555] Of the rib and other bones of St Bertin the abbot. Of the beard of St Cuthbert. Of the rib of St Ouen. Bones from these confessors: of the hand of St Martin, Nicholas, Sylvester, Gregory, Benedict, Maurus the abbot, Germanus the bishop, Augustine, Ambrose, Médard, Vedast and Amand, Gaugeric,[556] Winwaloe, Wandrille, Wilfrid, Columbanus, Samson, Hilary; the rib of St Swithun, Birinus, Malo, Sulpicius, Guthlac, Corentin, Judoc, Giles, Leonard, Anthony, Machar, Colum Cille;[557] a finger of Malo the witness.[558]

228. *Concerning the virgins.*[559]
Of the hairs of St Mary Magdalene. Of the head of St Cecilia and her finger. Of the hairs of St Lucy. Both arms and the jaw-bones with teeth of St Bathild. Of the bones of these virgins: Agatha; Agnes;

[554] On the relics of St Edward, king and martyr, being brought to Abingdon in the time of Cnut, see Bk. i, c. 116, Vol. i, c. B250 (*CMA* i. 442–3). Shaftesbury Abbey also claimed to possess the relics of St Edward, and—unlike Abingdon—was closely associated with his cult; see *Charters of Shaftesbury Abbey*, ed. S. E. Kelly (Oxford for the British Academy, 1996), pp. xiv–xv.

[555] See above, p. 68.

[556] A seventh-century bishop of Câteau-Cambrésis; see *Bibliotheca Hagiographica Latina*, nos. 3286–91.

[557] i.e. St Columba of Iona.

[558] See Vol. i, Introduction, 'Style', for the unusual word 'contestor'.

[559] For Mary Magdalene and Margaret, see also above, p. 70.

Agnetis, Margarite, Anastasie, Barbare, Genouefe, Eadburge, Gratiane.[560] Et de uestimentis sancte Brigide, Radegundis, Iuliane, Victorie.

229. *De morte pie memorie domni Faritii abbatis.*[561]

Cum igitur huius uiri uenerandi Faritii laudabili industria opes istius ecclesie multiplicate de die in diem augmentarentur, decidit in egritudinem, qua[a] ex luce subtractus, a laboribus suis beato fine quieuit, septimo decimo uidelicet regiminis sui anno, septimo kalendas Martii.[562] Post cuius discessum, omnes res siue redditus huius ecclesie mox describuntur, ac, trecentis libris fisco regali per
[ii. 159] singulos annos deputatis, reliqua usibus ecclesie conceduntur.[563] Fuimus autem sine abbate quatuor annis, omnem tamen habundantiam uictus et uestitus habentes. Prefuit uero huic domui quidam ex nostris [b]uir uenerabilis,[b] nomine Warengerius, qui a tempore Rainaldi abbatis prioris functus officio; strenue nos gubernauit, ac uelut benignissima mater sinceriter semper fouit. Erat enim uerus Dei seruus et uera caritate plenus.

230. *De decima Speresholt.*[564]

In secundo anno post obitum domni Faritii abbatis, Hugo dispensator regis in capitulo concessit huic ecclesie suam decimationem de omni pecunia, tam de mobilibus rebus quam immobilibus, de manerio
B fo. 157v Speresholt quod de ecclesia tenebat, | sua coniuge Helewisa fauente,[565] coram his testibus: Poidras[c] suo homine, et Anschitillo[d] suo preposito de predicta uilla, et multis aliis.

231. *De decima duarum hidarum in Scereng'.*[566]

Eodem anno Radulfus, camerarius abbatis Faritii, decimationem
C fo. 164v suam de omni pecunia sua | agrorum, uidelicet pecudum, lanee, et caseorum, de duabus hidis in Sceringeford, quas de feudo Roberti de Britteuilla[e] tenebat, concessit huic ecclesie; et conuentus illam
[ii. 160] delegauit loco refectorii, quatinus que opus erant infra ipsam

[a] quia *B* [b–b] uenerabilis uir *B* [c] *initial om. B* [d] sckitllo, *initial om. B*
[e] Brittewella *B*

[560] Eadburh appears in *Oxford Dictionary of Saints*, p. 118 *s.n.* Edburga. According to Durham relic lists, Gratiana was a virgin martyr; *Historiæ Dunelmensis scriptores tres*, ed. J. Raine (Surtees Soc., [ix], 1839), p. ccccxxix. However, no such St Gratiana can be traced; possibly she derived from St Gratianus.

[561] See also above, p. xlix, for the account of Faritius's death in *De abbatibus*; *CMA* ii. 290. For the date of his death, see also Cambridge, University Library, Kk. i 22, fo. 2r.

Margaret; Anastasia; Barbara; Genevieve; Eadburh; Gratiana.[560] And of the clothes of St Brigid, Radegund, Juliana, Victoria.

229. *Concerning the death of lord Abbot Faritius, of holy memory.*[561]
While, therefore, the wealth of this church was day by day being multiplied and increased by the praiseworthy toil of this venerable man, Faritius, he fell ill, was taken from this light, and rested from his toils with the blessed end of life, that is in the seventeenth year of his rule, on 23 February [1117].[562] Shortly after his death, all the possessions and rents of this church were listed, and £300 a year were designated to the royal treasury, the rest granted to the uses of the church.[563] Moreover, we were without an abbot for four years, but had every abundance of provisions and clothing. Indeed, a venerable man from amongst us, named Warenger, had charge of this house. He had enjoyed the office of prior from the time of Abbot Reginald, ruled us vigorously, and always tended us as single-mindedly as the kindest mother. For he was a true servant of God and full of true love.

230. *Concerning the tithe of Sparsholt.*[564]
In the second year after the death of lord Abbot Faritius, in the chapter, Hugh the king's dispenser, with his wife Helewise's approval, granted to this church his tithe of all his goods, both moveables and immoveables, from the manor of Sparsholt which he held from the church.[565] In the presence of these witnesses: Poidras his man, and Ansketel his reeve of the aforesaid village, and many others.

231. *Concerning the tithe of two hides in Shellingford.*[566]
In the same year, Ralph, Abbot Faritius's chamberlain, granted to this church his tithe of all his goods, that is of fields, livestock, wool, and cheeses, from two hides in Shellingford which he held from the fee of Robert de Bretteville. The convent delegated this to the refectory, so that what was needed within this house might be

[562] A similar passage appears in the Abingdon copies of the Worcester chronicle; John of Worcester, *Chronicle*, iii. 308.
[563] See above, p. lxxv; also Salter, 'Chronicle roll', p. 729.
[564] For Hugh and Sparsholt, see also above, p. 52.
[565] On Helewise, see above, p. xliii n. 179.
[566] *DB* i, fo. 59v, states that 'the abbey itself holds Shellingford [Berks.], and always held it'. The Gilbert who then held two hides from the abbot may be Gilbert de Bretteville, see above, pp. 43 n. 103, 210.

domum inde procurarentur, coram his testibus: Bernero et Turstino militibus, et multis aliis.

232. *De dominio huius ecclesie.*[567]

Anno tercio post obitum [a]abbatis Faritii,[a] cum adhuc abbatia hec in attentione abbatis fuisset, et[b] consideratione regia ad id adipiscendum, dominium ecclesie erat quietum a geldis que exigebantur in comitatu uniuerso. Sed tamen in comitatu Berchescira, a collectoribus amplius exigebatur quam debebatur de gildatione ecclesie contingenti, et hoc frequenter. Vnde clamore apud regiam iusticiam facto, decretum est ut aliquis de ecclesia[c] affidaret fide in comitatu predicto de quot hidis dominiis ecclesia deberet quietari, scilicet per episcopum Salebiriensem[d] Rogerum, et per episcopum[e] Lincolniensem Robertum, et Rannulfum cancellarium[568] (qui nominatim multum adiuuit inde), et Radulfum Basset. Itaque sedente comitatu apud Suttunam, et Willelmo de Bochelande[f] uicecomite existente, die lune post festum sancti Martini proximo, Rogerus de Harteluilla, homo ecclesie, pro ecclesia affidauit fidem in manu ipsius uicecomitis, uidente toto comitatu, quod de septies uiginti hidis de dominio deberet abbatia in Berchescira esse quieta, quando gildaretur.[569] Tunc erat collector comitatus Ædwinus presbiter de Celsi et ⟨S⟩amuel filius eius.[570] Ibi fuerunt de nostris Robertus sacrista, et
[ii. 161] Willelmus Brito, et alter Willelmus monachus, et Willelmus de Suuecurda, et Turstinus, et Radulfus camerarius, et multi alii.[571]

233. *De ecclesia Eadwardestune.*[g][572]

Anno quarto post obitum abbatis Faritii, Gillebertus filius Huberti de [h]Monte Canisi[h] recepit in capitulo societatem beneficiorum ecclesie huius,[573] et ibi concessit et affirmauit donum patris sui de ecclesia Eadwardestune, et de reliquis rebus a patre suo prius concessis tempore[i] domni Faritii abbatis. Et ita scilicet affirmauit, [j]textum sanctum[j] euuangeliorum loco pigneris in manum prioris

[a–a] Faricii abbatis *B* [b] a *add. B* [c] ecclesie *B C* [d] Salesberiensem *B* [e] *interlined before the preceding* et *B* [f] Bochlande *B* [g] Edwardestune *B* [h–h] Munte Kanesi *B* [i] tempo *B* [j–j] textu sancto *B C*

567 *RRAN* ii, no. 1211; *English Lawsuits*, no. 215.

568 Chancellor 1107–23; see Green, *Government*, p. 28, *RRAN* ii, p. ix.

569 Using 1086 hidage figures, *Domesday* indicates that about 165 hides were in demesne in 1086; conceivably 140 hides would be an accurate figure for just over thirty years later, although it is unclear how exactly the composer of the *History* came to this figure. R. C. Palmer, *The County Courts of Medieval England, 1150–1350* (Princeton, 1982), pp. 13–14,

procured therefrom. In the presence of these witnesses: the knights Berner and Thurstan, and many others.

232. *Concerning the demesne of this church.*[567]
In the third year after Abbot Faritius's death, while this abbey was still waiting to acquire an abbot by royal appointment, the demesne of the church was quit of the gelds which were being demanded throughout the county. However, in the county court of Berkshire the collectors demanded more than was owed from the geld-assessment of the church, and they did so repeatedly. Therefore, a claim was brought before royal justice, and through Roger bishop of Salisbury, and Robert bishop of Lincoln, and Ranulf the chancellor[568] (who specifically helped greatly concerning this), and Ralph Basset, it was decided that someone from the church should pledge his faith in the aforesaid county court regarding the number of demesne hides of which the church should be quit. Therefore, when the county court was meeting at Sutton, with William of Buckland present as sheriff, on the Monday after the feast of St Martin [17 Nov. 1119], Roger of Hardwell, a man of the church, pledged his faith in the hand of that sheriff on behalf of the church, with the whole shire court looking on, that in Berkshire the abbey ought to be quit from one hundred and forty hides of demesne when geld was taken.[569] The county collector then was Eadwine, priest of Cholsey, with Samuel his son.[570] Present there of our men were Robert the sacrist, and William *Brito*, and the other monk William, and William of Seacourt, and Thurstan, and Ralph the chamberlain, and many others.[571]

233. *Concerning the church of Edwardstone.*[572]
In the fourth year after Abbot Faritius's death, Gilbert son of Hubert de Montchesney received in the chapter the society of the benefits of this church,[573] and there he granted and affirmed his father's gift of the church of Edwardstone and of the other possessions previously granted by his father in the time of lord Abbot Faritius. And he affirmed it by placing the holy text of the Gospels as a pledge in the

notes that there was no set place for the meeting of the court of Berkshire; see also below, p. 310, for the court meeting at Farnborough. Hardwell was a dependency of Watchfield; Roger may have been a descendant of Gilbert de Colombières.

[570] *DB* i, fos. 56v–57r, shows that Cholsey was a royal possession; it remained so until Henry I granted it to Reading Abbey at its foundation.

[571] See above, pp. lviii, lxii.

[572] See above, p. 92.

[573] i.e. the confraternity of the house.

Warengerii ponendo, presente toto conuentu et militibus[a] huius ecclesie, Bernero et Warino.

234. *De abbate Vincentio.*[574]

Post quatuor annos, redeunte rege de Normannia, erat enim ibidem tanto tempore diuersis causis occupatus,[575] cum uenisset ad oppidum[b] quod[c] uulgo Windlesora[d] nuncupatur, mox accesserunt ad eum quidam ex fratribus, humiliter rogantes ut ecclesie pastore uiduate secundum Deum consuleret. Quos benigne consolans, iussit domum B fo. 158v redire, | precipiens[e] ut quinta die coram se apud Wintoniam cum priore adessent. Qui statuto die uenientes, coram rege ea que prius ceperunt rogare. Quibus, optimatum suorum consilio, tradidit in pastorem, coram episcopis et baronibus suis, quendam bone fame uirum nomine Vincentium, ex Gemmeticensi[f] ecclesia monachum, [ii. 162] cunctis qui aderant id laudantibus.[576] Quem fratres gaudenter suscipientes, peruenerat enim dudum fama bonitatis eius multociens ad eos, perduxerunt eum ad ecclesiam sibi commissam, comitante secum Rogero Salesbiriensi episcopo multisque aliis famosis uiris. A quibus in sede pastorali positus, domum sibi creditam sapienter gubernabat. Erat autem ualde benignus ac pietatis gratia plenus. Omnibus compatiebatur, omnes pio affectu deligebat.[g][577] De quo et tales litteras totius regni Anglie primoribus misit:

235. *Littere regis pro[h] abbate Vincentio.*[578]

Henricus rex Anglie archiepiscopis, episcopis, abbatibus, comitibus, baronibus, uicecomitibus, et omnibus fidelibus suis, Francis et C fo. 165r Anglis, | totius Anglie, salutem. Sciatis me dedisse et concessisse Vincentio abbati abbatiam de Abbendona, cum omnibus rebus abbatie ipsi pertinentibus. Et uolo et firmiter precipio ut bene et in pace et quiete et honorifice et libere teneat, cum saca et soca et toll[i] et team et infangenetheof,[j] in burgo et extra burgum. Hamsocnam uero et grithbriche et foresteal[k] super propriam

[a] milibus *C* [b] opidum *C, corrected to* oppidum *by interlin. of* p *in B* [c] qui *B C* [d] Windelesora *B* [e] principes *B* [f] Gemeticensi *B* [g] diligebat *B* [h] de *B* [i] tol *B* [j] infangeneþef *B* [k] forestal *B*

[574] For the account of Abbot Vincent in *De abbatibus* (*CMA* ii. 290), see above, p. li.

[575] Henry returned from Normandy on the night of 25/26 Nov. 1120, the occasion of the sinking of the White Ship. He was married at Windsor on 29 Jan. 1121, and was at Abingdon on 13 Mar. for the consecration of Robert bishop of Lichfield; Eadmer, *Historia novorum*, bk. vi, ed. Rule, p. 293, John of Worcester, *Chronicle*, iii. 148–50. This may well have been the occasion for the formal election of Vincent.

[576] A similar sentence appears in an Abingdon copy of the Worcester chronicle, the

hand of Prior Warenger, in the presence of the whole convent and of Berner and Warin, knights of this church.

234. *Concerning Abbot Vincent.*[574]
After four years, the king came back from Normandy, where he had been lengthily occupied by various affairs.[575] Soon after he came to the town which is commonly called Windsor, certain of the brethren approached him and humbly asked that, in accordance with God, he provide for the church, widowed of a pastor. He kindly consoled them and ordered that they return home, instructing that they and their prior appear before him at Winchester in five days time. They came before the king on the specified day and began to repeat their requests. By the counsel of his leading men, in the presence of his bishops and barons, with the approval of all present, he gave them as their pastor a certain man of good repute, named Vincent, a monk from the church of Jumièges.[576] The brethren received him joyfully, for frequent report of his goodness had reached them. Accompanied by Roger bishop of Salisbury and many other famous men, they took him to the church committed to him. He was placed by them in the pastoral seat, and he wisely governed the house entrusted to him. Moreover he was an extremely kind man and filled with the grace of piety. He felt compassion for all, and he loved all with pious affection.[577] Concerning him, the king sent the following letters to the leading men of the whole realm of England:

235. *Letters of the king for Abbot Vincent.*[578]
Henry king of England to his archbishops, bishops, abbots, earls, barons, sheriffs, and all his faithful men, French and English, of the whole of England. Know that I have given and granted to Abbot Vincent the abbey of Abingdon with everything pertaining to that abbey. And I wish and firmly order that he may hold well and in peace and undisturbed and honourably and freely, with sake and soke and toll and team and infangentheof, in borough and out of borough. I moreover grant him hamsocn and grithbriche and foresteal over all

manuscript of which is preserved in Lambeth Palace library; John of Worcester, *Chronicle*, iii. 308.

[577] Near identical sentences appear in an Abingdon copy of the Worcester chronicle, the manuscript of which is preserved in Lambeth Palace library; John of Worcester, *Chronicle*, iii. 308.

[578] *RRAN* ii, no. 1259; Lyell, no. 85; Chatsworth, no. 344; the writ almost certainly dates to soon after Vincent's formal election in 1121, on which see above, pp. xxviii, 228. For the privileges contained in the writ, see above, p. xcvii.

terram abbatie ei concedo, sicut aliquis antecessorum suorum unquam melius et quietius et honorificentius et liberius tenuit, cum omnibus aliis consuetudinibus suis. Testibus Rogero episcopo Saresbirie,[a] et Rannulfo cancellario, et Iohanne Baioc', et Willelmo de Pontearcharum. Apud Wdestocam.

[ii. 163] 236. *De foro Abbendonie*.[579]

In diebus huius patris, quidam maligni abeuntes ad regem, adulando suaserunt ei ut hundredum de Hornimere huic ecclesie abriperet, simul et mercatum huius uille interdiceret, affirmantes suis mendaciis quod nunquam abbas huius loci in propria potestate illud habuerit, uel mercatum antiquitus in hac uilla extiterit. Quorum adulationibus rex commotus, quibusdam iustisoribus suis precepit questionem inde mouere. Qui priusquam rem sicut erat indagarent, totam abbatiam in forisfactum regis posuerunt. Quod cernens uir prudentissimus, tam seue tempestati se uiriliter obiciens, regem adiit, priuilegium regis Eadwardi protulit, et ut cunctis legeretur rogauit.[580] Quod cum, rege iubente, Rogerus Salesbiriensis episcopus recitasset, cepit rex ab indignatione animum reuocare, leuius cum abbate loqui. At ille fauore baronum circumassistentium fultus, diligebatur enim ab omnibus eo quod esset munificus et largus, postulabat regem ut illud suo priuilegio et ipse confirmaret,[b] sigillo muniret, promittens ei trecentas marcas argenti se daturum, si deinceps sic hactenus[c] liceret sibi quiete et sine querela in propria illud potestate habere. Cuius
B fo. 158v precibus rex annuens, iussit que petebatur si|ne dilatione fieri. Sed et de mercatu uille, iussit similiter uoluntatem abbatis fieri, muniens ea que scribi precepit suo sigillo:[581]

[ii. 164] 237. *Carta regis Henrici de hundredo Hornimere*.[d][582]

Henricus rex Anglorum episcopo Salesb', et uicecomiti, et iusticiariis, et omnibus baronibus et fidelibus suis, Francis et Anglis, de Berchesira,[e] salutem. Sciatis me concessisse Deo, et ecclesie sancte Marie Abbendone, et abbati Vincentio, et omnibus abbatibus successoribus suis, et monachis ibidem Deo seruientibus hundredum de

[a] Salesbirie *B* [b] *the word* et *may have been omitted here* [c] actenus *B C* [d] de Hornemere *B* [e] Berchescira *B*

[579] *English Lawsuits*, no. 246; for the date, see below, p. 231 n. 582.

[580] This is may be Bk. i, c. 129 (*CMA* i. 465–6 = *Charters of Abingdon Abbey*, no. 149, a grant of Hormer hundred) or Bk. i, c. 127 (*CMA* i. 464–5 = *Charters of Abingdon Abbey*, no. 148, a grant of sake and soke etc.). Both are suspicious in their current form, and may indeed be products of the present dispute. See also above, p. xcvii.

[581] Both *De abbatibus* and an additional passage in MS B specify that Vincent broke up a

the abbey's own land, as best and most undisturbedly and honourably and freely as any of his predecessors ever held, with all his other customs. Witnesses: Roger bishop of Salisbury, and Ranulf the chancellor, and John de Bayeux, and William de Pont de l'Arche. At Woodstock.

236. *Concerning Abingdon market.*[579]
In the days of this father, some evil men went to the king and by flattery persuaded him to take away from this church the hundred of Hormer and at the same time to prohibit this town's market, for they mendaciously asserted that the abbot of this monastery never had that hundred in his own power, nor of old was there a market in this town. The king was swayed by their flattery and ordered some of his justiciars to start a plea concerning this. Before they ascertained the facts of the matter as they truly were, these men placed the whole abbey in the king's forfeiture. Vincent, a most prudent man, saw this and manfully opposed the wild storm. He went to the king, presented the privilege of King Edward, and asked that it be read to all.[580] When, at the king's order, Roger bishop of Salisbury had read it out, the king began to check his anger and to speak more mildly to the abbot. But, supported by all the barons present (for everyone loved him since he was munificent and generous), the abbot requested of the king that he confirm this by his privilege and fortify it with his seal, promising that he would give the king 300 marks of silver if he were henceforth, as hitherto, allowed to have this in his own power undisturbed and unchallenged. The king agreed to his requests and ordered that his petitions be fulfilled without delay. Also, he similarly ordered that the abbot's will be done concerning Abingdon market, reinforcing with his seal what he ordered to be written down:[581]

237. *Charter of King Henry concerning the hundred of Hormer.*[582]
Henry king of the English to the bishop of Salisbury, and his sheriff, and justiciars, and all his barons and faithful men, French and English, of Berkshire, greeting. Know that I have granted to God, and to the church of St Mary of Abingdon, and to Abbot Vincent, and to all his successors as abbot, and to the monks serving God there, the

retable or a panel which Æthelwold had made above the altar; *CMA* ii. 278, below, p. 338. This was worth 300 marks or more according to the passage in MS B, £300 according to *De abbatibus*.

[582] *RRAN* ii, no. 1477; Lyell, no. 90; Chatsworth, no. 341. The writ can probably be dated to 1126 × 1127; according to *RRAN* Nigel 'is not known to attest before 1126' and 'Ralph Basset does not attest English documents after Aug. 1127'.

Hornimera iure perpetuo tenendum et habendum eis et omnibus successoribus suis in legitima[a] et liberrima potestate sua et iusticia, sicut Eadwardus rex Anglorum dedit et concessit predicte ecclesie, et per cartam suam confirmauit, quam coram me et baronibus meis lectam esse testificor, et sicut pater meus Willelmus rex dona Eadwardi regis per cartam suam concessit et corroborauit. Et uolo et firmiter precipio ut abbas et monachi, presentes et futuri, predictum hundredum in pace et quiete et honorifice teneant, cum omnibus consuetudinibus et quietationibus suis cum quibus melius et honorabilius tenuerunt tempore predictorum regum, scilicet quod nullus uicecomes uel eorum ministri inde se quicquam intromittant, sed ipsi libere iusticiam suam habeant et faciant.[b] Testibus Rogero episcopo Sar', et Alexandro episcopo Linc', et Gaufrido cancellario, et Roberto de Sigillo, et Nigello[c] nepote episcopi, et Willelmo de
[ii. 165] Albini, et Roberto de Oili, et Radulfo Basset, et Gaufrido de Clint', et Willelmo de Pont', et Milone de Gloecestria,[d] et Albrico de Ver, et Willelmo de Albini Britone, et Ricardo Basset. Apud Lundoniam.

238. *De mercatu.*[e] [583]

Henricus rex Anglorum episcopo Sar',[f] et uicecomiti, et iusticiariis, et
C fo. 165v omnibus baronibus et fidelibus suis de Berchesira,[g] salutem. | Sciatis me concessisse ecclesie sancte Marie Abbendone, et abbati Vincentio, et monachis mercatum Abbendone, sicut ecclesia predicta et abbates et ipse Vincentius abbas melius unquam et liberius habuerunt, et die qua abbatiam predicto Vincentio dedi. Et bene et in pace et honorifice et quiete teneant. Testibus Rogero episcopo Sar', et Gaufrido cancellario, et Gaufrido de Clint', et Willelmo de Pont'. Apud Lundoniam.

239. *De curia abbatis apud Oxeneford.*[h] [584]

Henricus rex Anglorum Radulfo Basset, salutem. Precipio quod facias habere Vincentio abbati Abbendone curiam suam in Oxeneford, ita bene et plenarie sicut unquam ipsa ecclesia Abbendonensis uel aliquis antecessorum suorum melius et plenarius et honorificentius habuit. Et homines sui non placitent extra curiam suam, nisi abbas prius defecerit de recto in curia sua. Et sicut poteris inquirere per legales

[a] legittima *B* [b] faceant *B* [c] Nigellus *B* [d] Cloec' *B* [e] Abbend' *add. B* [f] Salesb' *B* [g] Berchescira *B* [h] Oxeneford' *B*

[583] *RRAN* ii, no. 1478; Lyell, no. 93; Chatsworth, no. 207; this may well be of the same date as the previous writ, and must be after Geoffrey became chancellor in 1123.

hundred of Hormer, for them and all their successors to hold and have by perpetual right in their lawful and most free power and justice, as Edward king of the English gave and granted to the aforesaid church and confirmed through his charter, which I witness was read in the presence of me and my barons, and as my father King William through his charter granted and strengthened the gifts of King Edward. And I wish and firmly order that the abbot and monks, present and future, hold the aforesaid hundred in peace and undisturbed and honourably, with all their customs and quittances with which they best and most honourably held in the time of the aforesaid kings; that is, that no sheriff or sheriff's officials interfere in anything therein, but they are to have and do their own justice freely. Witnesses: Roger bishop of Salisbury, and Alexander bishop of Lincoln, and Geoffrey the chancellor, and Robert *de Sigillo*, and Nigel the bishop's nephew, and William d'Aubigny, and Robert d'Oilly, and Ralph Basset, and Geoffrey of Clinton, and William de Pont de l'Arche, and Miles of Gloucester, and Aubrey de Ver, and William d'Aubigny *Brito*, and Richard Basset. At London.

238. *Concerning the market.*[583]
Henry king of the English to the bishop of Salisbury, and his sheriff, and justiciars, and all his barons and faithful men of Berkshire, greeting. Know that I have granted to the church of St Mary of Abingdon, and to Abbot Vincent, and to the monks the market of Abingdon, as the aforesaid church and its abbots and Abbot Vincent himself ever best and most freely had, and as on the day on which I gave the abbey to the aforesaid Vincent. And let them hold well and in peace and honourably and undisturbed. Witnesses: Roger bishop of Salisbury, and Geoffrey the chancellor, and Geoffrey of Clinton, and William de Pont de l'Arche. At London.

239. *Concerning the abbot's court at Oxford.*[584]
Henry king of the English to Ralph Basset, greeting. I order that you make Vincent abbot of Abingdon have his court in Oxford as well and fully as that church of Abingdon or any of his predecessors ever best and most fully and most honourably had it. And his men are not to plead outside his court, unless the abbot first fails with regard to justice in his court. And as you can discover through lawful men of

[584] *RRAN* ii, no. 1516; Lyell, no. 86 and note; *English Lawsuits*, no. 244. The writ dates between the start of Vincent's abbacy in 1121 and Henry's departure for Normandy in 1127. See also above, p. xcvi.

homines de Oxeneford, quod habere debeat curiam suam. Teste cancellario. Apud Wdestoca.

[ii. 166] **240.** *De ecclesia de Mercham.*[585]

B fo. 159r Cum ex hac uita migrasset, [a]uita adhuc dignior,[a] | uenerandus abbas Faritius, ecclesia hec (sicut supra memorauimus) annis quatuor abbate uacauit. Quo interuallo, Simon, regis Henrici dispensator, quia propinquus erat Willelmi Rainaldi[b] abbatis filii (qui dono patris sui ecclesiam de Mercheam[c] et alias quasdam possessiones uita tantum comite de ecclesia ista tenebat, et habitum monachi in hoc loco suscipiens, omnia quieta clamauerat), suggessit regi in Normannia ecclesiam et terram prefatam iure hereditario ad se pertinere.[586] Quod cum facile ei persuasisset, quia defuit qui resisteret, rege iubente, Simon terram cum ecclesia saisiauit, et tamdiu tenuit quousque abbas Vincentius huius loci pastor successit. Qui cum de re ista sicut de iniuste ablata coram rege calumpniam[d] moueret, Simonque cogitasset quam iniuste eam adeptus fuisset, talis tandem inter[e] abbatem et ipsum Simonem finis euenit:

241. *Descriptum conuentionis inter domnum abbatem Vincentium et dispensatorem regis Simonem.*

Iste Simon, pro timore et reuerentia Dei eiusque genitricis Domine nostre sancte Marie, et amore consilioque predicti abbatis Vincentii, et ut conuentum Abbendonensem sibi magis beniuolum efficeret, immo pro salute sue anime, ratione horum singulorum, et prudentia tam aliorum se in Deo et seculo diligentium quam sua propria, ad hoc deducente, omnia reliquit quieta que tenuerat de rebus ecclesie Abbendonensis ante aduentum eiusdem abbatis ad ipsam abbatiam:
[ii. 167] scilicet ecclesiam de Mercham et cuncta ei adiacentia, id est duas hidas in eadem uilla, cum uno molendino et unam wicam; apud Garaford unam hidam; item apud Middeltuna unam hidam, et aliam apud Eppelford;[f] capellam quoque in predicta uilla Middeltuna, cum dimidia hida eidem ecclesie adiacenti.[587] Et hec omnia clamauit quieta in perpetuum ecclesie Abbendonensi et monachis ibidem Deo seruientibus, tam de se quam de omnibus suis heredibus sibique pertinentibus. Deinde abbas uolens eundem Simonem, ut probum

[a–a] *the Latin here is ungrammatical, requiring a different case and perhaps a preposition, but the sense is clear* [b] Renaldi *B* [c] Mercheham *B* [d] calumniam *B* [e] iter *B* [f] Appelford *B*

[585] *English Lawsuits*, no. 222. Henry I was in Normandy until 25 Nov. 1120.
[586] See above, p. 58.

Oxford that he ought to have his court. Witness: the chancellor. At Woodstock.

240. *Concerning the church of Marcham.*[585]
When the venerable Abbot Faritius had migrated from this life for a still worthier one, this church lacked an abbot for four years, as we recorded above. In this interval, Simon, King Henry's dispenser, suggested to the king in Normandy that Marcham church and some other land belonged to him by hereditary right, since he was a relative of Abbot Reginald's son William (who by his father's gift had held the church and the other possessions from Abingdon only for as long as he lived, and had quitclaimed them all when he adopted the monk's habit in this monastery).[586] Simon easily persuaded the king of this, since there was no one there to provide resistance; on the king's order he seized the land with the church and held them for a long time until Abbot Vincent succeeded as pastor of this monastery [Mar. 1121]. When Vincent brought a claim before the king about the possession which had been unjustly taken in this way, and Simon thought how unjustly he had acquired it, at length the following settlement came about between the abbot and Simon:

241. *Record of the agreement between lord Abbot Vincent and Simon the king's dispenser.*
This Simon—for fear and reverence of God and of His mother our holy Lady Mary, and by the love and counsel of the aforesaid Abbot Vincent, and so that he might increase the good-will of the convent of Abingdon towards him, and still more for the salvation of his soul—led hither by reason of each of these considerations and both by the prudence of others who loved him in God and the world and by his own prudence, left quit everything he had held from the possessions of the church of Abingdon before Abbot Vincent came to the abbey: namely, the church of Marcham and everything belonging to it, that is two hides in the same village with one mill and one dairy-farm; at Garford one hide; likewise at Milton one hide and another at Appleford; also a chapel in the aforesaid village of Milton with half a hide belonging to this church.[587] And he quitclaimed all these things in perpetuity to the church of Abingdon and to the monks serving God there, both from himself and from all his heirs and from those connected to him. Then the abbot, wishing to keep Simon in the

[587] See above, p. 190. *DB* i, fo. 59r, states that 'the abbey itself holds Garford [Berks.], and always held it.'

et prudentem uirum, in seruitio et amore ecclesie retinere, concessit illi tres hidas et dimidiam apud Gersendunam, habere et tenere de ecclesia in feudo, sibi scilicet suisque post eum heredibus (quam terram ipse Simon, cum ceteris predictis et iam ecclesie relictis rebus,[a] antea tenuerat), ita uidelicet, ut debitum et solitum seruitium hactenus ecclesie impensum post hac quoque impenderetur. Preterea etiam abbas manerium quod Tademertun uocatur concessit | eidem
C fo. 166r et suis heredibus post eum, tenere de ecclesia in feudo firma pro quindecim libris singulis annis, ipsi ecclesie reddendis in Natiuitate scilicet Domini, in Pascha, et in kalendis Augustarum die sancti Petri ad Vincula, singulis his terminis centum solidos.[588] Et ut totius machinationis ecclesie in posterum nociue suspicio abscideretur, idem Simon, coram abbate, considente ibidem toto conuentu, et
B fo. 159r plurimis assistentibus laicis, super textum sacrum | euuangeliorum sanctorum iuramentum fecit, se aut suum heredem nunquam ingenium aliquod quesituros de eodem manerio aut de eadem firma tunc illic imposita quod ecclesie foret in detrimento. In hac quoque
[ii. 168] concessione hoc dispositum communi decreto fuit, ut si forte siue ipse Simon siue sui post eum heredes de firma huius manerii reddenda deficeret, ecclesia Abbendonie idem manerium Tademertun sine ullo contradicto in proprio dominio resaisiret, nec ultra alicui inde siue de supradictis rebus a predicto uiro ecclesie iuri relictis responsum ullum faceret. Cumque hec totius conuentus auctoritate confirmata fuissent, idem Simon cum monachis et laicis ecclesiam adiens, altare sancte Marie uadem horum omnium dictorum et factorum ita sese prosecuturum imposuit, et eadem prosequenda a suis heredibus. Pro predictis itaque feudis sibi concessis deinde abbati et ecclesie homagium cum fidelitate fecit. Et hi laici interfuerunt his uniuersis exhibitis[b] actibus pro testimonio:[589] ex parte abbatis Vincentii: prior suus Warengerius, et totum capitulum, Willelmus de Seuecurda, Bernerus cum filio suo Hugone, et multi alii; ex parte uero Simonis: Willelmus de Amfreuilla monachus, Willelmus magister de Gloecestria, Ansketillus uicecomes, Baldewinus clericus, et multi alii.[590] Hec circa Simonem gesta sunt. Verum ipse Simon

[a] retibus *B* [b] exibitis *B*

---

[588] See above, pp. lxxi–ii, 190.
[589] The phraseology, specifying that the witnesses were laymen, is peculiar, given the names that follow.

service and love of the church as an upright and prudent man, granted him three and a half hides at Garsington to have and hold from the church in fee, that is for him and his heirs after him. Simon had previously held this land with those other aforesaid possessions which were now left to the church. He was to hold in such a way that the due and accustomed service which had hitherto been paid to the church should also be paid hereafter. Further, the abbot also granted him and his heirs after him the manor called Tadmarton to hold from the church in fee farm for £15 each year to be rendered to this church, 100s. on the Nativity of the Lord, 100s. at Easter, and 100s. on 1 August on the day of St Peter's Chains.[588] And to remove forever suspicion of any scheming harmful to the church, Simon made an oath on the sacred text of the holy Gospels, in the presence of the abbot and with the whole convent sitting there and with very many laymen in attendance, that neither he nor his heir would ever attempt any ruse concerning this manor or the farm then imposed on it, to the detriment of the church. In this grant it was also laid down by common decision that if it happened that either Simon himself or his heirs after him failed to render the farm of this manor, the church of Abingdon would without contradiction reseise that manor of Tadmarton into its own demesne, and would make no further answer to anyone concerning this or the above-mentioned possessions left to the church's right by the aforesaid man. And when these matters had been confirmed by the authority of the whole convent, Simon came to the church with monks and laymen, and placed on the altar of St Mary a pledge of everything that had been said and done, that he would comply with them and that they would be complied with by his heirs. And so he then did homage with fealty to the abbot and church for the aforesaid fiefs granted to him. And these laymen were present as witness for all these deeds:[589] from Abbot Vincent's side: his prior Warenger and the whole chapter, William of Seacourt, Berner with his son Hugh, and many others; from Simon's side: William d'Amfreville the monk, Master William of Gloucester, Ansketel *uicecomes*, Baldwin the cleric, and many others.[590] These things were done with reference to Simon. In return, for this monastery

[590] William of Seacourt was Simon the dispenser's brother-in-law; see above, p. xliii. William the monk's place of origin is uncertain, as there is more than one Amfreville in Normandy. Ansketel's position is uncertain; he does not appear in Green, *Sheriffs*. He may be an otherwise unknown sheriff, a sub-sheriff, or even, perhaps, a *uicomte* in Normandy. One may speculate whether there was a connection with, or a confusion concerning, Ansketel, Hugh the dispenser's reeve of Sparsholt, above, p. 224.

econtra hunc locum de seipso istud fieri, in eodem capitulo, presentibus testibus hic annotatis, disposuit, ut si animus sibi habitum secularem mutandi uoluntatem per monachatum condonaret, existente se in Anglia, uel si sine hac commutatione de hac uita in ipsa Anglia decederet, non alias quam Abbendonie siue hunc monachatum[a] reciperet, seu decedens non alias quam hic sepeliretur, cum tota mobili sue partis pecunia; quod si extra Angliam uita[b] fungeretur,[c] eadem tamen sue partis huius patrie portio tota Abbendonensi loco cederet.[591]

[ii. 183] **242.** *De Waltero filio Hingam.*[592]

B fo. 161v Regnante autem rege Stephano, et presidente huic ecclesie domno Ingulfo abbate, predictus Simon dedit filiam suam in coniugium cuidam militi nomine Waltero filio Hingam, tradiditque ei supradictam uillam Tademertun, tali scilicet conditione qua et ipse eam tenuerat, id est ut quindecim libras abbati inde per singulos annos redderet. Qui uillam tenuit, sed nichil omnino pro ea reddidit. Quam ob causam abbas ad eandem uillam quendam ex monachis suis transmittens, resaisiauit eam in manu sua, reputans sibi in quantulumcumque lucri prouenire, saltem ipsam uillam (licet etiam aliquan-
[ii. 184] diu cum detrimento constituti redditus) obtinere, quam utroque simul, et uilla scilicet et solito eius redditu, destitui. Hoc autem factum memoratus Simon et Walterius gener eius necnon et filii eorum grauiter accipientes, multa circa nos deinceps malitia usi sunt, nobis semper prout ualebant aduersantes.

243. *De eadem ecclesia.*[d][593]

B fo. 162r Eo igitur anno quo | rex Stephanus et Henricus dux Normannie federati sunt, Turstinus filius eiusdem Simonis suggessit regi abbatem Abbendone quasdam hereditarii sui iuris possessiones iniusta et
C fo. 166v fraudulenta inuasione iam aliquandiu occupasse. Datis | ei pro restitutione earundem muneribus, rex ilico abbati per breue suum mandauit ut, remota omni dilatione, quicquid Turstinus suum dicebat saisiaret.[594] Quo audito, abbas non leue dampnum inspiciens,

[a] monacatum *B* [b] *om. B* [c] fungetur *B* [d] *first five words of next sentence erased at bottom of this column B*

[591] On burials, see above, p. lxix. The last two sentences refer to the portion of moveable goods which an individual could bequeath, on which see above, p. 182 n. 453. This example is cited by Sheehan, *Will in Medieval England*, p. 290 n. 273.

[592] A Walter son of Hingan appears in the 1166 *Carta* of Richard de Cormelles, for Herefordshire in Wales, *Red Book*, i. 285; see also e.g. *The Herefordshire Domesday, c. 1160–70*, ed. V. H. Galbraith and J. Tait (Pipe Roll Soc., New Series xxv, 1950), p. 78.

Simon laid down the following concerning himself, in the same chapter in the presence of the witnesses here recorded: that if his mind made him wish to change his worldly habit for the monastic while he was in England, or if he departed from this life in England without making this change, either he would receive the monastic habit nowhere else than at Abingdon, or after dying would be buried nowhere but here, with all his own portion of moveable goods; if he completed his life outside England, however, this same portion in this country would pass to the monastery of Abingdon.[591]

242. *Concerning Walter son of Hingam.*[592]

Moreover, when King Stephen was reigning and lord Abbot Ingulf ruling this church, the aforesaid Simon gave his daughter in marriage to a knight named Walter son of Hingam, and handed over to him the afore-mentioned village of Tadmarton, on the same condition by which he himself had held it, that is, that he render £15 a year therefrom to the abbot. Walter held this village but rendered nothing at all for it. For this reason, the abbot sent one of his monks to this village and reseised it into his possession, considering that however little profit would come to him, at least he was obtaining that village (even though for some time with a loss of the established rent), rather than being deprived of both at once, that is both the village and its accustomed rent. But Simon and Walter his son-in-law and also their sons were bitter about this, and henceforth engaged in many evil acts towards us, always opposing us as much as they could.

243. *Concerning the same church.*[593]

Therefore, in the year in which King Stephen and Henry duke of Normandy established a treaty [1153], Thurstan son of this Simon suggested to the king that the abbot of Abingdon had now for some time occupied by unjust and fraudulent invasion certain possessions of his hereditary property. Given gifts for their restitution, the king immediately instructed the abbot by his writ that he deliver without delay seisin of whatever Thurstan said was his.[594] When the abbot heard this, he saw that the damage was not light, nor did he agree

[593] *English Lawsuits*, no. 363; see above, p. 234; also H. A. Cronne, *The Reign of Stephen 1135–54* (London, 1970), pp. 261–2; G. J. White, *Restoration and Reform, 1153–65: Recovery from Civil War in England* (Cambridge, 2000), pp. 71–2, 174, 186–7, and more generally pp. 69–76 for treatment of Henry's actions between the peace treaty and the death of Stephen.

[594] This writ does not survive; see above, p. xxix. On Thurstan, see above, p. lxxi.

non leuiter consensit. Adunata[a] tamen curia sua, diem statuit quo, habita deliberatione, excogitaret quid super hoc responderet. Iam aderat dies statuta, et nondum consentiente abbate ut uel tunc Turstinus quod petebat acciperet, sicut primo sic secundo diem distulit, quo scilicet sapientiores de tali negotio consuleret. Quo contra Turstinus lucrum suum differri considerans, [b]renuit diem,[b] regem adiit, et quod iussa regis abbas implere noluerit mendaciter indicauit; insuper ut citius uoti compos efficeretur, regem regisque collaterales iam iterum muneribus sibi illexit. Rex autem causam Turstini iustam existimans, uicecomiti suo tunc temporis, Henrico de Oxeneford, precepit ut, ablato omni dilationis scrupulo, causam utramque secundum ius regium tractaret.[595] Vicecomes uero amore
[ii. 185] pecunie deprauatus, iustos possessores depredauit, et Turstinum in re non sua, quasi rege iubente et iure dictante, iniuste—ut ipse postea confessus est—introduxit. Turstinus ergo saisiatus re quam petebat, id est ecclesia de Mercham, et tribus hidis ad eandem pertinentibus, et una in Middeltun, una quoque in Eppelford,[c] contra ius ecclesiasticum agens, rem eandem detinuit. Sed non patitur Deus sicut iusta sic iniusta diu subsistere.

[ii. 186] Eodem[d] namque anno quo res ecclesie inuasit, Stephanus rex diem obiit, eique in regno Henricus iunior successit.[596] Quem adeuntes de congregatione fratres, rem prout erat peruerse tractatam monstrauerunt, supplicantes ut eorum iuste querele aurem accommodaret. Adquiescens uero rex fratribus quorum iustam querelam deprehendit, semel et iterum missis litteris precepit ut in comitatu Berchesire[e] causa utriusque—ecclesie Abbendonensis scilicet et Turstini—in medio proferretur, prolata examinaretur, examinata uel hinc uel inde terminaretur.[597] Sed Turstinus de culpa sibi conscius, nunc simulata[f] regis

[a] Aduna *B* [b–b] diem renuit *B* [c] Appelford *B* [d] *preceded by rubricated heading of minims B* [e] Berchescire *B* [f] simulato *B*

[595] Henry of Oxford was sheriff of Berkshire and Oxford *c.*1153–55; Green, *Sheriffs*, pp. 27, 70. E. Amt, *The Accession of Henry II in England* (Woodbridge, 1993), p. 57, argues that the sheriff must have been Duke Henry's nominee, that Thurstan son of Simon 'seems to have been an Angevin supporter', and that if 'Stephen was now disposed to make judgements in favour of Henry's men and to have one of them as sheriff, it would seem that some Angevin partisans were beginning to regain their Oxfordshire lands in the course of 1154.' For the sheriff himself, see further K. S. B. Keats-Rohan, 'The making of Henry of Oxford: Englishmen in a Norman world', *Oxoniensia*, liv (1989), 287–309. R. C. van Caenegem, *The Birth of the English Common Law* (2nd edn., Cambridge, 1988), p. 36, suggests that the decision that the case was to be heard 'according to royal law' may have arisen from the contempt of a royal writ. Cronne, *Stephen*, pp. 261–2, suggests the

to it lightly. However, he gathered his court and set a day when, after deliberation, he would devise what he should answer concerning this. When the set day came, the abbot would still not agree that Thurstan should even then receive what he sought. Just as on the first occasion, so on the second he put off the day, so he might consult the wiser men concerning this business. However, Thurstan, thinking that he was being delayed in obtaining his gains, refused the day set, went to the king, and mendaciously declared that the abbot was not willing to fulfil royal orders. In addition, he again used gifts to entice the king and the king's entourage to take his side, so that what he desired might more swiftly be accomplished. The king, furthermore, considered Thurstan's case to be just, and ordered his sheriff at that time, Henry of Oxford, that without the slightest delay he treat both sides' case according to royal law.[595] The sheriff, certainly corrupted by his love of money, despoiled the just possessors, and—as he later confessed—unjustly introduced Thurstan into a possession which was not his own, as if the king were ordering it and right dictating it. So Thurstan was seised of the possessions he sought, that is the church of Marcham and the three hides pertaining to it, and one hide in Milton and one in Appleford, and, acting against ecclesiastical law, he kept this possession. But God does not allow unjust things to persist long, as just ones do.

For in the same year as Thurstan invaded the church's possession, King Stephen ended his days and Henry the younger succeeded him in the kingdom.[596] Brethren of the congregation went to him, showed that the matter had been treated wrongly, and begged that he pay attention to their just complaint. The king indeed gave his agreement to the brethren, whose just complaint he grasped, and he twice sent letters ordering that the case of both sides—namely the church of Abingdon and Thurstan—be made public in the county court of Berkshire, that having been made public it be examined, and that having been examined it be decided one way or the other.[597] But Thurstan, aware of his guilt, circumspectly evaded the county court

presence of 'a strong feeling in this account that the royal writs deprived the abbot of Abingdon not only of property but of his lawful jurisdictional rights, which had to give way to the *jus regium* administered by the sheriff, acting *ad hoc*, it would seem, as a royal justice'; this seems to me to be reading too much into the text.

[596] Stephen died on 25 Oct. 1154; Henry II was crowned on 19 Dec. 1154. On Henry being referred to as Henry the younger, see above, p. xvii n. 2.

[597] These are probably two writs which appear only in MS B; see below, p. 348.

negotio, nunc infirmitate, nunc hac nunc illa occasione, per biennium et eo amplius comitatus caute subterfugit.[598] Quod intelligens abbas, laboris totiens inanis piguit, et assumptis secum fratribus ad regem, qui tunc apud Wdestoca morabatur, accessit, obnixe postulans ut sui misertus et laboris et cause finem imponeret. Annuit ilico rex, et conuocatis iusticiis suis, Gregorio scilicet Lundoniense, et Willelmo filio Iohannis, et Nigello de Brocco, ceterisque curie sue sapientibus, precepit ut abbatis et Turstini, qui tunc aderat, causam tractarent, asserens quicquid super hoc recte iudicarent, inconcusse teneri debere.[599] Qui inspecta rei ueritate, intellexerunt Turstinum sub-
B fo. 162v stantiam ecclesie in|iuste detinuisse, et abbatem pro tali dampno[a] iustam querelam mouisse.[b] Sed quamuis hoc iustum esset, non tamen de se presumebant ut hunc re quam inuaserat[c] priuarent, nisi prius
[ii. 187] audita ab ore regis sententia. Dicebant quippe solidius posse subsistere, quod ex ore regio prolata auctoritas studuerit confirmare. Nuntiauerunt interea prefati uiri regi de iudicio sibi commisso quid actum esset, orantes ut ipse uoluntatem suam inde[d] eis aperiret. Quibus precepit ut non solum quod Turstinus iniuste adeptus fuerat in dominium ecclesie reuerterent, uerum etiam dampnum quod interim ecclesie intulit restaurari iuberent, seruato quod, si idem Turstinus uellet, sicut pater eius, et ipse manerium Tademertun per singulos annos pro quindecim libris de abbate teneret. Quibus diligenter dampnum computantibus, dictum est parum esse si Turstinus pro dampno[e] de Tademertun[f] sexaginta marcas, pro dampno uero ecclesie de Mercham et quinque hidarum quas prediximus tres
C fo. 167r marcas abbati persolueret, nisi in | hoc idem abbas Turstino parcere uoluisset. Turstinus autem cognoscens quod ei imponebatur uires suas excedere, et uillam tenere et pro dampno quod iussus erat persoluere se non posse indicauit. Quod cum regi nuntiatum esset, iussit ut abbas sic uillam sicut ecclesiam et terram prefatam reciperet, et Turstino uel suis heredibus post illum diem nichil responderet. Sic ergo, Deo uolente, in pristinum statum rediit quicquid defraudator ille de rebus monasterii defraudauit.

[a] damno *B* [b] monuisse *B* [c] euaserat *B* [d] indem *C*, idem *B*
[e] damno *B* [f] Tadmertun *B*

---

[598] On essoins, see 'Glanvill', *Tractatus de legibus*, bk. i, cc. 11–29, ed. Hall, pp. 7–17. The passage of more than two years probably means that the hearing at Woodstock, Oxon., took place in 1157.

[599] On these royal justices, see D. M. Stenton, *English Justice between the Norman Conquest and the Great Charter 1066–1215* (Philadelphia, 1964), pp. 68–70; also White,

for more than two years, now pretending the king's business, now illness, now this circumstance, now that.[598] Realizing this, and irked by such repeated, fruitless toil, the abbot took some of the brethren, went to the king who was then staying at Woodstock, and resolutely demanded that the king show compassion and bring an end to his toil and the case. The king at once agreed, and when he had gathered his justices, that is Gregory of London and William son of John and Nigel de Broc, and the other wise men of his court, he ordered that they treat the case of the abbot and Thurstan (who was then present); the king asserted that whatever they justly adjudged concerning this should remain unshakeable.[599] When they had examined the truth of the matter, they understood that Thurstan had unjustly detained the church's property and that the abbot had moved a just claim concerning that loss. But although this was just, however they did not themselves presume to deprive Thurstan of the possession he had invaded, unless first the sentence was heard from the king's mouth. Rather, they said that something the king was concerned to confirm by his spoken authority would remain more secure. Meanwhile the aforesaid men announced to the king what had been done regarding the judgment entrusted to them, and praying that he should reveal to them his will concerning this. He ordered them that not only were they to return to the church's demesne what Thurstan had unjustly acquired, but also that they order that the damage which he had meanwhile done to the church be restored, saving that, like his father, Thurstan too might hold from the abbot the manor of Tadmarton for £15 each year, if he so wished. When they diligently calculated the damage, it was said that it would be too little if Thurstan paid the abbot sixty marks for the damage concerning Tadmarton and three marks for the damage concerning the church of Marcham and the five hides already mentioned, unless the abbot wished to spare Thurstan in this matter. Thurstan, however, realized that what was imposed on him exceeded his means and indicated that he could not hold the village and pay what had been ordered for the damage. When this was announced to the king, he ordered that the abbot should receive the village, like the church and the aforesaid land, and not answer in any regard to Thurstan and his heirs after that day. So, by God's will, he returned to its former state whatever that defrauder had defrauded from the monastery's possessions.

Restoration and Reform, pp. 187–8, on Gregory of London. It is uncertain whether this William son of John is the same man who appears below, pp. 248, 304.

244. *Item de eadem ecclesia.*[600]

Preterea tempore quo prefatus Turstinus rem, de cuius recuperatione mentionem fecimus, teneret, cuidam ex regis clericis, Radulfo scilicet de Tamewrða, ecclesiam de Mercham absque terra habendam
[ii. 188] donauit.[601] Dissaisiato uero illo, consequens fuit ne iste partem iniuste teneret, qui illam ab eo acceperat, qui totum iuste perdiderat. Solatium tamen amissionis sue uel locum recuperandi querens, frequenter regiis litteris et optimatum eius apportatis, abbatem et conuentum rogaturus conuenit, ut ei saltem sicut cuilibet alteri redditum persoluenti tenere concederent. Sed illis nequaquam consentientibus, ad Apostolicum se contulit, apostolicaque fultus auctoritate et litteris ad Walchelinum, Ingulfi successorem, non iam rogaturus, sed quasi uim facturus accessit, sperans a secundo quod a primo optinere non potuit. Sed non minori studio secundus quam primus ne hoc fieret restitit. Ad regem ergo accessit, et quam fraudulenter clericus suus contra ecclesiam Abbendonensem ageret ei indicauit. Rex itaque clerico indignatus, mandauit ei ut, si uellet in curia uel etiam in regno eius manere, cum ecclesia Abbendonensi studeret pacem habere. Sicque a rege prius restituta, et postea defensata, altari sancte Marie usque hodie iacet attitulata.

[ii. 169] **245.** *De quadam decima.*[602]
B fo. 159v Miles quidam, Iocelinus nomine, loci huius religione delectatus, dedit Deo et sancte Marie, in capitulo coram domno Vincentio abbate et toto conuentu, duas partes decime omnium rerum suarum quas in possessione quadam que Graua dicitur habebat, tam segetum quam pecorum,[a] uel omnium rerum quas iure decimare deberet. Post cuius obitum, Randulfus filius eius decimam quidem[b] segetum, quam auferre non potuit, concessit.[603] Pecorum uero siue ceterarum rerum, non solum ipse sed et patrem suum nunquam affirmabat concessisse. Audita tamen a pluribus rei ueritate, domni Walchelini abbatis tempore [c]in capitulum[c] uenit fratrum, et omnium rerum decimam quam pater eius dedit et ipse deuote concessit. Et quia ad

[a] peccorum *B* [b] quidæm *or corr. from* quidam *C,* quidam *B* [c–c] *om. B*

[600] *English Lawsuits*, no. 418; the events must pre-date the death of Walkelin on 10 Apr. 1164.

[601] Ralph was to act as an envoy from Henry II to Rome in 1166, as well as being archdeacon of Stafford; see *HKF* i. 62; *Charters in the British Museum*, ed. Warner and Ellis, no. 44.

[602] Chatsworth, no. 48 n., EPNS, *Oxfordshire*, i. 177, identify this as in Holton parish;

244. *Likewise, concerning the same church.*[600]

While the aforesaid Thurstan was holding the possession which we have just mentioned being recovered, he gave to one of the king's clerics, namely Ralph of Tamworth, the church of Marcham, to have without any land.[601] When Thurstan was disseised, a consequence was that Ralph should not hold unjustly a portion which he had received from Thurstan who had justly lost the whole. However, he sought compensation for his loss or the opportunity to recover it, and, bearing letters of the king and his great men, he frequently came to ask the abbot and convent that they at least allow him to hold like anyone else paying rent. But as they would not agree at all, he went to the pope, and strengthened with papal authority and letters he approached Walkelin, Ingulf's successor, not now to make a request but as if to make an assault, hoping to obtain from Walkelin what he could not get from Ingulf. But Walkelin resisted this outcome with no less ardour than had Ingulf. He went to the king and showed him how deceitfully his cleric was acting against the church of Abingdon. The king therefore was angry with the cleric and instructed him that if he wished to remain in his court or even in his kingdom, he should strive to make peace with the church of Abingdon. And so what had previously been restored and afterwards defended by the king, to this day lies assigned to the altar of St Mary.

245. *Concerning a certain tithe.*[602]

A certain knight named Jocelin, delighted with the religious life of this monastery, gave to God and to St Mary, in the chapter in the presence of lord Abbot Vincent and the whole convent, two parts of the tithe of all that belonged to him in a possession called Grove, both of corn and of livestock, and of all goods which ought rightly to pay tithe. After his death, Randulf his son granted the tithe of corn, which he could not take away.[603] But he asserted that neither he nor his father had ever granted the tithe of livestock and other goods. However, he heard the truth of the matter from very many people, and in the time of lord Abbot Walkelin came into the brethren's chapter and himself devoutly granted the tithe of all the goods his father had given. And since that tithe was assigned to

see also Chatsworth, no. 388, a confirmation by Jocelin's great grandson Thomas. *DB* i, fo. 158^{v}, shows that Holton belonged to Roger d'Ivry in 1086, but Grove is not specifically named in *Domesday Book*; see also *VCH*, *Oxfordshire*, v. 172.

603 For tentative identification of Randulf as Ralph, priest of St Martin's, and for further details of his family, see *Charters in Oxford Muniment Rooms*, ed. Salter, no. 77 n.

opus infirmorum fratrum decima illa deputata fuerat, super altare quod in oratorio infirmorum erat manu propria imposita perpetue confirmauit.

246. *De decima Winterburne.*[604]

Alius etiam miles quidam, Normannus appellatus, in Winterburna
B fo. 160r posses | sionem habens, filium suum, qui Eudo dictus est, in hac Abbendonensi ecclesia monachum[a] fieri postulauit tempore abbatis Vincentii. Et ut facilius quod uolebat optineret, decimam dominii sui
[ii. 170] de Winterburna,[b] quam cui placeret ecclesie libere donare poterat, una cum filio dono perpetuo contradidit.[605] Que sic concessa, sub manu[c] sacriste redacta est.

247. *De dimidia hida apud Mora.*[606]

Similiter miles huius ecclesie, Raibaldus[d] de Tubeneia, ex filiis suis unum Adelelmum nomine in hac eadem ecclesia habitum monachi induere postulauit. Quod et facile optinuit, data cum eo perpetuo absque calumpnia aliqua dimidia hida terre in loco qui uulgariter Mora dicitur, que et predicto abbate Vincentio ad officium sacristerii deputata est.

248. *De Radulfo Basset.*

Radulfus etiam cognomento Basset, in omni Anglie regno iusticie habens dignitatem, hanc Abbendonensem ecclesiam, ut | effectus
C fo. 167v probauit operis, speciali amauit delectione. Seipsum enim (quo nichil carius habet aliquis) fraternitati ecclesie sociauit, ubi et habitum mutare, et post uite transitum se sepeliri disposuit. Transacto uero cursus sui tempore, cum esset apud Northamtonam subita egritudine cepit detineri, et suspicans quia moreretur, monachorum sibi habitum indui postulauit. Requisitus uero cuius ei ecclesie religio placeret, non alibi quam ad fratres suos Abbendoniam uel deferri, uel se sepeliri si obiret, respondit, sicut ante promiserat. Diuisione etiam omnium rerum suarum sollenniter[e] facta, pecuniarum quantitatem non modicam secum Abbendonam deferendam segregauit; de prediis uero quibus large habundabat,

[a] h *interlin., in different ink B* [b] Winterburne *B* [c] *corr. from* manus *B*
[d] Rainbaldus *B* [e] sollempniter *B*

[604] Berks. Note that *DB* i, fo. 61v, has a tenant called Norman holding five hides in Winterbourne from Hascoit Musard. The donor here may be that Norman, or a descendant. A list in MS C in the same hand as the *History*, below, p. 397, places the tithe of Winterbourne amongst the revenues of the altar.

[605] On gifts accompanying monks entering Abingdon, see above, p. lxix.

the use of the sick brethren, he confirmed it perpetually with his own hand placed on the altar which is in the chapel of the sick.

246. *Concerning the tithe of Winterbourne.*[604]
Also, another knight, called Norman, had a possession in Winterbourne, and in Abbot Vincent's time he requested that his son, called Eudo, become a monk in this church of Abingdon. And to obtain more easily what he wished, he handed over as a perpetual gift, together with his son, the tithe of his demesne of Winterbourne, which he was able to give freely to whatever church he pleased.[605] The tithe granted thus was placed under the control of the sacrist.

247. *Concerning half a hide at Moor.*[606]
Similarly, a knight of this church, Rainbald of Tubney, requested that one of his sons, named Adelelm, assume the monk's habit in this church. He easily obtained this, after giving with Adelelm half a hide of land in the place which is commonly called Moor, perpetually free of any claim. This also was delegated by the aforesaid Abbot Vincent to the office of the sacristy.

248. *Concerning Ralph Basset.*
Ralph, surnamed Basset, who had the status of justice throughout the realm of England, also loved this church of Abingdon with special affection, as the outcome of his action proved. For he associated himself (than which no one holds anything more dear) with the fraternity of the house, and arranged to change his habit there [i.e. become a monk] and to be buried there after the span of his life. And indeed, when the period of his passage through life was completed, while he was at Northampton he began to be gripped by a sudden illness, and, suspecting that he would die, requested that he be endowed with the habit of monks. When indeed he was asked which church's religious life pleased him, he answered that he was to be taken nowhere except to his brethren at Abingdon, or—if he died—was to be buried there, as previously he had promised. When indeed all his possessions were solemnly divided up, he separated off not a small quantity of goods to be taken to Abingdon with him. Further, from the estates with which he was copiously supplied, he

[606] The location of this land is not certain, but it is probably in the same place as the Moor mentioned above, p. 192, that is Draycott Moor or Southmoor. See also below pp. 272, 397, for 8s. of the 'rents of the altar' coming from 'Mora'; *De abbatibus* records half a hide of 'Lamora' being among Vincent's endowment for the monks' baths; *CMA* ii. 290.

quatuor sui iuris hidas in Chedelswrtha[a] perpetue mansuras loco
[ii. 171] eidem concessit.[607] Decedens uero ibidem a luce presenti, cum honore maximo et magna populi frequentia ad Abbendonam, ut ipse iusserat, est delatus, et ab omni conuentu utpote frater eorum et multorum largitor (dum potuit) beneficiorum gratanter receptus, in eorum capitulo honorifice, ut talem decebat uirum, completo seruitio est sepultus.[608] Sicque quatuor hide de Chedeleswrtha in dominium ecclesie Abbendonensis sunt saisiate, et a cunctis filiis Radulfi omnes enim tunc presentes aderant confirmate. Hec enim gesta sunt tempore domni[b] Vincentii abbatis; que uero sequuntur in diebus successoris sui Ingulfi.

[ii. 188] **249.** *De Ricardo Basset.*[609]

B fo. 162ᵛ Ricardus itaque Basset, filius Turstini filii Radulfi predicti, cum patre
B fo. 163ʳ mortuo heres successisset, de supradictis quatuor hidis | calumpniam mouit, multa obiectione et curiositate agens, ut eas ad se, si quomodo posset, attraheret.[c] Versutias uero eius fratres agnoscentes, regem Henricum iuniorem, tunc temporis regnantem, adierunt, postulantes
[ii. 189] ut eis cum pace tenere faceret quod eis iuste donatum fuerat. Quorum petitioni benigne annuens, tale breue, sigillo suo munitum, Ricardo direxit:

250. *Carta regis Henrici iunioris.*[610]

Henricus rex [d]Anglorum et dux Normannorum et Aquitanie et comes Andegauorum[d] Ricardo Basset, salutem.[611] Precipio quod monachi mei de Abbendona teneant in pace et libere et quiete et iuste quatuor hidas terre de Chedeleswrtha, sicut eas tenuerunt tempore Henrici regis aui mei, et eisdem[e] libertatibus cum omnibus pertinentiis earum; et prohibeo ne quis eos inde iniuste ponat in placitum. Quod nisi feceris, iusticia mea faciat fieri, ne inde audiam clamorem pro penuria pleni recti uel firme iusticie. Teste Willelmo filio Iohannis. Apud Cliuam.

[a] Chedeleswrtha *B* [b] dompni *B* [c] attraeret *B* [d–d] Anglie et dux Normannie et Aquitanie et comes Andegauie *B* [e] eiusdem *B*

607 *DB* i, fo. 62ʳ, has Robert d'Oilly holding four hides at Chaddleworth, Berks.; this was one of various of Robert's estates which passed to the Bassets.

608 Ralph died at the end of the 1120s or early in 1130; see above, p. 111 n. 260. On burials, see above, p. lxix. See above, p. xxix, for an additional Basset document in the Abingdon cartularies.

granted to remain perpetually to that monastery four hides of his property in Chaddleworth.[607] Then, at Northampton, he departed from the present light, and with the utmost honour and accompanied by a great crowd of people he was brought to Abingdon as he had ordered, and was joyfully received by all the convent as their brother and (while he was able) the bestower of many benefits. He was buried honourably in their chapter-house, with a full service, as befitted such a man.[608] And so the four hides at Chaddleworth were seised into the demesne of the church of Abingdon, and confirmed by all Ralph's sons, for they were then all present. These events took place in the time of lord Abbot Vincent; those which follow, on the other hand, took place in the days of his successor Ingulf.

249. *Concerning Richard Basset.*[609]
When Richard Basset, son of Thurstan son of the aforesaid Ralph, succeeded as heir after his father's death, he moved a claim concerning the above-mentioned four hides. He employed many a charge and subtlety so that he might appropriate these hides for himself, if he could do so in any way. The brethren, however, recognized his cunning ploys and came to King Henry the younger, who was then reigning, and they requested that he make them hold peacefully what had been justly given to them. The king accepted their petition with good will and sent to Richard the following writ, strengthened with his seal:

250. *Charter of King Henry the younger.*[610]
Henry king of the English and duke of the Normans and of Aquitaine and count of the Angevins to Richard Basset, greeting.[611] I order that my monks of Abingdon may hold in peace and freely and undisturbed and justly the four hides of land at Chaddleworth, as they held them in the time of King Henry my grandfather, and with the same liberties, with all their appurtenances. And I forbid that anyone unjustly place them in plea concerning this. If you do not do this, my justice is to ensure that it is done, so that I do not hear complaint concerning this for want of full right or firm justice. Witness: William son of John. At King's Cliffe.

[609] *English Lawsuits*, no. 424; the precise date is uncertain.
[610] Lyell, no. 128, Chatsworth, no. 297. MS B repeated this document in its series of Henry II writs; see below, p. 350.
[611] See above, p. vii, on the forms of royal titles in MSS B and C.

Quo breue audito, Ricardus nec ualens in aliquo contradicere, sed et sciens se calumpniam mouisse, cirographum tale cum Abbendonensibus composuit:

251. *Cirographum de Chedeleswrtha.*[612]

Notum sit omnibus, tam presentibus quam futuris, quod ego Ricardus Basset, filius Turstini Basset, concessi in elemosinam perpetuam et firmiter confirmaui, in capitulo coram omni conuentu, et super altare signo cultelli [a]manibus propriis[a] posui, ecclesie Abbendone quatuor hidas de Chedeleswrtha[b] cum pertinentiis earum, in bosco, in plano, quas auus meus Radulfus Basset et pater meus Turstinus Basset dederant predicte ecclesie, tenendas liberas et absolutas ab omni seruitio militari et exactione preter commune
[ii. 190] geldum totius comitatus, ita tamen, si alie terre mee sunt quiete, et illa similiter sit quieta. De bosco autem quod predicte terre adiacet, cum fuero in prouincia, illa retineo ad focum coram me faciendum, et ad coquinam meam, et uirgas et palas ad faldos et sepes circa curiam meam faciendas, et arbores ad molendina mea de[c] Hledecumba,[d] si in
C fo. 168[r] bosco illo inueniri | poterunt.[613] Quod totum capietur per uisum forestarii monachorum, et sicut docuerit.[614] Et porci mei de Hledecumba[e] de dominio quieti sint de pasnagio. Presentibus testibus subscriptis: toto conuentu; de laicis: Adam uicecomite, Iordano de Sandford,[f] Iohanne de Sancta Helena, Gaufrido de Sunigewelle, Henrico de Pisi, Radulfo Britone, Radulfo placitore, et multis aliis.[615]

His ita terminatis, Ricardus, assumpta secum cirographi parte media, amicus factus, recessit ad propria.

[a–a] propriis manibus *B* [b] Cheleswrthe *B* [c] d *C* [d] Ledecumba *B* [e] Ledecumba *B* [f] Samford *B*

---

[612] The Abingdon cartularies include a later version with some minor verbal modifications, an additional clause recording the presence and consent of Thurstan Basset, and different witnesses; Lyell, no. 248, Chatsworth, no. 296. The first of the witnesses is 'domino Godefrido episcopo ipsius ecclesie prelato', that is Godfrey bishop of Asaph, guardian of Abingdon 1165–75.

[613] *DB* i, fo. 62[r], records Letcombe Basset, Berks., as an estate of Robert d'Oilly, including two mills at £3. The entry makes no mention of woodland, whereas that concerning Robert d'Oilly's holding of Chaddleworth, *DB* i, fo. 62[r], records 'woodland of ten pigs.'

[614] The monks' forester may be the same as the lignar, whose primary responsibility was the fuel supply but who certainly in the later middle ages had other responsibilities as well; see e.g. *Accounts of the Obedientiars of Abingdon Abbey*, ed. R. E. G. Kirk (Camden Soc., New Series li, 1892), pp. xxix–xxx, 5–11. Alternatively, he might be a lesser official with local responsibility; see e.g. Chatsworth, nos. 150, 162, 165, 224 for thirteenth-century charters witnessed by foresters; cf. below, p. 368, on the park-keeper.

When he heard the writ, Richard was unable to contradict it in any way. Aware that he had brought the claim, he agreed upon the following cirograph with the men of Abingdon:

251. *Cirograph concerning Chaddleworth.*[612]
Let it be known to all, both present and future, that I, Richard Basset, son of Thurstan Basset, have granted to the church of Abingdon in perpetual alms and have firmly confirmed in the chapter in the presence of all the convent, and have placed with my own hands on the altar by the symbol of a knife, the four hides at Chaddleworth with their appurtenances in wood and plain, which my grandfather Ralph Basset and my father Thurstan Basset had given to the aforesaid church, to be held free and exempt from any knight service and exaction, except the common geld of the whole county, in such a way, however, that if my other lands are quit, it likewise is to be quit. However, concerning the wood which belongs to the aforesaid land, when I am in that region I retain it for making a fire for myself and for my kitchen, and sticks and stakes for making folds and fences around my court, and trees for my mills of Letcombe, if they can be found in that wood.[613] All this is to be taken under the supervision of the monks' forester and as he instructs.[614] And my pigs of the demesne of Letcombe are to be quit of pannage. The witnesses recorded below were present: the whole convent; of laymen: Adam the sheriff, Jordan of Sandford, John of St Helen, Geoffrey of Sunningwell, Henry of Pusey, Ralph *Brito*, Ralph the pleader, and many others.[615]

After these things had been concluded thus, Richard took half the cirograph, was made a friend [of the church], and returned home.

[615] Adam of Catmore was sheriff of Berkshire from the seventh until half way through the sixteenth year of Henry II's reign. He may earlier have been under-sheriff, see *PR 2–4 HII*, pp. 34–5. The reference to Adam below, p. 280, in a witness list as sheriff in an incident of Stephen's reign may show that the writer in the 1160s thought of him as 'Adam the sheriff', or that he had indeed been sheriff in Stephen's reign. Jordan was probably the son of Robert of Sandford, above, p. 88. The 1166 Abingdon *Carta* records that he held four knights' fees of the abbey; *Red Book*, i. 305, below, p. 390. For John of St Helen, see also below, p. 390. See below, p. 360 for Geoffrey of Sunningwell's holding of Abingdon in Garford; also *CMA* ii. 302, for a Geoffrey of Sunningwell holding two hides at Boxford late in the twelfth century. He does not appear in the 1166 *Carta*; see below, pp. 390–1. A list in MS C, in a later hand, mentions a Henry of Sunningwell, who may be a relative; *CMA* ii. 311. The 1166 Abingdon *Carta* records that Henry of Pusey held one knight's fee of the abbey; *Red Book*, i. 306, below, p. 390. Ralph *Brito* may or may not be the same man who appears below, p. 296. A Ralph *Brito* witnessed a dispute settlement of 1169 × 81, *Charters in Oxford Muniment Rooms*, ed. Salter, no. 88; see also *Oseney*, i, no. 489, ii, nos. 1099, 1101, iv, no. 22.

[ii. 171] **252.** Venerabilis[616] itaque et Deo dignus abbas Vincentius omnia
B fo. 160r ministeria fratrum accreuit, ut absque murmure Deo possent seruire. Ad ministerium enim coquine dedit omnes redditus huius uille, quantumcumque deinceps creuissent, addens et quinque libras de suo marsupio, et uiginti solidos ad diuersa condimenta deputauit.[617] Solebat autem tunc temporis ista uilla quindecim libras reddere.
[ii. 172] Addidit et his molendinum super Hocke[a] positum, uiginti quinque solidos tunc reddens.[618] In die sui anniuersarii per singulos annos ad fercula et ad potum fratrum quadraginta solidos procurauit, ex his que propria industria ecclesie apud Oxeneford acquisiuit.[619] |

B fo. 160v Ad ministerium cellarii addidit uiginti sextaria mellis ad conficiendum ydromellum, que antecessores sui ad ministeria propria solebant habere. Ad hec addidit et quatuor libras ex prepositura Cudesdunæ[b] ad emendum uinum, unde fratres in precipuis festiuitatibus habeant caritatem.[620]

Ad ministerium refectorii uiginti solidos de quadam hida de Middeltuna dedit, ad emendum iustas, et ciphos, et coclearia, et salaria, et candelabra, et si que[c] minora fuerint necessaria.

Ad ministerium camere addidit quatuor hidas de Chedeleswrthe,[d] quas Radulfus Basset huic ecclesie dedit.[621] Ad ministerium altaris dedit ecclesiam de Wicham, reddentem quatuor libras.[622] Ad [e]lignarium fratrum[e] dedit sexaginta solidos de redditibus Cudesduna et Cernie.[623] Curiam honestis edificiis et muris uenustauit.[624] Pro fratre in isto loco professo de hac uita decedenti, a die sui transitus usque ad diem anniuersarii eiusdem anno integro reuoluto, eundem uictum quem uiuens et in refectorio residens habiturus esset, largiri constituit.[625] Hec et multa alia beneficia huic ecclesie largitus est.

[a] Ocke *B* [b] Cudesduna *B* [c] qua *B C* [d] Chedeleswrtha *B*
[e–e] lingnarium *B*

---

616 See Preface, p. viii, for MS C presenting this as a new section, despite the absence of a rubricated heading. In MS B, it is preceded by a section 'Concerning the ornaments of Abbot Vincent', below, p. 340.

617 See also a list in MS C in the same hand as the *History*, below, p. 395.

618 On this mill, see above, p. 94. *De abbatibus* attributes to Ingulf the gift of Ock Mill to the kitchen; *CMA* ii. 291. See also below, p. 395, which puts the rent at 36s.; *CMA* ii. 306, which puts it at 36s. 4d.

619 These lands are not mentioned elsewhere in the *History*'s account of Vincent's abbacy or in *De abbatibus*; cf. a list in MS C in the same hand as the *History*, below, p. 395. Special food (*ferculum*) would consist of meat or fish, as opposed to bread; *DMLBS*, fasc. iv, s.v. *ferculum*.

620 See also below, p. 395, for rents from Cuddesdon being attributed to the kitchen;

252. So Abbot Vincent,[616] venerable and worthy of God, increased all the offices of the brethren, that they could serve God without complaint. For to the office of the kitchen he gave all the rents of Abingdon, however much they increased thereafter, adding also £5 from his own purse, and he consigned 20s. for various seasonings.[617] At the time, moreover, that town was accustomed to render £15. He also added to these a mill situated on the Ock, then rendering 25s.[618] On the day of his anniversary every year, for the special food and drink of the brethren, he provided 40s. from those in Oxford which he acquired by his own toil for the church.[619]

To the office of the cellar he added twenty sesters of honey for making mead, which his ancestors were accustomed to have for their own. To these he added also £4 from the reeveship of Cuddesdon for buying wine from which the brethren are to have their special allowance on the main feast days.[620]

To the office of the refectory he gave 20s. from a hide at Milton, for buying flagons, and goblets, and spoons, and salt-cellars, and candlesticks, and any other lesser necessities.

To the office of the chamber he added four hides at Chaddleworth which Ralph Basset gave this church.[621] To the office of the altar he gave the church of Wickham, rendering £4.[622] To the fuel provision of the brethren he gave 60s. from the rents of Cuddesdon and Charney.[623] He made the court attractive with becoming buildings and walls.[624] For a brother who had professed in this monastery and who departed this life, he decided to bestow the same provisions as one living and present in the refectory would have, from the day of his passing to the day of his anniversary a full year later.[625] These and many other benefits he conferred on this church.

CMA ii. 312, 314–17, for lists of feast days on which wine was to be provided. On ordinary days, monks would normally have drunk ale. See Harvey, *Living and Dying*, p. 58.

[621] See above, p. 246; a list in MS C in the same hand as the *History*, below, p. 398, includes four pounds from Chaddleworth among the revenues of the chamber.

[622] See also Lyell, no. 164 and note; a list in MS C in the same hand as the *History*, below, p. 397, states that forty pounds of wax were rendered to the altar from the church of Wickham. Wickham is a hamlet close to Welford, Berks.; see *VCH*, *Berkshire*, iv. 116, 124–5.

[623] See also a list in MS C in the same hand as the *History*, below, pp. 394–5.

[624] For the area of the monastic precinct known as the court, see Plan, p. cv.

[625] Harvey, *Living and Dying*, p. 13 notes 'the universal practice of commemorating deceased monks by putting their portions of food and drink on the tables in the refectory at meal-times for a period after the decease, the whole to be given to the poor at the conclusion of the meal. Commonly, each monk was commemorated in this way for never less than thirty days after his death, and in some houses for a whole year.'

253. *De morte [a]abbatis Vincentii.[a]*

Regiminis uero sui anno decimo, ecclesie sue bono per omnia intentus, uir uenerabilis,[626] et merito suo huic ecclesie in euo memorandus, quieuit in Domino, bonis omnibus domum sibi creditam posteris relinquens habundantem.

[ii. 173] **254.** *De [b]abbate Ingulfo.[b]*

Successit autem ei in loco pastoris Ingulfus, prior Wintoniensis ecclesie, uir religiosus et scientia litterarum adprime instructus,[627] qui ecclesiam sibi commissam,[c] in diuersis persecutionibus positus, pro ut tempus ei sinebat, moderate regebat, que persecutiones post regis Henrici obitum ei nunquam defuerunt. Pro quo confirmando et in abbatem promouendo, idem rex primoribus Anglie tales litteras suo sigillo munitas direxit:

255. *Littere regis.*[d][628]

Henricus rex Anglorum,[e] archiepiscopis, episcopis, abbatibus, comitibus, uicecomitibus, baronibus, et omnibus fidelibus suis, Francis et Anglicis, totius Anglie, salutem. Sciatis me concessisse et dedisse Ingulfo abbati abbatiam de Abbendona, cum omnibus rebus ipsi abbatie pertinentibus. Et uolo et firmiter precipio quod bene et in pace et quiete et honorifice teneat et libere, cum saca et soca et toll[f] et tem et infangetheof,[g] et gritbruche et forstel et hamsocna et flemeneformthe, in burgo et extra burgum, in bosco et plano, in aquis et in riuis, et semitis, et in festo et sine festo, et cum omnibus aliis
C fo. 168v consuetudinibus suis, sicut | unquam aliquis antecessorum suorum melius et quietius et honorificentius et liberius tenuit. Testibus Rogero episcopo Sar', et Henrico episcopo Wint', et S.[h] cancellario,
[ii. 174] et Nigello nepote episcopi, et Willelmo de Pontearcarum, et Roberto de Oili, et Warino uicecomite. Apud Wintoniam.[i]

256. *De ecclesia sancti Aldadi.*[629]

Est in ciuitate Oxeneford monasterium quoddam sancti Aldadi episcopi uenerationi consecratum. Cuius omne beneficium duo clerici

[a–a] Vincentii abbatis *B* [b–b] Ingulfo abbate *B* [c] *first* s *interlin. in different ink B* [d] Henrici *add. B* [e] Anglie *B* [f] tol *B* [g] infangentheof *B* [h] *om. B* [i] Winc' *B*

[626] Vincent died in 1130; on 29 Mar. according to Cambridge, University Library, Kk. i 22, fo. 2v, and John of Worcester, *Chronicle*, iii. 194, 308.

[627] Ingulf probably became prior of Winchester in the mid–late 1120s; *Fasti: Monastic Cathedrals*, p. 88. He was elected abbot of Abingdon at Woodstock, and was blessed at Salisbury by Bishop Roger on Sunday 8 Jun. 1130; John of Worcester, *Chronicle*, iii. 194.

253. *Concerning the death of Abbot Vincent.*
In the tenth year of his rule, the venerable man found rest in the Lord.[626] He had been attentive to the good of his church in everything and is to be remembered for ever for his meritorious service to this church, leaving the house which had been entrusted to him abundant in all good things for those to come.

254. *Concerning Abbot Ingulf.*
His successor in the position of pastor was Ingulf, prior of the church of Winchester, a devout man, educated to the highest degree in the knowledge of letters.[627] He ruled the church entrusted to him with moderation, as far as circumstances permitted him, in that he was placed amidst various persecutions and was never free of them after King Henry's death. To confirm him and promote him to abbot, King Henry sent the following letters, strengthened with his seal, to the leading men of England:

255. *Letters of the king.*[628]
Henry king of the English to his archbishops, bishops, abbots, earls, sheriffs, barons and all his faithful men, French and English, of the whole of England, greeting. Know that I have granted and given to Abbot Ingulf the abbey of Abingdon with everything pertaining to this abbey. And I wish and firmly order that he may hold well and in peace and undisturbed and honourably and freely, with sake and soke and toll and team and infangentheof, and grithbrech and foresteal and hamsocn and flemenforthe, in borough and out of borough, in wood and plain, in waters and in streams and tracks, and in feast and without feast, and with all its other customs, as best and most undisturbedly and honourably and freely as any of his predecessors ever held. Witnesses: Roger bishop of Salisbury, and Henry bishop of Winchester, and [Geoffrey] the chancellor, and Nigel the bishop's nephew, and William de Pont de l'Arche, and Robert d'Oilly, and Warin the sheriff. At Winchester.

256. *Concerning the church of St Aldate.*[629]
There is in the city of Oxford a certain minster consecrated to the veneration of St Aldate, the bishop. Two clerics of that town, the

[628] *RRAN* ii, no. 1641; the writ dates to between Vincent's death on 29 Mar. 1130 and Henry's departure across the Channel in Aug. or Sept. of that year.

[629] See J. Blair, 'Saint Frideswide's monastery: problems and possibilities', *Oxoniensia*, liii (1988), 221–58, at pp. 233–5; Salter, *Medieval Oxford*, pp. 116–17. For St Frideswide's claim that Henry I gave half the church of St Aldate, see *RRAN* ii, no. 1342; however, it is

[*See p. 256 for n. 629 cont.*]

ex eadem uilla, fratres Robertus et Gillebertus, cum quodam Nicholao sacerdote eque[a] dimidiabant.[630] Contigit autem ut, uocante Deo, predicti duo fratres habitum monachi in hoc Abbendonensi cenobio, huius abbatis scilicet Ingulfi tempore, susciperent, et partem ecclesie que eis contingebat, cum terra et domibus infra ciuitatem hereditario iure sibi pertinentibus, huic ecclesie dono perpetuo contraderent. Quod uidens Nicholaus, alterius partis ecclesie dominus, abbatem simul et conuentum conuenit, postulans ut ei partem fratrum predictorum cum sua quamdiu uiueret tenere concederent, ita ut censum quem pars accepta exigebat, scilicet uiginti solidos annuatim, persolueret. Conditionem etiam talem interposuit, ut cum habitum mutare uellet, non nisi in ecclesia ista mutaret, uel etiam si in illo habitu quo tunc erat uitam finiret, pars dimidia ecclesie supradicte que sua erat, cum altera parte, in perpetuum isto loco remaneret. Rogante etiam Nicholao, in priuilegio Romano ista ecclesia posita est, quod tunc temporis renouabatur.[631] Reuersus ergo ad propria, duos solidos per annos singulos in recognitionem pacti prenotati, extra censum consuetum, dum uixit persoluit.

[ii. 175] Defluente uero postmodum aliquanto tempore, Nicholaus idem subita egritudine correptus, letali morbo se sensit detineri. Qui salutis proprie recordatus, ad fratres suos Abbendoniam nuntium transmisit, petens ut religionis habitum indueret, priusquam deficeret. Qui cum mortem eius nondum sic imminere putarent, et iccirco aliquantulum uenire tardarent, Nicholaus in exthasi detentus iacuit. Astantes autem sancte Fritheswithe canonici, iamque mortuum putantes, et idem fortasse propter lucrum suum desiderantes, nescienti habitum suum superposuerunt, sicque ad suam ecclesiam quadam ui et iniuria rapuerunt. Postea tamen reuocato spiritu ad se rediens, cum a Wigodo abbate Oseneie interrogaretur utrum ei habitus sic assumptus, aut ibi mori placeret, respondit se amplius in quodam uili specu uelle proici quam ibi detineri.[632] Dicebat enim bono suo se ibi non

[a] *B lacks a folio here, lost after the first numbering of folios; it seems likely that the folio was removed for the picture of King Stephen which it would have contained*

possible that the charter is interpolated, and the church is not mentioned in confirmations by Popes Honorius II and Innocent II; *Cartulary of St Frideswide*, i, nos. 8, 15. The Empress confirmed it to St Frideswide's in mid-1141, *RRAN* iii, no. 646. In 1148 or later, King Stephen ordered the bishop of Lincoln that he should not place the prior of St Frideswide's in plea concerning half the church of St Aldate and the church of St Edward, except in the king's presence. It is plausible that Abingdon was the other party to the dispute. A general confirmation by Hadrian IV for St Frideswide's included 'whatever you have in the church of St Aldate'; *Cartulary of St Frideswide*, i, no. 23. A further settlement

brothers Robert and Gilbert, used to share equally the benefice of that church with a priest, Nicholas.[630] But it happened in the time of this abbot, Ingulf, that, at God's calling, those two brothers adopted the monk's habit in this monastery of Abingdon, and they handed over to this church as a perpetual gift the part of the church which belonged to them, with the land and houses within the city which pertained to them by hereditary right. Seeing this, Nicholas, the lord of the other part of the church, came to the abbot and convent and demanded that they grant him the aforesaid brothers' part to hold with his own as long as he lived, thus that he would pay the required rent from the part he received, that is 20s. a year. He also set down the following condition, that when he wished to change his habit, he would not do so except in this church, or even if he finished his life in his current habit, his half of the above-mentioned church, with the other part, would remain to this monastery in perpetuity. Also at Nicholas's request, this church was placed in the Roman privilege which was being renewed at the time.[631] So he went home, and as long as he lived he annually paid 2s. above the accustomed rent in recognition of the above agreement.

Some while later, Nicholas was taken by a sudden sickness and felt himself gripped by a deadly illness. Mindful of his own salvation, he sent a messenger to his brethren at Abingdon, with a request to assume the habit of the religious life before he lost his strength. They did not think his death so imminent and therefore delayed a little in coming, while Nicholas lay unconscious. However, the canons of St Frideswide who were present thought him already dead, and they placed their own habit on him without his knowledge, possibly desiring him because of his wealth, and thereby wrongfully seizing him by force for their own church. Afterwards, however, his spirit was recalled, he came to, and when asked by Wigod abbot of Oseney whether he was pleased with the habit adopted thus or with dying there, he replied that he would rather be thrown into some vile cave than be kept at St Fridewide's.[632] For, he said, he could not for his

concerning presentation of the church was made in the time of Abbot Hugh (1189/90–1221); *Cartulary of St Frideswide*, i, no. 254. Conflict occasionally arose again (*Cartulary of St Frideswide*, i, no. 255), but *VCH*, *Oxfordshire*, iv. 373, shows the arrangement outlined in the following section in general working well up to the Dissolution.

[630] Nicholas the priest may be the same man mentioned in a charter of King Stephen for St Frideswide's; *RRAN* iii, no. 640.

[631] See above, pp. xxix, lii; also below, pp. 266, 272.

[632] Wigod was prior 1138–54; abbot 1154–68: *Heads of Religious Houses*, p. 179.

posse sepeliri, ubi sepultus fidem quam fratribus suis debuit probaretur mentiri; se potius ad eum locum deferendum quem, seu uiuus seu mortuus, elegerit inhabitandum. Detentus tamen ab his qui bonis suis inhiabant, presentis uite fine inibi interceptus, atque sepultus est. Partem uero ecclesie quam Nicholai diximus esse, et iam iure nostram, negligentibus circa rerum suarum defensione[a] prelatis,[b] usque hodie detinent, et perpetue detinere[c] nituntur; nobis tamen, cum parte iam nostra, personatus dignitate reseruata. Hec iccirco dixerim, ut quandoque per uirum a Deo datum, tanto citius perueniat eius iusta recuperatio, quanto inuenta fuerit scripta iniusta distractio.

[ii. 176] **257.** *Cirographum de wicha apud Oxeneford.*

Frater Ingulfus et totus conuentus, cui a Deo datus est in Abbendonia humilis minister, omnibus successoribus suis in Christo salutem. Notum sit uobis omnibus quod in pleno capitulo wichiam nostram que iuxta pontem Oxeneford iacet, Nicholao sacerdoti ac Roberto nepoti eius, iure hereditario possidendam, concessimus, retentis eiusdem consuetudinibus et conseruata nobis firma nostra, quadra-
C fo. 169r ginta uidelicet solidorum per annum, sub quibus | Ermenoldus et Godwinus eam prius tenuerant eam.[d][633] Pro hac autem sua hereditate, Nicholaus et Robertus homagium nobis in pleno capitulo fecerunt. In hoc autem simul sedimus ego frater Ingulfus et totus conuentus. Cum Nicholao et Roberto affuerunt Willelmus decanus, Rogerus filius Wigeri, et multi alii. Hoc autem pactum recordatum et confirmatum est in camera nostra, coram baronibus et multis uicinis nostris, qui in Natiuitate beatissime uirginis Marie, ut mos eorum est, apud nos conuenerant.[634]

258. *Cirographum de quadam terra in Gersendona.*[635]

Ego Adeliz et filius meus Hugo, annuente[e] domino meo Roberto, concessimus et iureiurando concessionem confirmauimus terram de Gersenduna, que fuit Gilleberti aui mei, quam dedit Willelmo de Botendona cum matre mea[f] Agnete, liberam et quietam ab omni calumpnia, Deo, et sancte Marie Abbendonie, et domno Ingulfo abbati,[636] quia et mater mea eam Faritio abbati reddiderat, ita et ego

[a] *for* defensionem ? [b] prolatis *C* [c] ditinere *C* [d] *either* eam *has been unnecessarily repeated, or possibly the first instance should read* iam [e] xiii *between columns C* [f] sua *C*

[633] See above, p. 204. [634] See above, p. c. [635] See also above, pp. 48, 130.

[636] See above, p. 48, for Agnes, one of the three daughters of Gilbert Latimer. Both that

own good be buried at that place, where his burial would prove that he had feigned the good faith which he owed his brethren [of Abingdon]; he should instead be taken to that monastery which he had chosen to inhabit, whether living or dead. However, he was detained by those who coveted his goods, and there he was snatched by the end of the present life and was buried. Moreover, with prelates neglecting the defence of their own possessions, the canons of St Frideswide withhold to this day, and strive to withhold forever, the part of the church which we have said belonged to Nicholas and now by right was ours. The honour of making the presentment, however, is reserved for us, together with our part. I have spoken for this reason, so that some day, through a man given by God, the just resumption of the other part should occur that much more swiftly, because the unjust seizure is found recorded in writing.

257. *Cirograph concerning a dairy-farm at Oxford.*
Brother Ingulf and the whole convent in Abingdon to whom he has been given by God as a humble minister, to all their successors in Christ, greeting. Let it be known to you all that in full chapter we have granted to Nicholas the priest and Robert his nephew our dairy-farm which lies next to the bridge at Oxford, to possess by hereditary right, retaining its customs and keeping for ourselves our farm, that is 40s. a year, under which Ermenold and Godwine had previously held it.[633] Moreover, Nicholas and Robert did homage to us in full chapter for this their inheritance. In this, moreover, I Brother Ingulf and the whole convent sat together. Present with Nicholas and Robert were William the deacon, Roger son of Wiger, and many others. This agreement, moreover, was recorded and confirmed in our chamber, in the presence of our barons and many of our neighbours, who had gathered in our presence on the Nativity of the most blessed Virgin Mary [8 Sept.], as is their custom.[634]

258. *Cirograph concerning certain land in Garsington.*[635]
I, Adeliza, and my son Hugh, with the agreement of my lord husband Robert, grant and confirm with an oath our grant to God, and to St Mary of Abingdon, and to lord Abbot Ingulf, free and quit of all claim, the land of Garsington which was Gilbert my grandfather's and which he gave to William of *Botendon* with my mother Agnes.[636] For my mother had given it back to Abbot Faritius, and so

passage, and the rest of the present cirograph, strongly suggest that Agnes was Adeliza's mother, despite the scribes' use of 'sua' in this sentence.

[ii. 177] et Hugo filius meus eam reddidimus. Huic concessioni interfuerunt testes ex utraque parte; ex parte abbatis: ipse domnus abbas, Walterus, Alerannus monachi, et ex militibus Rogerius de Mollesford cum Willelmo milite suo, et multi alii;[637] ex parte ipsius Adeliz: ipsa Adeliz, Robertus uir suus, Hugo filius suus, et multi alii.

[ii. 178] **259.** *De Stephano rege.*

Sexto igitur huius abbatis anno, Henricus rex in Normannia uita defungitur, cui successit in regnum Stephanus, nepos eius. Ortaque werra inter regem et imperatricem, filiam superioris regis, tota Anglie ecclesia diuersis tribulationibus pluribus annis ualde uexatur. Ecclesia etiam ista illo in tempore plurimarum rerum suarum detrimentum incurrit.

260. *Carta de hundredo.*[638]

Stephanus rex Anglorum episcopo Sar', et iusticiis, et uicecomiti, et omnibus baronibus et fidelibus suis, Francis et Anglis, de Berchesire, salutem. Sciatis me concessisse Deo, et ecclesie sancte Marie Abbendone, et abbati Ingulfo, et omnibus abbatibus successoribus suis, et monachis ibidem Deo seruientibus, hundredum de Hornimera iure perpetuo tenendum et habendum eis et omnibus successoribus suis in legitima et liberima potestate sua et iusticia, sicut
B fo. 161r Eadwardus rex Anglorum dedit et[a] | concessit, et per cartam suam confirmauit, quam coram me et baronibus meis lectam esse testificor, et sicut Willelmus rex auus meus et Henricus auunculus meus dona regis Eadwardi[b] per cartas suas concesserunt et corroborauerunt. Et uolo et firmiter precipio ut abbas et monachi, presentes et futuri, predictum hundredum in pace et quiete et honorifice et libere teneant, cum omnibus consuetudinibus et quietationibus suis cum quibus melius et honorabilius tenuerunt tempore predictorum regum,
[ii. 179] scilicet quod nullus uicecomes uel eorum ministri inde se quicquam intromittant, sed ipsi libere iusticiam suam habeant et faciant. Testibus comite Gaufrido, et Roberto de Ver, et Willelmo de Ipra.[c] Apud Oxeneford.[639]

[a] *B resumes here* [b] Edwardi *B* [c] et Waltero de Bocheland', et Adam de Belnaio, et Ricardo de Luci, Rainfenin' Britone, et Hugo de Bolebec *add. B and Chatsworth, no. 342*

[637] Moulsford was in the Slotisford hundred of Berkshire; EPNS, *Berkshire*, ii. 506, 527–8.

also I and my son Hugh give it back. At this grant were present witnesses from both sides; from the abbot's side: the lord abbot himself, the monks Walter and Aleran and, of the knights, Roger of Moulsford with William his knight, and many others;[637] from Adeliza's side: Adeliza herself, Robert her husband, Hugh her son, and many others.

259. *Concerning King Stephen.*

In this abbot's sixth year, in Normandy King Henry came to the end of his life, and his nephew Stephen succeeded him in the kingship. War broke out between the king and the empress, daughter of the previous king, and for many years the whole church of England was greatly troubled by various afflictions. At that time, too, this church incurred the loss of many of its possessions.

260. *Charter concerning the hundred.*[638]

Stephen king of the English to the bishop of Salisbury, and his justices, and sheriff, and all his barons and faithful men, French and English, of Berkshire, greeting. Know that I have granted to God, and to the church of St Mary of Abingdon, and to Abbot Ingulf, and to all his successors as abbot, and to the monks serving God there, the hundred of Hormer for them and all their successors to hold and have by perpetual right in their lawful and most free power and justice, as Edward king of the English gave and granted and confirmed through his charter, which I witness was read in the presence of me and my barons, and as my grandfather King William and my uncle Henry through their charters granted and strengthened the gifts of King Edward. And I wish and firmly order that the abbot and monks, present and future, hold the aforesaid hundred in peace and undisturbed and honourably and freely, with all their customs and quittances with which they best and most honourably held in the time of the aforesaid kings; that is, that no sheriff or sheriff's officials interfere in anything therein, but they are to have and do their own justice freely. Witnesses: Earl Geoffrey, and Robert de Ver, and William de Ypres. At Oxford.[639]

[638] *RRAN* iii, no. 4 , dating to *c.*1140 × 1143; Chatsworth, no. 342. Except for very minor changes, appropriate up-dating (e.g. William I is now referred to as the king's grand-father), and different witnesses, the document is identical to Henry I's charter, *RRAN* ii, no. 1477, above, p. 230.

[639] In MS B, two further writs are included here; see below, p. 340.

[ii. 180] **261.** [a]*De foro Abbendonensi.*[a] [640]

Stephanus rex Anglorum episcopo Sar', iusticiis, uicecomiti, baronibus, et omnibus ministris et fidelibus suis, Francis et Anglis, de Berchescira, salutem. Sciatis me concessisse Deo, et ecclesie sancte[b] Marie de Abbendona, et Ingulfo abbati, et monachis cum eo in ea Deo seruientibus mercatum in uilla de Abbendonia [c]ad diem Dominicam[c] [641] sicut predicta ecclesia et abbates et ipse [d]abbas Vincentius[d] unquam melius uel liberius tenuerunt, et die qua rex Henricus eis
[ii. 181] dedit et concessit abbatiam. Et uolo et firmiter precipio quod omnes
B fo. 161v homines illuc euntes, et ibidem morantes, | et inde redeuntes, plene habeant meam firmam pacem, ne super hec iniuste disturbentur, super decem libras forisfacture. Teste Willelmo de Ipra.[e] Apud Oxeneford.

262. [f]*De terris huius ecclesie.*[f] [642]

Stephanus rex Anglorum[g] iusticiis, uicecomiti, baronibus, ministris, et omnibus fidelibus suis, Francis et Anglis, de Oxenefordscira et de
C fo. 169v Berchesira,[h] salutem. | Precipio quod abbas et monachi de[i] Abbendona teneant et habeant omnes terras, et homines suos, et omnes res suas, ita bene[j] in pace et honorifice et libere et quiete, sicut tenuerunt die qua rex Henricus fuit uiuus et mortuus, et die qua primum coronatus fui, ne super hoc ponatur inde in placitum donec ueniam in prouinciam, quia nolo quod placitent nisi coram me. Teste Ricardo de Luci. Apud Lundoniam.

263. [k]*Vt non placitet abbas nisi coram rege.* [643]

Stephanus rex Anglorum iusticiis, et uicecomitibus, et baronibus, et
[ii. 182] ministris, et omnibus fidelibus suis, Francis et Anglis, de Oxenefordscira et de Berchesira, salutem. Sciatis quia warantizo abbati Abbendone ne ipse uel homines sui placitent de aliquo placito quod pertineat ad coronam meam nisi coram me et quando ero apud Oxeneford. Teste Willelmo de Ipra. Apud Londoniam.

[a–a] *om., but an entry, probably* De mercatu de Abbend' *in dry point in one of the hands providing guidance for the rubricator in margin B* [b] beate *B* [c–c] *these words have been erased in C; in B, only the last has been erased; they remain intact in Chatsworth, no. 353* [d–d] Vincentius abbas *B* [e] Willelmo de Caisn', et Ricardo de Luci, et Ricardo de Camuilla *add. B* [f–f] *om. B, erasure in margin* [g] Anglie *B* [h] Bercscira *B* [i] *om. B* [j] et *add. B* [k–264/a] *these two writs om. B*

[640] *RRAN* iii, no. 5, dating to 1139 × 1154, on the basis that Richard de Lucy was in

261. *Concerning Abingdon market.*[640]
Stephen king of the English to the bishop of Salisbury, and his justices, sheriff, barons, and all his officials and faithful men, French and English, of Berkshire, greeting. Know that I have granted to God, and to the church of St Mary of Abingdon, and to Abbot Ingulf, and to the monks there serving God with him in that church, the market in the town of Abingdon on Sunday,[641] as the aforesaid church and abbots and Abbot Vincent himself ever best and most freely held, and as on the day on which King Henry gave and granted the abbey to them. And I wish and firmly order that all men going to that place and staying there and returning thence should fully have my firm peace, lest they be unjustly disturbed contrary to this, on £10 of forfeiture. Witness: William de Ypres. At Oxford.

262. *Concerning the lands of this church.*[642]
Stephen king of the English to his justices, sheriffs, barons, officials, and all his faithful men, French and English, of Oxfordshire and Berkshire, greeting. I order that the abbot and monks of Abingdon may hold and have all the lands and their men and all their possessions, as well in peace and honourably and freely and undisturbed as they held on the day on which King Henry was alive and dead and on the day on which I was first crowned. And let the church not be brought to court on this matter contrary to this, until I come into the region, since I do not wish that they plead except in my presence. Witness: Richard de Lucy. At London.

263. *That the abbot is not to plead except in the king's presence.*[643]
Stephen king of the English to his justices, and sheriffs, and barons, and officials, and all his faithful men, French and English, of Oxfordshire and Berkshire, greeting. Know that I warrant to the abbot of Abingdon that neither he nor his men should plead concerning any plea which pertains to my crown, except in my presence and when I shall be at Oxford. Witness: William de Ypres. At London.

England; Chatsworth, no. 353. Compared with the previous document, this writ shows considerably greater changes from Henry I's equivalent grant of a market, above, p. 232.

[641] The subsequent deletion of the words 'on Sunday' reveals concern about markets being held on the sabbath; see R. J. Bartlett, *England under the Norman and Angevin Kings* (Oxford, 2000), pp. 637–9, and below, p. 308. Chatsworth, no. 353 gives the full reading.

[642] *RRAN* iii, no. 10, dating to 1139 × 54.

[643] *RRAN* iii, no. 3, dating to 1139 × 54.

264. *Item de hundredo.*[644]

Stephanus rex Anglorum Iord' de Podiis, salutem.[645] Precipio tibi quod permittatis abbatem de Abbendona tenere hundredum suum et omnes tenuras suas bene et in pace, sicut melius tenuit tempore regis Henrici, et sicut carte regum testantur quas inde habet, et cum omnibus libertatibus suis. Teste A. clerico. Apud Sanctum Albanum.[a][646]

[ii. 190] **265.** *De priuilegio Romano.*

B fo. 163r Videns itaque abbas Ingulfus regis litteras[b] ad munimen ecclesie cui preerat modicum aut nichil proficere, quia—propter regni discidium—diuersi principes diuersis ducibus obediebant, et quod unus confirmabat, alter irritum facere studebat, ad solatium capitis
B fo. 163v uni|uersalis ecclesie, quod ei potissimum (sicuti erat) uidebatur confugit.[647] Vnum ergo ex clericis suis ecclesie Romane, notum et in dicendo peritum, Gaufridum Trenchebisa[648] ad Romanam sedem direxit, apostolice supplicans dignitati ut res ecclesie sibi commisse
[ii. 191] auctoritate sua et litteris confirmaret, et ab hostium incursione qui iam imminebant defenderet. Cuius fauens petitioni, uenerabilis apostolicus Eugenius tercius, tunc sancte Romane ecclesie presidens, litteras huic Abbendonensi ecclesie in hec uerba direxit:[649]

266. *Priuilegium Eugenii pape tercii.*

Eugenius episcopus seruus seruorum Dei dilectis filiis Ingulfo, abbati monasterii sancte Marie de Abbendona, eiusque fratribus, tam presentibus quam futuris, regularem uitam professis, in perpetuum. Pie postulatio uoluntatis effectu debet prosequente compleri, quatinus et deuotionis sinceritas laudabiliter enitescat, et utilitas postulata uires indubitanter assumat.

Ea propter, dilecti in Domino filii, uestris iustis postulationibus clementer annuimus, et prefatam sancte Dei genitricis ecclesiam, in qua diuino mancipati estis obsequio, sub beati Petri et nostra

[b] *latter part of this word erased C*

---

[644] *RRAN* iii, no. 2, dating to 1136 × 54.

[645] Jordan witnessed a lost charter of Stephen, *RRAN* iii, no. 89. The identification of the toponym is uncertain, but Les Pieux (Dept. Manches) was always Latinized in such a way. *VCH*, *Oxfordshire*, xi. 197, gives this surname as 'Podio' or 'Putz'.

[646] In MS B, three further writs appear here; see below, p. 342.

[647] For such resort to the pope instead of the king during Stephen's reign, see e.g. Hudson, *Land, Law, and Lordship*, pp. 142–3.

[648] In the bottom right hand corner of the bull has been added the words 'Memoriale

264. *Likewise, concerning the hundred.*[644]
Stephen king of the English to Jordan de *Podiis*, greeting.[645] I order you that you allow the abbot of Abingdon to hold his hundred and all his tenures well and in peace, as best he held in the time of King Henry and as witnessed by the kings' charters which he has concerning this, and with all his liberties. Witness: A. the cleric. At St Albans.[646]

265. *Concerning the Roman privilege.*
Abbot Ingulf saw that the king's letters achieved little or nothing for the defence of the church of which he had charge, since different nobles followed different leaders because of the division of the realm, and what one confirmed the other strove to make ineffectual. He therefore fled for refuge to the comfort of the head of the universal church, which seemed to him most powerful (as it in fact was).[647] So he sent to the see of Rome Geoffrey *Trenchebisa*,[648] one of his clerics, known to the Roman church and experienced in speaking, begging the apostolic dignity that he confirm by his authority and letters the possessions of the church entrusted to him, and defend them from the assault of the enemies who were now threatening. The venerable Pope Eugenius III, who was then in charge of the holy Roman church, agreed to his request and sent letters in the following words to this church of Abingdon:[649]

266. *Privilege of Pope Eugenius III.*
Bishop Eugenius, servant of the servants of God, to his beloved sons Ingulf abbot of the monastery of St Mary of Abingdon and his brethren, both present and future, who have professed the regular life, in perpetuity. The request of a pious will ought to be fulfilled with the appropriate outcome, so that both the sincerity of devotion may shine forth in praiseworthy manner and the advantage requested may take effect without hesitation.

Therefore, sons beloved in the Lord, we have mercifully agreed to your just requests, and we take under the protection of St Peter and

magistri Galfridi trenchebise'. The hand is very similar to, and could be the same as, that of the scribe who wrote the *History*; see also Vol. i, Introduction, 'Composition'. Despite his importance here, I have been unable to discover more of Geoffrey.

[649] Eugenius III was elected on 15 Feb. 1145, consecrated three days later, and died 8 Jul. 1153; I. S. Robinson, *The Papacy 1073–1198* (Cambridge, 1990), p. 526. This document survives as an original in Lambeth Palace Library; for details, see J. Sayers, *Original Papal Documents in the Lambeth Palace Library* (*Bulletin of the Institute of Historical Research, Special Supplement no. 6*, London, 1967), p. 9.

protectione suscipimus, et presentis scripti priuilegio communimus. Statuentes ut quascumque possessiones, quecumque bona, inpresentiarum iuste et canonice possidetis aut in futurum concessione pontificum, liberalitate regum, largitione principum, oblatione fidelium, seu aliis iustis modis, prestante Domino, poteritis adipisci, firma uobis uestrisque successoribus et illibata permaneant.

In quibus hec propriis duximus exprimenda uocabulis. Ipsum
locum in quo monasterium uestrum fundatum est, hundredum de
Hornimera, Abbandonam,[a] et forum cum libertatibus et consuetudinibus omnibus, sicut reges Anglie eas uobis concesserunt, et per
cartas suas confirmauerunt, cum Cumenora[b] et Bertuna,[c] et omnibus
appenditiis[d] hundredi. Mercheham,[e] Middeltonam,[f] Draitonam,
C fo. 170r Saringeford, Wachenesfeld, cum omnibus | appenditiis suis. Eccle-
[ii. 192] siam sancte Marie de Colum cum pertinentiis suis. Ecclesiam de
Cinsentona[g] et duas hidas cum eis que adiacent. Ecclesiam sanctorum
Innocentum,[h] et hospicia uestra que iuxta ecclesiam sunt apud
Lundonias uia Westmonasterii. Ecclesiam sancti Martini, et ecclesiam
sancti Aldadi, et quicquid terre et iuris habetis apud Oxeneford.
Ecclesiam de Niweham. Ecclesiam de Suttuna,[i] Lacing, Gaing,[650]
Fernebergam, Witteham, Appelford, cum appenditiis suis. Offentonam, Gosi,[651] Wrdham,[j] Cerni, Weliford, Chiueleiam,[k] Winechefeld,[l]
Wisseleiam,[m] cum appenditiis suis. Culeham,[n] Cuthesdonam, Leoue-
chenoram, Thademertonam, Bedenam, Lechamstedam, Lewarto-
nam,[652] Tubbeneiam, Linfordam, Fageflor, cum omnibus que
adiacent. In Gloucestrechira:[o] Dumeltunam,[p] et Cirne cum appenditiis.[q][653] In Chiltona quinque hidas. In Pesi duas hidas. In Den-
cheswrtha[r] septem hidas. In Boclanda quinque hidas.[654] In
B fo. 164r Chade|leswrtha[s] quatuor hidas que fuerunt Radulfi Basset. In
Gersendona nouem hidas. In Cestretona unam hidam. In Hulla
duas hidas. In Bereford quinque hidas.[655] In Hernicota duas hidas.
In Suttuna[t] unam hidam, et molendinum de Henoura.[u] In Fencota
unam hidam. In Beneham[v] duas hidas ex dono Humfridi[w] de Bohum.

[a] Abbadonam *L* [b] Cummenora *L* [c] Bertona *L* [d] appendiciis *L* [e] Mercham *B* [f] Middeltunam *B* [g] Cinsentuna *B* [h] Innocentium *B* [i] Suttona *L* [j] Wurdham *L* [k] Chiueleam *B* [l] Winekefeld *B* [m] Wisseleam *B* [n] Chuleham *B* [o] Glouecestreschira *B* [p] Dumeltonam *L* [q] appendiciis *L* [r] Dencheswrda *L*; Dencheswrða *B* [s] Chadeleswrda *L*; Chadeleswrða *B* [t] Suttona *L* [u] Henouara *B* [v] Benneham *B* [w] Hunfridi *L*

650 *DB* i, fo. 59v, states that 'the abbey itself holds [West] Ginge, [Berks.], and always held it'.

ourselves, and we fortify by the privilege of the present document, the aforementioned church of the holy mother of God in which you are given over to divine service. We decree that whatever possessions and whatever goods you justly and canonically possess at present, or which you can in future acquire—with the Lord providing—by the grant of bishops, the liberality of kings, the generosity of princes, the offerings of the faithful, or in other just ways, remain to you and your successors firm and undiminished.

We have decided to describe these by their own names. The place itself in which your monastery was founded, the hundred of Hormer, Abingdon, and the market with all liberties and customs as the kings of England granted them to you and confirmed by their charters, with Cumnor and Barton and all appendages of the hundred. Marcham, Milton, Drayton, Shellingford, Watchfield, with all their appendages. The church of St Mary of Colne with its appurtenances. The church of Kensington and two hides with whatever belongs to it. The church of the Holy Innocents and your houses which are next to the church in London on the Westminster road. The church of St Martin and the church of St Aldate and whatever lands and rights you have in Oxford. The church of Nuneham. The church of Sutton, Lockinge, Ginge,[650] Farnborough, Wittenham, Appleford, with their appurtenances. Uffington, Goosey,[651] Longworth, Charney, Welford, Chieveley, Winkfield, Whistley, with their appendages. Culham, Cuddesdon, Lewknor, Tadmarton, Beedon, Leckhampstead, Leverton,[652] Tubney, Lyford, Fawler, with everything which belongs. In Gloucestershire, Dumbleton and Cerney with appendages.[653] In Chilton five hides. In Pusey two hides. In Denchworth seven hides. In Buckland five hides.[654] In Chaddleworth four hides which were Ralph Basset's. In Garsington nine hides. In Chesterton one hide. In Hill two hides. In Barford five hides.[655] In Arncott two hides. In Sutton one hide and the mill of Hennor. In Fencott one hide. In Benham two hides by gift of Humphrey de Bohun. In

[651] *DB* i, fo. 59[r], states that 'the abbey itself holds Goosey, [Berks.], and always held it'.

[652] *DB* i, fo. 59[r], states that 'Hezelin holds Leverton, [Berks.] from the abbot'.

[653] *DB* i, fo. 169[r], states that 'Walter [son Roger] holds [South] Cerney, [Glos.]. . . . This manor has been claimed for the church of St Mary of Abingdon, but the whole county has witnessed that Archbishop Stigand held it for ten years while King Edward was alive. Earl William gave this manor to Roger the sheriff, Walter's father.'

[654] *DB* i, fo. 59[v], states that 'the abbey itself holds Buckland [Berks.]. . . . Then and now five hides'.

[655] *DB* i, fo. 156[v], states that 'Wadard's son holds five hides in Barford [St Michael, Oxon.] from Roger, and he from the abbot [of Abingdon]'.

In Niweham unam pischariam cum appenditiis.[a] In Colebroc quicquid terre et iuris habetis ex dono Milonis Crispini et Roberti Gernun.[b] In Dumeltuna[c] unam hidam ex dono Willelmi Guizemboez, et dimidiam hidam ex dono Henrici regis. In Stretona[d] unam hidam et tres uirgatas ex dono Henrici de Albennieo.[e]

Obeunte autem te—nunc eiusdem loci abbate—uel tuorum quolibet successorum, nullus ibidem qualibet surreptionis astutia uel uiolentia preponatur, nisi quem fratres communi consensu, uel fratrum pars consilii sanioris, secundum Dei timorem et beati Benedicti regulam, canonice prouiderint eligendum. Prohibemus insuper ut nullus, post factam ibidem professionem, absque abbatis et fratrum suorum licentia de eodem monasterio audeat discedere,
[ii. 193] discedentem uero nullus audeat retinere. Statuimus quoque ut in monasterio uestro in quo fratres regularem uitam professi degunt, nulli omnino[f] liceat secundum beati Benedicti regulam ibidem constitutam[g] ordinem inmutare. Nullus etiam episcoporum futuris temporibus audeat eiusdem religionis fratres de monasterio uestro, abbate et fratribus inuitis, expellere. Sepulturam quoque [h]monasterii uestri[h] liberam esse concedimus, ut eorum, qui se illic sepeliri deliberauerint, deuotioni[i] et extreme uoluntati, nisi forte excommunicati sint, nullus obsistat.

Preterea libertates omnes et rationabiles monasterii uestri consuetudines a regibus Anglie et episcopis uestris uobis concessas et scriptis eorum confirmatas, sicut eas hactenus in pace habuistis et tenuistis, uobis in perpetuum confirmamus. Decernimus ergo ut nulli omnino hominum liceat prefatum monasterium temere perturbare, aut eius possessiones auferre, uel ablatas retinere, minuere, seu quibuslibet uexationibus fatigare. Sed omnia integra conseruentur, eorum pro quorum gubernatione et sustentatione concessa sunt usibus omnimodis profutura, salua sedis apostolice auctoritate, et diocesanorum episcoporum canonica iusticia et reuerentia.

Si qua igitur in futurum ecclesiastica secularisue persona, huius nostre constitutionis paginam sciens, contra eam temere uenire
C fo. 170v temptauerit, secundo tercioue[j] commonita, si non | reatum suum congrua satisfactione correxerit, potestatis honorisque sui dignitate careat, reamque se diuino iudicio existere de perpetrata iniquitate cognoscat,[k] et a sacratissimo corpore et sanguine Dei et Domini

[a] appendiciis *L* [b] Gernum *B* [c] Dumeltona *L* [d] Strattona *L* [e] Albenneio *B* [f] hominum *add. L* [g] constitutum *L* [h–h] uestri monasterii *L*; *om. B* [i] deuocioni *L* [j] tertioue *L* [k] agnoscat *B*

Nuneham one fishery with appendages. In Colnbrook whatever lands and rights you have by gift of Miles Crispin and Robert Gernon. In Dumbleton one hide by gift of William Goizenboded and half a hide by gift of King Henry. In Stratton one hide and three virgates by gift of Henry d'Aubigny.

Moreover, when you—now abbot of this monastery—or any of your successors die, no one is to be set in charge in that place by any craft or violence of deceit; rather the brethren by common consent, or the party of brethren of wiser counsel, are to choose him to be elected canonically, according to fear of God and the rule of St Benedict. In addition, we forbid that anyone, after having made their profession here, dare withdraw from this monastery without the abbot and his brethren's permission, or indeed that anyone dare to harbour someone who is withdrawing. We also lay down that, in your monastery in which brethren live the regular life they have professed, no one be permitted to change in the least the order constituted there according to the rule of St Benedict. Nor is any bishop in future to dare to expel the brethren of this religious life from your monastery, against the will of the abbot and brethren. We also grant that your monastery's right of burial be free, so that no one may obstruct the devotion and final will of those who resolve to be buried there, unless by chance they have been excommunicated.

Besides we confirm to you in perpetuity all the liberties and reasonable customs of your monastery granted to you by the kings of England and your bishops, and confirmed by their documents, as you have hitherto had and held them in peace. We accordingly decree that it be utterly forbidden to any man to disturb recklessly the aforementioned monastery or take away its possessions, withhold what has been taken away, or diminish or trouble them with any vexations. But everything is to be preserved whole, to be beneficial for all needs of those for whose direction and sustenance it was granted, save the authority of the apostolic see and the canonical justice and reverence of diocesan bishops.

If, therefore, in future, any ecclesiastical or secular person who has knowledge of this and recklessly attempts to go against it, after receiving a second and third warning, if he does not correct his offence with proper satisfaction, let him be deprived of the dignity of his power and honour, and let him learn that he stands in divine judgment guilty of the iniquity he perpetrated, and let him be separated from the most sacred body and blood of God and our

redemptoris nostri Iesu Christi aliena fiat, atque in extremo examine districte[a] ultioni subiaceat. Cunctis autem eidem loco sua iura
[ii. 194] seruantibus, sit pax Domini nostri Iesu Christi, quatinus | et hic
B fo. 164v fructum bone actionis percipiant, et apud districtum iudicem premia eterne pacis inueniant. Amen. Amen. Amen.

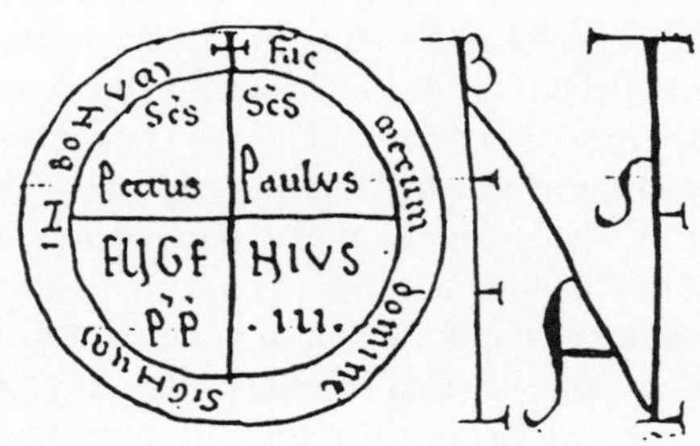

Ego[b] Eugenius catholice ecclesie episcopus subscripsi.[656]
Ego Conradus Sabinensis episcopus subscripsi.
Ego Ymarus Tusculanus[c] episcopus subscripsi.
Ego Gregorius presbiter cardinalis titulo Calixti subscripsi.
Ego Guido presbiter cardinalis titulo sancti Crisogoni subscripsi.
Ego Vbaldus presbiter cardinalis titulo sancte Crucis in Ierusalem subscripsi.
Ego Guido presbiter cardinalis titulo sanctorum Laurentii et Damasi subscripsi.
Ego Bernardus presbiter cardinalis titulo sancti Clementis subscripsi.
Ego Mansredus presbiter cardinalis titulo sancte Sauine subscripsi.
[ii. 195] Ego Iordanus presbiter cardinalis titulo sancte Susanne subscripsi.
Ego Odo diaconus cardinalis sancti Georgii ad Velum Aureum subscripsi.
Ego Iohannes diaconus cardinalis sancte Marie Noue subscripsi.
Ego Berardus[d] diaconus cardinalis[e] sancte Romane ecclesie subscripsi.
Ego Cinthius diaconus cardinalis sanctorum Sergii et Bachi subscripsi.
Datum Viterbi, per manum[f] Guidonis sancte Romane ecclesie diaconi cardinalis et cancellarii, decimo kalendas Ianuarii, indictione nona, incarnationis Dominice anno millesimo centesimo quadragesimo sexto, pontificatus uero domni Eugenii tercii pape anno secundo.

[a] directe *B* [b] Ego *in each case is preceded by a cross B* [c] Tuperculanus *B C, deriving from the form in the original* [d] Bernardus *B* [e] *om. B* [f] annum *B*

Lord Redeemer Jesus Christ, and let him in the Last Judgment be subject to severe punishment. But let all preserving that monastery's rights for it have the peace of our Lord Jesus Christ, and let them receive the fruit of their good deed, and find in the presence of the severe Judge the rewards of eternal peace. Amen. Amen. Amen.

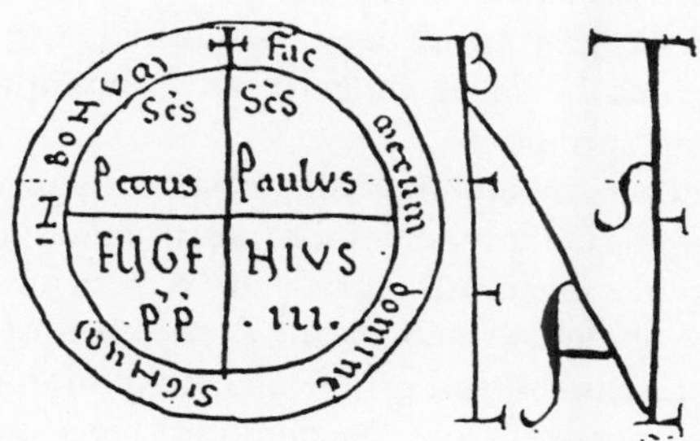

I Eugenius bishop of the Catholic church have subscribed.[656]
I Conrad bishop of Sabina have subscribed.
I Imar bishop of Tusculum have subscribed.
I Gregory cardinal priest of the title of Calissto have subscribed.
I Guy cardinal priest of the title of S. Grisogono have subscribed.
I Ubald cardinal priest of the title of S. Cruce in Gerusalemme have subscribed.
I Guy cardinal priest of the title of S. Lorenzo in Damaso have subscribed.
I Bernard cardinal priest of the title of S. Clemente have subscribed.
I Mansred cardinal priest of the title of S. Sabina have subscribed.
I Jordan cardinal priest of the title of S. Susanna have subscribed.
I Odo cardinal deacon of S. Giorgio in Velabro have subscribed.
I John cardinal deacon of S. Maria Nuova have subscribed.
I Berard cardinal deacon of the Roman church have subscribed.
I Cinthius cardinal deacon of SS. Sergio e Bacco have subscribed.

Given at Viterbo by the hand of Guy the cardinal deacon and chancellor of the Holy Roman church, on the tenth of the Kalends of January [23 Dec.], in the ninth indiction, in the year of our Lord 1146, and in the second year of the pontificate of lord Eugenius III the Pope.

[656] In the original, the names of the cardinal priests form a left-hand column, those of Eugenius, Conrad and Ymarus a central column, those of the cardinal deacons a right-hand column

267. *Item eiusdem Eugenii pape tercii aliud priuilegium de possessionibus huius ecclesie.*[657]

Eugenius episcopus seruus seruorum Dei dilectis filiis Ingulfo, abbati monasterii sancte Marie de Abbendona, eiusque fratribus, tam presentibus quam futuris, regulariter substituendis, in perpetuum. Quoniam sine uere cultu religionis, nec caritatis unitas potest subsistere, nec Deo gratum exhiberi[a] seruitium, expedit apostolice auctoritati religiosas personas diligere, et earum quieti, auxiliante Domino, salubriter prouidere.

Ea propter, dilecti in Domino filii, uestris iustis postulationibus clementer annuimus, et predecessoris nostri felicis memorie, pape Innocentii, uestigiis inherentes, prefatam ecclesiam, in qua diuino [ii. 196] mancipati estis obsequio, sub beati Petri et nostra protectione suscipimus, et presentis scripti priuilegio communimus.[658] Statuentes ut quascumque possessiones, quecumque bona, eadem ecclesia inpresentiarum iuste et canonice possidet, aut in futurum concessione pontificum, largitione regum uel principum, oblatione fidelium, seu aliis iustis modis, Deo propitio, poterit adipisci, firma uobis uestrisque successoribus et illibata permaneant.

In quibus hec propriis duximus exprimenda uocabulis. De redditibus[b] altaris:[659] ecclesiam sancti Martini; ecclesiam sancti Aldadi in Oxeneford; ecclesiam de Cumenora, cum capellis suis; ecclesiam de Niweham; ecclesiam de Offentona; ecclesiam de Witteham, cum molendino eiusdem uille; ecclesiam de Cuthesdona;[c] ecclesiam de Wicheham;[d] de ecclesia Kingestone, duos et triginta denarios; C fo. 171r dimidiam decimationem de Mercheham; | terram quam tenuit B fo. 165r Walman iuxta pontem Oxene|fordie;[660] decem acras in Hannie; mansos tres;[e] in Abbendona; quadraginta solidatas terre iuxta Coleham; decimationem lane et casei in Heldesleia de dominio; decimationem dominii in Winterburna; decimationem dominii in Westlachinga;[f] duo prata iuxta parcum; unum pratum in Niweham; unum mansum in Oxeneford, de dono Ermenoldi;[661] tres solidatas terre iuxta pontem eiusdem ciuitatis; duas oras in Draituna, et unam uirgatam terre; in Mora octo solidos; in Wintonia, foris Sudgatha, dimidiam marcam; decimationem de Middeltuna.

[a] exiberi *B* [b] reddibus *B* [c] Cudesdona *B* [d] Wicham *B* [e] *cf. Lyell, no. 24* iiij [f] Westlakinge *B*

[657] Lyell, no. 24.
[658] See above, p. xxix.

267. *Likewise another privilege of the same Pope Eugenius III concerning the possessions of this church.*[657]

Bishop Eugenius, servant of the servants of God, to his beloved sons Ingulf abbot of the monastery of St Mary of Abingdon and his brethren, both present and those in future taking their place according to the rule, in perpetuity. Since the unity of love cannot exist nor grateful service be rendered to God without the observance of true religion, it is right for the apostolic authority to love people of the religious life, and—with the Lord's help—to provide profitably for their freedom from disturbance.

Therefore, sons beloved in the Lord, we have mercifully agreed to your just requests, and, following closely in the footsteps of our predecessor of happy memory, Pope Innocent, we take under the protection of St Peter and ourselves and we fortify by the privilege of the present document the aforementioned church in which you are given over to divine service.[658] We decree that whatever possessions and whatever goods that church justly and canonically possesses at present, or in future can—God being merciful—acquire by the grant of bishops, the generosity of kings or princes, the offerings of the faithful, or in other just ways, remain to you and your successors firm and undiminished.

We have decided to describe these by their own names. Concerning the rents of the altar:[659] the church of St Martin; the church of St Aldate in Oxford; the church of Cumnor with its chapels; the church of Nuneham; the church of Uffington; the church of Wittenham with the mill of that village; the church of Cuddesdon; the church of Wickham; from the church of Kingston 32d.; half the tithe of Marcham; the land which Walman held next to the bridge of Oxford;[660] ten acres in Hanney; three messuages in Abingdon; land worth 40s. a year next to Culham; the tithe of wool and cheese from the demesne in Ilsley; the tithe of the demesne in Winterbourne; the tithe of the demesne in West Lockinge; two meadows next to the park; one meadow in Nuneham; one messuage in Oxford, by gift of Ermenold;[661] land worth 3s. a year next to the bridge of that city; two *ores* in Drayton and one virgate of land; in Moor 8s.; in Winchester outside the south gate half a mark; the tithe of Milton.

[659] Cf. the rents of the altar as described in a list in MS C in the same hand as the *History*, below, p. 397.

[660] This land cannot be precisely identified; for holdings next to the bridge of Oxford, see above, pp. 204, 258.

[661] See above, p. 204.

De communi: francum hundredum, uidelicet Abbendonam, Bertonam, Comenoram, cum omnibus appenditiis earum, et Coleham cum omni libertate quam hactenus dinoscuntur habuisse; ecclesiam de Suttuna, Mercheham, Wrdam,[a] Cerneiam, Goseiam, Offentonam, Saringeford, Wachenesfeldam, Lakingas utrasque, Fernebergam, Chiueleiam,[b] Bocsoram,[c] Walifordam,[d] Wicheham, cum omnibus appenditiis earum; Draitonam, Middeltonam, Appelfordam, Witteham, Wichenefeldam, Wischeleiam,[e] cum appenditiis earum.

[ii. 197] In episcopatu Linconiensi: quicquid terrarum et iuris habetis in Oxinefordio,[f] Leuechenoram, Cudesdonam,[g] cum appenditiis earum, Tademertuna et terram quam habetis in Hanweia;[662] [h]terram iuxta[h] Norhamtonam in Sitelhangar.[663] In Wigornensi episcopatu: Cernam et Dumeltunam, cum appenditiis suis. In [i]Cestrensi episcopatu:[i] Cestretonam.[j] In Londoniensi[k] episcopatu: cenobium quod appellatur Coles; in Londonia,[l] mansum unum ad hospicium abbatis, cum ecclesia sancte Marie que adiacet; ecclesiam iuxta Londoniam[m] de Chinsentuna. Decimationem uenationis totius foreste de Windleshora, que capitur in stabiliis regis.[664]

In parrochialibus quoque ecclesiis quas tenetis, liceat uobis honestos sacerdotes eligere et episcopis presentare, quibus, si idonei fuerint, episcopi parrochie curam animarum committant ut huiusmodi sacerdotes de plebis quidem cura episcopis respondeant, uobis uero pro rebus temporalibus debitam subiectionem exhibeant.

Obeunte uero te—nunc eiusdem loci abbate—uel tuorum quolibet successorum, nullus ibi qualibet surreptionis astutia seu uiolentia preponatur, nisi quem fratres communi consensu, uel pars consilii sanioris, secundum Deum et beati Benedicti regulam, prouiderint eligendum.

Decernimus ergo ut nulli omnino hominum liceat prefatum monasterium temere perturbare, aut eius possessiones auferre, uel ablatas retinere, minuere, uel aliquibus uexationibus fatigare, sed omnia integra conseruentur, eorum pro quorum gubernatione et sustentatione concessa sunt usibus omnimodis profutura, salua sedis apostolice auctoritate et diocesanorum episcoporum canonica iusticia.

[a] Wardam *B* [b] Chiueleam *B* [c] Boxoram *B* [d] Walingafordam *B* [e] Wischeleam *B* [f] Oxenefordio *B* [g] Cuthesdonam *B* [h–h] iuxta terram *B* [i–i] *written twice B* [j] Crestrentonam *B* [k] Lundoniensi *B* [l] Lundonia *B* [m] Lundoniam *B*

[662] In 1086 Hanwell, Oxon., had been held by Leofwine from the king; *DB* i, fo. 160[v].

Concerning the common fund: the free hundred, namely Abingdon, Barton, Cumnor, with all their appendages, and Culham, with all the liberty they are known to have enjoyed hitherto; the church of Sutton, Marcham, Longworth, Charney, Goosey, Uffington, Shellingford, Watchfield, both Lockinges, Farnborough, Chieveley, Boxford, Welford, Wickham, with all their appendages; Drayton, Milton, Appleford, Wittenham, Winkfield, Whistley, with their appendages.

In the see of Lincoln: whatever lands and right you have in Oxford; Lewknor, Cuddesdon, with their appendages; Tadmarton and the land you have in Hanwell;[662] the land next to Northampton in Shuttlehanger.[663] In the see of Worcester: Cerney, and Dumbleton with their appendages. In the see of Chester: Chesterton. In the see of London: the monastery which is called Colne. In London: one messuage at the abbot's residence with the church of St Mary which is nearby; the church of Kensington, next to London. The tithe of all game of Windsor forest, which is taken in the king's hunting enclosures.[664]

Also in the parish churches which you hold, you are to be permitted to choose worthy priests and present them to bishops. The bishops will entrust the cure of the souls of the parish to them, if they are suitable, so that priests of this sort may indeed answer to the bishops concerning the care of the people, but may show you due subjection with regard to temporal things.

Moreover, when you—now abbot of this monastery—or any of your successors die, no one is to be set in charge there by any craft or violence of deceit; rather the brethren by common consent, or the party of brethren of wiser counsel, are to choose the one to be elected, according to God and the rule of St Benedict.

We accordingly decree that it be utterly forbidden to any man to disturb recklessly the aforementioned monastery or take away its possessions, withhold what has been taken away, or diminish or trouble them with any vexations. But everything is to be preserved whole, to be beneficial for all the needs of those for whose direction and sustenance it was granted, save the authority of the apostolic see and the canonical justice of diocesan bishops.

In the twelfth century, according to *VCH*, *Oxfordshire*, ix. 115, it was 'probably in the possession of the Vernons.'

663 See above, p. 180.

664 'Stabiliis' probably refers to enclosures into which were driven game for hunting there; see Barlow, *William Rufus*, pp. 129–33.

[ii. 198] Siqua igitur in futurum ecclesiastica secularisue persona hanc
B fo. 165v nostre constitutionis paginam sciens contra eam temere ue|nire temptauerit, secundo tercioue commonita, si non satisfactione congrua emendauerit, potestatis honorisque sui dignitate careat, reamque se diuino iudicio existere de perpetrata iniquitate cognoscat, et a sacratissimo corpore ac sanguine Dei et Domini redemptoris nostri Iesu Christi aliena fiat, atque in extremo examine districte ultioni subiaceat. Cunctis autem eidem loco iusta seruantibus, sit pax
C fo. 171v Domini nostri Iesu Christi, quatinus et hic fructum | bone actionis percipiant, et apud districtum iudicem premia eterne pacis inueniant. Amen. Amen. Amen.

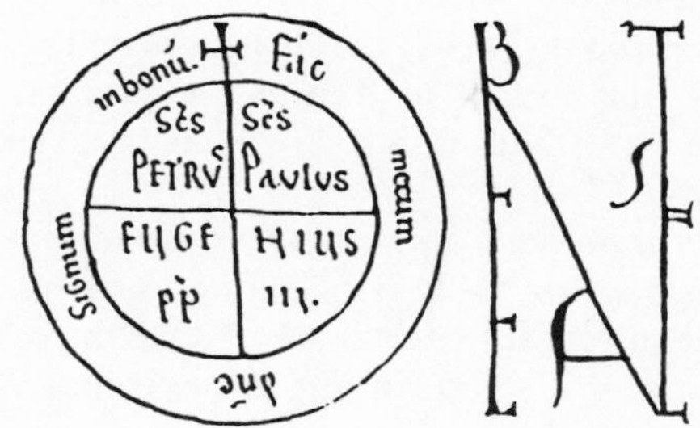

Ego[a] Eugenius catholice ecclesie episcopus subscripsi.
Ego Hugo Hostiensis episcopus subscripsi.
Ego Gregorius presbiter cardinalis titulo Calixti subscripsi.
Ego Hubaldus presbiter cardinalis titulo sancte Praxedis subscripsi.
Ego Iulius presbiter cardinalis titulo sancti Marcelli subscripsi.
Ego Bernardus presbiter cardinalis titulo sancti Clementis subscripsi.
[ii. 199] Ego Octauianus presbiter cardinalis titulo sancte Cecilie subscripsi.
Ego Rollandus presbiter cardinalis titulo sancti Marci subscripsi.
Ego Gerardus presbiter cardinalis titulo sancti Stephani in Celio Monte subscripsi.[b]
Ego Iohannes presbiter cardinalis sanctorum Iohannis et Pauli subscripsi.
Ego Cencius presbiter cardinalis titulo in Lucina[c] subscripsi.
Ego Henricus presbiter cardinalis titulo sanctorum Nerei et Achillei subscripsi.[d]

[a] Ego *in each case is preceded by a cross B* [b] *om., possibly because of lack of space B*

If, therefore, in future, any ecclesiastical or secular person who has knowledge of this document recording our decree recklessly attempts to go against it, after receiving a second and third warning, if he does not make amends with proper satisfaction, let him be deprived of the dignity of his power and honour, and let him learn that he stands in divine judgment guilty of the iniquity he perpetrated, and let him be separated from the most sacred body and blood of God and our Lord Redeemer Jesus Christ, and let him in the Last Judgment be subject to severe punishment. But let all preserving those things to which the monastery is entitled have the peace of our Lord Jesus Christ, and let them receive the fruit of their good deed, and find in the presence of the severe Judge the rewards of eternal peace. Amen. Amen. Amen.

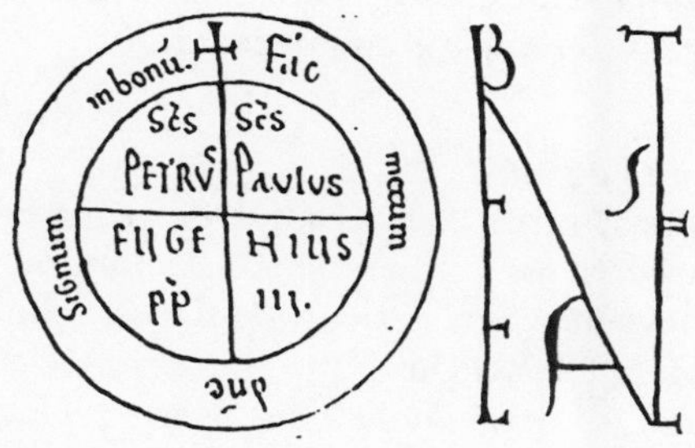

I Eugenius bishop of the Catholic church have subscribed.
I Hugh bishop of Ostia have subscribed.
I Gregory cardinal priest of the title of Callisto have subscribed.
I Hubaldus cardinal priest of the title of S. Prassede have subscribed.
I Julius cardinal priest of the title of S. Marcello have subscribed
I Bernard cardinal priest of the title of S. Clemente have subscribed.
I Octavianus cardinal priest of the title of S. Cecilia have subscribed.
I Rolland cardinal priest of the title of S. Marco have subscribed.
I Gerard cardinal priest of the title of S. Stefano in Monte Celio have subscribed.
I John cardinal priest of SS. Giovanni e Paolo have subscribed.
I Cencius cardinal priest of the title [of S. Lorenzo] in Lucina have subscribed.
I Henry cardinal priest of the title of SS. Nereo ed Achilleo have subscribed.

[c] Lucia *B* [d] *om., possibly because of lack of space, B*

Ego Otto diaconus cardinalis sancti Georgii ad Velum Aureum subscripsi.[a]
Ego Rodulfus diaconus cardinalis sancte Lucie in septa solis subscripsi.
Ego Gregorius diaconus cardinalis sancti Angeli subscripsi.
Ego Guido diaconus cardinalis sancte Marie in Porticu subscripsi.
Ego Iacinctus diaconus cardinalis sancte Marie in Cosmydyn subscripsi.
Ego Iohannes diaconus cardinalis sanctorum Sergii[b] et Bachi subscripsi.
Datum Signie, per manum Bosonis sancte Romane ecclesie scriptoris, septimo idus Aprilis, indictione quinta decima, incarnationis Dominice anno millesimo centesimo quinquagesimo secundo, pontificatus uero domni Eugenii tercii pape anno octauo.[665]

[ii. 200] **268.** *Item aliud priuilegium.*

Eugenius episcopus, seruus seruorum Dei, uenerabilibus fratribus Theodbaldo Cantuariensi archiepiscopo, Alexandro Lincoliensi, S. Wigornensi, et Iocelino[c] Saresbiriensi episcopis, salutem et apostolicam benedictionem.[666] Religiosorum fratrum Abbendonie grauem querelam accepimus, quod Willelmus Martel, Hugo de Bolebec, Willelmus de Bello campo, Iohannes Marescalus,[d] et eorum homines, et plures etiam alii parrochiani uestri, possessiones eorum uiolenter inuadunt, et bona ipsorum rapiunt et distrahunt,[e] et indebitas castellorum operationes ab eis exigunt.[667] Quia igitur nostri officii debitum nos compellit rerum[f] ecclesiasticarum[g] peruasores animaduersione debita cohercere, per apostolica uobis scripta precipiendo mandamus quatinus prefatos, et alios parrochianos uestros, qui bona ipsius monasterii inuadunt et diripiunt et iniustis exactionibus inquietant, districte commoneatis ut ablata eidem monasterio restituant, de dampnis et illatis iniuriis condigne satisfaciant, et ab eorum infestatione omnino desistant. Quod si contemptores extiterint, de

[a] *om., possibly because of lack of space B* [b] Gergii *B* [c] Iocellino *B* [d] Marescallus *B* [e] distraunt *B* [f] reum *B* [g] ecclesaisticarum *C*

[665] For Boso's title of *scriptor*, see Robinson, *Papacy*, pp. 95–6.

[666] Theobald was elected archbishop of Canterbury in 1138, consecrated in 1139, and died in 1161; Alexander was bishop of Lincoln 1123–48, Simon bishop of Worcester 1125–50, Jocelin bishop of Salisbury 1142–84; *Handbook of British Chronology*, pp. 232, 255, 278, 270.

[667] William Martel was Stephen's steward, and a very frequent witness of his charters;

I Otto cardinal deacon of S. Giorgio in Velabro have subscribed.
I Rodulf cardinal deacon of S. Lucia in Septisolio have subscribed.
I Gregory cardinal deacon of S. Angelo have subscribed.
I Guy cardinal deacon of S. Maria in Portico have subscribed.
I Iacinctus cardinal deacon of S. Maria in Cosmedin have subscribed.
I John cardinal deacon of SS. Sergio e Bacco have subscribed.
Given at Segni by the hand of Boso *scriptor* of the Holy Roman church, on the 7th of the Ides of April [7 Apr.], in the fifteenth indiction, in the year of our Lord 1152, and in the eighth year of the pontificate of lord Eugenius III the Pope.[665]

268. *Likewise, another privilege.*
Bishop Eugenius, servant of the servants of God, to the venerable brethren Archbishop Theobald of Canterbury, and Bishops Alexander of Lincoln, Simon of Worcester, and Jocelin of Salisbury, greeting and apostolic blessing.[666] We have received the serious complaint of the religious brethren of Abingdon that William Martel, Hugh de Bolbec, William de Beauchamp, John Marshal, and their men, and also many other men of your dioceses, are violently invading their possessions, and seizing and taking away their goods, and demanding from them castle-work services which are not owed.[667] Since therefore the duty of our office compels us to subdue usurpers of church possessions with fitting punishment, by ordering you through papal documents we instruct that you severely urge the aforementioned and other men of your dioceses, who invade and seize and vex with unjust exactions the goods of that monastery, that they restore to the monastery what they have taken away, and suitably compensate for the damage and the wrongs inflicted, and utterly desist from their assault. If they remain insubordinate, you are

see Cronne, *Stephen*, pp. 198–200. See *Red Book*, i. 308, *VCH*, *Berkshire*, iv. 288 n., for Martel interests in Hanney and Watchfield, and esp. below, p. 342, for a writ of Stephen which suggests that William may have been harming the abbey's lands at Whistley and Winkfield. Note also *Reading*, ii, no. 1268, for William making a restoration to Reading. He had died by 1166, as it was his son who sent in a *Carta*; *Red Book*, i. 217. Hugh de Bolbec was both a tenant-in-chief and a very significant tenant of the Giffard family; for his family, see *Red Book*, i. 312, 316–17; *Rotuli de dominabus*, pp. xxxix–xli. William de Beauchamp (I) succeeded his father, Walter, in 1131 and lived until 1170; Sanders, *Baronies*, pp. 69–70. He was sheriff of Worcester and closely linked to Waleran de Meulan, apart from a rupture in relations in 1141; Crouch, *Beaumont Twins*, pp. 38–40, 47, 51, 71, 85, 174, 209. For his oppression of the abbey of Evesham in Stephen's reign, see *Chronicon abbatiæ de Evesham ad annum 1418*, ed. W. D. Macray (London, 1863), pp. 99–100. For John Marshal in Stephen's reign, see D. B. Crouch, *William Marshal* (London, 1990), pp. 11–18; the threat may have come from his castle at Hamstead Marshal, Berks.

B fo. 166r ipsis canonicam iusticiam faciatis. | Datum Autisiodori, quinto decimo kalendas Augusti.[668]

269. *De decima in Hannie.*[669]

Rainaldus, quondam huius Abbendonensis ecclesie abbas, quandam [ii. 201] decimam de Hanni,[a] decem uidelicet acras possessionis ecclesie, cuidam sibi familiari presbitero dum uiueret tenere concessit, ita ut absque aliqua calumpnia ante obitum suum eandem restitueret huic ecclesie. Isdem[b] uero presbiter de abbatis gratia confidens, et per hoc deprauatus, decimam predictam cum quadam sua cognata iure dotis, quod de re ecclesie agere contra ecclesiam est, cuidam militi Rogero dicto donauit.[670] Hic, quia callidus erat, seruitia abbati sui temporis que poterat exhibebat, quatinus decimam quam acceperat, quia iure non poterat, gratia quadam sibi retineret; quod et quamdiu uixit optinuit. Sed Rogero ad finem adducto, Ingulfus—tunc huius abbas ecclesie—cum cognouisset[c] qualiter illam acceperit, eandem saisaiuit, et annis plus minus quatuor tenuit. Assiduis tamen postmodum C fo. 172r precibus Roberti, Rogeri | predicti filii, et amicorum eius qui tunc potentes[d] in werra erant, fatigatus, timens ne si petitioni eorum contrairet, illorum odium et maius ecclesie dampnum incurreret, decimam Roberto ad tempus tenere permisit. Robertus uero hanc se diu tenere posse diffidens, eam aliis uendere curauit. Sed qui ad emendum uocati erant, contra ecclesiam cuius erat decima inconsulte agere nolentes, emere recusabant. Istis ergo deficientibus, ad sacristam huius ecclesie, Ricardum nomine, se contulit, qui oportunum tempus aduenisse uidens quo decimam diu ablatam ecclesie restitueret,[671] quam iniuriose eam tenuerit Roberto demonstrauit, preces pro restitutione adiungens, et, ut ad summum proficeret, septem ei marcas animo bono donauit. Quibus acceptis, Robertus super magnum altare, filio suo quem heredem habuit astante et idem confirmante, absque[e] aliqua in posterum calumpnia perpetuo deci- [ii. 202] mam predictam concessit. Teste Hugone filio Berneri, Iohanne de Tubbeneia, Roberto de Wicham, Adam uicecomite, et aliis nonnullis quos nominare non est necesse.[672] Ricardus autem per hoc quod iam

[a] Hannie *B* [b] Hisdem *B C* [c] coonguisset *B* [d] potens *B* [e] abque *B*

[668] 1147; see *Papsturkunden in England*, ed. W. Holtzmann (3 vols., Berlin and Göttingen, 1930–52), iii. 193–203. [669] See also below, p. 397.

[670] Here, and below, p. 284, *dos* is used to mean dowry, that is, property given by a father to his son-in-law; in the chapter after this one, below, p. 282, it is used to mean dower, that is, land assigned to a wife by her husband, or land deemed to be the equivalent

to do canonical justice concerning these matters. Given at Auxerre on the fifteenth of the Kalends of August [18 Jul.].[668]

269. *Concerning the tithe in Hanney.*[669]
Reginald, once abbot of this church of Abingdon, granted a tithe of Hanney, that is ten acres, which belonged to the church, to a priest who was close to him, to hold as long as he lived, in such a way that before his death he would restore it to this church without any claim. This priest, however, corrupted by his trust in the good grace of the abbot, gave the aforesaid tithe with a kinswoman of his to a knight named Roger, by right of dowry, thereby acting against the church concerning the church's possession.[670] Since he was crafty, Roger did the abbot of his time those services he could, so that by abbatial favour he might retain the tithe he had received, since he could not retain it by right; and this he achieved as long as he lived. But Roger reached the end of his life, and when Ingulf—then abbot of this church—learnt how Roger had acquired that tithe, he seized it and held it for approximately four years. Afterwards, however, he was worn down by the persistent prayers of Robert, Roger's son, and his friends, who then were powerful in war, and fearing that if he opposed their request he would incur their hatred and greater harm to the church, he allowed Robert to hold that tithe for a while. Robert then doubted that he would be able to hold it for long and took steps to sell it to others, but those called upon to buy it were unwilling to act ill-advisedly against the church, whose tithe it was, and declined to buy. They defaulted and Robert therefore went to the sacrist of this church, named Richard, who saw that an opportune time had arrived for restoring to the church the long lost tithe.[671] He showed Robert how wrongfully he held it, added prayers for its restitution, and good-heartedly gave him seven marks so that he might attain complete success. Robert accepted these, and on the great altar granted the aforesaid tithe forever, with no claim in future, with his son whom he held as his heir present and confirming this. Witness: Hugh son of Berner, John of Tubney, Robert of Wickham, Adam the sheriff, and some others whom it is not necessary to name.[672] Moreover, when Richard had secured this outcome in

of such an assignment. See also 'Glanvill', *Tractatus de Legibus*, bk. vi, c. 1, bk. vii, c. 1, ed. Hall, pp. 58–9, 69 for these two meanings.

[671] On the place of Richard the sacrist within the *History*, see above, p. lviii.

[672] On John of Tubney, see above, p. lxiv. Robert's surname may be from Wickham, Berks.

diximus de patre securus effectus, suspicans ne per filium in posterum peruerse quid accideret, zonam ei ceruinam optimam dedit et nummos duodecim, et in capitulo, coram conuentu, super sacras reliquias iurare fecit quod nunquam, per se neque per alterum, quereret quo pactio iam facta minus firma consisteret.

270. *De dimidia hida*[a] *in Boreshulla.*[673]

Idem preterea Robertus dimidiam hidam[b] terre in Boreshulla[c] post patris decessum, quorumdam amicorum suorum adiutus auxilio, ui detinebat, quam abbas Vincentius patri suo Rogero, dum uiueret et non aliter, aut dedit aut tenere concessit.[674] Abbas autem Ingulfus terre predicte perditionem non leuiter ferens, Robertum in curia sua[d] euocatum, ad hoc tandem, quamuis laboriose, perduxit, quod dimidiam illam hidam ipse cum herede suo abbati quietam omnino |
B fo. 166v clamauit, et manu in manum reddidit.[e] Quam ita recuperatam abbas sacriste Ricardo dedit, osculata sibi manu ab ipso. Ne tamen Robertus aliquando super hoc graue ferret, aut peruersum moueret, dedit ei Ricardus solidos uiginti, preter alios quinquaginta quos ei prius super terram eandem, pro spe recuperandi, accomodauerat. Sicque factum est ut ipse Robertus, toto astante conuentu, dimidiam illam hidam super magnum altare, absque omni in posterum reclamatione, confirmaret. Postea tamen Roberti uxor asserens hanc in dotem sibi
[ii. 203] fuisse donatam, a rege Henrico iuniore, qui post Stephanum regnauit, breue quoddam abbati Ingulfo detulit, sensum habens ut super hac calumpnia rectum [f]abbatem et mulierem[f] examinaret. Breui autem perlecto, astante muliere, communi sapientium plurimorum qui uocati erant consideratione, ostensum est de terra ad eam nil pertinere. Et muliere quidem ad propria reuertente, causa hec [g]ita finita est.[g]

271. *De decima in Westlakinge.*[675]

Cooperante eodem Ricardo, miles quidam, Giralmus de Curzun, decimam triginta acrarum de Westlakinge, quam parentes sui prius concesserant, et ipse altari sancte Marie concessit, addens de porcellis, siue agnellis, aut caseis, et rebus aliis que decimari solent, decimam, quam priores sui minime dederant. Hanc uero donationem super altare sancte Marie deuotus optulit, trium tantum acrarum

[a] hidam *B* [b] *om. B* [c] Boreshilla *B* [d] *om. B* [e] reddit *B*
[f–f] *for* abbatis et mulieris ? [g–g] est ita finita *B*

673 Berks. *English Lawsuits*, no. 378. See also below, p. 397.
674 The phrase 'either given or granted' is peculiar. It may signify that the chronicler

relation to the father, he feared lest in future some wrong might occur through the son, so he gave him an excellent deerskin belt and twelve penny coins, and made him swear on sacred relics in the chapter in the presence of the convent that he would never seek, through himself or another, that the current agreement be weakened.

270. *Concerning half a hide in Boars Hill.*[673]
After his father's death, the same Robert, aided and assisted by some of his friends, forcibly detained half a hide of land in Boars Hill, which Abbot Vincent had either given or granted to Roger his father to hold as long as he lived and not otherwise.[674] But Abbot Ingulf, not bearing the loss of that land lightly, summoned Robert to his court, and after much time and labour achieved the following result: Robert with his heir entirely quitclaimed that half hide to the abbot, and gave it back, placing his hand in the abbot's. The abbot gave the land thus recovered to Richard the sacrist, who kissed his hand. However, lest Robert at some time feel resentful about this or proceed to do wrong, Richard gave him 20s., besides the other 50s. which he had previously loaned him on the land in the hope of regaining it. And so it happened that Robert, in the presence of the whole convent, confirmed that half hide on the great altar, without any future claim. However, Robert's wife afterwards asserted that this had been given to her in dower, and brought to Abbot Ingulf a writ from King Henry the younger, who reigned after Stephen, to the effect that, concerning this claim, he would examine the abbot and woman as to their right. The writ, then, was read in the woman's presence and, by the common decision of the large number of wise men who had been summoned, it was shown that nothing from that land pertained to her. And the woman returned home, and so this case ended.

271. *Concerning the tithe of West Lockinge.*[675]
With the co-operation of the same Richard, a certain knight, Giralmus de Curzon, himself granted to the altar of St Mary the tithe of thirty acres of West Lockinge, which his parents previously had granted, and added the tithe of piglets, lambs, cheeses, and other goods which are accustomed to be tithed, which his predecessors had not given in the slightest. Moreover, he devoutly offered this gift on the altar of St Mary, keeping back from the

was uncertain whether Abbot Vincent had made the initial grant to Roger, or had merely allowed him to continue in existing possession for the remainder of his life.

[675] See also above, p. 44.

decima de triginta ecclesie de Wanetinge reseruata. Hanc eandem quoque donationem suam Giralmus, in capitulo coram omni conuentu, presente abbate Ingulfo, confirmauit, teste Sarico coco et aliis pluribus.[676] Sacrista uero ei decem solidos tunc in testimonium uice
C fo. 172v caritatis dedit. Hic[a] idem tamen Giralmus, | causa nescio qua postea deprauatus, decimam predictam in horreo reposuit, sed a Ricardo redargutus, penitentiam agens, horrei seras manu propria confregit et decimam ecclesie reddidit, nichilque tale se amplius facturum iuramento confirmans. Aliquanto uero postea euoluto tempore, optinuit
[ii. 204] Giralmus a sacrista ut ei septem[b] solidos accomodaret tempore statuto absque dilatione reddendos. Sed termino prefinito adueniente, altero quoque necnon et tercio, sacrista quod accomodauerat adquirere nequiuit. Insuper iterum Giralmus decimam in horreo reposuit, ut dum utrumque negaret, si unum redderet, alterum quomodocumque[c] retineret. Ricardus namque cum eo uerbis confligens, hoc tandem ab eo extorsit, ut si ei septem[d] solidos quos accomodauerat condonaret, et decimam quam acceperat gratis concederet, tres ei quartarios frumenti cum gratiarum actione daret, et decimam absque ulla reclamatione perpetuo concederet et testibus confirmaret. Ricardus autem petitionibus eius consentiens, coram his et multis aliis testibus confirmari idem[e] fecit: Petro de Vernun, Hugone filio Ricardi, Osmundo de Graua, Simone de Churlintuna.[f][677] Hoc ergo tandem ita se habuit et talem exitum accepit. |

B fo. 167r **272.** *De una uirgata terre in Draituna.*

Quidam, Radulfus uocabulo, uirgatam unam terre in Draituna tenebat, que altari sancte Marie triginta duos denarios omni anno reddebat, quam idem Radulfus cuidam Rogero cum filia sua in dotem donauit.[678] Cum autem obisset Rogerus, filius eius Thomas, fauente sibi matre, cum annis pluribus debitum altari persoluere non posset, ad Ricardum sacristam se contulit, petens ut ei aliquid supra quod debebat[g] conferret, quatinus ei uirgatam illam animo bono omnino habendam concederet. Cumque eidem Thome in denariis et rebus

[a] *initial om. C* [b] *om. B* [c] quocumque *B* [d] vi. *B* [e] *om. B*
[f] Churlintune *B* [g] debeat *B*

[676] See below, p. 396, for a list of the kitchen's rents in the same hand as the *History*, which mentions a Saric.

[677] For a Vernun family with lands in Oxfordshire and Berkshire, see *Anglo-Norman Families*, p. 110, *HKF* ii. 276; Peter may have been a member of this family. A monk called Peter de Vernun witnessed C.H., no. 1a, which dates from 1165 × 1175. For a Hugh son of Richard active in Faritius's time, see above, pp. 158, 216. The 1166 *Carta* of the honour of

thirty only the tithe of three acres for the church of Wantage. Giralmus also confirmed this gift of his in the chapter before all the convent in Abbot Ingulf's presence, with Saric the cook and many others as witness.[676] The sacrist then gave him 10s. as a free gift in testimony. However, this Giralmus was afterwards led astray by I know not what cause, and once more placed the aforesaid tithe in his barn. But rebuked by Richard, he did penance and with his own hands broke the bolts of the barn and gave the tithe back to the church, confirming with an oath that he would do nothing similar again. After some time had passed, however, Giralmus obtained from the sacrist that he would lend him 7s., to be repaid without delay at a fixed time. But when the set time arrived, the sacrist could not acquire what he had lent, nor could he do so on a second or even a third occasion. Furthermore, Giralmus again placed the tithe in his barn, so that—while he refused to give either the loan or the tithe—if he gave back one he would retain the other no matter what. But Richard spoke and reasoned with him and at length extracted from him that if Richard excused Giralmus the 7s. loaned, and freely granted him the tithe which he had taken, Giralmus would give him three quarters of corn in thanks, and would grant and by witnesses confirm the tithe in perpetuity without any further challenge. Richard agreed to Giralmus's requests and had this confirmed in the presence of the following and many other witnesses: Peter de Vernun, Hugh son of Richard, Osmund of Grove, Simon of Charlton.[677] This therefore went on for a long time thus and had the above outcome.

272. *Concerning one virgate of land in Drayton.*

A certain man named Ralph was holding one virgate of land in Drayton, which each year rendered 32d. to the altar of St Mary. Ralph gave this virgate to a certain Roger as a dowry with his daughter.[678] But after Roger died, his son Thomas was for very many years unable to pay what was due to the altar, so, supported by his mother, he went to Richard the sacrist and sought that Richard might confer on him something in addition to what he owed, so that he would good-heartedly grant Richard that virgate to have completely. And when Richard had compensated Thomas with pennies

Wallingford records a Hugh son of Richard owing two knights; *Red Book*, i. 309. Simon and Osmund were probably of Charlton, about one mile from West Lockinge, and Grove a further mile away; both are in Berkshire.

[678] For a Ralph holding land in Drayton, see below, p. 387.

ceteris satisfecisset, predicta uirgata a Ricardo libere saisiata, in officium sacristerii est redacta.

[ii. 205] 273. *De quadam domo.*

Huius quoque Ricardi adquisitione sollerti, quidam Robertus, presbiter de Mercham, domum[a] quandam, quam sibi liberam et omnino quietam parauerat, Deo et altari sancte Marie donauit. Et quia ille[b] ultima infirmitate iam laborabat et illuc ire non poterat, cuidam Waltero de Coleshulle, cognato suo, uice sua domum eandem super magnum altare offerre precepit, omni astante conuentu, clericis quoque et laicis pluribus.[679] Quod postquam ut uoluit factum est, ipse a uita presenti decessit. Postea tamen quidam Willelmus, cognomento Pincun, quia pars aliqua predicte domus supra terram suam nam proxima erat fundata uidebatur, calumpniam mouit et frequenter in litigium uenit. Cuius importunitatem sacrista deuitans, assidua prece[c] eiusdem et aliorum amicorum eius plurimorum, domum eandem pro duodecim nummis per annos singulos Willelmo tenere permisit, ita ut idem Willelmus domum erga prepositum acquietaret, et si quid aliud reddendum pro ea contingeret.[d][680]

274. *De domibus Scalegrai in ista uilla.*[681]

Ricardo adhuc persuadente, quidam 'Scalegrai' uulgariter nominatus de domibus suis ecclesiam heredem facere cogitauit. Quod cum duo eius propinqui audirent, Robertus uidelicet de Lakinge et alius quidam Robertus, hereditariam super domos illas[e] calumpniam
[ii. 206] mouerunt. Qui causa in communi hallimot ad hoc tandem perducta est, ut uterque calumpniator, quia ibi nichil iuris habebat, uacuus a spe sua, ut iustum erat, recederet. Sicque predictus Scalegrai domos suas uoluntarie huic ecclesie donauit, et quia iter longinquum transire habebat, sacrista noster marcam unam libenter ei ad uiaticum largitus est, et causam istam domibus ad se receptis taliter terminauit.

275. *Item de alia quadam terra.*[682] |

C fo. 173r Mulier iterum quedam Beliardis dicta, Sturnelli cuiusdam uxor, huius Ricardi industria prouocata, post uiri sui decessum domos suas altare sancte Marie attitulare disposuit. Sed et talia cogitanti, calumpniatores[f] quidam, qui iuris ibi[g] aliquid se habere

[a] donum *B* [b] illæ *C* [c] *ends with half completed* s *C*; preces *B* [d] continget *B* [e] alias *B* [f] calumniatores *B* [g] sibi *B*

[679] Walter was presumably associated with Coleshill, Berks.

and other things, the aforesaid virgate was freely seized by Richard and restored to the office of the sacristy.

273. *Concerning a certain house.*

Also through Richard's skilled procurement, a certain Robert, priest of Marcham, gave to God and to the altar of St Mary a house which he had obtained for himself free and entirely undisturbed. And since he was now suffering his final illness and could not go there, in his place he ordered his kinsman, Walter of Coleshill, to offer that house on the great altar, with all the convent present and also very many clerics and laymen.[679] After this was done as he wished, he departed the present life. However, afterwards a certain William, surnamed Pincun, moved a claim and frequently brought lawsuits that part of the aforesaid house appeared to rest on his adjoining land. The sacrist ignored his insistence, but William and very many other friends of his were persistent in their requests, so Richard allowed William to hold that house for twelve penny coins each year, in such a way that William acquitted the house regarding the reeve and if there were anything else which ought to be rendered for it.[680]

274. *Concerning the houses of Scalegrai in this place.*[681]

Also at the Richard's urging, a man named in the vernacular Scalegrai considered making the church heir of his houses. When two of his relatives, namely Robert of Lockinge and another Robert, heard this, they moved a hereditary claim on those houses. At length this case was held in the common hallmoot with the following result, that both claimants left emptied of hope, as was just since they had no right there. And so the aforesaid Scalegrai of his free will gave his houses to this church, and since he had a long distance to travel, our sacrist gladly gave him one mark for his travelling expenses. Thus, after receiving the houses for himself, he brought this case to an end.

275. *Likewise, concerning certain other land.*[682]

Roused again by the labours of this Richard, a certain woman called Beliardis, wife of one Sturnell, following the death of her husband, decided to consign her houses to the altar of St Mary. But some claimants, who thought they had some right there, rose against her as

680 A list in MS C in the same hand as the *History*, below, p. 397, includes 12d. from the land of William Pincun among the revenues of the altar.

681 *English Lawsuits*, no. 379; see also below, p. 397, a list in MS C in the same hand as the *History*.

682 *English Lawsuits*, no. 380; see also above, p. xciii.

putabant, insurrexerunt; sed ueritatis inuestigatione a sapientibus, qui causam utramque tractabant, utpote calumpniam iniustam
B fo. 167v inferentes, | postmodum, ut rectum erat, repulsi sunt. Mulier autem iam libera utens potestate domos suas altari sancte Marie animo bono concessit, eique Ricardus quatuordecim solidos pro hac concessione in manum posuit, et domos taliter a muliere donatas recepit. Nec pretereundum quod quidam canonicus transmarinus, Sturnelli predicti filius, calumpniam mouens aduenit, sed ubi se nichil proficere posse attendit, ad locum unde uenerat recessit, nec ulterius ut calumpniam moueret rediit.[a]

276. *De terra Rogeri Haliman.*[683]

Rogerius quidam sacerdos de Walingefor,[b] cui cognomen erat Hali-
[ii. 207] man, cum filio nomine Thoma, in ista ecclesia Abbendonensi habitum monachi suscipiens,[684] mansiones duas[c] domorum sui iuris pertinentes altari sancte Marie donauit, sed in werra ui militum in eodem castello manentium per aliquod tempus fuerunt alienate. Facta autem pace sub rege Henrico iuniore, omnes barones simul congregatos illius oppidi una cum Henrico filio Geroldi, tunc quidem oppidano illius castelli, Ricardus sacrista adiit, et in tantum coram eis profecit, quod miles, Ricardus nomine, qui terram eandem tenebat, coram omnibus ecclesiam istam saisiaret.[685] Sed quia idem miles nouas domos super iam dictam terram fecerat, interuentu eorum qui ibi congregati erant, iterum eum resaisiauit, recepturus ab eo aut qui ibi manserit annuatim sex denarios, et pro domo altera in qua manebat quidam Gerardus Rufus, iterum alios sex denarios.

277. *De terra quadam in Walingaford.*

Similiter quidam de uilla eadem desiderium habens, Æilwinus dictus,[686] ut cum filio paruulo in hac ecclesia monachus fieret, inter cetera domos suas cum terra altari sancte Marie optulit, que in werra, ueluti multe res[d] alie, parum utilitatis ecclesie contulerunt. Sed werra cessante, quia domus predicte confracte erant, terram eandem sacrista cuidam burgensium pro duodecim denariis per annum dimisit.

[a] reddit *B* [b] Walingeford *B* [c] suas *B* [d] *corr. from* rex *C*; rex *B*

683 See also below, p. 397.

684 On priests with children, see C. N. L. Brooke, 'Gregorian reform in action: clerical marriage in England, 1050–1200', *Cambridge Historical Journal*, xii (1956), 1–21. For this gift, see also *Testa de Nevill*, i. 110.

685 Henry son of Gerold was also Henry II's chamberlain; see further Amt, *Accession of Henry II*, pp. 60–1, *Boarstall Cartulary*, p. 309. The 1166 *Carta* for Wallingford includes

she was considering these matters. However, as one might expect for those bringing forward an unjust claim, they were afterwards repulsed, as was just, through investigation of the truth by the wise men who were treating both sides' case. Moreover, the woman used her unrestricted power and granted her houses good-heartedly to the altar of St Mary, and for this grant Richard placed 14s. in her hand, and received the houses given thus by the woman. And it should not be passed over that a canon from overseas, the son of the aforesaid Sturnell, came and moved a claim, but when he recognized that he could make no progress, he returned to the place whence he had come and never came back to move a claim again.

276. *Concerning the land of Roger Haliman.*[683]
A certain Roger, priest of Wallingford, who had the surname Haliman, assumed the monk's habit in this church of Abingdon, together with his son named Thomas.[684] He gave to the altar of St Mary two holdings of houses which were his property, but during the war they were alienated for a time by the force of the knights who were resident in Wallingford castle. But when peace had been made under King Henry the younger, Richard the sacrist came to a gathering of all the barons of that fortress, together with Henry son of Gerold, then castellan of that castle, and in their presence he achieved such success that the knight named Richard, who was holding the land concerned, seised the church in the presence of all.[685] But since that knight had built new houses on the aforesaid land, the sacrist reseised him again on the intervention of those gathered there, and in future would receive from him or whoever lived there 6d. a year, and again another 6d. for another house in which a certain Gerard Rufus lived.

277. *Concerning certain land in Wallingford.*
Likewise a man of that town, called Æilwin,[686] desired to become a monk in this church, together with his little son, and offered to the altar of St Mary his houses with land, amongst other things. During the war, these, like many other possessions, brought negligible advantage to the church. But with the war ending, the sacrist bestowed that land on one of the burgesses for 12d. a year, since the aforesaid houses had been destroyed.

more than one knight named Richard; *Red Book*, i. 308–11. Lyell, no. 255 gives Richard the surname 'le Blunt'.

[686] This is probably the Æilwin son of Wulfreuen mentioned in *Testa de Nevill*, i. 110, as making a gift when he became a monk. See also below, p. 397, and above, n. 541, on the name form.

278. *De festiuitate reliquiarum.*[687]

Considerans hic idem sacrista Ricardus quia in ecclesia ista[a] multe
[ii. 208] sanctorum reliquie reseruantur, quorum tunc temporis nulla celebrabatur memoria, consensu abbatis et totius conuentus, diem Martis qui primo post quindecim dies Pasce occurrit, quo omnium reliquiarum huius ecclesie habetur memoria primus instituit, quadraginta solidorum redditum proprio labore adquisitum adiungens, quo inter festa principalia dies ille honorifice, ut dignum est, perpetuo celebretur.

279. *De organis.*

Organa[b] quoque, de sumptu proprio, idem Ricardus in ecclesia ista constituit, de adquisitione sua redditum attitulans, quo in posterum reparari aut manuteneri[c] possent. Genuas[d] similiter ex ferro decenter compositas, primus in ecclesia hac fabricari fecit. In uasis uero argenteis aut metalli alterius, candelabris uel campanis,
B fo. 168r uel rebus pluribus ad ornatum ecclesie pertinentibus, mag|na habetur in hac ecclesia istius uiri memoria. Hec de iam mortuo enarraui, nec me suspicabitur aliquis uelle adulari cineribus. Ex hinc ad alia transeamus.[688]

280. *De Suinlea.*[e][689]

Abbatis istius Ingulfi tempore, quedam ecclesie possessiones, quasi[f] sub specie recti quia abbate uolente, iniuste tamen quia ad ecclesie dampnum, sunt distracte. In werra enim terra quedam ecclesie, Swinleia dicta, possessoribus predantium metu eam tenere non
C fo. 173v ualentibus, sicuti | plures et ipsa deserta iacebat. Quod uidentes, monachi albi de Stretford abbatem Ingulfum adierunt, tam prece
[ii. 209] quam pretio ab eo nitentes optinere, ut ipsis sex solidos per annum reddentibus terram illam habere concederet.[690] Quorum uerbis et muneribus abbas adquiescens, consentientibus sibi aliquibus fratribus[g] quos monachi predicti munere placauerant, terram quam petebant eis tradidit, et litteris suis et sigillo ecclesie contra conuentus uoluntatem confirmauit. Sigillum enim ecclesie sub potestate propria detinebat, et quod uolebat illo confirmabat. Vnde etiam factum est, ut

[a] *om. B* [b] *initial contains small picture of organ with pipes C* [c] manu teneri *B*
[d] *I take* genuas *to be intended as a version of* ianuas [e] Suuinlea *B* [f] quas *B*
[g] fribus *B*

[687] See above, p. cvi.

[688] Richard appears to have died after the coronation of Henry II, 19 Dec. 1154, but before the death of Ingulf, 19 Sept. 1158.

278. *Concerning the festival of the relics.*[687]
The same sacrist Richard contemplated that there were preserved in this church many relics of saints of whom no commemoration was then celebrated. With the consent of the abbot and the whole convent, he was the first to institute the Tuesday immediately after the Easter fortnight as the day on which the commemoration of all this church's relics is held, and added 40s. rent, acquired by his own toil, whereby that day would be honourably celebrated for ever amongst the principal feasts, as is fitting.

279. *Concerning the organs.*
That Richard also set organs in place in this church at his own expense, consigning from his own acquisition rent by which they could be repaired or maintained in future. Similarly he was the first to have suitably formed iron doors constructed in this church. Also in this church vessels of silver or other metal, candlesticks, bells, and a great many other things which adorn the church preserve the great memory of this man. I have related these matters concerning a man now dead, and no one will suspect me of wishing to flatter ashes. Let us pass hence to other matters.[688]

280. *Concerning Swinley.*[689]
In Abbot Ingulf's time, some of the church's possessions were taken away with a veneer of propriety, in that the abbot so wished, but unjustly, in that it harmed the church. For during the war, some of the church's land, called Swinley, lay abandoned; like many others, its possessors were unable to hold it out of fear of predators. Seeing this, the White Monks of Stratford came to Abbot Ingulf, striving to obtain from him by both prayer and payment that he grant to them to have that land, in return for rendering 6s. a year.[690] The abbot agreed to their words and gifts, and, with the consent of certain of the brethren whose favourable disposition the monks of Stratford had gained with gifts, handed over to them the land which they sought, confirming this by his letters and the church's seal, against the will of the convent. For he kept the seal of the church under his own control and confirmed with it what he wished. Therefore after his death it

[689] Swinley was in Winkfield; *VCH*, *Berkshire*, iii. 87. On the writer's attitude to Ingulf, see above, p. lii.

[690] The Cistercian house at Stratford Langthorne, Essex, had been founded on 25 Jul. 1135; *Heads of Religious Houses*, p. 144.

post eius obitum [a]pleraque sigilla ab eo inutiliter facta,[a] frangerentur. Monachi uero terram prefatam recipientes, sic detinent, et in perpetuum detinere nituntur.[691]

281. *De Hachamste.*[b]

Iterum quidam clericus de Luuechenora, Ansgerus[c] dictus, uillam eandem de abbate Ingulfo diu tenuit, eique seruitia que potuit exhibuit. Qui cum in abbatis fauorem uenisset, tam prece quam pretio ab eo optinuit in feudo et hereditate quoddam membrum de Luuechenora, Hachamstede[d] dictum, pro solidis quadraginta tenere, quod antea quinquaginta reddere solebat.[692] Quod contra uoluntatem et utilitatem conuentus factum est, et abbatis litteris et ecclesie sigillo quod (ut diximus) in manu propria habebat confirmatum.

282. *De terra quadam apud Bertuna.*

Similiter huius abbatis concessu, Hugo filius Berneri terram, que a Bertuna curiam uersus itinerantibus dextrorsum est (quam ueneran-
[ii. 210] dus abbas Faritius a predicto Bernero escambiauit pro terra que Blachegraua[e] dicitur pro .[f] solidos per annum) optinuit sine conuentus assensu, reddentem undeuiginti solidos, sine aliis consuetudinibus, et nouem denarios.[693]

Item[g] huius abbatis dono Willelmus, cognomento Paulinus, nouem acras de dominio de Bertona adeptus est, et contra ecclesiam[h] istam detinet. Talibus modis possessiones ecclesie debilitantur, donec per uirum a Deo datum iterum aliquando unde sublate sunt restituantur.

283. *De pecunia quam rex in ecclesia ista accepit.*

Non solum autem in exterioribus possessionibus magnum detrimentum ecclesia ista illo tempore passa est, uerum etiam in interioribus. Nam pecuniam permaximam quam ipse abbas congregauerat, et quicquid in ecclesia custodiendi causa depositum fuerat, per[i] proditionem quorundam abbatis amicorum ad exercitus sui stipendia rex Stephanus depredauit. Postea uero, circa finem abbatis, quicquid

[a–a] plerique sigilli ab eo inutiliter facti *B C* [b] Hachamsted' *over erasure B* [c] Angerus *B* [d] Hacamsteda *B* [e] Blakegraua *B* [f] x *erased C* [g] *preceded by rubricated heading of minims B* [h] ecclesia *B C* [i] *probably corr. from* pro *C*; pro *B*

[691] See *Monasticon Anglicanum*, ed. W. Dugdale, J. Caley *et al.* (6 vols. in 8, London, 1817–30), v. 588, for a charter of Henry II confirming to the monks of Stratford grants of various donors, including the grange at Swinley, with its appurtenances, which they have from the monks of Abingdon; Lyell, no. 362, for a final concord between the abbots of

was ensured that many seal impressions harmfully made by him were broken. But the monks who received the aforementioned land still withhold it thus and strive to withhold it for ever.[691]

281. *Concerning Ackhamstead.*
Again, a certain cleric of Lewknor, called Ansger, long held that village from Abbot Ingulf and did him what service he could. When he came into the abbot's favour, by both prayer and payment he obtained from him a member of Lewknor, called Ackhamstead, to hold in fee and inheritance for 40s., which previously was accustomed to render 50s.[692] This was done contrary to the will and interests of the convent, and was confirmed by the abbot's letters and the church's seal, which, as we have said, he had in his own possession.

282. *Concerning certain land at Barton.*
Likewise, by grant of this abbot, without the assent of the convent, Hugh son of Berner obtained the land which is to the right for travellers from Barton towards the court and renders 19s. 9d. without any other customs. The venerable abbot Faritius had received this in exchange from the aforesaid Berner for the land which is called Blagrove for [blank] shillings a year.[693]

Likewise, William surnamed Paulinus acquired nine acres of the demesne of Barton by this abbot's gift and retains it against this church. In such ways the possessions of the church are impaired, until, through a man given by God, they may sometime be restored again whence they have been taken away.

283. *Concerning the money which the king seized in this church.*
Moreover, this church suffered great loss at that time not only in external possessions, but also internal ones. For through the treachery of some of the abbot's friends, King Stephen plundered, for his army's pay, the vast amount of money which Abbot Ingulf had gathered and whatever had been deposited in the church for safekeeping. Later, moreover, around the time of the abbot's end, almost

Abingdon and Stratford concerning land at Swinley; the document can be dated to 1189 × 1197.

[692] On Ackhamstead, see above, p. 140.

[693] See above, p. 202, for the exchange. For the area of the monastic precinct known as the court, see Plan, p. cv.

pene auri et argenti in scriniis sanctorum uel uasis in ecclesia
B fo. 168v repertum est pro reddendis | debitis ipsius distractum.[694]

284. [a]*De Henrico rege iuniore.*

Interea rege Stephano defuncto anno nonodecimo regni sui, Henricus iunior successit in regnum, cessauitque mirabilis werra totius Anglie.[a]

[ii. 211] **285.** *Carta de decima Ciltune.*[b]

Notum sit presentibus et futuris, testimonio huius scripti sigillo mei signati, quod ego Nicholaus filius Turoldi de Estuna, pro salute anime mee parentumque meorum, et pro eo quod licitum mihi esset[c] ab ecclesia de Abbendona cimiterium haberi capelle mee de Winterburna, concessi firmiter et finaliter dedi predicte ecclesie Abbendonensi singulis annis in perpetuum habendas decimas terre mee quam in dominio meo teneo in uilla Chiltune; in blado scilicet ad ostium grancie mee suscipiendo, et in caseis et in uelleribus et agnis et porcellis, et in omnibus que decimari solent.[695] Insuper firmiter statui ecclesiam de Chiuelea singulis annis de duabus acris[d] ex dominio meo in Winterburna, unus[e] frumenti et alius auene, uel duobus solidis, recognoscendam in electione mei post discessum Helie clerici, et ita quod deinceps ego prefate capelle de Winterburna seruiende perso-
C fo. 174r nam eligam | et ponam, saluo iure rerum[f] episcopalium. Hec donatio facta est in die sancti Laurentii, in capitulo Abbendonensi, anno secundo Henrici regis, presente Ingulfo abbate, et Waltero priore, ceterisque fratribus.[696] His testibus etiam subscriptis: Rogero archidiacono, magistro Rannulfo, Helia clerico de Chiuelea, Ricardo fratre eiusdem Nicholai, Hamone Pirun, Ricardo de Henreda,[g] Iohanne de Tubbeneia, Henrico de Pisia.[697]

[ii. 212] Concedente itaque abbate, predicta decima ad usum pauperum et peregrinorum consignata est, ipso Nicholao astante et magnopere[h] gratias agente, quod elemosinam suam ad tale negotium deputasset.[698]

[a–a] *om. B* [b] *heading erased B* [c] esse *B C* [d] *the text here appears to be flawed; the addition of a phrase such as* decimas recepturam *would start to restore the sense* [e] unius *B C* [f] uerum *B* [g] Henereda *B* [h] magnoopere *B*

---

[694] See above, p. liv, for the different account of Stephen's plundering of Abingdon in *De abbatibus*; *CMA* ii. 291–2.

[695] Nicholas's toponymic surname was from Aston Tirold, Berks.; on this family, tenants of the earls of Warwick, see *VCH*, *Berkshire*, iii. 453, iv. 63–4, *Red Book*, i. 326. Lyell, nos. 356, 484, Chatsworth, no. 83 (= *English Lawsuits*, no. 617), show Nicholas in dispute with Abingdon in 1186 × 9 over the advowson of the church of Winterbourne. On the tithe, see also *CMA* ii. 327, a list concerning rents due to the almoner, in a hand different from that of the *History*.

[696] For Walter, see above, p. lvii.

all the gold and silver found in the saints' reliquaries and in the church vessels was removed to pay his debts.[694]

284. *Concerning King Henry the younger.*
Meanwhile, King Stephen died in the nineteenth year of his reign, Henry the younger succeeded to the kingdom, and the extraordinary war ceased throughout England.

285. *Charter concerning the tithe of Chilton.*
Let it be known to men present and future, by testimony of this document sealed with my seal, that I, Nicholas son of Thorold of Aston, for the salvation of my soul and of my parents, and in return for it being allowed me by the church of Abingdon that my chapel of Winterbourne have a cemetery, have granted firmly and definitively have given to the aforesaid church of Abingdon to have each year in perpetuity the tithes of my land which I hold in my demesne in the village of Chilton; that is, in corn to be received at the door of my grange, and in cheeses and fleeces and lambs and piglets, and in everything which is accustomed to be tithed.[695] In addition, I have firmly laid down that the church of Chieveley each year receive tithes from two acres of my demesne in Winterbourne, one of wheat, the other of oats, or 2s., for recognizing my choice after the death of the cleric, Helias, in such a way that henceforth I may choose and install the parson to serve the aforementioned chapel of Winterbourne, save the right of episcopal matters. This gift was made on the day of St Laurence in the chapter at Abingdon, in King Henry's second year, in the presence of Abbot Ingulf and Walter the prior and the other brethren [10 Aug. 1156].[696] Also with the following witnesses: Roger the archdeacon, Master Ranulf, Helias the cleric of Chieveley, Richard brother of this Nicholas, Hamo Piron, Richard of Hendred, John of Tubney, Henry of Pusey.[697]

Therefore, the aforesaid tithe was assigned by the abbot's grant to the use of the poor and pilgrims, with Nicholas present and particularly giving thanks that his alms were assigned to such business.[698]

[697] Roger was archdeacon of Berkshire at least from 1150 × 7 Sept. 1151; *Fasti: Salisbury*, p. 29. A Master Ralph, conceivably the same as the Master Ranulf mentioned here, witnessed *Oseney*, vi, no. 1068, a charter of Robert bishop of Lincoln, in 1163 × 6. Hamo Piron lived at least until the later 1160s, when he was succeeded by his son, Henry; see *Boarstall Cartulary*, p. 316. On Richard of Hendred's family, see *VCH*, *Berkshire*, iv. 303.

[698] See above, p. xl on the abbot's oath to preserve the possessions of the church, the wording of which the present text may echo.

286. *Cirographum de quadam terra in Oxeneford.*

Nouerint presentes et futuri, clerici et laici, Franci et Angli, quod ego Ingulfus, Dei gratia abbas Abbendone, totusque conuentus noster concessimus Radulfo Britoni terram unam tenendam de nobis iure hereditario, infra forum Oxeneford sitam, quam Gaufridus filius M⟨at⟩ilde tenuit, que ad altare ecclesie nostre pertinet, pro uiginti solidis singulis annis sacriste nostro reddendis.[699] Et insuper acquietabit eandem terram erga regem, per sexdecim denarios secundum consuetudinem uille Oxeneford, et ut ita bene et libere ipse Radulfus et heredes eius teneant sicut ullus ante eum melius et liberius prefatam terram de nobis tenuerat.

287. *Testamentum domni Ingulfi abbatis.*

Notum sit presentibus et futuris quod ego Ingulfus abbas Abbendonie concessi et finaliter[a] concedo conuentui nostro omnes consuetudines quas habuit in singulis obedientiis suis, sicut melius et plenius stabilite fuerunt tempore predecessoris mei domni Vincentii abbatis, et sicut eas inueni; uidelicet in cellario, in refectorio, in elemosinario, in mandato, in sacristario, in domo infirmorum, in coquina, in camera, in consuetudine seruientium, in curia, in hospitibus susci-
[ii. 213] piendis, in lignagio, et in operibus ecclesie. Insuper concedo in perpetuum ad sagimen fratrum Wisselegam et Winekefeld, cum
B fo. 169r omnibus redditibus suis.[700] Et | presenti scripto, sub conditione anathematis, potestate quam habeo, confirmo ut nullus successorum meorum supradictam dispositionem nostram in aliquo diminuat, nec donationes nostras subtrahat quas nos ecclesie dedimus, scilicet sacristerie quadraginta solidos, in Middeltona[b] uiginti solidos, et de monasterio sancti Aldadi de Oxeneford uiginti solidos, et in Wechenesfeld redditum molendini, ad celebranda festa sanctorum Swithuni et Æthelwoldi.[c][701]

[ii. 215] **288.** *De Walchelino abbate.*

B fo. 169v Anno igitur uicesimo nono regiminis sui, uir Deo deuotus, senex et plenus dierum,[702] domnus Ingulfus abbas egritudinem incurrit. In

[a] familiariter *B* [b] Middeltuna *B* [c] Adthelwoldi *B*

[699] See below, p. 397, a list in MS C in the same hand as the *History*, for the land which Ralph *Brito* holds in Oxford owing 20s. in rent for the altar. Salter, *Medieval Oxford*, p. 28 identifies the land as that which later was 58–61 Cornmarket; in the Hundred Rolls, it paid 16d.

[700] *De abbatibus* records that Ingulf gave to the monks' kitchen Whistley, Winkfield, Shippon, and the mills of Ock and Watchfield; *CMA* ii. 291. See also below, p. 395, and above, above, p. lxxxvii.

286. *Cirograph concerning certain land in Oxford.*

Let men present and future, cleric and lay, French and English, know that I, Ingulf, by the grace of God abbot of Abingdon, and our whole convent have granted to Ralph *Brito* one piece of land to be held from us by hereditary right, situated within the market-place of Oxford, which Geoffrey son of M⟨at⟩ilda held, which pertains to the altar of our church, in return for 20s. each year to be rendered to our sacrist.[699] In addition, he will acquit this land towards the king for 16d. according to the custom of the town of Oxford, so that Ralph himself and his heirs are thus to hold as well and freely as anyone before him had best and most freely held the aforementioned land from us.

287. *Testament of lord Abbot Ingulf.*

Let it be known to men present and future that I Ingulf, abbot of Abingdon, have granted and definitively grant to our convent all the customs which it had in each of its offices, as they were best and most fully established in the time of my predecessor lord Abbot Vincent and as I found them; that is, in the cellar, in the refectory, in the almonry, in the maundy, in the sacristy, in the house of the sick, in the kitchen, in the chamber, in the custom of servants, in the court, in the receiving of guests, in the provision of wood, and in the works of the church. In addition, I grant Whistley and Winkfield with all their rents in perpetuity for the brethren's provision of fat.[700] And by the present document I confirm, under condition of anathema, by the power I have, that none of my successors may diminish in anything our aforesaid arrangement, nor take away our gifts which we have given to the church, that is 40s. to the sacristy, in Milton 20s., and from the minster of St Aldate of Oxford 20s., and in Watchfield the rent of a mill, for celebrating the feasts of Saints Swithun [2 Jul.] and Æthelwold [1, 2 Aug.].[701]

288. *Concerning Abbot Walkelin.*

Therefore, in the twenty-ninth year of his period of rule, lord Abbot Ingulf, a man devoted to God, 'old and full of days',[702] fell ill. During

[701] Cf. above, p. 255 n. 629; see also below, p. 395 for the mill at Watchfield, p. 397 for income from Milton and St Aldate's. *De abbatibus* specifies that Ingulf gave the sacrist the church of St Aldate and 20 shillings in Drayton; *CMA* ii. 291. Cf. above, p. lxxxvi. In MS B there follow sections concerning pasture in Uffington and the ornaments of Abbot Ingulf; below, p. 344. For celebration at Abingdon of the feasts of St Swithun and St Æthelwold, the latter on two days, see *Benedictine Kalendars*, i. 25–6.

[702] Gen. 35: 29.

qua diu laborans, in capitulo fratrum se deduci fecit, pre egritudine[a] enim ire non poterat, ibique omnes sibi subiectos a peccatis suis absoluit, humiliter rogans ut siquid[b] et ipse in eis peccauerat ipsi pro Deo dimitterent. Sicque eis ultimum ualefaciens et benedicens, paucis post diebus e mundo migrauit, tercio decimo kalendas Octobris, anno uidelicet quarto Henrici regis iunioris.[703] Cui a rege, in loco pastoris, substituitur Walchelinus, ecclesie Eoueshamnensis monachus,[c] uir circa possessiones ecclesie sibi commisse fidelis et
[ii. 216] prudens, in reuocandis quoque priorum pastorum negligentia perditis studiosus. Qua de causa a rege plurimum dilectus, de eo iam in abbatem promoto primoribus Anglie talia scripta transmisit:

289. [d]*Littere regis de eodem abbate.*[704]

Henricus rex Anglorum et dux Normannorum et Aquitanorum et comes Andegauorum, archiepiscopis, episcopis, abbatibus, comitibus, baronibus, iusticiis, uicecomitibus, ministris, et omnibus fidelibus
C fo. 174v suis, Francis et Anglicis, totius Anglie, salutem. | Sciatis me concessisse et dedisse Walchelino abbati abbatiam de Abbendona, cum omnibus rebus ipsi abbatiæ[e] pertinentibus. Et ideo uolo et firmiter precipio quod predictus abbas predictam abbatiam habeat et teneat cum omnibus pertinentiis suis, bene et in pace, libere et quiete, plenarie et integre et honorifice, cum saca et soca et toll et them et infangenetheof, et gritbruche et forstel et hamsocna et flemeneformthe, in burgo et extra burgum, in bosco et plano, in pratis et molendinis, in aquis et riuis, in uiis et semitis, in festo et sine festo, et cum omnibus aliis consuetudinibus, sicut unquam aliquis ante-
B fo. 170r cessorum suorum | melius et liberius, quietius et honorificentius tenuit tempore regis Henrici aui mei, et sicut carta ipsius testatur. Testibus episcopo Ebroic', et episcopo Baioc', et Willelmo de Caisneto. Apud Rothom'.

290. *Littere regis Henrici iunioris de hundredo.*[705]

Henricus rex Anglorum et dux Normannorum et Aquitanorum[f]
[ii. 217] et comes Andegauorum episcopo Saresb', baronibus, iusticiis, uicecomiti, ministris, et omnibus fidelibus suis, Francis et Anglicis,

[a] *four lines written over erasure in B* [b] at ipsi pro Deo dimitterent. Sicque eis *in margin in brown ink in one of the hands providing guidance for the rubricator B* [c] monacus *B* [d] *illustration of Henry II B* [e] abbatie *B* [f] Aquitanie *B*

[703] See also Cambridge, University Library, Kk. i 22, fo. 5v. The Winchester annals mention Ingulf's death *s.a.* 1159; *Annales monastici*, ii. 56.

his lengthy struggle with illness, he had himself brought into the brethren's chapter, for the illness prevented him walking, and there he absolved of their sins all subject to him, humbly asking that they remit in God's name any sin he had committed towards them. And a few days after he had thus said good-bye and blessed them for a last time, he departed from the world, on 19 September, in the fourth year of King Henry the younger [1158].[703] The king replaced him in the position of pastor with Walkelin, a monk of the church of Evesham, a man faithful and prudent concerning the possessions of the church entrusted to him, and also diligent in recalling what had been lost by the negligence of previous pastors. For this reason he was greatly loved by the king, who sent to the leading men of England the following letters about Walkelin, now promoted to abbot:

289. *Letters of the king concerning this abbot.*[704]
Henry king of the English and duke of the Normans and Aquitainians and count of the Angevins to his archbishops, bishops, abbots, earls, barons, justices, sheriffs, officials, and all his faithful men, French and English, of the whole of England, greeting. Know that I have granted and given to Abbot Walkelin the abbey of Abingdon with everything pertaining to this abbey. And so I wish and firmly order that the aforesaid abbot may have and hold the aforesaid abbey with all its appurtenances, well and in peace, freely and undisturbed, fully and completely and honourably, with sake and soke and toll and team and infangentheof, and grithbrech and foresteal and hamsocn and flemenforthe, in borough and out of borough, in wood and plain, in meadows and mills, in waters and streams, on roads and tracks, in feast and without feast, and with all the other customs, as best and most freely and undisturbedly and honourably as any of his predecessors ever held in the time of King Henry my grandfather, and as his charter witnesses. Witnesses: the bishop of Evreux, and the bishop of Bayeux, and William de Chesney. At Rouen.

290. *Letters of King Henry the younger concerning the hundred.*[705]
Henry king of the English and duke of the Normans and Aquitainians and count of the Angevins to the bishop of Salisbury, his barons, justices, sheriff, officials, and all his faithful men, French and English,

[704] The editors of the *Acta of Henry II* suggest the date ?May 1159 for this and the following seven writs; Lyell, no. 92; Chatsworth, no. 346. Henry was south of the Channel from Aug. 1158 until Jan. 1163. *De abbatibus* says that Henry appointed Walkelin at the urging of Queen Eleanor; *CMA* ii. 292; also above, p. liv. The exact date of his appointment in 1159 is not certain.

[705] Lyell, no. 91, Chatsworth, no. 343.

de Berchesira,[a] salutem. Sciatis me concessisse Deo, et ecclesie sancte Marie Abbendone, et abbati Walchelino, et omnibus abbatibus successoribus suis, et monachis ibidem Deo seruientibus, hundredum de Hornimera iure perpetuo tenendum et habendum eis et omnibus successoribus suis in legitima[b] et liberima potestate sua et iusticia, sicut Eadwardus rex [c]et Willelmus rex[c] et Henricus rex auus meus predicte ecclesie concesserunt et cartis suis confirmauerunt. Et uolo et firmiter precipio ut predictus abbas Walchelinus et monachi de Abbendona predictum hundredum in pace et quiete et honorifice teneant, cum omnibus consuetudinibus suis et quitantiis suis cum quibus melius et honorabilius tenuerunt temporibus predictorum regum, scilicet quod nullus uicecomes uel eorum ministri inde se quicquam intromittant, sed ipsi libere iusticiam suam habeant et faciant, sicut carta Henrici regis aui mei testatur. Testibus episcopo Ebroic',[d] et Philippo episcopo Baioc', et Willelmo de Caisneto. Apud Rothom'.

291. *De mercatu Abbendonie.*[706]

Henricus rex Anglorum et dux Normannorum et Aquitanorum et comes Andegauorum, episcopo Saresb', baronibus, iusticiis, uicecomiti, ministris, et omnibus fidelibus suis de Berchesira,[e] salutem. Sciatis me concessisse ecclesie sancte Marie de Abbendona, et abbati
[ii. 218] Walchelino, et monachis ibidem Deo seruientibus, mercatum Abbendone, sicut ecclesia predicta et antecessores sui abbates unquam melius et liberius habuerunt tempore regis Henrici aui mei, et sicut carta illius testatur. Et teneant predictum mercatum bene et in pace, libere et quiete, integre et honorifice. Testibus episcopo Ebroic', et episcopo Baioc', et Willelmo de Caisneto. Apud Rothom'.

292. *De theloneo.*[707]

Henricus rex Anglorum et dux Normannorum et Aquitanorum et comes Andegauorum, iusticiis, uicecomitibus, ministris, et omnibus bailliuis suis totius Anglie et portuum maris, salutem. Precipio quod monachi de Abbendona sint quieti de[f] theloneo, de passagio, de pontagio, de lestagio, et de omnibus consuetudinibus per omnes terras meas et portus maris, de omnibus rebus quas homines sui poterunt affidare esse suas proprias, sicut carta Henrici regis aui mei

[a] Berchescira *B* [b] legittima *B* [c–c] *om. B* [d] Eboric' *B*
[e] Berchescira *B* [f] omni *add. B*

[706] Lyell, no. 94; Chatsworth, no. 208.

of Berkshire, greeting. Know that I have granted to God, and to the church of St Mary of Abingdon, and to Abbot Walkelin, and to all his successors as abbot, and to the monks serving God there, the hundred of Hormer, for them and all their successors to hold and have by perpetual right in their lawful and most free power and justice, as King Edward, and King William, and King Henry my grandfather granted and by their charters confirmed to the aforesaid church. And I wish and firmly order that the aforesaid Abbot Walkelin and the monks of Abingdon hold the aforesaid hundred in peace and undisturbed and honourably with all their customs and their quittances, with which they best and most honourably held in the times of the aforesaid kings; that is, that no sheriff or sheriff's officials interfere in anything therein, but they are to have and do their justice freely, as the charter of King Henry my grandfather witnesses. Witnesses: the bishop of Evreux, and Philip bishop of Bayeux, and William de Chesney. At Rouen.

291. *Concerning the market of Abingdon.*[706]
Henry king of the English and duke of the Normans and Aquitainians and count of the Angevins to the bishop of Salisbury, his barons, justices, sheriff, officials, and all his faithful men of Berkshire, greeting. Know that I have granted to the church of St Mary of Abingdon, and to Abbot Walkelin, and to the monks serving God there, the market of Abingdon, as the aforesaid church and his predecessors as abbot ever best and most freely had in the time of King Henry my grandfather and as his charter witnesses. And let them hold the aforesaid market well and in peace, freely and undisturbed, completely and honourably. Witnesses: the bishop of Evreux, and the bishop of Bayeux, and William de Chesney. At Rouen.

292. *Concerning toll.*[707]
Henry king of the English and duke of the Normans and Aquitainians and count of the Angevins to his justices, sheriffs, officials, and all his bailiffs of the whole of England and the sea-ports, greeting. I order that the monks of Abingdon be quit of toll, of transport due, of bridge-due, of lastage, and of all customs throughout all my lands and sea-ports, concerning all goods which their men can pledge their faith to be their own, as the charter of King Henry my grandfather

[707] Lyell, no. 98. See above, p. 116 for Henry I's charter. MS B mistakenly repeats this writ at fo. 171[r].

testatur. Et prohibeo ne quis eos uel homines eorum disturbet, super decem libras forisfacture. Testibus Arnulfo Lux' episcopo, Willelmo de Kesneto, Willelmo de Hastinguis.[a] Apud Rothom'.

293. *De decima uenationis foreste Windlesores.*[b][708]

Henricus rex Anglorum et dux Normannorum et Aquitanorum et comes Andegauorum iusticiis, uicecomitibus, forestariis, et omnibus ministris suis de foresta de Windesora, salutem. Sciatis me con-
C fo. 175r cessisse et confirmasse Deo et ecclesie | sancte Marie de Abbendona
B fo. 170v totam | decimam de uenatione que capta fuerit in foresta de Win-
[ii. 219] desora, sicut Henricus auus meus eis concessit et carta sua confirmauit. Testibus Rotroldo episcopo Ebroic', et Philippo episcopo Baioc', et Willelmo de Caisneto. Apud Rothom'.

294. *De siluis Cumenore*[c] *et Bachelee.*[d][709]

Henricus rex Anglorum et dux Normannorum et Aquitanorum et comes Andegauorum episcopo Saresb', baronibus, iusticiis, uicecomiti, forestariis, ministris, et omnibus fidelibus suis, Francis et Anglis, de Berchesira, salutem. Sciatis me concessisse et confirmasse Deo, et ecclesie sancte Marie de Abbendona, et abbati, et monachis ibidem Deo seruientibus, in perpetuam elemosinam habendam in custodia eorum siluam de Cumenora et de Bagelega,[e] et omnes capreolos quos ibi inuenire poterint accipiant. Et ceruos et ceruas non capiant nisi mea licentia, et ego nemini dabo licentiam ibi uenandi nisi illis, et omnes foresfacturas sartorum condono eis, sicut rex Henricus auus meus eis concessit, et sicut carta ipsius eis testatur. Testibus Rotroldo episcopo Ebroic', et Philippo episcopo Baioc', et Willelmo de Caisneto. Apud Rothom'.

295. *De warennis huius ecclesie.*[710]

Henricus rex Anglorum et dux Normannorum et Aquitanorum et comes Andegauorum iusticiis, uicecomitibus, forestariis, et omnibus
[ii. 220] ministris suis Anglie, salutem. Concedo quod abbas de Abbendona habeat warennas in omnibus terris suis in quibus antecessores sui warennas habuerunt tempore regis Henrici aui mei. Et prohibeo ne quis in eis fuget uel leporem capiat sine eius licentia super decem

[a] Hastingis *B* [b] Windelesores *B* [c] Cumenor *B* [d] Bacchelea *B* [e] Bageleia *B*

[708] Lyell, no. 83.

[709] Lyell, no. 77; *The Cartæ Antiquæ, Rolls 11–20*, ed. J. Conway Davies (Pipe Roll Soc.,

witnesses. And I forbid that anyone disturb them or their men, on £10 of forfeiture. Witnesses: Arnulf bishop of Lisieux, William de Chesney, William of Hastings. At Rouen.

293. *Concerning the tithe of the game of the forest of Windsor.*[708]
Henry king of the English and duke of the Normans and Aquitainians and count of the Angevins to his justices, sheriffs, foresters, and all his officials of the forest of Windsor, greeting. Know that I have granted and confirmed to God and to the church of St Mary of Abingdon the entire tithe of the game which is taken in the forest of Windsor, as Henry my grandfather granted and confirmed to them by his charter. Witnesses: Rotrou bishop of Evreux, and Philip bishop of Bayeux, and William de Chesney. At Rouen.

294. *Concerning the woods of Cumnor and Bagley.*[709]
Henry king of the English and duke of the Normans and Aquitainians and count of the Angevins to the bishop of Salisbury, his barons, justices, sheriff, foresters, officials, and all his faithful men, French and English, of Berkshire, greeting. Know that I have granted and confirmed to God, and to the church of St Mary of Abingdon, and to the abbot, and to the monks serving God there, to have in their custody in perpetual alms the wood of Cumnor and of Bagley, and they may take all the roe deer which they can find there. And they are not to take red deer stags and hinds except by my permission, and I shall give no one permission to hunt there except them. And I pardon them all forfeitures concerning assarts, as King Henry my grandfather granted them and as his charter witnesses for them. Witnesses: Rotrou bishop of Evreux, and Philip bishop of Bayeux, and William de Chesney. At Rouen.

295. *Concerning the warrens of this church.*[710]
Henry king of the English and duke of the Normans and Aquitainians and count of the Angevins to his justices, sheriffs, foresters, and all his officials of England, greeting. I grant that the abbot of Abingdon may have warrens in all his lands in which his predecessors had warrens in the time of King Henry my grandfather. And I forbid that anyone may hunt in them or take a hare without his permission, on

New Series xxxiii, 1960), no. 573 (where it is wrongly dated to 1105, presumably on account of the royal title, which must have been abbreviated).

[710] Lyell, no. 99, Chatsworth, no. 352.

libras forisfacture. Testibus episcopo Ebroic', et episcopo Baioc'. Apud Rothom'.

296. *Confirmatio possessionum huius ecclesie.*[711]
Henricus rex Anglorum et dux Normannorum et Aquitanorum et comes Andegauorum archiepiscopis, episcopis, abbatibus, comitibus, baronibus, iusticiis,[a] uicecomitibus, ministris, et omnibus fidelibus suis, Francis et Anglicis, totius Anglie, salutem. Sciatis me concessisse et presenti carta confirmasse Deo, et ecclesie sancte Marie Abbendone, et Walchelino abbati et omnibus successoribus suis abbatibus, et monachis ibidem Deo seruientibus, hundredum de Hornimera iure perpetuo tenendum et habendum in legitima[b] et liberima potestate sua et iusticia. Preterea concedo eis habendam in custodia eorum siluam de Cumenora et de Bagelea,[c] et quod capiant omnes capreolos quos ibi inuenire poterint, et ceruos et ceruas non capiant nisi mea licentia, et nemini do licentiam ibi uenandi nisi illis, et omnes[d] forisfacturas sartorum condono eis. Concedo etiam eis totam decimam de uenatione que capta fuerit[e] in foresta mea de Windesores. Et concedo eis habendum libere et tenendum mercatum de Abbendona. Quare uolo et firmiter precipio quod predicta ecclesia et abbates et monachi omnia hec predicta habeant et teneant bene et
[ii. 221] in pace, libere et quiete, integre et plenarie et honorifice, cum omnibus libertatibus et liberis consuetudinibus suis in omnibus locis et in omnibus rebus, sicut unquam melius et liberius, quietius et honorificentius habuerunt et tenuerunt tempore regis Henrici aui
B fo. 171r mei, et sicut ipse eis concessit et cartis suis confirma|uit. Testibus Rotroldo episcopo Ebroic', et Philippo episcopo Baioc', et Willelmo de Caisneto, et Willelmo filio Iohannis, et Huberto de Vaus. Apud Rothom'.

297. *Quot porcos [f]abbas debeat[f] habere in Kingesfrid.*[712]
Henricus rex Anglorum et dux Normannorum et Aquitanorum et comes Andegauorum Ricardo de Luceio et forestariis de Windesores, salutem.[713] Precipio quod sine dilatione faciatis recognosci per sacramenta legalium hominum de hundredo quot porcos quietos de

[a] *om. B* [b] legittima *B* [c] Bageleia *B* [d] omnis *del. by expunction dot, with* omnes *added in central margin in brown ink in one of the hands providing guidance for the rubricator B* [e] erat *B* [f-f] debeat abbas *B*

[711] Lyell, no. 95, Chatsworth, no. 340.
[712] *English Lawsuits*, no. 400, dating to 1159 × 62. 'Kingsfrid' means 'king's wood', see EPNS, *Berkshire*, i. 35, iii. 862, 870. For its location in the parish of Old Windsor, see

£10 of forfeiture. Witnesses: the bishop of Evreux and the bishop of Bayeux. At Rouen.

296. *Confirmation of the possessions of this church.*[711]
Henry king of the English and duke of the Normans and Aquitainians and count of the Angevins to his archbishops, bishops, abbots, earls, barons, justices, sheriffs, officials, and all his faithful men, French and English, of the whole of England, greeting. Know that I have granted and by the present charter confirmed to God, and to the church of St Mary of Abingdon, and to Abbot Walkelin, and to all his successors as abbot, and to the monks serving God there, the hundred of Hormer to hold and have by perpetual right in their lawful and most free power and justice. Besides, I grant to them to have in their custody the wood of Cumnor and of Bagley, and that they may take all roe deer which they can find there, and that they are not to take red deer stags and hinds except by my permission, and I give no one except them permission to hunt there, and I pardon them all forfeitures concerning assarts. Also I grant to them the entire tithe of game taken in my forest of Windsor. And I grant to them to have freely and to hold the market of Abingdon. Wherefore I wish and firmly order that the aforesaid church and abbots and monks may have and hold all these aforesaid things well and in peace, freely and undisturbed, completely and fully and honourably, with all their liberties and free customs in all places and in all possessions, as ever they had and held best and most freely, most undisturbedly and most honourably, in the time of King Henry my grandfather, and as he granted them and confirmed by his charters. Witnesses: Rotrou bishop of Evreux, and Philip bishop of Bayeux, and William de Chesney, and William son of John, and Hubert de Vaux. At Rouen.

297. *How many pigs the abbot ought to have in Kingsfrid.*[712]
Henry king of the English and duke of the Normans and Aquitainians and count of the Angevins to Richard de Lucy and the foresters of Windsor, greeting.[713] I order that you without delay cause to be recognized by oath of lawful men of the hundred how many pigs the

Calendar of the Patent Rolls preserved in the Public Record Office. Edward III (16 vols., London, 1891–1916), xiii. (1364–7), p. 95. See *DB* i, fo. 56^{v}, for references to pannage under the king's holding at Windsor.

[713] Richard de Lucy was a prominent administrator of Stephen and justiciar of Henry II; see W. L. Warren, *Henry II* (London, 1973), esp. pp. 54–5; E. Amt, 'Richard de Lucy, Henry II's justiciar', *Medieval Prosopography*, ix (1988), 61–87. During the period of this writ, he accounted as keeper of Windsor and its forest.

pasnagio abbas de Abbendona solebat habere in foresta mea que Kingesfrid uocatur, tempore regis Henrici aui mei. Et sicut |
C fo. 175ᵛ recognitum fuerit, ita Walchelino abbati de Abbendona et monachis ibidem Deo seruientibus iuste habere faciatis. Teste Manassero Biset dapifero. Apud Rothom'.[714]

[ii. 225] **298.** | *De porcis in Kingesfrid.*
B fo. 171ᵛ Secundum itaque preceptum regis, per legales homines de hundredo sacramento recognitum est abbatem Abbendonie in foresta Kingesfrid trecentos porcos habere sine pasnagio antiquitus solere, et regis Henrici tempore habuisse. Quod et ita Walchelino abbati et successoribus suis ex regis iussu concessum et confirmatum est.

299. *De militibus huius ecclesie.*[715]
Alienor regina Anglorum ducissa Normannorum et Aquitanorum et comitissa Andegeuorum militibus et hominibus qui de abbatia de Abbendona terras et tenuras tenent, salutem. Precipio quod iuste et sine dilatione faciatis Walchelino abbati de Abbendona plenarie seruitium suum quod antecessores uestri fecerunt antecessoribus suis tempore regis Henrici aui domini regis. Et nisi feceritis, iusticia regis et mea faciat fieri. Teste Ioscelino de Bailol.[a] Apud Wintoniam, per breue regis de ultra mare.

300. [b]*De decima de Mercheham.*[b][716]
B fo. 172ʳ Tempore quo Turstinus Simonis | filius terram et ecclesiam de Mercham, ut supra diximus, iniuste tenebat, decimam quoque
[ii. 226] eiusdem uille saisiauit, que ad ecclesiam illam non pertinebat, sed ad luminare altaris huius ecclesie.[717] Ea de causa quidam ex fratribus ad regem trans mare dirigitur, ut per eius iusticiam et auctoritatem rectum suum ecclesie restitueretur. Quod et ita factum est, rediens enim frater qui missus fuerat breue a rege transmissum in hec uerba reportauit:[718]

Henricus rex Anglorum[c] et dux Normannorum et Aquitanie et comes Andegauorum uicecomiti suo et ministris suis de Berchesira, salutem. Si ecclesia de Abbendona habuit decimam de Mercham ad luminare

[a] Baillol *B* [b–b] *om. B* [c] *om. B*

[714] In MS B, this is followed by nine further writs, of which two have already appeared in the text; see above, pp. 249 n. 610, 301 n. 707, below, pp. 346–52.

[715] J. C. Holt, *Colonial England 1066–1215* (London, 1997), p. 79, dates this writ to Aug. × Dec. 1158.

abbot of Abingdon was accustomed to have quit of pannage in my forest which is called Kingsfrid, in the time of King Henry my grandfather. And as it is recognized, so you are to make Abbot Walkelin of Abingdon and the monks serving God there have justly. Witness: Manasser Biset the steward. At Rouen.[714]

298. *Concerning the pigs in Kingsfrid.*
Therefore, according to the king's order, it was recognized on oath through lawful men of the hundred that the abbot of Abingdon was accustomed of old to have, and in King Henry's time had, 300 pigs in the forest of Kingsfrid without pannage. And by the king's order it was granted and confirmed thus to Abbot Walkelin and his successors.

299. *Concerning the knights of this church.*[715]
Eleanor queen of the English, duchess of the Normans and Aquitainians, and countess of the Angevins to the knights and men who hold land and tenures from the abbey of Abingdon, greeting. I order that justly and without delay you do fully to Walkelin abbot of Abingdon his service which your ancestors did to his predecessors in the time of King Henry, grandfather of the lord king. And if you do not, the king's and my justice is to ensure that it is done. Witness: Jocelin de Balliol. At Winchester. Through writ of the king from beyond the sea.

300. *Concerning the tithe of Marcham.*[716]
During the time when, as we have said above, Thurstan son of Simon was unjustly holding the land and church of Marcham, he also seized the tithe of that village, which pertained not to that church but to the lighting of the altar of this church [of Abingdon].[717] One of the brethren was sent overseas to the king concerning this matter, so that the church of Abingdon's own right be restored by his justice and authority. And this occurred, for the brother who had been sent brought back on his return a writ sent from the king in these words:[718]

Henry king of the English and duke of the Normans and of Aquitaine and count of the Angevins to his sheriff and his officials of Berkshire, greeting. If the church of Abingdon had the tithe of Marcham for the

[716] *English Lawsuits*, no. 442. See also *Royal Writs*, ed. van Caenegem, pp. 168–9 n. 5, 203 n. 4, and no. 98. See above, p. 238.
[717] See above, p. 244, and note also below, p. 272.
[718] See above, p. xvii n. 1, on the dating of this writ.

ecclesie tempore Henrici regis aui mei, et anno et die qua fuit mortuus et uiuus, et post, et inde sit dissaisita iniuste et sine iudicio, tunc precipio quod sine dilatione inde eam resaisiatis. Et ita bene et in pace et libere et iuste tenere faciatis, sicut melius et liberius tenuit tempore Henrici regis aui mei. Et precipio quod quando Turstinus filius Simonis redierit in Angliam,[a] abbas Abbendonie plenum rectum habeat de terra quam predictus Turstinus filius Simonis tenet de feudo abbatie. Et si abbas poterit disrationare quod non defecerit de recto predicto Turstino in curia sua, abbas inde ei in curia sua rectum teneat. Teste magistro Iohanne de Oxeneford. Apud Turon'.

Cum uero perlectum esset regis breue in pleno comitatu, et manifeste compertum totius comitatus testimonio quoniam prefata decima ad luminare altaris sancte Marie pertineret, et quod eam Turstinus iniuste tenebat, uicecomes ex parte regis illum dissaisiauit, et eam altari cui adiacebat restituit. Qualiter autem ecclesia cum terra coram rege disrationata fuerit, superius in gestis uenerandi abbatis Vincentii memorauimus.[719]

[ii. 227] **301.** *De foro Abbendonie.*[720]

In primo tempore aduentus abbatis Walchelini ad hanc ecclesiam, adierunt regem istum Henricum iuniorem Walingefordenses cum his de Oxenefordia, de foro ei Abbendonensi suggerentes quoniam aliter esset quam esse deberet, uel Henrici regis aui sui tempore fuerit. Multa preterea uerborum dolositate et fallaciis insistebant, ut regis assensum de foro defendendo adquirerent. Quibus cum rex credendum putaret, precepit quidem interim mercatum defendi preter parua uenalia que ibi uendi solebant quousque ipse de transmarinis partibus (ad quas tunc properabat) reuerteretur, et super hoc causam subtilius examinaret.[721] Illi uero accepta potestate a fori defensione, donec rex
C fo. 176r transfreta|ret[b] abstinuerunt, sed postea quasi libero utentes malitie sue impetu, assumpto secum regis constabulario de Walingeford, [c]die Dominico[c] Abbendoniam aduenerunt, ex regis uerbo[d] omnes qui uenalia sua illuc detulerant abire precipientes, rusticisque uim

[a] Anglia *B C. Both C and B follow this word by repeating* quod *unnecessarily* [b] *C damaged, text completed from B* [c–c] *erased in B* [d] *corr. from* uerba *B C*

[719] See above, p. 234. See above, p. xxxi, on such cross-referencing.
[720] *English Lawsuits*, no. 406.

lighting of the church in the time of King Henry my grandfather, and on the year and day on which he was dead and alive, and afterwards, and has been disseised thereof unjustly and without judgment, then I order that you reseise it thereof without delay. And make the church hold as well and in peace and freely and justly, as it best and most freely held in the time of King Henry my grandfather. And I order that when Thurstan son of Simon returns to England, the abbot of Abingdon is to have full justice concerning the land which the aforesaid Thurstan son of Simon holds of the abbey's fee. And if the abbot can prove that he did not default concerning justice to the aforesaid Thurstan in his own court, let the abbot do justice to him in his court concerning this. Witness: Master John of Oxford. At Tours.

The king's writ was read out in the full county court and it was manifestly found by the testimony of the whole county that Thurstan was holding the afore-mentioned tithe unjustly, since it pertained to the lighting of the altar of St Mary. The sheriff on the king's behalf disseised him and restored it to the altar to which it belonged. Moreover, we recorded above, among the deeds of the venerable Abbot Vincent, how Marcham church with the land was deraigned in the king's presence.[719]

301. *Concerning the market at Abingdon.*[720]
Soon after Abbot Walkelin came to this church, the men of Wallingford, together with those of Oxford, went to King Henry the younger and made the following complaint to him concerning Abingdon market: that it was held in a way other than it should be and other than it had been in the time of King Henry his grandfather. With great verbal deceitfulness and with lies, they strove to acquire the king's assent to the banning of the market. Since the king thought he should believe them, he indeed ordered that the market should be forbidden provisionally, except the small goods which were customarily sold there. The ban was to last until he would return from overseas (where he was then hastening) and examine the case in greater detail.[721] However, those men, after receiving the power to forbid the market, refrained from doing so until the king made his crossing, but afterwards they gave free rein to their malice and, taking with them the king's constable of Wallingford, they went to

[721] Henry crossed to Normandy in Aug. 1158; R. W. Eyton, *Court, Household, and Itinerary of King Henry II* (London, 1878), p. 40.

inferentes.[722] Abbendonenses autem fori sui defensionem grauiter ferentes, assumpta nescio unde audatia, omnes qui aduenerant aduersarios cum dedecore a uilla longius abegerunt. Qua repulsione
B fo. 172v amplius aduersarii ad malum | instigati, regis in patriam aduentum non expectantes, ad eum ubi erat uenerunt, et qualiter eis non sine iniuria regis euenerit, multa super addentes uana, retexerunt. Importunitati quorum cum legis equitate satisfacere uolens, quodam eis breue tradito, repatriare permisit. Reuertentes uero, et prorsus fori
[ii. 228] Abbendonensis euersionem in litteris contineri putantes, ad iusticiam Anglie, Robertum uidelicet comitem Legecestrie, peruenerunt.[723] Lectum [a]est ergo[a] coram iusticia, abbate Walchelino assistente, breue huiusmodi habens sensum:

Henricus rex Anglorum[b] et dux Normannorum et Aquitanorum et comes Andegauorum Roberto comiti Legecestrie, salutem.[724] Precipio ut, conuocato omni comitatu Berchesire,[c] quatuor et uiginti homines de senioribus, qui Henrici regis aui mei tempore fuerunt, eligere facias. Qui si iurare poterint quod in diebus eius plenum mercatum in Abbendonia fuerit, ita sit et nunc. Si uero nec uiderint nec iurare poterint, ut rectum est prohibeatur, ne amplius inde clamorem audiam.

Quo perlecto, confusi sunt a spe sua qui portauerant, utpote de ueritate sibi conscii. Precipiente tamen comite, Adam uicecomes comitatum plenum apud Ferneburgam congregans, homines, qui secundum regis preceptum iurare deberent, electos constituit. Qui cum iuramento asseruerunt se rerum omnium uenalium mercatum plenissimum inibi uidisse et interfuisse. His ita finem habentibus, et rege ad regnum proprium reuertente, conuenerunt ad eum iurgatores predicti.[725] Fingentes iuramentum falsum factum fuisse, et quia quidam eorum qui iurauerant de abbatia[d] erant, quod eis utile uidebatur et non quod rei ueritas docebat protulisse. His uerbis rex

[a–a] ergo est *B*   [b] Anglie *B*   [c] Berchescire *B*   [d] abbatie *C*

[722] The identity of this constable is not absolutely certain; *PR 6 HII*, p. 21, and *PR 7 HII*, p. 53, have a William Salnarius rendering account for Wallingford, which was in royal hands from early in Henry II's reign; Sanders, *Baronies*, p. 93. See above, p. 263 n. 641, on markets being held on Sundays.

[723] Robert, earl of Leicester 1118–68, was a leading figure in the reigns of Henry I, Stephen, and Henry II, under the last of whom he was justiciar; see Crouch, *Beaumont Twins*.

[724] This writ, preserved in neither cartulary, is diplomatically odd in its lack of witnesses and place date.

Abingdon on a Sunday.[722] On the king's word, they ordered to go away all who had brought to that place their goods for sale, and attacked the country people. But the men of Abingdon took bitterly the banning of their market, and with an audacity acquired from I know not where, they drove away from the town, in a state of shame, all their opponents who had come there. The opponents were inspired to further evil by this rebuff. They did not wait for the king's arrival in the country, but went to him where he was and, adding many falsehoods, revealed to him what had happened to them and the harm to the king it involved. Wishing to satisfy their insistence with the equity of the law, he handed over a writ and allowed them to go home. They moreover returned and, thinking that the complete destruction of Abingdon market was contained in the letters, went to the justiciar of England, namely Robert earl of Leicester.[723] Therefore the writ, with the following content, was read out before the justiciar and in Abbot Walkelin's presence:

Henry king of the English and duke of the Normans and Aquitainians and count of the Angevins to Robert earl of Leicester, greeting.[724] I order that, after summoning together all the county of Berkshire, you are to choose twenty-four of the older men who were alive in the time of King Henry my grandfather. If these men can swear that in his days there was a full market in Abingdon, let it be so now. But if they neither saw nor can swear to this, let it be forbidden as is just, so that I do not hear further complaint concerning this.

When this had been read through, those who had brought the writ were confounded in their hope, as they were aware of the truth. However, at the earl's order, Adam the sheriff gathered the full county court at Farnborough and ordained that the men who had been chosen according to the king's order should swear. They asserted with an oath that they had seen and been present at the fullest market there, with all types of goods for sale. Faced with this outcome, the aforesaid litigious men went to the king, who had returned to his own kingdom.[725] They pretended that a false oath had been made, and that since some of those who had sworn were men of the abbey, they had expressed what seemed advantageous to them and not what the truth of the matter taught. The king was somewhat

[725] The following events took place in the early months of 1163; see Eyton, *Henry II*, pp. 58–62.

aliquantulum commotus, precepit ut apud Oxenefordam iterum Walingefordenses et omnis comitatus Berchesire coram iusticiis suis conuenirent, et ex utraque parte seniores uiri eligerentur, qui secundum quod eis uerum uideretur pro foro Abbendonensi iurarent, ita tamen ut de abbatia nullus de iurantibus esset, ne suspicarentur aliqua de causa uelle peiurare. Quod cum precepisset, rex ad Saresbiriam profectus est, omnibus iusticiis suis ad audien-
[ii. 229] dum relictis. Congregati sunt ergo, ut rex iusserat, uniuersi, et segregati qui iurarent, diuersis opinionibus causam suam confundebant. Walingefordenses[a] enim nunquam Henrici regis senioris tempore, preter panem uel ceruisiam, uendi in Abbendonia iurabant; Oxenefordenses uero (nam et ipsi iurabant) se mercatum inibi ampliorem ceteris, non autem plenum, ut in nauibus onerariis et quadrigis, uidisse dicebant. Qui uero de comitatu iurabant, plenum omnium rerum mercatum uidisse se asserebant, de nauibus tantum onerariis per aquam Tamisie currentibus dubitabant, abbate tamen nauibus suis ad ea que uellet utente. Comes autem Legecestrie, qui iusticia et iudex aderat, eorum uidens opiniones uariare, nichil super hoc iudicare presumpsit, sed ad regem profectus ei que gesta
B fo. 173r fu|erant indicauit. Ne tamen rex de rei huius ueritate inscius dubitaret, idem comes plenum Henrici regis tempore se testatus
C fo. 176v est uidisse[b] | mercatum, et, quod ulterius est, cum adhuc puer esset et apud Abbendonam nutriretur regis Willelmi tempore. Rex autem tanti uiri testimonio delectatus plus soli uerum dicenti credendum sentiuit, quam multis per contentionem a ueritate discordantibus.[c] Interea rege apud Radingam existente, conuenerunt ad eum prefati calumpniatores, dicentes se eius uillas minime tenere posse si mercatum, ut ceperat, in Abbendonia permaneret. Quibus pro male mentis pertinatia rex indignatus, eosdem a se turbulenter abegit. Precepitque ut a die illo mercatum plenissimum ibi esset, nauibus tantum exceptis, abbate tantummodo suis utente. Et ne aliquis dissipare niteretur quod Henrici regis aui sui tempore dispositum constabat, et ipse tunc confirmabat, calumpniantibus silentium imponens, perpetuum interdixit. Tamen antequam res hec ad hunc finem perueniret, non modicum pertulit abbas Walchelinus laborem.

[a] Walinkefordenses *B* [b] uidisse *rep. at start of fo. 176v C* [c] *corr. from* discordentibus *B C*

shaken by these words and ordered that the men of Wallingford and all the county court of Berkshire should again come together before his justices at Oxford; older men from each side should be chosen, who would swear according to what seemed true to them concerning the market of Abingdon, in such a way, however, that none of the abbey's men be among the oath-takers, lest they be suspected of wishing to commit perjury for any reason. When he had ordered this, the king set out for Salisbury, leaving behind all his justices for the hearing. Therefore everyone gathered as the king had ordered, and those who were to swear were separated off, but confused their case by the diversity of their opinions. For the men of Wallingford swore that in the time of King Henry the elder there was never anything sold in Abingdon except bread and beer; but the men of Oxford (for they also swore) said that they had seen there a relatively large-scale market but not a full one, as in cargo boats and carts. But the men of the county who swore maintained that they had seen a full market of all goods, and only had doubts about cargo boats coming on the waters of the Thames, although the abbot used his own boats for whatever he wanted. Now when the earl of Leicester, who was present as justice and judge, saw that their opinions varied, he presumed to make no judgment on this, but went to the king and told him what had happened. However, so that the king was not left in doubt through ignorance of the truth of the matter, Earl Robert testified that he had seen a full market in the time of King Henry, and, what's more, when he was still a boy and was being raised at Abingdon in the time of King William. The king, moreover, was delighted with the testimony of such a great man and felt he should believe one man speaking what was true rather than many who, through strife, were at variance with truth. Meanwhile the aforementioned claimants went to the king who was at Reading, saying that they could hardly maintain his towns if the market continued in Abingdon as it had begun. The king was angry with them for the persistence of their evil minds, and he violently sent them from him. He ordered that from that day the fullest market should exist at Abingdon, with the sole exception of boats, the abbot only using his own. And he imposed silence on the claimants and forbade forever that anyone seek to weaken what it was agreed had been settled in the time of King Henry his grandfather, and what he was then confirming. However, before this matter reached such a conclusion, Abbot Walkelin had expended no little effort.

[ii. 230] 302. *De centum solidis male uicecomiti datis.*[726]

Ingulfus itaque abbas, predecessor huius Walchelini, quia dierum et prouecte erat etatis et comitatus sequi non poterat, centum solidos per annos singulos plurimo tempore uicecomiti de Berchesira dare consueuit, ea de causa ut abbatie homines lenius tractaret, et eos in placitis et hundredis, siquid necesse haberent, adiuuaret. Quod postquam processu temporis in consuetudinem uersum est, centum quidem solidos de abbatia uicecomes, ac si de redditu suo essent, accipiebat, ipsis uero pro quibus dabantur prorsus nichil proficiebat. Cuius noticia cum ad abbatem Walchelinum perueniret, pro tali ecclesie dampno doluit, et post annum aduentus sui ad abbatiam primum solidos dare distulit.[727] Requisitus autem quare non illos centum solidos persoluisset, respondit ne usus malus contra ecclesiam suam inoleret, cum utique priscis temporibus ita minime fuisse. Iubente uero rege,[a] inquisita est rei ueritas si ita Henrici regis aui scilicet sui tempore fuisset. Quod cum ita non fuisse in comitatu iuramento manifestatum[b] esset, prohibuit rex solidos reddi uel a quoquam in posterum exigi. Sicque abbas Walchelinus centum ad se solidos, male ante annuatim perditos, retraxit, et ad usum ecclesie amplius profuturum deputauit.

303. *De quodam molendino.*[728]

Eo tempore quo seditio orta inter regem Stephanum et ducem
[ii. 231] Henricum pro regno optinendo, utrimque seuiebant, Willelmus Boterel constabularius de Walingeford, pecunia accepta a domno Ingulfo abbate, res ecclesie Abbendonensis a suo exercitu se defensurum promisit. Sponsionis ergo sue inmemor, in uillam Culeham, que huic cenobio adiacet, quicquid inuenire potuit depredauit.[729] Quo audito, abbas quosdam de fratribus ad eum direxit, suppliciter
B fo. 173v postulans ut predam | restitueret, admirans quomodo quod tueri deberet, fure nequior diripuisset. Quibus domum redeuntibus, nichil preter responsum quod predam reddere noluisset reportauerunt. Coactus itaque abbas Ingulfus, iubente Theodbaldo Cantuariorum archiepiscopo et Iocelino[c] Saresbiriensi episcopo, ad uindictam sancte ecclesie confugit, et Willelmum anathematis uinculo dampnauit.[730]

[a] *C damaged, text completed from B* [b] manifestum *B* [c] Iocellino *B*

[726] *English Lawsuits*, no. 390.

[727] Walkelin's first year as abbot ended at some point in 1160.

[728] The mill is in Benson, Oxon. *DB* i, fo. 154v, mentions that the king's holding at Benson in 1086 included two mills, value 40s. Lyell, no. 341, Chatsworth, no. 385 is Peter's charter concerning this gift; see also Chatsworth, no. 386, for a later confirmation.

302. *Concerning 100s. wrongly given to the sheriff.*[726]
Since Abbot Ingulf, Walkelin's predecessor, was of advanced age and could not attend the county courts, he was long accustomed to give annually 100s. to the sheriff of Berkshire for the following reason, that he treat the abbey's men more leniently and help them in pleas and hundreds, if they had any need. Afterwards, the progress of time turned this into a custom, and the sheriff used indeed to receive from the abbey the 100s. as if they were his rent, but this brought no profit at all for those on whose behalf the money was given. When Abbot Walkelin heard of this, he was upset by such damage to the church, and after his first year in the abbacy, he refrained from giving the shillings.[727] Asked why he had not paid those 100s., he answered that it was to prevent an evil usage growing up against his church, since it had not been so at all in earlier times. At the king's order, indeed, the truth of the matter was sought, as to whether it was so in the time of King Henry, that is his grandfather. When it was made clear by oath in the county court that it had not been so, the king forbade that the shillings be rendered or demanded by anyone in future. And thus Abbot Walkelin took back for himself the 100s. a year which had earlier been wrongly lost, and assigned them for the more profitable use of the church.

303. *Concerning a certain mill.*[728]
At the time when violent discord arose between King Stephen and Duke Henry over possession of the kingdom, and both sides were behaving with ferocity, William Boterel the constable of Wallingford received money from lord Abbot Ingulf and promised that he would protect the possessions of the church of Abingdon from his troops.[729] Then, oblivious of his promise, he seized as plunder whatever he could find in the village of Culham which belongs to this monastery. When the abbot heard this, he sent some of the brethren to him, asking humbly that he restore the plunder, and wondering how he, more depraved than a thief, could loot what he ought to protect. When they came home, they brought back nothing save the answer that he was unwilling to give back the plunder. Thus compelled, Abbot Ingulf, at the order of Theobald archbishop of Canterbury and Jocelin bishop of Salisbury, resorted to the retribution of the holy Church and condemned William to the bond of anathema.[730] Yet,

[729] William Boterel witnesses charters associated with knights of Wallingford in the 1150s; *Eynsham*, i, no. 127, *Oseney*, vi, no 1086.

[730] No archiepiscopal or episcopal documents recording such an order survive, and the *History* need not imply that a written order ever existed.

Dampnatus autem, de commisso ueniam uel de anathemate[a] absolutionem usque ad diem exitus sui postulare neglexit. Tandem uero iusto Dei iudicio, in prenominata seditione letale uulnus accepit, quod ei protinus loquelam extorsit, et deinceps ad auxiliandum siue nocendum inutilem reddidit, qui et desperatus est. Cuius miserie condolens frater eius Petrus Boterel abbatem supplex[b] pro fratre rogaturus adiit, ut ueniam morienti impetraret.[731] Promittente quoque eo se quicquid depredatum fuerat redditurum, frater eius Willelmus (quem desperatum diximus) absolutus et defunctus est.
C fo. 177r Post cuius decessum, Petrus litteris ac|ceptis[c] a duce Henrico ad abbatem uenit, orans ut pro ducis amore sibi quid debebat condonaretur.[732] Abbas uero litteris ducis contradicere metuens, petitioni, quamuis non ex corde bono, ad tempus tamen adquieuit. Transeunte autem aliquanto tempore, uoluebat in animo idem Petrus parum uel nichil fratri suo mortuo profuisse, quod tam graue dampnum nulla
[ii. 232] restitutione, nisi sola condonatione, emendatum esset. Veniens igitur in capitulum fratrum, in presentia abbatis Walchelini et totius conuentus, molendinum quoddam de Bensintuna,[d] iuxta Walingeford,[e] quinque solidos per annum reddens, quasi in restitutione dampni[f] predicti, optulit. Abbas uero utilius iudicans aliquid uel parum accipere, quam parum negligendo totum perdere, molendinum accepit, et ad necessaria fratrum infirmorum, ipso Petro concedente et manum super altare ponente, in perpetuum concessit.[733]

304. *De quodam Ricardo.*

Contigit etiam ut quidam, Ricardus nomine, de Warwicsira[g] quodam pro negotio quod cum Willelmo de Lega, milite istius ecclesie, habebat, Abbendoniam ueniret.[734] Sine consensu enim ecclesie Abbendonensis, de cuius feudo erat terra quam Willelmus tenebat et quod ab eo accipere debuit, causam suam consummare non potuit. Residente autem abbate Walchelino cum fratribus in capitulo, predictus Ricardus, accepta fratrum societate, assensum eorum[h] in

[a] anathemathe *B C* [b] suppex *B* [c] *C damaged, text completed from B*
[d] Bensingtuna *B* [e] Walingaford *B* [f] damni *B* [g] Wareuuikescira *B*
[h] *om. B*

[731] *PR 11 HII*, p. 72, shows that Peter had died by 1165. *Testa de Nevill*, i. 117 (a 1212 inquiry), says Peter Boterel held Chalgrove after the first coronation of Henry II.

[732] These letters do not survive. For Henry's governmental activities in England before he became king, see White, *Restoration and Reform*, pp. 45–55, 69–76.

[733] Cf. *De abbatibus*, which attributes to Abbot Ingulf the grant of the mill to the infirmary; *CMA* ii. 291.

despite this condemnation, until the day of his death he neglected to seek forgiveness concerning his misdeed or absolution concerning the anathema. But at long last, by God's just judgment, he received in the aforementioned war a deadly wound, which immediately took away his speech, and rendered him henceforth useless for giving aid or doing harm, and he was despaired of. Feeling compassion for his misery, his brother Peter Boterel came as a supplicant to the abbot, to ask on his brother's behalf that he might obtain forgiveness for the dying man.[731] Peter also promised that he would give back to the abbot whatever had been plundered, and then his brother (whom we have said had been despaired of) was absolved and died. After William's death, Peter received letters from Duke Henry and went to the abbot, praying that for love of the duke he be pardoned what he owed.[732] The abbot indeed feared to contradict the duke's letters and temporarily agreed to the request, although unhappily. Some time later, however, Peter was turning over in his mind that he had done little or no good for his dead brother, because such a great sin had been corrected not by restitution but only by a pardon. Therefore he came into the brethren's chapter and, in the presence of Abbot Walkelin and the whole convent, offered a mill at Benson, next to Wallingford, rendering 5s. a year, as it were in restitution for the aforesaid damage. The abbot judged that it would certainly be more profitable to accept something or a little, rather than to lose everything by neglecting the little. He therefore accepted the mill and granted it in perpetuity to the needs of the sick brethren, with Peter himself granting and placing his hand on the altar.[733]

304. *Concerning a certain Richard.*
It also happened that a certain man named Richard, from Warwickshire, came to Abingdon about some business which he had with William of Bessels Leigh, a knight of this church.[734] For he could not achieve his purpose without the consent of the church of Abingdon, of whose fee was the land which William held and what Richard should receive from William. But when Abbot Walkelin was in the chapter with the brethren, the aforesaid Richard received the society of the brethren, and then requested

[734] The 1166 Abingdon *Carta* records that William of 'Lega', i.e. Bessels Leigh, owed two knights; *Red Book*, i. 305, below, p. 390. See also Lyell, nos. 253, 254 for two of his grants to Abingdon; *CMA* ii. 329, for 5s. due to the infirmarer from a tithe from William. A deed recording a grant of his made in 1165 × 1175 survives; C.H., no. 1a.

negotio suo postulauit, et ut facilius adquiescerent, duodecim nummos super analogium posuit, et totidem per singulos annos in recognitionem quod de ecclesia teneret se suosque heredes, uel quicumque in posterum tenuerit quod ipse tunc a Willelmo accepit, ad domum infirmorum daturum promisit et perpetue confirmauit.

[ii. 233] 305. *De una hida in Appelford.*

Quidam, Paganus nomine, homo ecclesie huius, in uilla Appelford unam hidam tenendam pro uiginti solidis singulis annis, ad coquinam
B fo. 174r mona | chorum reddendis, acceperat.[735] Sed per tempus multum, prelatis sui temporis sibi fauentibus, reddere differebat. Quod animaduertens abbas Walchelinus, frequenter cum eodem Pagano egit, ut ecclesie restitueret quod iniuste annuatim auferebat. Quod quamuis Paganus graue ferret, ad hoc tamen constantia huius abbatis adductus est, ut in capitulum fratrum, cum filio quem heredem habuit, ueniret, et pro illa terra, et alia quam in Stoches[a] de ecclesia tenebat, cum abbate et conuentu[b] talem pactionem confirmaret.[736] Pro dampno uero preterito in misericordiam abbatis se posuit. Cirographum autem taliter se habet:

306. *Cirographum.*

Sciant tam futuri quam presentes quod ego Walchelinus, Dei gratia abbas Abbendonie, totusque conuentus eiusdem ecclesie concessimus Pagano de Apelford[c] et heredibus suis iure hereditario tenendam de ecclesia nostra inperpetuum tenaturam suam de Appelford et de Stoches, excepta omni purprestura,[d] pro uiginti solidis singulis annis coquinario ecclesie nostre reddendis pro omni seruitio, scilicet ad festum sancti Michaelis decem solidos, et ad Annuntiationem sancte Marie decem solidos. Et ut hec conuentio firmior et stabilior
[ii. 234] haberetur, nos prefato Pagano cirographum[e] sigillis nostris munitum contradidimus, et ipse Paganus et Robertus filius suus ex sua parte, in presentia totius capituli et plurimorum clericorum et multorum laicorum, iurauerunt se et suos heredes sine omni simulatione prefatam conuentionem esse seruaturos. His testibus subscriptis:

[a] Steches *B* [b] conuentui *B C* [c] Appelford *B* [d] purpestura *B C*
[e] cirgraphum *B*

[735] Pain is recorded as holding a hide at Appleford in a list of tenants from Henry I or Stephen's time, below, p. 394. It seems plausible that this is the same hide which had been held by William son of Abbot Reginald, Simon the dispenser of Henry I, and Thurstan son of Simon, see above, pp. 190, 234, 240. Pain may even have been sub-tenant of this land when it was under the dispensers' control. They may well be the great men who favoured

their assent in his business. He placed twelve penny coins on the lectern so they might agree more easily, and promised and perpetually confirmed that each year he and his heirs, or whoever in future held what he then received from William, would give equally much to the house of the sick, in recognition that he held from the church.

305. *Concerning one hide in Appleford.*
A certain man of this church, named Pain, received one hide in the village of Appleford to hold for 20s. to be rendered annually to the monks' kitchen.[735] But for a long period, when the great men of his time were favouring him, he refrained from rendering the rent. Noticing this, Abbot Walkelin frequently raised with Pain that he restore to the church what he was unjustly taking away each year. Even though Pain took this badly, still he was brought by the abbot's constancy to come to the brethren's chapter with the son whom he held as his heir, and to confirm the following agreement with the abbot and convent for that land and the other land which he was holding from the church in Stoke.[736] And indeed he placed himself in the abbot's mercy for the past wrong. The cirograph is of the following form:

306. *Cirograph.*
Let men both future and present know that I Walkelin, by the grace of God abbot of Abingdon, and the whole convent of that church have granted to Pain of Appleford and his heirs to hold by hereditary right from our church in perpetuity his tenure of Appleford and of Stoke, except all purpresture, for 20s. to be rendered annually to the kitchener of our church for all service, that is 10s. at the feast of St Michael [29 Sept.] and at the Annunciation of St Mary [25 Mar.] 10s. And so that this agreement be firmer and more stable, we have given in return to the aforementioned Pain a cirograph strengthened by our seals, and Pain and Robert his son, on their side, have sworn in the presence of the whole chapter and of very many clerics and many laymen that they and their heirs will preserve the aforementioned convention, without any dissimulation. With the following witnesses:

him. See also a list of revenues devoted to the kitchen, in MS C in the same hand as the *History*, below, p. 395, which mentions 20s. from Appleford.

[736] I have not been able to identify this place with certainty; North Stoke, Oxon., or another of the nearby Stokes is a possibility. See also above, p. 180, for Stoke Bruern, Northants.

Clemente decano, Radulfo de Sancto Martino et Rogero filio suo, Martino presbitero et Helia clerico, Adam uicecomite, Nicholao filio Turoldi, Iohanne de Tureberuilla,[a] Roberto de Seuecurða[b] et Willelmo filio suo, Iohanne de Tubeneia et Ricardo filio suo, Willelmo de Lega,[c] Bomundo de Bed', Rannulfo de Morles, Henrico de Luuechenora, et multis aliis.[737]

[a] Turberuilla *B* [b] Seuecurð *B* [c] Leia *B*

[737] Ralph of St Martin is presumably Ralph, priest of St Martin's, a rural dean of Oxfordshire for over twenty years; see *Charters in Oxford Muniment Rooms*, ed. Salter, no. 77. Helias may be the clerk of Chieveley, mentioned above, p. 294. *Red Book*, i. 338 records a John de 'Turbelvulle' having had one knight's fee from William earl of Ferrers. He may have held East Hendred from Abingdon; *VCH*, *Berkshire*, iv. 297. A John de 'Turberville' also witnessed *Oseney*, iv, no. 424A, concerning Pusey. For the Seacourt family, see above, p. lxii. The 1166 Abingdon *Carta* mentions a 'Buamundus de Leges',

Clement the deacon, Ralph of St Martin and Roger his son, Martin the priest and Helias the cleric, Adam the sheriff, Nicholas son of Thorold, John de Turbeville, Robert of Seacourt and William his son, John of Tubney and Richard his son, William of Bessels Leigh, Bomund of Beedon, Ranulf of *Morles*, Henry of Lewknor, and many others.[737]

Red Book, i. 306, below, p. 390. *PR 13 HII*, p. 9, records that 'Bedena Boamundi redd' comp' de dimidia m'. In thesauro liberauit. Et quietus.' The fact that he owed three knights, and was associated with Beedon, suggests that he was the successor of Walter and Jocelin de Rivers, but a later list of knights in MS C has a W. de Rivers holding eleven hides in Beedon, *CMA* ii. 312. See also below, p. 397, for a Ralph of *Morles* appearing in a list in MS C in the same hand as the *History*. A Ranulf and a William of *Morles* witnessed C.H., no. 1a, a charter dating from 1165 × 1175. Their toponymic surname may relate to the land of *Morelese* or *Morehelese* at Abingdon, Lyell, no. 188, EPNS, *Berkshire*, ii. 442; it may derive from Mosles (Dept. Calvados) in Normandy.

APPENDIX I: ADDITIONS IN MS B

This appendix gives the additional passages which appear in MS B, up to the end of the period covered in MS C. MS B's continuation thereafter appears as Appendix II. In the present appendix I indicate the location of the passage first by reference to the manuscript, and second by a number which marks where in the main text the addition should be inserted; for example sections no. 5a and no. 5b below follow section no. 5 in the main text.

(i) MS B, fos. 120v–121r

[ii. 4] **5a.** *Hii sunt milites tenentes de Abbendonia.*

fo. 120v Gueres de Palences: iiiior. milites, pro Samford et Leowartune vii. hidas, in Chiltune v. hidas, in Dentune ii. hidas,[1] in Wateleia i. hidam, in Baiwrðe et Suningewelle iiii. hidas.

Reginaldus de Sancta Helena: iii. milites, pro v. hidis in Gerstune, et pro iiiior. hidis in Frileford, et iii. hidis in Liford, et ii. hidis in Henreþe.[2]

Ansgil: ii. milites, pro Seuecurt, et v. hidis in Baiuurþe, et i. hida in Mercham.[3]

Warinus: iiii. hidas in Suggeƿurþe, pro seruitio dimidii militis.[4]

Hubertus: i. militem, pro v. hidis in Witham.[5]

Raimbaldus: militem et dimidium, pro ii. hidis in Sunningeuuelle, et in Kenitune iii. hidis, in Gareford ii. hidis, in Boxore ii. hidis, in Cumenore ii. hidis et terram de Blachegraue, et in Frileford i. hida quam dedit Bernerus Turstino de Sancta Helena, in ƿurþa i. hida.[6]

[ii. 5] Raimbaldus: i. militem, pro Tubbeneia.[7]

Aschetillus: ii. milites, pro Leia et Cestretunæ.[8]

[1] Denton, Oxon., is not named in *Domesday*; it lies between two other Abingdon possessions, Cuddesdon and Garsington. Gueres does not appear elsewhere in the *History*, nor does he appear in *Domesday Book*, unless—as was suggested by Stenton, *VCH, Oxfordshire*, i. 381—he is to be identified with the Wenric who held Chilton and Sandford-on-Thames from the abbey, *DB* i, fos. 59r, 156v. However, no connection is apparent with the other estates in *Domesday*.

[2] *DB* i, fos. 58v, 59r, confirms Reginald as tenant of these lands in Frilford and Lyford; *Domesday* does not link him with lands in Garsington or Hendred. *Domesday* does not mention any Abingdon land in Hendred, but see below, p. 388, for another reference to

APPENDIX I: ADDITIONS IN MS B

(i) MS B, fos. 120^{v}–121^{r}

5a. *These are the knights holding from Abingdon.*

Gueres de Palences: four knights, for Sandford and Leverton seven hides, in Chilton five hides, in Denton two hides,[1] in Wheatley one hide, in Bayworth and Sunningwell four hides.

Reginald of St Helen: three knights, for five hides in Garsington, and for four hides in Frilford, and three hides in Lyford, and two hides in Hendred.[2]

Anskill: two knights for Seacourt, and five hides in Bayworth, and one hide in Marcham.[3]

Warin: four hides in Sugworth, for the service of half a knight.[4]

Hubert: one knight, for five hides in Wytham.[5]

Raimbald: a knight and a half, for two hides in Sunningwell, and in Kennington three hides, in Garford two hides, in Boxford two hides, in Cumnor two hides and the land of Blagrove, and in Frilford one hide which Berner gave to Thurstan of St Helen, in Longworth one hide.[6]

Raimbald: one knight, for Tubney.[7]

Ansketel: two knights, for Bessels Leigh and Chesterton.[8]

Hendred in a list of Abingdon tenants; note also the discussion in *Charters of Abingdon Abbey*, pp. 224–5.

[3] *DB* i, fo. 58^{v}, confirms Anskil as tenant of these lands. *DB* i, fo. 59^{r}, also attributes Fawler to him, which this list attributes to Baldwin de Colombières.

[4] *DB* i, fo. 58^{v}, confirms Warin as tenant of these lands.

[5] *DB* i, fo. 58^{v}, confirms Hubert as tenant of these lands.

[6] On Blagrove, see above, p. 202; on Rainbald's lands, see also above, p. lxiii.

[7] *DB* i, fo. 58^{v}, confirms Rainbald as tenant of one hide in Tubney.

[8] *Domesday* does not mention Ansketill as a tenant of Abingdon.

Herebertus filius Hereberti: i. militem, pro Lechamstede x. hidas.[9]

Walterus de Riparia: ii. milites et dimidium, pro Bedena.[a][10]

Pro Bradeleia, dimidium militem.[11]

Walterus Giffard: i. militem, pro Liford vii. hidas.[12]

Hugo de Boclande: i. militem, pro Boclande x. hidas.[13]

Gillebertus de Culumbers: ii. milites, pro Horduuelle et vi. hidis in Offentune.[14]

Gillebertus: i. militem, pro duabus hidis in Pusie, et ii. in Mora et in Draicote, et i. hida in Lakinges.[15]

Baldeuuinus de Culumbers: i. militem, pro Flauflor.[16]

Raerus de Aure: i. militem, pro Sudcote.[17]

Henricus filius Oini: i. militem, pro iii. hidis in Abbendonia et ii. hidis in Hulle.[18]

Gillebertus Marescal: vii. hidas et dimidium in Gersentune, et Sueting auus Mathie in Wateleia i. hidam et dimidium, pro seruitio unius militis.[19]

5b. *Hec sunt nomina eorum qui tenent minutas partes que pertinent ad cameram domni abbatis.*

Walterus de Gersindon': dimidium militis.

Benedictus de Westona: dimidium militis.

Petrus de Aldebiri: v. partem unius militis.[20]

[a] s⟨ecundum⟩ alios iii. m⟨ilites⟩ *added at top of this column in brown ink in one of the hands used to provide guidance for the rubricator*

---

[9] *DB* i, fo. 58[v], attributes these lands to Rainbald. The Abingdon list derived from *Domesday*, below, p. 381, attributes them to Herbert the chamberlain, on whom see also above, pp. 126, 196. Herbert son of Herbert was a tenant of Abingdon in the mid-twelfth century; *PR 2–4 HII*, p. 35, and the Abingdon *Carta* of 1166, *Red Book*, i. 306, and below, p. 390, reveals him owing one knight.

[10] *DB* i, fo. 58[v], confirms Walter as tenant of Beedon; it also specifies that he held two hides in Benham; see also above, p. 188.

[11] This is probably Bradley in Chieveley, see above, p. 188.

[12] *DB* i, fo. 59[r], confirms Walter as tenant of these lands.

[13] Cf. *DB* i, fo. 59[v], which states that 'the abbey itself holds Buckland', for five hides. See below, p. 393, for William of Buckland holding five hides there; also above, p. 266.

[14] On Hardwell as a dependency of Watchfield, see above, p. 227; *DB* i, fo. 59[r], confirms Gilbert as tenant of the lands in Uffington, and attributes to him three hides and one virgate in Watchfield. Note, however, that the Abingdon *Carta* of 1166 also records a later Gilbert de Colombières owing Abingdon two knights in 1166; *Red Book*, i. 306, and below, p. 390.

Herbert son of Herbert: one knight, for Leckhampstead ten hides.[9]

Walter de Rivers: two and a half knights, for Beedon.[10]

For Bradley, half a knight.[11]

Walter Giffard: one knight, for Lyford seven hides.[12]

Hugh of Buckland: one knight, for Buckland ten hides.[13]

Gilbert de Colombières: two knights, for Hardwell and six hides in Uffington.[14]

Gilbert: one knight, for two hides in Pusey, and two in Moor and in Draycott, and one hide in Lockinge.[15]

Baldwin de Colombières: one knight, for Fawler.[16]

Raer de *Aure*: one knight, for Southcote.[17]

Henry son of Oini: one knight, for three hides in Abingdon and two hides in Hill.[18]

Gilbert Marshal: seven and a half hides in Garsington, and Sueting grandfather of Matthias one and a half hides in Wheatley, for the service of one knight.[19]

5b. *These are the names of those who hold very small portions which pertain to the chamber of the lord abbot.*

Walter of Garsington: half a knight.

Benedict of Weston: half a knight.

Peter of *Aldebiri*: one fifth of a knight.[20]

[15] *DB* i, fo. 59[r–v], confirms Gilbert as tenant of two hides in Pusey, and attributes to him one hide in Draycott, and one hide and a church with half a hide in Lockinge.

[16] Baldwin was not a *Domesday* tenant of Abingdon. The Abingdon *Carta* of 1166 records a Baldwin of Fawler owing Abingdon one knight; *Red Book*, i. 306, and below, p. 390.

[17] The Abingdon *Carta* of 1166 records a 'Raerus de Alra' owing Abingdon one knight; see *Red Book*, i. 305, and below, p. 390. A 'Reherius de Aura' was joint custodian of Glastonbury Abbey in 1186–87; *PR 33 HII*, p. 27. A list of hidages, below, p. 388, specifies that Ralph de *Alra* was tenant of seven hides in Denchworth. Another list in MS C, in a later hand, has a Ralph de *Aura* holding six hides in Southcote; *CMA* ii. 311. See also Lyell, no. 213, *Testa de Nevill*, i. 294, ii. 844, 847, 852. Southcote, or Circourt, is in Denchworth, EPNS, *Berkshire*, ii. 473, *VCH*, *Berkshire*, iv. 281. I have not been able to identify the family toponym with any certainty; one English possibility might be Awre, Glos., where in 1221 a man named Ralph held land (*VCH*, *Gloucestershire*, v. 26), while in 1220 a Ralph held four carucates in Southcote (*Testa de Nevill*, i. 294).

[18] On Henry, see above, p. 202; he was not a *Domesday* tenant of Abingdon.

[19] *DB* i, fo. 156[v], confirms Gilbert and Sueting as tenants of these lands.

[20] *Red Book*, i. 306, has Peter contributing to making up one and a half knights owed to Abingdon in 1166; the Abingdon version of the *Carta*, below, p. 391, does not specify the

Petrus de Gosie: v. partem unius militis.[21]

Iohannes filius Roberti: apud Hanni, quintam partem unius militis.[22]

Robertus Francolanus de Lakinges: quintam partem unius militis.[23]

Filie Willelmi Grim: apud Mercham et apud Westuuike, quintam partem unius militis.[24]

Terra que fuit Galfridi de Samford: sextam partem unius militis.[25]

fo. 121^{r} Ricardus Gernun de Wateleia: sextam partem unius militis.[26] |

[ii. 6] Terra que fuit Willelmi Chaumum apud Wichtham: quartam partem unius militis.[27]

Wuillelmus de Suttuna: quintam partem unius militis, tempore huius abbatis.[28]

Item Iohannes filius Roberti: apud Abbendun, vi. partem unius militis.

Sed isti duo, Willelmus et Johannes, dant scuagium et non faciunt wardam.

Wuillelmus de Wanci: in Kenintona, quintam partem unius militis.[29]

(ii) MS B, fos. 122^{v}–123^{v}

[ii. 12] **15a.** *Quomodo Robertus de Oili reddidit ecclesie Abbendonie Tademertun.*[30]
fo. 122^{v} Eius[a] temporibus,[b][31] et temporibus duorum regum, scilicet Willelmi qui Anglos deuicerat et filii eius Willelmi, erat quidam constabulus

[a] *corr. from* Eiusdem. *There is also a* b *above the* u, *to indicate that this should follow the next section, which is marked with an* a, *but be before the next but one, which is marked with a* c [b] teporibus *MS*

amount of his contribution. The hidage list below, p. 394, has a Robert of *Aldebiri* holding one and a half hides. The name may relate to part of Chieveley, EPNS, *Berkshire*, i. 245.

[21] *Red Book*, i. 306, has Reginald of Goosey contributing to making up one and a half knights owed to Abingdon in 1166; the Abingdon version of the *Carta*, below, p. 391, specifies that his contribution was one fifth of a knight.

[22] John was a late twelfth- to early thirteenth-century tenant of Abingdon; see e.g. Lyell, nos. 205, 256. He may have been the son of the Robert mentioned in connection with Boars Hill, above, p. 282. *Red Book*, i. 306, has a Robert son of the *dapifer* contributing to making up one and a half knights owed to Abingdon in 1166; the Abingdon version of the *Carta*, below, p. 391, specifies that his contribution was one sixth of a knight; cf. Lyell, no. 205. Another list in MS C, in a later hand, has John son of Robert holding one hide in Hanney and two hides in Abingdon; *CMA* ii. 311.

[23] Another list in MS C, in a later hand, has a John 'Frankelannus' holding one hide in Sandford; *CMA* ii. 311. This is an earlier instance of Francolanus apparently being used as a surname than any of those which appear in *DMLBS*, fasc. iv., s.v. *franclingus*.

[24] *Red Book*, i. 306, has William Grim contributing to making up one and a half knights owed to Abingdon in 1166; the Abingdon version of the *Carta*, below, p. 391, specifies that

Peter of Goosey: one fifth of a knight.[21]

John son of Robert: at Hanney, one fifth of a knight.[22]

Robert Franklin of Lockinge: one fifth of a knight.[23]

The daughters of William Grim: at Marcham and at West Wick, one fifth of a knight.[24]

The land which was Geoffrey of Sandford's: one sixth of a knight.[25]

Richard Gernun of Wheatley: one sixth of a knight.[26]

The land which was William *Chaumum*'s at Wytham: a quarter of a knight.[27]

William of Sutton: one fifth of a knight, in the time of this abbot.[28]

Likewise John son of Robert: at Abingdon, one sixth of a knight.

But these two Williams and John give scutage and do not do guard service.

William de *Wanci*: in Kennington, one fifth of a knight.[29]

(ii) MS B, fos. 122ᵛ–123ᵛ

15a. *How Robert d'Oilly gave back Tadmarton to the church of Abingdon.*[30]

In his [Abbot Reginald's][31] time, and in the times of two kings, that is of William who had conquered the English and of his son, William,

his contribution was one fifth of a knight. See also below, p. 397, for the rents of the altar including three shillings from the tithe of William Grim. See below, p. 387, for Roger Grim holding half a hide in Hinksey; this could be the same as West Wick, if the latter is a dairy farm just south of Oxford.

[25] *Red Book*, i. 306, has Geoffrey contributing to making up one and a half knights owed to Abingdon in 1166; the Abingdon version of the *Carta*, below, p. 391, specifies that his contribution was one fifth of a knight.

[26] *Red Book*, i. 306, has Richard contributing to making up one and a half knights owed to Abingdon in 1166; the Abingdon version of the *Carta*, below, p. 390, specifies that his contribution was one sixth of a knight.

[27] See above, p. 123.

[28] See below, pp. 388, 394, for Edward of Sutton holding one hide.

[29] *Testa de Nevill*, i. 292, 297, has a William de *Wancy* acting as collector of carucage in Berkshire in 1220, and holding lands in Leverton and Compton. *Testa de Nevill*, ii. 843, has a Geoffrey de *Wancey* holding one fee in Leverton; ii. 846, 853, have Geoffrey de *Wancy* and the prioress of Littlemore holding one fee in Leverton from the fee of the abbot of Abingdon. Note that Leverton is in the south of Berkshire, Kennington in the north. A possible origin of the family toponym may be Wanchy (Dept. Seine Maritime), but this cannot be certain. For East Anglian Domesday tenants of the honour of Warenne from Wanchy, see *Anglo-Norman Families*, p. 111.

[30] Cf. above, pp. lxx, 32.

[31] The rearrangement of sections marked in the manuscript indicates that this section was meant to follow that on the coming of Abbot Reginald.

Oxonie, Robertus de Oili dictus, in cuius custodia erat illo tempore prouincia illa, in preceptis et in factis, adeo ut de ore regis proferretur[a] illi accio. Diues enim ualde erat, diuiti nec pauperi parcebat exigere ab eis pecunias sibique gazas multiplicari, sicut qui breui uersiculo de similibus comprehendit, dicens 'Crescit amor nummi, quantum pecunia crescit.'[32] Ecclesias uero cupiditate pecuniarum infestabat ubique, maxime abbatiam Abbendonie, scilicet possessiones abstracte, et frequenter in placitis grauare, quandoque [ii. 13] in misericordiam regis ponere. Inter cetera mala, pratum quoddam extra muros Oxonie situm, consentiente rege, a monasterio abstraxit et in usum militum castelli deputauit. Pro quo dampno contristati sunt fratres Abbendonenses magis quam pro aliis malis. Tunc simul congregati ante altare sancte Marie, quod dedicauerat sanctus Dunstanus archiepiscopus et sanctus Aþeluualdus episcopus, cum lacri- fo. 123r mis prostrati in terram, deprecantes | de Roberto de Oili monasterii depredatore uindictam facere, aut illum ad satisfactionem conuertere.[33]

Interea dum sic per dies et noctes beatam Mariam inuocassent, decidit ipse Robertus in egritudine ualida, in qua laborabat multis diebus inpenitens, donec uidebatur ei quadam nocte in palatio cuiusdam regis magni insistere, et hinc inde multitudinem magnatuum hominum assistere, et in medio illorum quandam gloriosam supra tronum sedere in muliebri habitu speciosam ualde, et ante illam stare duos fratres ex congregatione predicti cenobii, quorum nomina cognouit. Et cum ipsi duo uidissent illum in palatium intrare, flectabant genua ante illam dominam dicentes cum [b]magno suspirio[b] 'Ecce, domina, iste est qui possessiones ecclesie tue sibi usurpat et pratum, unde clamorem facimus, nuper a monasterio tuo abstraxit.' At illa, commota aduersus Robertum, illum iussit foras eicere et ad pratum ducere, quod a monasterio abstraxit, ibique illum torqueri. Ad cuius preceptum surrexerunt duo iuuenes ex circumastantibus et duxerunt eum in predictum pratum, ibique eum fecerunt sedere. Et statim conuenerunt ibi turpissimi pueri, portantes fenum de ipso prato super humeros suos, irridentes et ad inuicem dicentes 'Ecce, karissimus noster. Ludamus cum eo.' Tunc fasciculos de humeris suis

[a] profereretur *MS*   [b–b] *corr. from* magna suspiria, *or vice versa*

[32] Juvenal, *Sat.* xiv. 139.

[33] Dunstan was archbishop of Canterbury 959–88; see *St Dunstan. His Life, Times, and Cult*, ed. N. Ramsay, M. Sparks, and T. Tatton-Brown (Woodbridge, 1992). For his involvement in the dedication of Abingdon, see Bk. i, c. 71 (*CMA* i. 349); for Æthelwold's involvement, see Wulfstan, *Life of Æthelwold*, ed. Lapidge and Winterbottom, p. 24.

there was a certain constable of Oxford called Robert d'Oilly, who then had custody of that region regarding orders and deeds, to such an extent that directions for action came to him from the king's own mouth. For he was extremely rich, and used to spare neither rich nor poor from demanding their money and multiplying his own treasure, as is dealt with in the brief verse concerning similar people, saying 'The love of riches grows as much as wealth grows.'[32] Indeed, he vexed churches everywhere with his greed for wealth, especially the abbey of Abingdon; he took away its possessions and frequently oppressed it in pleas, sometimes placing it in the king's mercy. Amongst his other evils, with the king's consent he took away from the monastery a meadow situated outside the walls of Oxford, and assigned it to the use of the knights of the castle. The brethren of Abingdon were more distressed by this loss than by the other evils. Then all gathered before the altar of St Mary, which St Dunstan the archbishop had dedicated with St Æthelwold the bishop, and with tears they prostrated themselves on the ground, praying that St Mary take vengeance concerning Robert d'Oilly, or persuade him to make amends.[33]

Meanwhile, as they were thus invoking the blessed Mary day and night, Robert himself fell into a severe illness, in which he—impenitent—suffered for many days, until it seemed to him one night that he was standing in the palace of some great king. A multitude of important men stood on both sides, and in the middle of them a glorious woman sat on a throne, extremely splendid in female clothing. Before her stood two brethren from the congregation of the aforesaid monastery, whose names he knew. And when these two saw him enter the palace, they genuflected before that lady, saying with a great sigh, 'Behold, lady, that is the man who usurps for himself the possessions of your church, and has recently taken away from your monastery the meadow regarding which we complain to you.' Enraged with Robert, she ordered him to be thrown outside and led to the meadow which he had taken from the monastery, and to be tortured there. At her order, two young men from amongst those in attendance rose to their feet, led him into the aforesaid meadow, and made him sit there. And at once the most disgusting boys gathered there, bearing on their shoulders hay from that meadow, mocking, and saying to one another 'Behold, our dearest friend. Let's play with him.' Then they put down the

deponentes et desuper mingebant, igne subposito, et sic fumigauerunt eum. Quidam ex eis tortas de illo feno faciebant, et in fatiem eius
[ii. 14] iactabant. Alii barbam eius inflammauerunt. Ille uero in tali angustia positus, clamare cepit, adhuc [a]sopori detento:[a] 'Sancta Maria, indulge mihi, iam moriar.' Vxor autem eius iuxta lectulum eius iacebat et euigilauit illum, dicens 'Domine, euigila, graue enim dormis.' At ille expergefactus a sompno, dixit 'Vere graue, quia in medio demonum erat.' Illa respondit, dicens 'Dominus custodiat te ab omni malo.'[34]

Tunc ille narrauit sompnium uxori sue, et illa 'Dominus flagellat omnem filium quem recipit.'[35] Post paucos uero dies, cogente eum uxore sua, ad Abbendoniam eum nauigare fecit, et ibi ante altare, coram abbate Reginaldo et omni congregatione[b] fratrum et amicorum suorum circumastantium, Tademertune decem librarum reditum, quas Aþelelmi abbatis illuc usque dono exegerat, omni⟨n⟩o[c] remittens, contestatur suarum post se rerum possessiones,[d] ne inde quicquam exactionis ultra queretur;[e] simul et amplius quam centum librarum summam, suorum pro emendatione preteritorum commissorum, sinuanda[f] quoque monasterii reedificatione quod nuper antea abbas Reginaldus ampliari inchoauit, super altare optulit tunc ad presens. Qui adeo monasterii[g] renouationi intendit tunc, ut illud toto illo anno sine penuria fabricare accelerarent.

fo. 123v Post predictam autem uisionem quam uiderat, iussu Dei ge|nitricis se a satellitibus malis torqueri, non tantum ecclesiam sancte Marie de Abbendonia curabat erigere, uerum etiam alias parrochianas ecclesias dirutas, uidelicet infra muros Oxonefordie et extra, ex
[ii. 15] sumptu suo reparauit.[h] Nam sicut ante uisionem illam depredator ecclesiarum et pauperum erat, ita postea effectus est reparator ecclesiarum et recreator pauperum, multorumque bonorum operum patrator. Inter cetera pons magnus ad septemtrionalem plagam Oxonie per eum factus est.[36] Qui mense Septembrio obiens, in capitulo Abbendonensi in parte aquilonis sepulturam meruit. Vxor autem eius in sinistra eius condita requiescit.

[a–a] *for* sopore detentus ? [b] abbate *in margin in different but possibly contemporary hand, which also appears e.g. at fo. 113r* [c] *cf. above, p. 32* [d] *for* possessores, *as above, p. 32* [e] *for* quereretur, *as above, p. 32* [f] *for* pro iuuanda, *as above, p. 32* [g] *corr. from* monasterium [h] raparauit *MS*

---

[34] Cf. Ps. 120 (121): 7, 'Dominus custodit te ab omni malo.'

[35] Cf. Heb. 12: 6, 'Quem enim diligit dominus, castigat: flagellat autem omnem filium, quem recipit.'

bundles from their shoulders, urinated on them, and, by setting fire to them from below, thus engulfed him in smoke. Some of them made coils from the hay and threw them in his face. Others set fire to his beard. Placed in such affliction, he began to cry out whilst still fast asleep, 'St Mary, forgive me as I'm dying now.' His wife, who was lying beside him on his bed, woke him up, saying 'Lord husband, awake, for you are sleeping badly.' Then he awoke from his sleep, and said 'Truly badly, since it was in the midst of demons.' She answered him, saying '"The Lord shall preserve you from all evil."'[34]

Then Robert told his dream to his wife, and she said '"The Lord scourgeth every son whom he receiveth."'[35] So, after a few days, at his wife's instigation, he had himself taken by boat to Abingdon, and there, before the altar, in the presence of Abbot Reginald and with all the congregation of the brethren and his friends in attendance, he entirely remitted the £10 rent from Tadmarton which until then he had demanded by gift of Abbot Adelelm, and solemnly declared that those possessing his property after him would henceforth seek no exaction therefrom. At the same time, he for the moment offered on the altar a sum of more than £100 to emend for his past misdeeds, and to help the rebuilding of the monastery which Abbot Reginald had recently begun to enlarge. So enthusiastic was he then about the rebuilding of this church that throughout that year those building it were able to speed up the work without any shortages.

Moreover, after seeing the aforesaid vision in which he was tortured by evil attendants on the order of the mother of God, he not only took steps to erect the church of St Mary of Abingdon, but also repaired at his own expense other ruined parish churches, that is within and outside the walls of Oxford. For, just as he had been a plunderer of churches and the poor before that vision, so afterwards he was made a repairer of churches and a reviver of the poor and a perpetrator of many good works. Amongst other things, the great bridge to the north bank at Oxford was built by him.[36] He died in September, and deserved burial in the northern part of the chapter of Abingdon. Moreover his wife lies at rest there, buried on his left.

[36] Folly Bridge. Lennard, *Rural England*, p. 71 suggests that 'the sentence in the chronicle which describes the bridge as *ad septemtrionalem plagam Oxoniae* . . . must be a slip for *australem plagam*'; however, from the perspective of Abingdon, the bridge might be seen as spanning to the northern side at Oxford.

(iii) MS B, fos. 154v–155v

[ii. 146] **214a.** *De operibus Faricii abbatis et maxime de ecclesia.*

fo. 154v Quodam tempore uenerabili patre Faritio fundamenta edificii Abbendonensis cenobii magna et pulcherrima iaciente, dum more solito opus uisitans, operarios opera indulgere sedulus ammoneret, quidam ex comfratribus adulatorie dixit ei 'O pater uenerabilis, quam magna sunt fundamenta que iacis, que proculdubio non sine sumptu premaximo opus efficient consummatum. Si igitur uestre placitum dilecte fuerit paternitati, panis nostri communis[a] (quadraginta[b] libras statere appendentis), quartam uobis partem ad opus consummandum inceptum uoluntate unanimi libentissime concederemus.' Quibus auditis, uir per omnia mansuetissimus super hiis responsum ad presens dare dissimulauit. Sequenti uero die, fratrum conuentu in capitulo more solito coadunato, abbas polliciti non inmemor, conuentus super hiis requirit consensum, quod una uoce uniuersi qui aderant dignum fieri gaudenter acclamarunt. Perpendens igitur pastor benignus commissi sibi gregis animum deuotissimum, uultu ut semper erat iocundo, huiusmodi confestim erupit in uerbis: 'O fratres
[ii. 147] et commilitones in Christo carissimi, testem uobis propono altissimum me nec predicti panis uestri stateram[c] sed neque aliarum consuetudinum uestrarum, quamdiu me uitalis carpserit aura,[37] quouis modo infringere tenorem; quin immo domus mihi credite, in quantum potero, dispersa restaurans,[38] et restaurata sollicite conseruans, ad prefatam panis mensuram dimidie marce pondus augebo, ut quicquid cenantibus fuerit residuum in opus misericordie egenis erogandum reseruetur.' Quod donum, ne quis sibi in posterum abbatum succedentium presumeret infringere, sub Dei omnipotentis nomine prohibuit, et omnes infringentes in conuentu sollempniter anatematizauit.

Succedente uero temporis interuallo, cum idem uenerabilis pater Faritius, commissa sibi ecclesia, bonorum operum polleret studiis, instinctu diaboli (qui bonorum omnium semper est emulus) agentibus quibus eidem patri nostro insidiantibus, Willelmo uidelicet

[a] comunis *MS* [b] *figure over erasure* [c] staterem *MS*

[37] Vergil, *Aen.* i. 387–8; see also below p. 354, and Vol. i, c. B44 (*CMA* i. 56).

[38] See above, Introduction, p. xl, on the abbot's vow to regather the unjustly dispersed possessions of the church.

(iii) MS B, fos. 154^{v}–155^{v}

214a. *Concerning the works of Abbot Faritius and especially concerning the church.*

At the time when the venerable father Faritius was laying the substantial and very fine foundations of the building of the monastery of Abingdon, and was visiting the building work, as he was accustomed to do, he diligently urged the workers to devote themselves to the works. One of the brethren flatteringly said to him 'O venerable father, how great are the foundations you are laying, which doubtless will become the completed work . . . but not without great expense. Therefore, if it pleases your beloved fatherhood, our unanimous wish is that we would most willingly grant to you a quarter of our common bread, weighing forty pounds.' When he had heard this, that most gentle man refrained from answering them for the time being. But on the following day, when the convent of brethren had gathered in the chapter as usual, the abbot, who was not forgetful of the promise, sought the convent's consent on these matters. With one voice, all who were present gladly acclaimed that this was a fitting action. The kind shepherd, therefore, carefully assessed the very devout character of the flock entrusted to him, and—as ever with an agreeable expression—immediately spoke out in words of the following kind: 'O dearest brethren and fellow soldiers in Christ, I place before you the Highest as witness that I will not infringe in any way either the weight of your bread or the terms of your other customs so long as I "draw the breath of life".[37] But rather by restoring, as far as I can, the dispersed possessions of the house entrusted to me,[38] and carefully conserving what has been restored, I will add the weight of half a mark to that measure of bread, so that whatever is left over by those dining is reserved for the charitable work of giving food allowances to the needy.' Under the name of Omnipotent God, he forbade that any of the abbots succeeding him in future presume to infringe this gift, and in the convent he solemnly anathematized all those infringing it.

In the following time, however, when that venerable father Faritius, to whom the church was entrusted, was devoting his energies to good works, a general grumbling arose in the convent about that venerable man, at the instigation of the devil, who is always envious of everything good. The ring-leaders were certain men who were making a treacherous attack on our father Faritius—that is

precentore eidem ecclesie et Pondio,[39] circa eundem uirum uenerabilem in conuentu generalis est exorta murmuratio; eo quod frusta[a] casei, ut eis uisum fuerat, ab institutione sancti patris nostri Adelwoldi immutata asserent et inminorata,[40] quod ad noticiam regis Henrici, fama crebrescente, est diuulgatum.

Rex igitur, ut semper erat pacis amator, ut predicta fratrum commotio totaliter intingueretur,[b] Radulfum Cantuariensem archiepiscopum, et Rogerum episcopum Saresbiriensem, et Hugonem de Boclande Abbendoniam destinauit;[41] quos pater uenerabilis susceptos
fo. 155r honorifice, | coram omni congregatione in capitulo sic est allocutus:
[ii. 148] 'Vestram, uiri, fratres, domini, nolo[c] lateat excellentiam, me numquam, post pastoralis officii honus susceptum, institutiones sancti Adeluuoldi, ut mihi obiectum est, infregisse; sed neque res ecclesiasticas intrinsecus seu forinsecus diminuisse, uerum in his augendis toto mentis annisu, post susceptum[d] regiminis officium, semper elaborasse. Non enim ad hoc misit me Dominus, ut congregata dilapidarem, sed ut dilapsa coadunarem; quod et feci, fratrum numero a me primitus ibidem inuento, quinquaginta duo fratres adiciens, exceptis tribus peregrinis pauperibus, quos in redemptoris nostri memoriam, per dies singulos eodem pane et potu quem conuentus dabat, cum frustis casei et duobus pulmentis, a tribus fratribus manibus deuote lotis et pedibus, refocillari constitui.'[42]

Tunc archiepiscopus: 'His[e] omnibus nostrum prebemus assensum, et inperpetuum a posteris obseruari diiudicamus. De frustis tamen

[a] frustra *MS* [b] *for* extingueretur ? [c] uolo *MS* [d] suscepti, *with the last two letters on a different line from the rest of the word, thereby perhaps encouraging the mistaken agreement with* regiminis. *An alternative emendation might be* suscepi *but this would destroy the parallel with the phrase earlier in the sentence* [e] Is *MS*

[39] For this dispute, see Introduction, pp. xxxviii, xlvii.

[40] Note Vol. i, c. B207 (*CMA* i. 345–7) for food arrangements associated with Æthelwold. These lay down that every five days a 'pondus Abbendunense' (an 'Abingdon wey'), that is 22 stones of cheese was to be distributed. According to the *De obedientiariis* (*CMA* ii. 404), the weight of a wey should be eighteen stones. Such inconsistency in calculation of weights is not unusual, but may have encouraged disputes. For 'weys', see Zupko, *Weights and Measures*, pp. 434–8.

Doubt has been cast upon the authenticity of the arrangements attributed to Æthelwold, e.g. Knowles, *Monastic Order*, pp. 716–17, in part because they only appear in MS B, and in a somewhat different form in *De abbatibus*; *CMA* ii. 279. Likewise, Brett, *English Church*, p. 133, feels that the account of the dispute under Faritius should be treated with suspicion, because it only appears in MS B. However, M. Lapidge, 'Æthelwold as scholar and teacher', *Bishop Æthelwold*, ed. Yorke, pp. 89–117, at 106 n. 105 points out 'that the information as transmitted [in MS B] includes a number of Old English words and expressions (e.g. *bolla Æthelwoldi*) which are unlikely to have been fabricated by a

William, precentor for this church, and Pondius.[39] This was the issue: they asserted that the portions of cheese, as it seemed to them, had been changed and diminished from the disposition of our holy father Æthelwold.[40] As news of this spread, it was brought to the notice of King Henry.

The king, therefore, as he was always a lover of peace, sent Ralph archbishop of Canterbury, and Roger bishop of Salisbury, and Hugh of Buckland to Abingdon in order that this dissension among the brethren be totally doused.[41] These men were honourably received, and the venerable father spoke thus in the chapter, in the presence of the whole congregation: 'Men, brethren, lords, I do not wish it to be concealed from your excellence that, after undertaking the burden of pastoral office, I have never broken the dispositions of St Æthelwold, as I have been accused; nor have I diminished the church's internal or external possessions, but have always striven with every effort of my mind to increase them, after I undertook the office of the abbacy. For the Lord did not send me to squander what has been gathered, but to gather together what has been squandered, and I have done this, adding fifty-two brethren to the number of brethren first found by me here; not counting the three poor pilgrims whom, in memory of our Redeemer, I have established to be refreshed with the same bread and drink each day which the convent used to give, with pieces of cheese and two dishes of pottage, and with their hands and feet devoutly washed by three of the brethren.'[42]

Then the archbishop said 'We give our assent to all these things, and decree that they should be observed in perpetuity by men to come. Nevertheless, concerning the portions of cheese about which

thirteenth-century chronicler.' Moreover, according to the *De abbatibus*, Æthelwold specified that 'a wey of cheese' ('pondus casei') was to be distributed every ten days; *CMA* ii. 279. Then Faritius specified that the amount of cheese which Æthelwold fixed for forty-three monks for ten days was to be granted to eighty monks every five days; *CMA* ii. 287. This fits better with the present text, and the consistency is the more significant if these sections of *De abbatibus* pre-date the first manuscript of the *History*; see above, p. xxii.

[41] Ralph's election as archbishop 26 Apr. 1114 gives a *terminus post quem* for the royal intervention; *Handbook of British Chronology*, p. 232.

[42] For the 'three poor pilgrims', cf. *Regularis Concordia*, ed. T. Symons (NMT, 1953), p. 61: 'without fail the service of the Maundy may be rendered to three poor men chosen from among those who are wont to receive their support from the monastery; and let the same foods of which the brethren partake that day be given to them.' See also *De obedientiariis* for the washing of the feet of three poor men every day; *CMA* ii. 405. *Pulmenta*, here translated as 'pottage', were dishes of vegetable or cereal foods, sometimes served in addition to the common monastic dishes, sometimes as substitutes for them; for 'generals', 'pittances', and '*pulmenta*', see Harvey, *Living and Dying*, pp. 10–12.

casei, pro quibus mota est altercatio, quid uestro supersederit animo nobis insinua.' Abbas ad hec: 'Vestre non fiat ignotum sanctitati institutionem sancti Adelwoldi ad hec non sufficere, ut talia sint frusta, cum per Dei uoluntatem fratrum numerus sit multiplicatus, qualia fuerunt cum essent multo pauciores. Verumptamen si in commune cunctis placuerit, ut pondus, quod prius diebus decem distribuebatur, nunc, pro augmento congregationis, quinque diebus attituletur, cucullatis dumtaxat in refectorio necnon et infirmario, cum tribus pauperibus prenominatis, te uolente,[a] peroptime procurabimus in perpetuum obseruari. Refectorarius igitur die quinto
[ii. 149] prefatum pondus ex more suscipiens, illis solummodo quos prenominauimus diebus quinariis, ut dictum est, distribuet.' Tunc archiepiscopus: 'Hec omnia laudanda necnon et obseruanda diiudicaremus, si mensa abbatis, hospitum, et fratrum quos inuitauerit, predicto pondere non participaret.'[b] Cui abbas: 'Successoribus meis abbatibus in tantum prouidi, ut quadraginta sex pondera ad mensam suam annuatim possideat.'[43] Tunc demum archiepiscopus et Rogerus Saresbiriensis, cum omnibus qui aderant, abbatis prouidentiam simul et beniuolentiam erga conuentum considerantes, hec omnia, ut prefata sunt, a posteris inperpetuum firmiter obseruari, sine aliqua omnimodo diminutione, auctoritate sua diiudicarunt. Rogatu igitur abbatis Faritii et tocius conuentus assensu unanimi, Radulfus uenerabilis Cantuariensis archiepiscopus et Rogerus pontifex Saresbiriensis, idem quoque pater prefatus, cum totius conuentus [c]sacerdotibus stolis indutis,[c] candelis accensis, huius institutionis tenorem omnes inposterum uiolatores seu diminutores solempni perculerunt[d] anathemate, ceteris fratribus, ordinis inferioris, uoce submissa, 'Fiat, fiat, fiat' acclamantibus.

fo. 155v Iste[e] sunt wike que tot pisas inue|nire debent:[44] De Sellingeford, xxx. pondera.[45] De wika Roberti, vi. pondera. De Lakinges, decem pondera. De Tropa, iiii. pondera.[46] De duabus wikis de

[a] obuolente *MS, my emendation being speculative but fitting the sense* [b] participarent *MS* [c–c] sacerdotili stolis induti *MS*; *this form does not make good grammatical sense. A more limited emendation, simply replacing* sacerdotili *with* sacerdotes *might be possible, but is still somewhat awkward* [d] pertulerint *MS* [e] De wichis abbatie, *in dry-point in margin in one of the hands providing guidance for the rubricator. This was the intended heading. The last word is hard to decipher*

[43] *VCH*, *Berkshire*, i. 306 n. 1, suggests that the forty-six weys constituted one wey a week, except for the six weeks of Lent.

[44] See also above, Introduction, p. lxxxii; *VCH*, *Berkshire*, i. 306.

this dispute arose, make known to us what remains upon your mind.' To these words the abbot replied 'Let it not be unknown to your holiness that the disposition of St Æthelwold does not suffice for these arrangements, as there are only as many portions now when by God's will the number of brethren has multiplied, as there were when there were many fewer brethren. Nevertheless if it pleases everyone in common, and you so wish, we will provide most clearly that it be for ever observed that the weight which previously was distributed every ten days be now assigned every five, because of the increase in the congregation, at least for the cowled monks in the refectory and also in the infirmary, together with the three poor men specified above. Therefore, the refectorer on the fifth day is customarily to receive the afore mentioned weight, and to distribute it, as has been said, every five days, solely to those specified above.' Then the archbishop said 'We adjudge all these arrangements praiseworthy and they are to be observed, if the table of the abbot, the guests, and the brethren whom he invites there, does not share in the aforesaid weight.' To this the abbot replied 'I have provided for my successors as abbot in as much as he may each year possess for his table forty-six weys.'[43] Then at last the archbishop and Roger of Salisbury and all who were present, bearing in mind the prudence of the abbot along with his good will towards the convent, decreed by their authority that all these arrangements, as mentioned above, should be firmly observed in perpetuity by those to come, with no diminution in any way. Therefore, at the request of Abbot Faritius and with the unanimous assent of the whole convent, Ralph, the venerable archbishop of Canterbury, and Roger bishop of Salisbury, and also the afore mentioned father, together with the priests of the whole convent put on their stoles, and, with candles lit, struck with solemn anathema all who in future violated or diminished the terms of this decree, with the other brethren, in lesser orders, expressing their approval in a low voice, 'so be it, so be it, so be it.'

These are the dairy-farms which ought to find the following number of weys:[44] From Shellingford, thirty weys.[45] From Robert's wick, six weys. From Lockinge, ten weys. From Thrupp, four weys.[46] From

[45] Note also the entry for Shellingford, *DB* i, fo. 59^{v}: '£4 16s. 8d. from the custom of cheeses'.

[46] Thrupp, Berks., is just east of Abingdon.

Goseie, xxviii. pondera. De wika de Cerneia, xvi. pondera. Et de Herbalduna, x. pondera.[47]

214b. *Summa sticarum anguillarum.*[48]

[ii. 150] De Culeham, xx.[a] sticas. De Ascelino, duodecim sti⟨c⟩as. De Trope,
septem sticas. De Alexandro Blundel, viii. De Swineford, xvi. sticas.[49] De Witeleie, uiginti iiii. sticas.[50] De Herwaldun, viii. sticas.

214c. *De operibus Faricii abbatis.*[51]

Nec est obliuioni tradendum quod memoratus abbas Faricius illam partem ecclesie que nauis ecclesie appellatur, cum duabus turribus, et capella sanctæ Marie Magdalene, locutorium cum capitulo, dormitorium cum refectorio, cameram abbatis cum capella, claustrum cum coquina, temporibus suis construi fecit. Ad omnia edificia que fecerat abbas predictus, trabes et tigna de regione Walensium uenire fecit, cum magno sumptu et graui labore. Sex enim plaustra ad hoc habebat, et ad unumquodque illorum xii. boues. Sex uel septem ebdomadarum iter erat eundi et redeundi, nam iuxta Salopesberiam transire oportuit.

(iv) MS B, fo. 155[v]

[ii. 151] **216a.** [b]Dedit etiam duo magna dossaria, que pendent in choro in
fo. 155 precipuis festiuitatibus, unum decem[c] uirginibus,[52] alterum de
historia Job.[b]

(v) MS B, fo. 158[v]

[ii. 163] **236a.** Tunc abbas Vincentius tabulam sancti Aþelwoldi, ex auro et
fo. 158[v] argento fabrefactam, penitus eruderauit;[53] e cuius precio trecentas
[ii. 164] marcas et eo amplius collectas, abbas dedit regi in confirmatione sue
libertatis, ne, si forte tempore succedente et malitia hominum

[a] *followed by space caused by figure being written over erasure* [b–b] *this passage also appears in brown ink in one of the hands providing guidance for the rubricator, at bottom of column. In the main text it is written over an erasure* [c] de decem *in version at bottom of column*

[47] Harrowdown Hill, Berks., near Longworth; EPNS, *Berkshire*, ii. 393–4.

[48] A stick consisted of twenty-five eels; Zupko, *Weights and Measures*, pp. 389–90. See also above, Introduction, p. lxxxii; below, p. 396, a list in MS C in the same hand as the *History*; also *CMA* ii. 308, in a later hand.

[49] Swinford, Berks., is not named in *Domesday Book*, but probably formed part of Abingdon's manor of Cumnor; see *VCH*, *Berkshire*, iv. 400.

the two wicks of Goosey, twenty-eight weys. From the wick of Charney, sixteen weys. And from Harrowdown, ten weys.[47]

214b. *Total of sticks of eels.*[48]
From Culham, twenty sticks. From Ascelin, twelve sticks. From Thrupp, seven sticks. From Alexander Blundel, eight. From Swinford, sixteen sticks.[49] From Whistley, twenty-four sticks.[50] From Harrowdown, eight sticks.

214c. *Concerning the works of Abbot Faritius.*[51]
And it should not be consigned to oblivion that the above-mentioned Abbot Faritius had built in his times that part of the church which is called the nave of the church, with two towers, and a chapel for St Mary Magdalene, and the parlour with the chapter house, and the dormitory with the refectory, and the abbot's chamber with a chapel, and the cloister with the kitchen. For all the buildings which that abbot made, he had beams and timber brought from the region of the Welsh, at great expense and with severe toil. He had six wagons for this and for each of them twelve oxen. The outward and return journey lasted six or seven weeks, as it was necessary to cross near Shrewsbury.

(iv) MS B, fo. 155ᵛ

216a. He also gave two large hangings, which hang in the choir on the main feast days, one depicting the ten virgins,[52] the other depicting the story of Job.

(v) MS B, fo. 158ᵛ

236a. Then Abbot Vincent thoroughly stripped St Æthelwold's retable, fashioned from gold and silver.[53] 300 marks and more were received for the price of this, and the abbot gave this money to the king in confirmation of his liberty, in case, by chance with the passing of time and the growing wickedness of men, knights or men

[50] *DB* i. 59ʳ, mentions a mill at 5s. and 250 eels, and a fishery at 300 eels at Whistley.
[51] See Introduction, p. cii.
[52] See Matt. 25: 1–13.
[53] On this, see also above, pp. xxxix, 230, and Vol. i, c. B207 (*CMA* i. 344); *English Lawsuits*, no. 246. *De abbatibus* specifies that on the retable the twelve apostles were sculpted from pure gold and silver; *CMA* ii. 278.

crescente, milites uel homines hundredi et mercatus libertatem propter adiutorium quasi suum proprium sibi uendicarent emptiticium.

(vi) MS B, fo. 160r

[ii. 171] fo. 160r **251a.** [a]*De ornamentis Vincentii abbatis.*[a] [54]
In diebus aduentus sui ad abbatiam, dedit casulam purpuream, quam Robertus sacrista, sicut adhuc patet, auro obtexuit obrizo. Deinde maiorem turrem ecclesie construi fecit, curiam forinsecis domibus uariis et necessariis, uidelicet aula hospitum cum camera, gernario, bracino, pistrino,[b] dupplici stabulo, elemosinaria cum tribus magnis turribus decenter ornauit. Campanas quoque duas dedit, que priuatis diebus ad horas pulsantur.

(vii) MS B, fo. 161r

[ii. 179] fo. 161r **260a.** Stephanus[c] rex Anglie episcopo Salesb', et iusticiis, et uicecomitibus, et baronibus, et ministris, et omnibus fidelibus suis Anglie, salutem.[55] Sciatis me concessisse et confirmasse donationem illam quam Willelmus rex Anglie auunculus meus fecit ecclesie sancte Marie de Abbendonia et monachis ibidem Deo seruientibus de ecclesia Suttone, cum terris, et decimis, et aliis rebus et consuetudinibus eidem pertinentibus ecclesie. Quare precipio quod predicta ecclesia et monachi ecclesiam Sudtone, cum omnibus pertinentiis suis, bene et in pace et libere et quiete teneant, sicut illam melius tenuerunt tempore predecessorum meorum regum Anglie, sicut testantur eorum carte. Testibus W. Mart' et Ricardo de Luci. Apud Wareng'.

260b. Stefanus[d] rex Anglie episcopo Linc', et iusticiis, et uicecomitibus, et baronibus, et ministris, et omnibus fidelibus suis, salutem.[56]
[ii. 180] Sciatis me concessisse et confirmasse ecclesie sancte Marie de Abbendonia et monachis ibidem Deo seruientibus tenere et habere in perpetua elemosina ecclesiam de Neweham, cum una hida terre, et cum tota decima eiusdem manerii, et cum una piscaria cum omnibus sibi pertinentibus, et cum prato et cum pastura, sicut Willelmus de

[a–a] *in margin* [b] *interlin.* [c] De ecclesia de Suttune *at bottom of column in dry-point, in one of the hands providing guidance for the rubricator* [d] De ecclesia de New' *at top of column in dry-point, in one of the hands providing guidance for the rubricator*

[54] See Introduction, p. ciii.

might claim for themselves the liberty of the hundred and market as if their own purchase, on account of a payment.

(vi) MS B, fo. 160^r

251a. *Concerning the ornaments of Abbot Vincent.*[54]
At the time of his coming to the abbacy, he gave a purple chasuble, which Robert the sacrist covered with pure gold, as can still be seen. Then he had built the larger tower of the church, and fittingly adorned the court with various and apt out buildings, that is the hall of the guests with a chamber, a granary, a brew-house, a bake-house, a double stable, an almonry with three great towers. He also gave two bells, which are struck at the hours on weekdays.

(vii) MS B, fo. 161^r

260a. Stephen king of England to the bishop of Salisbury, and his justices, and sheriffs, and barons, and officials, and all his faithful men of England, greeting.[55] Know that I have granted and confirmed that gift which William king of England, my uncle, made to the church of the Blessed Mary of Abingdon and to the monks serving God there, of the church of Sutton, with the lands and tithes and other possessions and customs pertaining to that church. Therefore I order that the aforesaid church and monks may hold the church of Sutton with all its appurtenances well and in peace and freely and undisturbed, as best they held it in the time of my predecessors as king of England, as their charters witness. Witnesses: William Martel and Richard de Lucy. At Wallingford.

260b. Stephen king of England to the bishop of Lincoln, and his justices, and sheriffs, and barons, and officials, and all his faithful men, greeting.[56] Know that I have granted and confirmed to the church of St Mary of Abingdon and to the monks serving God there to hold and have in perpetual alms the church of Nuneham, with one hide of land and with the whole tithe of that manor, and with one fishery with everything pertaining to it, and with meadow and with pasture, as William de Courcy the steward gave and

[55] *RRAN* iii, no. 12, dating to 1139 × 1154. For William II's grant of the church of Sutton, see above, p. 36.

[56] *RRAN* iii, no. 11, dating to one of the recorded sieges of Wallingford, 1139, 1146, and 1152–3. See also above, pp. 78–80, for William de Courcy's grant of the church of Nuneham to Abingdon, and his son's confirmation charter.

Curci dapifer illa eis dedit et concessit, et sicut Willelmus de Curci filius eius illa eis reddidit et carta sua confirmauit, et sicut carta regis Henrici testatur. Et precipio quod predicta ecclesia et monachi omnes illas tenuras bene et in pace et libere et quiete teneant, sicut melius et liberius tenent alias elemosinas ecclesie sue pertinentes. Testibus Willelmus Mart', et comite Albrico, et Baldwino filio Gilleberti. Apud Wareng', in obsidione.

(viii) MS B, fo. 161^{v}

[ii. 182] fo. 161^{v} **264a.** Stephanus rex Anglie Willelmo Mart' et omnibus fidelibus suis, Francis et Anglis, salutem.[57] Sciatis quia reddidi et concessi Deo et abbatie et monacis de Abbendonia terram suam de Wisselega et de Winkefeld; et terra illa, et omnes alie terre sue, et omnes res sue, sunt in mea tutela et proteccione. Quare uolo et precipio quod sint bene et in pace, ita ne quisquam eis forisfaciat, nec quicquam inde capiat, quia uolo quod omnes res sue sint ita bene custodite, sicut mee dominice, in omnibus rebus. Teste Adam de Beln'. Apud Oxen'.

[ii. 183] **264b.** Stephanus rex Anglie iusticiis, et uicecomitibus, et baronibus, et omnibus ministris et fidelibus suis Anglie et portuum maris, salutem.[58] Precipio quod totum corredium et omnes res abbatis et monachorum sancte Marie de Abbendonia, quas homines sui affidauerint suas esse proprias sint, quiete de theloneo et passagio[a] et omni consuetudine, ne super hoc iniuste disturbentur,[b] super decem libras forisfacture. Testibus Willelmo de Ipra et Ricardo de Luci.

264c. Stephanus rex Anglie Ingulfo abbati Abbendonie, salutem.[59] Mando uobis et precipio quod faciatis wardam uestram ad castellum meum de Windesor, ita bene et plenarie sicut unquam melius et plenius ibidem fecistis, et non alibi. Teste Willelmo de Ipra. Apud Oxen'.

[a] pasnagio *MS* [b] distribuentur *MS*

[57] *RRAN* iii, no. 7, dating to 1136 × 1154.
[58] *RRAN* iii, no. 8, dating to 1139 × 1154.

granted those things to them, and as William de Courcy his son gave back these things to them and confirmed by his charter, and as the charter of King Henry witnesses. And I order that the aforesaid church and monks hold all those tenures well and in peace and freely and undisturbed, as best and most freely they hold the other alms pertaining to their church. Witnesses: William Martel, and Earl Aubrey, and Baldwin son of Gilbert. At Wallingford, during the siege.

(viii) MS B, fo. 161^{v}

264a. Stephen king of England to William Martel and all his faithful men, French and English, greeting.[57] Know that I have given back and granted to God and the abbey and the monks of Abingdon their land of Whistley and of Winkfield. And that land and all their other lands and all their possessions are in my guardianship and protection. Therefore I wish and order that they be well and in peace thus that no one harm them nor take anything therefrom, since I wish that all their possessions be as well guarded as my demesnes, in all possessions. Witness: Adam de Beaunay. At Oxford.

264b. Stephen king of England to his justices, and sheriffs, and barons, and all his officials and faithful men of England and the sea-ports, greeting.[58] I order that the entire provisions and all the goods of the abbot and monks of St Mary of Abingdon, which his men will have pledged their faith to be their own, be quit of toll and transport-due and all custom, and that they are not to be unjustly disturbed contrary to this, on £10 of forfeiture. Witnesses: William de Ypres and Richard de Lucy.

264c. Stephen king of England to Abbot Ingulf of Abingdon, greeting.[59] I instruct and order you that you do your guard-service at my castle of Windsor, as well and fully as ever you best and most fully did it there, and not elsewhere. Witness: William de Ypres. At Oxford.

[59] *RRAN* iii, no. 6, dating to 1139 × 1154. The abbot was presumably being pressed by the king's opponents to provide castle-guard elsewhere, for example at Wallingford, to the detriment of the guarding of Windsor.

(ix) MS B, fo. 169[r–v]

[ii. 213] **287a.** *De quadam pastura in Vffentona.*[60]
fo. 169[r] Item tempore Ingulfi abbatis orta est contentio inter hordarium Wintoniensem et ipsum abbatem, super quadam pastura inter Offentonam et Wlfrichestun, que uocatur Sumerlese.[61] Que causa tamdiu[a] est uentilata, donec memorata pastura per duellum est sopita, et per uictoriam pugilis abbatis huic domui secundum consuetudinem regni est adiudicata.

287b. *De ornamentis Ingulfi abbatis.*
Hec sunt ornamenta que contulit abbas Ingulfus ecclesie Abbendonie uidelicet: quatuor cappe meliores; dalmatica nobilissima; pallium, ad magnum altare, cum leonibus; et quinta cappa, quam in oblatione contulit. Dedit etiam duas cortinas que Gallice 'dossers' uocantur,[62] unam uidelicet de Incarnatione Christi, alteram de Apocalipsi, que etiam in precipuis festiuitatibus pendent in choro.
[ii. 214] Preter hec bona et alia quam plurima que nos latere non dubitamus, fecit infirmariam cum duobus capellis, cameram similiter maiorem que prioris dicitur.[63]

Accidit etiam tempore illius abbatis, ingruente necessitate, pauperes Christi in partibus istis famis seuissima clade periclitari. Qua de re, memoratus abbas pietate motus ac dolore cordis uehementi intrinsecus tactus, cepit erogare quicquid potuit preter ea que monachorum suorum uictui forent neccessaria. Quid multa? Deficiente abbatis substantia inualescente, etiam de die in diem famis pestilentia ad hanc abbatiam pauperum multitudo istius prouincie confluebat infinita. Quod cum uidisset predictus abbas, totus, ut affluebat misericordie uisceribus, ue⟨he⟩m⟨en⟩ter condolere cepit super contricione Ioseph.[64] Dumque deliberasset quid cautius super huiuscemodi infortunio agere posset, de consensu et pari uoluntate fratrum suorum, tecam sancti Vincentii penitus eruderauit, et in usus pauperum largiter infudit.

[a] tam *interlin. at start of this word*

[60] *English Lawsuits*, no. 381. 'Sumerlese' means 'summer pasture'; see EPNS, *Berkshire*, ii. 381.
[61] The hoarder was a monastic treasurer at Winchester; see *DMLBS*, fasc. iv, s.v. *hordarius*.
[62] i.e. dossals; see *Anglo-Norman Dictionary*, fasc. ii, s.v. *dosser*, and above, p. lii.
[63] See Introduction, p. ciii.

(ix) MS B, fo. 169^{r-v}

287a. *Concerning a certain pasture in Uffington.*[60]
Likewise, in Abbot Ingulf's time there arose a dispute between the hoarder of Winchester and the abbot over a certain pasture between Uffington and Woolstone, which is called *Sumerlese*.[61] This case was discussed at length, until that pasture was settled by judicial duel, and by the victory of the abbot's champion was adjudged to this house according to the custom of the realm.

287b. *Concerning the ornaments of Abbot Ingulf.*
These are the ornaments which Abbot Ingulf conferred on the church of Abingdon, that is: four copes of higher quality; a most superior dalmatic; an altar cloth, with lions, for the great altar; and a fifth cope, which he conferred in an offering. He also gave two hangings which in French are called 'dossers',[62] one depicting the Incarnation of Christ, the other depicting the Apocalypse, which indeed hang in the choir on the principal feast days. Besides these good deeds and very many others which we do not doubt are hidden from us, he made the infirmary with two chapels, and likewise the greater chamber which is called the prior's.[63]

There also occurred in that abbot's time a most savage disaster of starvation which threatened the poor of Christ in those areas, as scarcity bore down on them. Concerning this matter, Abbot Ingulf was moved by pity and in his heart was touched with intense grief, and he began to bestow on the poor whatever he could, besides what was necessary for the food of his monks. What's more, with the abbot's resources failing, and also the plague of starvation growing stronger from day to day, an infinite crowd of the poor of this province converged on the abbey. When that aforesaid abbot saw this, as he was abounding with 'the bowels of mercy', like Joseph, all of him began to feel intense compassion for the affliction.[64] And while he was deliberating what he could do particularly prudently concerning such misfortune, by the consent and corresponding will of his brethren he thoroughly stripped the reliquary of St Vincent and generously employed it for the use of the poor.

[64] The allusion is to Gen. 43: 30, 'Festinauitque, quia commota fuerant uiscera eius super fratre suo' ['And Joseph made haste; for his bowels did yearn upon his brother']. The phrase 'uiscera misericordie' appears in Luke 1: 78, Col. 3: 12; note also Vol. i, c. B16 (*CMA* i. 19), and Wulfstan of Winchester, *The Life of St Æthelwold*, ed. M. Lapidge and M. Winterbottom (OMT, 1991), p. 50.

Contigit etiam hiis temporibus, regnante piissimo rege Stephano, ut quidam miles istius abbatie, nomine Ricardus de Sancta Helena, peccatis suis exigentibus, regiam grauiter incurreret offensam.[65] Qui cum ex precepto regis exeredari debuisset per abbatem Ingulfum, perpropere properauit, rogans attencius quatinus abbas ei super huiuscemodi negotio consilium preberet propensius et auxilium. Cuius peticioni abbas maturius satisfatiens, duodecim tecas ex auro puro et argento coopertas iterum eruderauit, utilius diiudicans aurum et argentum pro redemptione militis et libertate ecclesiastica in fisco
fo. 169v regio[a] ad horam exaggerare, quam seruitium eius | dem terre penitus
[ii. 215] amittere, et iacturam ignominiosam diutius sustinere. Reuocans iterum ad memoriam memoratus abbas Ingulfus qualiter tecas eruderasset, et quasi quodammodo reliquias sanctorum in eis reconditas sua spoliasset pulcritudine, uolens eas iterum argento cooperire pariter et auro, quingentas marcas argenti et quadraginta nouem auri ad id faciendum coadunauit. Verum quo thesauro sic coadunato, accesserunt quidam proditores de secreto eius consilio ad regem, alter eum[b] accusantes super huiuscemodi pecunia, quasi illiciter adquisita. Quo audito, rex nuncios suos misit, et in proprios usus sibi addixit thesaurum quem uir Dei ad honorem sanctarum reliquiarum, non sine magno sudore studiosius adquisierat.

(x) MS B, fo. 171^{r-v}

[ii. 221] **297a.** Henricus rex Anglie et dux Normannie et comes Andegauie,
fo. 171r iusticiis, uicecomitibus, ministris, et omnibus bailliuis suis tocius Anglie et portuum[c] maris, salutem.[66] Precipio quod monachi de Abbendona sint quieti de theloneo, de passagio, de pontagio, de
[ii. 222] lestagio, et de omnibus consuetudinibus per omnes terras meas et portus maris, de omnibus rebus quas homines sui poterunt affidare esse suas proprias, sicut carta Henrici regis aui mei testatur. Et prohibeo ne quis eos uel homines eorum inde disturbet, super decem libras forisfacture. Testibus Arnulfo Lex' episcopo, Willelmo de Kelneto, Willelmo de Hasting. Aput Rotomatum.

297b. Henricus[d] Dei gratia rex Anglie et dux Normannie et Aquitanie et comes Andegauie iusticiis suis in quorum bailliis abbas[e] de

[a] *over erasure, with* regio *in margin* [b] *corr., possibly from* alterius. *The sense is unclear, and the word* alter, *remaining from* alterius, *perhaps should be omitted; such has been the basis of my translation* [c] portium *MS* [d] Quod abbas Abbend' mittat senescallum suum uel aliquem alium ad assisas et placita *in margin in dry-point, in one of the hands providing guidance for the rubricator* [e] habbas *MS*

It also happened in that period, when the most pious King Stephen was reigning, that a certain knight of this abbey, Richard of St Helen by name, incurred severe royal animosity, as his sins demanded.[65] When he ought by the king's order to have been disinherited through Abbot Ingulf, he hurried in haste to beg earnestly that the abbot very favourably counsel and aid him in this business. The abbot speedily complied with his request and thoroughly stripped twelve more reliquaries covered with pure gold and silver, judging it more profitable to pile up in the royal treasury for the moment gold and silver for the redemption of a knight and for ecclesiastical liberty, than to lose totally the service of that land and to sustain an ignominious loss for a longer time. Remembering again how he had stripped the reliquaries and, as it were, had despoiled of their beauty the relics of the saints stored therein, Abbot Ingulf wished to cover them again in the same manner with silver and gold, and gathered five hundred marks of silver and forty-nine of gold for doing this. But when this treasure had been gathered thus, some betrayers of his secret counsel went to the king, accusing him as if he had acquired this money improperly. When the king heard this he sent his messengers and assigned to himself for his own uses the treasure which the man of God had acquired for the holy relics very zealously and not without considerable exertion.

(x) MS B, fo. 171^{r-v}

297a. Henry king of England and duke of Normandy and count of Anjou to his justices, sheriffs, officials, and all his bailiffs of the whole of England and the sea-ports, greeting.[66] I order that the monks of Abingdon be quit of toll, of transport-due, of bridge-due, of lastage, and of all customs throughout all my lands and sea-ports, concerning all goods which their men can pledge their faith to be their own, as the charter of King Henry my grandfather witnesses. And I forbid that anyone disturb them or their men concerning this, on £10 of forfeiture. Witnesses: Arnulf bishop of Lisieux, William de Chesney, William of Hastings. At Rouen.

297b. Henry by the grace of God king of England and duke of Normandy and Aquitaine and count of Anjou to his justices in whose

[65] See Introduction, pp. liv, lxv.

[66] This writ has already appeared in both manuscripts; see above, p. 300.

Abbendonia habet terras, salutem.[67] Permitto quod abbas de Abbendonia mittat senescallum suum, uel aliquem alium, in loco suo ad assisas uestras et ad placita. Et ideo precipio quod recipiatis senescallum suum, uel alium, quem ad uos miserit loco suo. Teste Ricardo Britone clerico. Apud Wdest'.[68]

297c. Henricus rex Anglie et dux Normannie et Aquitanie et comes Andegauie H. de Oxeneford uicecomiti et ministris suis, salutem.[69] Precipio uobis quod, si abbatia de Abbendonia iniuste dissaisiata est de ecclesia de Mercheham et pertinentiis suis, et de una hida terre et dimidia in Middeltuna, et de una hida in Appelford, sine dilatione eam inde resaisiatis, et in pace tenere faciatis, sicut melius tenuit tempore Henrici regis aui mei. Et nisi feceritis, iusticia mea faciat. Teste Warino filio Giroldi. Apud Wdest'.[70]

[ii. 223] **297d.** Henricus[a] rex Anglie et dux Normannie et Aquitanie et comes Andegauie bailliuis suis de Wicu, salutem.[71] Precipio uobis quod sine dilatione et iuste reddatis monachis meis de Abbendonia salem suum, sicut solebant habere tempore regis Henrici aui mei. Et nisi feceritis, uicecomes meus de Wirecestresira faciat, nec inde amodo clamorem audiam pro penuria recti. Teste Iohanne Oxon'. Apud Wdestoc'.

297e. Henricus rex Anglie et dux Normannie et Aquitanie et comes Andegauie Ricardo de Canuill' uicecomiti de Berchescira, salutem.[72] Si abbas de Abbendonia iniuste et sine iuditio dissaisiatus[b] est de terra sua de Mercheham, et de Mideltona, et de Appelford, tunc precipio
fo. 171v quod eum inde sine dilatione et iuste resai | sias, et teneat ita bene et in pace et iuste, sicut ecclesia de Abbendonia melius eam tenuit tempore Henrici regis aui mei. Et catalla, que in terra illa iniuste ablata sunt, iuste eis reddere facias. Et nisi feceris, iusticia mea faciat fieri. Teste comite Reginaldo. Apud Windesor'.[73]

[a] De sale de Wic *in margin in dry-point, in one of the hands providing guidance for the rubricator* [b] dissaitus *MS*

[67] The editors of the *Acta of Henry II* suggest a date of ?July 1174 × 1184, with the king's return to England in July 1174 and the promotion of Richard *Brito* as archdeacon of Coventry providing the termini.

[68] *English Lawsuits*, no. 528; Lyell, no. 87, omits the witnesses and gives the place of issue as Westminster. It also uses the words 'our assizes', 'assisas nostras', not 'your assizes'; see also Richard I's charter, below, p. 374, which uses the phrase 'assisas et placita regis'. The writ can probably be dated to after 1172/3, if the original contained 'Dei gratia' in the address, and certainly before 1188 and perhaps before 1181; see *English Lawsuits*.

[69] The editors of the *Acta of Henry II* suggest a date of 1155 × July 1158.

jurisdictions the abbot of Abingdon has lands, greeting.[67] I allow that the abbot of Abingdon may send his steward or someone else in his place to your assizes and to the pleas. And I so order that you receive his seneschal or someone else whom he sends to you in his place. Witness: Richard *Brito*, the cleric. At Woodstock.[68]

297c. Henry king of England and duke of Normandy and Aquitaine and count of Anjou to Henry of Oxford the sheriff and his officials, greeting.[69] I order you that, if the abbey of Abingdon has been unjustly disseised of the church of Marcham and its appurtenances, and of one and a half hides of land in Milton and of one hide in Appleford, you are to reseise the abbey of them and make it hold in peace, as best it held in the time of King Henry my grandfather. And if you do not, my justice is to do so. Witness: Warin son of Gerold. At Woodstock.[70]

297d. Henry king of England and duke of Normandy and Aquitaine and count of Anjou to his bailiffs of Droitwich, greeting.[71] I order you that without delay and justly you give back to my monks of Abingdon their salt, as they were accustomed to have in the time of King Henry my grandfather. And if you do not, my sheriff of Worcestershire is to, so that I may henceforth hear no claim concerning this for want of justice. Witness: John of Oxford. At Woodstock.

297e. Henry king of England and duke of Normandy and Aquitaine and count of Anjou to Richard de Camville sheriff of Berkshire, greeting.[72] If the abbot of Abingdon has been unjustly and without judgment disseised of his land of Marcham and of Milton and of Appleford, then I order that you reseise him thereof without delay and justly, and let him hold as well and in peace and justly, as the church of Abingdon best held it in the time of King Henry my grandfather. And ensure that they are given back justly the chattels which were unjustly taken away on that land. And if you do not, my justice is to ensure that it is done. Witness: Earl Reginald. At Windsor.[73]

[70] For a probable mention of this and the next writ but one, see above, p. 240; if so, they date to 1155 × 1157, and such dating fits with the sheriffs addressed.

[71] This writ can probably be dated to 1155 × 1157; see also above, p. xvii n. 1.

[72] This writ can be dated to September 1155 × September 1157, Richard de Camville's period as sheriff. The editors of the *Acta of Henry II* suggest Oct./Nov. 1155, as the date of Henry II's only recorded visit to Windsor in this period.

[73] See above, p. 240.

297f. Henricus rex Anglie et dux Normannie et Aquitanie et comes Andegauie uicecomiti Lundonie, et uicecomiti de Hamtesii',[a] et uicecomiti de Gloec', salutem.[74] Precipio uobis quod permittatis monachos de Abbendonia emere uictualia sua in bailiis uestris, et deferre ad Abbendoniam per carreium uel quocumque modo uoluerint, que homines sui poterint affidare esse ad opus mona-
[ii. 224] corum. Et non disturbentur propter prohibitionem quam inde feci pro hoc exercitu meo Wallie. Teste Iohanne de Oxenef'. Apud Wirhalam.

297g. Henricus[b] rex Anglie et dux Normannie et Aquitanie et comes Andegauie iusticiis, uicecomitibus, et omnibus ministris suis Anglie, salutem.[75] Precipio quod omnes res monachorum de Abbendonia, quas homines sui affidauerint suas esse proprias ad uictum et uestitum eorum, sint quiete de theloneo, et passagio, et omni consuetudine. Et nullus eos iniuste inde disturbet, super decem libras forisfacture. Teste Willelmo filio Iohannis. Apud Wdestoc'.

297h. Henricus rex Anglie et dux Normannie et Aquitanie et comes Andegauie Rialfo de Suession', salutem.[76] Si monachi de Abbendonia sunt dissaisiti[c] iniuste et sine iuditio de terra Nigelli de Colebroc, quam clamant, tunc precipio quod iuste et sine dilatione eos[d] inde resaisias, sicut inde saiti[e] fuerunt tempore regis Henrici aui mei. Et nisi feceris, iusticia uel uicecomes meus faciat fieri. Teste Willelmo filio Iohannis. Apud Wdestoc'.[77]

297i. Henricus rex Anglie et dux Normannie et Aquitanie et comes Andegauie Ricardo Basset, salutem.[78] Precipio quod monachi mei de Abbendona teneant in pace et libere et quiete et iuste quatuor hidas terre de Chedeleswrð, sicut eas tenuerunt tempore regis Henrici aui

[a] *for* Hamtescira ? [b] Item carta regis de teloneo *in margin in dry-point, in one of the hands providing guidance for the rubricator* [c] *corr. from* dissaisiati [d] eas *MS* [e] saisiti *in margin in dry-point, in one of the hands providing guidance for the rubricator*

[74] Henry II had expeditions to Wales in 1157, 1163, and 1165, Davies, *Age of Conquest*, pp. 51–3. Eyton, *Henry II*, pp. 82–3, identifies the place of issue as Wirhall, near Chester, *Acta of Henry II* takes it as The Wirral. This probably rules out 1163, as in that year the expedition was to south Wales. 1157 might be a possibility, although that might be rather early for John of Oxford to be witnessing; however, see above, p. xvii n. 1.

[75] The editors of the *Acta of Henry II* suggest a date of 1155 × Aug. 1158; Chatsworth, no. 354.

[76] The editors of the *Acta of Henry II* suggest a date of 1155 × Aug. 1158.

[77] For land in Colnbrook, see above, p. 142. Riulf was from Cesson-sur-Seiche (Dept.

297f. Henry king of England and duke of Normandy and Aquitaine and count of Anjou to the sheriff of London, and the sheriff of Hampshire, and the sheriff of Gloucestershire, greeting.[74] I order you that you permit in your jurisdictions the monks of Abingdon to buy their food-stuffs which their men can pledge their faith to be for the monks' use, and to take them to Abingdon by cart or in whatever way they wish. And they are not to be disturbed on account of the prohibition I made concerning this on behalf of my army for Wales. Witness: John of Oxford. At Wirhall.

297g. Henry king of England and duke of Normandy and Aquitaine and count of Anjou to his justices, sheriffs, and all his officials of England, greeting.[75] I order that all the possessions of the monks of Abingdon which their men can pledge their faith to be their own for their food and clothing be quit of toll and transport-due and every custom. And let no one disturb them unjustly concerning this, on £10 of forfeiture. Witness: William son of John. At Woodstock.

297h. Henry king of England and duke of Normandy and Aquitaine and count of Anjou to Riulf de Cesson, greeting.[76] If the monks of Abingdon have been disseised unjustly and without judgment of the land of Nigel of Colnbrook which they claim, then I order that justly and without delay you reseise them of it, as they were seised thereof in the time of King Henry my grandfather. And if you do not, my justice or sheriff is to ensure that it is done. Witness: William son of John. At Woodstock.[77]

297i. Henry king of England and duke of Normandy and of Aquitaine and count of Anjou to Richard Basset, greeting.[78] I order that my monks of Abingdon may hold in peace and freely and undisturbed and justly the four hides of land at Chaddleworth, as they held them in the time of King Henry my grandfather, and

Ille-et-Vilaine). Early in Henry II's reign he held lands at Iver, Bucks., and Aston Rowant, Oxon.; see *Testa de Nevill*, i. 116, *Boarstall Cartulary*, pp. 307, 314, *VCH*, *Buckinghamshire*, iii. 287, *VCH*, *Oxfordshire*, viii. 20. The lands in Iver were close to Colnbrook. By 1161 Hugh de la Mare was rendering farm for Riulf's lands, suggesting he was dead by then; *PR 7 HII*, p. 54. The writ can therefore probably be dated to between 1154 and 1158 when Henry left for the Continent. Riulf witnessed a charter of Peter Boterel for Abingdon, Chatsworth, no. 385. Note also his witnessing of *Eynsham*, i, no 127, *Oseney*, vi, no. 1086, in association with Wallingford knights. The 1166 *Carta* of the honor of Wallingford refers to Stephen son of Riulf and another man jointly owing half a knight; *Red Book*, i 310.

[78] This writ has already appeared in both manuscripts; see above, p. 248.

mei, et eisdem libertatibus cum omnibus pertinentiis earum; et
[ii. 225] prohibeo ne quis eos inde iniuste ponat in placitum. Quod nisi feceris, iusticia mea faciat fieri, ne inde audiam clamorem pro penuria pleni recti uel firme iusticie. Teste Willelmo filio Iohannis. Apud Cliuam.

with the same liberties, with all their appurtenances. And I forbid that anyone unjustly place them in plea concerning this. If you do not do this, my justice is to ensure that it is done, so that I do not hear complaint concerning this for want of full right or firm justice. Witness: William son of John. At King's Cliffe.

APPENDIX II: CONTINUATION IN MS B FOS. 174r–177v

[ii. 234] *De Godefrido episcopo.*

fo. 174r Wualkelino abbate uiam uniuerse carnis ingresso,[1] Godefridus episcopus de Sancto Asaph, quem Henricus secundus istius domus constituit procuratorem, nouem annis et dimidio uicem gerens abbatis in omnibus tam in ordine intrinsecus quam in procuratione forinseca. Cuius constitutionis[a] littere regis subsequentes perhibent testimonium ueritatis, quarum tenor hic est:

Henricus rex Anglie et dux Normannie et Aquitanie et comes Andegauie omnibus, tam clericis quam laicis, tenentibus de abbatia Abbend', salutem. Precipio quod intendatis Godefrido episcopo, cui commendaui abbatiam de Abbendona, tanquam abbati de omnibus que pertinent ad ipsam abbatiam. Et faciatis ei fidelitatem et seruitia
[ii. 235] ita plenarie et integre sicut facere solebatis predecessoribus suis. Et nisi feceritis, uicecomites in quorum bailliis estis uos iusticient donec faciatis.[2] Teste Iohanne decano Sar'. Apud Wdestoc'.[3]

Godefrido[b] ab abbatia amoto, successit ei abbas Rogerus, qui nouem annis et dimidio prefuit huic domui.[4] Iste uero Rogerus, dum adhuc
fo. 174v uitales carperet au|ras,[5] de fugitiuis domus Abbendonie litteras ab ipso rege impetrauit, hanc formam continentes:

Henricus[c] Dei gratia rex Anglie et dux Normannie et Aquitanie et comes Andegauie iusticiis, uicecomitibus, et omnibus bailliuis suis Anglie, salutem. Precipio uobis quod iuste et sine dilatione faciatis

[a] coistitutionis *MS* [b] De Rogero abbate *added in margin in dry point, in one of the hands providing guidance for the rubricator* [c] fugitiuis ecclesie *added in margin in dry point in one of the hands providing guidance for the rubricator; presumably originally preceded by* De, *but the edge of the manuscript has been cut off*

[1] The phrase 'ingredi uiam uniuerse carnis' is quite common in mediaeval writings. It has Biblical roots, although it is not a quotation from the Bible: note esp. Gen. 6: 13 'finis uniuersae carnis'; Josh. 23: 14 'ingredior uiam uniuersae terrae'; 3 Kgs. (1 Kgs.) 2: 2 'ingredior uiam uniuersae terrae'. Walkelin died on 10 Apr. 1164; Cambridge, University Library, Kk. i 22, fo. 3r; *Heads of Religious Houses*, p. 25. For the income from Abingdon during the vacancy, see Introduction, p. lxxv. Godfrey had been consecrated bishop of St Asaph in 1160, was suspended by pope in 1170, and resigned on 18 May 1175; *Handbook of British Chronology*, p. 295.

APPENDIX II: CONTINUATION IN MS B FOS. 174r–177v

Concerning Bishop Godfrey.
When Abbot Walkelin had gone the way of all flesh,[1] Bishop Godfrey of St Asaph, whom Henry II appointed guardian of this house, ruled in all matters for nine and a half years in place of an abbot, both concerning internal order and external stewardship. Of his appointment, the following letters of the king bear witness of the truth, the terms of which are here:

Henry king of England and duke of Normandy and Aquitaine and count of Anjou to all men, both cleric and lay, holding from the abbey of Abingdon, greeting.[2] I order that you submit to the authority of Bishop Godfrey, to whom I have entrusted the abbey of Abingdon, as to an abbot, concerning everything which pertains to that abbey. And you are to do him fealty and services as fully and completely as you were accustomed to do his predecessors. And if you do not, let the sheriffs in whose jurisdictions you are distrain you until you do so.[3] Witness: John deacon of Salisbury. At Woodstock.

When Godfrey had been removed from the abbacy, there succeeded to him Abbot Roger who ruled this house for nine and a half years.[4] While indeed this Roger was still 'drawing the breath of life',[5] he obtained from the king himself letters concerning the fugitives of the house of Abingdon, containing this text:

Henry by the grace of God king of England and duke of Normandy and Aquitaine and count of Anjou to his justices, sheriffs, and all his bailiffs of England, greeting. I order you that justly and without delay

[2] The editors of *Acta of Henry II* suggest a date of May 1165 × May 1166, and preferring the start of this period.

[3] For *iusticiare* being used to mean 'distrain', see e.g. 'Glanvill', *Tractatus de legibus*, bk. ix. c. 8, ed. Hall, p. 112; Hudson, *Land, Law, and Lordship*, pp. 30–1, 36–40.

[4] According to Ralph Diceto in his *Ymagines historiarum*, in *Opera historica*, ed. W. Stubbs (2 vols., London, 1876), i. 401, Abingdon was still vacant on 8 Jul. 1175. Roger was elected in the latter part of that year. *Annales monastici*, i. 51, London, British Library, Cotton Cleopatra A. VII, fo. 12r (Tewkesbury, s. xiii) has 'Reg*inaldus*' receive Abingdon in 1175; this is presumably an error for an abbreviation of Roger.

[5] Vergil, *Aen.* i. 387–8; see also above, p. 332, and Vol. i, c. B44 (*CMA* i. 56).

habere Rogero abbati de Abbendonia omnes natiuos et fugitiuos suos cum catallis suis ubicumque inuenti fuerint in bailliis uestris, nisi sint in dominio meo, qui fugerunt de terra sua post mortem regis Henrici aui mei. Et prohibeo ne quis eos iniuste detineat, super forisfacturam meam. Teste Humfrido de Buun. Apud Oxeneford'.[6]

Tempore[a] etiam istius abbatis Rogeri orta est controuersia inter
[ii. 236] Willelmum Turpinum camerarium regis et domum Abbendonie super una hida in Dumeltune, quam clamabat per breue de recto tenere de domo Abbendonie;[7] que controuersia, cum inter memoratum Willelmum Turpinum et domum Abbendonie diu esset uentilata tandem in curia regis hoc fine et tenore est sopita, sicut attestatur carte regis Henrici secundi[b] subsequens inscriptio:[8]

Henricus[c] Dei gratia rex Anglie et dux Normannie et Aquitanie et comes Andegauie archiepiscopis, episcopis, abbatibus, comitibus, baronibus, iusticiis, uicecomitibus, ministris, et omnibus fidelibus suis, Francis et Anglis, tocius Anglie, salutem. Sciatis me concessisse et presenti carta confirmasse Willelmo Turpino camerario meo et heredibus suis terram de Fencota, quam Rogerus abbas Abbendonie, communi assensu tocius conuentus ipsius abbatie, coram me concessit ei,[d] tenendam pro duobus solidis annuatim reddendis camerario abbatis ad festum sancti Michælis pro omni seruitio ad ecclesiam Abbendonie pertinente, ita quod abbas terram illam ei warantizabit. Et prefatus Willelmus Turpinus totam terram quam clamabat in Dumbeltuna quietam clamauit ecclesie de Abbendonia, et warantizabit illam de omni parentela sua et contra totam progeniem Helie per quem ipse clamabat; et si eam warantizare non poterit, ipse uidelicet uel sui, ecclesia de Abbendonia recipiet terram suam de Fenchote liberam et quietam de Willelmo et suis, sicut cirographum inde inter eos factum et carta abbatis et conuentus testatur.[9] Quare uolo et

[a] ⟨Car⟩ta de Fencote *added in margin in dry point, in one of the hands providing guidance for the rubricator* [b] primi *MS* [c] ⟨Confirm⟩atio regis de Fencote *added in margin in dry point, in one of the hands providing guidance for the rubricator* [d] *corr. from* eis

[6] *Royal Writs*, no. 122; the writ cannot securely be dated more precisely than to those periods between 1175 and 1185 when Henry was in England. On such writs concerning fugitives, see above, p. 120 and fn. 283; for *natiui*, here translated 'villeins', see Hyams, *Kings, Lords, and Peasants*, pp. 228–9.

[7] *English Lawsuits*, no. 481; the case can be dated to the time when John was bishop elect of Norwich, 26 Nov.–14 Dec. 1175. I have not been able to establish with certainty the identity of 'the offspring of Helias', through whom William made his claim. William Turpin was a chamberlain of Henry II; see J. E. A. Jolliffe, *Angevin Kingship* (London,

you make Roger abbot of Abingdon have all his villeins and fugitives with their chattels, wherever they are found in your jurisdictions (unless they are in my demesne), who fled from his lands after the death of King Henry my grandfather. And I forbid that anyone unjustly detain them, on my forfeiture. Witness: Humphrey de Bohun. At Oxford.[6]

Also during the time of that Abbot Roger a dispute arose between William Turpin, the king's chamberlain, and the house of Abingdon, over one hide in Dumbleton which William was claiming by writ of right to hold from the house of Abingdon.[7] When this dispute between that William Turpin and the house of Abingdon had been discussed for a long time, at length it was settled in the king's court by this fine and on these terms, as the following text of King Henry II's charter witnesses:[8]

Henry by the grace of God king of England and duke of Normandy and Aquitaine and count of Anjou to his archbishops, bishops, abbots, earls, barons, justices, sheriffs, officials, and all his faithful men, French and English, of the whole of England, greeting. Know that I have granted and by the present charter confirmed to William Turpin my chamberlain and his heirs the land of Fencott which Roger abbot of Abingdon, by the common assent of the whole convent of that abbey, granted him in my presence, to be held for 2s. to be rendered annually to the chamberlain of the abbot, at the feast of St Michael, for all service pertaining to the church of Abingdon, thus that the abbot will warrant that land to him. And the aforementioned William Turpin quitclaimed all the land he was claiming in Dumbleton to the church of Abingdon, and will warrant it concerning all his relations, and against all the offspring of Helias through whom he made his claim; and if he, that is he or his men, cannot warrant it, the church of Abingdon is to take back its land of Fencott, free and quit of William and his men, as the cirograph made between them concerning this, and the charter of the abbot and convent, witness.[9] Therefore I wish

1955), pp. 70, 243, 257–8. For a charter recording Abbot Roger's grant of land in Fencott to William Turpin in return for land in Dumbleton, see *English Register of Godstow*, p. 327; the land subsequently passed to Godstow, pp. 327–30. For the writ of right, see 'Glanvill', *Tractatus de legibus*, bk. xii, cc. 1–5, ed. Hall, pp. 136–8; also e.g. Hudson, *Formation of the Common Law*, p. 127.

[8] See also Lyell, no. 115, the heading to which states that this was the land at Fencott mentioned above, p. 108.

[9] These documents do not appear in the *History* or the cartularies.

firmiter precipio quod idem Willelmus Turpinus et heredes sui predictam terram de Fenchota habeant et teneant in feudo et
[ii. 237] hereditate de ecclesia de Abbendonia et de abbate et successoribus suis per predictum seruitium bene et in pace, libere et quiete, integre et plenarie et honorifice, in bosco et plano, in pratis et pasturis, in aquis et piscariis, in uiis et semitis, et in omnibus aliis locis et aliis rebus ad eam pertinentibus, et cum omnibus libertatibus et liberis consuetudinibus suis, sicut coram me concessum fuit et conuentionatum. Testibus J.[a] electo id est Northw', Adam de Sancto Asaph episcopis, Ricardo de Luci, Willelmo filio Aldelini dapifero, Radulfo filio Stephani camerario. Apud Winton'.

Rogero abbate Abbendonie mortuo, transmisit rex Henricus |
fo. 175r Thomam de Hisseburna ad custodiam abbatie, alterum scilicet Rapsacen, non dico Sennacherib intentione.[10] A quo adueniente mox exiit edictum ut describeretur uniuersus locus, et ibant omnes ut profiterentur singuli de re ad se pertinente.[11] Replebant uillani angulos curie et compita uille, tractantes et conferentes quid nouo domino requisiti responderent. Et facta questione quid singuli ministrorum perciperent, quid ad singula ministeria pertinerent, hec descriptio prima facta est a presidente abbatie clerico prenotato.

Petrus[b] portarius duo conredia habet,[12] panem monachi et iios.
[ii. 238] coronatos[13] et iio. fercula per diem, et ceruisiam, unam mensuram de promtuario abbatis et aliam de cellario aule.[14] Scepinga[15] eius iiii.

[a] G. *MS* [b] consuetudinibus abbatie *added at bottom of column in dry point, in one of the hands providing guidance for the rubricator*

[10] Roger died on 30 Mar. 1185; *Heads of Religious Houses*, p. 25, Cambridge, University Library, Kk. i 22, fo. 2v. Sennacherib, the king of Assyria, sent Rabshakeh to Jerusalem with a great army; Isa. 36. The Latin is very compressed, but the writer seems cautiously to be making clear that he is not attacking Henry II, but only his official.

A longer version of events under Thomas of Hurstbourne appears in MS C in a different hand from that of the *History*, and is printed in *CMA* ii. 297–9 (= *English Lawsuits*, no. 570); it too is followed by sections on the customs of the abbey, although interspersed with other documents in a variety of hands. For Thomas, see above, p. lvi; for income during the vacancy, see above, p. lxxv.

[11] Cf. Luke 2: 1–3, 'Factum est autem in diebus illis, exiit edictum a Caesare Augusto ut describeretur universus orbis. Haec descriptio prima facta est a praeside Syriae Cyrino: et ibant omnes ut profiterentur singuli in suam civitatem.' I follow the Authorized Version translation for the verbal parallels, although it is unclear whether the Latin 'describeretur' and 'profiterentur' really should be taken to mean 'taxed' rather than 'described' and 'declare' respectively. 'Describere' and 'descriptio', which is used later in the paragraph, may also have reminded readers of the language used of the *Domesday* survey and *Book*; e.g. John of Worcester, *Chronicle*, iii. 44, a work which Abingdon possessed.

and firmly order that the same William Turpin and his heirs have and hold the aforesaid land of Fencott in fee and inheritance from the church of Abingdon and from the abbot and his successors through the aforesaid service, well and in peace, freely and undisturbed, completely and fully and honourably, in wood and plain, in meadows and pastures, in waters and fisheries, on roads and tracks, and in all other places and other things pertaining to it, and with all their liberties and free customs, as was granted and agreed in my presence. Witnesses: Bishops John, that is the elect of Norwich, and Adam of St Asaph, Richard de Lucy, William son of Aldelin the steward, Ralph son of Stephen the chamberlain. At Winchester.

When Abbot Roger of Abingdon had died, King Henry sent Thomas of Hurstbourne for custody of the abbey, another Rabshakeh, not I say a Sennacherib in intention.[10] Following this man's arrival, soon from him 'there went out a decree that all the place be taxed, and all went to be taxed, every one' concerning what pertained to him.[11] The inhabitants filled the extremities of the court and the cross-roads of the town, debating and discussing their answer to their new lord about what they had been asked. And when it had been enquired what each of the officials received, and what pertained to each office, this was the first description made by that cleric who was presiding over the abbey:

Peter the door-keeper has two corrodies,[12] the bread of a monk, and two crowned loaves,[13] and two dishes of cooked food each day, and beer, one measure from the abbot's store, and the other from the cellar of the hall.[14] His allotment[15] four acres in Milton and two acres

[12] For the servant's corrody or allowance, see Harvey, *Living and Dying*, p. 182: 'it always included a daily allowance of bread and ale, although often of the inferior kinds commonly given to lower servants. How much food it included depended on the rank of the servant whom the monks and their corrodians had in mind.'

[13] The sense of 'coronatos' with reference to bread is not entirely clear.

[14] Peter's allowance is a significant one, suggesting that he did not spend his days sitting in the abbey's gate-house. An agreement in 1202 allowed Andrew de Scaccario the position for life; see *Fines sive pedes finium*, ed. J. Hunter (2 vols., London, 1835–44), i. 118, N. Denholm-Young, *Collected Papers* (Cardiff, 1969), pp. 201–2. More generally on Benedictine door-keepers, see J. Kerr, 'Monastic Hospitality: the English Benedictines *c.*1070–1245', Ph.D. thesis (St Andrews, 2000), pp. 162–3. Peter also witnessed C.H., no. 1; see further Lyell, nos. 251, 267 (which mentions his wife, Matilda), Chatsworth, nos. 34, 83, 258.

[15] 'Scepinga' and related forms are very unusual. They may relate to the Old English *scyp*, meaning a patch of cloth, and by analogy a patch of land; see Lambrick, 'Administration', p. 170.

acras in Mideltuna, et ii. acras in Wthona, et in Gareford ii. acras de feudo Galfridi de Suningewella. Et habet oblationem iiiior. denariorum et oboli in Natali[a] Domini, ipse et homo suus, et in Pascha ii. denariorum, et pro puingn'[16] quod solebat habere. Scipinga abbatis de Witteham viii. acras.[17]

Cappellanus de sancto Nicholao ii. coronatos, et i. ferculum, et ceruisiam de cellario abbatis.[18]

Dapifer comedet in aula et xx. solidos habebit pro stipendio de Willelmo de Cumba. Et famulus suus comedet in aula. Et habet dapifer iiii. denarios et obolum in oblationem in Natali et ii. denarios in Pascha.

Lardenarius habet panem monachi, et i. ferculum, et ceruisiam de aula. Scipinga eius iiiior. acras in Appelford uno anno, et alio iii. acras de decima, et vi. pelles ouinas[b] in festo sancti Martini, et flotin de socio quod coquitur in lardario;[19] et in Natali Domini iii. denarios de oblatione et in Pascha ii. denarios.

Cocus abbatis ii. panes paruos, et pro companagio iii. obolos, et ceruisiam in aula. Scipinga eius ii. acras in Mideltuna, et iii. obolos in oblatione in Natali, et i. denarium in Pascha.

Bo. cocus monachorum ii. paruos panes, et i. ferculum, et ceruisiam de aula. Scipinga eius iiii. acras in Wechenesfeld, et in Natali iii. obolos in oblatione et in Pascha i. denarium.

Wuillelmus albus v. ambras de blado.[20] Scippe eius ii. acras de decima in Suttuna, et i. arietem uel iiii. denarios in Natali Domini.

Reginaldus Kiwel v. ambras. Scippe eius [c]acram et dimidiam[c] in
[ii. 239] Draituna in cultura rusticorum et i. acram in Suttuna de decima
Reginaldi de Curten', et in Natali i. arietem uel iiii. denarios.[21]

Hostiarius v. ambras bladi. Scippe eius ii. acras in Bertuna de decima, et in Natali Domini i. arietem uel iiii. denarios.

[a] *corr. from Natale* [b] ouine *MS* [c–c] acra et dimidia *MS*

[16] 'Puingn'' is most likely an Old French word, 'puignee' or 'poignee', meaning handful; see *Anglo-Norman Dictionary*, fasc. v, s.v. *poignee*. However, it is unclear of what Peter was accustomed to have a handful.

[17] It is just possible that this should be Wytham, the place-name form not being quite conclusive.

[18] The chapel of St Nicholas is at the abbey gate. It does not appear in Eugenius III's confirmations, and was probably very new at the time of this survey; cf. Lyell, no. 21.

[19] *Flotin* is probably a vernacular form, although it does not appear in the *Anglo-Norman Dictionary*. The Latin varied; see *DMLBS*, fasc. iv, s.v. *flotagium*, *flotiscum*, *flotimen*. I have

in Wootton, and in Garford two acres from the fee of Geoffrey of Sunningwell. And he has an offering of 4½d. at the birth of the Lord, he and his man, and at Easter 2d., and for the handful[16] which he was accustomed to have. Allotment of the abbot, from Wittenham, eight acres.[17]

The chaplain of St Nicholas two crowned loaves, and one dish of cooked food, and beer from the cellar of the abbot.[18]

The steward eats in the hall, and will have 20s. for a stipend from William of Coombe. And his servant eats in the hall. And the steward has 4½d. as an offering at Christmas and 2d. at Easter.

The larderer has the bread of a monk, and one dish of cooked food, and beer from the hall. His allotment four acres in Appleford one year, and the other year three acres of tithe, and six sheep-skins on the feast of St Martin [11 Nov.], and the skimmings of fat from the *socio* which is cooked in the larder;[19] and at the birth of the Lord 3d. from the offering and at Easter 2d.

The abbot's cook two small loaves of bread, and for the accompanying food 1½d., and beer in the hall. His allotment two acres in Milton, and 1½d. as an offering at Christmas and 1d. at Easter.

Bo. the monks' cook two small loaves of bread, and one dish of cooked food, and beer from the hall. His allotment four acres in Watchfield, and at Christmas 1½d. as an offering and at Easter 1d.

William the fair five measures of corn.[20] His allotment two acres of tithe in Sutton, and one ram or 4d. at the birth of the Lord.

Reginald Kiwel five measures. His allotment an acre and a half in Drayton in the peasants' tillage, and one acre in Sutton from the tithe of Reginald de Courtenay, and at Christmas one ram or 4d.[21]

The usher five measures of corn. His allotment two acres in Barton from the tithe, and at the birth of the Lord one ram or 4d.

been unable to establish the meaning of *socius* | *socium*. One possibility, deriving from the word in its form in the text, would be for it to mean 'common-pot', but in that case 'coquitur' would have to mean 'is used for cooking', rather than the usual 'is cooked'. Another possibility would be to see it as an unusual spelling of—or perhaps a scribal error for—a word such as 'salcius', i.e. salted food. The fat would be skimmed from the surface of the pot in which such food was slowly cooked, as one might now skim (and then most likely throw out) the fat from the top of a pan in which one was gently boiling a ham or bacon joint.

[20] An *ambra* or amber was a dry measure, which sometimes can be fixed at four bushels; *DMLBS*, fasc. i, s.v. *ambra*, Zupko, *Weights and Measures*, pp. 8–9.

[21] A charter of Henry II records him giving Sutton to Reginald de Courtenay; *Berks., Bucks. and Oxfordshire Arch. Journal*, xxv (1919–20), p. 99n. The editors of the *Acta of Henry II* suggest a date of Dec. 1175 × Apr. 1179.

A. scutellarius v. ambras. Scippe eius ii. acras in Suttuna de decima Reginaldi de Curt', et i. arietem uel iiii. denarios.

Amus cocus de familia ii. paruos panes, et ceruisiam de aula, et companagium de lardario. Sep' eius iiii. acras in Cudesduna, et in Natali Domini iii. obolos de oblatione et unum denarium in Pascha.

Ricardus de infirmario:[22] sep' ii. acras de Bertona, i. arietem uel iiii. denarios.

Galfridus de infirmario:[23] iii. solidos de camera abbatis.

Reinbaldus: xii. denarios.

Seruiens refectorii: v. ambras. Sep' eius ii. acras in Suttuna, in Natali i. arietem uel iiii. denarios.

Idem seruiens cellarii, et quando faciet medonem monachorum, habebit panem et ceruisiam de cellario monacorum et companagium de lardario.

Seruiens sacriste habebit ii. panes in aula, et ceruisiam de aula, et companagium de lardario.

Idem Adam.

fo. 175v Henricus: v. ambras, i. arietem uel iiii. denarios. Sep' eius | ii. acras in Wechenesfeld de decima.

Gerin comedet iiii. diebus Natalis, Pasche, et i. die Pentecostes in aula, et die Natiuitatis[a] sancte Marie.

[ii. 240] Seruiens de bracin[24] habebit ii. panes in aula et companagium in lardario. Sep' eius iiii. acras in Wechenesfeld de decima, in Natali Domini iii. obolos in oblatione et i. denarium in Pascha.

Duo alii famuli Ærwardus et H. comedent iiii. diebus Natalis, et Pasche, et i. Pentecostes in aula.

Seruiens de gardino W. habebit sep' in Wtona ii. acras, [b]cibum de elemosina.[b25]

W. Pucin habet ii. panes et ceruisiam in aula, et companagium in lardario.

[a] natiuiuitatis *MS, the repetition being caused by a change of line* [b–b] *in margin in main hand, with corresponding mark in text where should be inserted;* helemosina *MS*

[22] Richard also witnessed C.H., no. 1; see further Chatsworth, nos. 375, 388.

[23] Geoffrey also witnessed C.H., no. 1; see further Lyell, nos. 292, 293, Chatsworth, nos. 255, 388.

A. the scullery officer five measures. His allotment two acres in Sutton from the tithe of Reginald de Courtenay, and one ram or 4d.

Amus the cook of the household two small loaves of bread, and beer from the hall, and the accompanying food from the larder. His allotment four acres in Cuddesdon, and at the birth of the Lord 1½d. from the offering and 1d. at Easter.

Richard from the infirmary:[22] allotment two acres from Barton, one ram or 4d.

Geoffrey from the infirmary:[23] 3s. from the abbot's chamber.

Reinbald: 12d.

The servant of the refectory: five measures. His allotment two acres in Sutton, at Christmas one ram or 4d.

The servant of the cellar the same, and when he makes the monks' mead, he will have bread and beer from the monks' cellar and the accompanying food from the larder.

The servant of the sacrist will have two loaves of bread in the hall, and beer from the hall, and the accompanying food from the larder.

Adam the same.

Henry: five measures, one ram or 4d. His allotment two acres in Watchfield from the tithe.

Gerin eats in the hall on four days at Christmas, at Easter, and one day at Pentecost, and the day of the Nativity of St Mary.

The servant of the brew-house[24] will have two loaves of bread in the hall, and the accompanying food in the larder. His allotment four acres in Watchfield from the tithe, at the birth of the Lord 1½d. as an offering and 1d. at Easter.

Two other servants, Ærward and H., eat in the hall on four days at Christmas, and at Easter, and one at Pentecost.

W., the servant of the orchard, will have as an allotment two acres at Wootton, bread from the alms.[25]

W. Pucin has two loaves of bread and beer in the hall, and the accompanying food in the larder.

[24] 'Bracin' is an Old French word; *Anglo-Norman Dictionary*, fasc. i, s.v. *bracin*.

[25] 'Gardinum' may mean orchard or garden, *DMLBS*, fasc. iv, s.v. *gardinum*. I translate it as orchard here to distinguish its servant from the 'seruientes orti', translated below, p. 365, as 'servants of the garden'.

W. Sexi comedet iiii. diebus Natalis, Pasche, et i. Pentecostes.

Seruiens de pistrino, Mar', habet ii. panes coronatos in pistrino, et ceruisiam in aula, et companagium in lardario.[26] Sep' eius iiii. acras in Wttona et dimidiam acram in Kenitona, et in Natali iii. obolos et in Pasca i. denarium in oblatione.

Martinus habet v. famulos ad custum suum. Isti comedent in aula sicut alii superius.

Calefactor furni habet unum panem in pistrino, et v. ambras et i. arietem uel iiii. denarios. Sep' ii. acras in Culeham.

Vanator: vii. ambras, et in Natali i. arietem uel iiii. denarios.

Seruiens de camera, Robertus tallator, habet ii. panes, et ceruisiam in aula, et companagium in lardario. Sep' eius ii. acras in Bertona.

Robertus coruesarius: ii. panes, et ceruisiam in aula, et companagium in lardario. Sep' eius iiii. acras in Mercham,[a] et in Natali i. iuuenem porcum.

T. filius Salomonis habet sep' ii. acras in Bertona, et comedet sicut alii, et i. arietem in Natali uel iiii. denarios.[27]

Paganus: v. ambras et i. arietem uel iiii. denarios, et comedet sicut alii.

Rogerus filius Pag', Gal', et Mart' comedent sicut alii.

Randulfus habet v. ambras et i. arietem uel iiii. denarios, et in oblatione iii. obolos in Natali et i. denarium in Pascha.

Adam parimentarius: v. ambras et i. arietem uel iiii. denarios in Natali, et secundam falcaturam prati de Brewerin.[28] Sep' eius ii. acras in Gareford.

Seruiens de lauendrie: v. ambras, et ii. arietes in Natali, oblationem in
[ii. 241] Natali, ii. denarios pro iiobus. ministris et i. in Pascha. Sep' eius iiii.
acras de decima in Suttuna.

Seruientes elemosine vi. comedent in aula sicut alii.

Seruientes orti iii. habebunt singuli v. ambras, et in Natali singuli[b] arietem uel iiii. denarios. Sep' eorum x. acras diuidendas inter eos, scilicet iiii. acras in Gareford, et iiii. in Goseia, et ii. in Suttuna.

[a] *corr. from* Merham *by interlin. of* c *in brown ink in one of the hands providing guidance for the rubricator* [b] singulos *MS*

[26] Martin the baker also witnessed C.H., nos. 1, 2.

[27] On Thomas, see also *CMA* ii. 330, a list of rents owed to the hostillar or guest-master.

W. Sexi eats on four days at Christmas, at Easter, and one at Pentecost.

The servant of the bakehouse, Mar[tin], has two crowned loaves of bread in the bakehouse, and beer in the hall, and the accompanying food in the larder.[26] His allotment four acres in Wootton, and half an acre in Kennington, and at Christmas 1½d. and at Easter 1d. as an offering.

Martin has five servants at his own expense. They eat in the hall, like the others above.

The heater of the oven has one loaf of bread in the bakehouse, and five measures, and one ram or 4d. Allotment two acres in Culham.

The winnower: seven measures, and at Christmas one ram or 4d.

The servant of the chamber, Robert the tailor, has two loaves of bread, and beer in the hall, and the accompanying food in the larder. His allotment two acres in Barton.

Robert the cordwainer: two loaves of bread, and beer in the hall, and the accompanying food in the larder. His allotment four acres in Marcham, and at Christmas one young pig.

T[homas] son of Salomon has as an allotment two acres in Barton, and eats like the others, and one ram at Christmas or 4d.[27]

Pain: five measures, and one ram or 4d., and he eats like the others.

Roger son of Pain, Geoffrey, and Martin eat like the others.

Randulf has five measures and one ram or 4d., and as an offering 1½d. at Christmas and 1d. at Easter.

Adam the parmenter: five measures and one ram or 4d. at Christmas, and the second day's mowing service of the meadow of Bruney Mead.[28] His allotment two acres in Garford.

The servant of the laundry: five measures and two rams at Christmas, an offering at Christmas, 2d. for two subordinates, and 1d. at Easter. His allotment four acres from the tithe in Sutton.

The six servants of alms eat in the hall, like the others.

The three servants of the garden will each have five measures, and at Christmas each a ram or 4d. Their allotment ten acres to be divided between them, that is four acres in Garford, and four in Goosey, and two in Sutton.

[28] For Bruney Mead, see EPNS, *Berkshire*, ii. 440.

Carpentarius Simon habet iiii. acras et dimidium de terra rusticorum [a]in Draitun[a] ad eleccionem.[29] Et habebit conredium in curia quando operatur in curia, et i. porcum in Natali.

Reginaldus habebit i. panem in aula pro guteriis parandis. Sep' eius uno anno v. acras et alio iiii. acras et dimidiam de decima in Appelford, et i. porcum in Natali.

Summonitor v. ambras et companagium de lardario. Sep' eius duas acras in Bertona. De unoquoque manerio i. denarium de pannagio ad Natiuitatem sancte Marie.

Porcarius: v. ambras. Sep' eius ii. acras in Suttuna de decima, et iii. obolos in Natali, et in Pascha i. obolum, et summonitor i. denarium. Et de omni porco qui nutritur in curia, fructum de cauda habebit porcarius.

Stabularius: panem in aula, et ceruisiam et companagium in lardario. Sep' eius ii. acras in Suttuna de decima, et oblatio iii. obolorum in Natali et i. denarii in Pascha.

Vacarius habebit panem et ceruisiam in aula. Sep'. eius i. acram de dominio de Culeham.

Quatuor famuli de lignario comedent in aula sicut alii.[30]

[ii. 242] Cuuarius, quando operatur, habebit panem de aula, et companagium
fo. 176r de | lardario, et ceruisiam de cellario, et oblationem i. denarii in Natali et oboli in Pascha.

Passarius de Sunninches habet ii. summa frumenti et ii. caseos pro passare abbatem, si uenerit, uel suos uel sua.

La weite[b] habet conredium in aula, et oblationem i. denarii in Natali et oboli in Pascha, et pannos de abbate.[31]

Lauenderia habet conredium in aula quando portat mappas lauandas, et iterum quando reportat.[32]

Duo molendinarii comedent in aula sicut alii.

Custos posterne conredium in aula, et oblationem[c] in Natali i. denarii et oboli in Pascha, et pannos de abbate.

[a–a] *interlin.* [b] *corr. by interlin. from* wete [c] *corr. from* obbo

[29] The phrase 'ad eleccionem' is obscure. Professor P. D. A. Harvey (personal communication) suggests that it may mean Simon had first choice of strips within fields either cultivated communally or else regularly re-allocated; however, this would be a very late instance of such a process of re-allocation. Simon the carpenter and his wife Reinild

Simon the carpenter has four acres and half of the land of the peasants in Drayton, at his choice.[29] And he will have a corrody in the court when he works in the court, and one pig at Christmas.

Reginald will have one loaf of bread in the hall, for gutter work. His allotment one year five acres and the other four acres and a half of the tithe of Appleford, and one pig at Christmas.

The summoner five measures and the accompanying food from the larder. His allotment two acres in Barton. From each manor 1d. from pannage at the Nativity of St Mary.

The swineherd: five measures. His allotment two acres in Sutton from the tithe, and 1½d. at Christmas and ½d. at Easter, and the summoner 1d. And from each pig which is raised in the court, the swineherd will have the benefit of the tail.

The stable-man: bread in the hall, and beer, and the accompanying food in the larder. His allotment two acres in Sutton from the tithe, and an offering of 1½d. at Christmas and 1d. at Easter.

The cowherd will have bread and beer in the hall. His allotment one acre from the demesne of Culham.

The four servants of the lignar eat in the hall like the others.[30]

The cooper, when he works, will have bread from the hall, and the accompanying food from the larder, and beer from the cellar, and an offering of 1d. at Christmas and ½d. at Easter.

The ferry man of Sonning has two pack-horse loads of corn and two cheeses for ferrying the abbot if he comes, or his men or his things.

The watchman has a corrody in the hall, and an offering of 1d. at Christmas and of ½d. at Easter, and clothes from the abbot.[31]

The laundress has a corrody in the hall when she carries cloths for washing, and again when she brings them back.[32]

The two millers eat in the hall, like the others.

The guardian of the postern gate a corrody in the hall, and an offering at Christmas of 1d. and of ½d. at Easter, and clothes from the abbot.

are recorded in C.H., no. 1 (dating from 1175 × 1185) as having been involved in a dispute with William of Seacourt over a messuage in Abingdon. See also Lyell, no. 351, Chatsworth, nos. 246, 247.

[30] For the lignar, see above, p. 250 n. 614.

[31] 'La waite' is an Old French word; *Anglo-Norman Dictionary*, fasc. iii, s.v. *gaite*.

[32] 'Mappe' means table-cloths, towels, etc.; i.e. what we would call household linen.

Seruiens de Bertona habet conredium in aula, et oblationem i. oboli in Natali et oboli in Pascha.

Seruiens de Mercham: idem.

Grenetarius habet conredium in aula.

Pincerna: conredium.

Prior habebit unum hominem ad conredium in aula et prebendam ad unum equum.

Camerarius, sacrista, lignarius, coquinarius, magister operum: tantumdem.

Duo famuli de lauendaria habebunt ii. conredia in aula tribus uicibus quando monachi balneant.

[The remainder of this line, and the three following lines are blank]

Omnes isti famuli quos prenominauimus comedent in aula iiiior. diebus in Natali, et iiiior. in Pascha, et i. die Pentecostes, et habebunt liuresun[33] in aula in Natiuitate sancte Marie.

[ii. 243] Parcarius habebit ii. homines ad conredium predictis diebus. Wuillelmus de Tropa: i. hominem.

Edulfus, Ainulfus,[a] Wualterus de Hannie: singuli istorum i. hominem.

Isti etiam habebunt prebendam equorum et conredium suum quotiens equos adduxerint uel redierint.

Wicarii x. habent conredium quando primo portant caseum et quando ultimo redierint.[b]

Omnes isti habebunt lifreisun[c] in Natiuitate sancte Marie. xiii. piscatores, quando portabunt anguillas in capite ieiunii, habebunt singuli ii. paruos panes de aula.

Auaragii, quando redeunt de uia, habebunt singuli i. paruum panem de aula.

Omnes autem famuli domus habebunt feria iii. ante Cineres singuli singula frusta[d] carnis.

Executa itaque procuratione domus Abbendonie a prefato Thoma, ipse Londonias perrexit et de statu domus iustitiario domini regis

[a] *corr. from* Alnulfus [b] rediderint *MS* [c] *second* i *interlin.* [d] frustra *MS*

The servant of Barton a corrody in the hall, and an offering of ½d. at Christmas and ½d. at Easter.

The servant of Marcham: the same.

The granary-keeper has a corrody in the hall.

The butler: a corrody.

The prior will have one man at a corrody in the hall and a provender for one horse.

The chamberlain, the sacrist, the lignar, the kitchener, the master of works: the same amount.

The two servants of the washerwoman will have two corrodies in the hall on the three occasions when the monks take a bath.

[The remainder of this line, and the three following lines are blank]

All these servants whom we have named above eat in the hall on four days at Christmas, and four at Easter, and one day at Pentecost, and will have provisions[33] in the hall on the Nativity of St Mary.

The park-keeper will have two men at corrody on the aforesaid days. William of Thrupp: one man.

Edulf, Ainulf, Walter of Hanney: each one man.

These men will also have a provender of horses and their corrody as often as they bring horses or go back.

The ten dairy-farmers have a corrody when they first bring cheese and when they last go back.

All these men will have provisions on the Nativity of St Mary. The thirteen fishermen, when they will bring eels on Ash Wednesday, will have small loaves of bread from the hall.

Those owing transport service, when they return from the road, will each have one small loaf of bread from the hall.

Moreover all the servants of the house will each have individual pieces of meat on the Tuesday before Ash Wednesday.

Therefore, when the administration of the house of Abingdon had been carried out by the afore-mentioned Thomas, he went to London

[33] 'Livresun' or 'lifreisun' is an Old French word; *Anglo-Norman Dictionary*, fasc. iii, s.v. *liveresun*.

Rannulfo de Glanuilla innotuit, quod auena tocius domus Abbendonie solis equis monachorum per annum non sufficeret; nec hoc solum, uerum etiam dixit quod tota Berchesira non sufficeret ad caseum et lac monachorum inueniendum.[34] Quibus auditis a quibusdam confratribus nostris, scilicet[a] Nicholao priore, et Anchetillo priore de Colum, et Willelmo camerario cum aliis monachis, ad scaccarium tunc presentibus, responsum est quod domus Abbendonie diues est de bono frumento omnibus diebus, et qui habet frumentum potest emere auenam. Super caseo et lacte, sic ab eisdem fratribus responsum est quod wike a temporibus sancti Adelwoldi sunt preuise ad memoratum caseum et lac inueniendum. Que uero institutio ne in
[ii. 244] posterum uocaretur in irritum, beatus Adeluuoldus cum coepiscopis
fo. 176v Anglie | sollempniter excommunicauit omnes illos per quos prefata institutio foret adnichilata. Tunc precepit Rannulfus de Glanuilla iusticiarius domini regis magistro Thome de Husseburne ut nullum de antiquis domus Abbendonie consuetudinibus dum procurator esset aliquatenus diminueret, et maxime de caseo et[b] lacte et auena, timens ne si secus faceret beati Adeluuoldi et coepiscoporum Anglie grauiter incurreret sententiam.

De Alfredo abbate.[35]

Amoto itaque Toma a procuratione domus istius, rex Henricus dedit abbatiam Abbendonie Alfredo priori Rouecestrie.

[ii. 245] *De morte Henrici regis.*[36]

Itaque mortuo Henrico illustri rege Anglorum, gloriosus comes Pictauie Ricardus filius eius suscepit regni gubernacula. Iste uero rex Ricardus, leonina ut erat ferocitate, tam strenue et tam potenter se habebat in regni moderamine, ut fama eius de die in diem crescente, non solum reges Christiani sed et pagani, qui de eo loqui audiebant, generaliter eum timebant.[37]

De Hugone abbate.

Eodem mense quo illustris rex Ricardus coronatus est, abbas Alfredus cessit in fatum,[38] et successit ei Hugo abbas, uir bone memorie, qui,

[a] *interlin.* [b] *interlin.*

---

[34] Ranulf de Glanville was justiciar in the last decade of Henry II's reign; see *DNB* entry by F. W. Maitland.

[35] Alfred or Alvred was appointed in 1186; *Heads of Religious Houses*, p. 25. See Introduction, p. lvi, for the description of his abbacy in *De abbatibus*.

[36] Henry died on 6 Jul. 1189.

and informed the lord king's justiciar, Ranulf de Glanville, concerning the state of the house, saying that the oats of the whole house of Abingdon did not suffice each year for the monks' horses alone, and not only this but also he said that the whole of Berkshire would not suffice for finding the monks' cheese and milk.[34] After some of our fellow brethren,—that is Nicholas the prior, and Anchetill prior of Colne, and William the chamberlain, together with other monks then present at the exchequer—heard these things, the response was made that the house of Abingdon is always rich in good wheat, and he who has wheat can buy oats. On cheese and milk, it was answered by the same brethren that dairy-farms had been provided for finding the above-mentioned cheese and milk from the times of St Æthelwold. Indeed lest in future this disposition be declared void, the blessed Æthelwold, with his fellow bishops of England, excommunicated all those through whom that provision be brought to nothing. Then Ranulf de Glanville, the lord king's justiciar, ordered Thomas of Hurstbourne that while he was guardian he was to diminish nothing at all of the old customs of the house of Abingdon, and especially with regard to cheese and milk and oats, fearing that if he did otherwise, he would gravely incur the sentence of the blessed Æthelwold and his fellow bishops of England.

Concerning Abbot Alfred.[35]
So, when Thomas was removed from the administration of that house, King Henry gave the abbey of Abingdon to Alfred, prior of Rochester.

Concerning the death of King Henry.[36]
So, when Henry, the illustrious king of the English was dead, the glorious count of Poitou, Richard, his son, undertook the governance of the kingdom. Indeed this king Richard, like a lion as he was in ferocity, behaved so vigorously and so powerfully in controlling the kingdom that, as his fame grew from day to day, not only Christian kings but also pagans who heard mention of him universally feared him.[37]

Concerning Abbot Hugh.
In the same month in which the illustrious King Richard was crowned, Abbot Alfred yielded to death,[38] and to him succeeded

[37] Cf. J. Gillingham, *Richard Coeur de Lion* (London, 1994), p. 184, on the legend linking Richard with a lion's heart.

[38] Alfred died in Sept. 1189, and Richard was crowned on 3 Sept. *De abbatibus* says that Hugh was a monk of Abingdon; *CMA* ii. 293. See also above, Introduction, p. lvi.

eodem anno quo curam suscepit pastoralem, tempore Paschali transfretauit et priuilegium omnes libertates domus Abbendonie comprehendens pariter et confirmans ab illustri rege prospere Ricardo et[a] feliciter impetrauit. Cuius priuilegii tenor hic est:

Carta quam domnus Hugo abbas apud dominum regem Ricardum obtinuit.[b][39]

Ricardus Dei gratia rex Anglie, dux Normannie et Aquitanie, comes
[ii. 246] Andegauie archiepiscopis, episcopis, abbatibus, comitibus, baronibus, iusticiis, uicecomitibus, et omnibus ministris et fidelibus suis tocius Anglie, salutem. Sciatis nos concessisse et presenti carta nostra[c] confirmasse Deo, et ecclesie beate Marie de Abbendonia, et abbati Hugoni, et omnibus successoribus suis, et monachis ibidem Deo seruientibus omnes terras et possessiones eidem ecclesie collatas, sicut carte regum predecessorum nostrorum eis confirmant et aliorum donatorum scripta testantur. Et uolumus et firmiter precipimus quod predictus abbas Hugo et omnes successores sui et[d] monachi de Abbendonia habeant et teneant in perpetuam elemosinam hundredum de Hornimere cum omnibus que ad hundredum pertinent, in legittima et liberrima potestate et iusticia sua; uidelicet quod nullus uicecomes uel eorum ministri inde se quicquam intromittant, uel placitent, uel aliquid exigant nec de dominico ipsius abbatis uel
fo. 177r monachorum ubicumque terras habent, sed ipsi libere ius|ticiam suam habeant et faciant. Volumus etiam et firmiter precipimus quod abbas et monachi de Abbendonia de predicto hundredo de Hornimere et de omni dominico suo, in quocumque comitatu terras habent, de hidagio et de omni dono uicecomitum[40] et de omni exactione et seculari seruitio sint inmunes in perpetuum et quieti. Preterea
[ii. 247] uolumus quod idem abbas Hugo et successores sui et monachi habeant et teneant iure perpetuo in predicto hundredo et in tota abbatia et in omnibus pertinentiis eius bene et in pace, libere et quiete, plene et[e] integre et honorifice sacham et socham et tol et them et infongeneþeof, et utfongeneþeof[41] et grithbreche et forstall et hamsochne et fleomenefremthe, in burgo et extra burgum, in bosco et plano, in pratis et molendinis, in aquis et riuis, in uiis et

[a] *interlin.* [b] *an illustration of Henry II appears at the head of the next column* [c] *interlin.* [d] *interlin.* [e] recte *scored out*

[39] Lyell, no. 100, Chatsworth, no. 349; note also Lyell, nos. 139, 141, 549. Another copy appears in MS C, but not in the hand of the *History*, and so I have not included variants

Abbot Hugh, a man of blessed memory, who at Easter time in the same year in which he undertook the pastoral care crossed the sea and successfully and happily obtained from the illustrious King Richard a privilege embracing and confirming all the liberties of the house of Abingdon. These are the terms of this privilege:

Charter which lord Abbot Hugh obtained in the presence of lord King Richard.[39]

Richard by the grace of God king of England, duke of Normandy and Aquitaine, count of Anjou to his archbishops, bishops, abbot, earls, barons, justices, sheriffs, and all officials, and his faithful men of the whole of England, greeting. Know that we have granted and by our present charter confirmed to God, and to the church of the blessed Mary of Abingdon, and to Abbot Hugh, and to all his successors, and to the monks serving God there, all the lands and possessions conferred on that same church, as the charters of our predecessors as king confirm to them, and the documents of other donors witness. And we wish and firmly order that the aforesaid Abbot Hugh and all his successors and the monks of Abingdon have and hold in perpetual alms the hundred of Hormer with everything which pertains to the hundred, in their lawful and most free power and justice; that is, that no sheriff or sheriff's official interfere in anything therein, or demand anything, neither from the demesne of the abbot himself nor of the monks, wherever they have lands, but they are to have and do their own justice freely. We also wish and firmly order that the abbot and monks of Abingdon be immune in perpetuity and quit of hidage and all gift of sheriffs[40] and of all exaction and secular service concerning the aforesaid hundred of Hormer and concerning all their demesne in whatever county they have lands. Besides, we wish that the same Abbot Hugh and his successors and the monks may have and hold by perpetual right in the aforesaid hundred and in the whole abbacy and in all its appurtenances, well and in peace, freely and undisturbed, fully and completely and honourably, sake and soke and toll and team and infangentheof, and utfangentheof[41] and grithbrech and foresteal and hamsocn and flemenforthe, in borough and out of borough, in wood and plain, in meadows and mills, in waters and streams, in

here. For further copies see *Cartæ Antiquæ, Rolls 11–20*, no. 470; PRO, C.47/, Chancery Miscellanea, 12/8, 82.

40 'Hidage' and 'sheriff's gift' were customary payments to sheriffs, although not with a universal rate; see Neilson, *Customary Rents*, pp. 124–9; J. A. Green, 'The last century of danegeld', *EHR* xcvi (1981), 241–58, at pp. 255–7.

41 See above, p. xcvii.

semitis, in festo et sine festo, cum omnibus aliis consuetudinibus suis. Confirmamus etiam Deo et ecclesie beate Marie de Abbendonia ecclesiam de Colum, cum omnibus pertinentiis, in liberam et[a] perpetuam elemosinam; uidelicet quod abbas et monachi de Abbendonia plenissimam potestatem habeant in ecclesiam de Colum et in omnibus pertinentiis suis, sicut habent in suo proprio dominico. Confirmamus etiam eis ecclesiam de Chinsentum, et ecclesiam de Suttun, ecclesiam de Niwenham, cum omnibus que ad easdem ecclesias pertinent, in liberam et perpetuam elemosinam. Concedimus preterea et confirmamus abbati et monachis de Abbendonia siluam de Cumenore et de Baggelea in libera custodia eorum perpetuo habendam, et omnes capreolos quos ibi inuenire poterunt[b] accipiant, et ceruos et ceruas non accipiant nisi nostra licentia; et omnes forisfacturas sartorum de Cumenore et de Baggelea eis condonamus. Et concedimus eis habendum et tenendum libere et quiete, bene et in
[ii. 248] pace, integre et honorifice, mercatum de Abbendonia. Concedimus eis preterea totam decimam de uenatione que capta fuerit in foresta nostra de Windleshores. Precipimus etiam quod abbas Hugo et omnes successores sui et monachi quieti sint[c] de theloneo, de passagio, de pontagio, de lestagio, et de omnibus consuetudinibus per omnes terras nostras et portus maris de omnibus rebus quas homines sui poterunt[d] affidare esse suas proprias. Et concedimus quod habeant warennas, et capiant lepores et uulpes in omni Berchescire et in omnibus terris suis, et prohibemus ne quis in terris suis[e] fuget uel leporem capiat sine eorum licentia. Concedimus preterea quod habeant curiam suam in Oxeneford et quod homines sui de Oxeneford non placitent extra curiam suam, nisi abbas et monachi prius defecerint de recto in curia sua. Permittimus etiam quod abbas mittat senescallum suum uel aliquem alium in loco suo ubique ad assisas et placita regis, et quod ille quem miserit loco suo pro ipso recipiatur. Volumus etiam quod habeant consuetudines in nauibus transeuntibus, scilicet in allecibus accipiendis et mercatis faciendis.
fo. 177v Prohibemus | preterea ne aliquis disturbet ullo modo careiam sancte Marie de Abbendonia, nec aliquid aliud quod sit dominicum abbatis uel monachorum, per terram uel per aquam impediat, sed in pace eat et redeat quietus quicumque rem suam siue aliquid aliud quod[f] ad opus ecclesie pertineat conduxerit.[42] Prohibemus etiam quod nullus detineat natiuos uel fugitiuos ecclesie de Abbendonia,

[a] *added in margin* [b] *for* poterint ? [c] *corr. from* sunt [d] *for* poterint ?
[e] *interlin.* [f] *interlin.*

roads and tracks, in feast and without feast, with all their other customs. We confirm also to God and the church of the blessed Mary of Abingdon the church of Colne with all appurtenances in free and perpetual alms, that is that the abbot and monks of Abingdon have the fullest power in the church of Colne and in all its appurtenances as they have in their own demesne. We also confirm to them the church of Kensington, and the church of Sutton, and the church of Nuneham, with everything which pertains to these same churches in free and perpetual alms. Besides, we grant and confirm to the abbot and monks of Abingdon the wood of Cumnor and of Bagley to have in their free and perpetual custody, and they may take all the roe deer which they can find there, but they are not to take red deer stags and hinds, except by our permission. And we pardon them all forfeitures concerning assarts from Cumnor and Bagley. And we grant them to have and hold freely and undisturbed, well and in peace, completely and honourably, the market of Abingdon. Besides we grant to them the entire tithe of game which is taken in our forest of Windsor. We also order that Abbot Hugh and all his successors and monks be quit of toll, of transport-due, of bridge-due, of lastage, and of all customs throughout all our lands and sea-ports, concerning all goods which their men can pledge their faith to be their own. And we grant that they have warrens and take hares and foxes in all Berkshire and in all their lands, and we forbid that anyone in their lands hunt or take a hare without their permission. Besides, we grant that they have their court in Oxford, and that their men of Oxford not plead outside their court, unless the abbot and monks previously fail with regard justice in their court. Also we allow that the abbot may send his steward or someone else in his place anywhere to the assizes and pleas of the king, and that he whom he sends in his place is to be received on his behalf. We also wish that they may have customs in passing ships, that is in receiving herrings and making purchases. Besides we forbid that anyone disturb in any way transport of St Mary of Abingdon, or impede anything else which may belong to the lordship of the abbot or monks, by land or by water, but whoever collects their property, or anything else which pertains to the use of the church, may go and return quit in peace.[42] We also forbid that anyone detain the villeins or fugitives of the church of

[42] Cf. above, p. 116.

ubicumque inuenti fuerint, nisi in dominio nostro. His testibus:
domino Baldeuuino Cantuariensi archiepiscopo, Hugone Dunelmensi, Huberto Saresbiriensi, Hugone Cestrensi, Reginaldo Bath-
[ii. 249] oniensi episcopis; Willelmo comite de Arundel, Willelmo de Humaz,
Albrico de Ver, Rannulfo de Glanuilla, ⟨J⟩ohanne de Alescun,
Wigano de Cheleburc. Datum per manum Willelmi de Longo
Campo cancellarii nostri Eliensis episcopi. Anno primo regni nostri,
uicesima nona die Marcii, apud Gisorz.

Abingdon, wherever they are found, except in our demesne. These witnesses: Lord Baldwin, archbishop of Canterbury, Bishops Hugh of Durham, Hubert of Salisbury, Hugh of Chester, Reginald of Bath, William earl of Arundel, William de Humez, Aubrey de Ver, Ranulf de Glanville, John de Alençon, Wigan de Cherbourg. Given by the hand of William de Longchamp, our chancellor, the bishop of Ely. In the first year of our reign on the twenty-ninth day of March, [1190] at Gisors.

APPENDIX III: ADMINISTRATIVE LISTS IN MS C

INTRODUCTION

This appendix prints those sections of MS C, except the Anglo-Saxon charter bounds, which follow the *History* in the manuscript and are in the same hand as the *History*. They appear in a single quire, fos. 187r–194v, and are followed by the Anglo-Saxon charter bounds in another quire. I note, but do not edit, entries in other hands. As these are administrative lists, I have left unextended place names, personal names, and other words where the endings are uncertain. I have left numbers as numerals or words according to the manuscript form. The entries are as follows:

1. A list of hidages for Berkshire, headed 'Concerning the hundreds and hides of the church of Abingdon in Berkshire, as the writing of the king's treasury contains them, arranged by each hundred'. Whilst the hidages coincide with those for the time of King Edward in *Domesday Book*, it should also be noted that there is some evidence for these figures rather than those for 1086 continuing to be used with reference to Berkshire lands, or for payment having to be made for the use of the reduced 1086 figure.

2. An abbreviated form of *Domesday*, with hidages for the time of King Edward and 1086, for all the counties in which Abingdon held lands. This list is headed 'Also, in the other book of the king's treasury in the time of King William who acquired England, written by his order, is contained an abbreviation of hides and a description, as follows.' The greater detail than in the list at fo. 187v may suggest that fos. 187v–189r drew directly upon *Domesday Book*. On the other hand, the Abingdon text states to which hundred lands belonged, even in the case of Oxfordshire for which *Domesday Book* does not provide hundreds. It seems most probable that *Great Domesday* itself is the 'book in the king's treasury' to which the heading refers, and that the Oxfordshire hundred names were added. The list also includes two gifts of land in Oxfordshire, both made during the abbacy of Faritius.

3. A list which gives hidages of estates and names of tenants within those estates, together with hidages of their holdings. This list is headed 'Those who hold lands of this church of Abingdon'. Most but not all the hidages correspond to those for the 'the time of King Edward' in *Domesday*. It is probably from the 1120s, 1130s, or early 1140s. It most likely slightly predates list no. 6. For convenience of comparison I have footnoted those men

who appear in this list, but not in no. 6. The footnotes to list no. 6 allow comparison of the holdings of men who appear in both lists.

4. A version of the 1166 Abingdon *Carta* somewhat different from that preserved in the Exchequer records. Notably, it specifies the fractions of knights' fees owed by those whom the *Red Book* version simply lists as together owing one and a half knights.

5. Another list of Berkshire hidages, some relating to the figure for the time of King Edward, some to 1086, and some not based on *Domesday*, either because the place is not named in *Domesday*—as in the case of Abingdon—or because it relates to a post-*Domesday* gift. The list must date from after the acquisition of Chaddleworth, above, p. 246. The hidages should also be compared with those given in the list of tenants printed as no. 3 in this Appendix. The rubricator failed to add initials on fo. 191ʳ, and was presumably also meant to give an explanatory heading.

6. A list of tenants and the hidages, but only very occasionally the names, of their holdings. It is probably from the 1120s, 1130s, or early 1140s. It most likely slightly post-dates no. 3. For convenience of comparison I provide cross-references to list no. 3.

7. Lists of dues owed to various monastic offices or 'obediences'.

For further comment, and evidence supporting the above summaries, see above, Introduction, p. xxiii.

TEXT

[Fo. 187ʳ has three entries, none in the main hand; the first hand is probably late twelfth century, the other two late medieval.]

1. *De hundredis et de hidis ecclesie Abbendonensis in Berchescire sicut scriptura thesauri regis continet per hundreta singula dispositis.* fo. 187ᵛ

Hornimere

In Hornimere hundreto. Cumenore: pro quinquaginta hidis. Bertone: pro lx. hidis.

In Roeberge hundreto. Ciuilea: pro xxvii. hidis. Waliford: pro l. hidis. De terra huius manerii Waliford tenet Rainbaldus Lechamstede x. hidas. Et Willelmus iiiior. hidas in Westuna. Et Bernerus ii. hidas in Boxore. Has tenuerunt Brichtwinus et Aluricus et quidam prepositus de abbatia; nec potuerunt recedere. Bedene: pro x. hidis. In Benneham ii. hide.

Mercham

In Mercheham hundreto. Merceham pro xx. hidis. Frieleford: pro x. hidis. In ⟨T⟩obbenei i. hida. Lege: pro i. hida. Gareford: pro x. hidis. Hannelei: pro x. hidis. Gosei: pro xvii. hidis. Linford: pro vii. hidis. Ibidem: iii. hide. Draicote: pro x. hidis.

Suttune

In Suttune hundreto. Appelford: pro v. hidis. Middeltun: pro xxviii. hidis.[1] In Suttune i. hida. Witteham: pro x. hidis.

Riplesmere

In Riplesmere hundreto. Winekefeld: pro x. hidis. De hac terra sunt iiiior. hide in foresta.

In Cerledone hundreto. Wiscelea: pro x. hidis.

Nachedesdore

In Nachedesdorne hundreto. Ferneburge: pro x. hidis. Milledone: pro v. hidis.

Chenetesberie

In Cheneteberie hundreto. Lawartone: pro vi. hidis et dimidia.

Scriueham

In Scriueham hundreto. Wacenesfeld: pro xx. hidis.

Hilleslaue

In Hilleslaue hundreto. Offenton: pro xl. hidis. Speresholt: pro x. hidis.[2]

Gamenesfeld

In Gamenesfeld hundreto. Wrdam: pro xxx. hidis. Cernie: pro ii. uirgatis. Item: dimidia hida. Scarengeford: pro xii. hidis. Pesei: pro ii. hidis.

In Wanetinz

In Wanetinz hundreto. Lachinz: pro x. hidis. Gainz: pro x. hidis. Item: ii. hide. Bochelande: pro v. hidis.

2. *Item in alio libro thesauri regis tempore Willelmi regis, qui Angliam suo adquisiuit imperio, scripto abreuiatio hidarum et descriptio taliter continetur.*

Abbatia de Abbendona tenet in Hornimere hundreto Cumenora. Tempore regis Eadwardi se defendit pro l. hidis, modo uero pro

[1] *DB* i, fo. 59^{r}, has Milton before Appleford.

[2] *DB* i, fo. 59^{r}, refers to these ten hides as Fawler; see above, p. 52 n. 124.

xxx. hidis. Ibi est ecclesia. De l. hidis predictis tenet Anskil v. hidas. Norman tenuit tempore regis Eadwardi pro i. manerio, Seuechwrda uocatur, et non potuit ire quo uoluit; et pro v. hidis geldauit cum superioribus. In Wihteham tenet Hubertus de abbate v. hidas de terra uillanorum et geldauerunt[a] cum predictis hidis. In Cumenora tenet Osbernus ii. hidas et dimidiam ex supradictis, et pro tanto geldauerunt cum aliis. Duo alodiarii tenuerunt de abbate. Rainaldus tenet i. hidam in Cumenore, et geldauit cum aliis predictis.

Bertuna

Ipsa abbatia tenet Bertone. Tempore regis Eadwardi se defendit pro lx. hidis, modo pro xl. hidis. De his lx. hidis tenet Rainaldus de abbate in uadimonio i. manerium, Sipene. Eadnod Stalre tenuit tempore regis Eadwardi, et non fuit tunc in abbatia. Sed Hugo comes dedit abbati. Tunc se defendit pro v. hidis, modo pro i. hida. Isdem tenet ibidem de abbate iii. hidas. Alfwardus presbiter et Leofwinus aurifaber tenuerunt de abbate, nec poterant recedere. Tunc et modo se defendit pro iii. hidis. Hugo cocus tenet de abbate in Bertone i. hidam et dimidiam, et in Sandford ii. hidas. Lewinus et Normannus tenuerunt, sed recedere non potuerunt. Ex supradictis lx. hidis tenent Anskil et Gillebertus in Baiwrda x. hidas de abbate. Wluricus tenuit, et recedere non potuit. He x. hide pro viii. se | defendit. De eodem manerio et de eadem terra tenet Warinus iiii. fo. 188r
hidas in Sogoorde, et Bernerus v. hidas in Soningewelle et in Cheniton, et Alfwinus i. hidam in Chenitona. Sex Anglici tenuerunt, et ab ecclesia recedere non potuerunt, et cum aliis hidis geldauerunt.

Roeberge

Ipsa abbatia tenet in In Roeberge hundreto Ciuelei.[b] Tempore regis Eadwardi se defendit pro xxviii. hidis, modo pro vii. et dimidia. De hac terra tenet Willelmus de abbate v. hidas, et Godefridus i. hidam et dimidiam.

Waliford

Ipsa abbatia tenet Waliford. Tempore regis Eadwardi se defendit pro l. hidis, modo pro xxxvii.[c] De hac terra tenet Herbertus camerarius x. hidas in Lechamstede,[3] et Willelmus iiii. hidas in Westona, et Bernerus ii. in Bocsora. Has tenuerunt Brichwinus et Aluricus et

[a] *ending supplied from DB* [b] *the disorderly form of this entry reflects the arrangement in DB, although DB does not repeat the word* in [c] *corr. by erasure from* xxxviii.

[3] *DB* i, fo. 58v, attributes these ten hides to Rainbald.

quidam prepositus de abbate, nec potuerunt recedere. Et Walterus de Riuera tenet de abbate Bedenam. Norman tenuit, et non potuit ire quo uoluit. Tunc se defendit pro x. hidis, modo pro viii., tamen fuit pro xv. hidis se⟨d⟩ rex Eadwardus condonauit xi.[4] hidas, ut dicunt. De ipsa terra tenet quidam miles ii. hidas. Isdem Walterus in Benneham tenet ii. hidas. Edgit tenuit tempore Eadwardi regis, et pro tanto se defendit tunc et modo.

Mercham

Ipsa abbatia tenet in Mercham hundreto Mercham. Tempore Eadwardi se defendit pro xx. hidis, modo pro x. De hac terra tenet Anskil i. hidam. Alfwinus tenuit de abbate.

Frigeleford

Ipsa abbatia tenet Frigeleford. Tempore Eadwardi et modo se defendit pro x. hidis. De hac terra tenet Rainaldus iiii. hidas, et Rainbaldus i. hidam, et Salui i. hidam. Quinque taini tenuerunt de abbate, nec potuerunt recedere quo uoluerunt. Rainbaldus tenet de abbate i. hidam in Tobeneia. Norman et Aluricus tenuerunt. Tempore regis Eadwardi et modo se defendit pro i. hida. Willelmus tenet de abbate Leie. Norman tenuit tempore regis Eadwardi. Tunc et modo se defendit pro una hida.

Gareford

Ipsa abbatia tenet Gareford. Tempore regis Eadwardi se defendit pro x. hidis, modo pro vi. Abbas habet viii. hidas, et Bernerus tenet de eo ii. hidas.

Hanlea

Ipsa abbatia tenet Hanleam. Tempore regis Eadwardi et modo se defendit pro x. hidis. De hac terra tenet Wlwi iii. hidas que fuerunt de dominico uictu monachorum tempore regis Eadwardi. Et Nicholaus tenet i. hidam de abbate, quam tenuit Edwinus presbiter, et non potuit ab eo recedere.

Gosei

Ipsa abbatia tenet Gosei. Tempore regis Eadwardi se defendit pro xvii. hidis, modo pro xi. hidis. De hac terra tenet Hermerus vii. hidas, et sunt de dominico uictu monachorum.

Linford

Walterus Giffar tenet de abbate Linford. Tempore regis Eadwardi tenuerunt filii Eliert de abbate, nec poterant alias ire absque licentia.

[4] *DB* i, fo. 58v: 'pro xi.'

Et tamen commendauerunt se Walterio sine abbatis precepto. Tunc et modo se defendit pro vii. hidis. Rainaldus tenet de abbate iii. hidas in eadem uilla. Limbaldus monachus tenuit de abbatia. Et pro iii. hidis se defendit tunc et modo.

Draicote

Ipsa abbatia tenet Draicote. Tempore regis Eadwardi et modo se defendit pro x. hidis. De hac terra tenet Gislebertus i. hidam, et quidam Anglicus dimidiam hidam.

Suttun'

Ipsa abbatia tenet in Suttun hundreto Middeltune. Tempore regis Eadwardi se defendit pro xxviii. hidis, modo pro xxiii. De eadem terra tenet Atselinus ii. hidas et unam uirgatam de abbate. Et Rainaldus iii. hidas.

Appelford

Ipsa abbatia tenet Appelford. Tempore regis Eadwardi et modo se defendit pro v. hidis. De hac terra tenet Robertus i. hidam.

De i. hida Suttune

In Suttuna tenet Alwi presbiter i. hidam de abbate. Pater eius tenuit, et tunc et modo pro tanto se defendit.

Witteham

Ipsa abbatia tenet Witteham. Tempore regis Eadwardi se defendit pro x. hidis, modo pro v. hidis.

Riplesmere hund' |

Ipsa abbatia tenet in Riplemere hundreto Winechefeld. Tempore fo. 188v
regis Eadwardi se defendit pro x. hidis, modo pro iii.[a] hidis et dimidia. Et unus homo tenet dimidiam hidam absque uoluntate abbatis et iniuste facit. De terra huius manerii sunt in foresta regis iiii. hide.

Cerledone

Ipsa abbatia tenet in Cerledone hundredo Wiscelea. Tempore regis Eadwardi se defendit pro x. hidis, modo pro vii. hidis.

Nachetedorne

Ipsa abbatia tenet in Nachethedorne hundredo Ferneburga. Tempore regis Eadwardi se defendit pro x. hidis, modo pro iiii. hidis et dimidia. Henricus tenet de abbate Cilletone. Blacheman presbiter

[a] *corr. by erasure from* iiii.

tenuit de Haroldo comite in alodium, et potuit ire quo uoluit. Tunc et modo se defendit pro v. hidis.

Cheneteberie hundredo[a]
Ietselinus tenet in Cheneteberie hundredo Lawertona de abbate. Blacheman tenuit in feudo. Tempore regis Eadwardi se defendit pro vi. hidis et dimidia, modo pro iiii. hidis et dimidia.

Scriueham
Ipsa abbatia tenet in Scriueham hundredo Wecenesfeld. Tempore regis Eadwardi se defendit pro xx. hidis, modo pro x. hidis. De hac terra tenet Gislebertus iii. hidas et i. uirgatam de abbate, et Wimundus i. hidam.

Hilleslaue
Ipsa abbatia tenet in Hilleslaue hundredo Offentuna. Tempore regis Eadwardi se defendit pro xl. hidis, modo pro xiii. hidis. De hac terra tenet Gislebertus vi. hidas de abbate.

Anskil tenet Speresholt de abbate. Edric tenuit in alodium de rege Eadwardo, et potuit ire quo uoluit. Tunc et modo se defendit pro x. hidis.

Gamenesfeld
Ipsa abbatia tenet in Gamenesfeld hundredo Wordam. Tempore regis Eadwardi se defendit pro xxx. hidis, modo pro viii. hidis.

Cernei
Ipsa abbatia tenet Cernei. Tempore regis Eadwardi et modo se defendit pro ii. uirgatis terre. Warinus tenet de abbatia dimidiam hidam. Wlwinus tenuit tempore regis Eadwardi de abbate. Tunc et modo se defendit pro dimidia hida.

Sceringeford
Ipsa abbatia tenet Sceringaford. Tempore regis Eadwardi se defendit pro xii. hidis, modo pro ii. hidis et i. uirgata. De hoc manerio tenet Gislebertus ii. hidas de abbate, et Wimundus i. hidam. Gislebertus tenet de abbate Pesei. Aluredus tenuit de abbate tempore regis Eadwardi. Tunc et modo pro ii. hidis se defendit.

Wanetinz hund'
Ipsa abbatia tenet in Wanetinz hundredo Laking. Tempore regis Eadwardi pro x. hidis se defendit, et modo pro vi. hidis et i. uirgata.

[a] hundredro *MS*

De hac terra tenet Gislebertus i. hidam de abbate, et i. ecclesiam cum dimidia hida.

Gaing

Ipsa abbatia tenet Gaing. Tempore regis Eadwardi se defendit pro x. hidis, modo pro ii. hidis et i. uirgata. Rainaldus tenet de abbate ii. hidas. Norman tenuit tempore regis Eadwardi de abbate. Tunc et modo pro ii. hidis se defendit.

Bochelanda

Ipsa abbatia tenet Bochelande. Elmarus tenuit tempore regis Eadwardi. Tunc et modo se defendit pro v. hidis.

Summa d. hid' et xii. hid' et dim'. Et de his sunt v. hide in elemosina ad Wordam.

[gap of 4 lines]

De terris in Oxeneford comitatu huius ecclesie

In Oxenefordscira abbatia de Abbendona tenet Leuecanore. Ibi sunt xvii. hide. De his sunt in dominio iiii. hide et dimidia.

Cudesduna

Eadem abbatia tenet Cudesdonam. Ibi sunt xviii. hide. De his sunt in dominio iiii. hide, et requirit Bolendone hund'.

Sandford

Henri tenet de abbatia Sanford.[5] Ibi sunt x. hide. De his sunt iiii. hide in dominio. In eadem uilla tenent Robertus et Rogerus i. hidam de abbate. Siwardus tenuit et ab ecclesia recendere non potuit. Similiter istud manerium requirit Bolendone hundr'.

Bereford |

Filius Wadardi tenet de Rogero, et ipse Rogerus de abbate, v. hidas in fo. 189^{r}
Bereford, sed et hoc manerium requirit Bolendone hund'.

Gersendune

Gillebertus tenet de abbate vii. hidas et dimidiam in Gersendune. Ibi est i. hida de inland que nunquam geldauit. In eadem uilla tenet Sueting i. hidam et dimidiam de abbate. Et hoc manerium requirit Bolendone hund'.

[5] *DB* i, fo. 156^{v}, calls the tenant 'Wenricus'; see above, p. 322. There is nothing in the form of the letter 'W' in the manuscript of *Domesday* which may have led to the substitution of an 'H'. It may be that the scribe's confusion arises in part from the fact that a tenant called Henry held land in a different Sandford, Dry Sandford, Berks., see above, p. 203, below, p. 387.

Tademertona.
Ipsa abbatia tenet xx. hidas in Tademertona. De his sunt vi. hide in dominio. De hac terra tenet i. miles v. hidas de abbate. Hoc manerium requirit hund' de Bloxan.

Ernicote
Robertus de Oili et Rogerus de Iuri tenent de abbate in Ernicote ii. hidas de feudo ecclesie.

Fencota i. hida[6]
Eadem ecclesia tenet i. hidam in Faincota de feudo Atheline d'Iureio. Eadem abbatia tenet ecclesiam de Niweham et totam decimam ipsius manerii, cum i. piscatione que Anglice tunc uocabatur Sotieswere, et terram que eidem adiacet.[7]

Brochestan
Eadem abbatia tenet ii. hidas in Brochestan de feudo Milonis Crispini, et Willelmus Clemens tenet ipsas in gablo de abbate.

[long gap to bottom of column]

De terris huius ecclesie in Warewicscira

[top of new column]

In Werewicscira tenet abbatia de Abbendona in Meretun hund' ii. hidas in Hylle, quas emit abbas Adelelmus de feudo Turkilli, et Warinus tenet de abbate. Et i. hidam in Cestretuna.

[gap of 7 lines]

De terris in comitatu Gloecestrec'
In Gloecestrescira tenet ecclesia de Abbendona in Grestestan hund' Dumeltun. Ibi sunt vii. hide et dimidia.

[long gap to bottom of column]

fo. 189[v] 3. *Qui sint qui tenent terras huius ecclesie Abbend'.*

In Bertona sunt xl. hide geldantes. Ex his tenet Willelmus de Seuekewrða vi. hidas in Baiwrda. Et in eadem tenet Robertus de Sandford iiii. hidas. Hugo filius Berneri tenet in Sunningewelle ii. hidas et in Cenituna iii. hidas. In eadem Kenituna tenet Atzo cocus i.

[6] The remaining Oxfordshire entries in the list do not appear in *Domesday Book*, but relate to post-1086 gifts; see above, pp. 106, 78, 158.

[7] See above, p. 78.

hidam et Edricus i. aliam. In Suggewrda tenent Robertus et soror eius iii. hidas.[8] In Sandford tenet Henricus filius Oini i. hidam. Et in eadem Fernoldus tenet i. hidam. In Hansteseie tenet Rogerus Grim dimidiam hidam.[9] Summa xxii. hid' et dim'.

In Sandford tenent uillani viii. hidas. Et in Scerpenhylla vi. hid' et dimid'. Et in Hansteseia ii. hid' et dimid'.

In dominio dimidia hida.

In Hanneia x. hide. Ex his tenent rustici vi. hidas. Osbertus iii. hidas.[10] Et Warinus i. hidam.

In Linford x. hide. Ex his tenet Radulfus de Langetot vii. hidas.[11] Et Turstanus iii. hidas.

In Gareford x. hidĕ. Ex his tenet Hugo ii. hidas. Et rustici tenent vi. hidas et i. uirgatam. Et abbas in dominio i. hidam et dimidiam et i. uirgatam.

In Mercham xx. hide. Ex his tenet Willelmus de Seuechewrda i. hidam. Et Rogerus camerarius dimidiam hidam.[12] Et rustici abbatis viii. hidas et dimidiam. Et cotsetli iii. hidas, v. acras minus. Et abbas in dominio vii. hidas et i. cotsetli.

In Frigelford x. hide. Ex his tenet Turstanus iiii. hidas. Et Iohannes ii. hidas.[13] Et rustici iiii. hidas.

In Tubbeneia i. hida.

In Appelford v. hide. Ex his tenet Paganus i. hidam. Et rustici iiii. hidas.

In Witteham x. hide et i. uirgata. Ex his tenent rustici v. hidas. Et in dominio v. hide et i. uirgata.

In Middeltuna x. hide et dimidia. Ex his in dominio v. hide. Et rustici v. hidas et dimidiam.

In Dreituna xviii. hide. Ex his tenet Radulfus i. hidam et i. uirgatam.[14] Et Turstanus i. hidam. Henricus i. hidam.[15] Et rustici xiiii.[a] hidas et iii. uirgatas.

[a] *corr. from* iiii.

---

[8] Below, p. 393, does not mention Robert's sister.
[9] William but not Roger Grim appears below, p. 393.
[10] See below, p. 393 for Osbert of Hanney.
[11] Ralph does not appear in the list below, pp. 392–4.
[12] See below, p. 394, for Ralph the chamberlain.
[13] This may be John of Tubney, see above, p. lxiv.
[14] This is probably not one of the Ralphs who appear in the list below, pp. 392–4.
[15] This is probably Henry son of Oini; see above, p. 202.

Turstanus de Sancta Helena tenet v. hidas in Gerstuna. Et ii. hidas in Henreda.[a] Et Eadwardus de Sutt' i. hidam.

In Cildetona v. hide de feudo Roberti de Sandford.

In Offentuna xl. hide. Ex his tenet Michael de Culumb' vi. hidas. Et sacerdos i. hidam.[16] Et Ricardus filius Sefug' i. hidam et i. uirgatam.[17] Et rustici viii. hidas. Et in dominio xxiiii. hide.

In Speresholt Hugonis dispensatoris x. hide.[18]

In Gosei x. hide. In dominio v. hide. Et rustici v. hidas.

In Denceswrde vii. hide. Radulfus de Alre tenet.

In Ferneberge x. hide. Ex his tenet Radulfus i. hidam.[19] Et rustici tenent ix. hidas.

In Laking x. hide. Hedewlfus tenet i. hidam.

In Gaingia x. hide.

In Cumenora li. hide. Ex his tenet Willelmus de Seuekurða v. hidas. Robertus de Wihteham v. hidas. Ricardus Calmunt i. hidam et dimidiam.[20] Walterus i. hidam.[21] Simon ii. hidas et dimidiam.[22] Robertus de Lie i. hidam. Robertus filius dapiferi dimidiam hidam. Et rustici tenent xxix. hidas. Et in dominio vi. hide et dimidia.

In Scelengeford xii. hide. Ex his tenent rustici xii. hidas. Et Michael de Columb' ii. hidas. Et in dominio ii. hide.

In Wecenesfeld xx. hide. Ex his sunt in dominio x. hide. Et rustici tenent vii. hidas. Et Willelmus de Pont' Arch' iii. hidas et i. uirgatam.

In Wrda xxv. hide. Ex his sunt in dominio xv. hide. Et homines tenent x. hidas.

In Cernei i. hida et i. uirgata.[b]

In Pesi ii. In Bochelande v. hide.

[a] *corr. from* Henrede [b] uergata *MS*

[16] The priest is not named in the list below, pp. 392–4.
[17] Richard does not appear in the list below, pp. 392–4.
[18] Hugh does not appear in the list below, pp. 392–4.
[19] This is probably not one of the Ralphs who appear in the list below, pp. 392–4.
[20] See also above, pp. 122, 327, below, pp. 390, 393.
[21] This is probably not one of the Walters who appear in the list below, pp. 392–4.
[22] Simon does not appear in the list below, pp. 392–4.

In Lechamstede x. hide. Ex his tenet Fulco frater abbatis ii. hidas et i. uirgatam.[23] Et Herebertus filius Hereberti viii. hidas et iii. uirgatas.[24]

In Waliford xl. hide. Ex his sunt x. hide in Weston'. Willelmus de Pont' Arch' tenet iiii. hidas. Et sacerdos i. hidam ad ecclesiam. Turstanus de Sancta Helena dimidiam hidam. | Et rustici iiii. hidas fo. 190r
et i. uirgatam. Et in dominio i. uirgata.

In Estona x. hide. Homines tenent.

In Boxora x. hide. Ex his Hugo filius Berneri tenet ii. hidas. Et homines tenent v. hidas et i. uirgatam. Et in dominio ii. hide et iii. uirgate.

In Benneham x. hide. Ex his tenet Ansgerus ii. hidas.[25] Et homines iiii. hidas. Et in dominio iiii. hide.

In Ciuelea xxvii. hide. Ex his tenet Iohannes i. hidam et i. uirgatam.[26] Et Eldel' i. hidam.[27] Et ecclesia i. hidam. Et homines xvii. hidas et iii. uirgatas. Et in dominio vii. hide.

In Bradelea v. hide. Engelardus camerarius episcopi Wint' tenet.[28] In Wisselea x. hide.

In Winekefeld x. hide.

In Leofwaratone vi. hide et dimidia. Robertus de Sandford tenet.

In Budene xi. hide.

In Abbendune xv. hide.

[Followed by 3 further short entries, not in the same hand as the above list. The first two reproduce almost verbatim the *Domesday* entries for Winkfield and Whistley. The third is in English, in a post-medieval hand.]

4. Presidente huic ecclesie iure abbatis domno Godefrido episcopo, rex Henricus iunior scire uolens quot in Anglia milites de ueteri aut de nouo fæfamento essent, precepit uicecomitibus suis omnibus ut hoc idem diligenter inuestigarent et presentie sue intimarent. Quod,

[23] Fulk does not appear in the list below, pp. 392–4.

[24] There appears to be a slip in the figures in this entry. Herbert son of Herbert does not appear in the list below, pp. 392–4.

[25] Ansger does not appear in the list below, pp. 392–4.

[26] The only John who appears in the list below, pp. 392–4, is John of Tubney, on whose lands see above, p. lxiv.

[27] This man does not appear in the list below, pp. 392–4.

[28] Engelard does not appear in the list below, pp. 392–4.

cum de hac abbatia sicut et de ceteris fieri iussum fuisset, inquisitum est sollicite sicut rex preceperat, et eorum nomina cum sigillo ecclesie regi sunt per scriptum transmissa. Quod scriptum taliter se habuit:

Hec sunt nomina militum tenentium de ecclesia Abbendonensi de ueteri fæfamento.

Iordanus de Sanford milites[i]	iiii.
Robertus de Seuechewrda[29]	ii.
Vincentius militem	i.
Rainaldus de Sancto Walerio	i.
Willelmus de Lega	ii.
Raerius de Alra	i.
Hugo filius Berneri	i. et dimidium
Iohannes de Tubenei	i.
Iohannes de Sancta Helena	iii.
Gillebertus de Culumb'	ii.
Hugo de Bochelanda	i.
Herebertus filius Hereberti	i.
Willelmus de Bradelega	i.[30]
Beomundus de Ledis	iii.[31]
Henricus de Pisia	i.
Rogerus de Chelesburgo	dimidium
Gillebertus filius Iohannis	dimidium
Paganus filius Henri et Rogerus de Hulla	i.[32]
Turstinus filius Simonis	dimidium
Gaufridus filius Willelmi	i.
Rogerus filius Hemingi	i.
Baldewinus de Fageflora	i.
Robertus de Pontearchis	dimidium
Willelmus de Watelega	dimidium
fo. 190v | Ricardus Calmunt[33]	quarta pars militis

[i] *? corr. from* miles

[29] *Red Book*, i. 305, gives just the place name.

[30] *Red Book*, i. 306, gives the figure as half a knight.

[31] *Red Book*, i. 306, mentions two hides which Humphrey de Bohun had taken away; see also above, p. xxv; *CMA* ii. 304; Lyell, no. 108, Chatsworth, no. 299, a writ of Henry II (dating to 1165x1175) ordering Humphrey to do justice ['rectum teneas'] to the monks of Abingdon concerning two hides at Benham which his grandfather had given them.

[32] *Red Book*, i. 306, mentions that William Giffard had taken away a third part of a knight's fee in Hill. Pain may be the son of Henry son of Oini, on whose holding at Hill see above, p. 203; Pain also witnessed C.H., no. 1, a charter of Abbot Roger (1175–1185).

[33] See also above, pp. 122, 327, 388, below, p. 393.

Ricardus Gernun	i. hid' et defendit se pro vi.ta parte militis
Robertus filius dapiferi	vi. parte militis
Gaufridus de Sanford	v.ta pars militis
Willelmus Grim	v.ta pars militis
Rainaldus de Goseia	v.ta pars militis

Petrus de Aldebira. Henricus de Lachingis. vi.ta pars militis. Et hida de Hanneia que est in manu episcopi que se defendit pro v.ta parte militis.[34]

Omnes isti pro i. milite se defendunt.[35]

Summa uero militum: xxxiii. milites.

5. ⟨B⟩ertona	xl.	fo. 191r
⟨A⟩bbendona	xv.	
⟨S⟩cipene	v.	
⟨C⟩umenora	l. et i.	
⟨M⟩erceham	lx. et i.	
⟨M⟩iddeltuna	l. et iii.	
⟨S⟩arenegford	xxx. et ii.	
⟨L⟩achinge	xxx.	
⟨O⟩ffentuna	xl.	
⟨G⟩osei	xx. et vii.	
⟨W⟩aliford	xl.	
⟨C⟩iuelea	xx. et vii.	
⟨W⟩isseleie	x.	
⟨W⟩enechefeld	v.	
⟨P⟩esi	ii.	
⟨B⟩edene	xi.	
⟨L⟩iwaretona	vi. hid' et dim'	
⟨L⟩echamstede	x.	
⟨B⟩echeland	v.	
⟨C⟩edelewrda	iiii.	

[34] *Red Book*, i. 306, seems to refer to this as the land of Geoffrey de *Raverches*. For Peter, see also above, p. 324.

[35] The arithmetic is here obscure, although the text is clearly saying that the various tenants perform one knight's service or, more likely, pay scutage for one knight's fee. However, the fractions do not add up, and moreover the version in the *Red Book*, i. 306, simply lists the names from 'Ricardus Calmunt' and says they make 'one and a half knights' [service].'

⟨I⟩n ⟨C⟩umenora	vi. hid' et dim'
⟨I⟩n ⟨B⟩ertona	dim' hid'
⟨I⟩n ⟨S⟩cipene	ii. hid'
⟨I⟩n ⟨M⟩erceham	ix. hid'
⟨I⟩n ⟨M⟩iddeltuna	x. hid' et i. virg'
⟨I⟩n ⟨O⟩ffentona	xx. et iii. hid'
⟨I⟩n ⟨L⟩achinge	x. hid'
⟨I⟩n ⟨S⟩caringeford	xii. hid'
⟨I⟩n ⟨W⟩rda	xv. hid'
⟨I⟩n ⟨W⟩aliford	vii. hid'
⟨I⟩n ⟨C⟩iueleia	vii. hid'
⟨I⟩n ⟨W⟩isseleia	vii. hid'
⟨I⟩n ⟨C⟩edelewrda	ii. hid'

⟨S⟩umma: c. hid' et i. uirg'.

⟨I⟩n ⟨C⟩umenora	xxx. hid' et dim'
⟨I⟩n ⟨B⟩ertona	xviii.
⟨I⟩n ⟨A⟩bbendona	x.
⟨I⟩n ⟨S⟩cipene	ii.
⟨I⟩n ⟨M⟩erceham	xxvii. hid' et iii. uirg'
⟨I⟩n ⟨M⟩iddeltona	xxix. hid' et i. uirg'
⟨I⟩n ⟨O⟩ffentuna	xiii. hid'
⟨I⟩n ⟨S⟩ceringeford	xv. hid'
⟨I⟩n ⟨L⟩achinge	xviii. hid'
⟨I⟩n ⟨W⟩rda	xxi. hid' et i. uirg'
⟨I⟩n ⟨W⟩aliford	xxiii. hid' et dim'
⟨I⟩n ⟨C⟩iuelea	xiii. hid'
⟨I⟩n ⟨W⟩isseleia	xiiii. hid'
⟨I⟩n ⟨C⟩edelewrda	ii. hid'

⟨S⟩umma: cc. hid' et xliii. hid'.

6. ⟨T⟩urstinus xv. hidas et dimidiam.[36]
⟨R⟩otbertus de Santford xv. hidas et dimidiam.[37]
⟨W⟩illelmus de Seuechewrda xii. hidas.[38]

[36] See above, p. 387, for a Thurstan holding 3 hides in Lyford, 4 hides in Frilford, 1 hide in Drayton; above, p. 388, for Thurstan of St Helen holding 5 hides in Garsington, 2 hides in Hendred, and, p. 389, half a hide in Welford, making a total of fifteen and a half hides.

[37] See above, pp. 386–8, for Robert holding 4 hides in Barton, 5 hides in Chilton, 6.5 hides in Leverton, making a total of fifteen and a half hides.

[38] See above, pp. 386–8, for William holding 6 hides in Bayworth, 5 hides in Cumnor, 1 hide in Marcham, making a total of twelve hides.

⟨M⟩ichael de Culumb' xi. hidas et i. uirgatam.[39]
⟨R⟩obertus de Leie i. hidam .[40]
⟨H⟩ugo filius Bernerii xi. hidas.[41]
⟨W⟩alterus de Riuere xi. hidas et in Benham ii. hidas.
⟨S⟩persolt x. hidas. ⟨L⟩echamsted' x. hidas.
⟨W⟩alterus Giffar vii. hidas. ⟨R⟩adulfus de Alra vii. hidas.[42]
⟨R⟩obertus de Wihtham v. hidas.[43] ⟨B⟩radelea v. hidas.
⟨W⟩illelmus de Bechelanda v. hidas.[44] ⟨W⟩illelmus de Pontearcis iiii. hidas.[45]
⟨J⟩ohannes de Tubenea iiii. hidas.[46] ⟨P⟩ichot de Pesi iiii. hidas.[47]
⟨O⟩sbernus de Hanni iii. hidas.[48] ⟨H⟩enricus filius Idini iii. hidas.[49]
⟨R⟩obertus de Suggevrð' ii. hidas.[50] ⟨R⟩icard de Calmunt i. hidam et dimidiam.[51]
⟨H⟩ydwlfus i. hidam.[52] ⟨R⟩einaldus de Gosi i. hidam.[53]
⟨W⟩arinus de Dencheswrda i. hidam.[54] ⟨F⟩ernoldus.[55]
⟨W⟩illelmus Grim i. hidam.[56] ⟨R⟩otbertus filius dapiferi i. hidam et dimidiam.[57]

39 See above, p. 388, for Michael holding 6 hides in Uffington and 2 hides in Shellingford.

40 See above, p. 388, for Robert holding 1 hide in Cumnor.

41 See above, pp. 386, 389, for Hugh holding 2 hides in Sunningwell, 3 hides in Kennington, and 2 hides in Boxford. That Berner was still alive in 1121, above, p. 236, helps to date the present list.

42 See above, p. 388, for Ralph holding 7 hides in Denchworth.

43 See above, p. 388, for Robert holding 5 hides in Cumnor.

44 Buckland, but no tenant, is mentioned in the list above, p. 388.

45 See above, pp. 388–9, for William holding 3 hides in Watchfield, 4 hides in Welford. William may have died in the mid-late 1140s (Green, *Government*, p. 267), helping to date the present list.

46 See above, pp. lxiv, 389.

47 This could be Picot the son-in-law of Gilbert Latimer, above, p. 48. In 1086 a Gilbert held Pusey from the abbot; *DB* i, fo. 59^{v}. Pusey, but no tenant, is mentioned in the list above, p. 388.

48 See above, p. 387, for 'Osbert' holding 3 hides in Hanney.

49 See above, p. 387, for Henry son of Oini holding 1 hide in Sandford; he is also probably the Henry listed as holding 1 hide in Drayton, above, p. 387.

50 See above, p. 387, for Robert and his sister holding 2 hides in Suggeworth.

51 See above, p. 388, for Richard holding 1.5 hides in Cumnor, possibly at Wytham; also above, p. 123, for his family.

52 See above, p. 388, for Hedewlfus holding 1 hide in Lockinge.

53 Goosey, but no tenant, is mentioned in the list above, p. 388.

54 See above, p. 387, for a Warin holding 1 hide in Hanney.

55 See above, p. 387, for Fernoldus holding 1 hide in Sandford.

56 See above, p. 387, for Roger Grim holding half a hide in Hinksey. A William Grim appears in the Abingdon *Carta* of 1166, above, p. 391, *Red Book*, i. 306. He is probably the successor of Roger, and if so this list post-dates that printed above, pp. 386–9.

57 See above, p. 388, for Robert holding half a hide in Cumnor. He may be the person

⟨R⟩obertus de Aldebiri i. hidam et dimidiam.[58] ⟨E⟩adward de Suttona i. hidam.[59]

⟨P⟩aganus de Appelford i. hidam.[60] ⟨R⟩adulfus camerarius i. hidam.[61]

⟨A⟩tzo cocus i. hidam.[62]

⟨S⟩umma: c. et lxiii. hid' et i. uirg'.

[ii. 321] 7. *De consuetudine lignandi.*

fo. 191v Domnus abbas Faritius hanc instituit consuetudinem lignandi, prout melius sibi uisum, tum ut facilius per officina[a] curie ignis haberetur, tum ut rustici uillarum id leuius paterentur. Soliti enim fuerant idem dare suas decimas per omnem abbatiam ad opus ecclesie reedificande faciendum. Ad ligna quoque ecclesie ministranda nummos inueniebant. Vnde eis abbas compatiens sic eorum grauamen, temperauit ut partim de decimis suis predictis, partim de nummis quos antea dabant lignorum consuetudinem inueniendorum constituerat, preter decimas de Cumenore et Bertune, quas operi ecclesie dimisit. Itaque ita determinatum est:

De Cumenore xxx. solidos.

De Bertune xxx. solidos.

De Merceham xl. ex decima, et de consuetudine, quam solebant pro lignis emendis reddere, xx. solidos.

De Middeltun et Appelford et Witteham xl. solidos.

De Laking et Ferneberga xxv. solidos de decima, et de consuetudine lignandi xx. solidos.

De Scaringeford et Wecenesfeld xv. solidos de consuetudine lignandi.

De Cerni et Wrda xx. solidos de decima, et de consuetudine lignandi xx. solidos.

De Offentuna xxx. solidos de decima, et xx. de consuetudine lignandi.

[a] *rectius* officinas

involved in the dispute over half a hide in Cumnor during Stephen's reign; if so, it would seem that his father died in Ingulf's time, that is 1130–58, again suggesting a possible date for this list.

[58] Robert does not appear in the list above, pp. 386–9. For a Peter of *Aldebiri*, see above, pp. 324, 391.

[59] See above, p. 388, for Edward holding 1 hide.

[60] See above, p. 387, for Pain holding 1 hide in Appleford.

[61] Cf. above, p. 387, for a Roger the chamberlain.

[62] See above, p. 386, for Atzo holding 1 hide in Kennington; for Atzo see also *CMA* ii. 306.

De Culeham inter decimam et consuetudinem lignandi xxx. solidos. [ii. 322]

De Cudesduna xxx. solidos de decima, et de consuetudine lignandi xx. solidos.

De Leuechenore l. solidos de consuetudine lignandi.

Summa: xxii. libre

De coquina monachorum.
De Abbendona xvi. libras. Ad festum sancti Michaelis iiii. libras. Ad Purificationem iiii. libras. Ad Hochedei iiii. libras. Et ad Aduincula sancti Petri iiii. libras. Super hoc Willelmus cocus ii. solidos.

De Sipene ix. libras et iv. solidos de curia.

De molendinis in curia iiii. libras.

De molendino super Eocha xxxvi. solidos.

De molendino Iohannis de Sancta Helena x. solidos.

De Wisele et Winekefeld x. libras et c. scutellas in Natali Domini, et c. in Pascha, et c. in Natiuitate sancte Marie. Ad sagimen iste x. libre.

De[a] Rehenere xx. solidos de gablo et v. solidos pro decima sua.

De Berwine xx. solidos de gablo et xxx. denarios pro decima sua. De Osmundo xx. solidos et xxx. denarios pro decima sua. De hida in Æppelford xx. solidos.

De pischaria eiusdem uille x. solidos. [ii. 323]

De Cudesdun' c. solidos ad cenam.

De decima rusticorum de Sanford xxiiii.[b] solidos ad diuersa condimenta. De pischaria de Culeham iii. solidos. De Niweham Wlfwine Porman xii. solidos.

De pischaria de Witteham xvii. solidos. De Ciuele xxxi. solidos. De molendino de Wecenesfeld xxv. De Oxeneford iii. libras et x. solidos. De Hugone de Sunnigewelle xxiiii.[c] denarios.

De Bertona xlv. solidos et xi. denarios, et tria milia oua, et centum et xxxvi. gallinas. Et vi. ambras leguminis. Similiter de Cumenora, Merceham, Cernei, Offentuna, Middeltuna, Scarengenford, Laking, Witteham. De Cudesduna medietatem, uidelicet xxii. solidos et x. denarios et obolum. Et sic ceterarum rerum quas supra nominauimus medietatem.

[a] *an entry beginning* De *is erased before this entry* [b] iiii. *interlin. in green ink above* xx.
[c] iiii. *interlin. in blue ink above* xx.

De supradictis uero maneriis debet habere coquinarius summagias ter in anno ad uoluntatem suam, scilicet tres homines cum equis eorum
fo. 192r de unoquoque[a] manerio | qui pergant de suo proprio sumptu longe aut prope ubi illis preceptum fuerit. Si autem coquinaria placuerit magis accipere nummos, dent ei prout gratiam potuerint inuenire.

In capite ieiunii redduntur iste anguille:
Ælfricus de Witelea xxx. sticas.
Alfricus de Herewaldinduna viii.
Turkillus de Culeham xx.
Ærnulfus xii.
Leofricus Cuceafoc x.
Adelwinus Quirc de Cumenora xvi. Et abbati viii.
De Tropo vii. De Wisselea xvi.
Ad coquinam abbatis. De Swinford Saricus xiiii. Haskillus vi. Godricus de Eockaford iiii.

Summa denariorum ad coquinam monachorum pertinentium quater uiginti libre et l. solidi.
Summa ouorum uiginti nouem milia et cccc. et l.
Summa gallinarum cccxliii.
[ii. 324] *Summa pisarum uel fabarum lvii. ambre.*
Summa de sumagiis quater xx. et v. et dimidium.
Si denarios pro sumagiis acceperit, summa illorum denariorum est.[b]
Summa anguillarum ad coquinam monachorum centum xix. stichæ.
Summa ad coquinam abbatis xxxii. stiche.

Coquinarius etiam monachorum habere debet de cellario x. panes cotidie quales ipsi habent in refectorio, et ceruisiam ad salsamentum faciendum, de pipere aut cimino. Quando uero mollas escas uoluerit facere, de ceruisia monachorum sufficienter debet habere.
In aduentu uero Domini quotiens fratres non comedunt sagimentum, xiii. panes debet habere tres uidelicet ad pulmentum. Similiter a Septuagesima ad Pascha et omni tempore ferie vi. et quatuor temporum, et si uoluerit, accipiat farinam in pistrino pro panibus suis.

[Second column of fo. 192r is blank, except for the bottom four lines, which contain an entry in a different hand concerning the refectorer; printed *CMA* ii. 324]

[a] unoquodque *MS* [b] *figure erased*

De redditu altaris. fo. 192v
De ecclesia de Mercham v. libras.
De ecclesia de Offentuna xx. solidos.
De ecclesia de Cumenora x. solidos.
De capellis de Tubbenei et Lega v. solidos. [ii. 325]
De ecclesia sancti Martini de Oxenef' xxv. solidos.
De ecclesia sancti Aldadi xx. solidos.
De ecclesia de Niweham xxx. solidos.
De ecclesia de Witteham.
De ecclesia de Wicham xl. libras cere.
De Redelea cereum.
De decima de Hanneia xxii.
De decima Westlakinge xx. solidos.
De decima de Middeltuna xx. solidos.
De decima de Winterburna.
De decima Radulfi de Morles unum marcum.
De decima Willelmi Grim iii. solidos.
De Wicha xxii. solidos.
De terra quam Radulfus Brito ten' in Oxen' xx. solidos.
De Mora dimidia hida viii. solidos.
De Boreshulla xii. solidos.
De terra Walman unum marcum.
De Kigestuna xxxii. denarios.
De terra Rogeri Haliman et Æilpini in Walingaf' ii. solidos.
De terra Roberti Vinet' iii. solidos.[63]
De terra Willelmi Pincun xii. denarios.
De terra Ædiue xii.[a] denarios.
De terra Piliard xi. denarios.
De terra Ælfrici iii. denarios.
De terra Scalegrai.
De terra Willelmi Blut vi. denarios.
De quodam prato.
De cellarario ceram de lii. sextariis mellis.
De Cudesduna i. marcum.
De terra apud Wint'.

[a] *corr. from* xx.

[63] A Robert the vintner witnessed C.H., no. 2.

[ii. 326] *De redditu camere.*
De Weliford xxxvii. libras.
Coquinario xxxi. solidos.
De Ciuele xvi. libras, et ex his reddet camerarius [figure missing].
De Chedeleswrda iiii. libras.
De Bedeford' xxv. solidos.
De Fencota xx. solidos.
Terre in Hensteseia xxv. solidos.
De molendino de Langeford cum una uirgata.
De Colebroc v. solidos.
De Abbendona iiii. solidos et iii. denarios.
De maneriis abbatie, que[a] faciunt ix. menses et dimidium, lii. solidos et iii. denarios.
In Middeltuna dimidium marcum.
Decimam de Betrintuna.
Decimam de Hordwella. Et omnes unctos porcorum, scilicet illorum maneriorum que[a] reddunt firmam monachorum, debet camerarius accipere ad sotulares monachorum unguendos.

Et ad omnes pelles conficiendos, siue sint cattorum siue agnorum, accipiet camerarius bladum de Bertuna, et sal in coquina monachorum, et chretam de Lakinge.

Et debet habere etiam unam carretam feni de Culeham ad lectulos monachorum faciendos per singulos annos. Et fenum unius insule ad usum balneorum, quando balneant monachi.

Et prebendam et fenum duorum equorum et conredium unius hominis in aula abbatis.

[ii. 327] Et si camerarius uadit ad feiram de Winchelcumba, homines de Dumbeltuna debent adducere quicquid ibi mercatum fuerit.

Et si uadit ad feiram de Wintonia, tenura de Weliford debet adducere quicquid ibi mercatum fuerit, licet manerium sit traditum ad firmam.

Francolanus etiam de Hanneia debet ire ad submonitionem camerarii cum eo ad negocia ecclesie facienda. Et si camerarius mercatus fuerit alicubi choria boum tanneta et sale opus habuerit, accipere debet de coquina monachorum quantum opus fuerit. |

[fo. 193^{r-v} is in a different hand, and has entries concerning the rents due to the almoner (*CMA* ii. 327–8); a bull of Alexander III (Lyell,

[a] qui *MS*

no. 21); the rents due to the precentor, the infirmarer, and the fabric of the house (*CMA* ii. 328–9). Then fos. 193^{v}–194^{r} in a further hand again has rents due to the hostillar (*CMA* ii. 329–30). The remainder of the first column of fo. 194^{r} is blank, and the second column and fo. 194^{v} are in later medieval hands (*CMA* ii. 330–4).]

INDEX OF QUOTATIONS AND ALLUSIONS

INDEX

To avoid providing many entries for undifferentiated personal names, a brief, generally formulaic, indication of each individual's place in the *History* has been included. The word 'witness' following a personal name indicates that the individual appears in the *History* only as a witness to a document or transaction.